BLADE
OF THE IMMORTAL

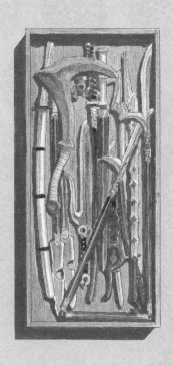

Final Curtain

publisher
Mike Richardson

editor
Philip R. Simon

assistant editor
Roxy Polk

collection designer
Kat Larson

digital production
Ryan Jorgensen

Dedicated to Toren Smith.

**Special thanks to Michael Gombos,
Annie Gullion, Dana Lewis, and Rich Powers.**

BLADE OF THE IMMORTAL Vol. 31: FINAL CURTAIN
Blade of the Immortal © 2013 by Hiroaki Samura. All rights reserved. First
published in Japan in 2013 by Kodansha Ltd., Tokyo. English translation
rights arranged through Kodansha Ltd. This English-language edition ©
2015 by Dark Horse Comics, Inc. All other material © 2015 by Dark Horse
Comics, Inc. Dark Horse Manga™ is a trademark of Dark Horse Comics,
Inc. All rights reserved. No portion of this publication may be reproduced
or transmitted, in any form or by any means, without the express written
permission of Dark Horse Comics, Inc. Names, characters, places, and inci-
dents featured in this publication either are the product of the author's imag-
ination or are used fictitiously. Any resemblance to actual persons (living or
dead), events, institutions, or locales, without satiric intent, is coincidental.

Dark Horse Manga
A division of Dark Horse Comics, Inc.
10956 SE Main Street
Milwaukie, OR 97222

DarkHorse.com

To find a comics shop in your area, call the
Comic Shop Locator Service toll-free at 1-888-266-4226.

First edition: March 2015
ISBN 978-1-61655-626-6

1 3 5 7 9 10 8 6 4 2

Printed in the United States of America

MIKE RICHARDSON president and publisher NEIL HANKERSON
executive vice president TOM WEDDLE chief financial officer RANDY
STRADLEY vice president of publishing MICHAEL MARTENS vice president of book trade sales SCOTT ALLIE editor in chief MATT PARKINSON
vice president of marketing DAVID SCROGGY vice president of product
development DALE LaFOUNTAIN vice president of information
technology DARLENE VOGEL senior director of print, design, and
production KEN LIZZI general counsel DAVEY ESTRADA editorial director CHRIS WARNER senior books editor DIANA SCHUTZ
executive editor CARY GRAZZINI director of print and development
LIA RIBACCHI art director CARA NIECE director of scheduling
MARK BERNARDI director of digital publishing

BLADE
OF THE IMMORTAL

art and story
HIROAKI SAMURA

translation
Kumar Sivasubramanian

English adaptation
Tomoko Saito and Philip R. Simon

lettering and retouch
Tomoko Saito

Final Curtain

DARK HORSE MANGA

ABOUT THE TRANSLATION

The Swastika

The main character in *Blade of the Immortal*, Manji, has taken the "crux gammata" as both his name and his personal symbol. This symbol is also known as the *swastika*, a name derived from the Sanskrit *svastika* (meaning "welfare," from *su* — "well" + *asti* — "he is"). As a symbol of prosperity and good fortune, the swastika was widely used throughout the ancient world (for example, appearing often on Mesopotamian coinage), including North and South America, and has been used in Japan as a symbol of Buddhism since ancient times. To be precise, the symbol generally used by Japanese Buddhists is the *sauvastika*, which moves in a counterclockwise direction, and is called the *manji* in Japanese. The sauvastika generally stands for night, and often for magical practices. The swastika, whose arms point in a clockwise direction, is generally considered a solar symbol. It was this version (the *hakenkreuz*) that was perverted by the Nazis. It is important that readers understand that the swastika has ancient and honorable origins, and it is those that apply to this story, which takes place in the eighteenth century (ca. 1782–83). *There is no anti-Semitic or pro-Nazi meaning behind the use of the symbol in this story. Those meanings did not exist until after 1910.*

The Artwork

The author of *Blade of the Immortal* requested that we make an effort to avoid mirror imaging his artwork. Some manga are first copied in a mirror image in order to facilitate the left-to-right reading of the pages. However, Mr. Samura decided that he would rather see his pages reversed via the technique of cutting up the panels and repasting them in reverse order. While we feel that this often leads to problems in panel-to-panel continuity, we place primary importance on the wishes of the creator. Therefore, most of *Blade of the Immortal* has been produced using the "cut and paste" technique. There are, of course, some sequences where it was impossible to do this, and mirror-imaged panels or pages were used instead.

The Sound Effects & Dialogue

Since some of Mr. Samura's sound effects are integral parts of the artwork, the decision was made to leave those in their original Japanese. When it was crucial to the understanding of the panel that the sound effect be in English, however, Mr. Samura chose to redraw the panel. We hope readers will view the unretouched sound effects as essential portions of Mr. Samura's extraordinary artwork. In addition, Mr. Samura's treatment of dialogue is quite different from that featured in average samurai manga and is considered to be one of the things that has made *Blade of the Immortal* such a huge hit in Japan. Mr. Samura has mixed a variety of linguistic styles in this fantasy story, where some characters speak in the mannered style of old Japan, while others speak as if they were street-corner punks from a bad area of modern-day Tokyo. The anachronistic slang used by some of the characters in the English translation reflects the unusual mix of speech patterns from the original Japanese text.

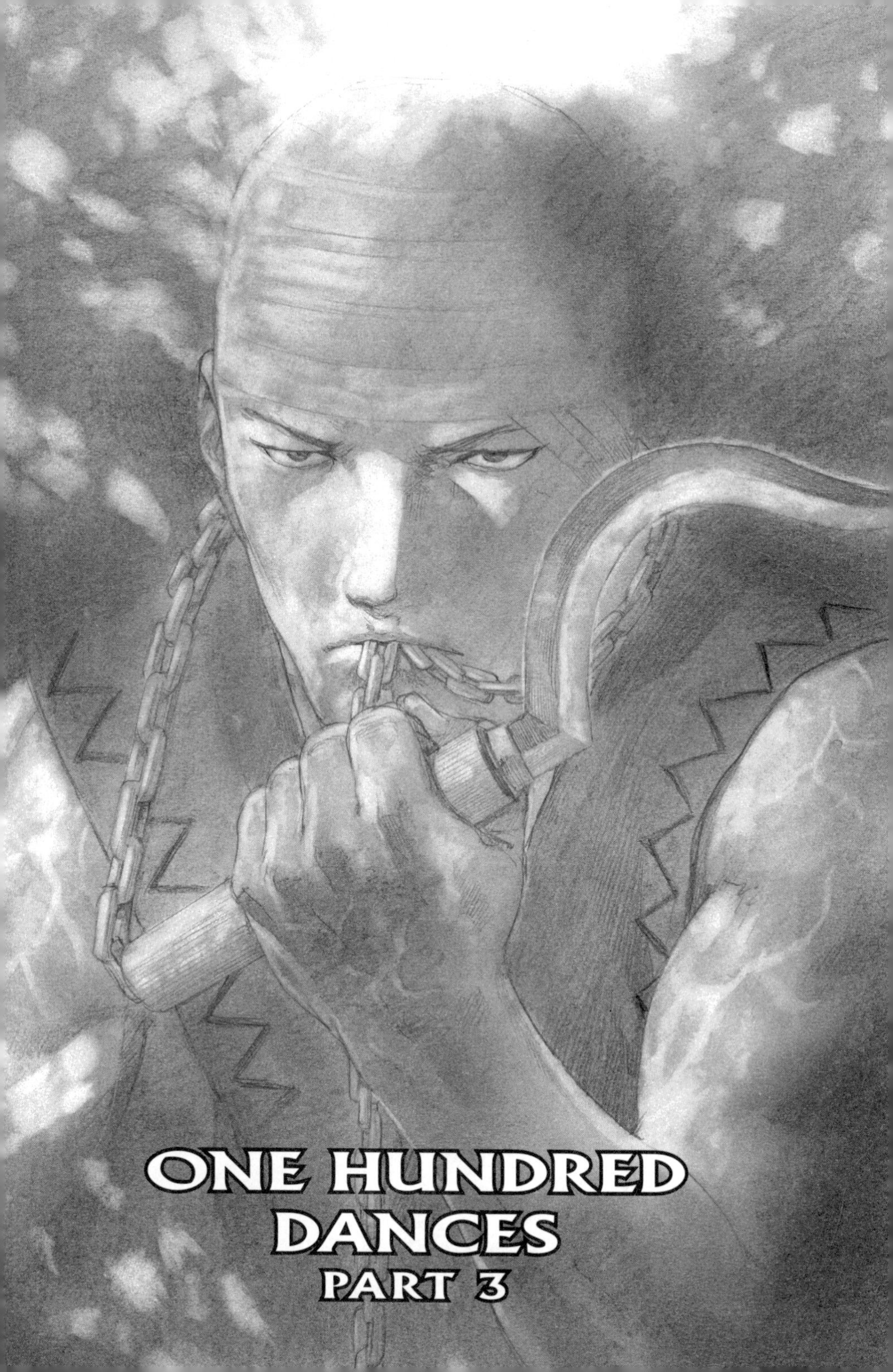
ONE HUNDRED
DANCES
PART 3

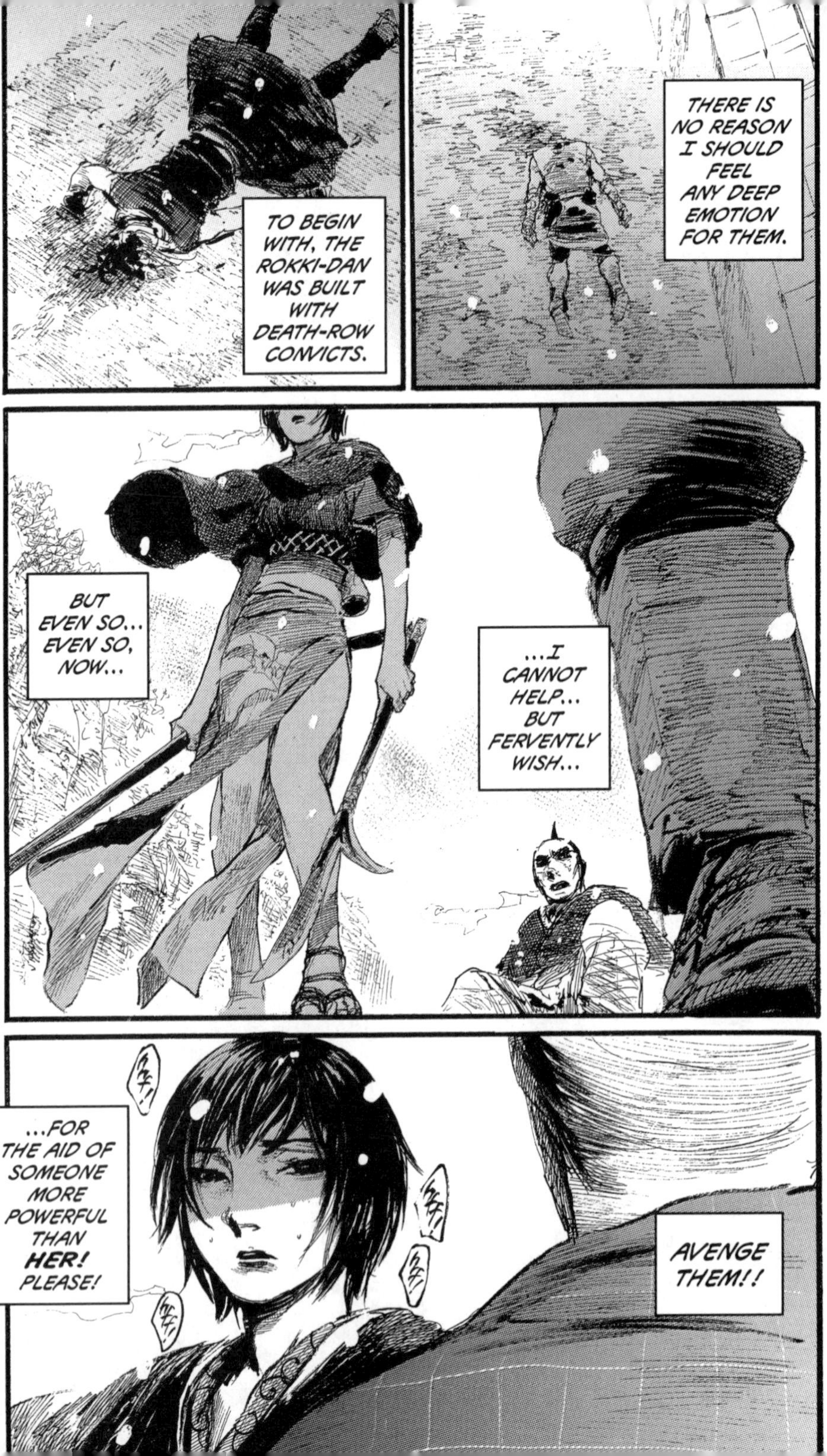
TO BEGIN WITH, THE ROKKI-DAN WAS BUILT WITH DEATH-ROW CONVICTS.
THERE IS NO REASON I SHOULD FEEL ANY DEEP EMOTION FOR THEM.
BUT EVEN SO... EVEN SO, NOW...
...I CANNOT HELP... BUT FERVENTLY WISH...
...FOR THE AID OF SOMEONE MORE POWERFUL THAN **HER!** PLEASE!
AVENGE THEM!!

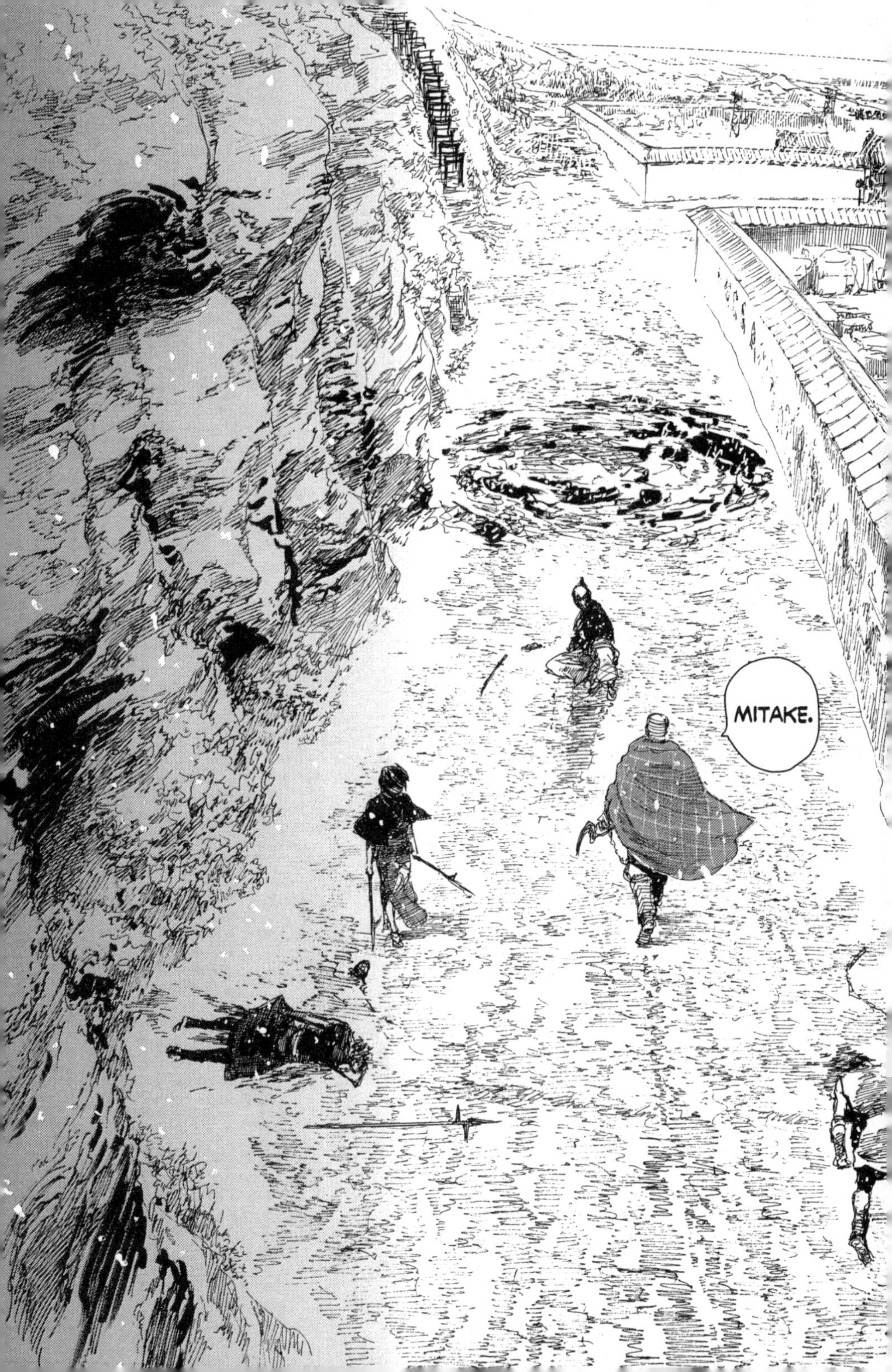
MITAKE.

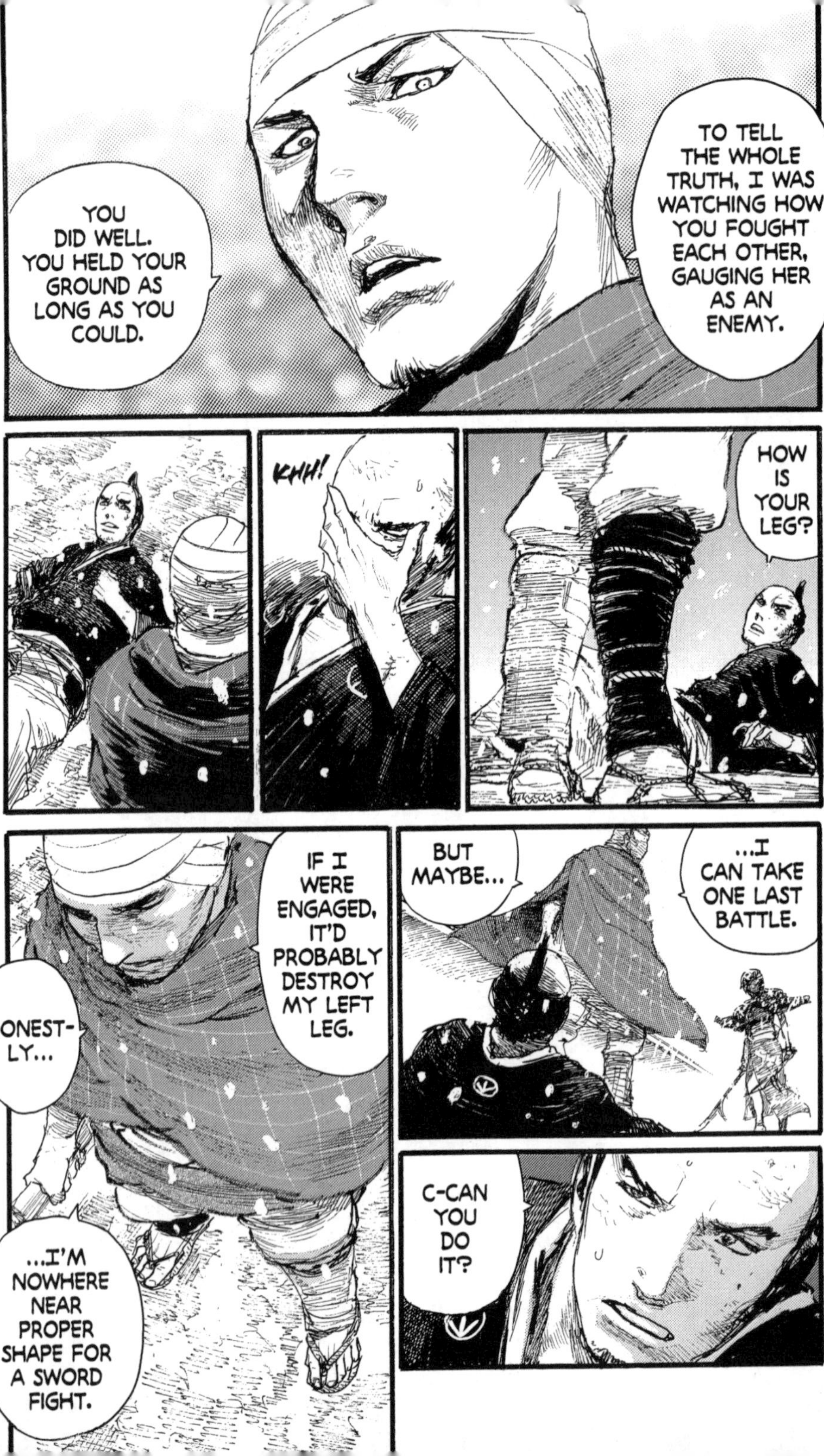
YOU DID WELL. YOU HELD YOUR GROUND AS LONG AS YOU COULD.
TO TELL THE WHOLE TRUTH, I WAS WATCHING HOW YOU FOUGHT EACH OTHER, GAUGING HER AS AN ENEMY.
KHH!
HOW IS YOUR LEG?
HONEST-LY...
...I'M NOWHERE NEAR PROPER SHAPE FOR A SWORD FIGHT.
IF I WERE ENGAGED, IT'D PROBABLY DESTROY MY LEFT LEG.
BUT MAYBE...
...I CAN TAKE ONE LAST BATTLE.
C-CAN YOU DO IT?

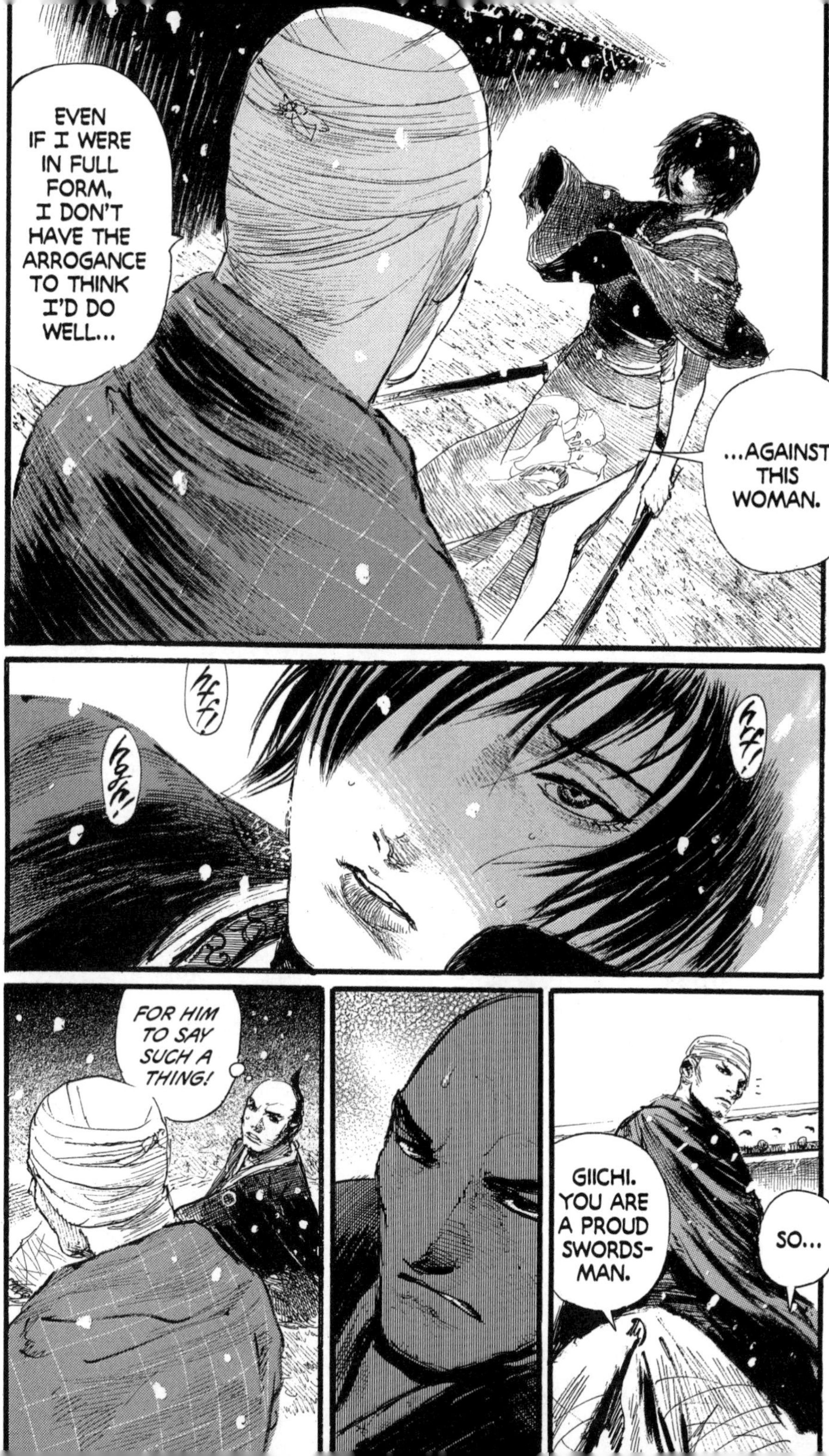
EVEN IF I WERE IN FULL FORM, I DON'T HAVE THE ARROGANCE TO THINK I'D DO WELL...
...AGAINST THIS WOMAN.
hff!
hngh!
hff!
FOR HIM TO SAY SUCH A THING!
GIICHI. YOU ARE A PROUD SWORDS-MAN.
SO...

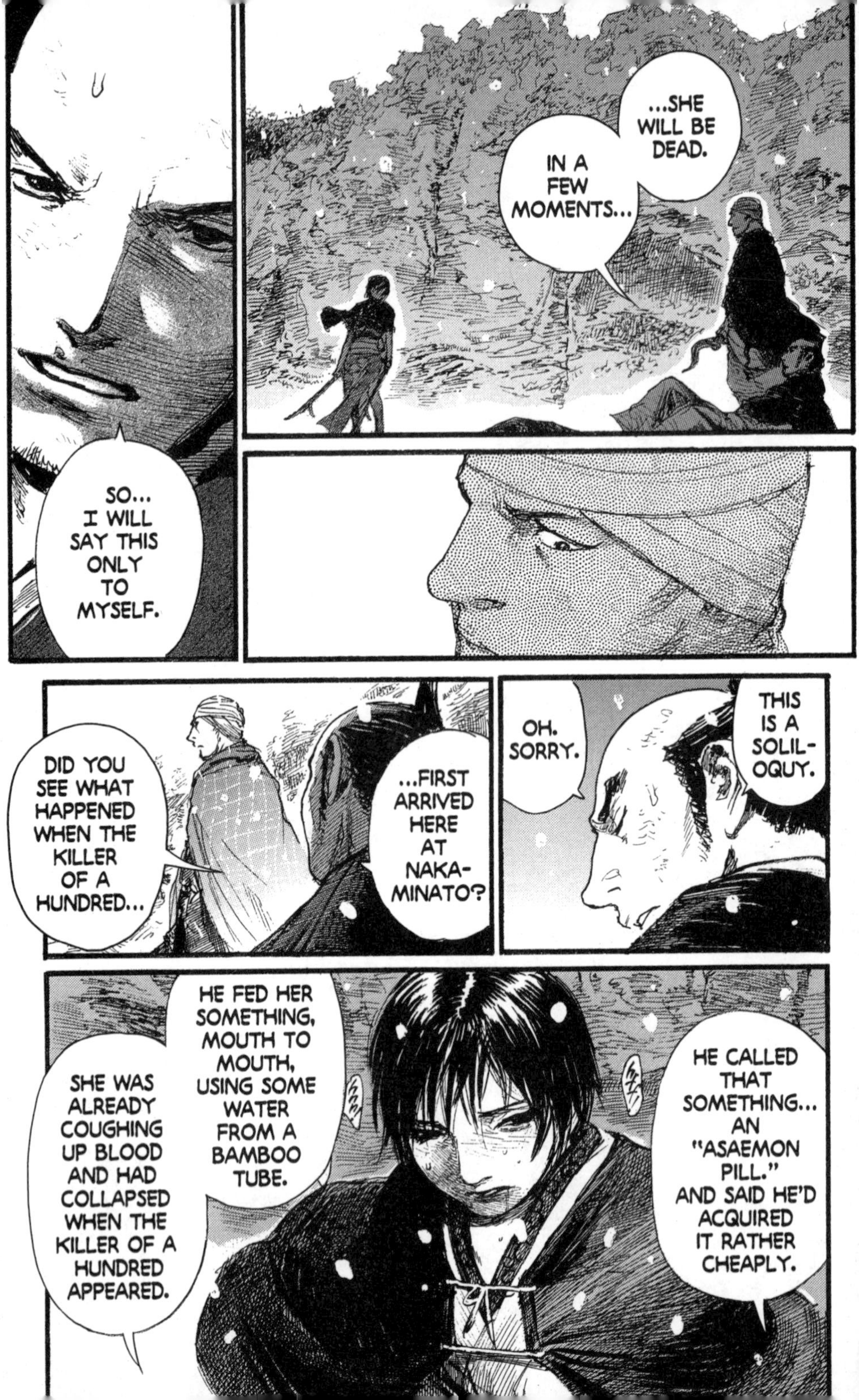
SO... I WILL SAY THIS ONLY TO MYSELF.
IN A FEW MOMENTS...
...SHE WILL BE DEAD.
DID YOU SEE WHAT HAPPENED WHEN THE KILLER OF A HUNDRED...
...FIRST ARRIVED HERE AT NAKA-MINATO?
OH. SORRY.
THIS IS A SOLIL-OQUY.
SHE WAS ALREADY COUGHING UP BLOOD AND HAD COLLAPSED WHEN THE KILLER OF A HUNDRED APPEARED.
HE FED HER SOMETHING, MOUTH TO MOUTH, USING SOME WATER FROM A BAMBOO TUBE.
HE CALLED THAT SOMETHING... AN "ASAEMON PILL." AND SAID HE'D ACQUIRED IT RATHER CHEAPLY.

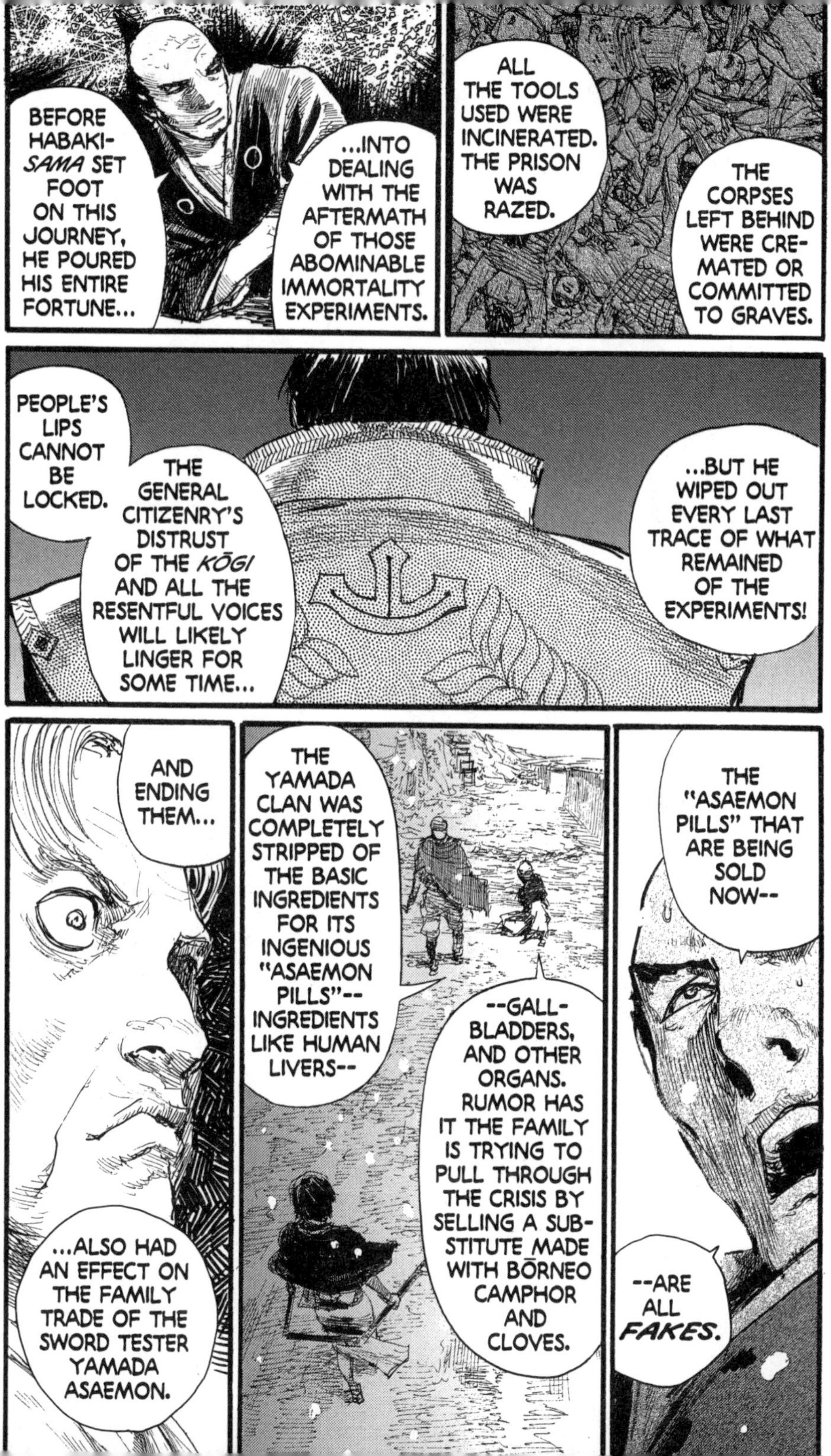
BEFORE HABAKI-*SAMA* SET FOOT ON THIS JOURNEY, HE POURED HIS ENTIRE FORTUNE...
...INTO DEALING WITH THE AFTERMATH OF THOSE ABOMINABLE IMMORTALITY EXPERIMENTS.
ALL THE TOOLS USED WERE INCINERATED. THE PRISON WAS RAZED.
THE CORPSES LEFT BEHIND WERE CRE-MATED OR COMMITTED TO GRAVES.
PEOPLE'S LIPS CANNOT BE LOCKED.
THE GENERAL CITIZENRY'S DISTRUST OF THE *KŌGI* AND ALL THE RESENTFUL VOICES WILL LIKELY LINGER FOR SOME TIME...
...BUT HE WIPED OUT EVERY LAST TRACE OF WHAT REMAINED OF THE EXPERIMENTS!
AND ENDING THEM...
...ALSO HAD AN EFFECT ON THE FAMILY TRADE OF THE SWORD TESTER YAMADA ASAEMON.
THE YAMADA CLAN WAS COMPLETELY STRIPPED OF THE BASIC INGREDIENTS FOR ITS INGENIOUS "ASAEMON PILLS"--INGREDIENTS LIKE HUMAN LIVERS--
--GALL-BLADDERS, AND OTHER ORGANS. RUMOR HAS IT THE FAMILY IS TRYING TO PULL THROUGH THE CRISIS BY SELLING A SUB-STITUTE MADE WITH BŌRNEO CAMPHOR AND CLOVES.
THE "ASAEMON PILLS" THAT ARE BEING SOLD NOW--
--ARE ALL ***FAKES***.

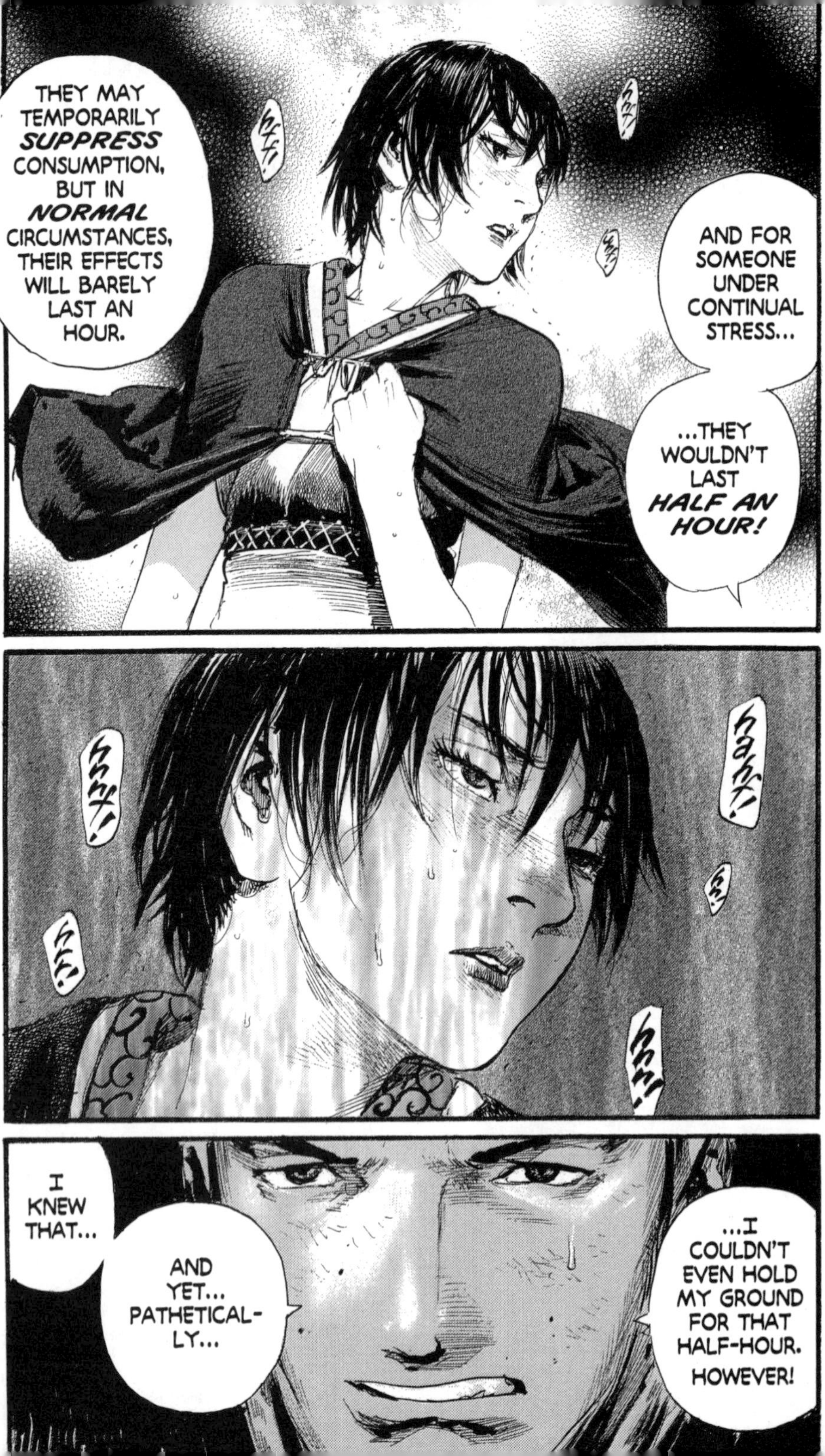
THEY MAY TEMPORARILY ***SUPPRESS*** CONSUMPTION, BUT IN ***NORMAL*** CIRCUMSTANCES, THEIR EFFECTS WILL BARELY LAST AN HOUR.
AND FOR SOMEONE UNDER CONTINUAL STRESS...
...THEY WOULDN'T LAST ***HALF AN HOUR!***
hnnf!
hahhf!
hnn!
I KNEW THAT...
AND YET... PATHETICAL-LY...
...I COULDN'T EVEN HOLD MY GROUND FOR THAT HALF-HOUR.
HOWEVER!

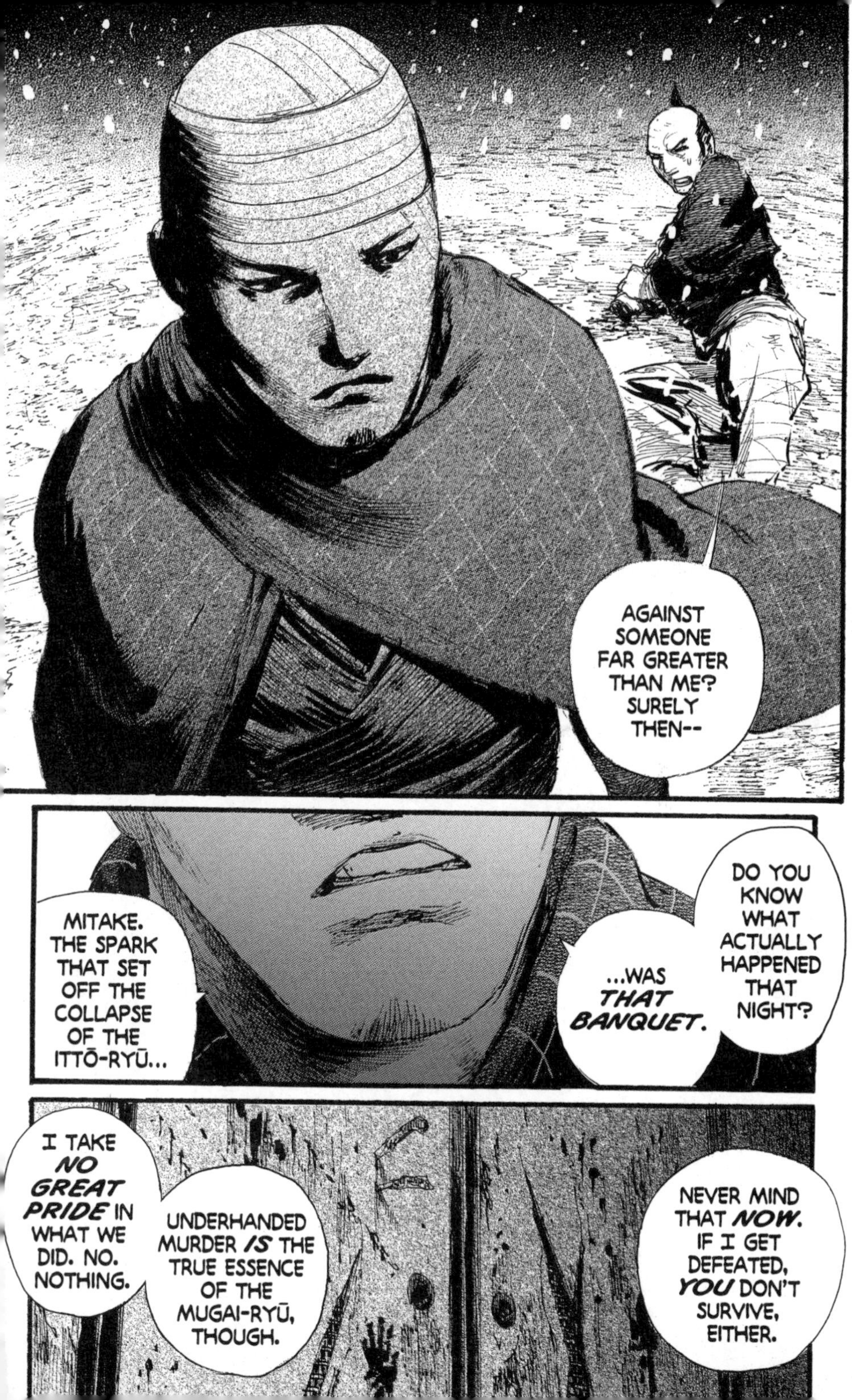
AGAINST SOMEONE FAR GREATER THAN ME? SURELY THEN--
MITAKE. THE SPARK THAT SET OFF THE COLLAPSE OF THE ITTŌ-RYŪ...
...WAS *THAT BANQUET*.
DO YOU KNOW WHAT ACTUALLY HAPPENED THAT NIGHT?
I TAKE *NO GREAT PRIDE* IN WHAT WE DID. NO. NOTHING.
UNDERHANDED MURDER *IS* THE TRUE ESSENCE OF THE MUGAI-RYŪ, THOUGH.
NEVER MIND THAT *NOW*. IF I GET DEFEATED, *YOU* DON'T SURVIVE, EITHER.

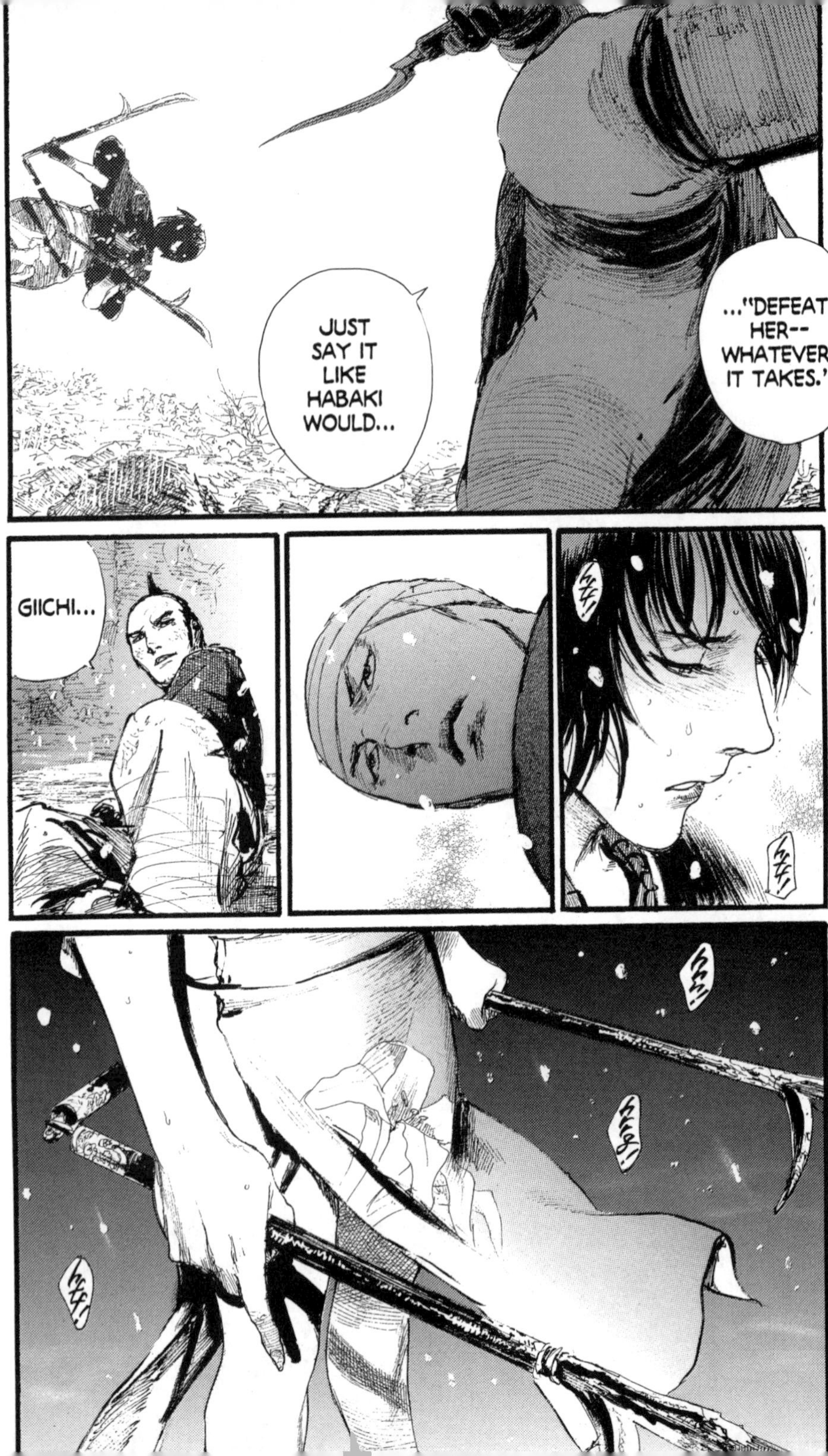
JUST SAY IT LIKE HABAKI WOULD...
..."DEFEAT HER-- WHATEVER IT TAKES."
GIICHI...

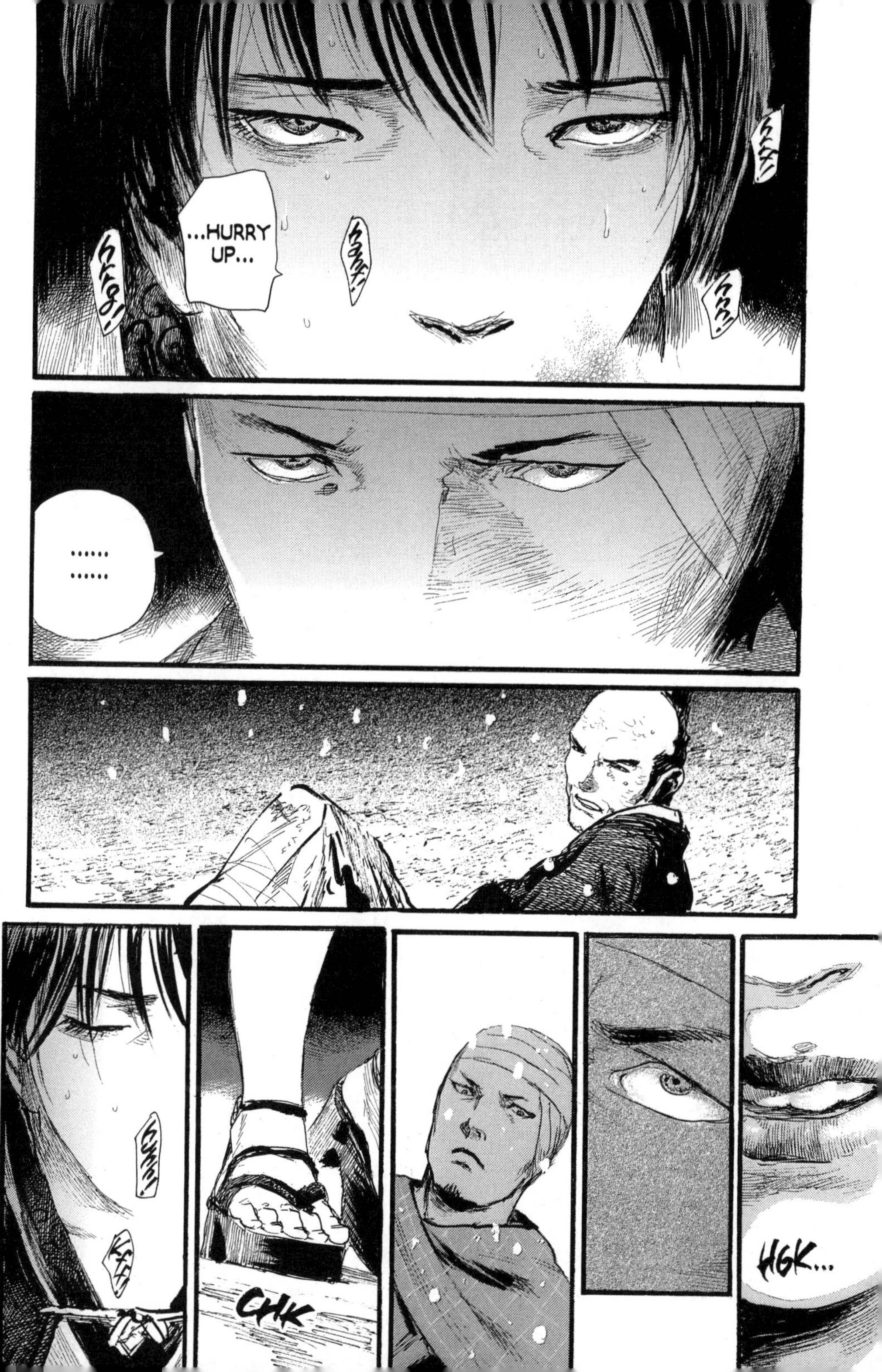
...HURRY UP...
......
......
CHK
HGK...

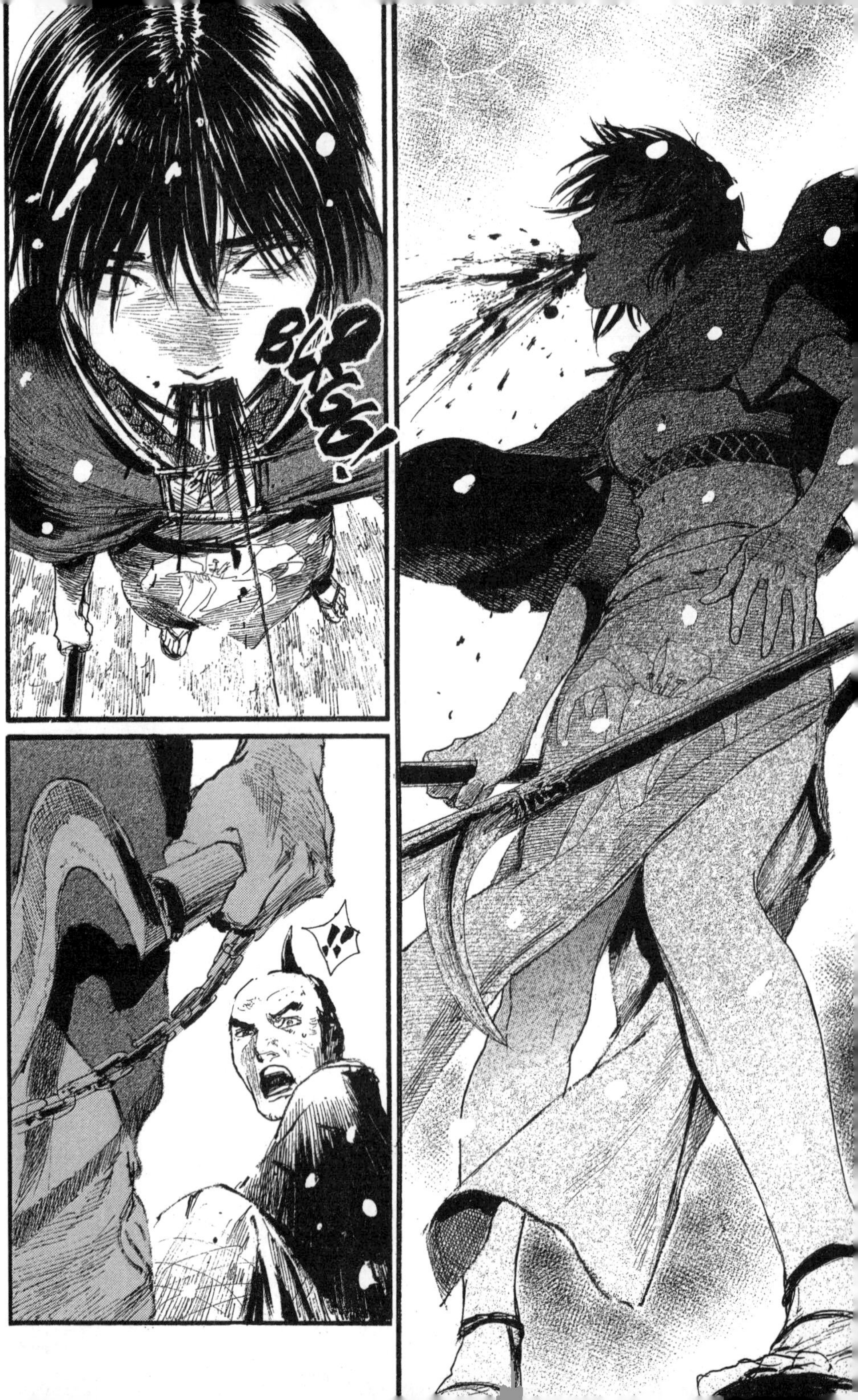
BLAGG!
!!

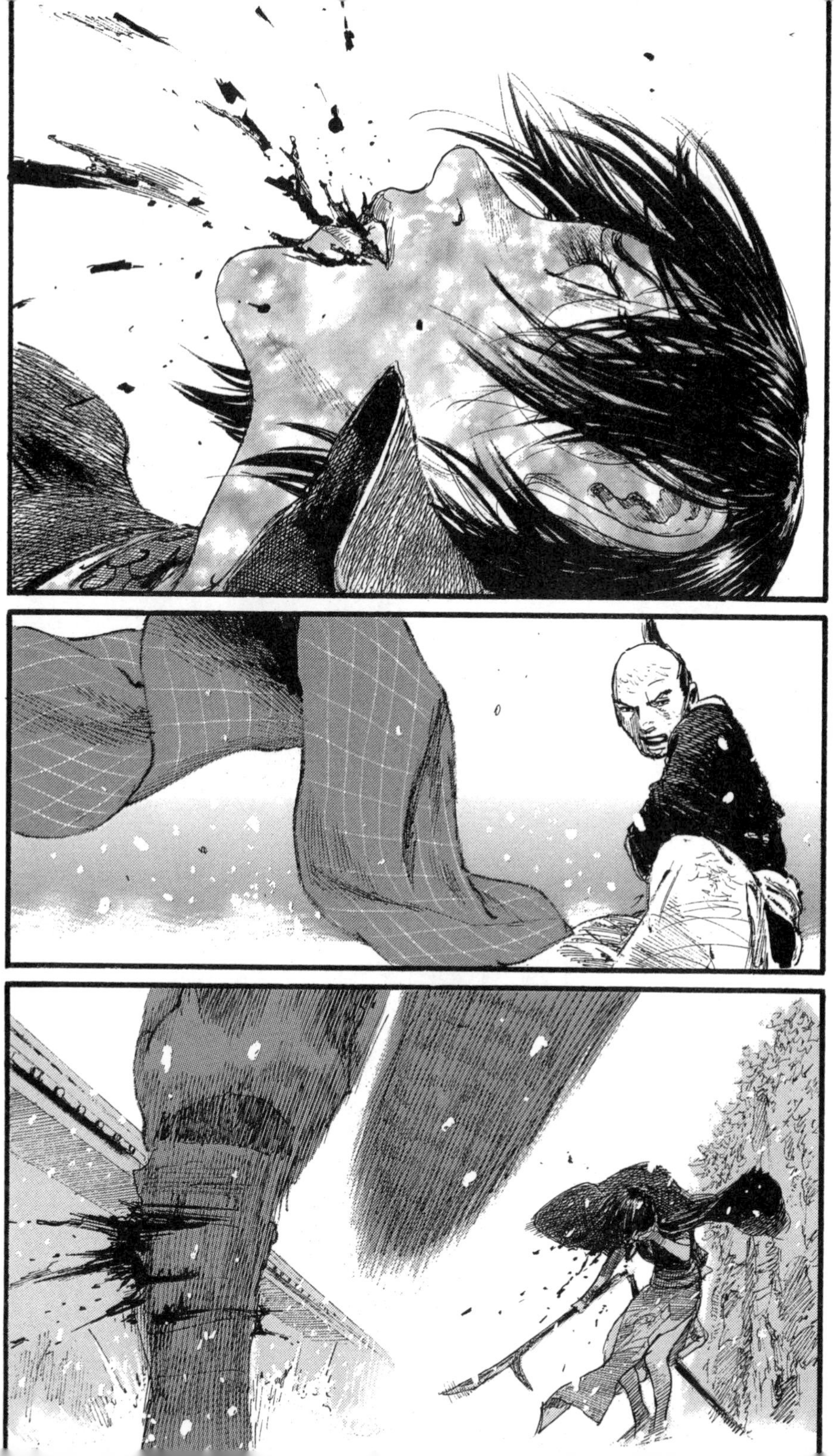

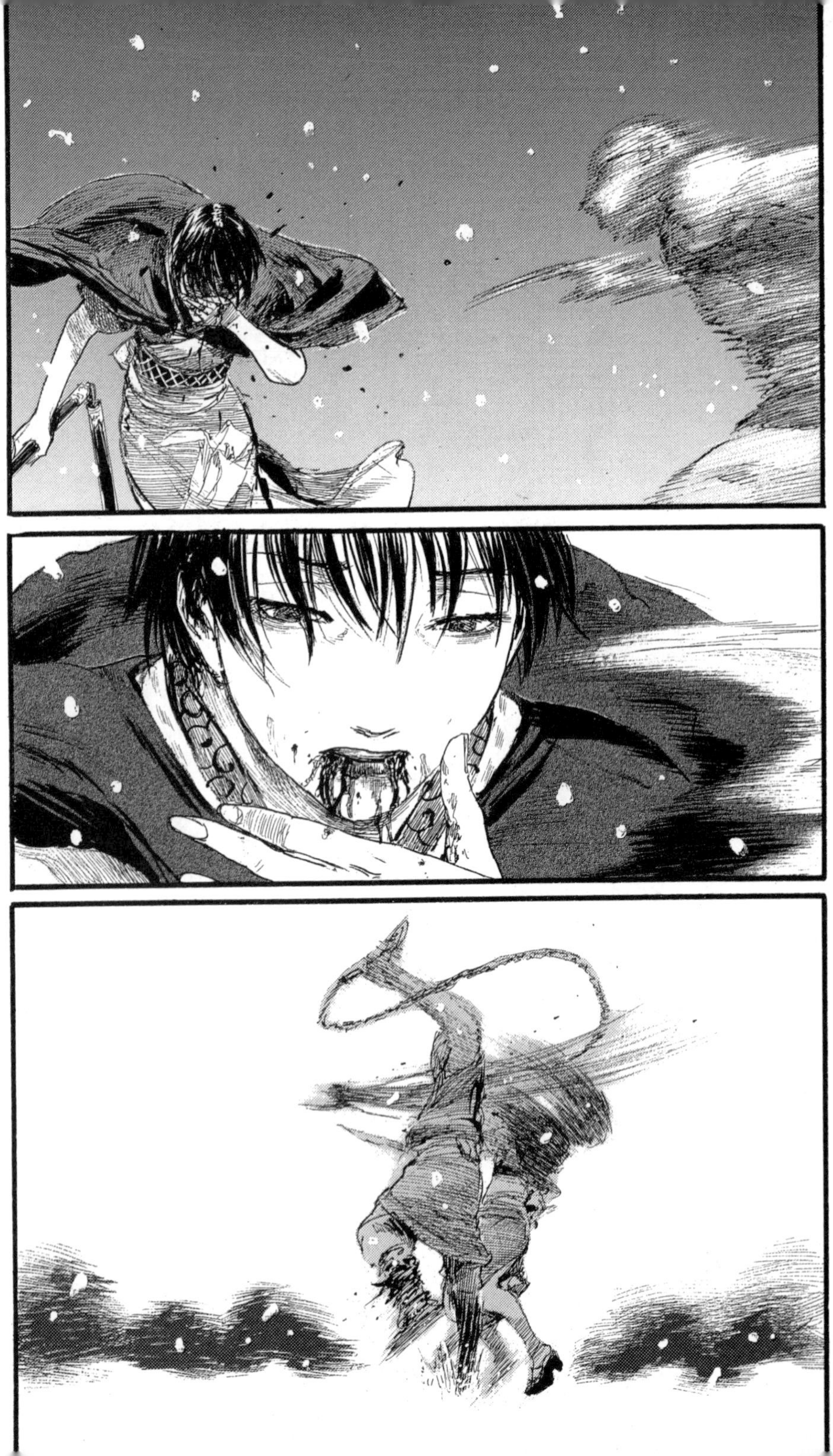

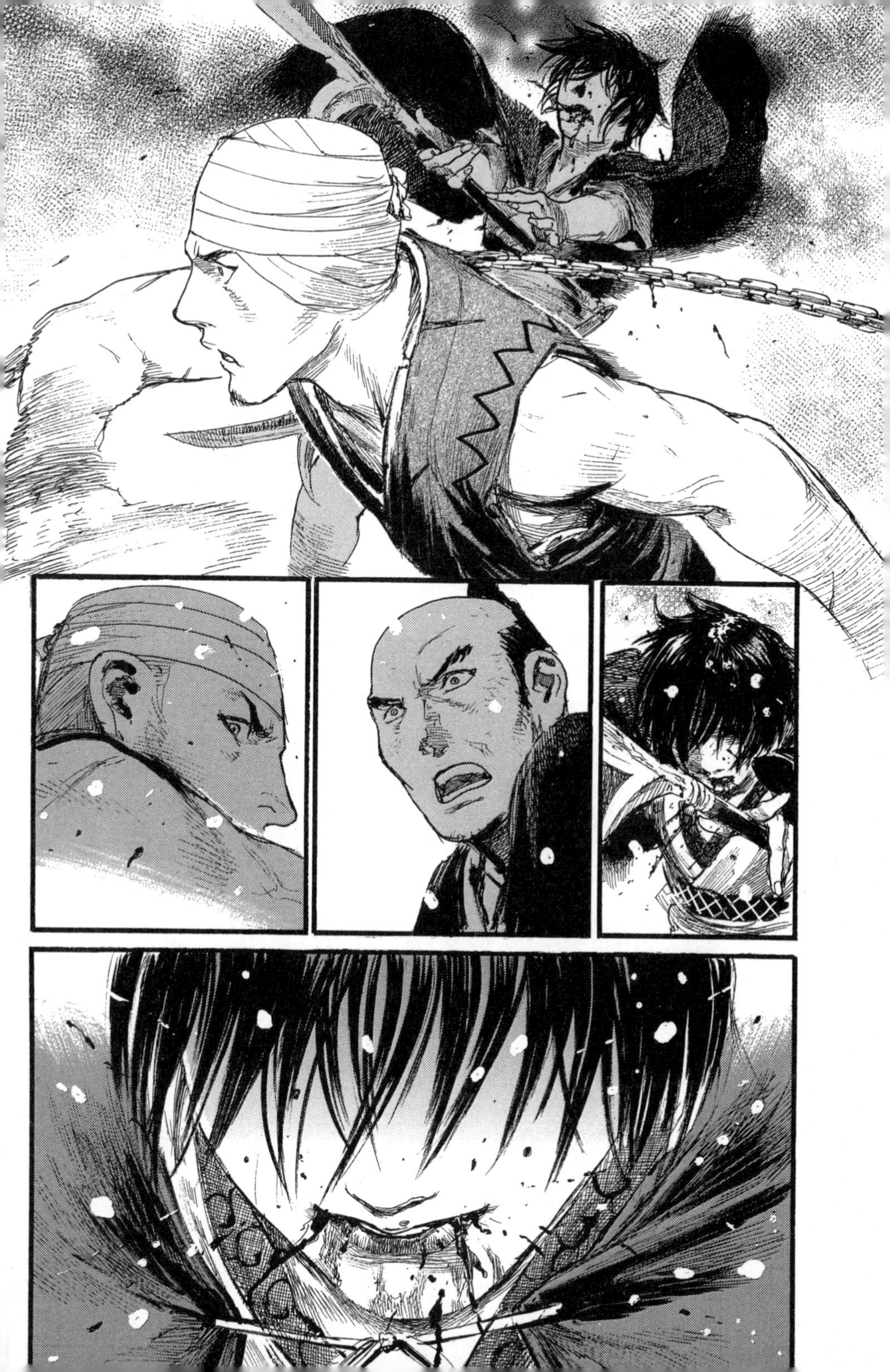

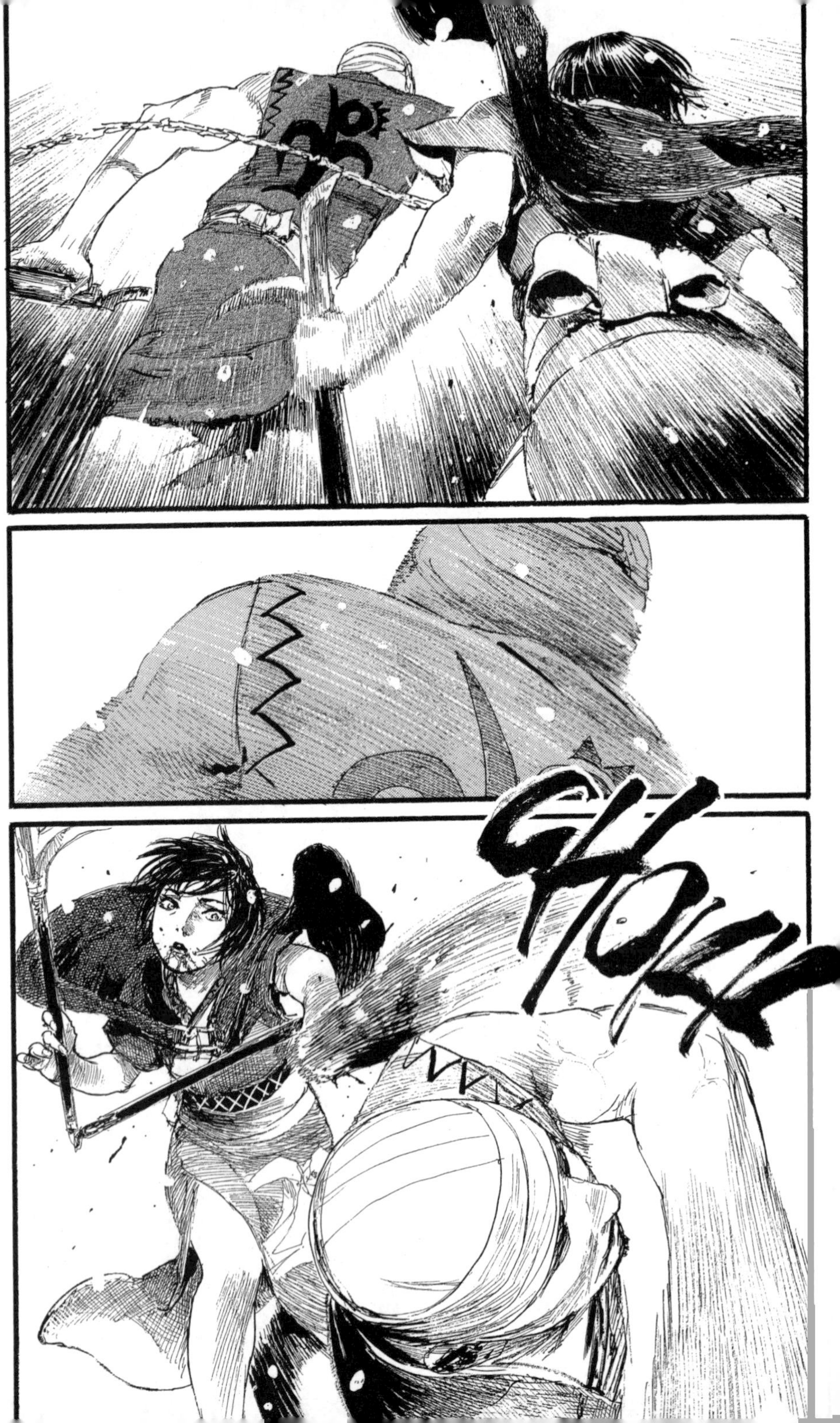
CHONK

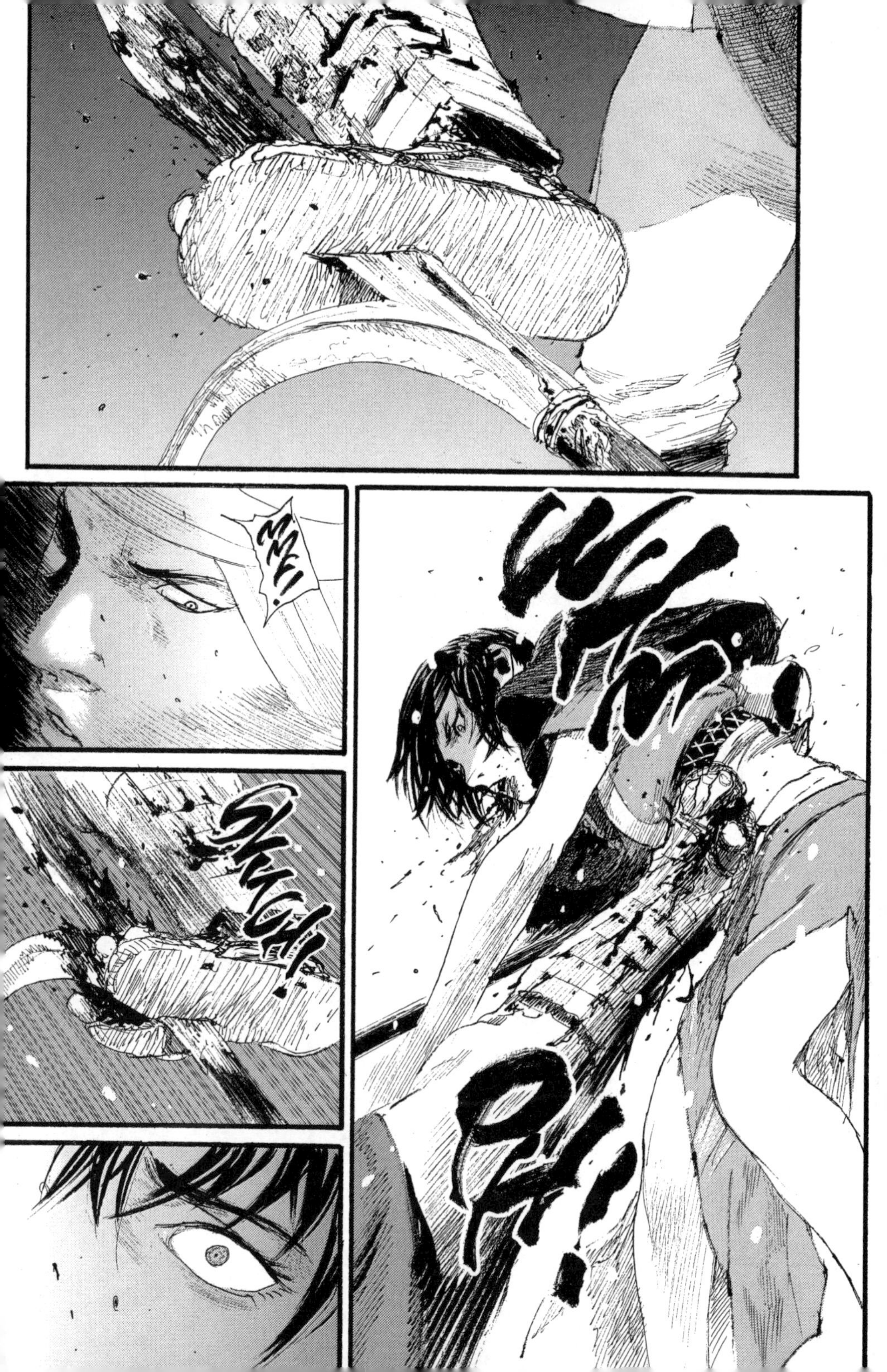
NNN!!
SHUNCH!!

THC KK!

KK!

SSSOI!

CHFCHF

KSHF HFF

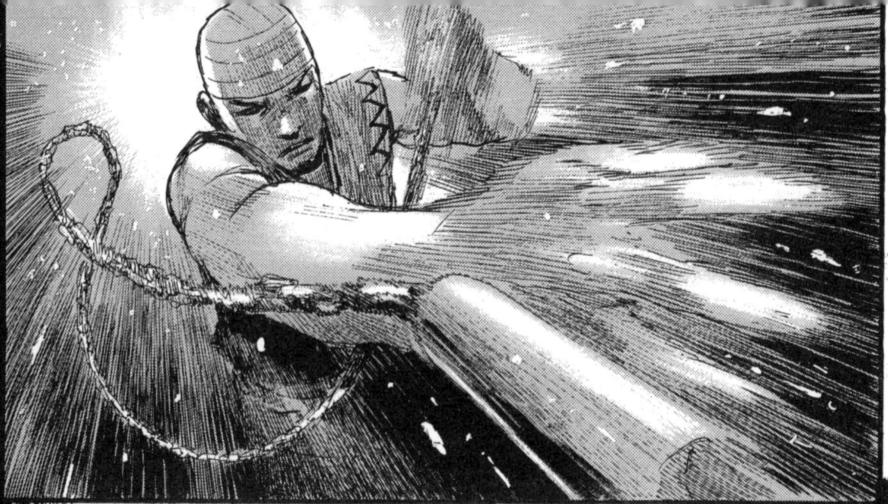
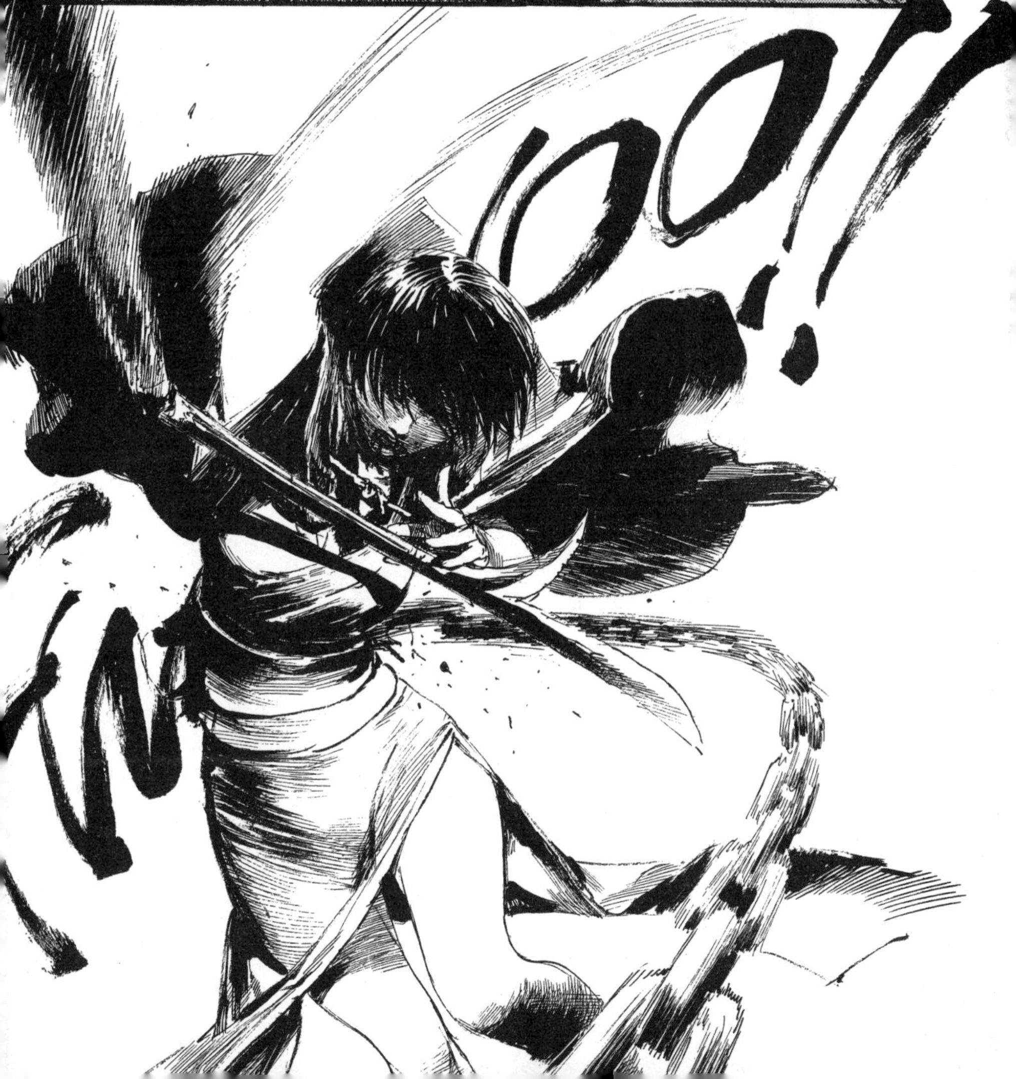

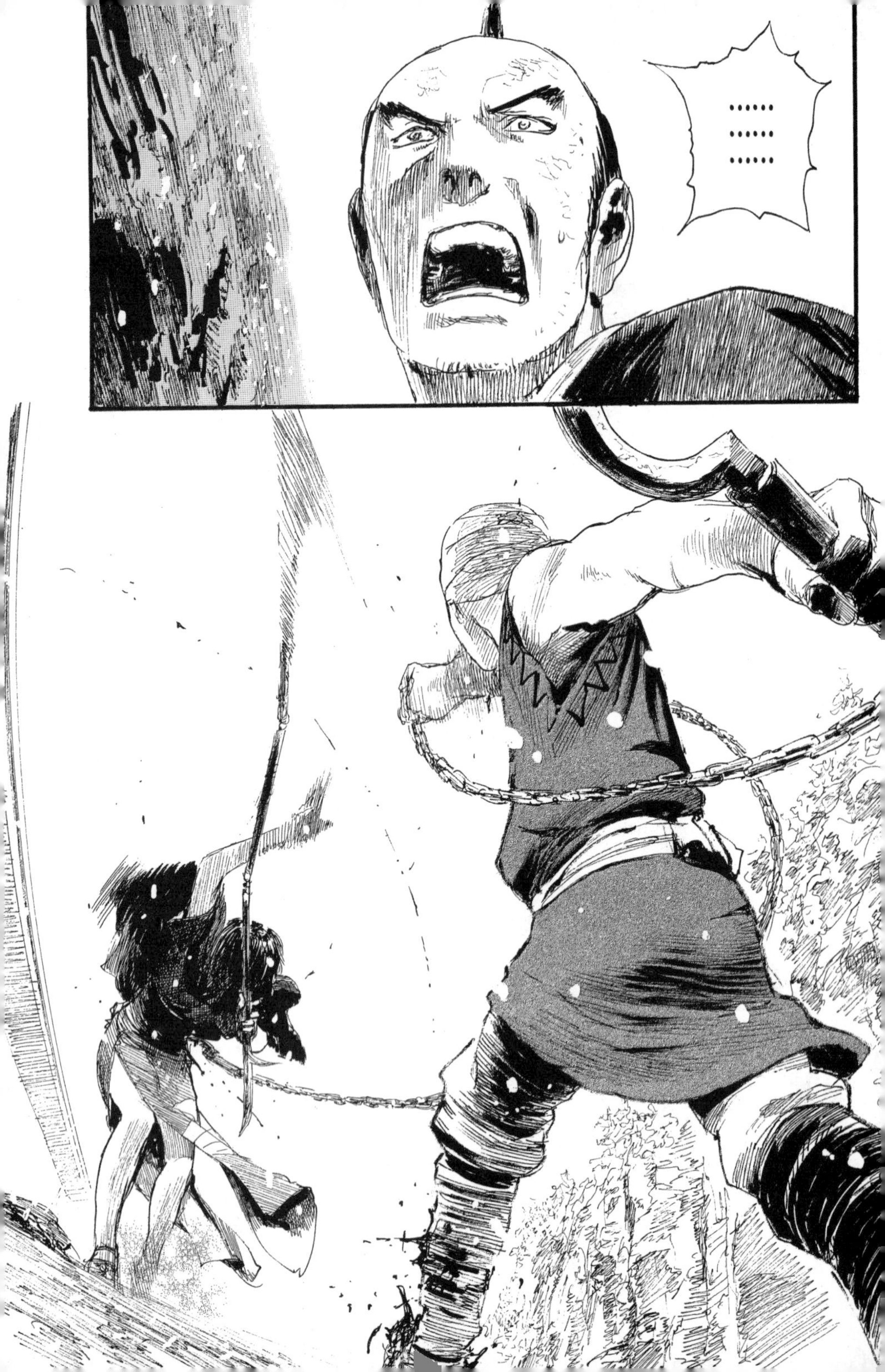
....

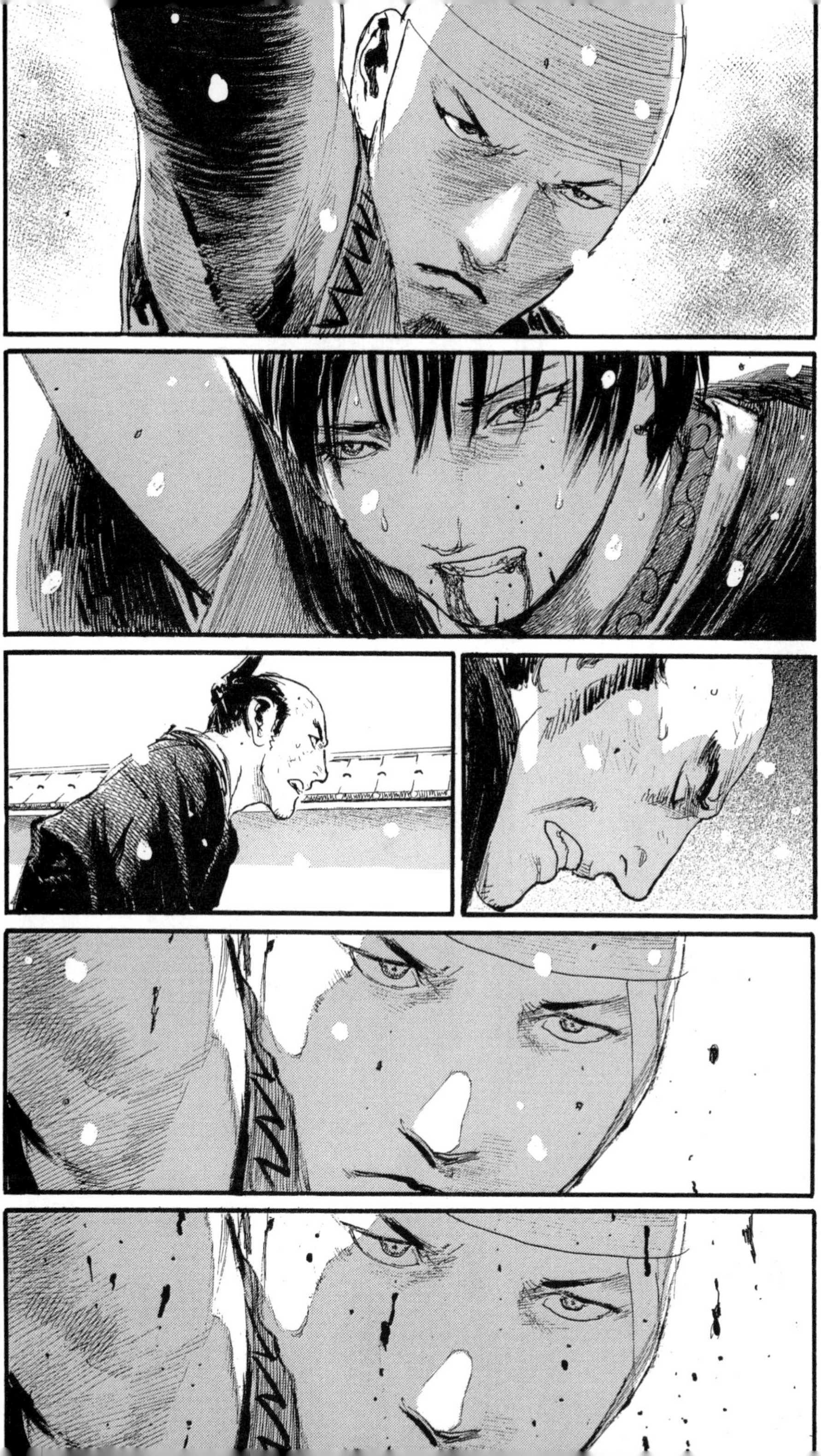

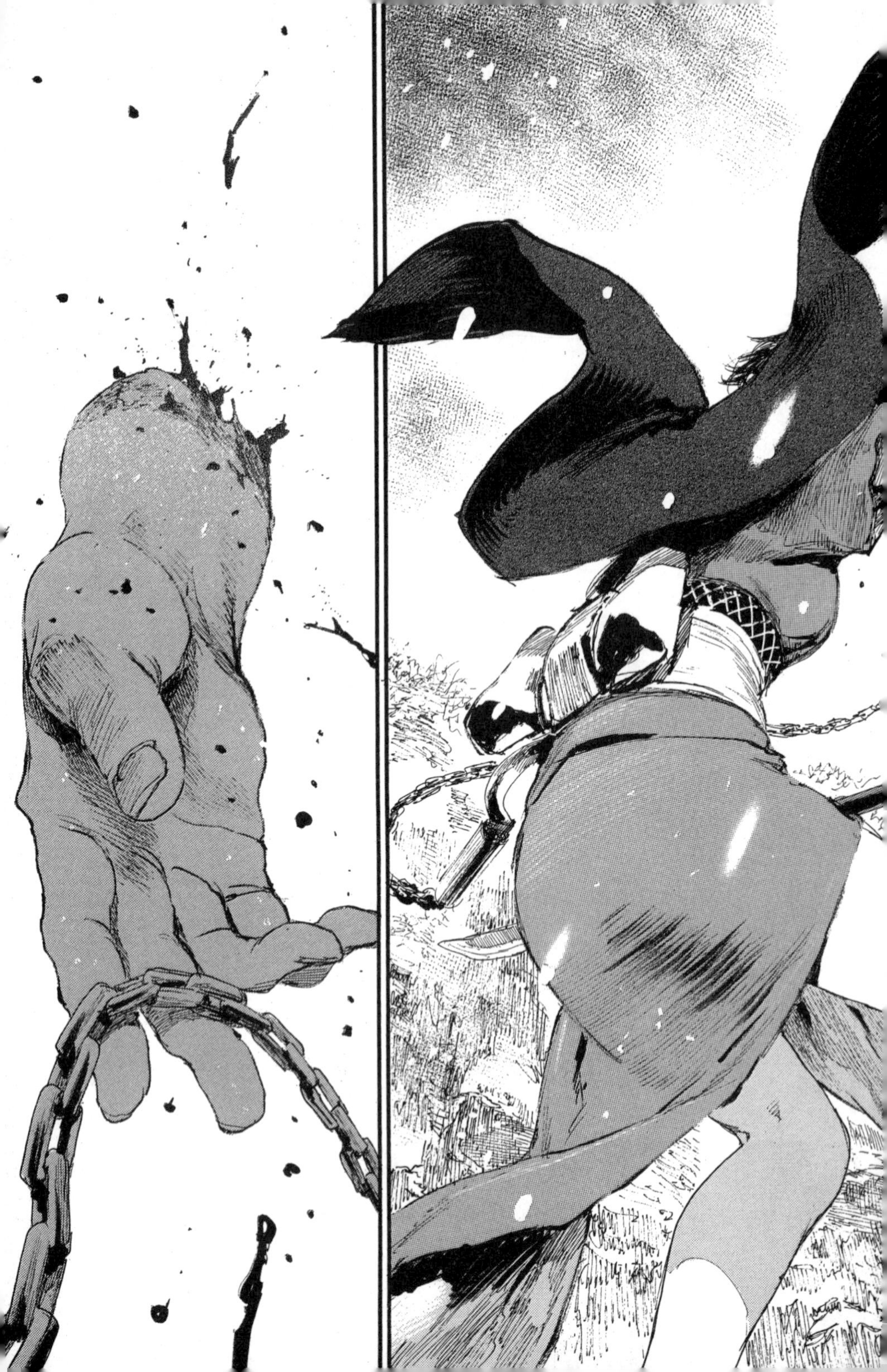

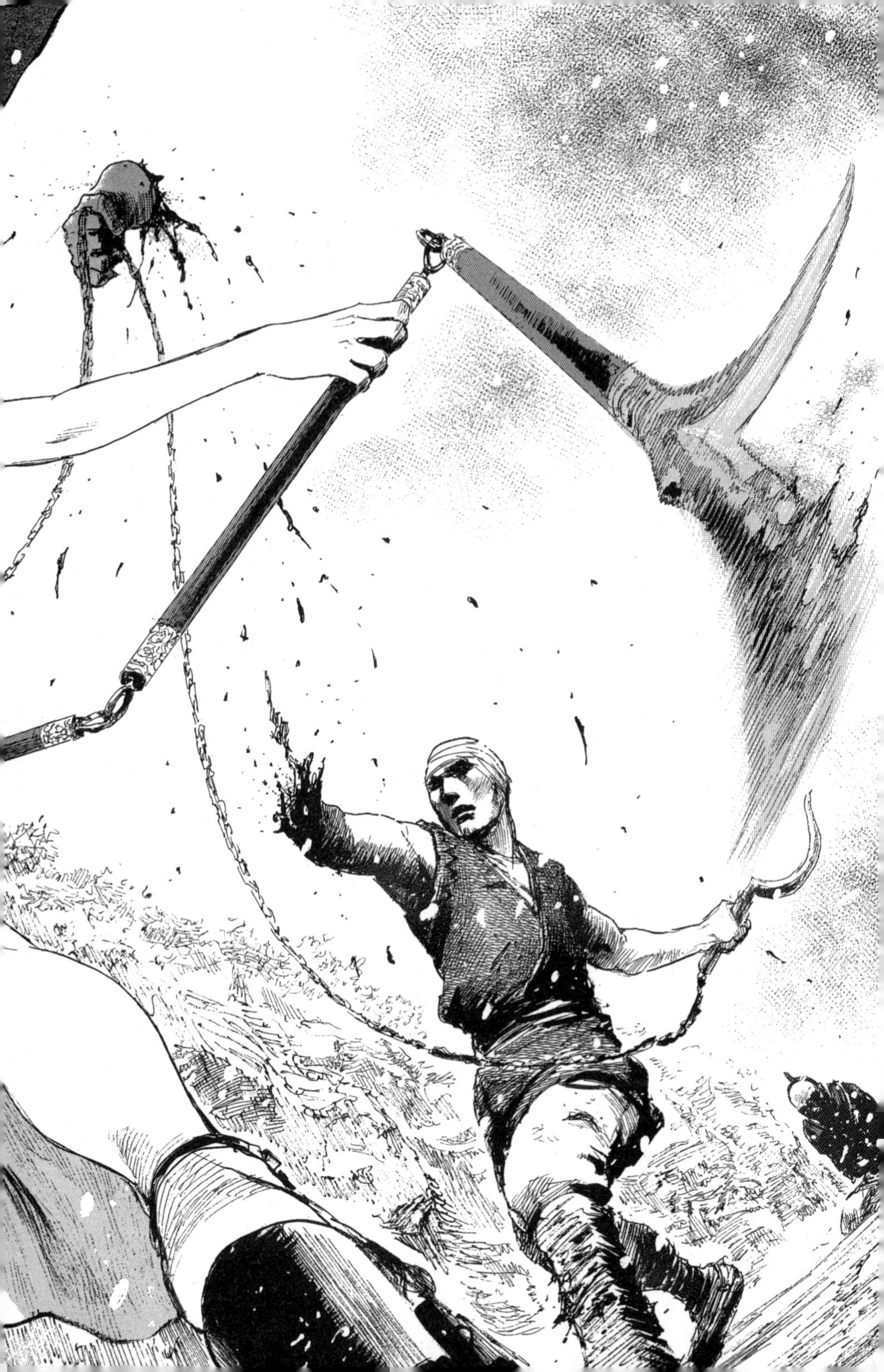

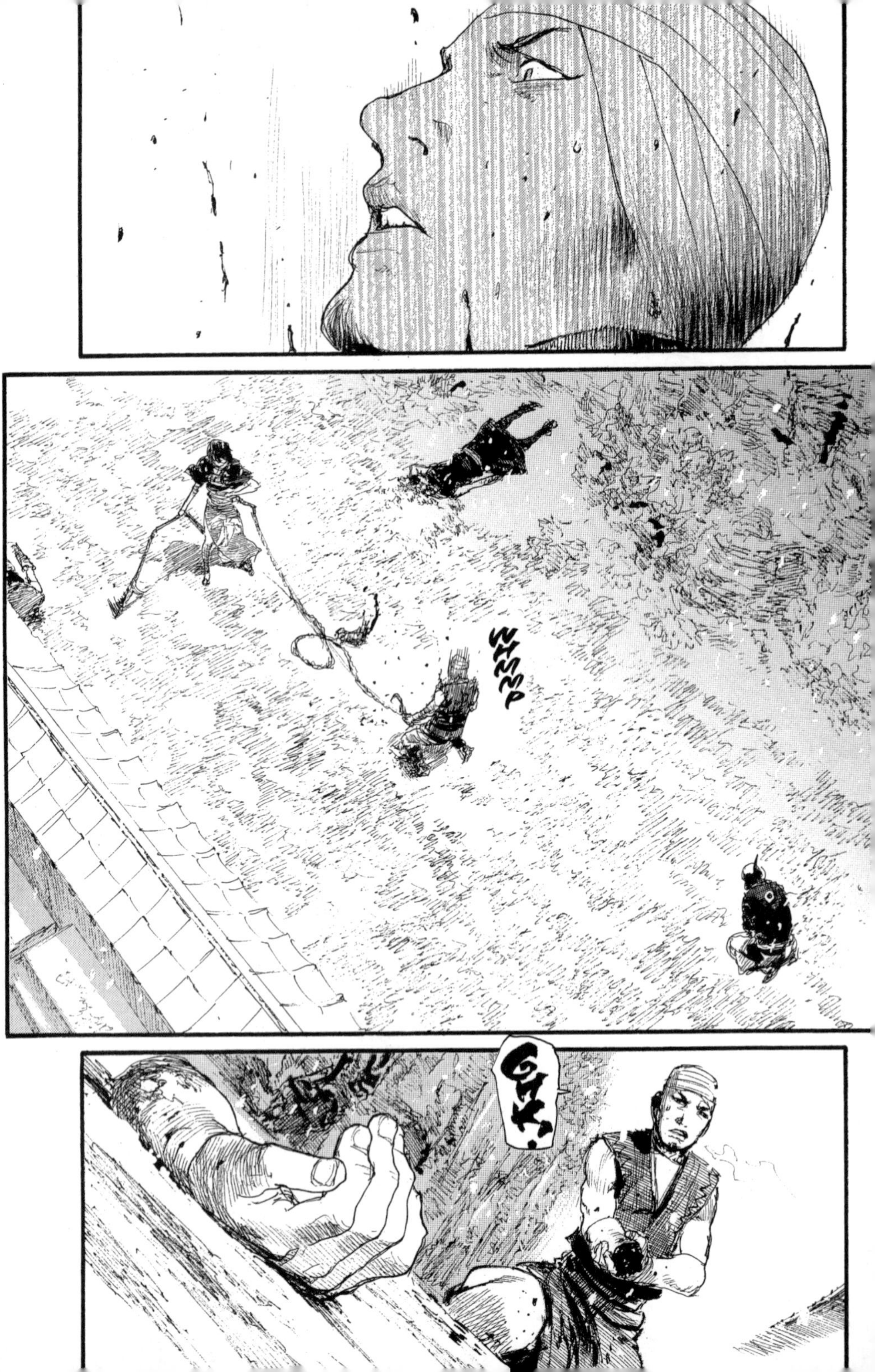
WHMMP
GNK!

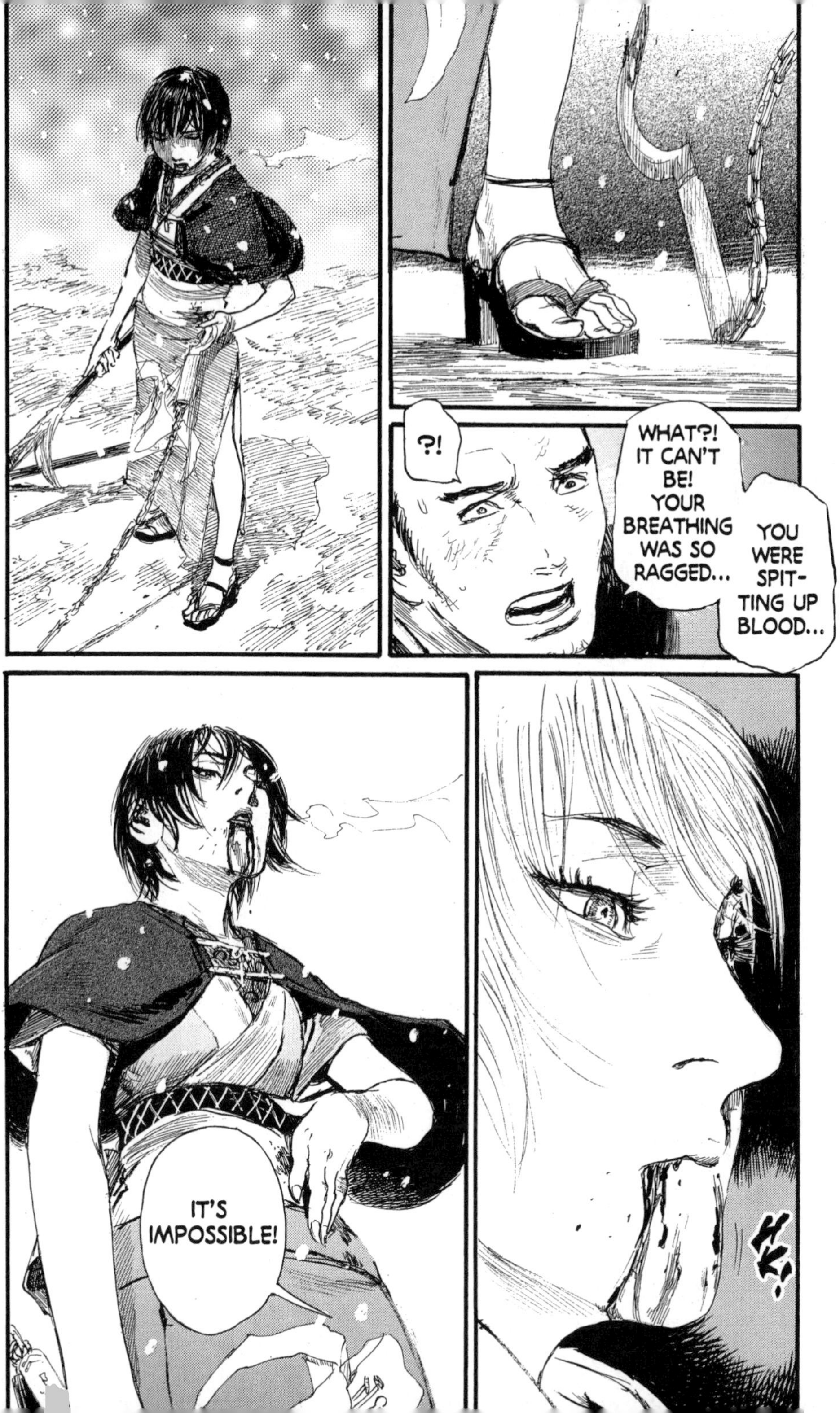
?!
WHAT?! IT CAN'T BE! YOUR BREATHING WAS SO RAGGED...
YOU WERE SPIT-TING UP BLOOD...
IT'S IMPOSSIBLE!
HK!

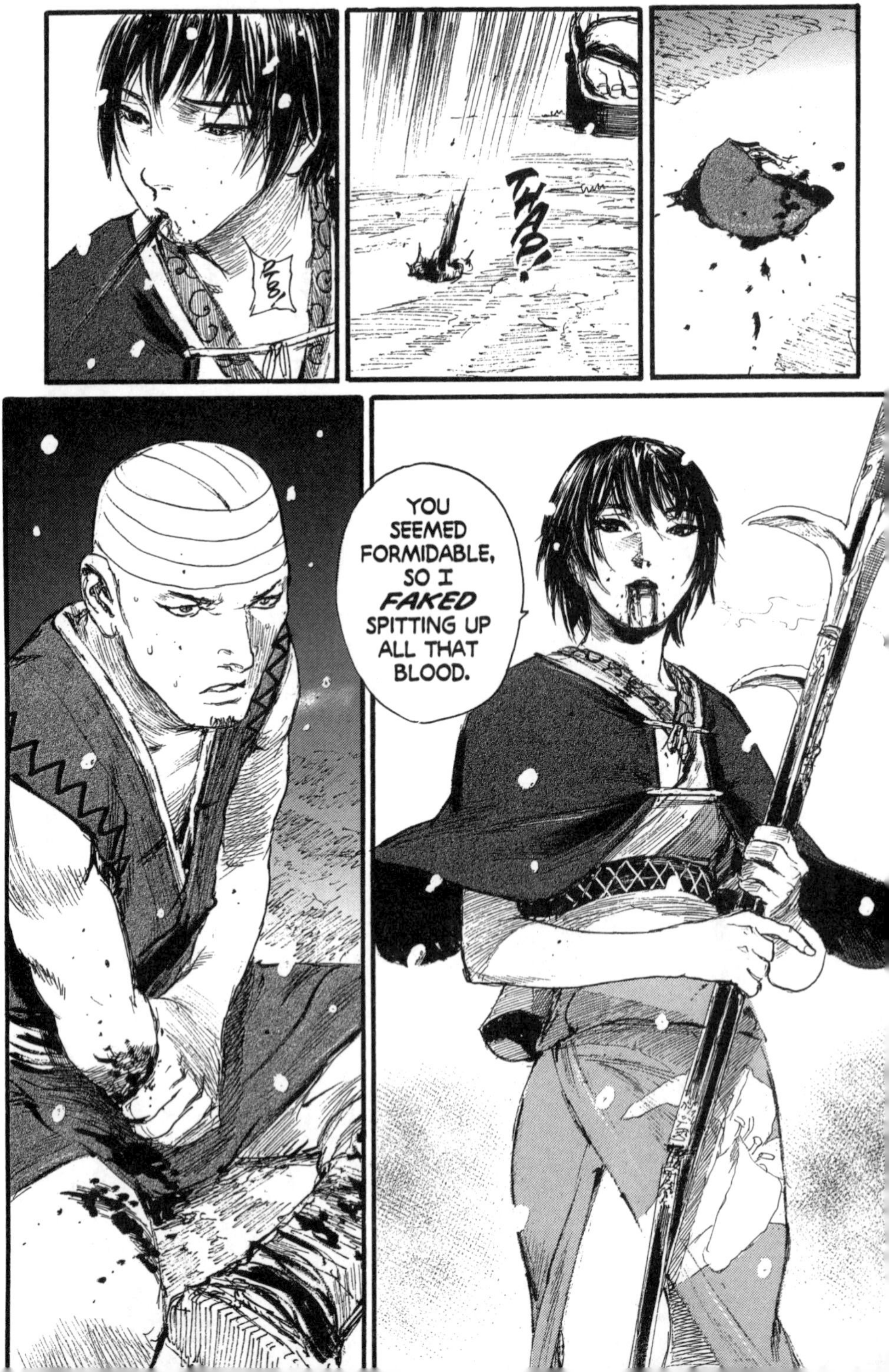
PTOO!
THAP!
YOU SEEMED FORMIDABLE, SO I *FAKED* SPITTING UP ALL THAT BLOOD.

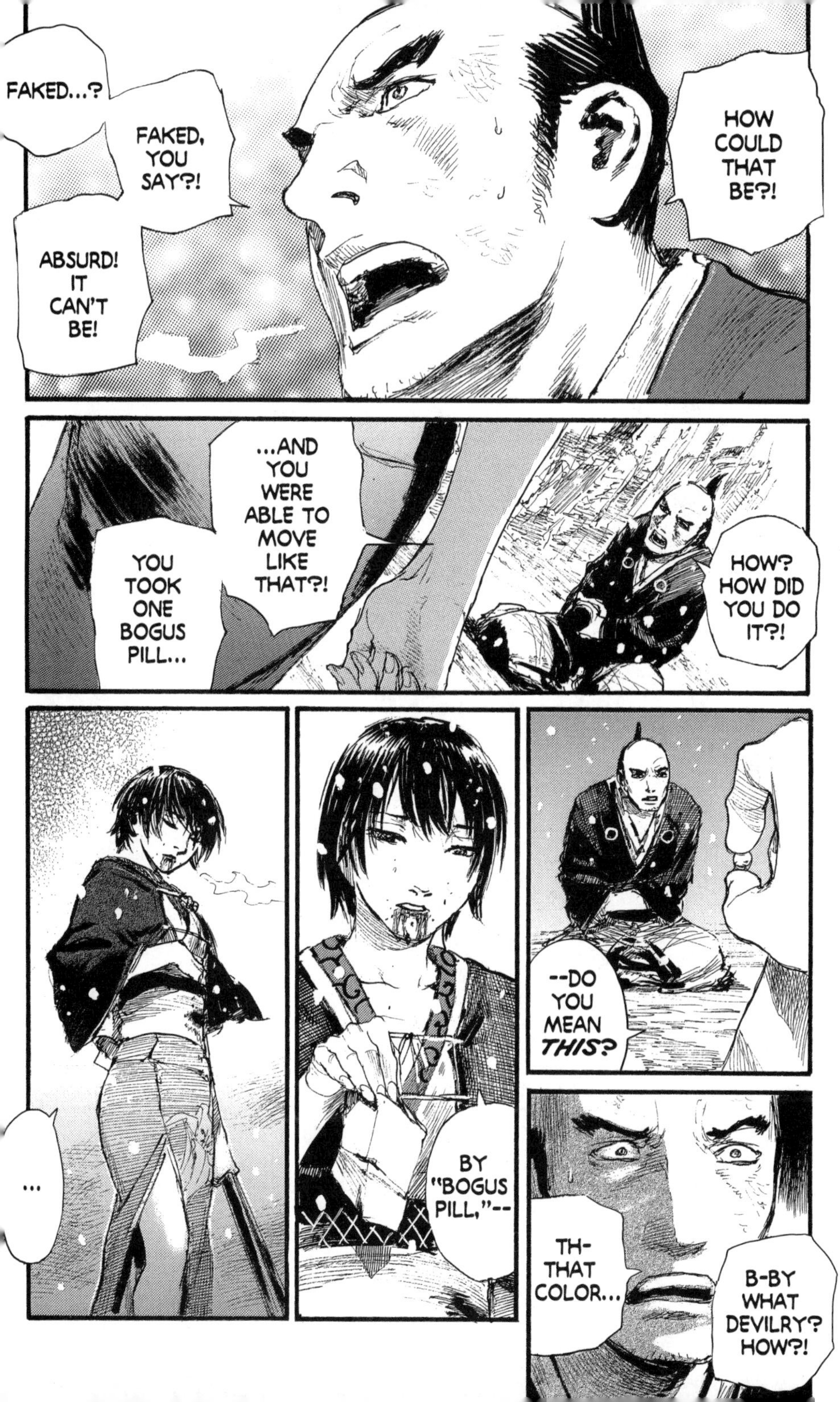
FAKED...?
FAKED, YOU SAY?!
ABSURD! IT CAN'T BE!
HOW COULD THAT BE?!
YOU TOOK ONE BOGUS PILL...
...AND YOU WERE ABLE TO MOVE LIKE THAT?!
HOW? HOW DID YOU DO IT?!
...
BY "BOGUS PILL,"--
--DO YOU MEAN *THIS*?
TH-THAT COLOR...
B-BY WHAT DEVILRY? HOW?!

YOU! HOW DID YOU GET A REAL ONE?! HOW COULD IT BE? TO SEE ONE NOW?!

THEY WERE ALL DESTROYED!

THIS GIFT WAS GIVEN TO ME BY ITTŌ-RYŪ *TŌSHU* ANOTSU KAGEHISA...

...AROUND THE TIME OF THE *TORI NO MACHI* FAIR.

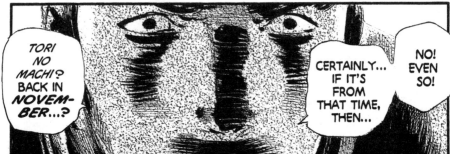

TORI NO MACHI? BACK IN *NOVEMBER*...?

CERTAINLY... IF IT'S FROM THAT TIME, THEN...

NO! EVEN SO!

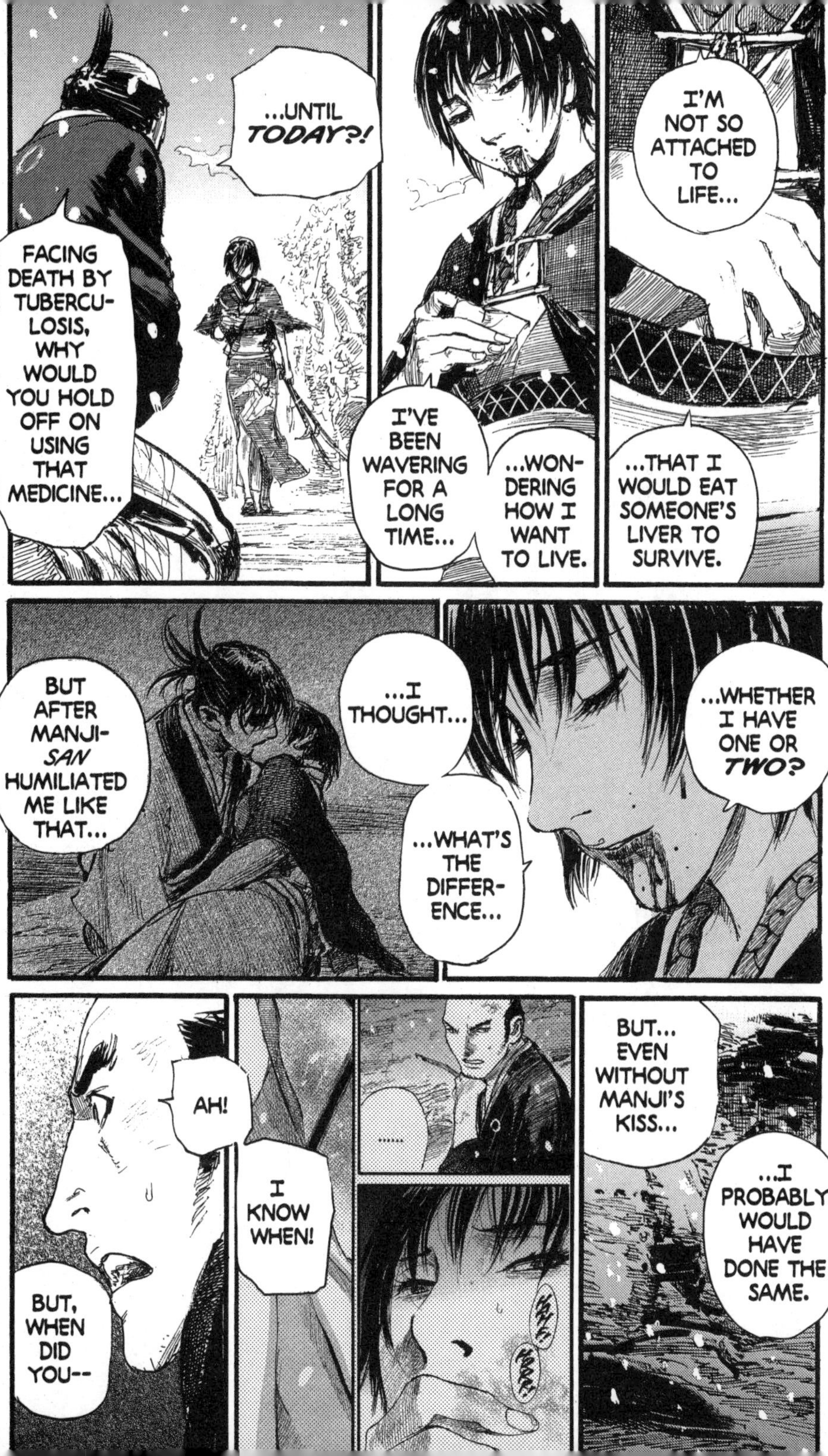
FACING DEATH BY TUBERCULOSIS, WHY WOULD YOU HOLD OFF ON USING THAT MEDICINE...
...UNTIL *TODAY?!*
I'VE BEEN WAVERING FOR A LONG TIME...
...WONDERING HOW I WANT TO LIVE.
I'M NOT SO ATTACHED TO LIFE...
...THAT I WOULD EAT SOMEONE'S LIVER TO SURVIVE.
BUT AFTER MANJI-*SAN* HUMILIATED ME LIKE THAT...
...I THOUGHT...
...WHAT'S THE DIFFERENCE...
...WHETHER I HAVE ONE OR *TWO?*
BUT, WHEN DID YOU--
AH!
I KNOW WHEN!
......
BUT... EVEN WITHOUT MANJI'S KISS...
...I PROBABLY WOULD HAVE DONE THE SAME.

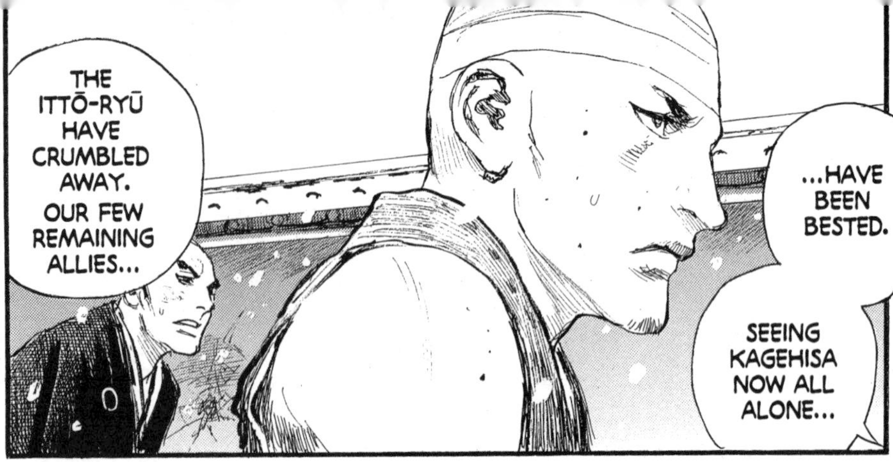
THE ITTŌ-RYŪ HAVE CRUMBLED AWAY. OUR FEW REMAINING ALLIES...
...HAVE BEEN BESTED.
SEEING KAGEHISA NOW ALL ALONE...
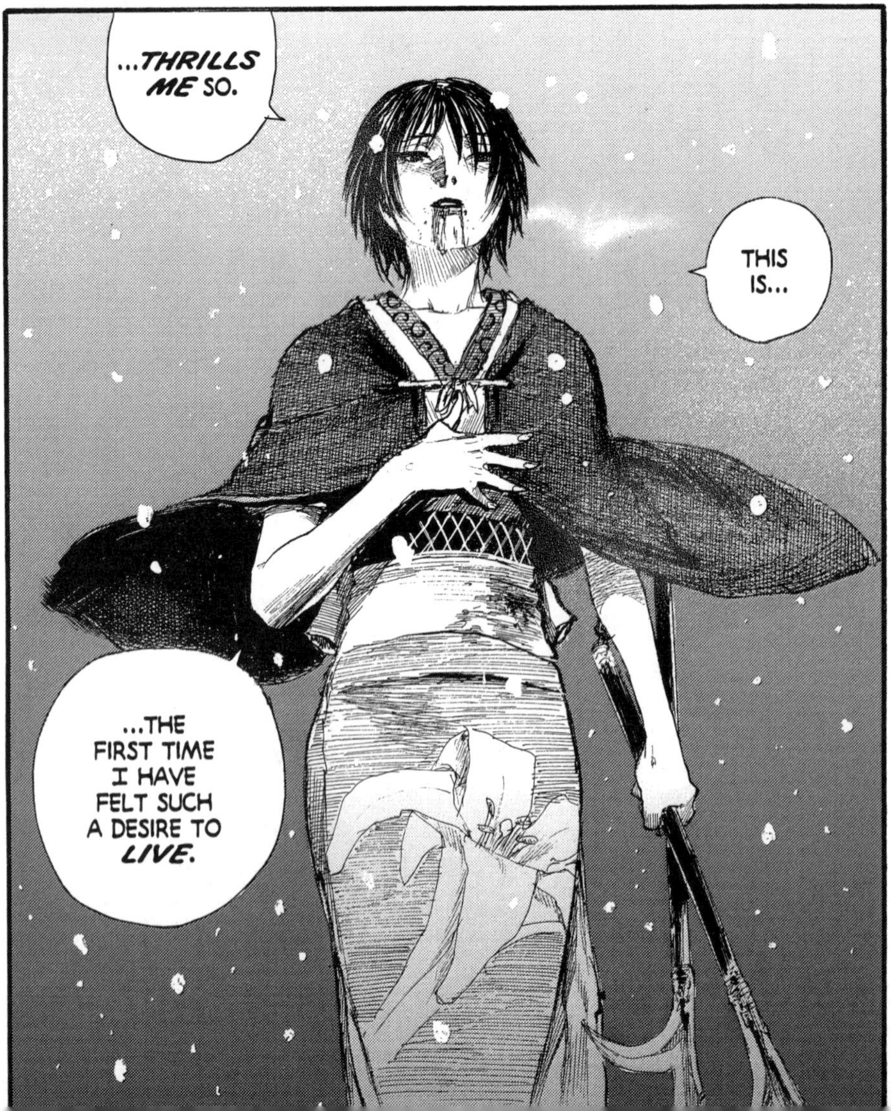
...*THRILLS ME* SO.
THIS IS...
...THE FIRST TIME I HAVE FELT SUCH A DESIRE TO *LIVE*.

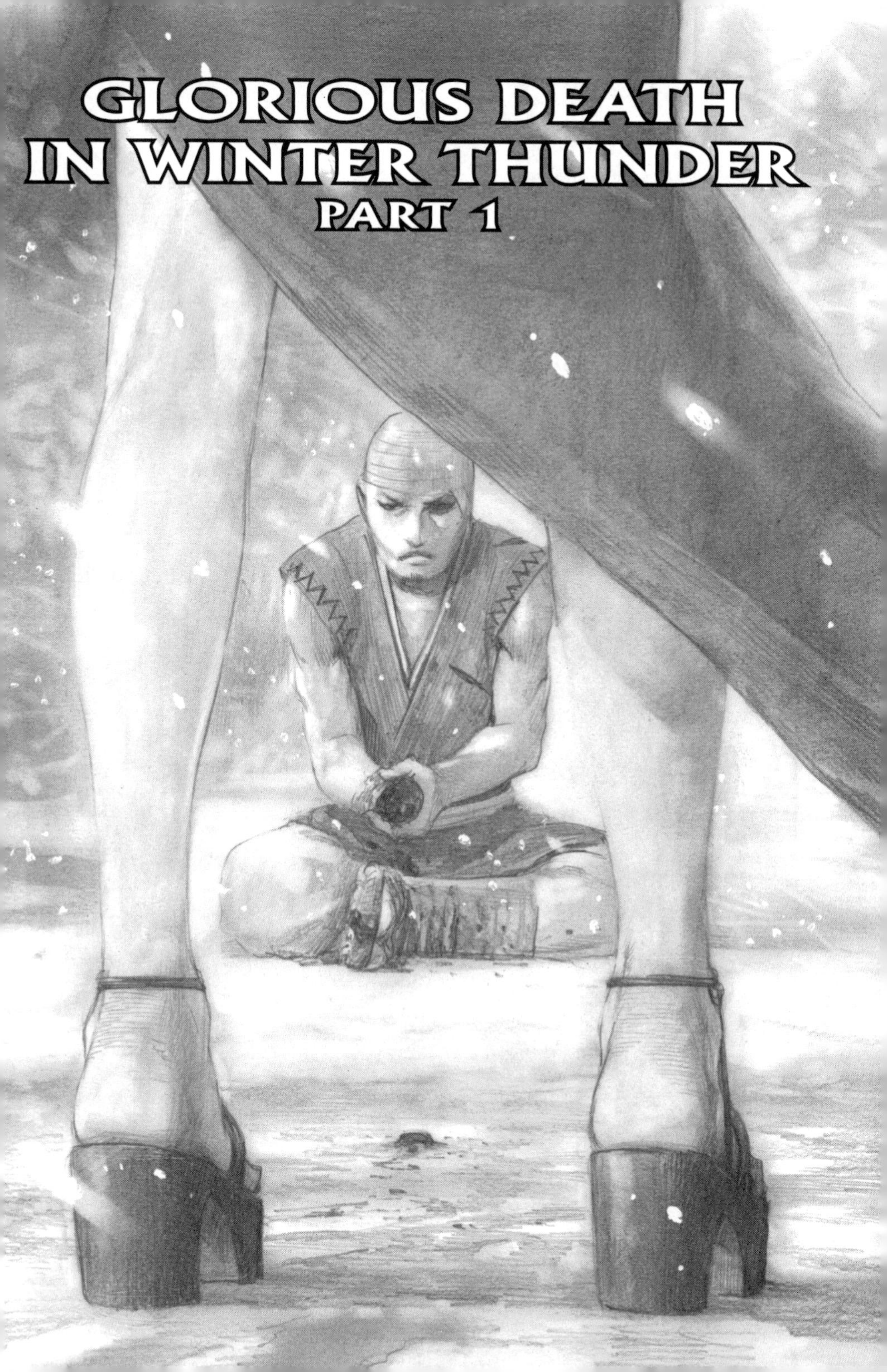
GLORIOUS DEATH
IN WINTER THUNDER
PART 1

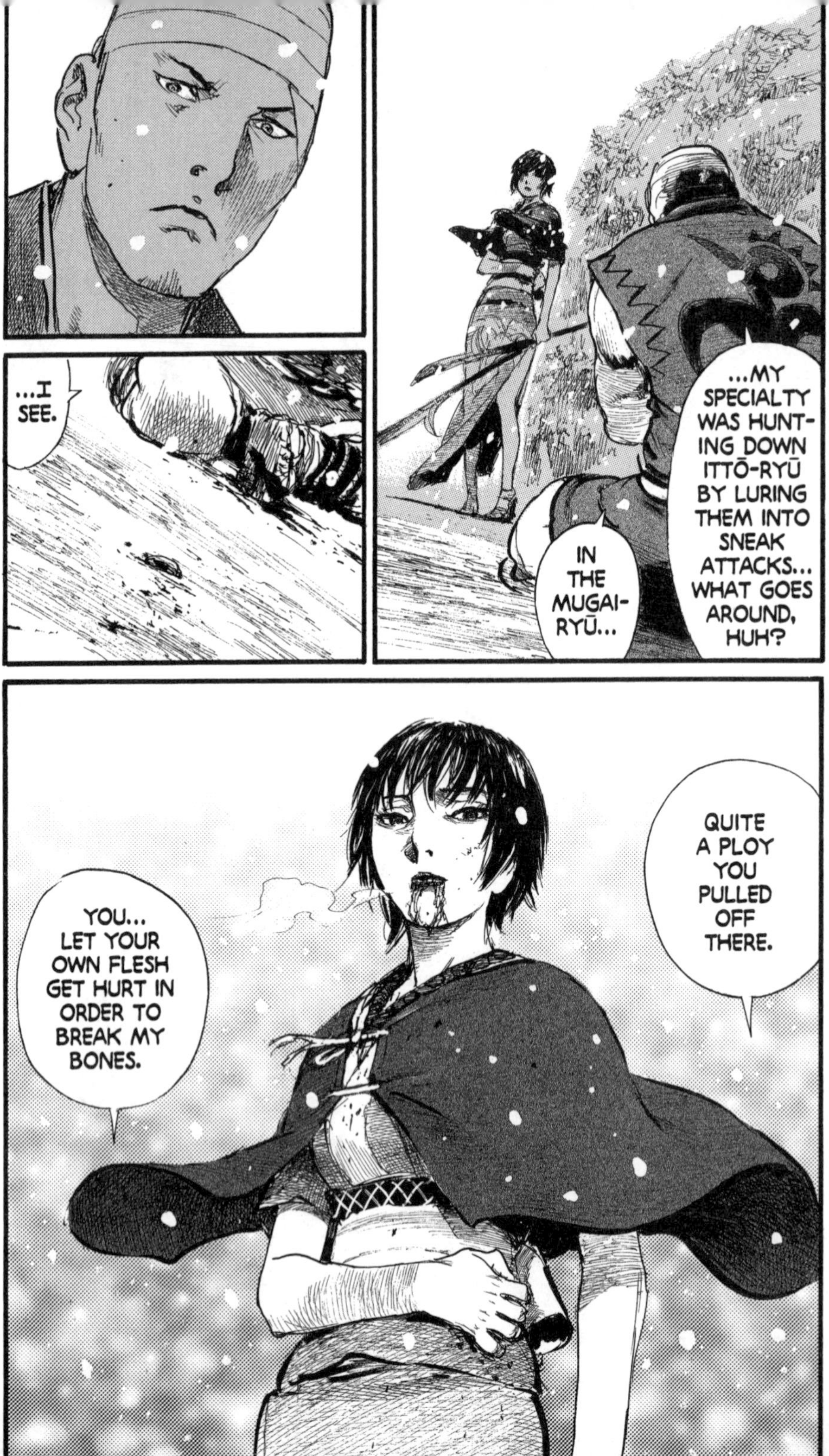

...I SEE.
IN THE MUGAI-RYŪ...
...MY SPECIALTY WAS HUNTING DOWN ITTŌ-RYŪ BY LURING THEM INTO SNEAK ATTACKS... WHAT GOES AROUND, HUH?
QUITE A PLOY YOU PULLED OFF THERE.
YOU... LET YOUR OWN FLESH GET HURT IN ORDER TO BREAK MY BONES.

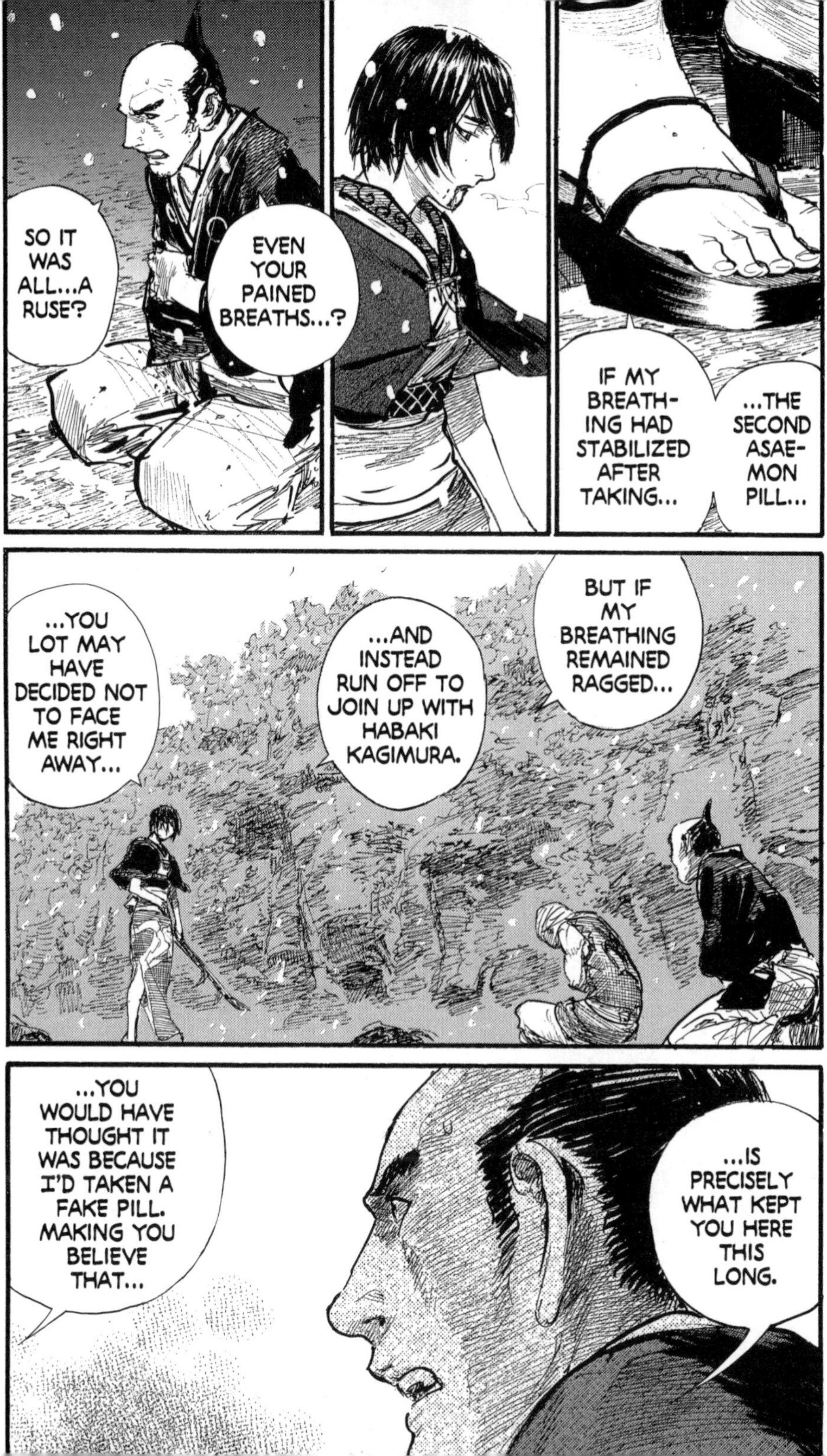
SO IT WAS ALL...A RUSE?
EVEN YOUR PAINED BREATHS...?
IF MY BREATH-ING HAD STABILIZED AFTER TAKING...
...THE SECOND ASAE-MON PILL...
...YOU LOT MAY HAVE DECIDED NOT TO FACE ME RIGHT AWAY...
...AND INSTEAD RUN OFF TO JOIN UP WITH HABAKI KAGIMURA.
BUT IF MY BREATHING REMAINED RAGGED...
...YOU WOULD HAVE THOUGHT IT WAS BECAUSE I'D TAKEN A FAKE PILL. MAKING YOU BELIEVE THAT...
...IS PRECISELY WHAT KEPT YOU HERE THIS LONG.

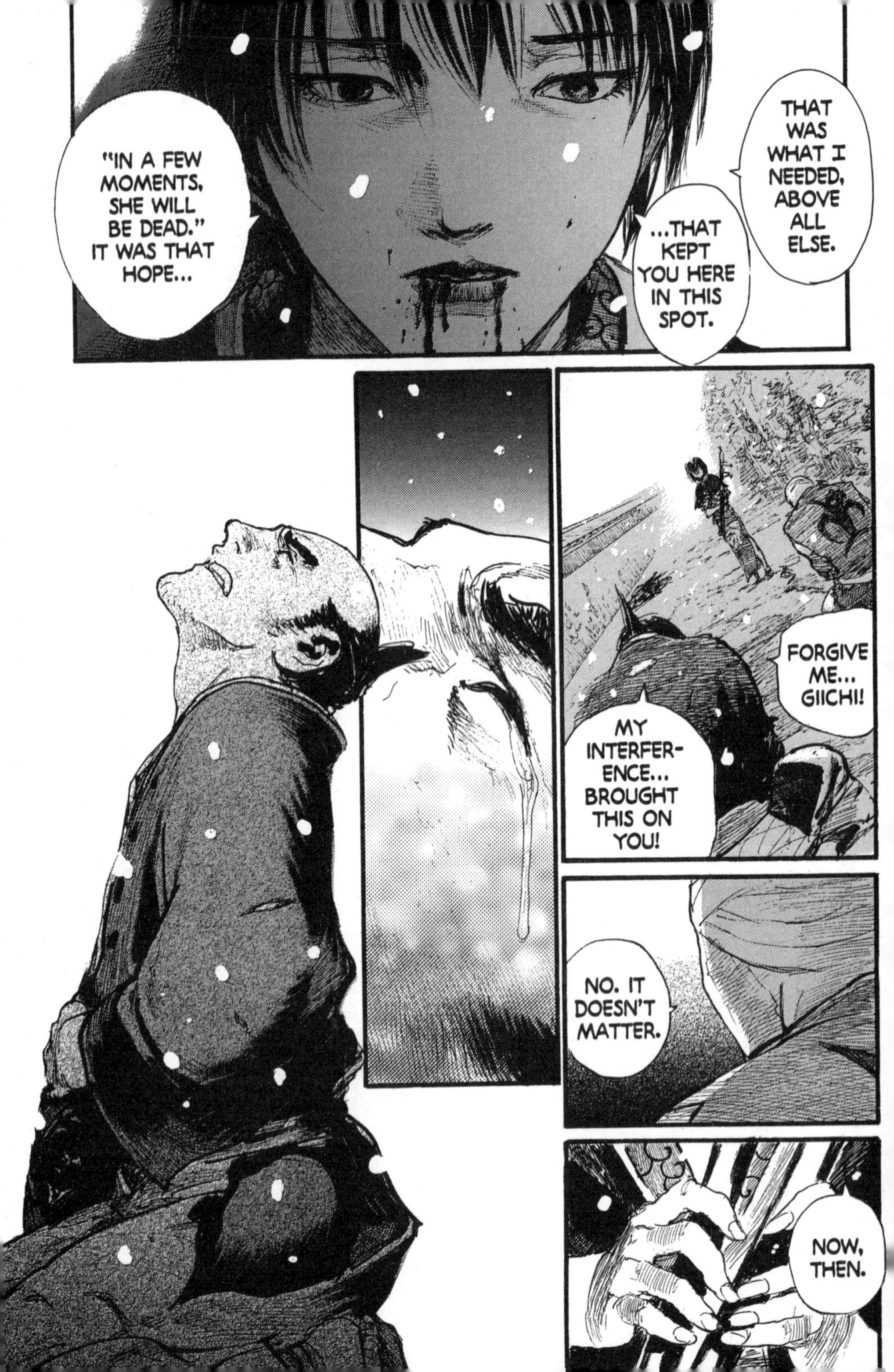
"IN A FEW MOMENTS, SHE WILL BE DEAD." IT WAS THAT HOPE...
...THAT KEPT YOU HERE IN THIS SPOT.
THAT WAS WHAT I NEEDED, ABOVE ALL ELSE.
FORGIVE ME... GIICHI!
MY INTERFERENCE... BROUGHT THIS ON YOU!
NO. IT DOESN'T MATTER.
NOW, THEN.

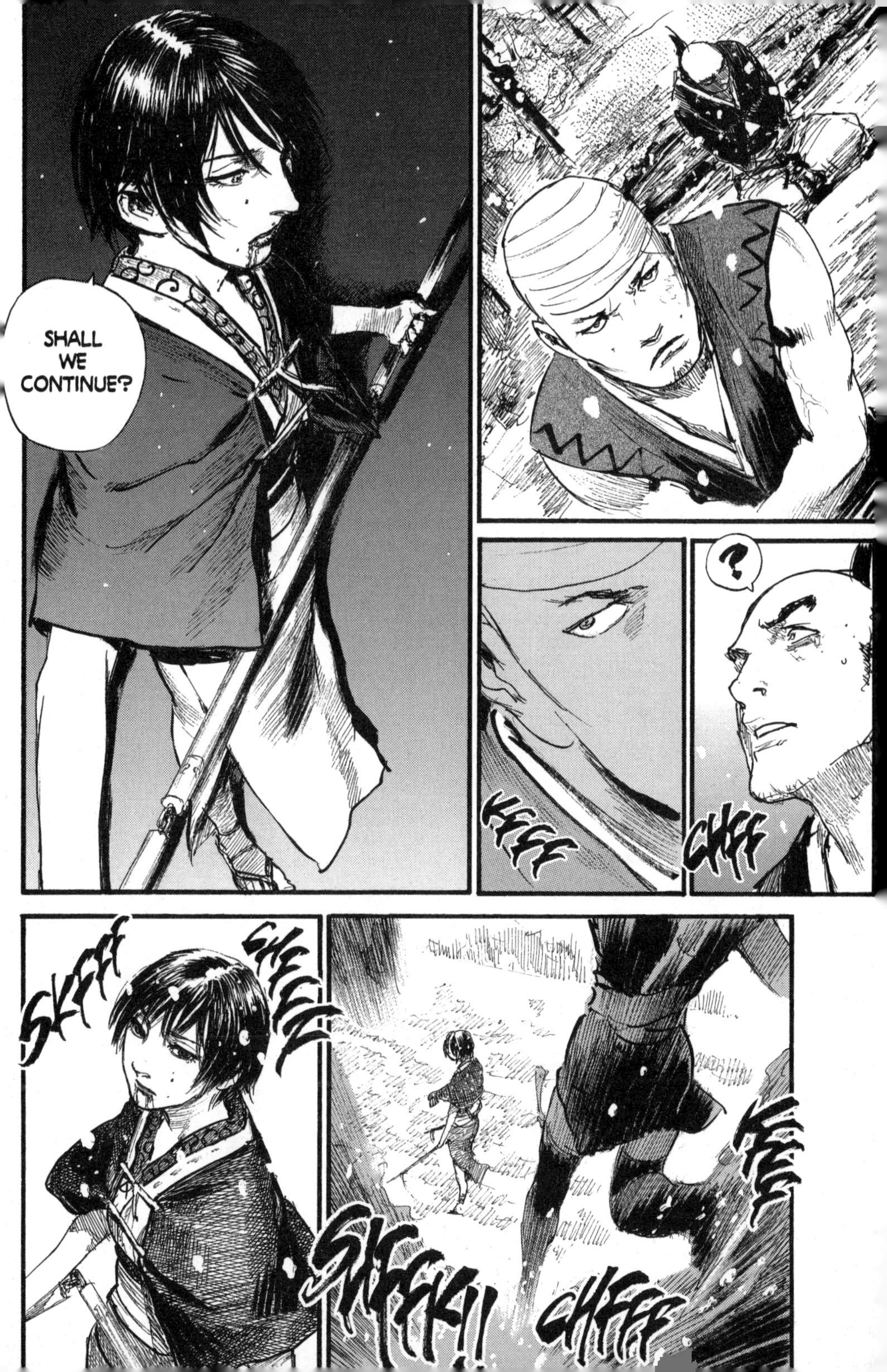
SHALL WE CONTINUE?
KFFF
?
CHFF
SKFFF
SHEEEN
SHEEK!!
CHFFF
KFFF

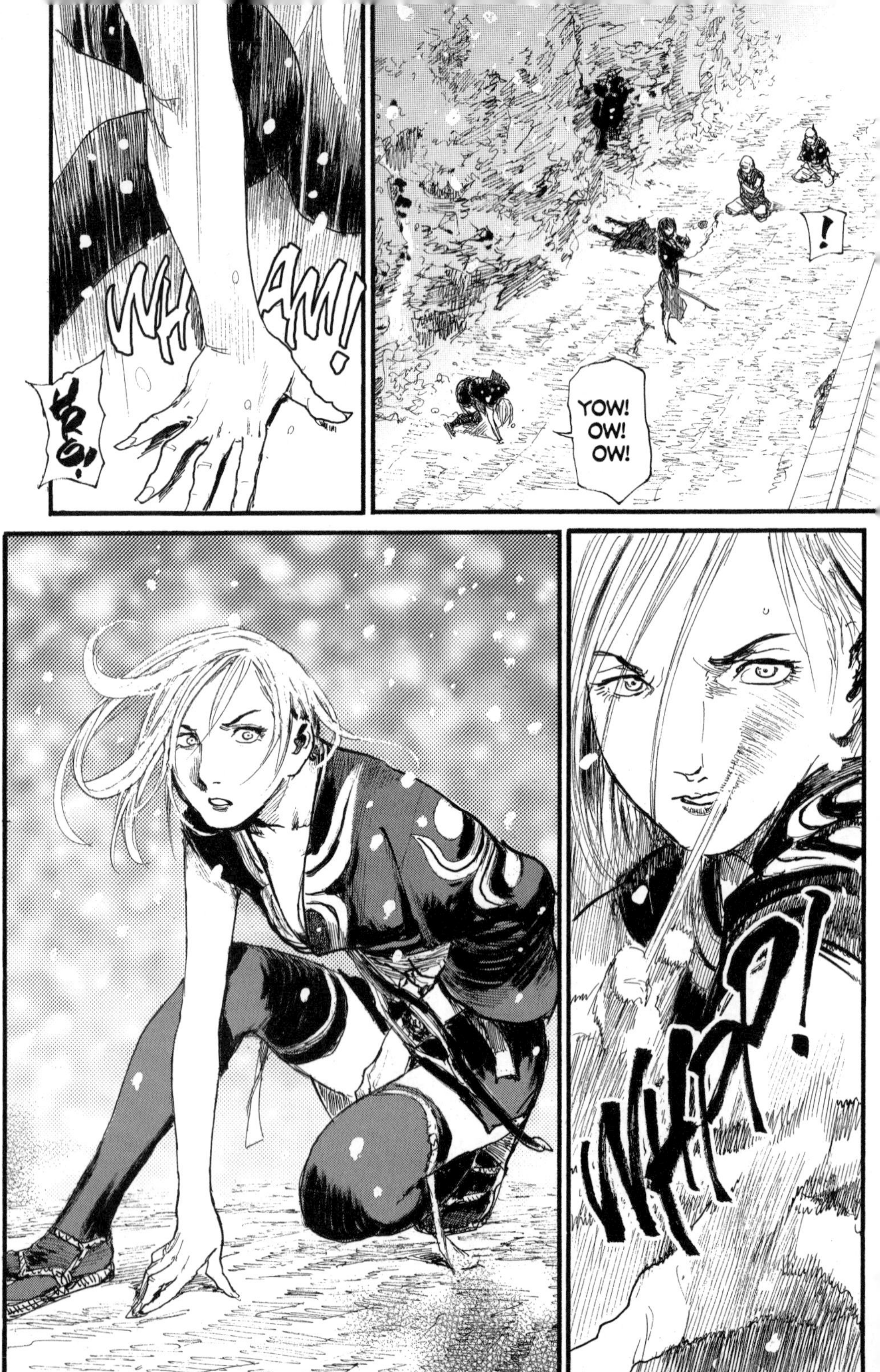
WHAM!
!
YOW! OW! OW!

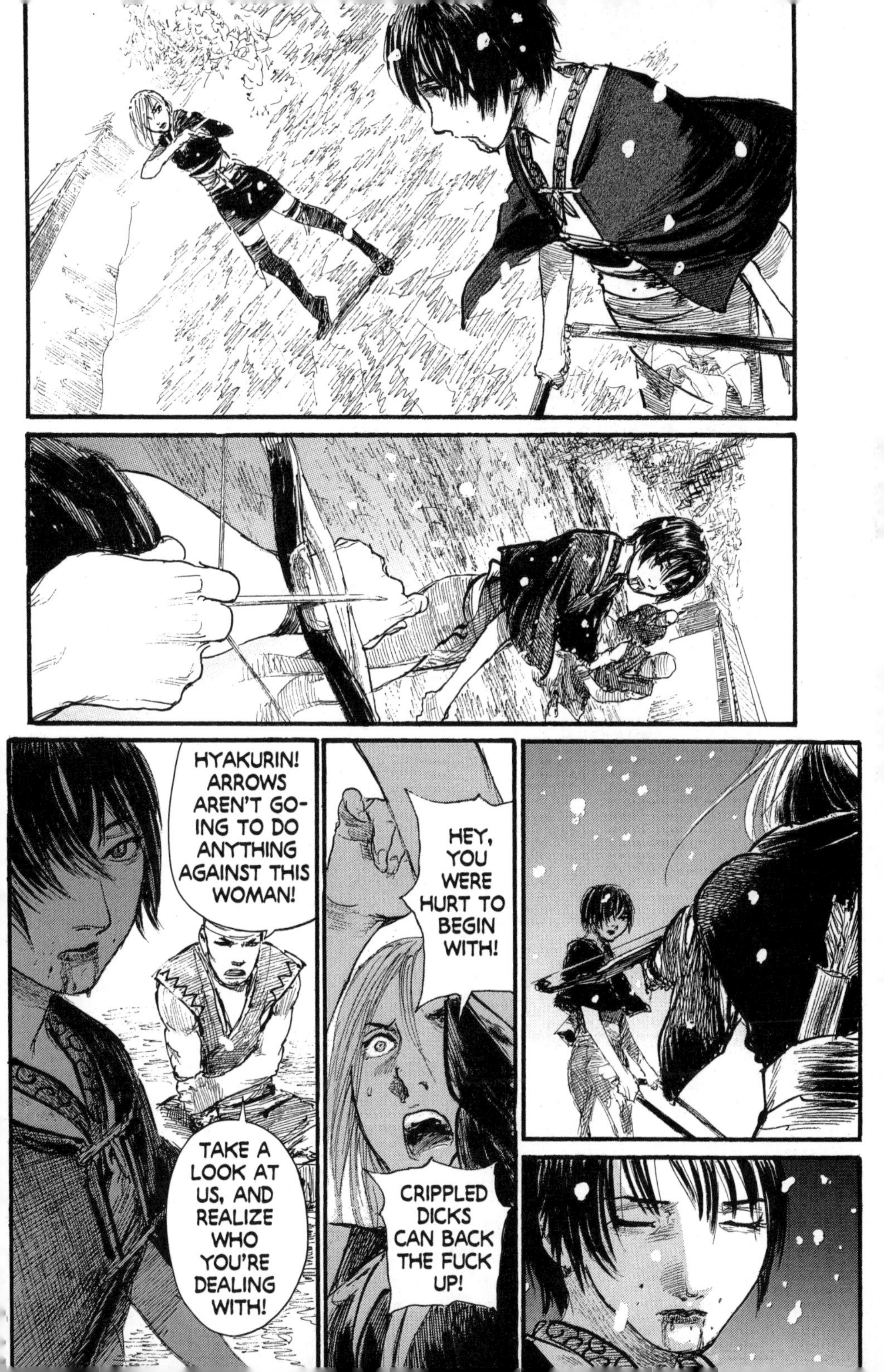
HYAKURIN! ARROWS AREN'T GO-ING TO DO ANYTHING AGAINST THIS WOMAN!
TAKE A LOOK AT US, AND REALIZE WHO YOU'RE DEALING WITH!
HEY, YOU WERE HURT TO BEGIN WITH!
CRIPPLED DICKS CAN BACK THE FUCK UP!

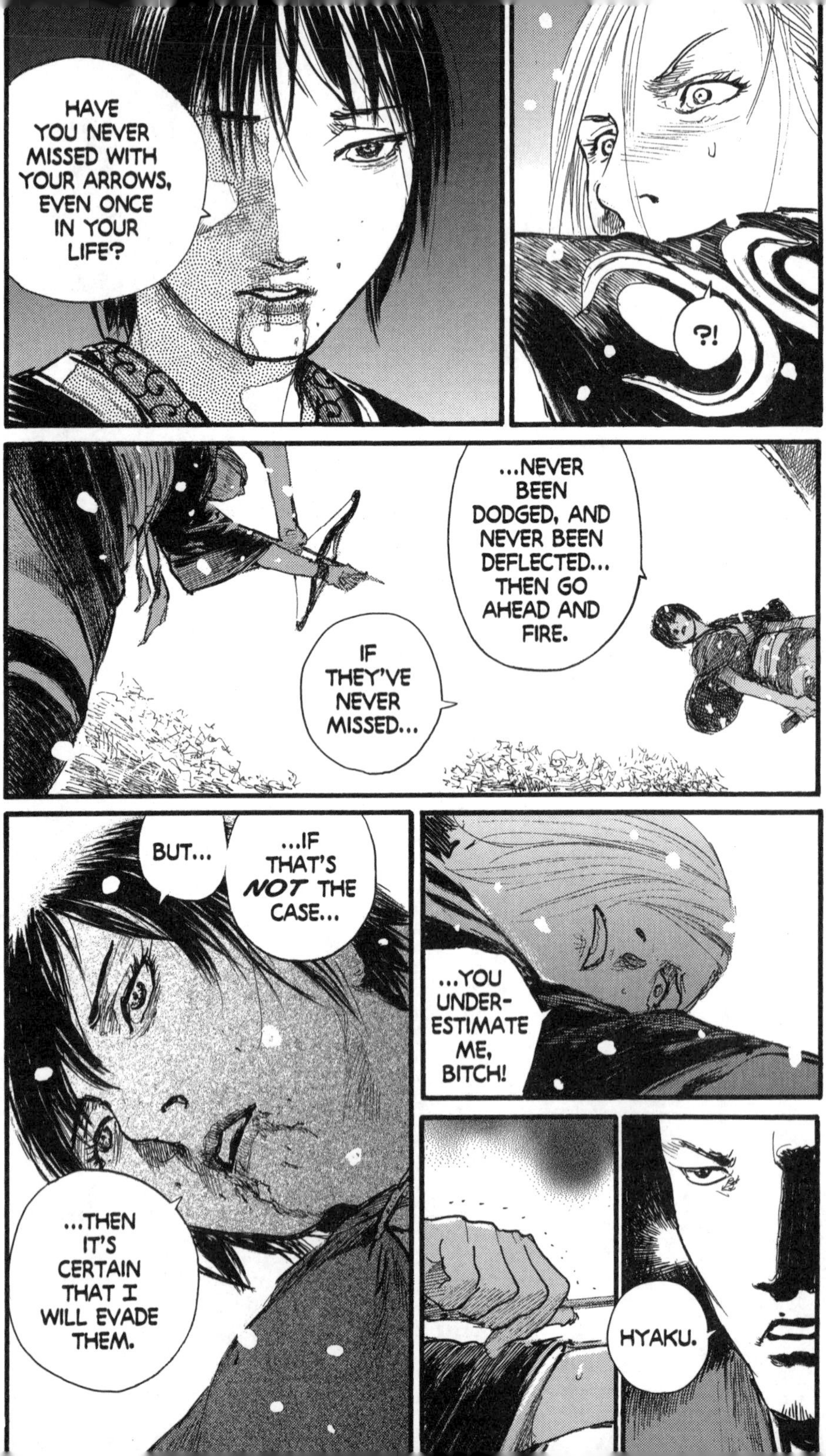
HAVE YOU NEVER MISSED WITH YOUR ARROWS, EVEN ONCE IN YOUR LIFE?
?!
IF THEY'VE NEVER MISSED...
...NEVER BEEN DODGED, AND NEVER BEEN DEFLECTED... THEN GO AHEAD AND FIRE.
BUT...
...IF THAT'S *NOT* THE CASE...
...THEN IT'S CERTAIN THAT I WILL EVADE THEM.
...YOU UNDER-ESTIMATE ME, BITCH!
HYAKU.

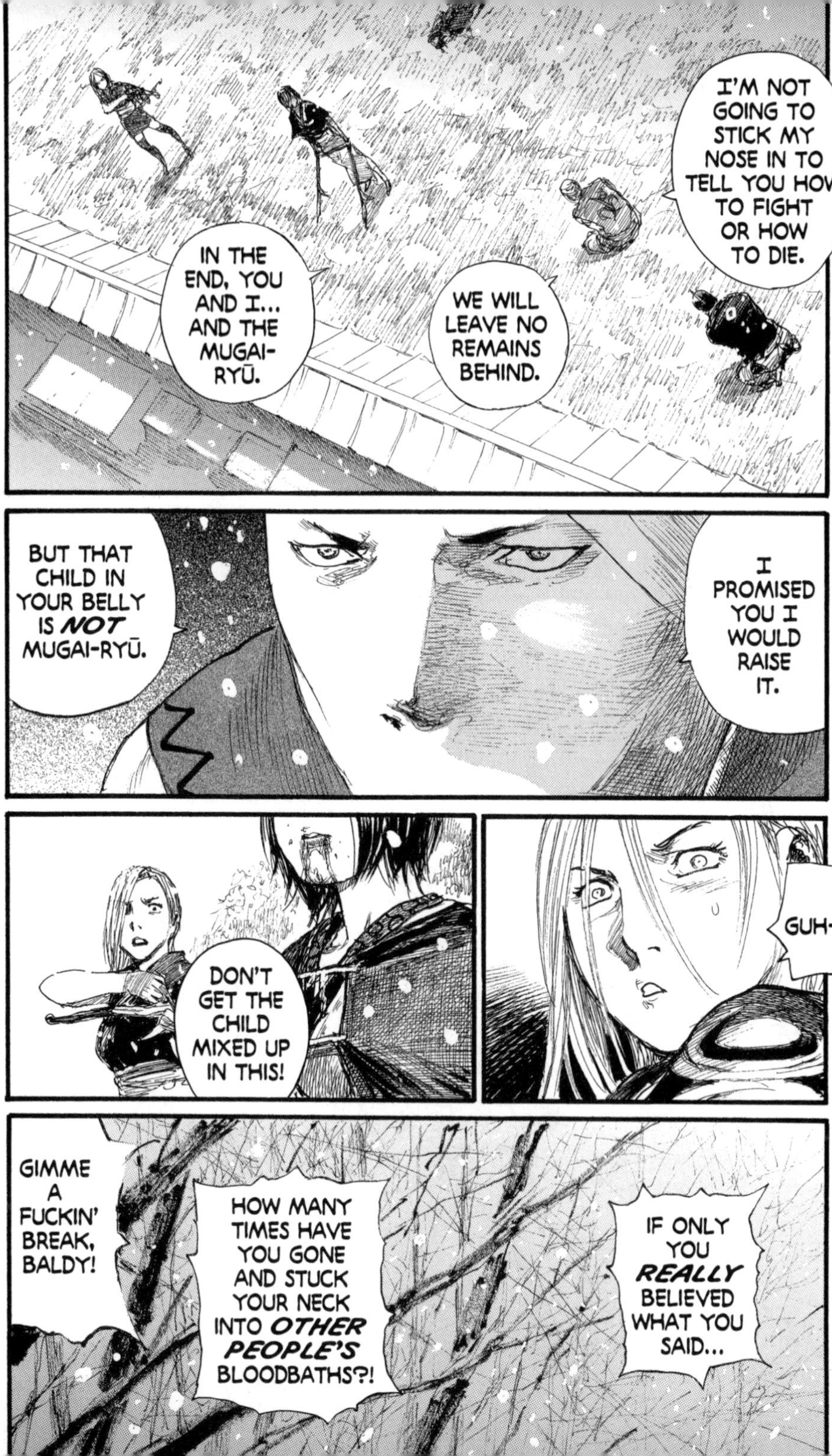
IN THE END, YOU AND I... AND THE MUGAI-RYŪ.
WE WILL LEAVE NO REMAINS BEHIND.
I'M NOT GOING TO STICK MY NOSE IN TO TELL YOU HOW TO FIGHT OR HOW TO DIE.
BUT THAT CHILD IN YOUR BELLY IS *NOT* MUGAI-RYŪ.
I PROMISED YOU I WOULD RAISE IT.
DON'T GET THE CHILD MIXED UP IN THIS!
GUH--
GIMME A FUCKIN' BREAK, BALDY!
HOW MANY TIMES HAVE YOU GONE AND STUCK YOUR NECK INTO *OTHER PEOPLE'S* BLOODBATHS?!
IF ONLY YOU *REALLY* BELIEVED WHAT YOU SAID...

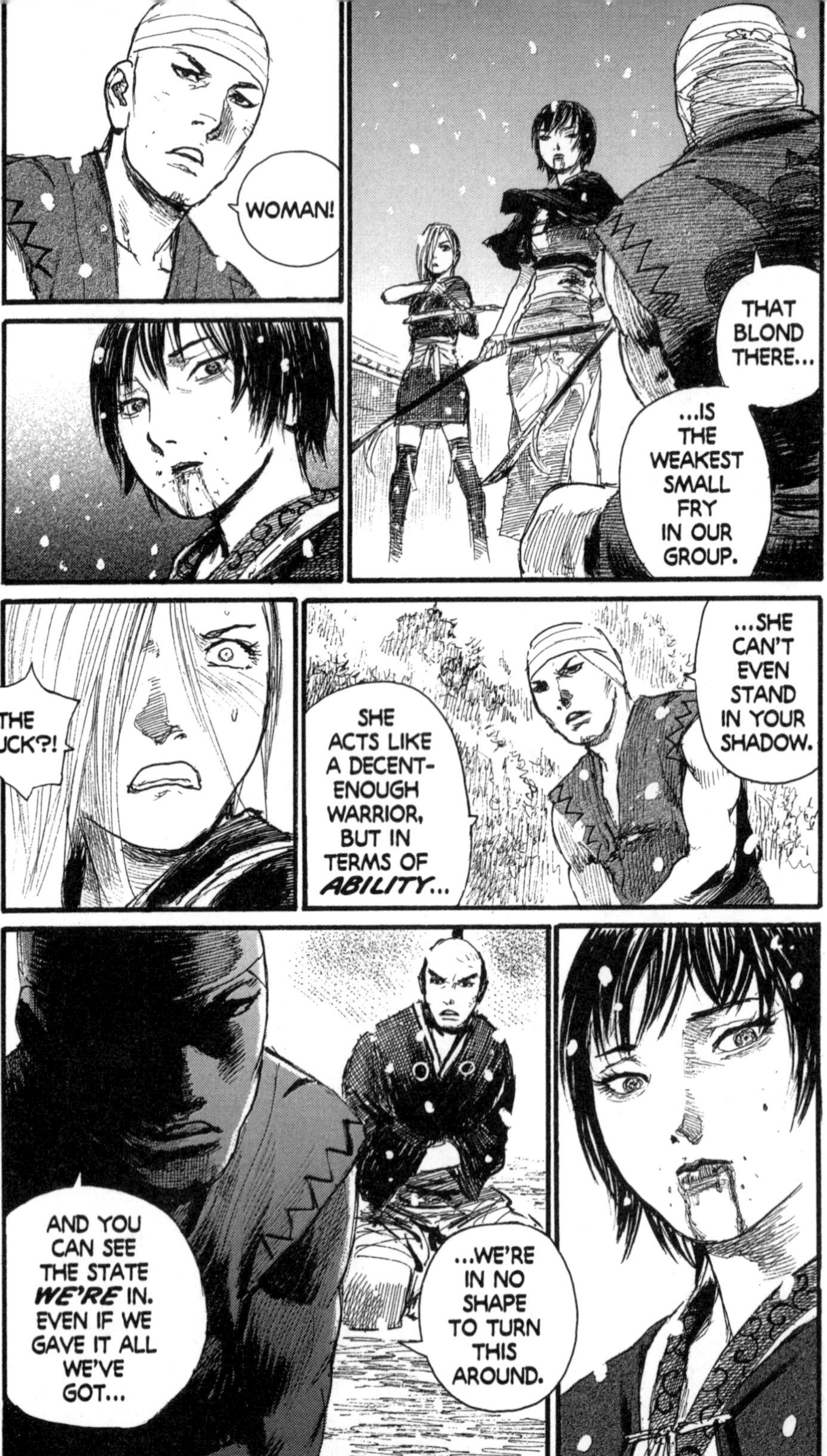

WOMAN!
THAT BLOND THERE...
...IS THE WEAKEST SMALL FRY IN OUR GROUP.
THE FUCK?!
SHE ACTS LIKE A DECENT-ENOUGH WARRIOR, BUT IN TERMS OF *ABILITY*...
...SHE CAN'T EVEN STAND IN YOUR SHADOW.
AND YOU CAN SEE THE STATE *WE'RE* IN. EVEN IF WE GAVE IT ALL WE'VE GOT...
...WE'RE IN NO SHAPE TO TURN THIS AROUND.

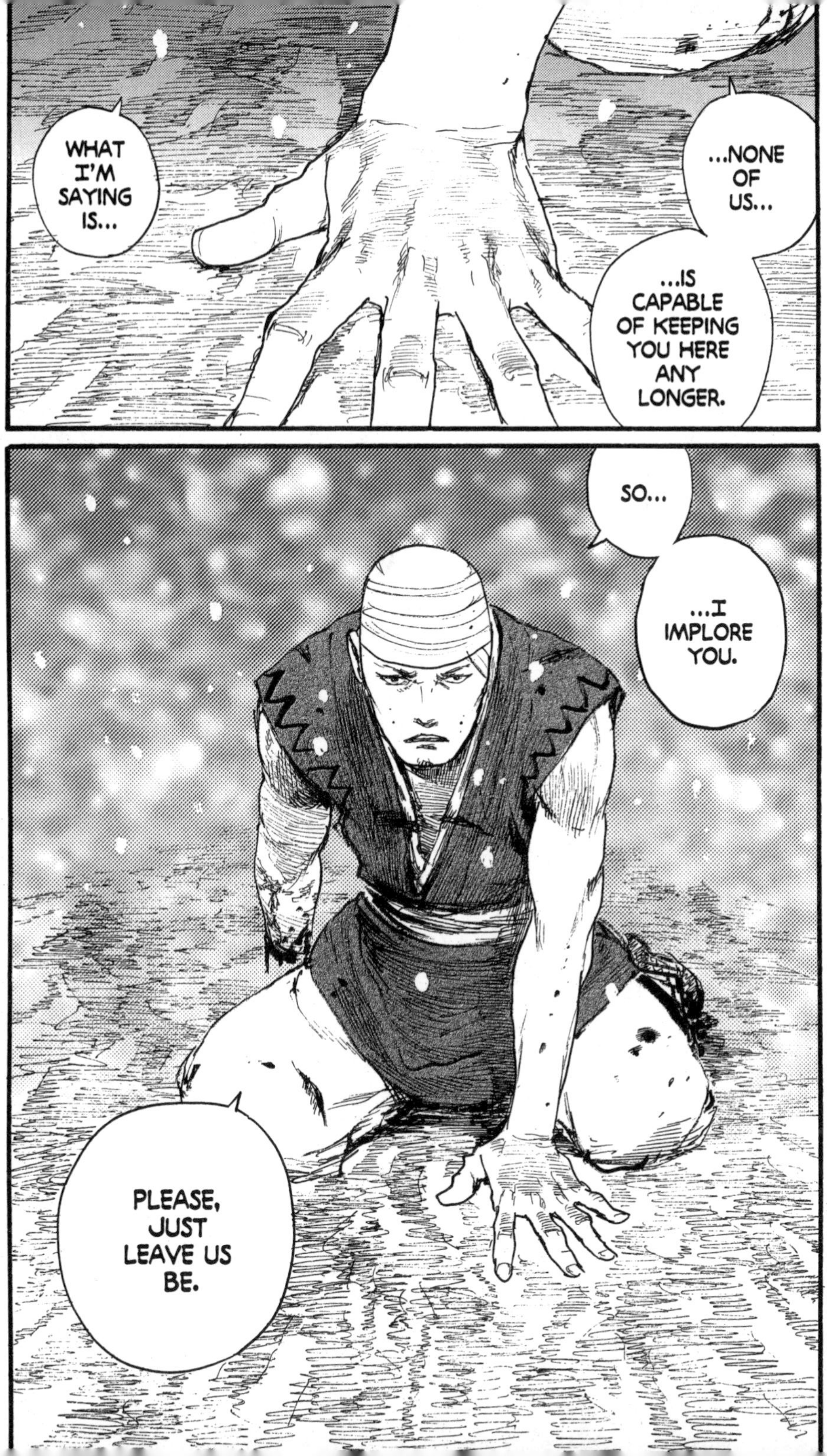
WHAT I'M SAYING IS...
...NONE OF US...
...IS CAPABLE OF KEEPING YOU HERE ANY LONGER.
SO...
...I IMPLORE YOU.
PLEASE, JUST LEAVE US BE.

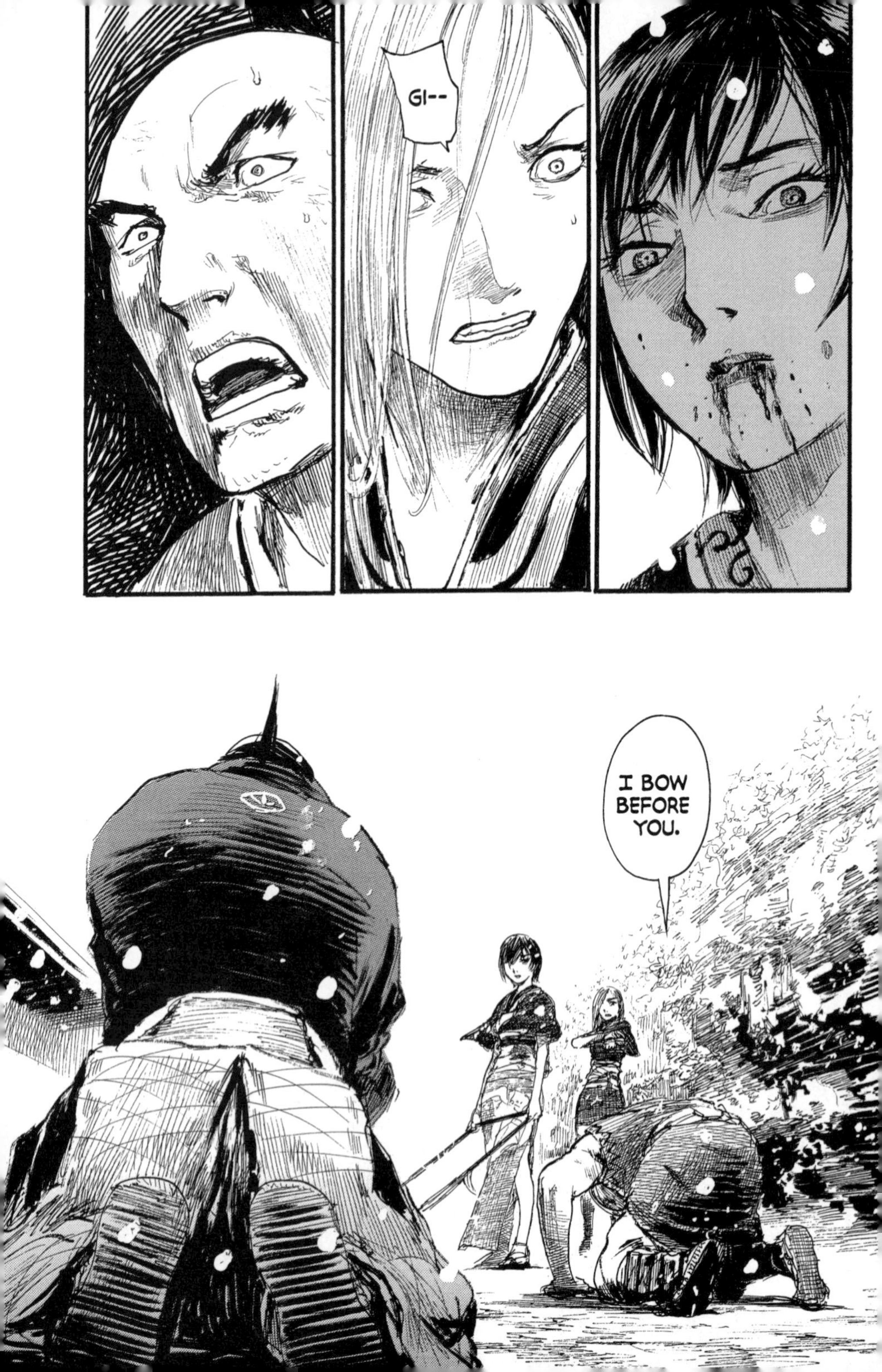
GI--
I BOW BEFORE YOU.

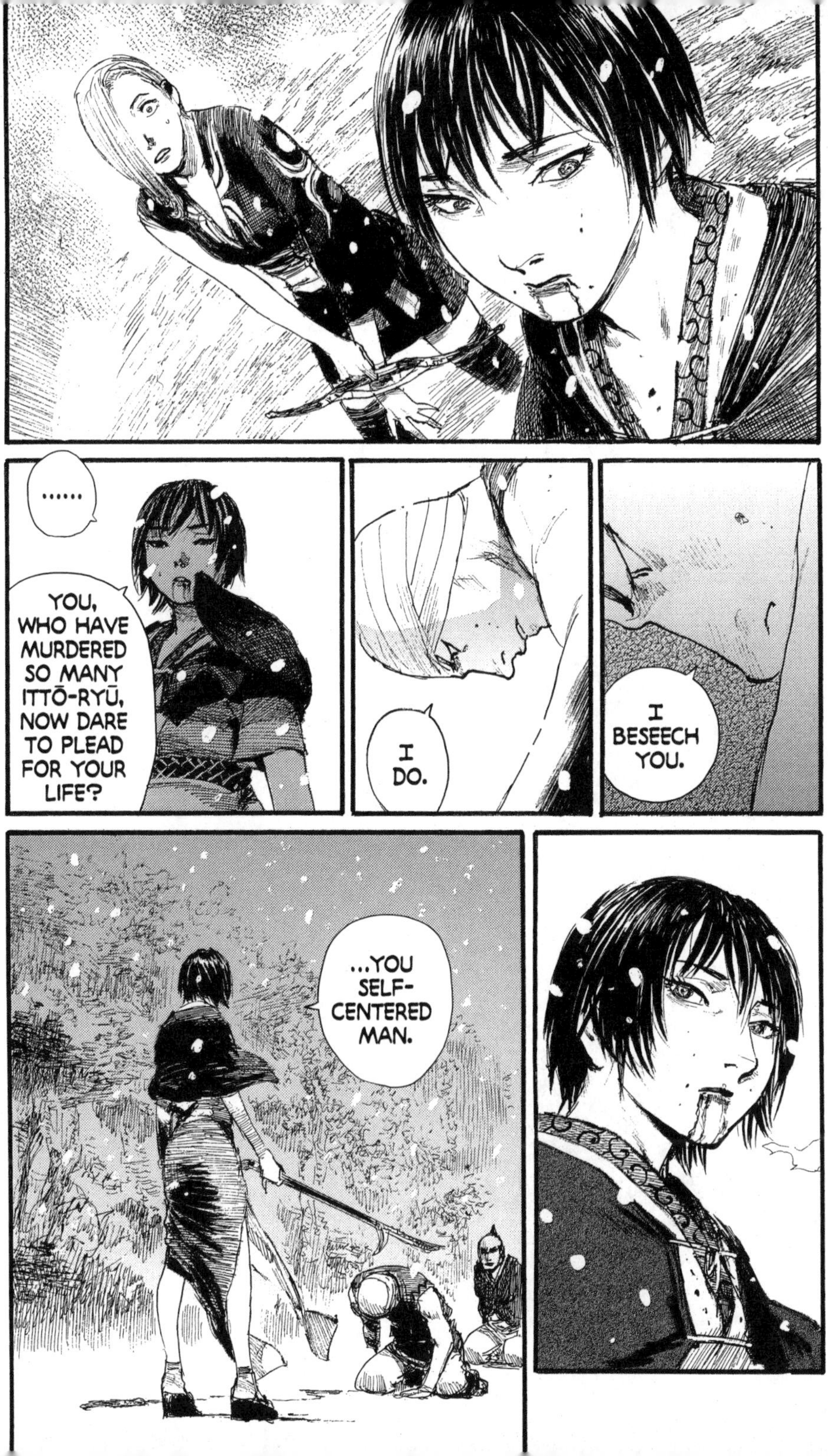
......
YOU, WHO HAVE MURDERED SO MANY ITTŌ-RYŪ, NOW DARE TO PLEAD FOR YOUR LIFE?
I DO.
I BESEECH YOU.
...YOU SELF-CENTERED MAN.

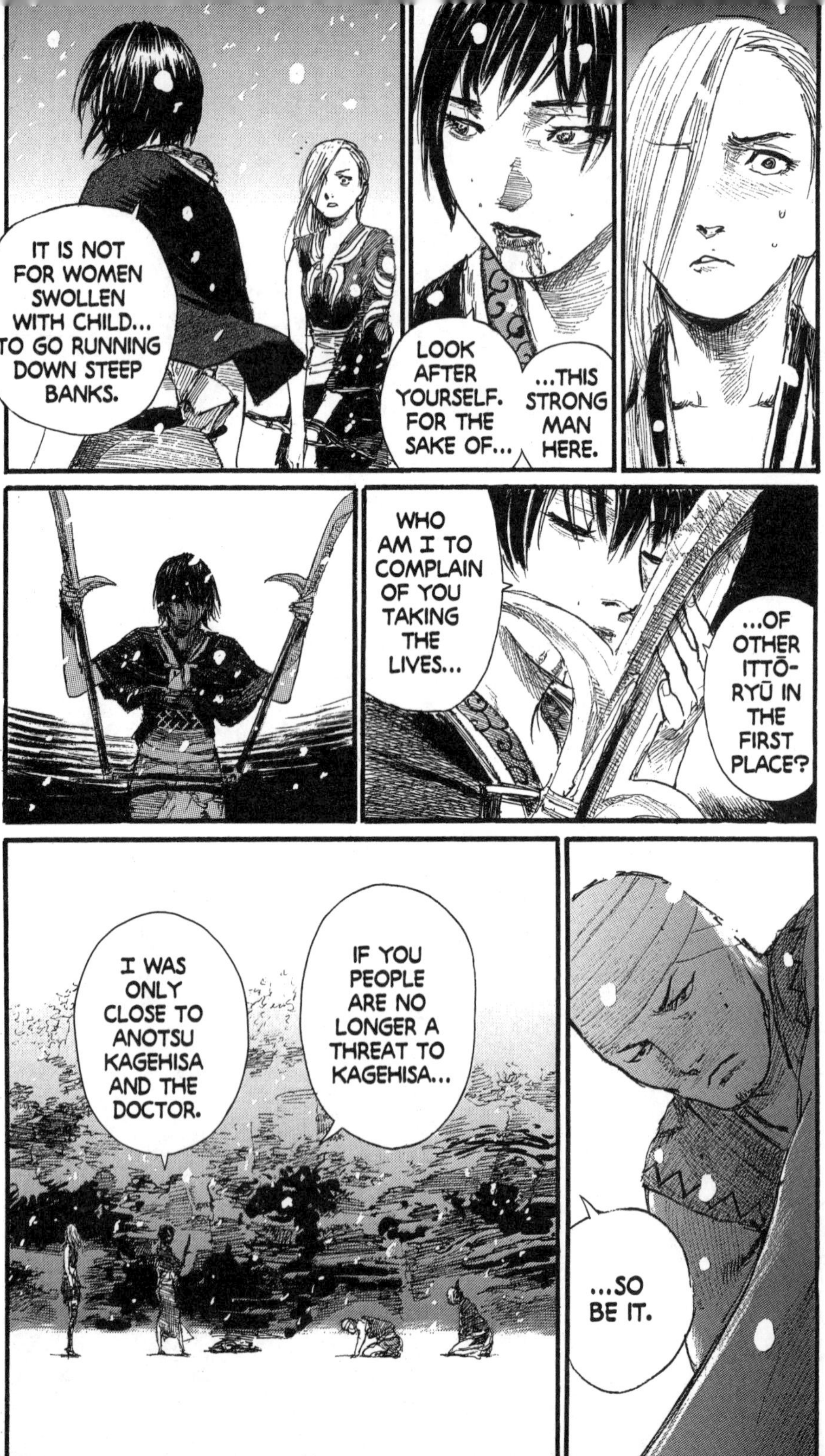
IT IS NOT FOR WOMEN SWOLLEN WITH CHILD... TO GO RUNNING DOWN STEEP BANKS.
LOOK AFTER YOURSELF. FOR THE SAKE OF...
...THIS STRONG MAN HERE.
WHO AM I TO COMPLAIN OF YOU TAKING THE LIVES...
...OF OTHER ITTŌ-RYŪ IN THE FIRST PLACE?
I WAS ONLY CLOSE TO ANOTSU KAGEHISA AND THE DOCTOR.
IF YOU PEOPLE ARE NO LONGER A THREAT TO KAGEHISA...
...SO BE IT.

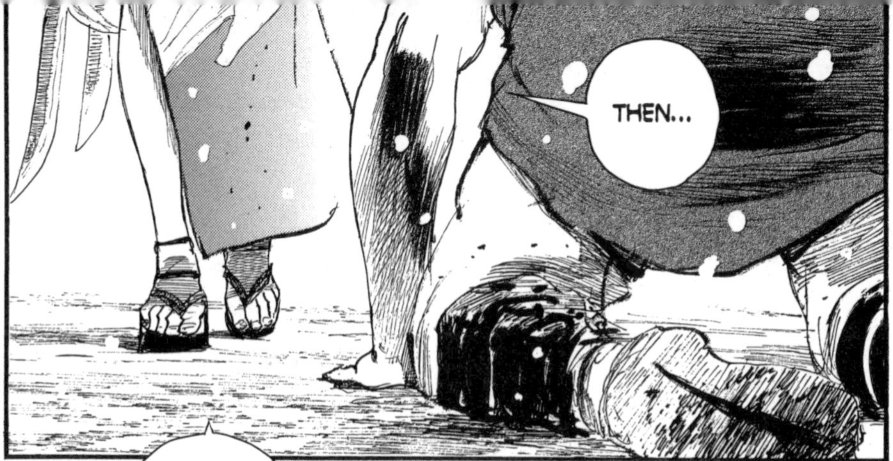
THEN...

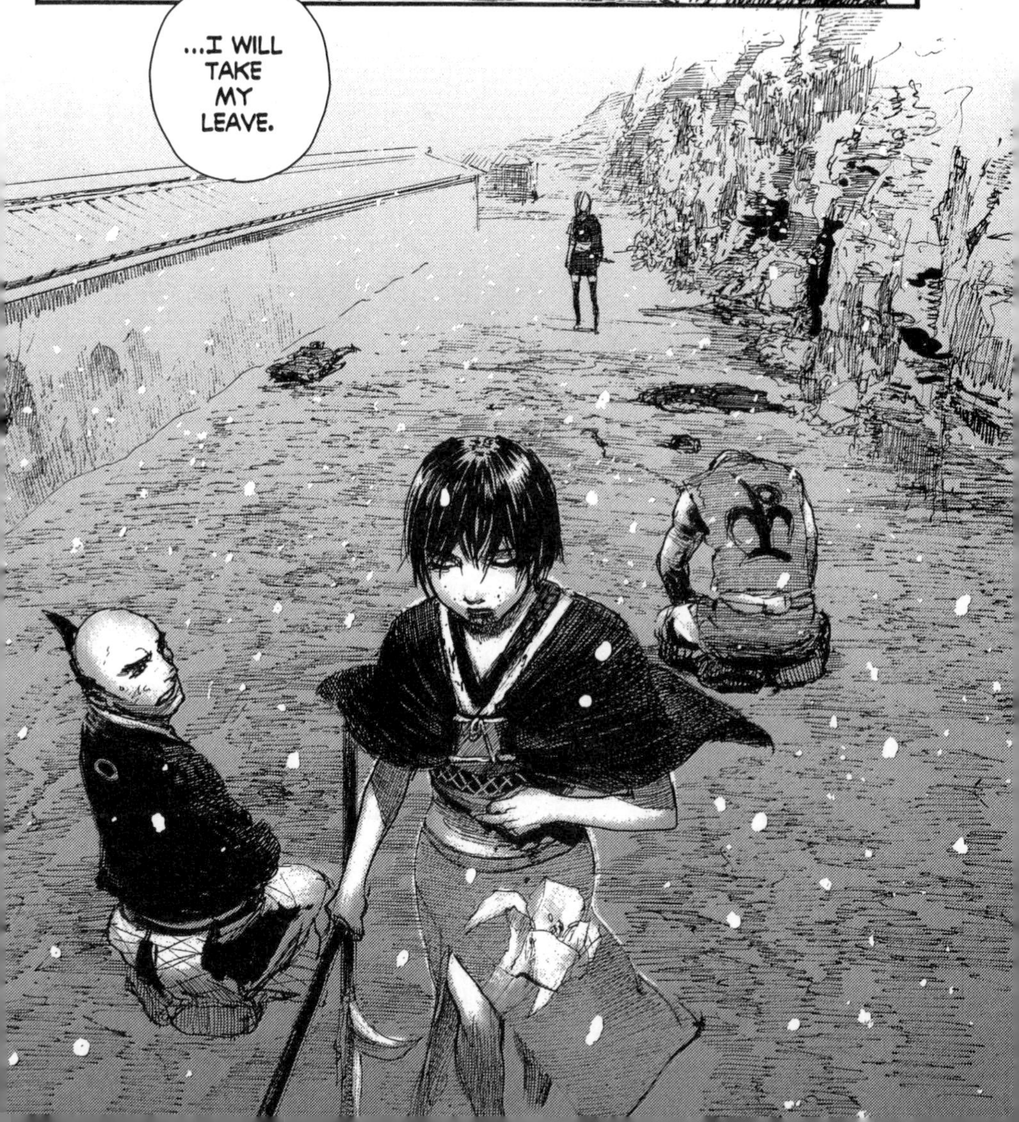
...I WILL TAKE MY LEAVE.

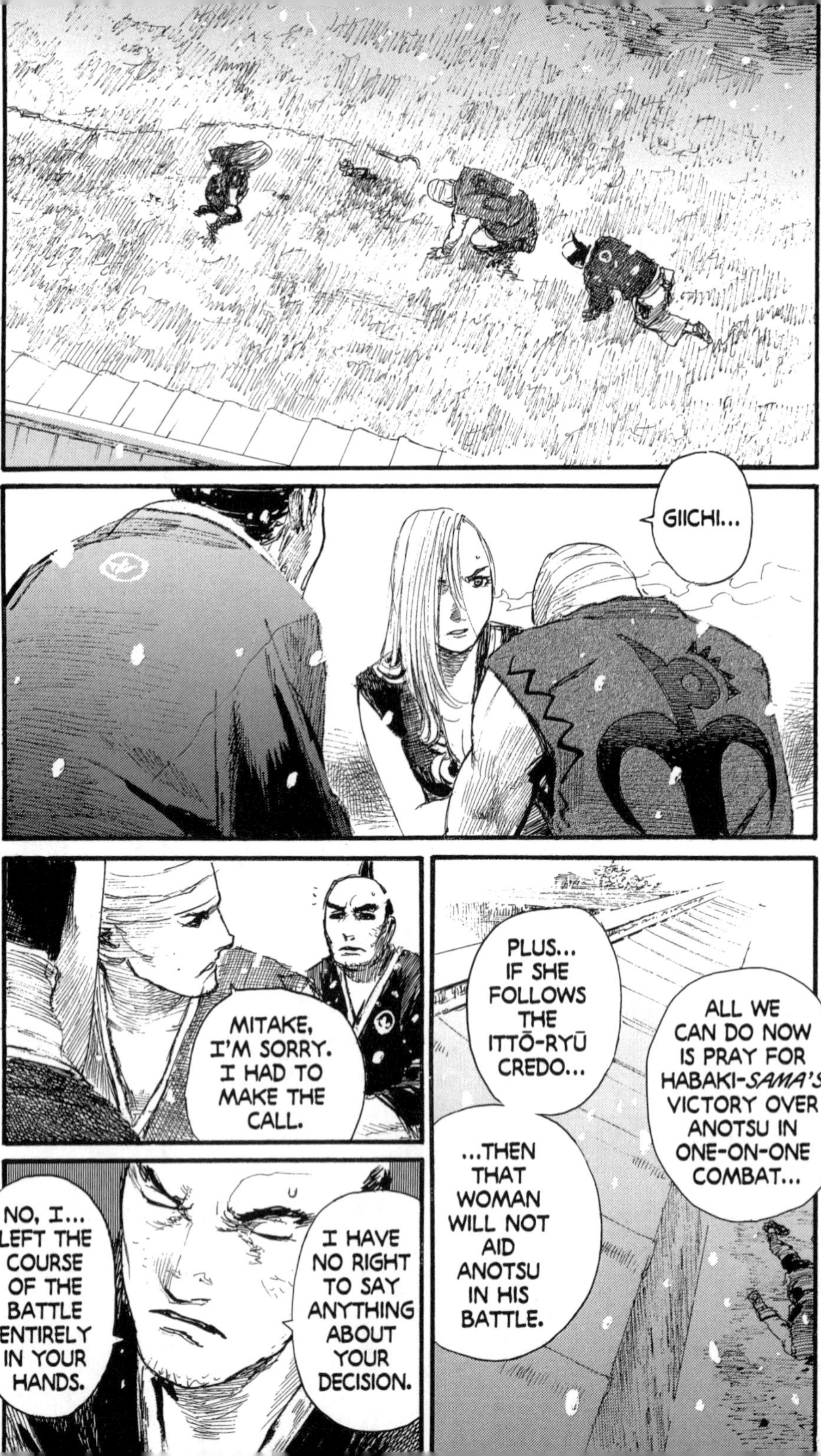
GIICHI...
MITAKE, I'M SORRY. I HAD TO MAKE THE CALL.
NO, I... LEFT THE COURSE OF THE BATTLE ENTIRELY IN YOUR HANDS.
I HAVE NO RIGHT TO SAY ANYTHING ABOUT YOUR DECISION.
PLUS... IF SHE FOLLOWS THE ITTŌ-RYŪ CREDO...
...THEN THAT WOMAN WILL NOT AID ANOTSU IN HIS BATTLE.
ALL WE CAN DO NOW IS PRAY FOR HABAKI-*SAMA'S* VICTORY OVER ANOTSU IN ONE-ON-ONE COMBAT...

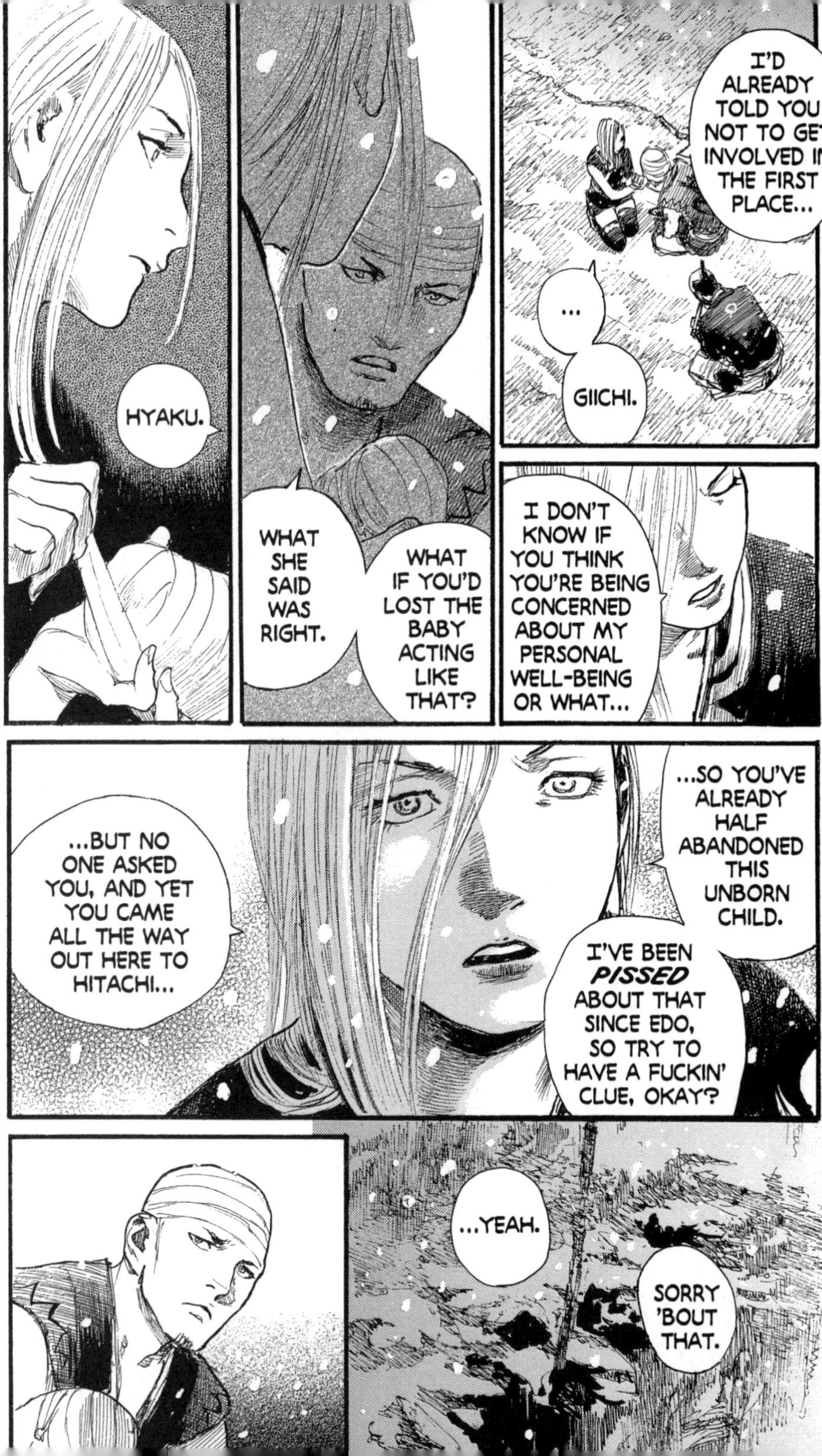
HYAKU.
WHAT SHE SAID WAS RIGHT.
WHAT IF YOU'D LOST THE BABY ACTING LIKE THAT?
I'D ALREADY TOLD YOU NOT TO GET INVOLVED IN THE FIRST PLACE...
...
GIICHI.
I DON'T KNOW IF YOU THINK YOU'RE BEING CONCERNED ABOUT MY PERSONAL WELL-BEING OR WHAT...
...BUT NO ONE ASKED YOU, AND YET YOU CAME ALL THE WAY OUT HERE TO HITACHI...
...SO YOU'VE ALREADY HALF ABANDONED THIS UNBORN CHILD.
I'VE BEEN *PISSED* ABOUT THAT SINCE EDO, SO TRY TO HAVE A FUCKIN' CLUE, OKAY?
...YEAH.
SORRY 'BOUT THAT.

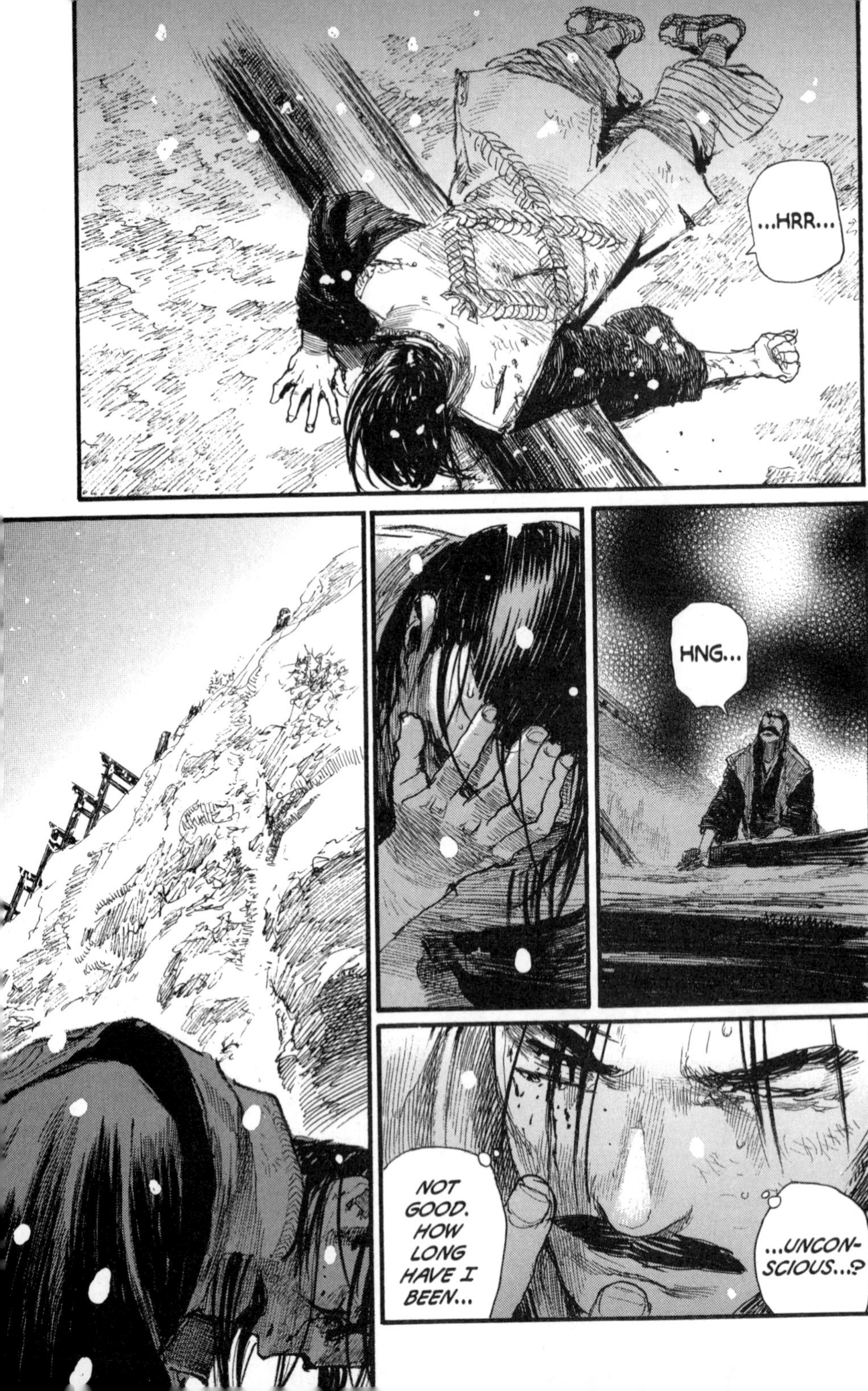
...HRR...
HNG...
NOT GOOD. HOW LONG HAVE I BEEN...
...UNCON-SCIOUS...?

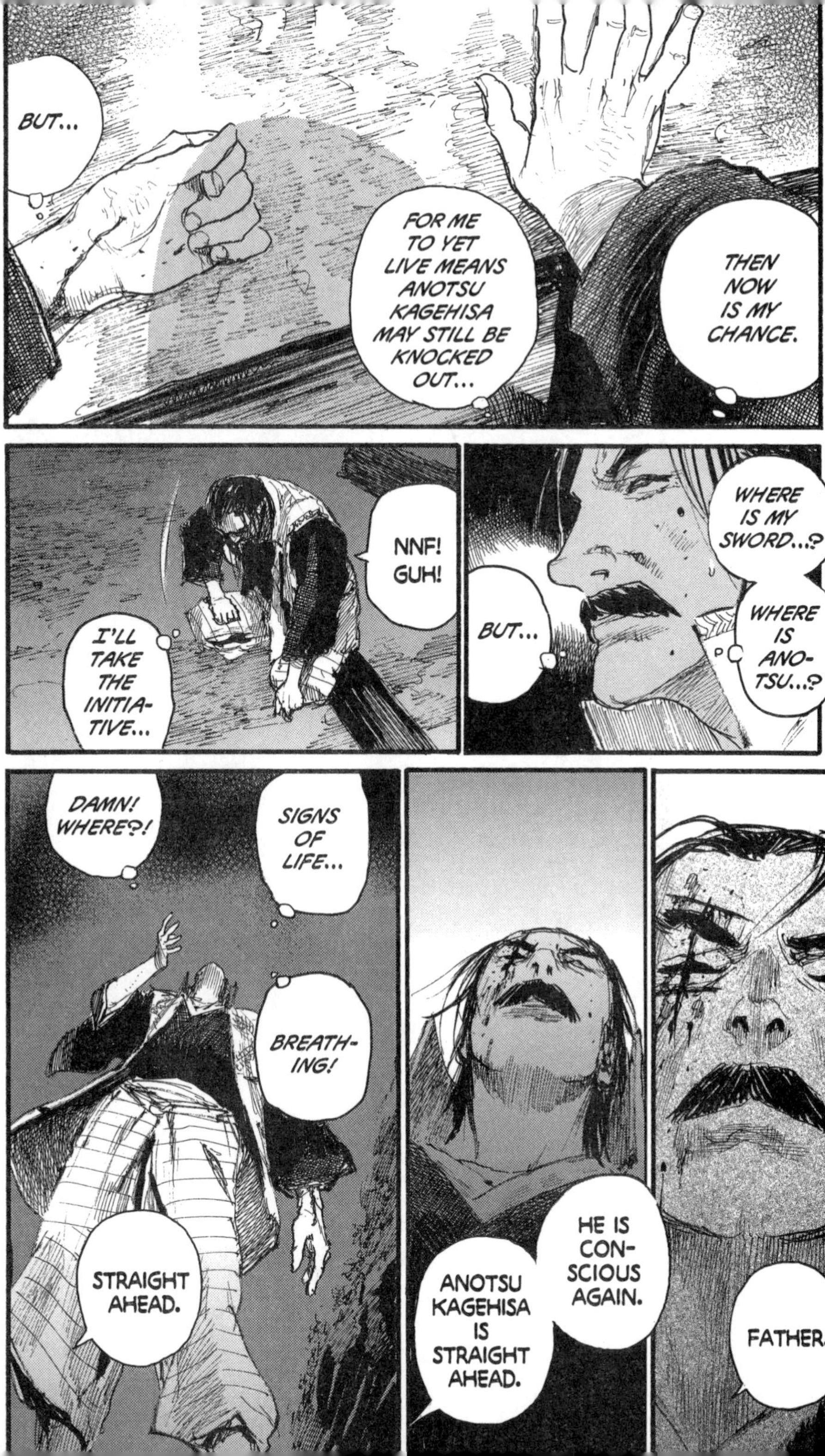
BUT...
FOR ME TO YET LIVE MEANS ANOTSU KAGEHISA MAY STILL BE KNOCKED OUT...
THEN NOW IS MY CHANCE.
NNF! GUH!
I'LL TAKE THE INITIA-TIVE...
WHERE IS MY SWORD...?
BUT...
WHERE IS ANO-TSU...?
DAMN! WHERE?!
SIGNS OF LIFE...
BREATH-ING!
STRAIGHT AHEAD.
HE IS CON-SCIOUS AGAIN.
ANOTSU KAGEHISA IS STRAIGHT AHEAD.
FATHER.

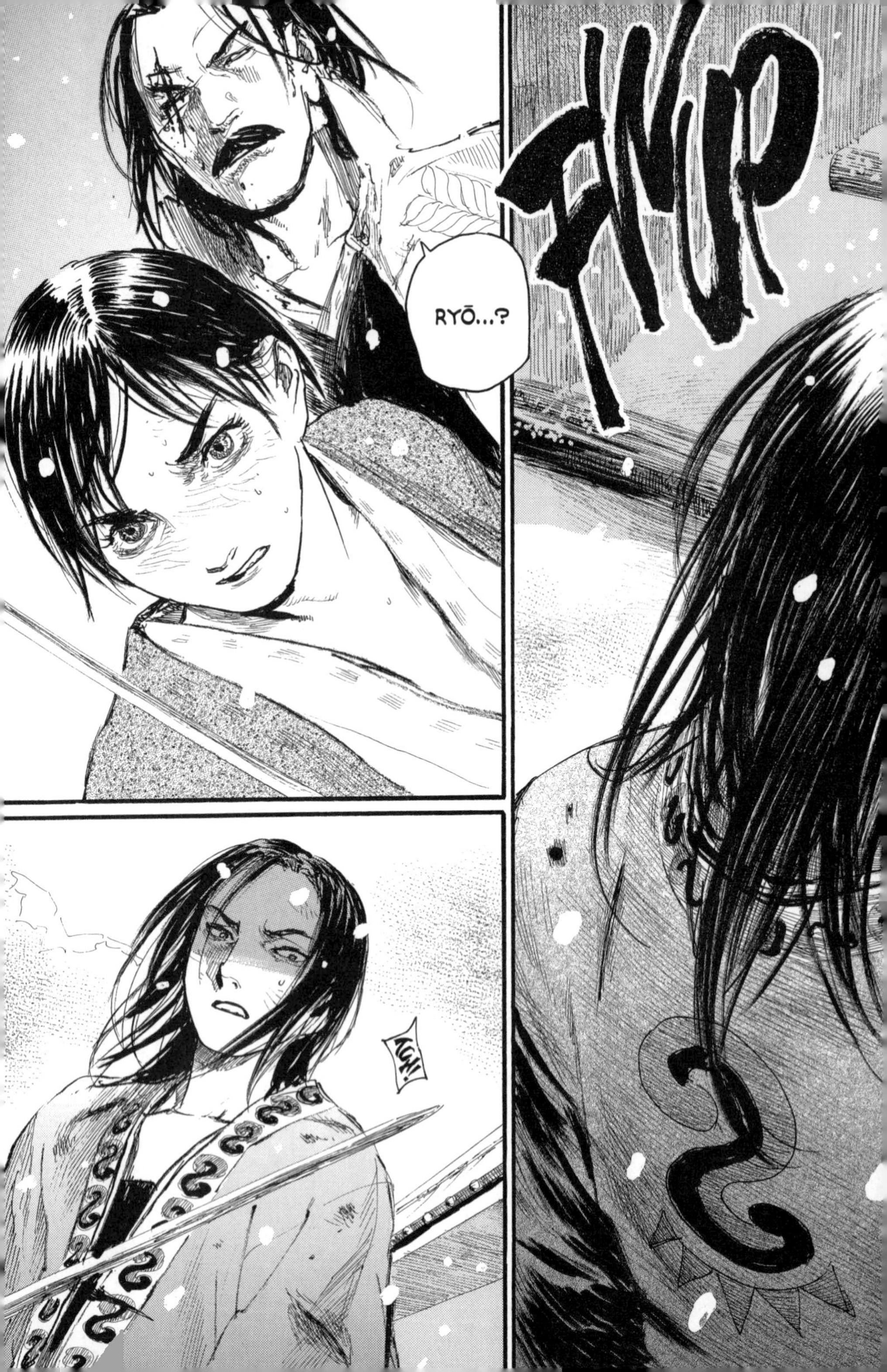
RYŌ...?
FWUP

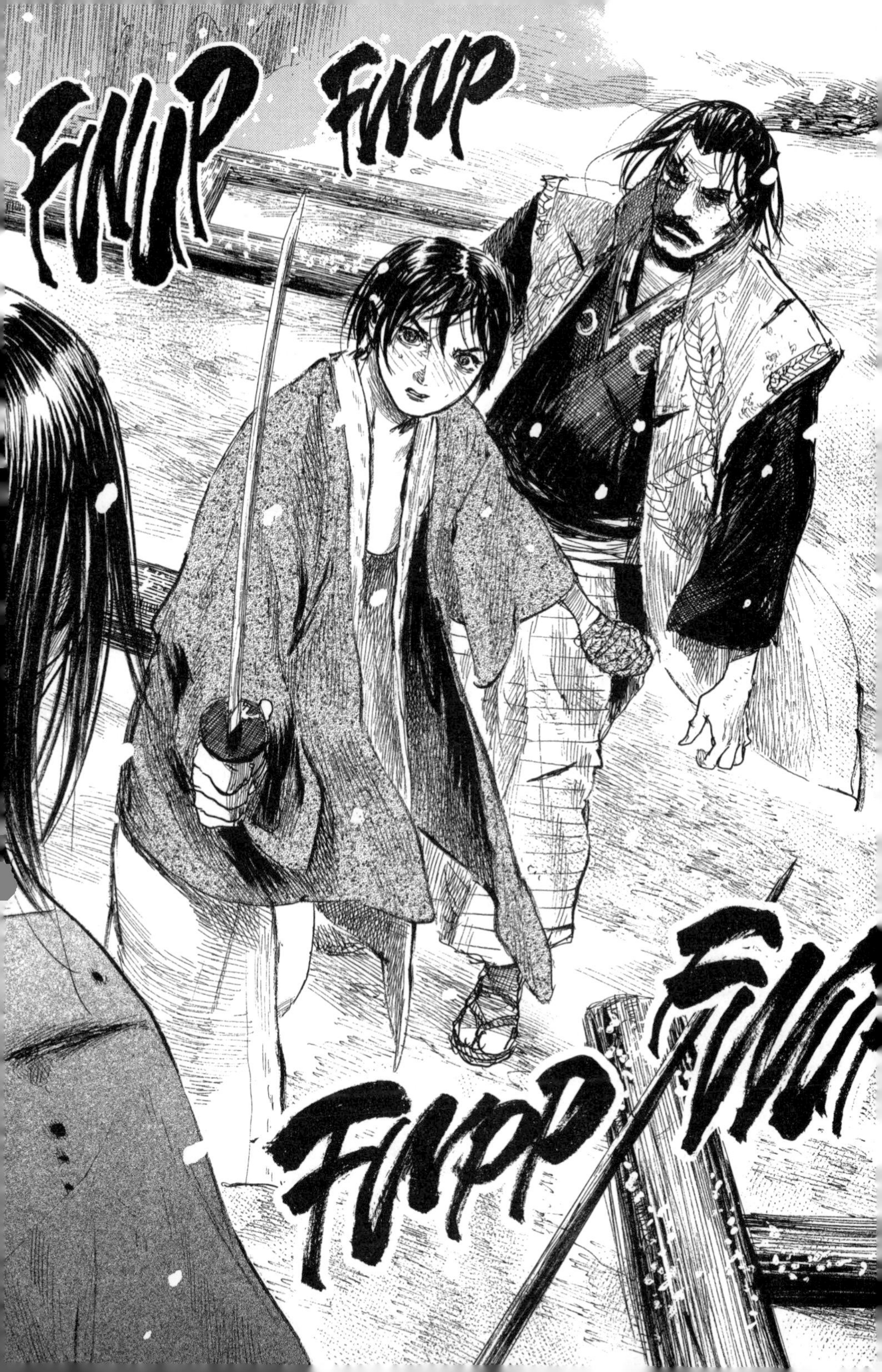
FWUP
FWUP
FWOP

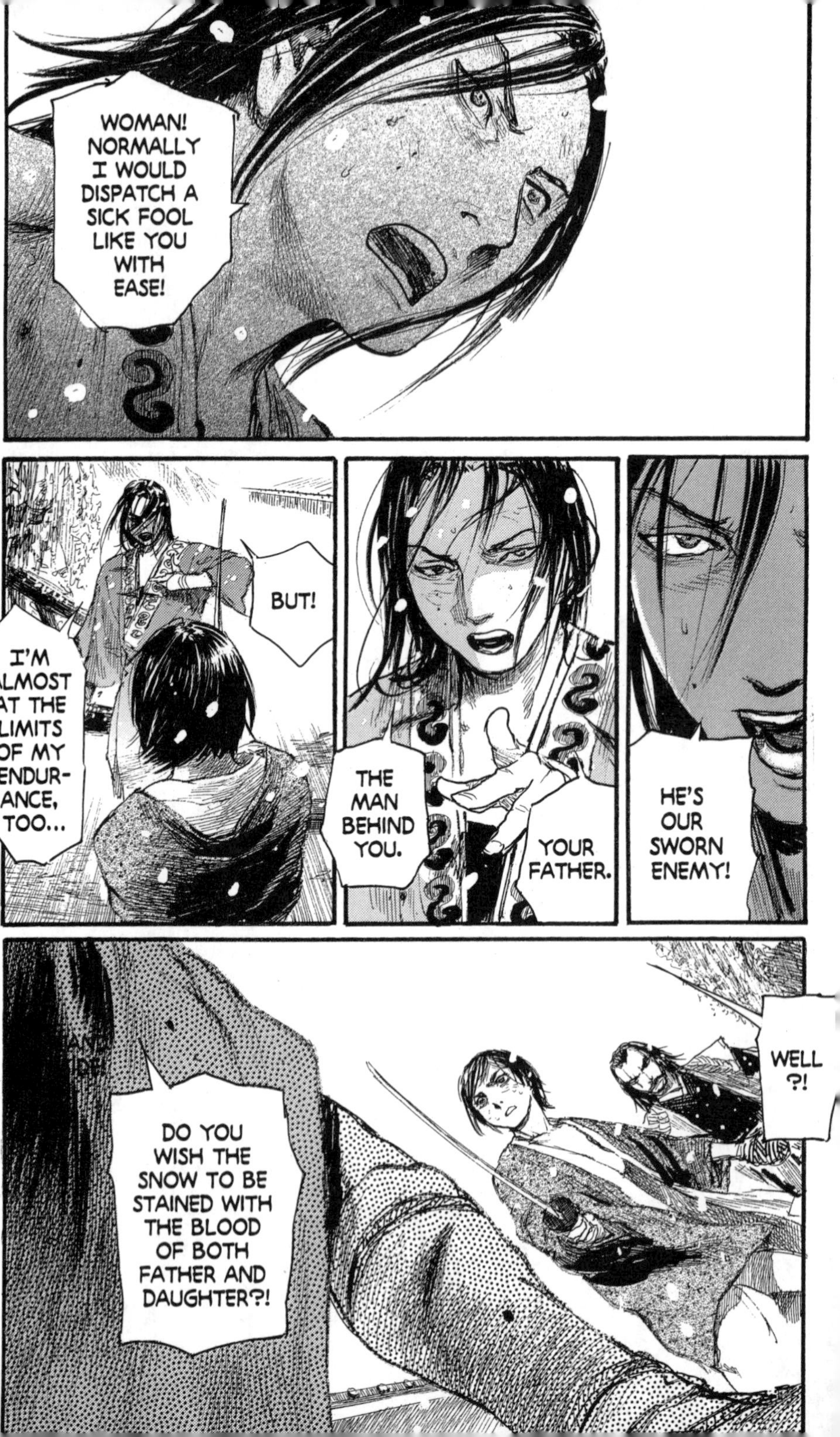
WOMAN! NORMALLY I WOULD DISPATCH A SICK FOOL LIKE YOU WITH EASE!
BUT!
I'M ALMOST AT THE LIMITS OF MY ENDURANCE, TOO...
THE MAN BEHIND YOU.
YOUR FATHER.
HE'S OUR SWORN ENEMY!
DO YOU WISH THE SNOW TO BE STAINED WITH THE BLOOD OF BOTH FATHER AND DAUGHTER?!
WELL ?!

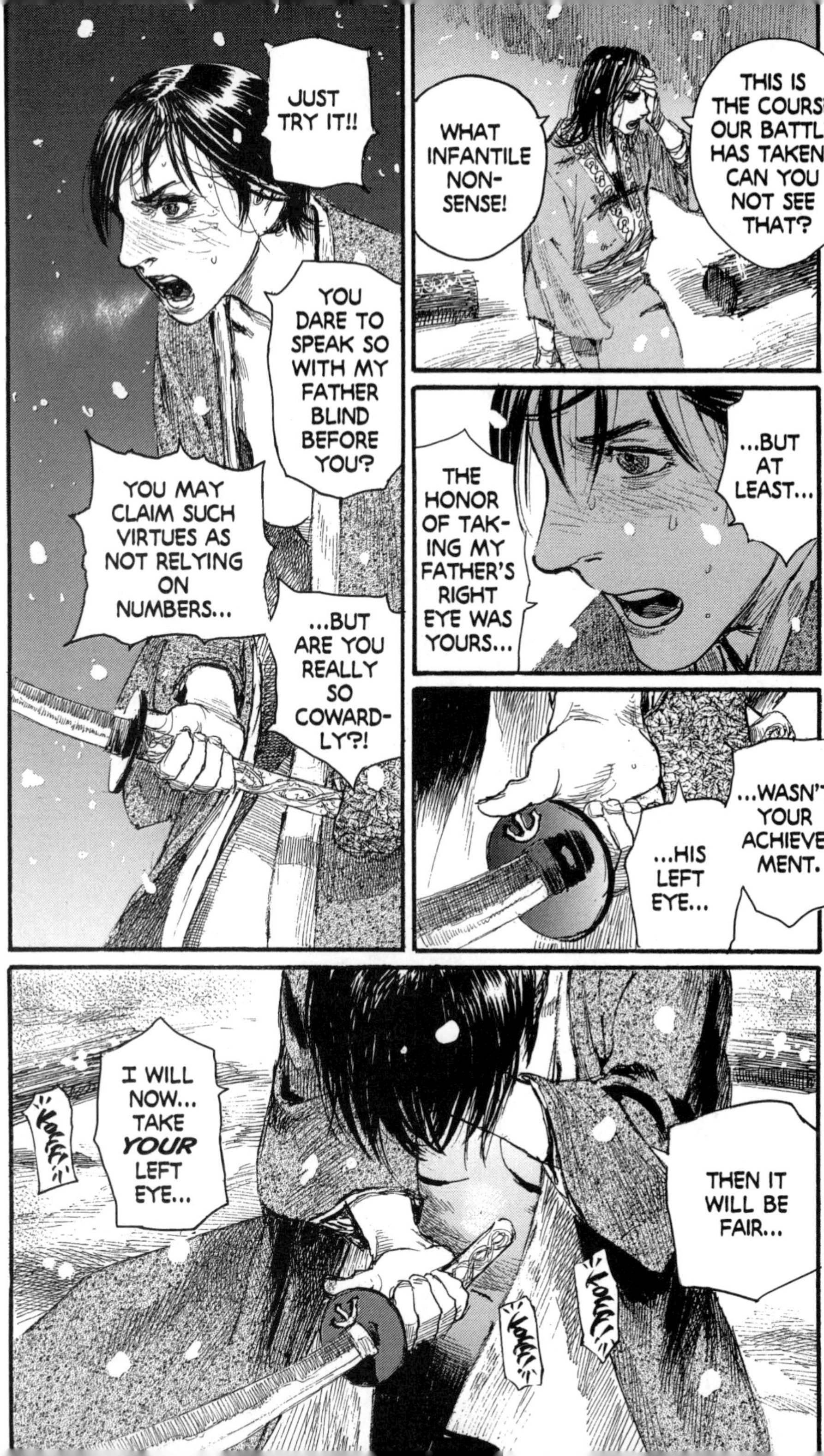
JUST TRY IT!!
YOU DARE TO SPEAK SO WITH MY FATHER BLIND BEFORE YOU?
YOU MAY CLAIM SUCH VIRTUES AS NOT RELYING ON NUMBERS...
...BUT ARE YOU REALLY SO COWARDLY?!
WHAT INFANTILE NON-SENSE!
THIS IS THE COURSE OUR BATTLE HAS TAKEN... CAN YOU NOT SEE THAT?
THE HONOR OF TAK-ING MY FATHER'S RIGHT EYE WAS YOURS...
...BUT AT LEAST...
...HIS LEFT EYE...
...WASN'T YOUR ACHIEVE-MENT.
I WILL NOW... TAKE *YOUR* LEFT EYE...
THEN IT WILL BE FAIR...

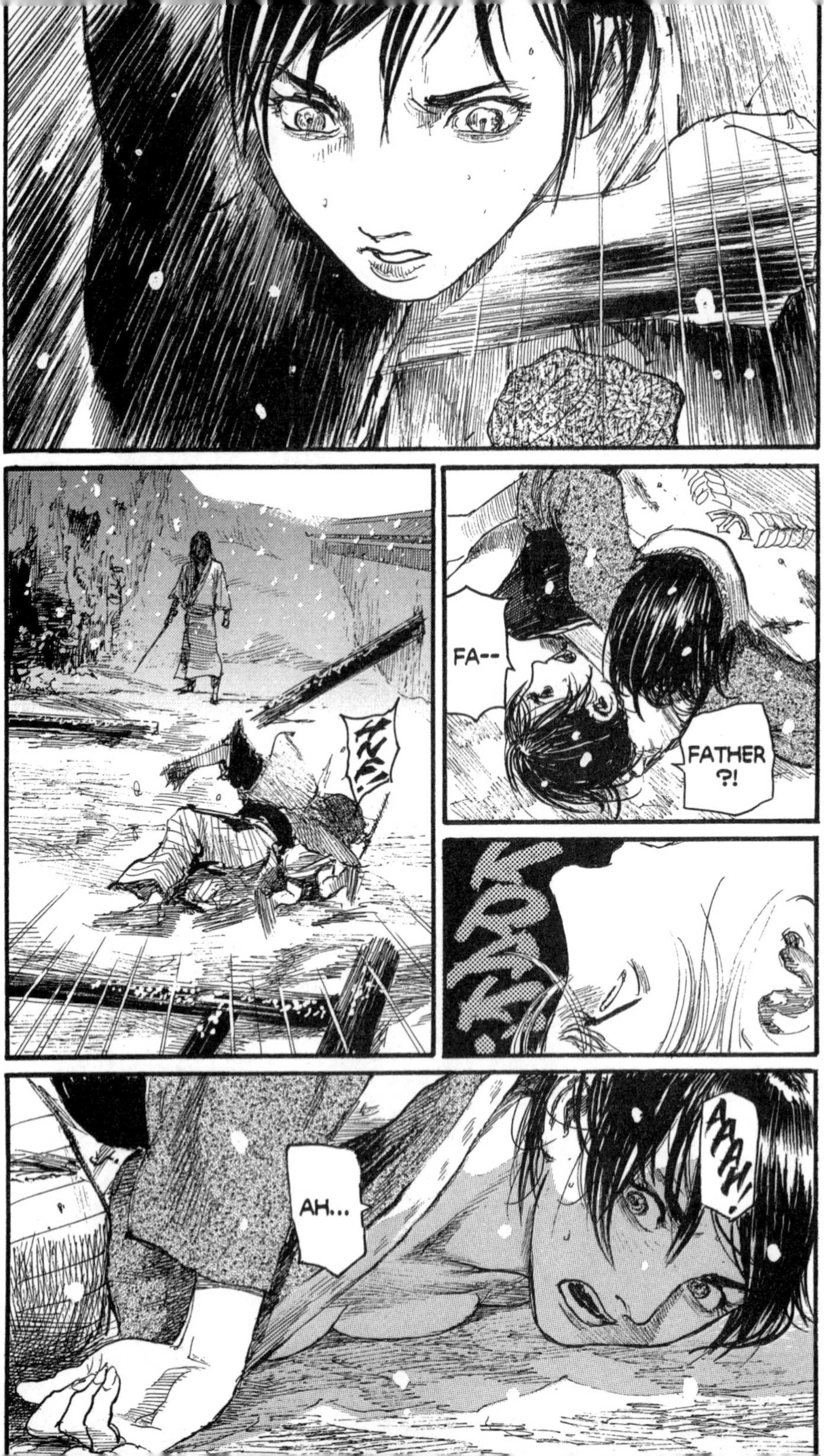
FA--
FATHER ?!
AH...

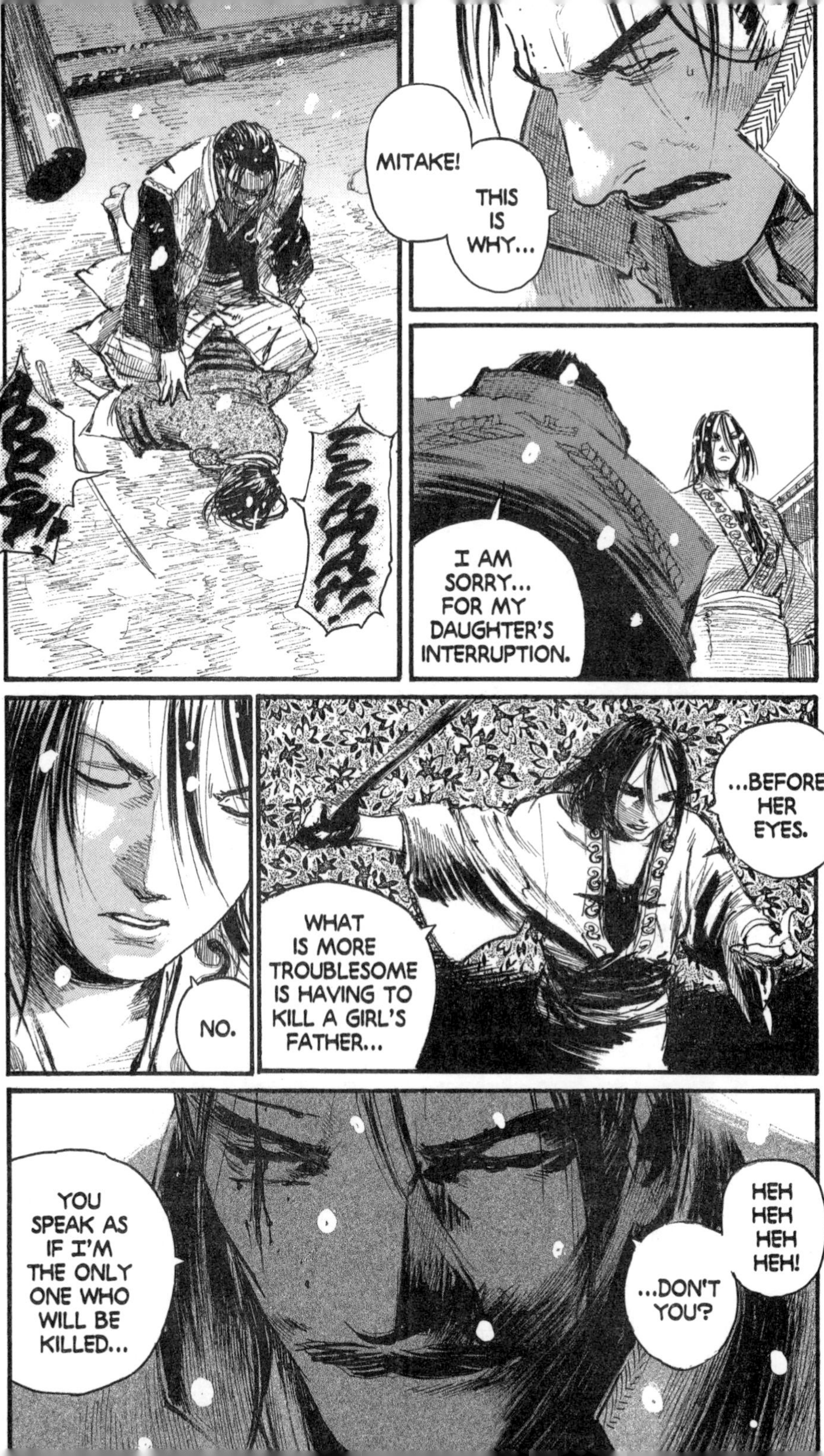
MITAKE!
THIS IS WHY...
I AM SORRY... FOR MY DAUGHTER'S INTERRUPTION.
NO.
WHAT IS MORE TROUBLESOME IS HAVING TO KILL A GIRL'S FATHER...
...BEFORE HER EYES.
YOU SPEAK AS IF I'M THE ONLY ONE WHO WILL BE KILLED...
...DON'T YOU?
HEH HEH HEH HEH!

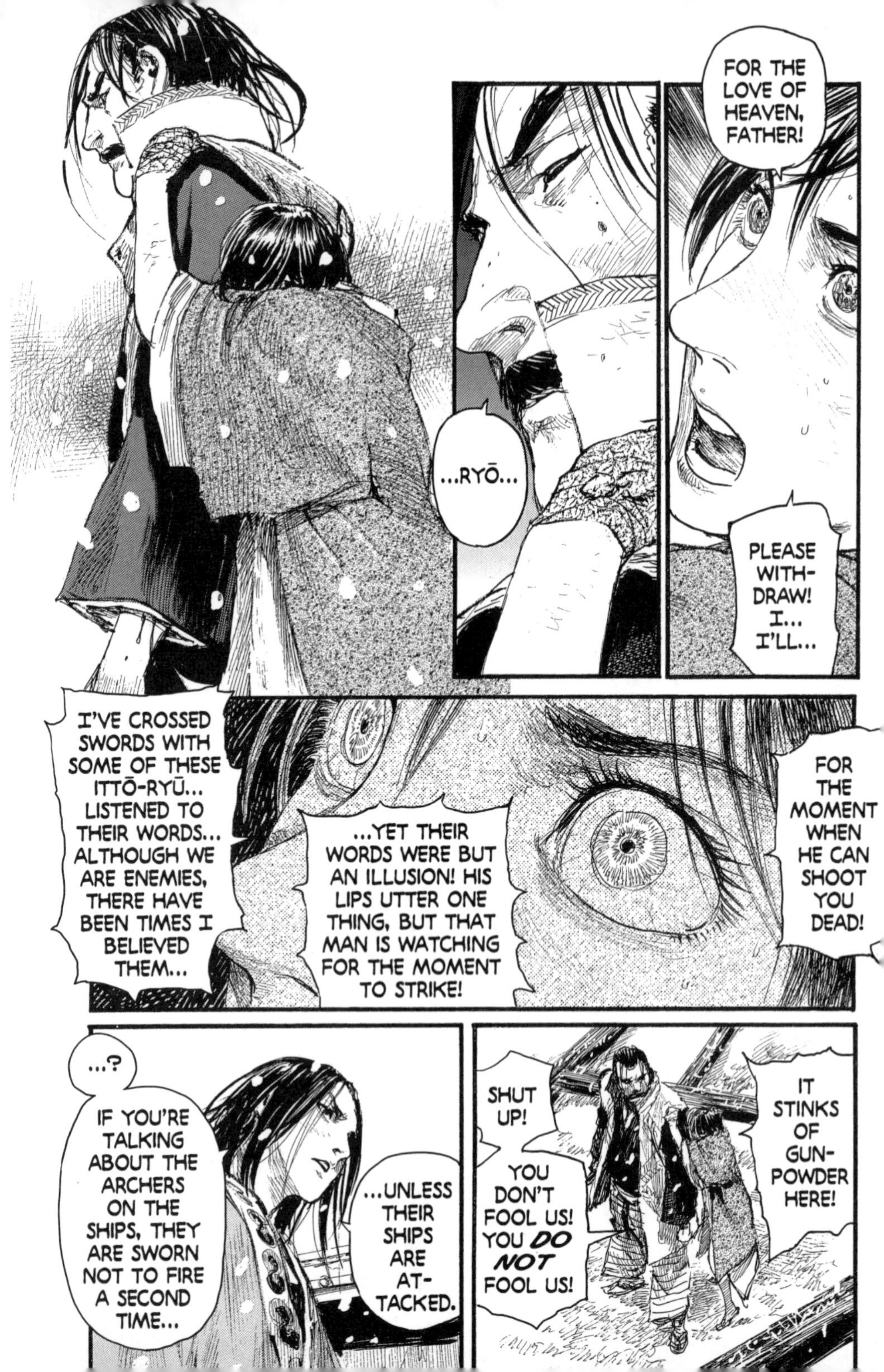
...RYŌ...
FOR THE LOVE OF HEAVEN, FATHER!
PLEASE WITH-DRAW! I... I'LL...
I'VE CROSSED SWORDS WITH SOME OF THESE ITTŌ-RYŪ... LISTENED TO THEIR WORDS... ALTHOUGH WE ARE ENEMIES, THERE HAVE BEEN TIMES I BELIEVED THEM...
...YET THEIR WORDS WERE BUT AN ILLUSION! HIS LIPS UTTER ONE THING, BUT THAT MAN IS WATCHING FOR THE MOMENT TO STRIKE!
FOR THE MOMENT WHEN HE CAN SHOOT YOU DEAD!
...?
IF YOU'RE TALKING ABOUT THE ARCHERS ON THE SHIPS, THEY ARE SWORN NOT TO FIRE A SECOND TIME...
...UNLESS THEIR SHIPS ARE AT-TACKED.
SHUT UP!
YOU DON'T FOOL US! YOU *DO NOT* FOOL US!
IT STINKS OF GUN-POWDER HERE!

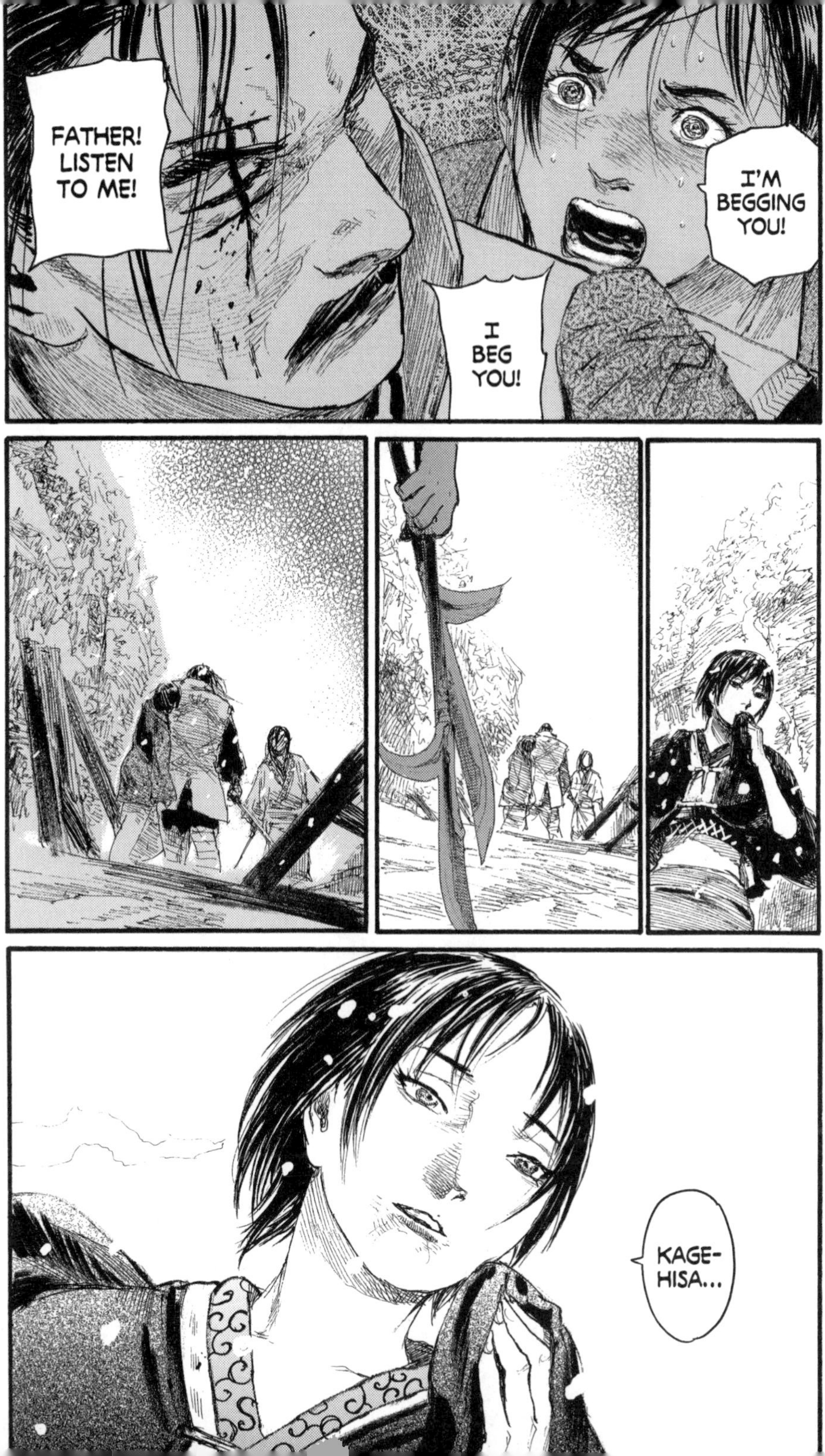
FATHER! LISTEN TO ME!
I'M BEGGING YOU!
I BEG YOU!
KAGE-HISA...

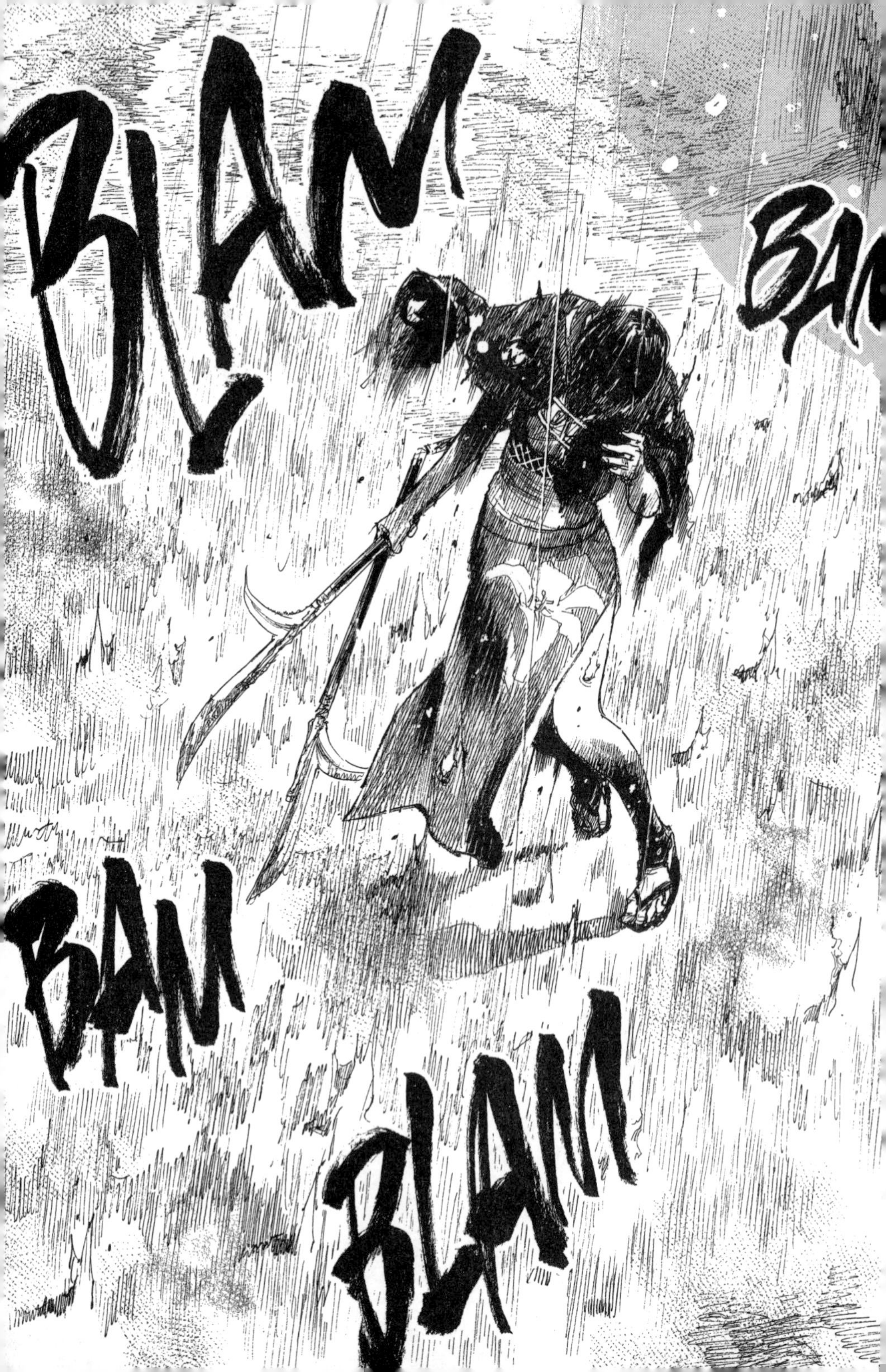
BLAM
BAM
BAM
BLAM

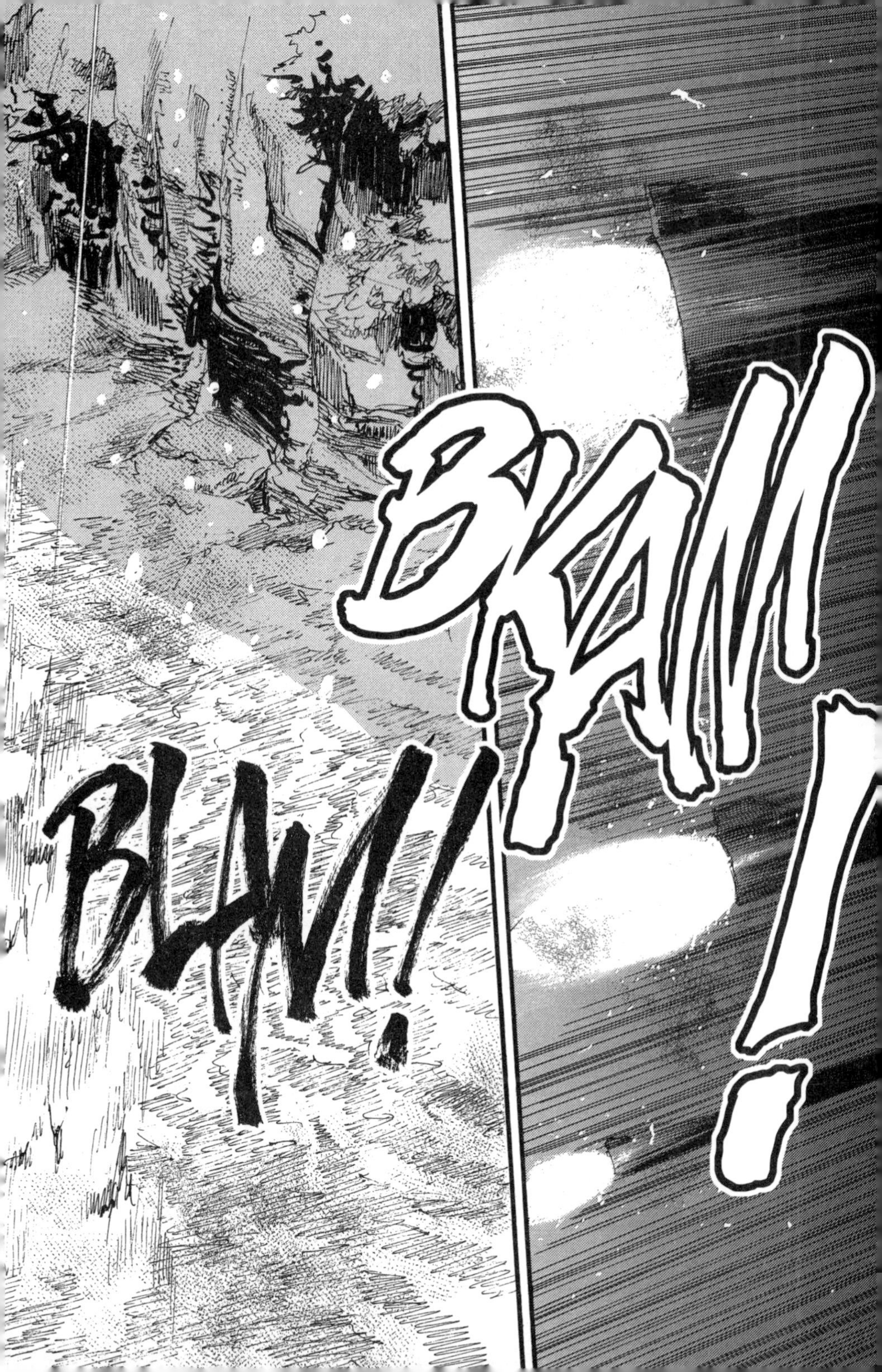
BLAM!
BLAM!!

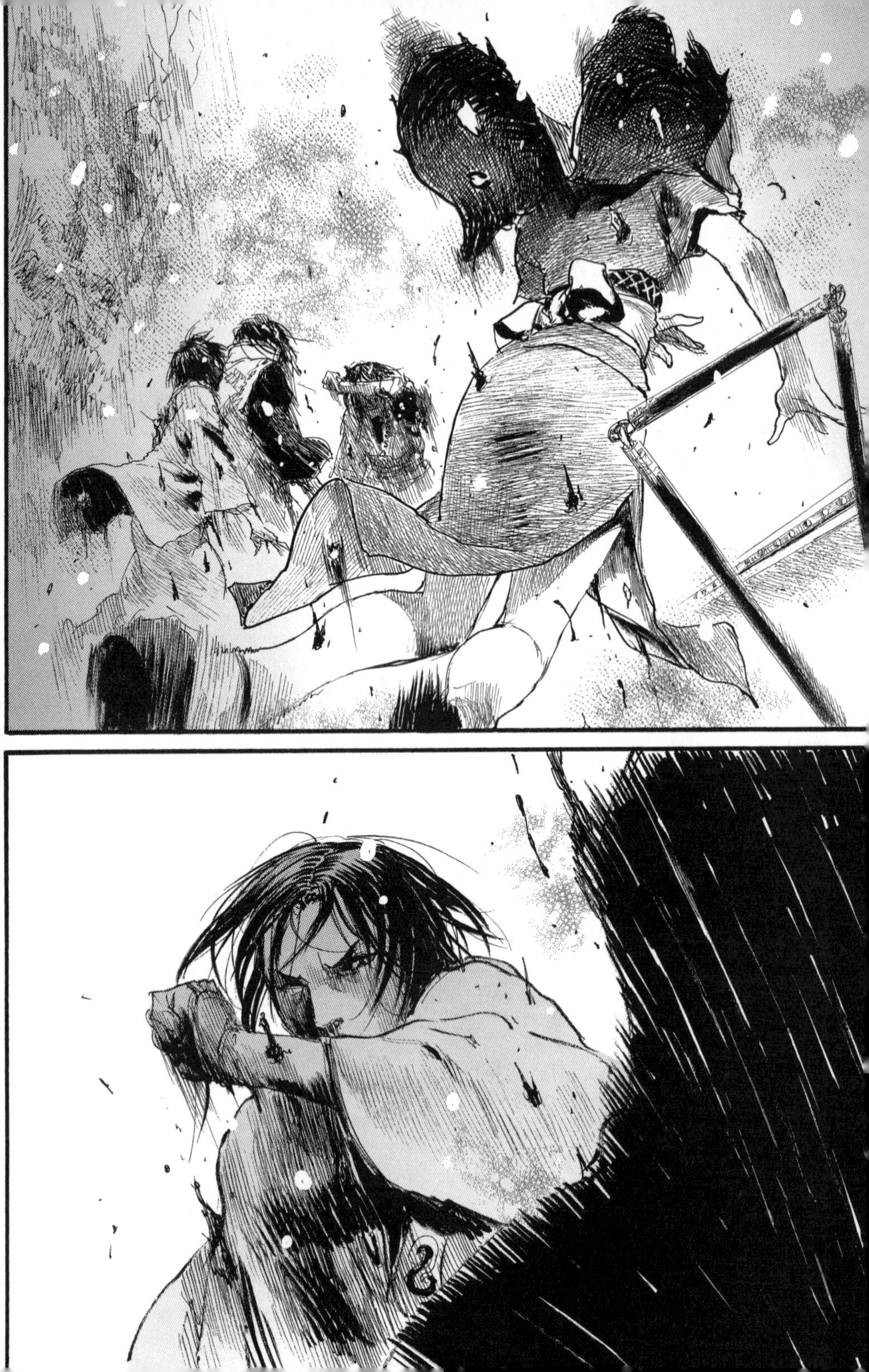

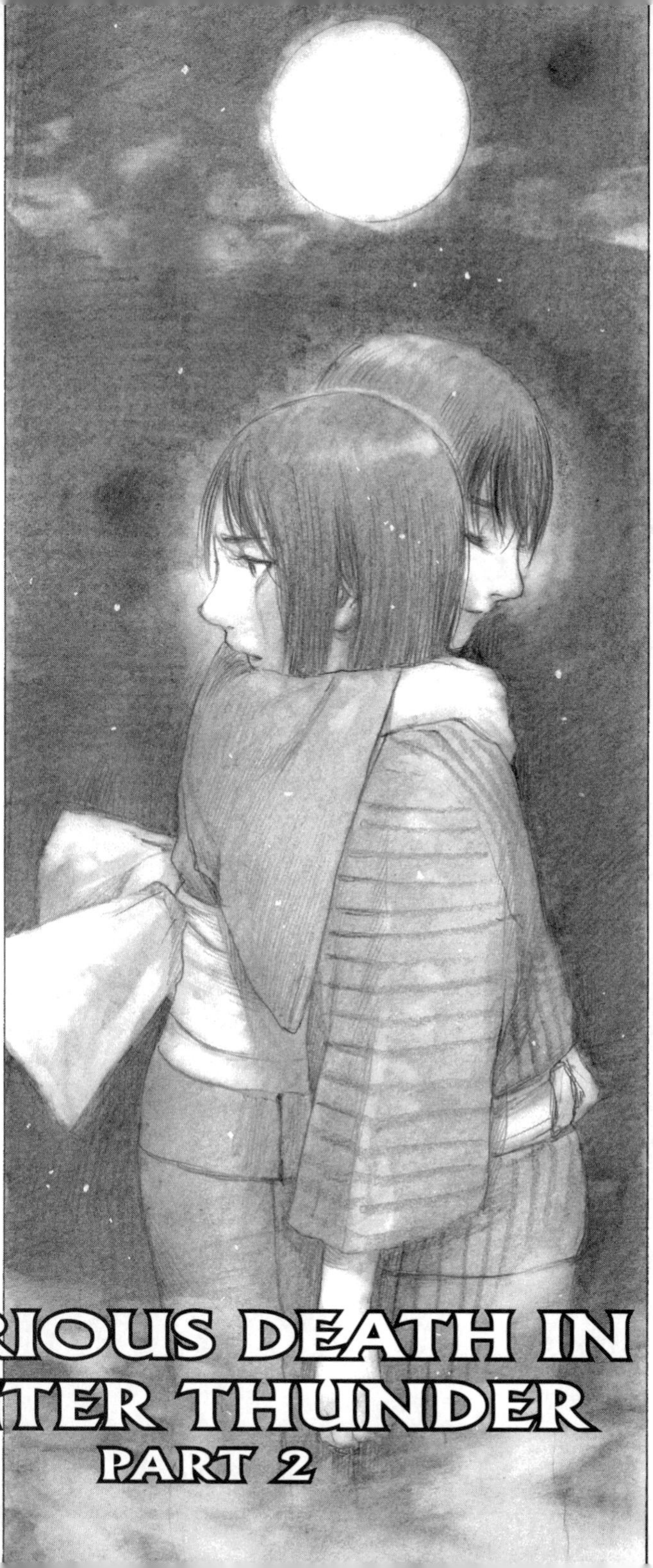

GLORIOUS DEATH IN WINTER THUNDER

PART 2

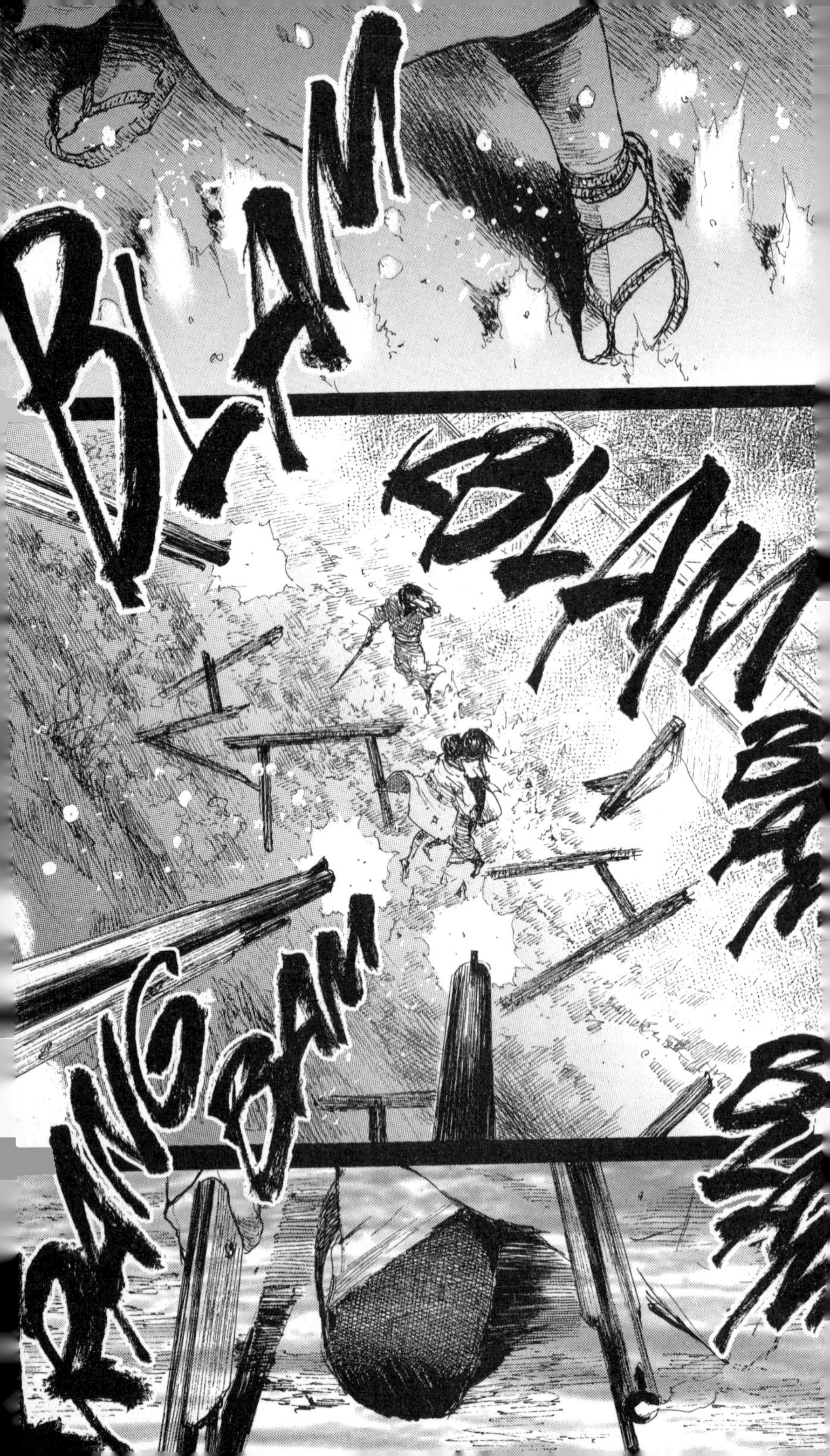
BLAM
BLAM
BANG
BLAM

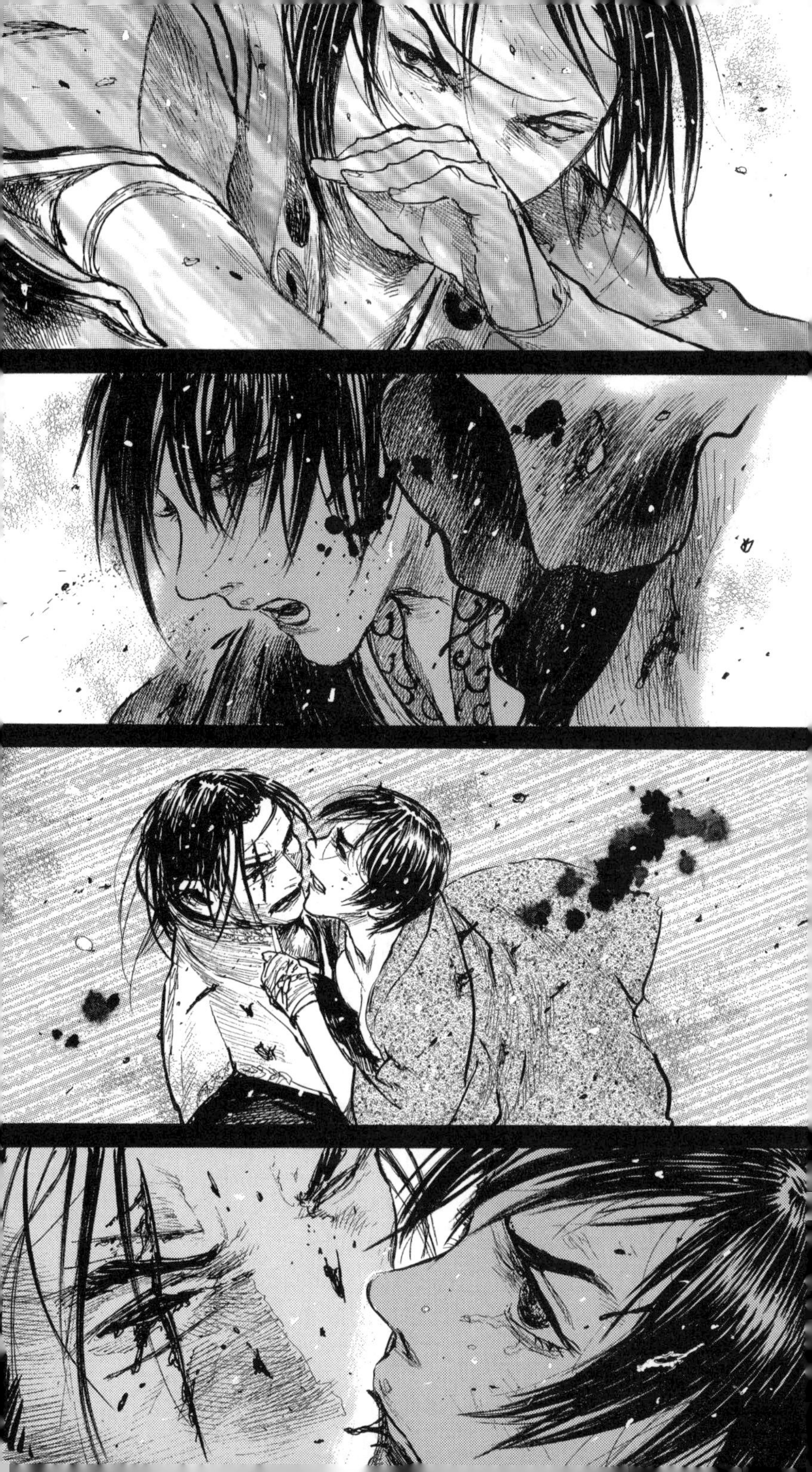

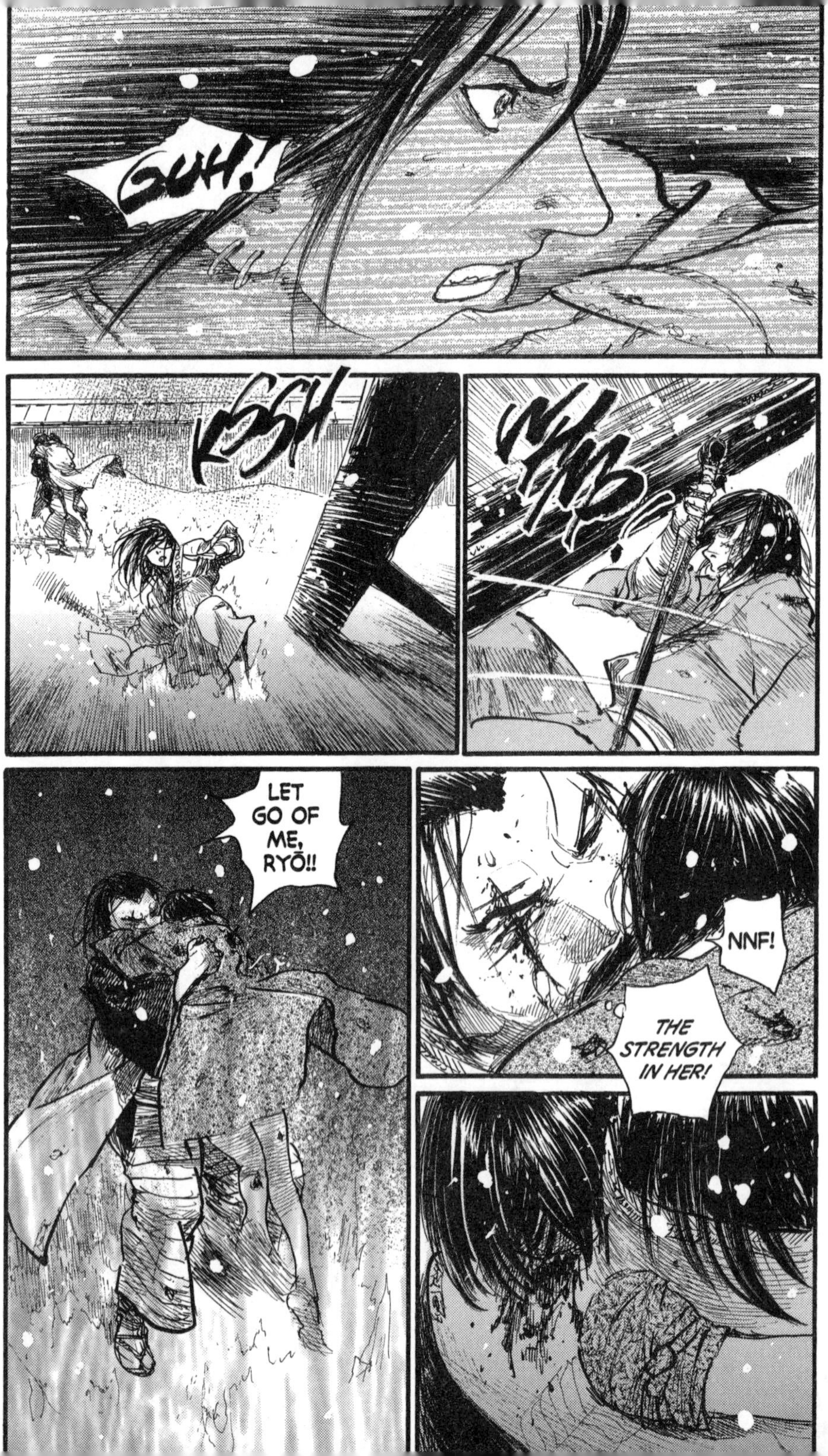
GUH!
KSSH
LET GO OF ME, RYŌ!!
NNF!
THE STRENGTH IN HER!

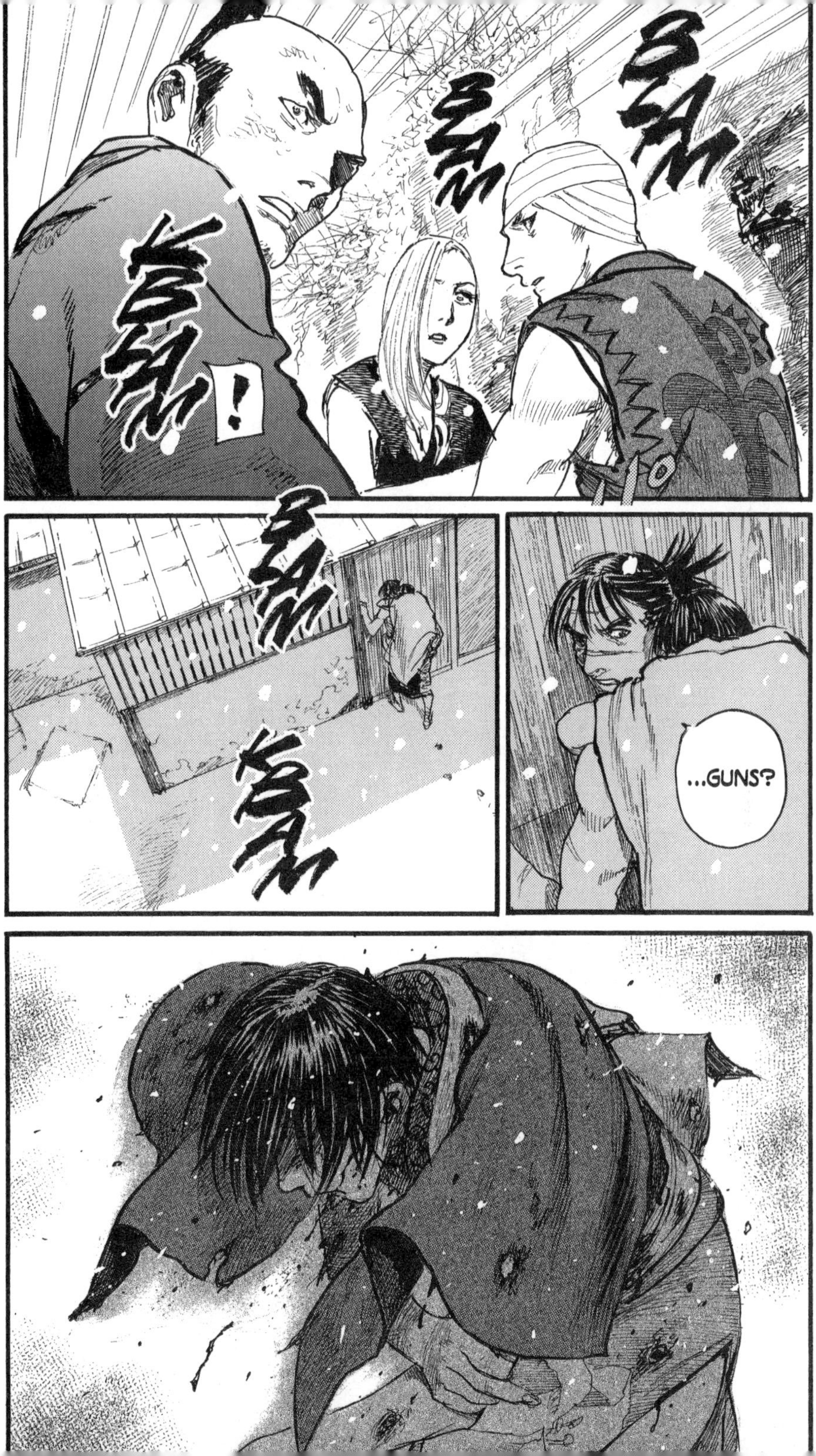
BAM
BAM
BAM
!
BAM
BAM
...GUNS?

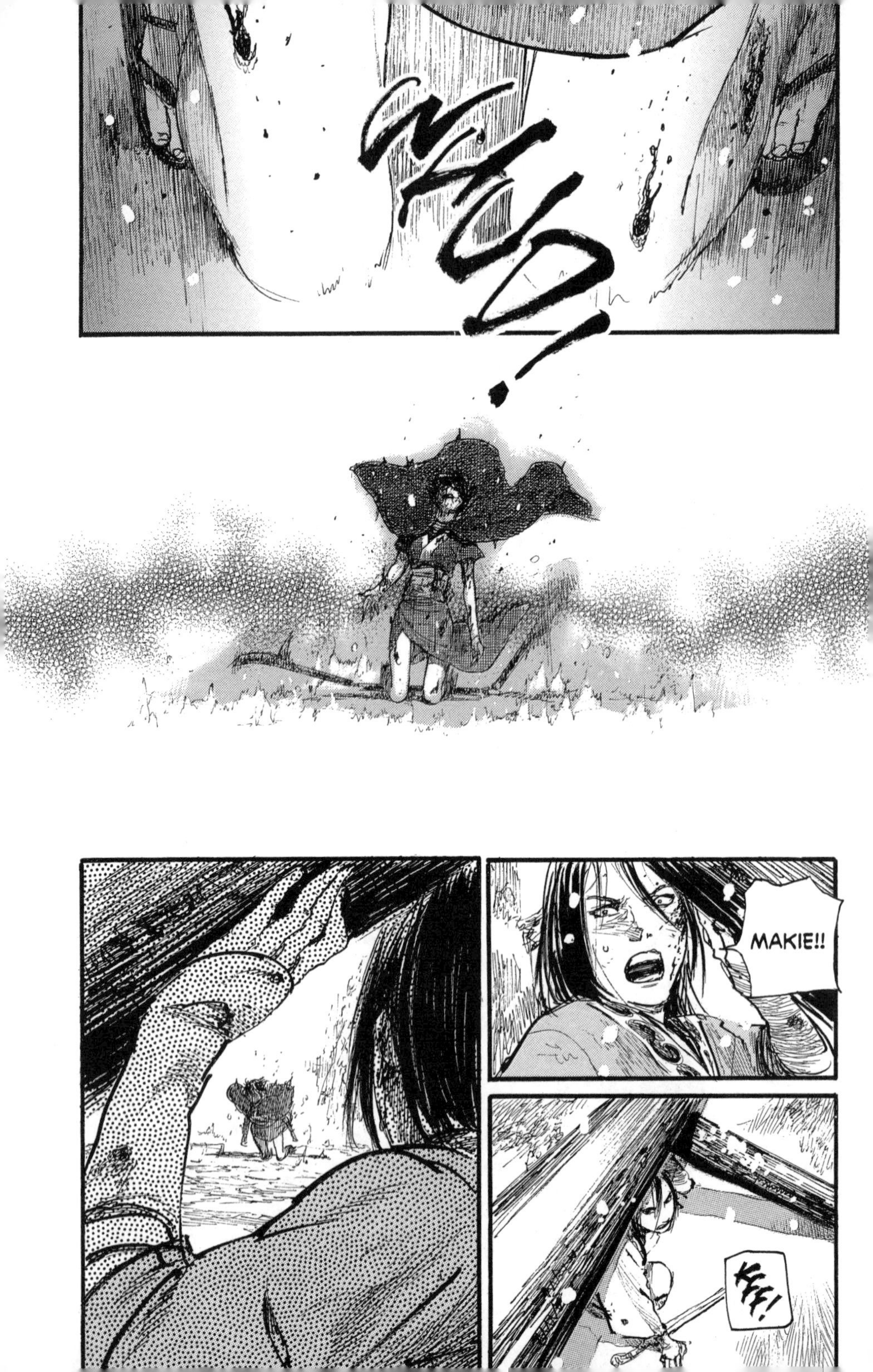
WHUD!
MAKIE!!
KFF!

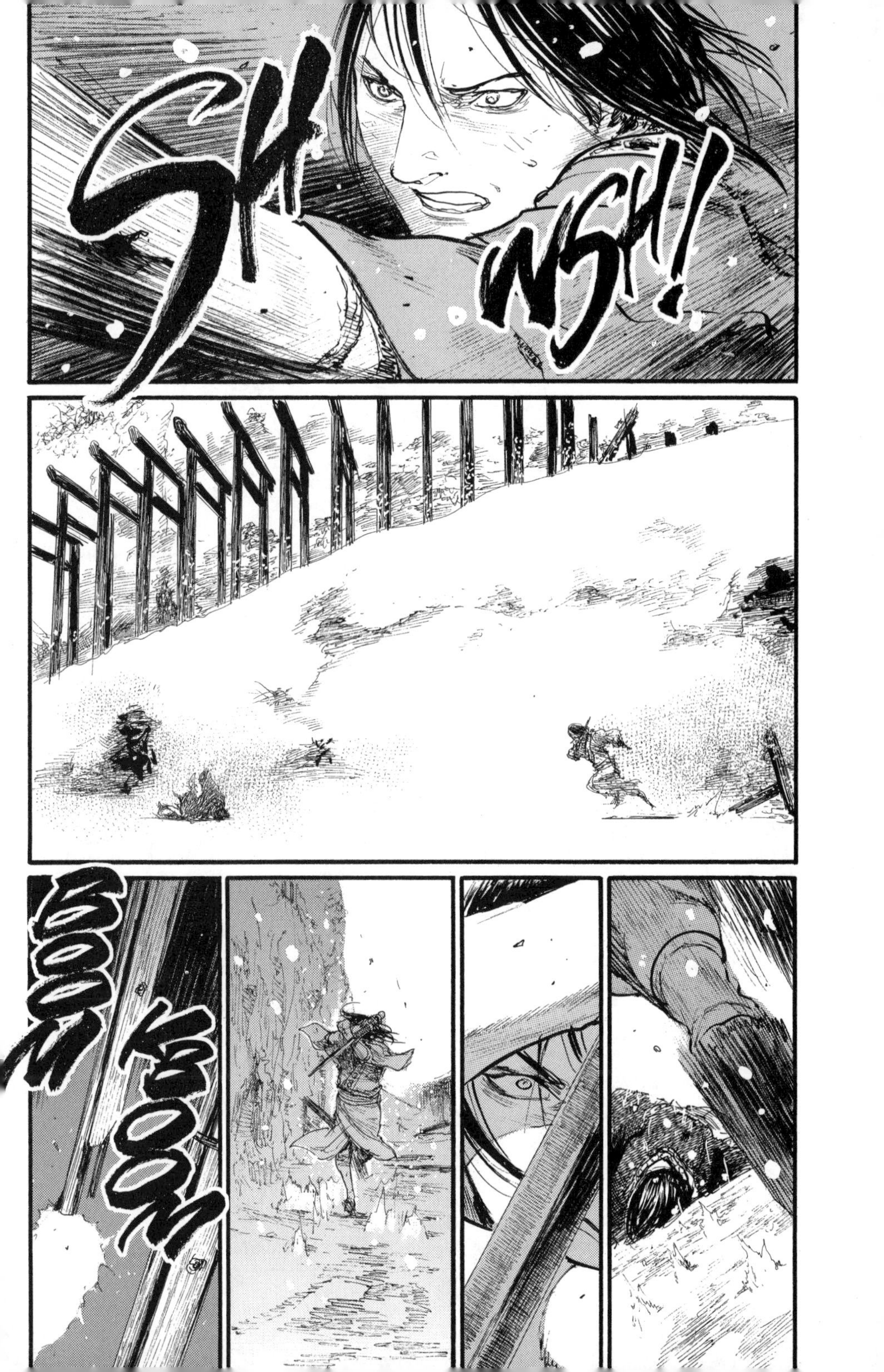
SHWSH!
BOOOM
KBOOM

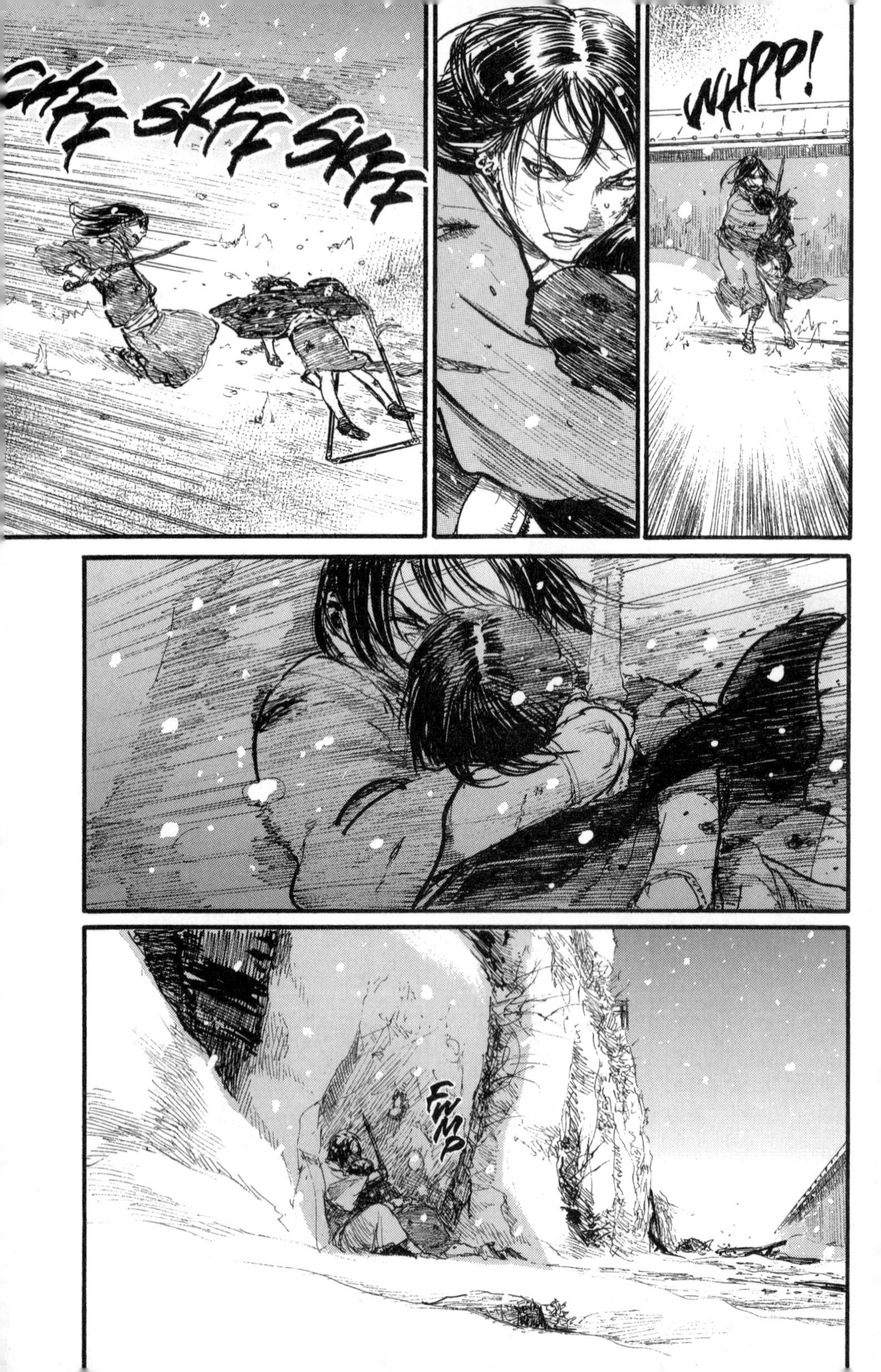
SKFF SKFF SKFF
WHPP!
FWMP

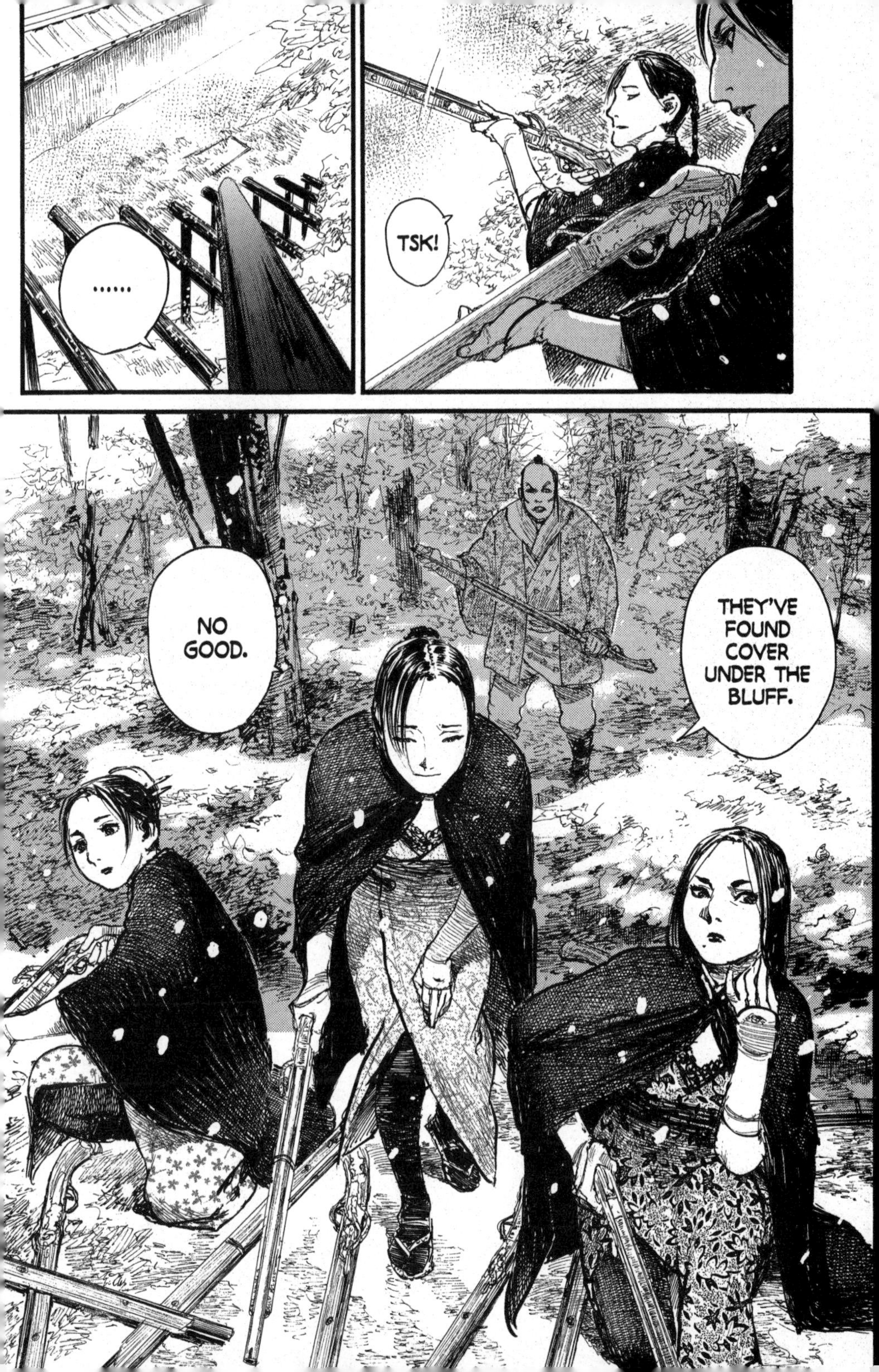
......
TSK!
NO GOOD.
THEY'VE FOUND COVER UNDER THE BLUFF.

Y-YOU'RE SAYING YOU FAILED TO KILL HIM...?!

TO KILL ANOTSU KAGEHISA...?!

DESPITE ALL THAT SHOOTING...?!

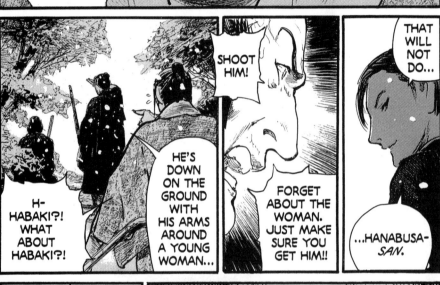

SHOOT HIM!

H-HABAKI?! WHAT ABOUT HABAKI?!

HE'S DOWN ON THE GROUND WITH HIS ARMS AROUND A YOUNG WOMAN...

FORGET ABOUT THE WOMAN. JUST MAKE SURE YOU GET HIM!!

THAT WILL NOT DO...

...HANABUSA-*SAN.*

AS CORRUPT AS A *KŌGI* MAY BE...

...CAN HE FIRE ON A FELLOW *KŌGI* WITHOUT EXCUSE... JUST BECAUSE THE *KŌGI* IS NEAR SOME ANTI-*BAKUFU* ITTŌ-RYŪ?

KHH!

AND WHAT ABOUT WHEN THE *KŌGI* HAS BEEN ORDERED TO COMMIT *SEPPUKU?*

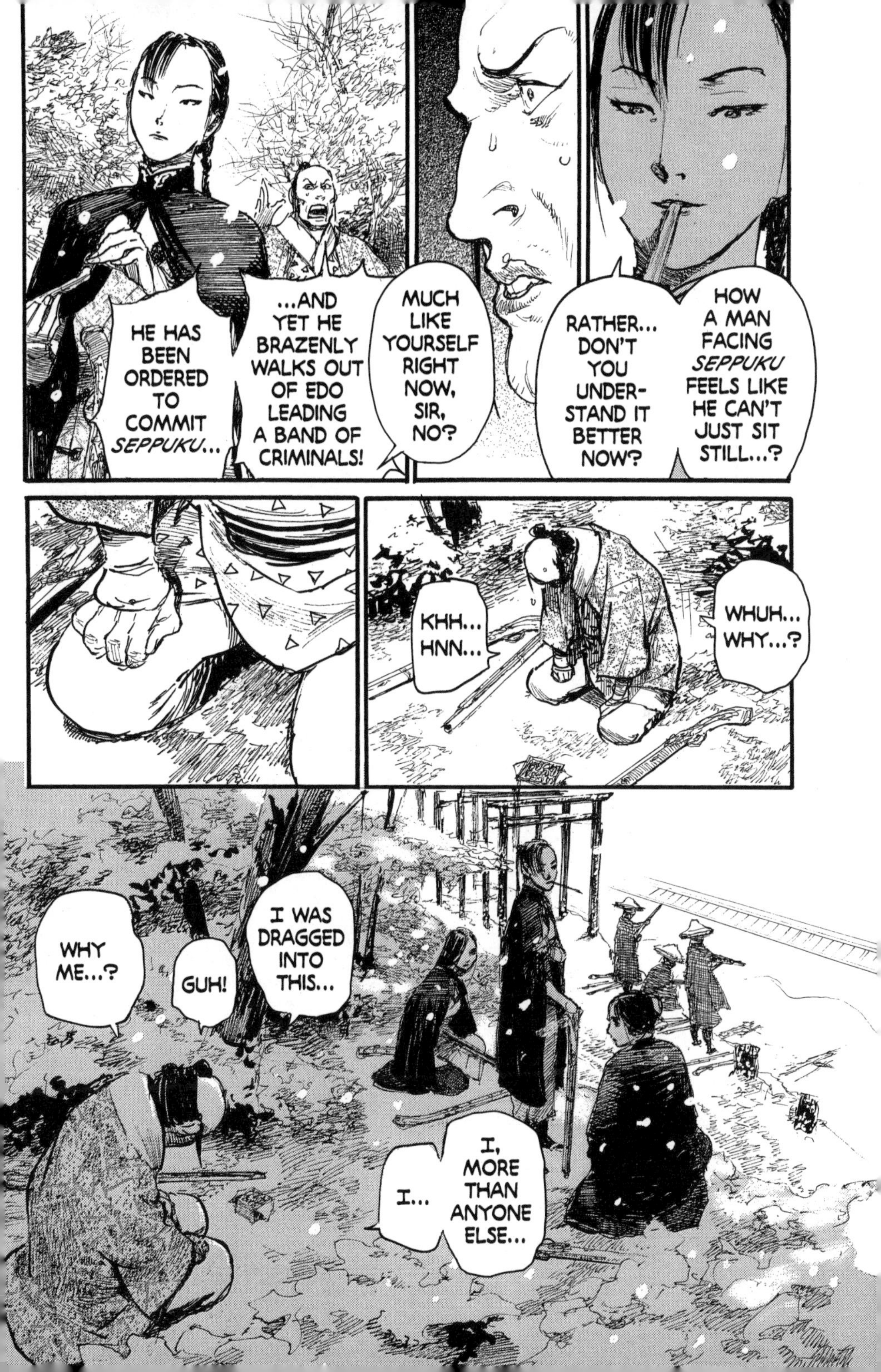
HE HAS BEEN ORDERED TO COMMIT *SEPPUKU*...
...AND YET HE BRAZENLY WALKS OUT OF EDO LEADING A BAND OF CRIMINALS!
MUCH LIKE YOURSELF RIGHT NOW, SIR, NO?
RATHER... DON'T YOU UNDER-STAND IT BETTER NOW?
HOW A MAN FACING *SEPPUKU* FEELS LIKE HE CAN'T JUST SIT STILL...?
KHH... HNN...
WHUH... WHY...?
WHY ME...?
GUH!
I WAS DRAGGED INTO THIS...
I...
I, MORE THAN ANYONE ELSE...

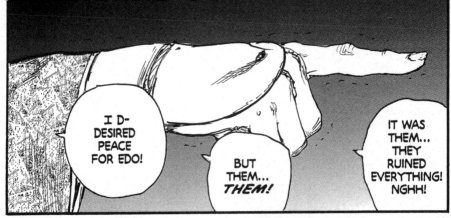

I D-DESIRED PEACE FOR EDO!

BUT THEM... *THEM!*

IT WAS THEM... THEY RUINED EVERYTHING! NGHH!

BUT HOW TREMENDOUSLY SWIFT YOU WERE, HANABUSA-*SAN.*

GETTING HOLD OF TWENTY RIFLES *AND* MAKING IT HERE SO FAST...

RUMOR HAS IT THAT ONE OF HABAKI-*SAN'S* SUBORDINATES WENT AROUND AND KILLED THE HORSES IN EVERY POST TOWN...

...SO YOU HAD THAT AS A DISADVANTAGE, TOO.

WHY ARE ALL THE TORII KNOCKED DOWN AROUND HERE?

THE HELL...?

...FIFTY *RYŌ*...

HN?

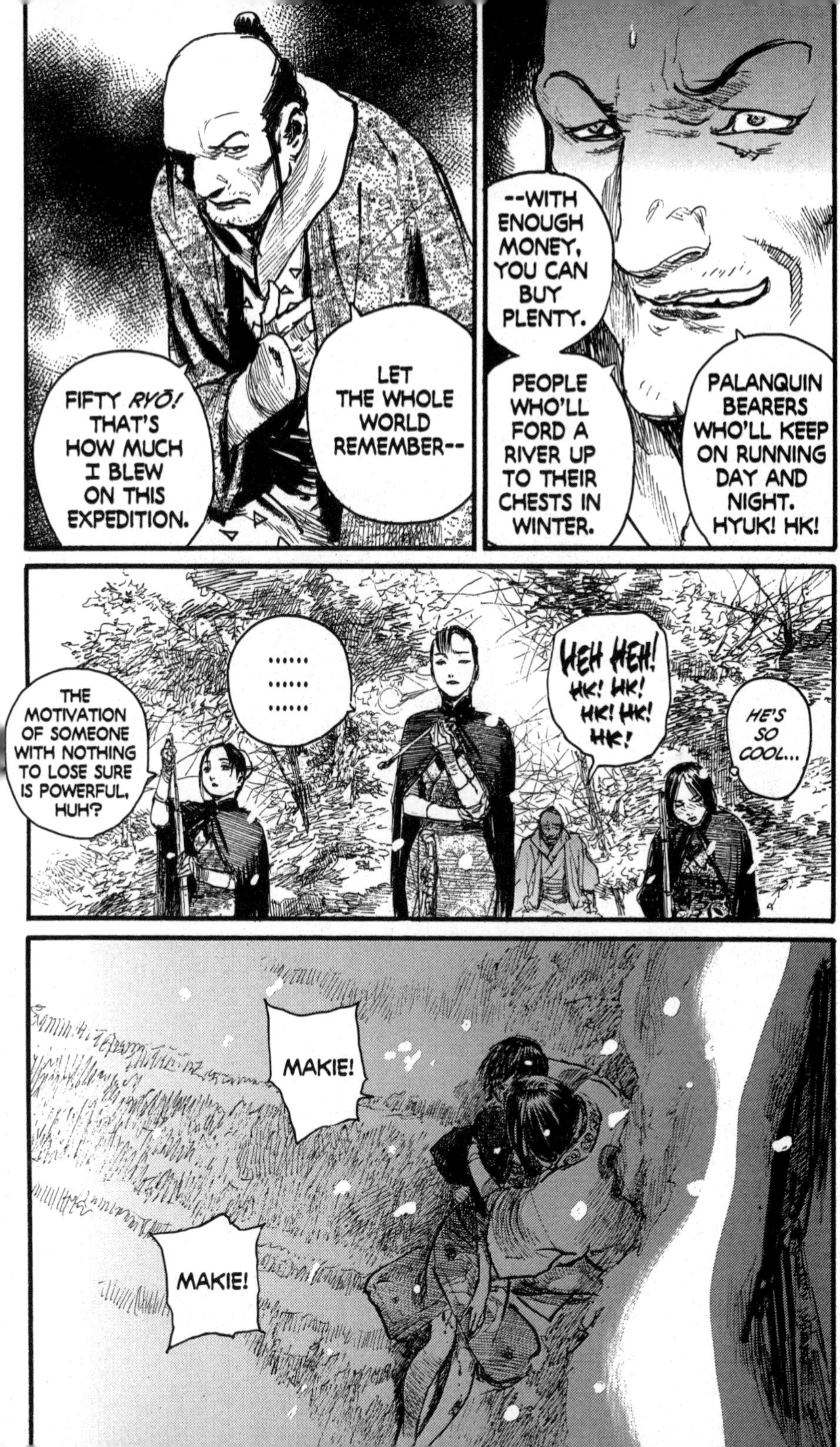
FIFTY *RYŌ!* THAT'S HOW MUCH I BLEW ON THIS EXPEDITION.
LET THE WHOLE WORLD REMEMBER--
--WITH ENOUGH MONEY, YOU CAN BUY PLENTY.
PEOPLE WHO'LL FORD A RIVER UP TO THEIR CHESTS IN WINTER.
PALANQUIN BEARERS WHO'LL KEEP ON RUNNING DAY AND NIGHT. HYUK! HK!
THE MOTIVATION OF SOMEONE WITH NOTHING TO LOSE SURE IS POWERFUL, HUH?
....
HEH HEH! HK! HK! HK! HK! HK!
HE'S SO COOL...
MAKIE!
MAKIE!

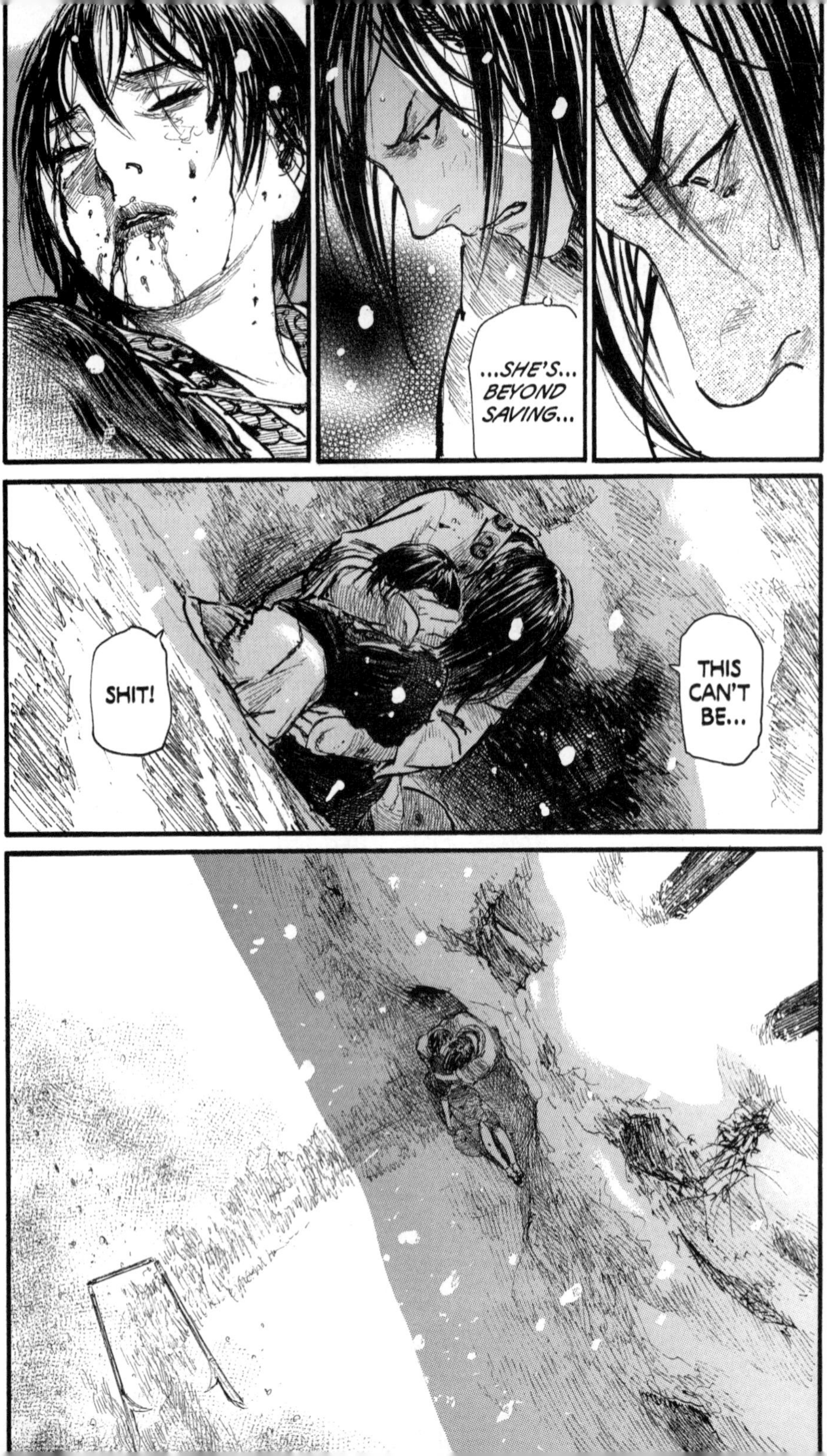
...SHE'S... BEYOND SAVING...
SHIT!
THIS CAN'T BE...

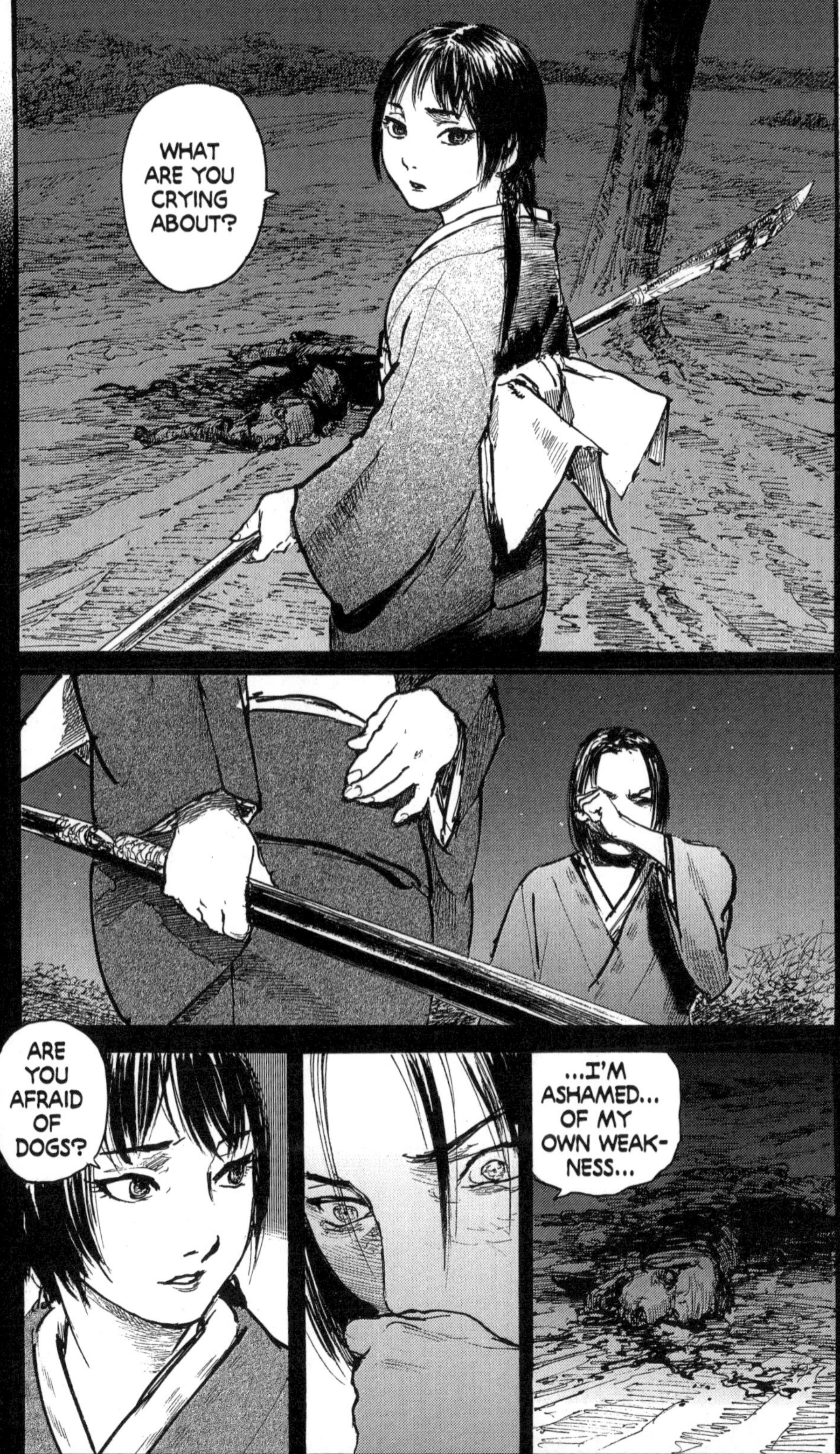
WHAT ARE YOU CRYING ABOUT?
ARE YOU AFRAID OF DOGS?
...I'M ASHAMED... OF MY OWN WEAK-NESS...

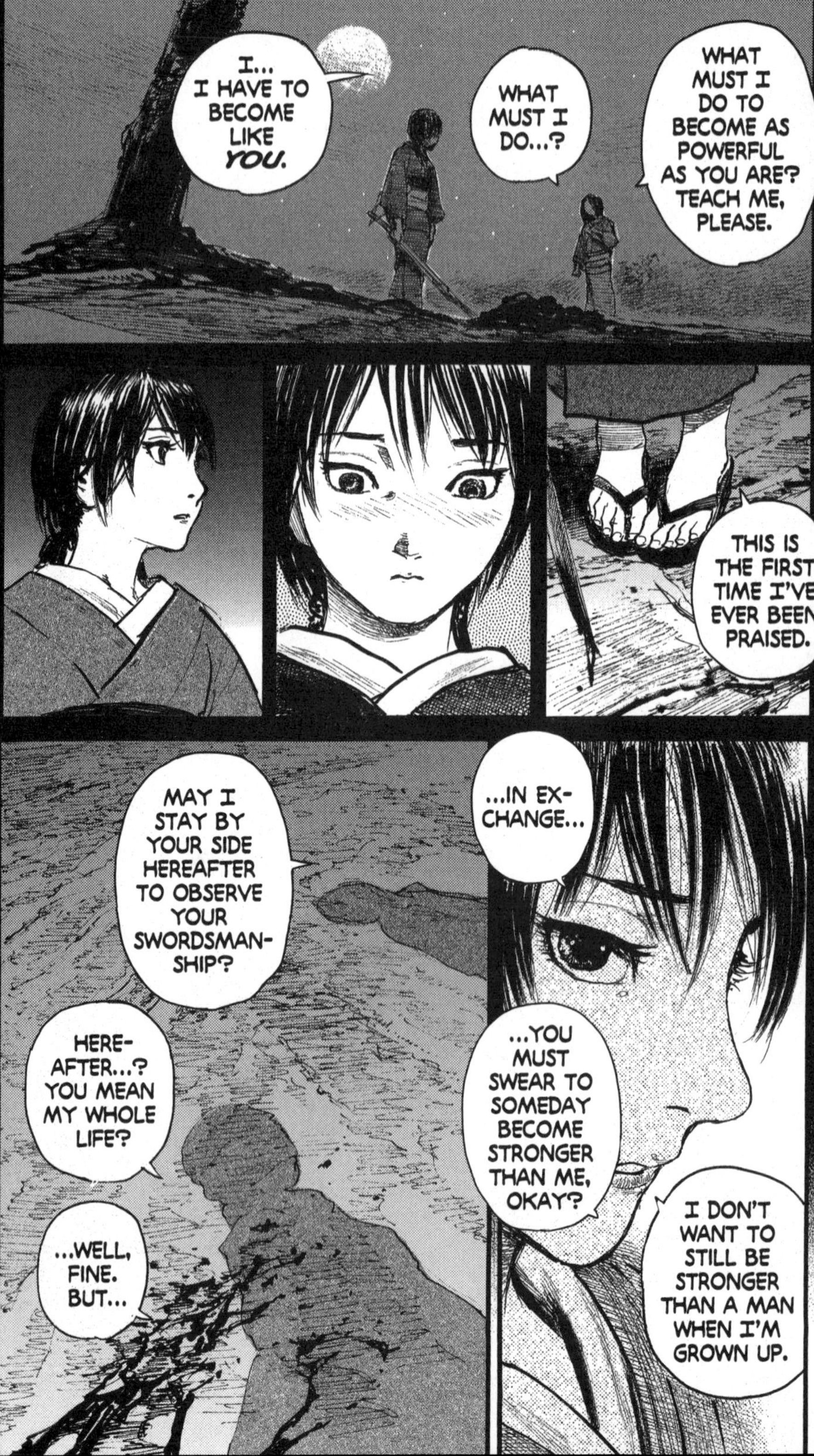
I... I HAVE TO BECOME LIKE YOU.
WHAT MUST I DO...?
WHAT MUST I DO TO BECOME AS POWERFUL AS YOU ARE? TEACH ME, PLEASE.
THIS IS THE FIRST TIME I'VE EVER BEEN PRAISED.
MAY I STAY BY YOUR SIDE HEREAFTER TO OBSERVE YOUR SWORDSMAN-SHIP?
HERE-AFTER...? YOU MEAN MY WHOLE LIFE?
...WELL, FINE. BUT...
...IN EX-CHANGE...
...YOU MUST SWEAR TO SOMEDAY BECOME STRONGER THAN ME, OKAY?
I DON'T WANT TO STILL BE STRONGER THAN A MAN WHEN I'M GROWN UP.

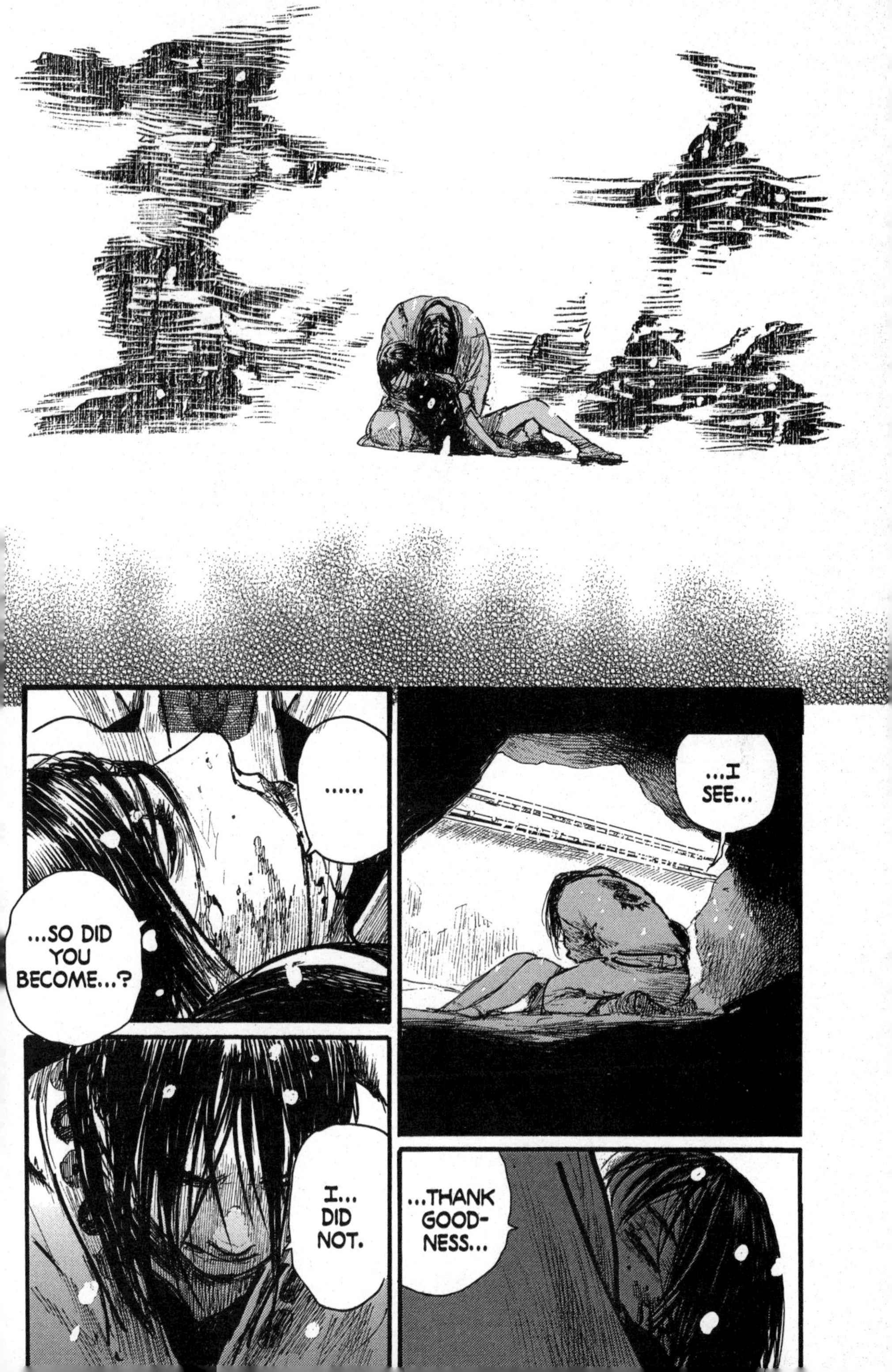

......
...SO DID YOU BECOME...?
I... DID NOT.
...I SEE...
...THANK GOODNESS...

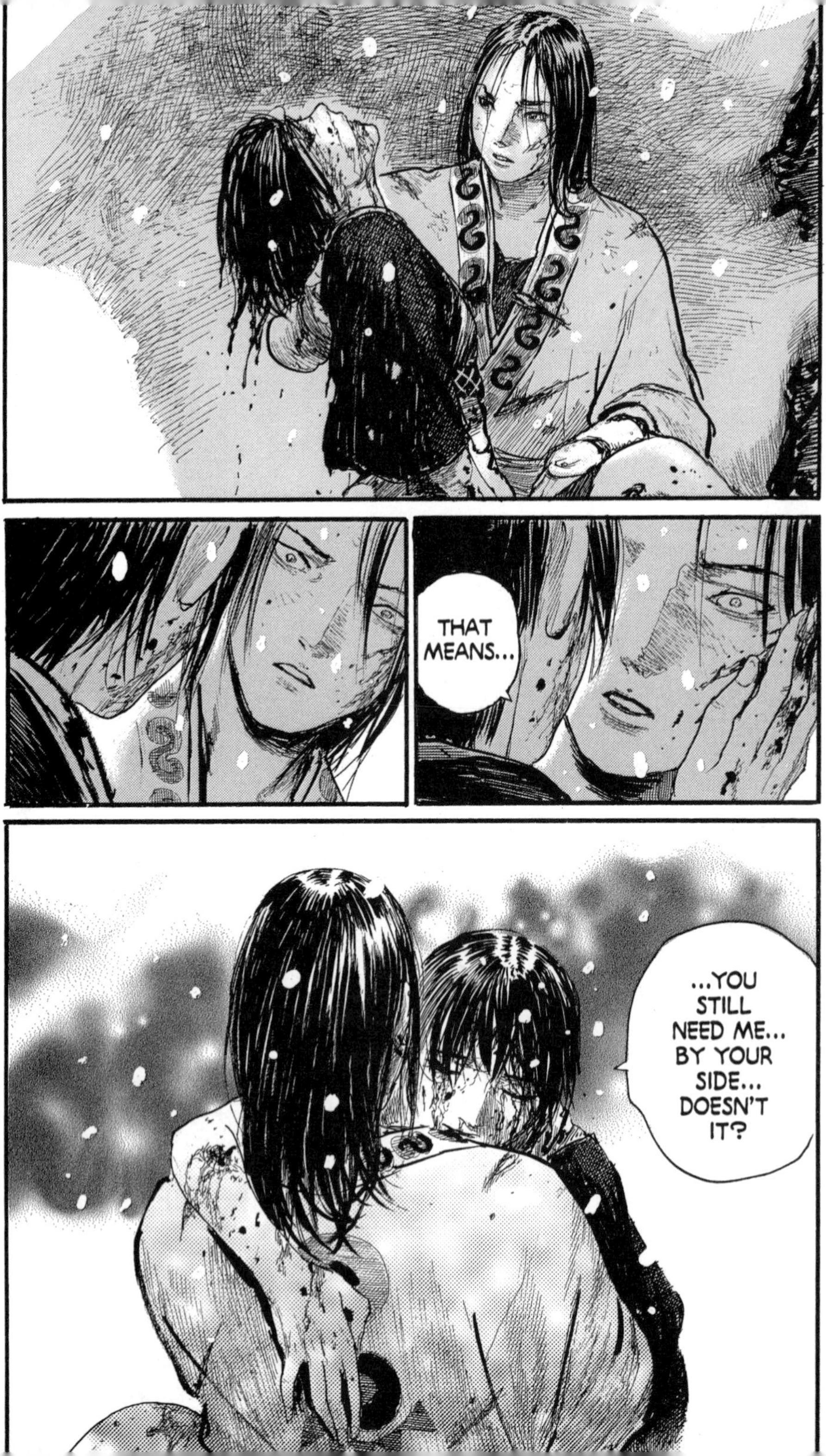
THAT MEANS...
...YOU STILL NEED ME... BY YOUR SIDE... DOESN'T IT?

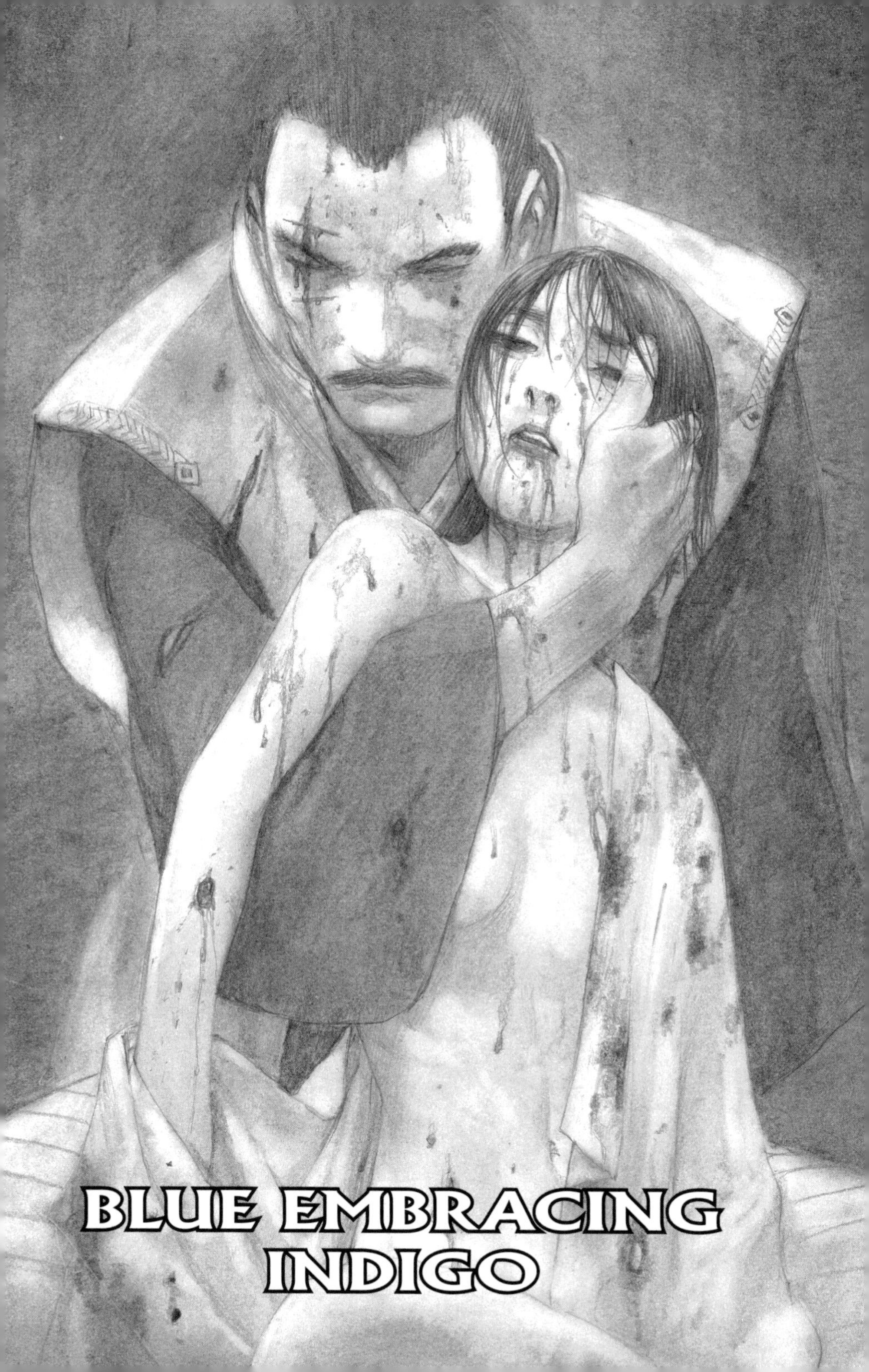
BLUE EMBRACING
INDIGO

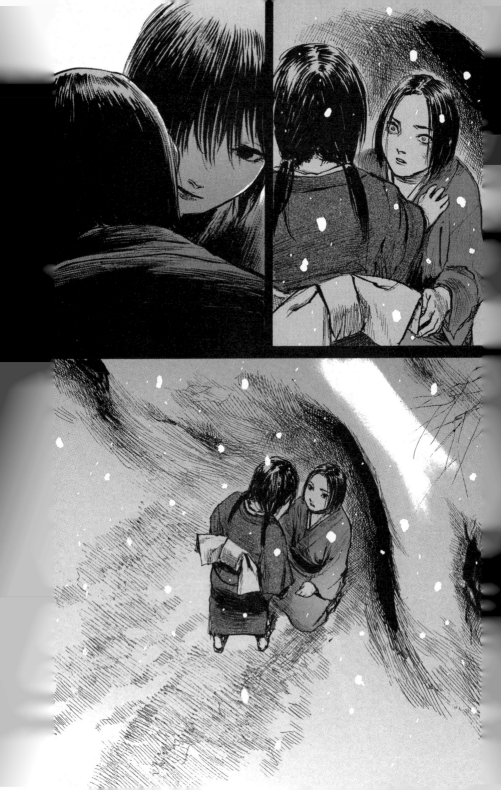

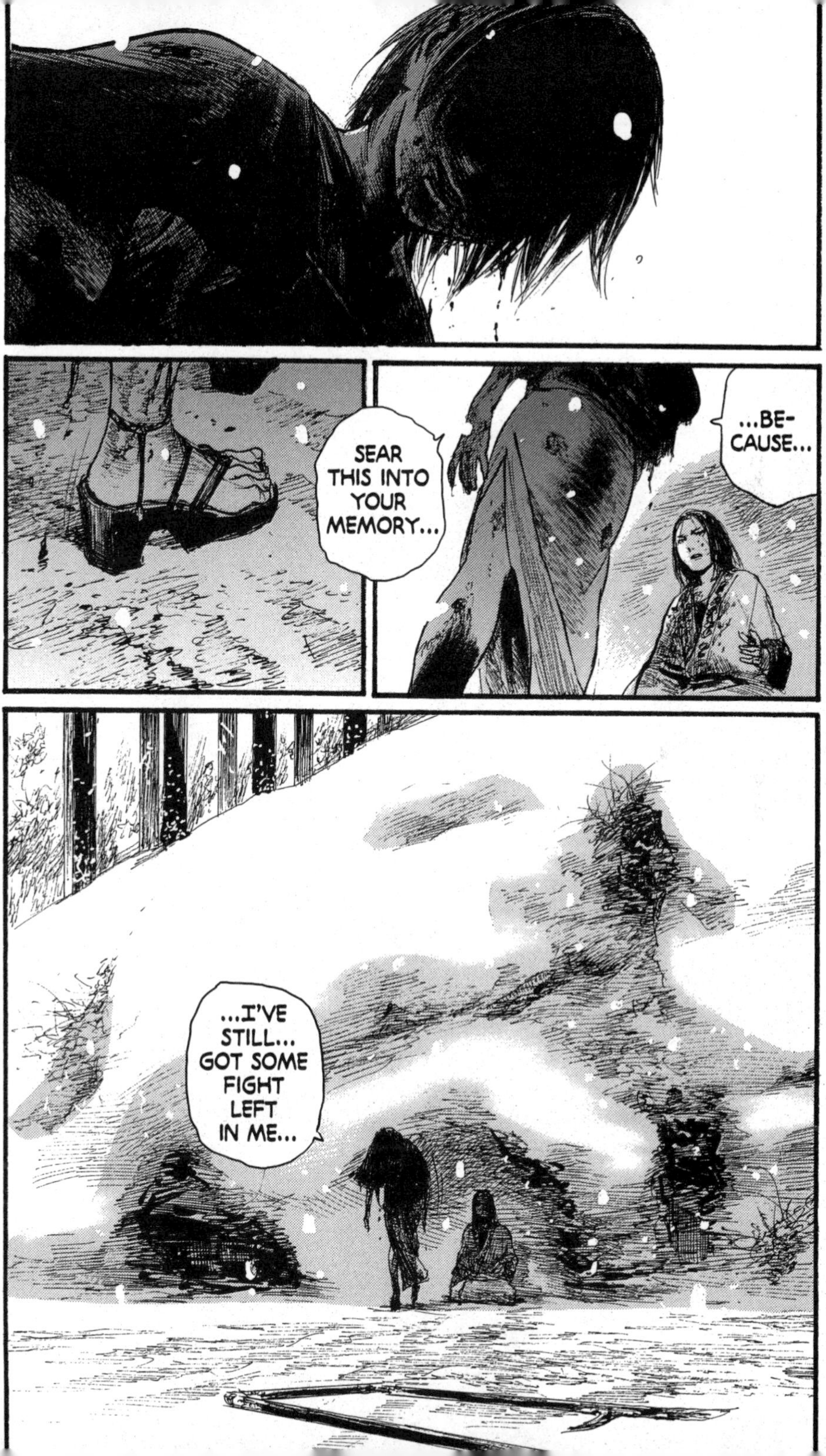
SEAR THIS INTO YOUR MEMORY...
...BE-CAUSE...
...I'VE STILL... GOT SOME FIGHT LEFT IN ME...

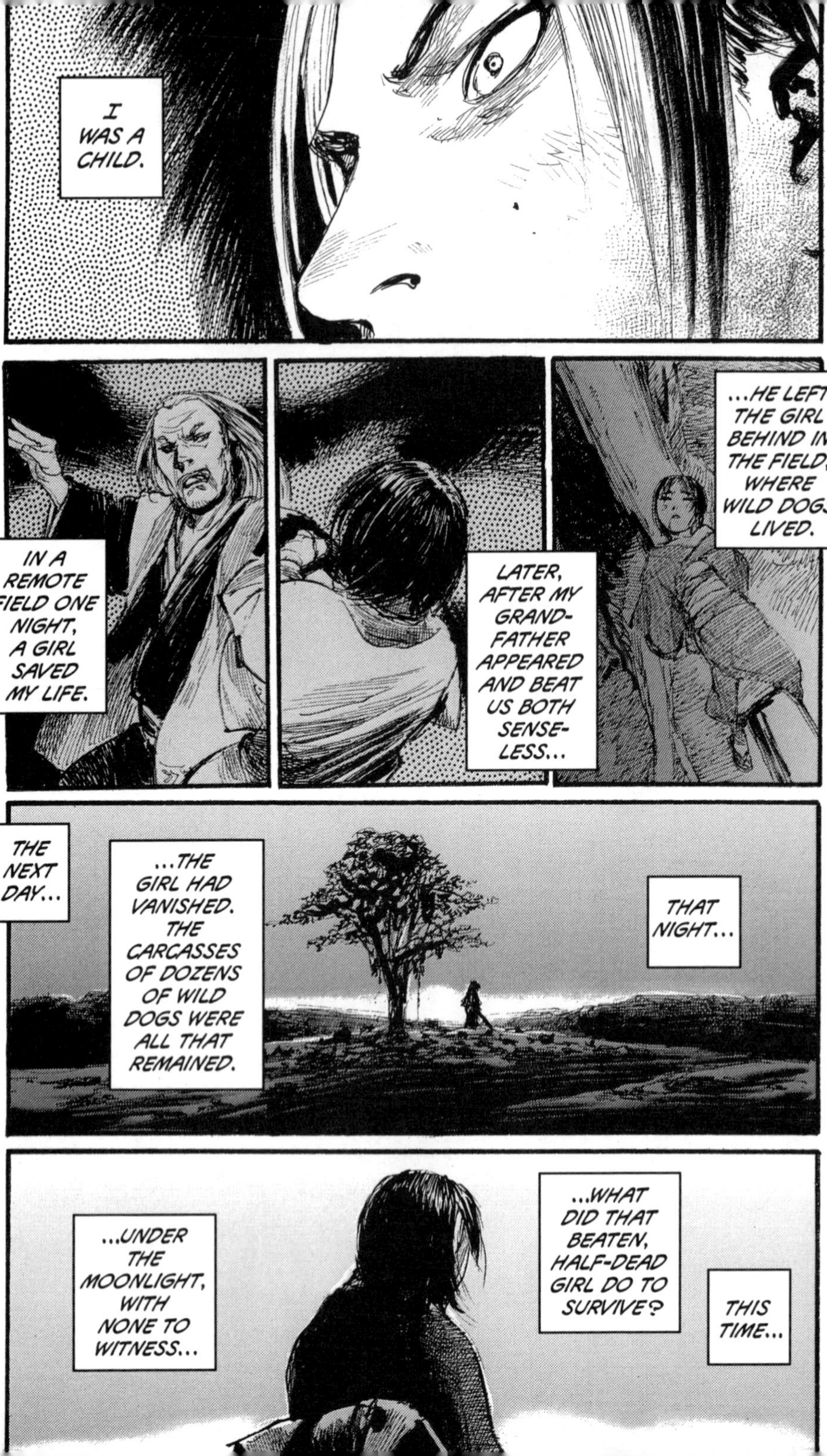
I WAS A CHILD.
IN A REMOTE FIELD ONE NIGHT, A GIRL SAVED MY LIFE.
LATER, AFTER MY GRAND-FATHER APPEARED AND BEAT US BOTH SENSE-LESS...
...HE LEFT THE GIRL BEHIND IN THE FIELD, WHERE WILD DOGS LIVED.
THE NEXT DAY...
...THE GIRL HAD VANISHED. THE CARCASSES OF DOZENS OF WILD DOGS WERE ALL THAT REMAINED.
THAT NIGHT...
...UNDER THE MOONLIGHT, WITH NONE TO WITNESS...
...WHAT DID THAT BEATEN, HALF-DEAD GIRL DO TO SURVIVE?
THIS TIME...

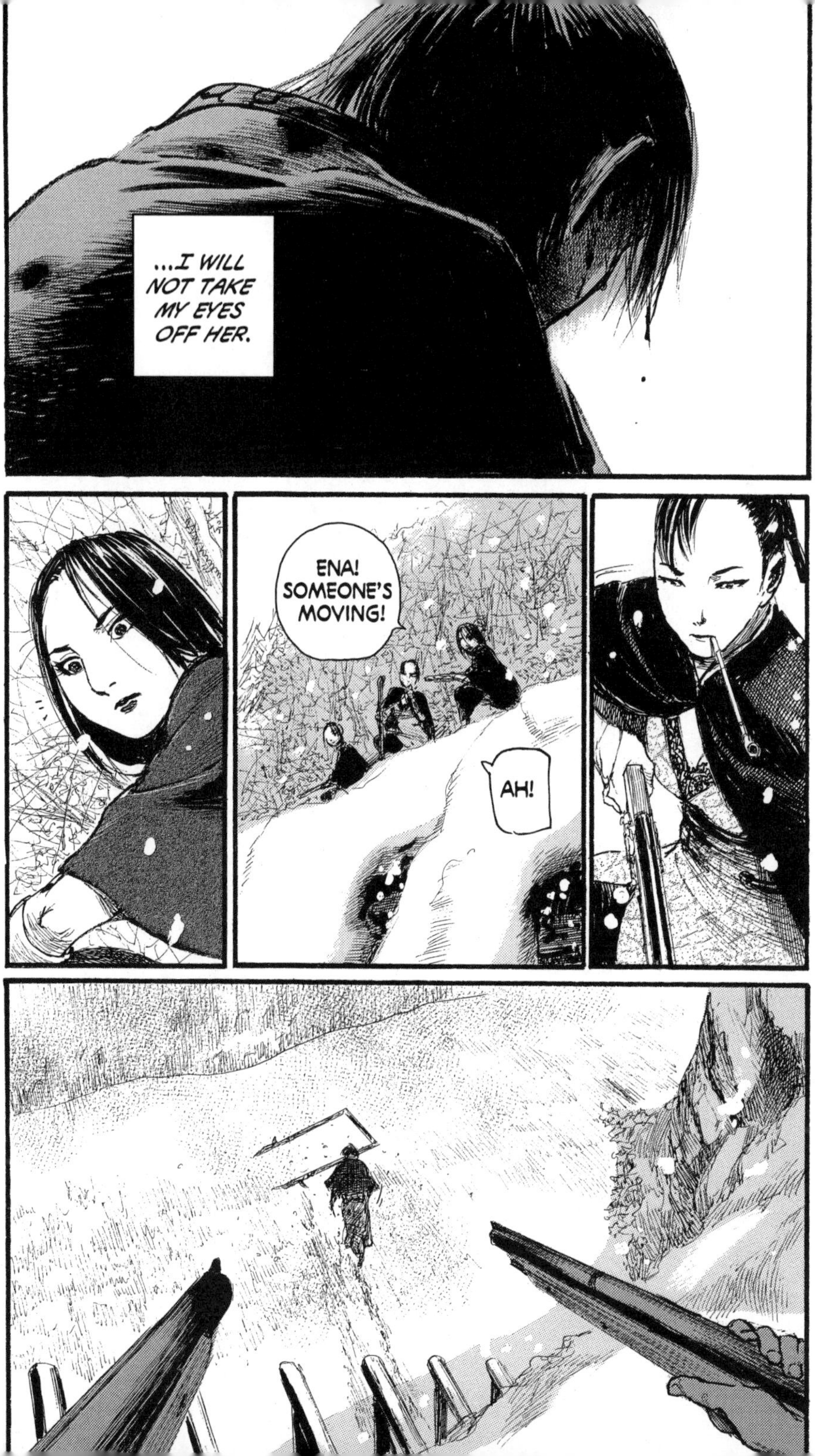
...I WILL NOT TAKE MY EYES OFF HER.
ENA! SOMEONE'S MOVING!
AH!

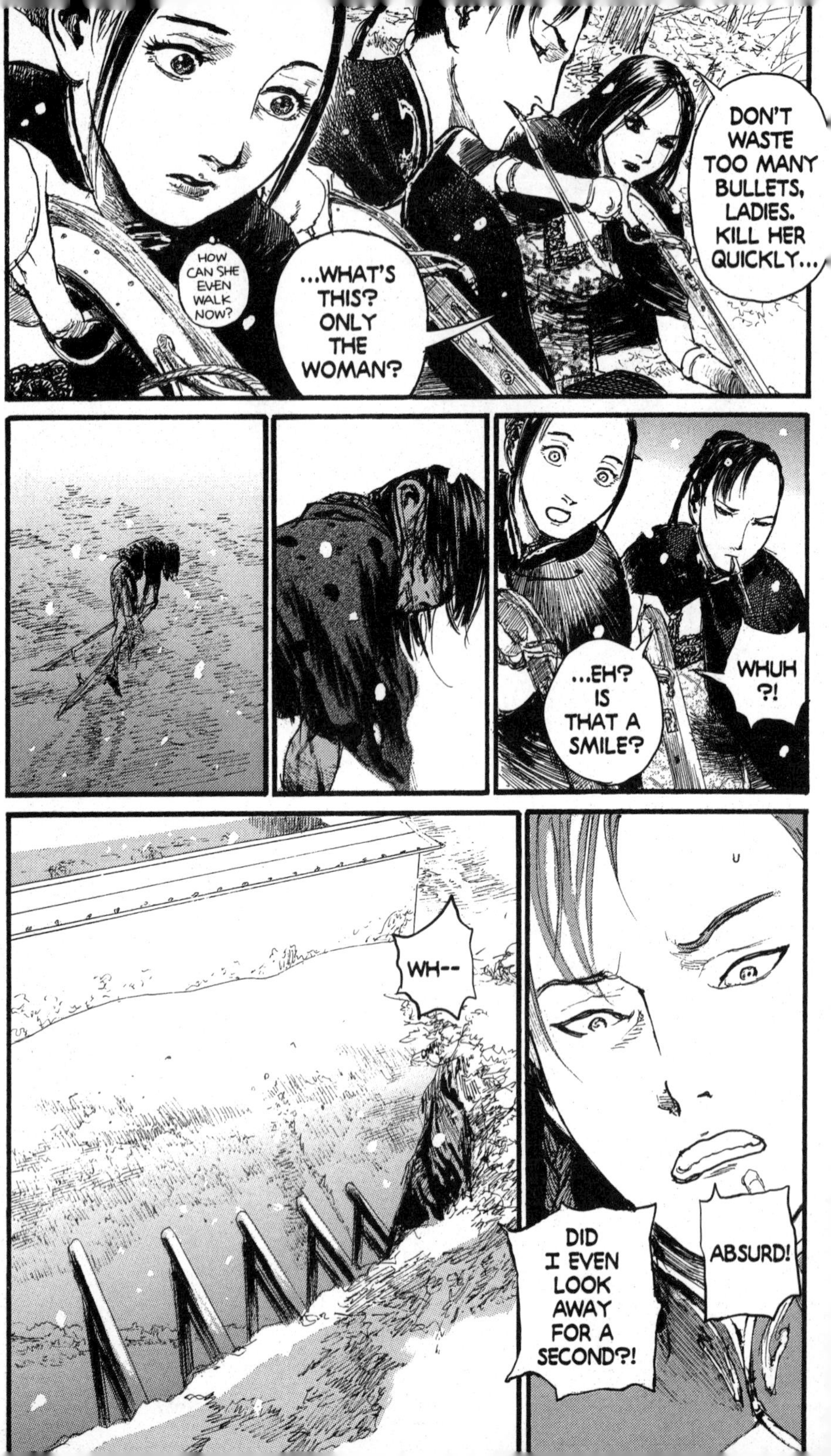
HOW CAN SHE EVEN WALK NOW?
...WHAT'S THIS? ONLY THE WOMAN?
DON'T WASTE TOO MANY BULLETS, LADIES. KILL HER QUICKLY...
...EH? IS THAT A SMILE?
WHUH ?!
WH--
DID I EVEN LOOK AWAY FOR A SECOND?!
ABSURD!

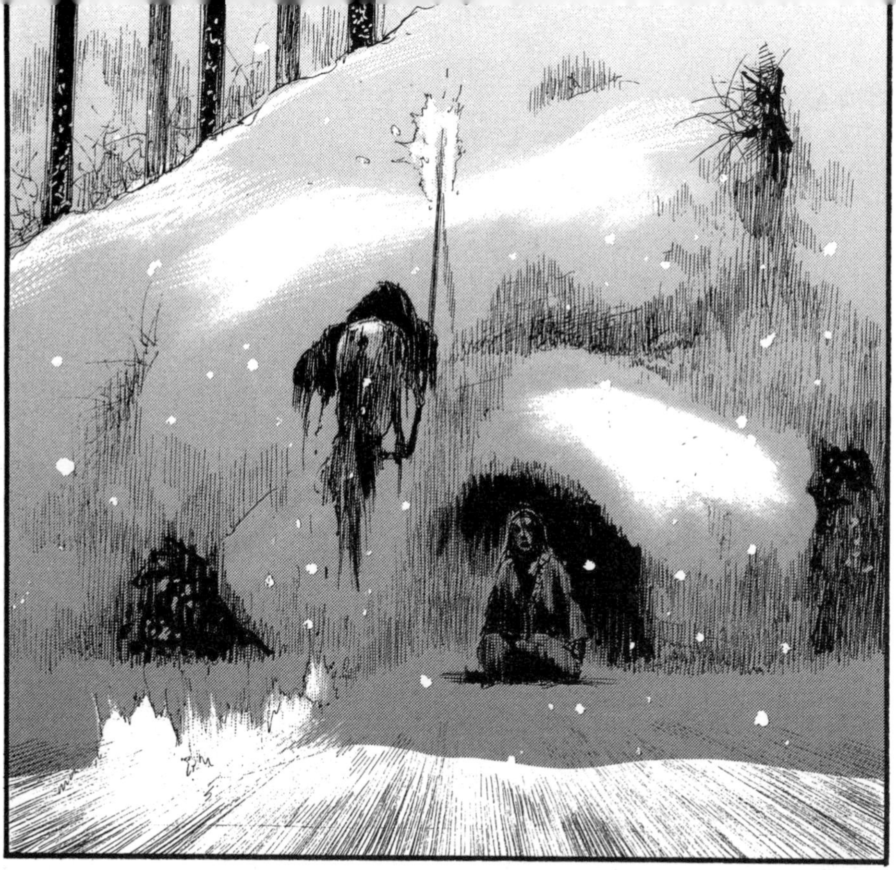
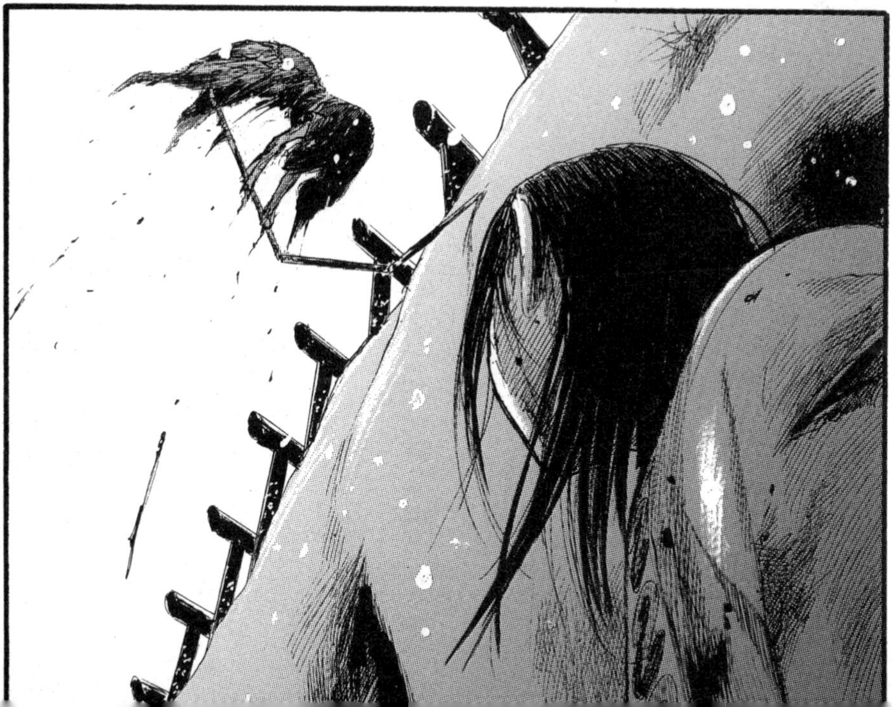

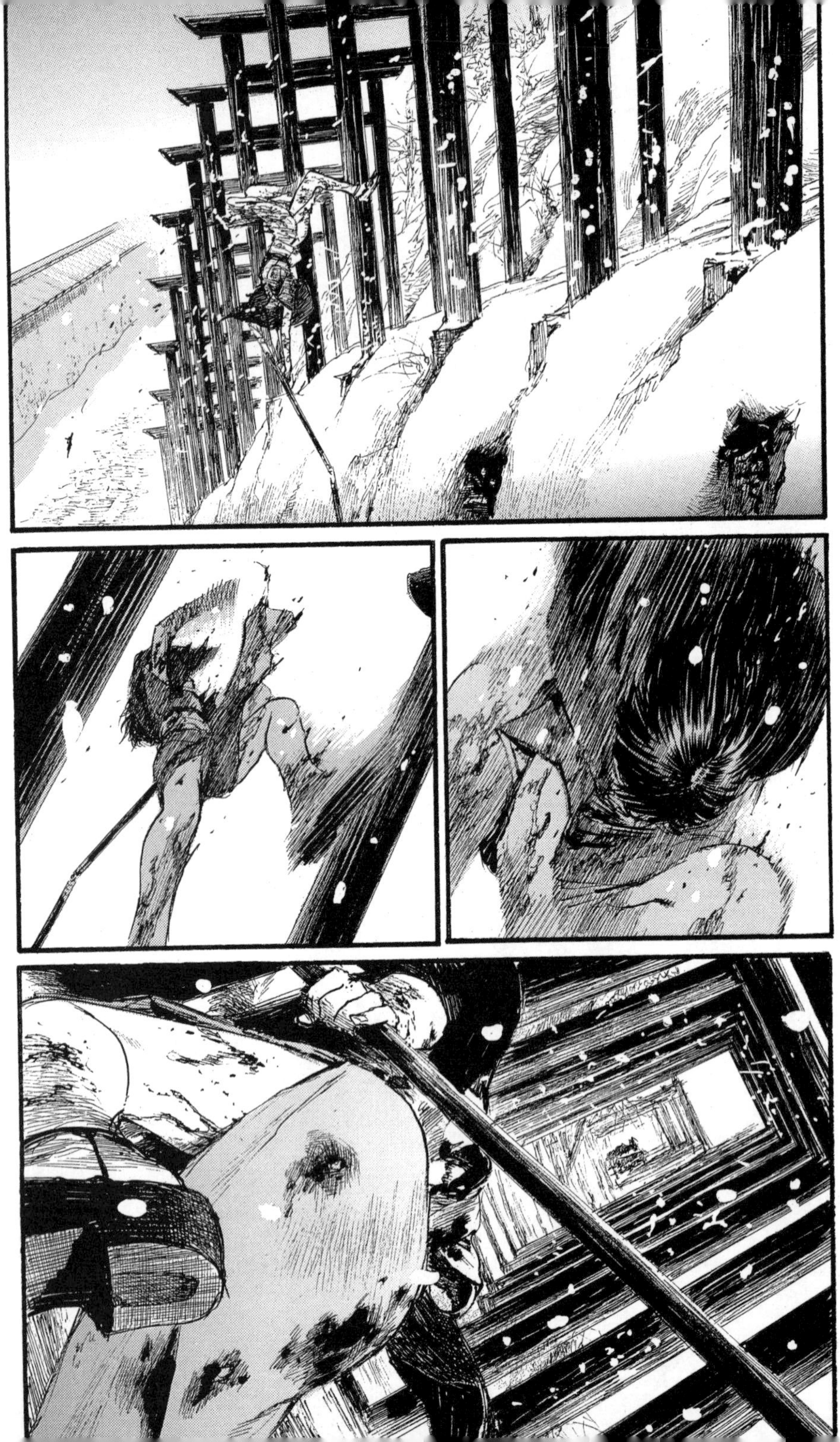

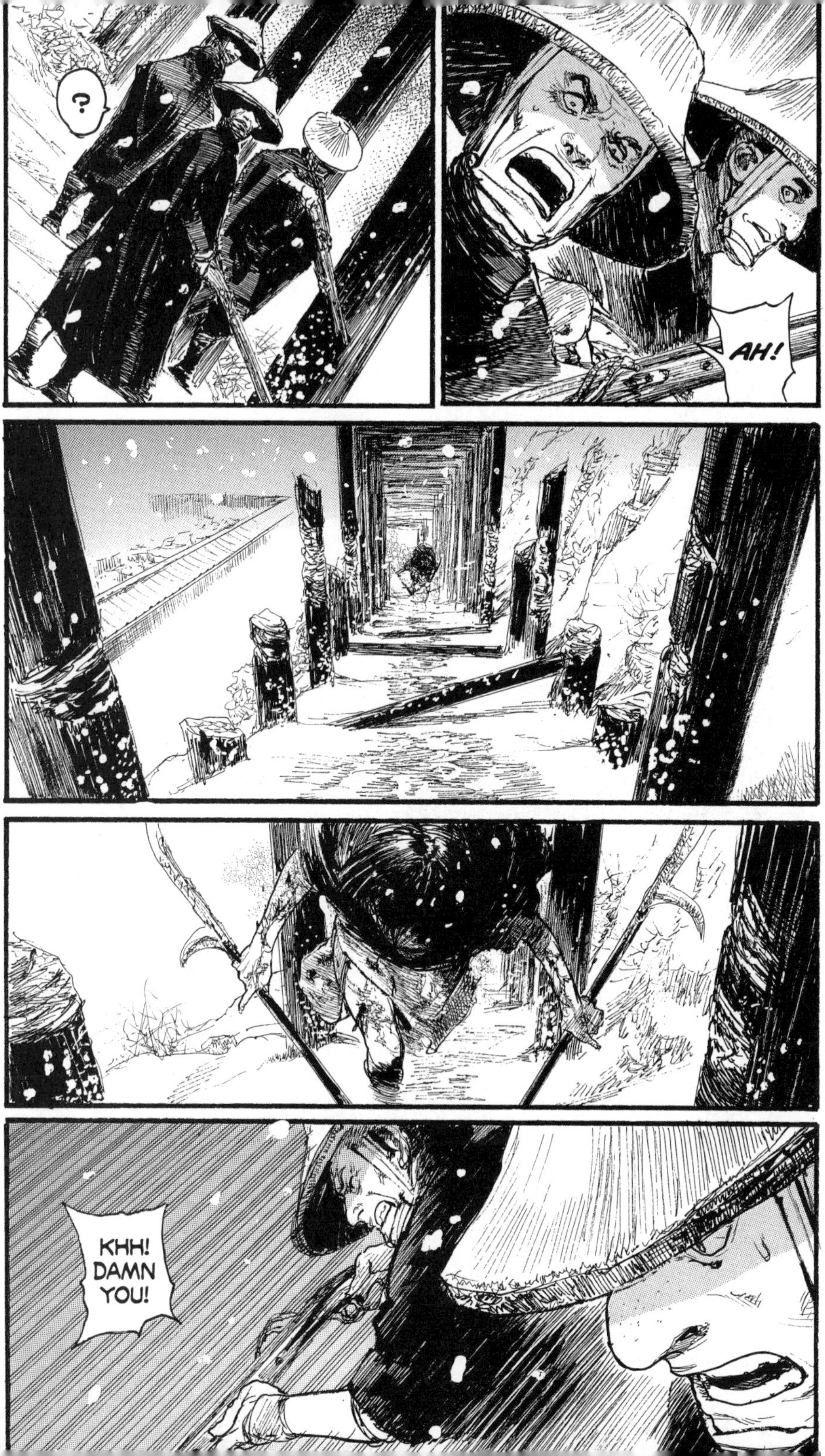
?
AH!
KHH! DAMN YOU!

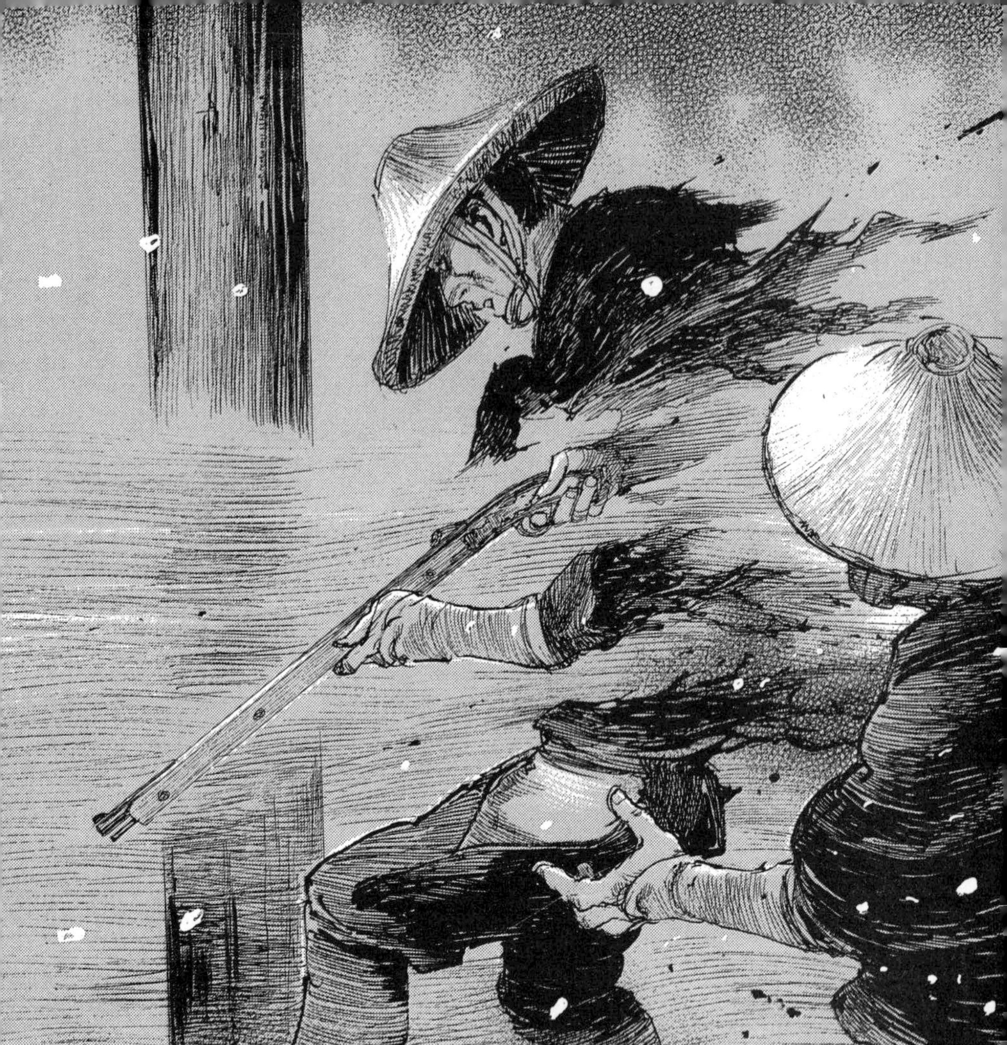
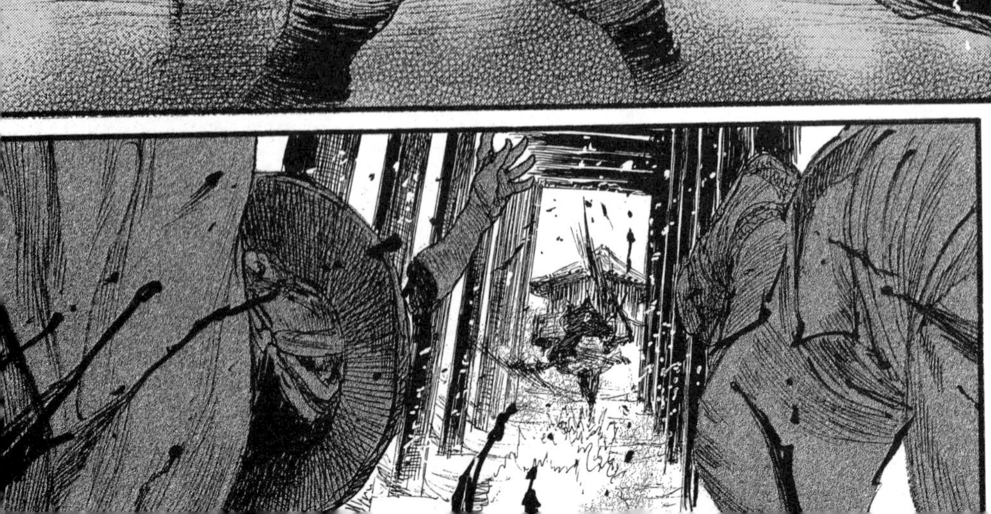

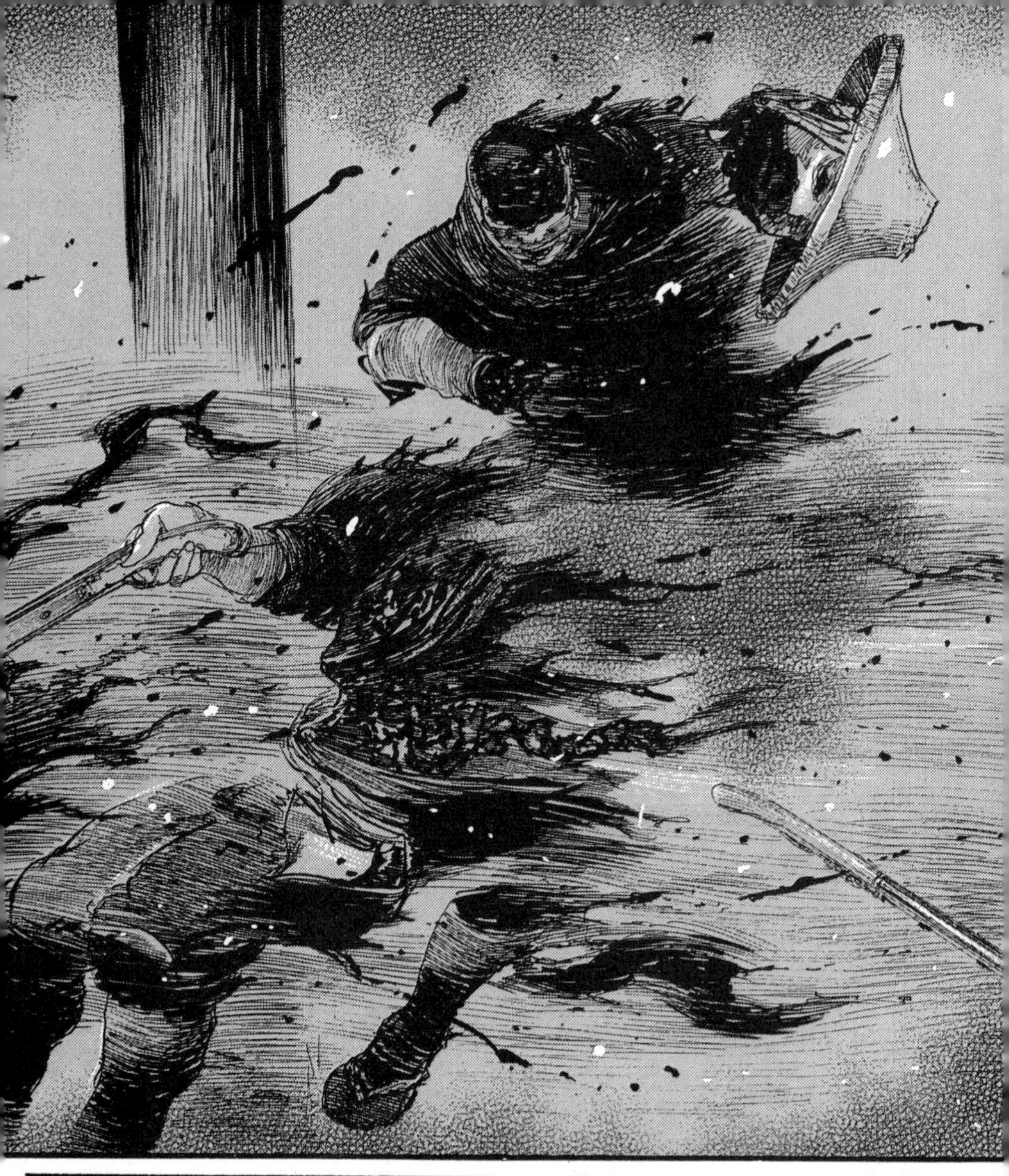
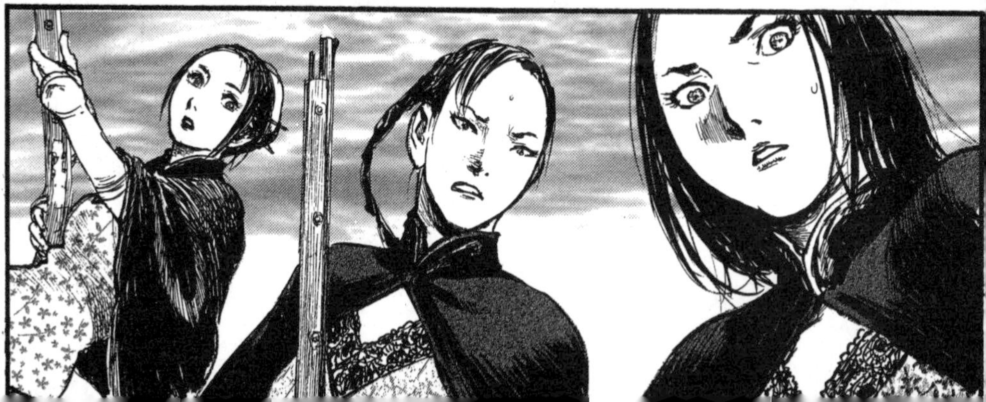

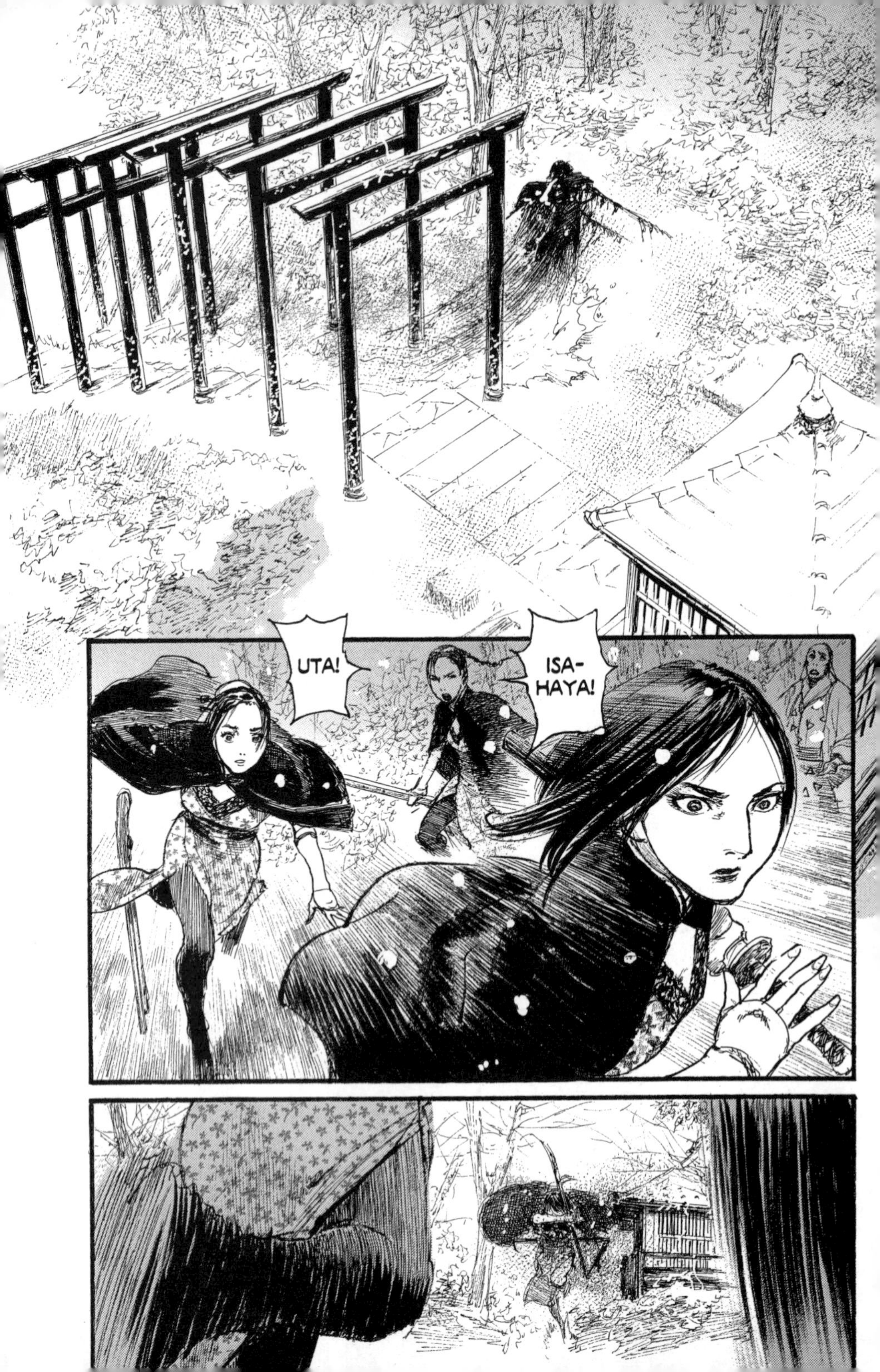
UTA!
ISA-
HAYA!

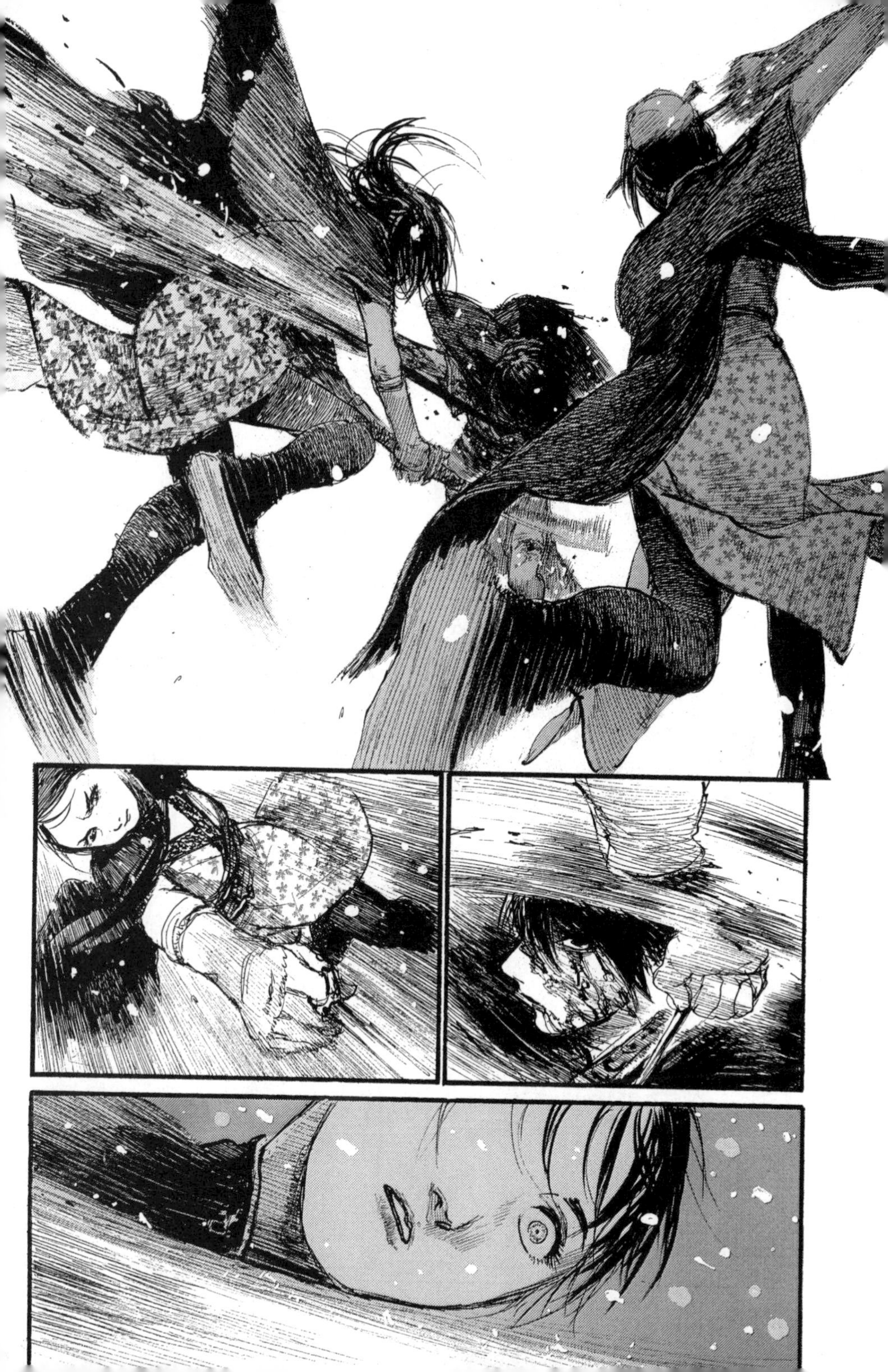

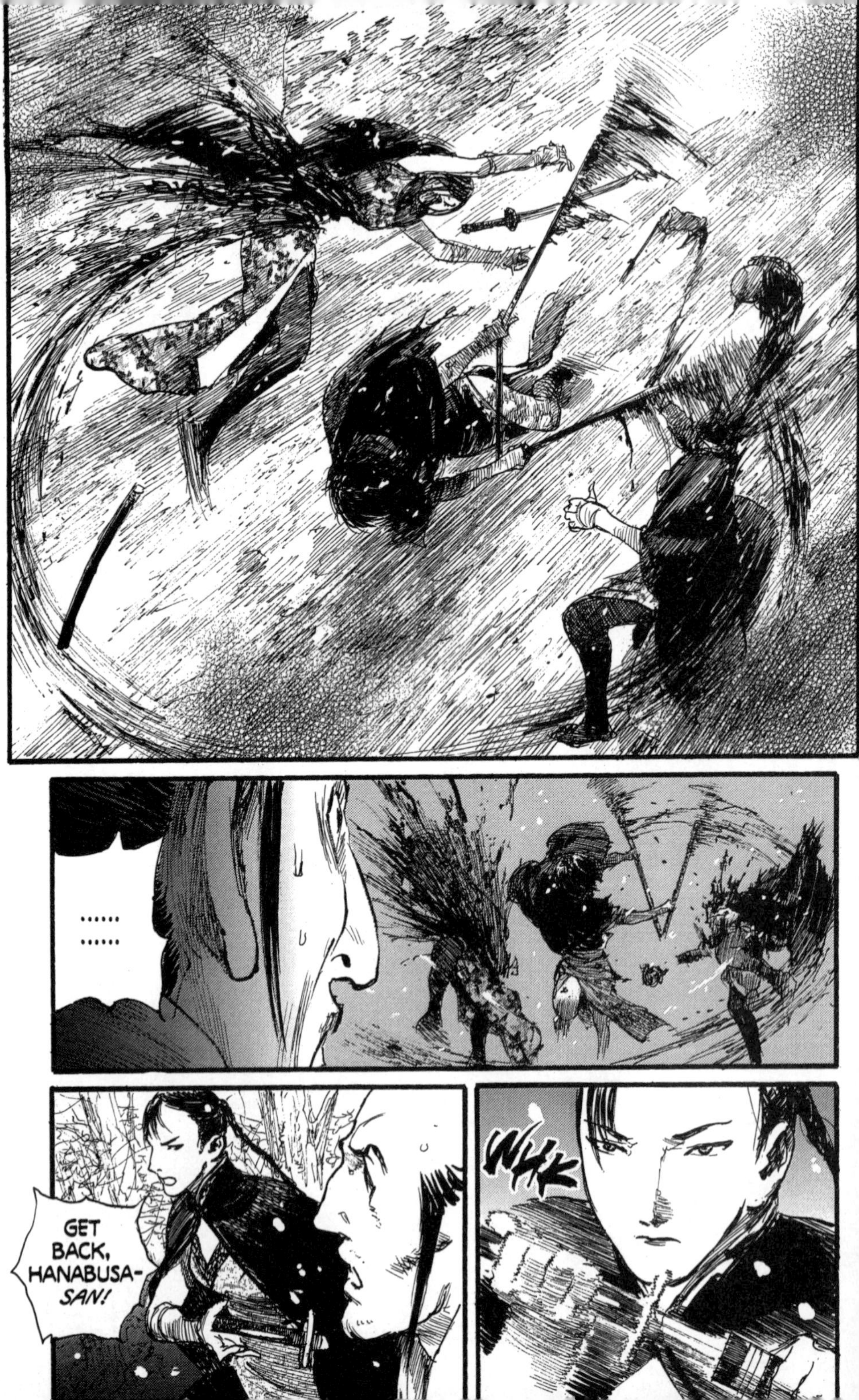
......
......
WHK
GET BACK, HANABUSA-SAN!

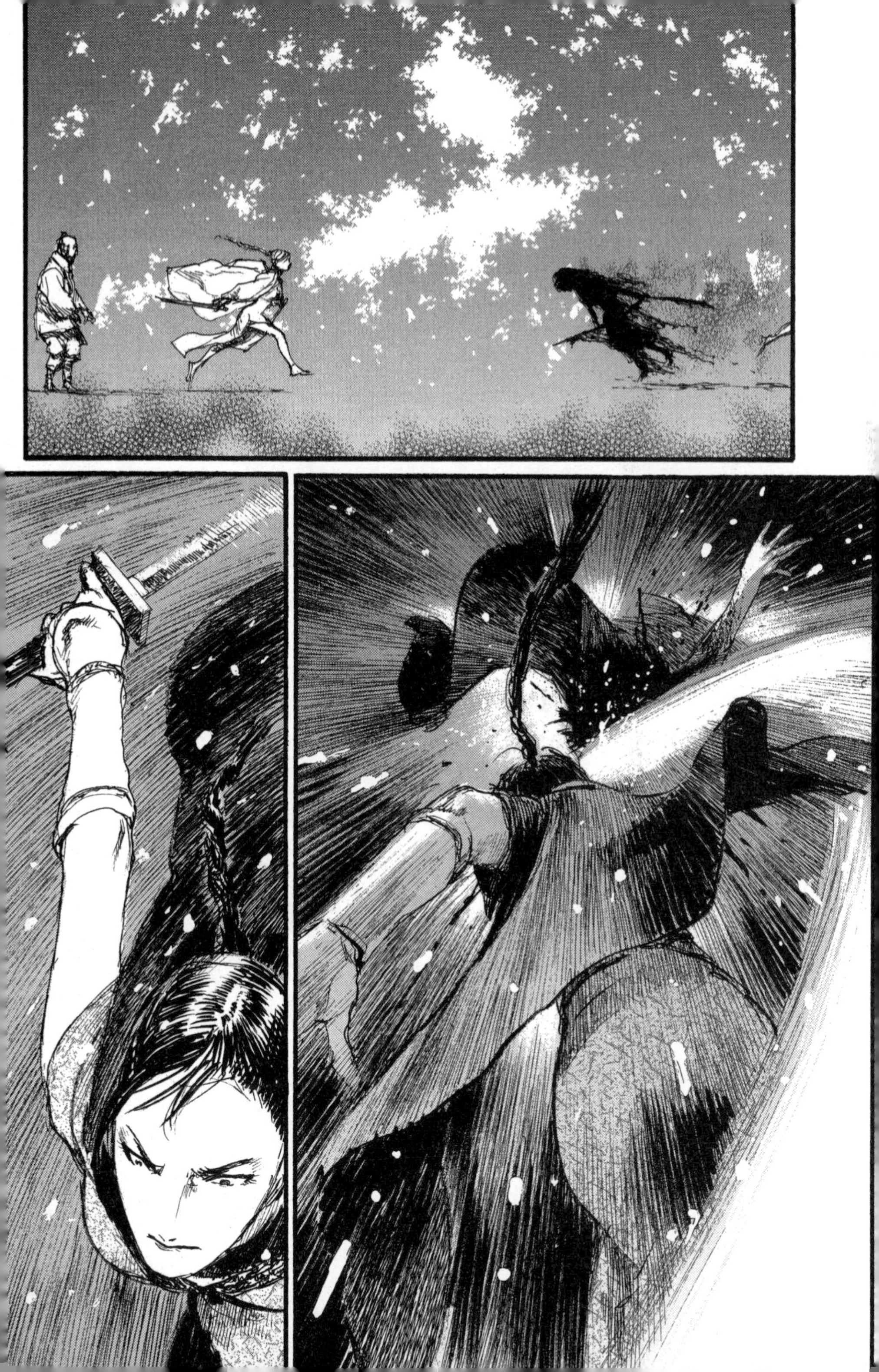

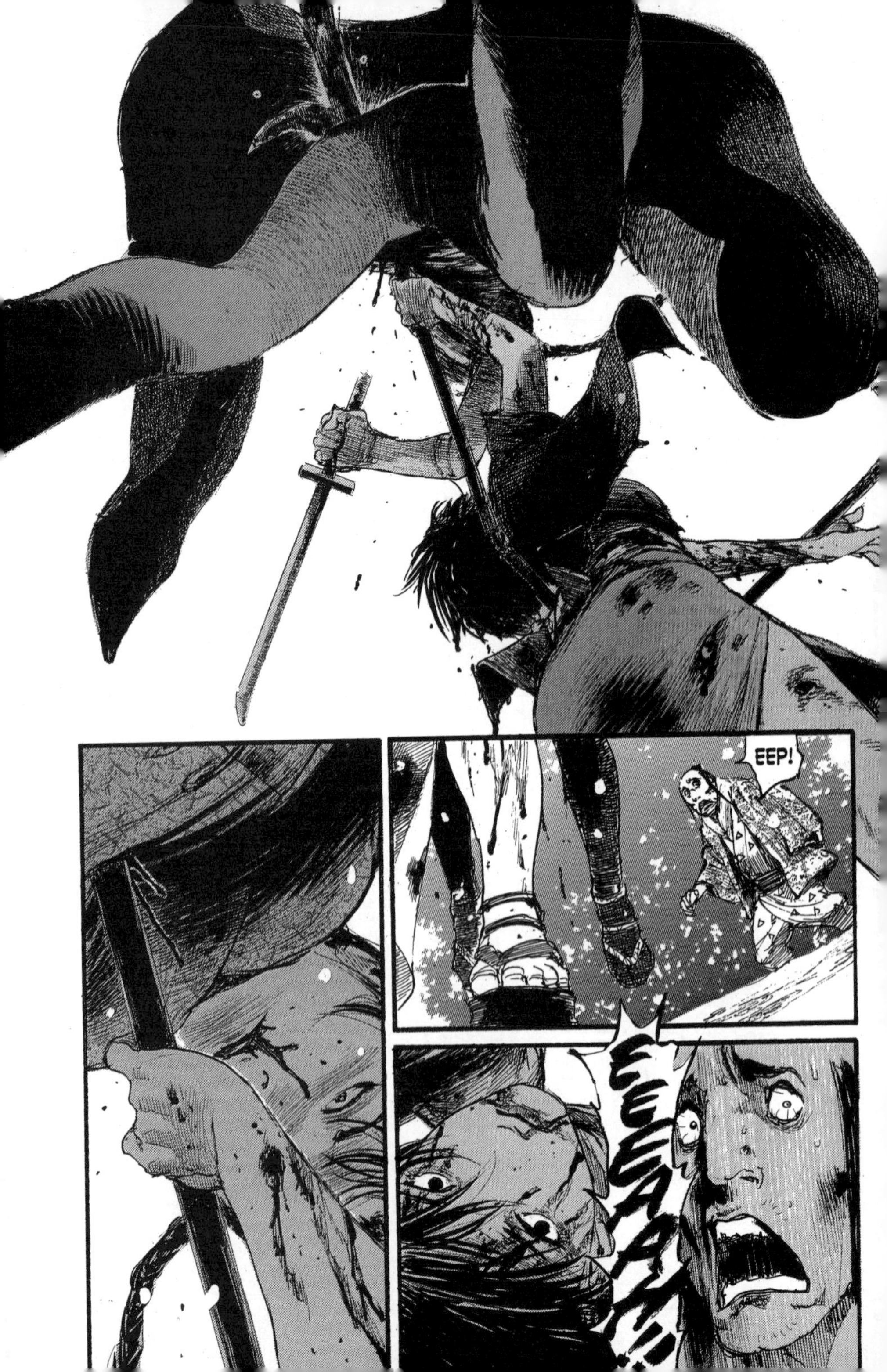
EEP!
EEEAAA!!

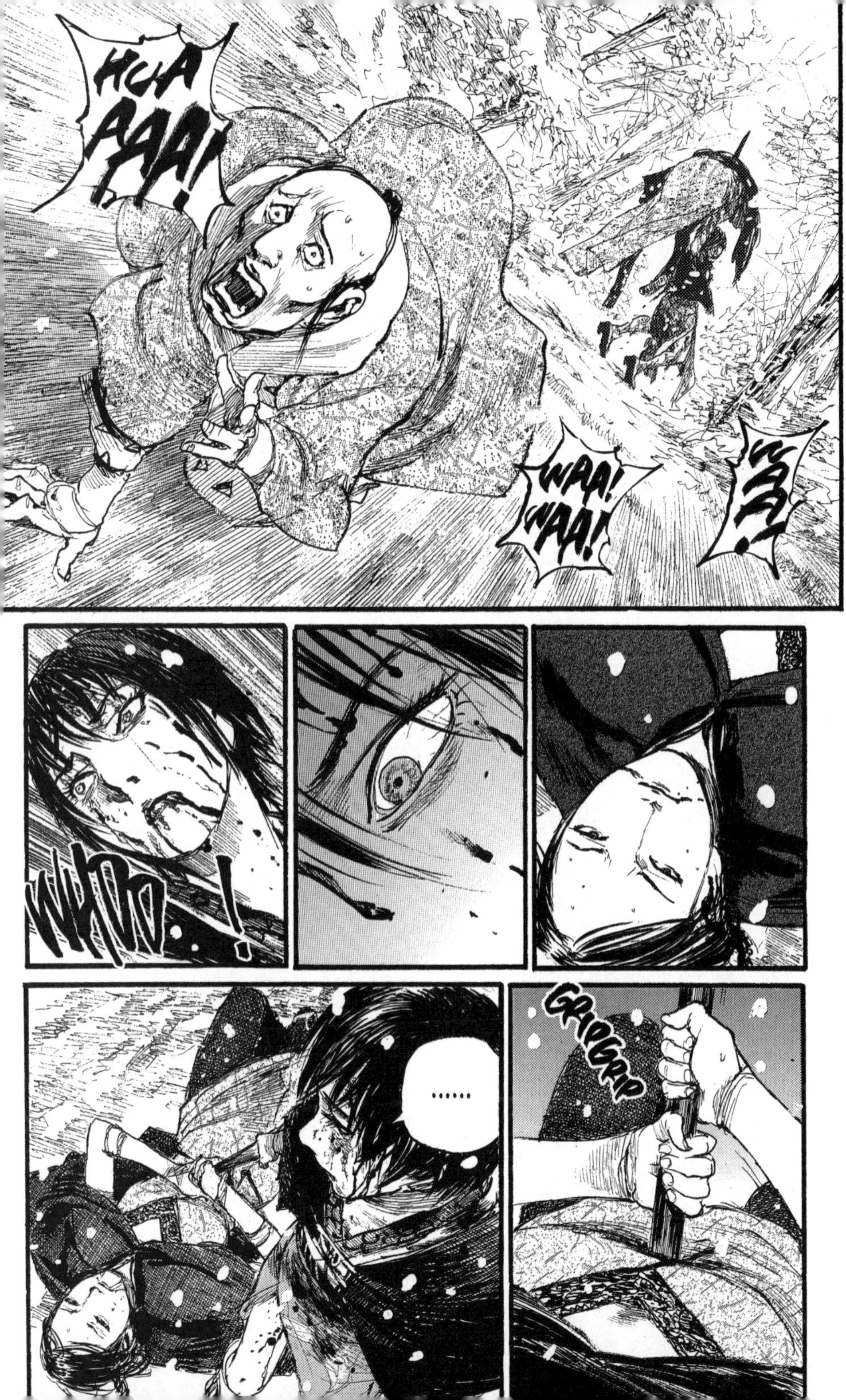
HUA AAA!
WAA! WAA!
WAA!
WHOO..!
......
GRIPGRIP

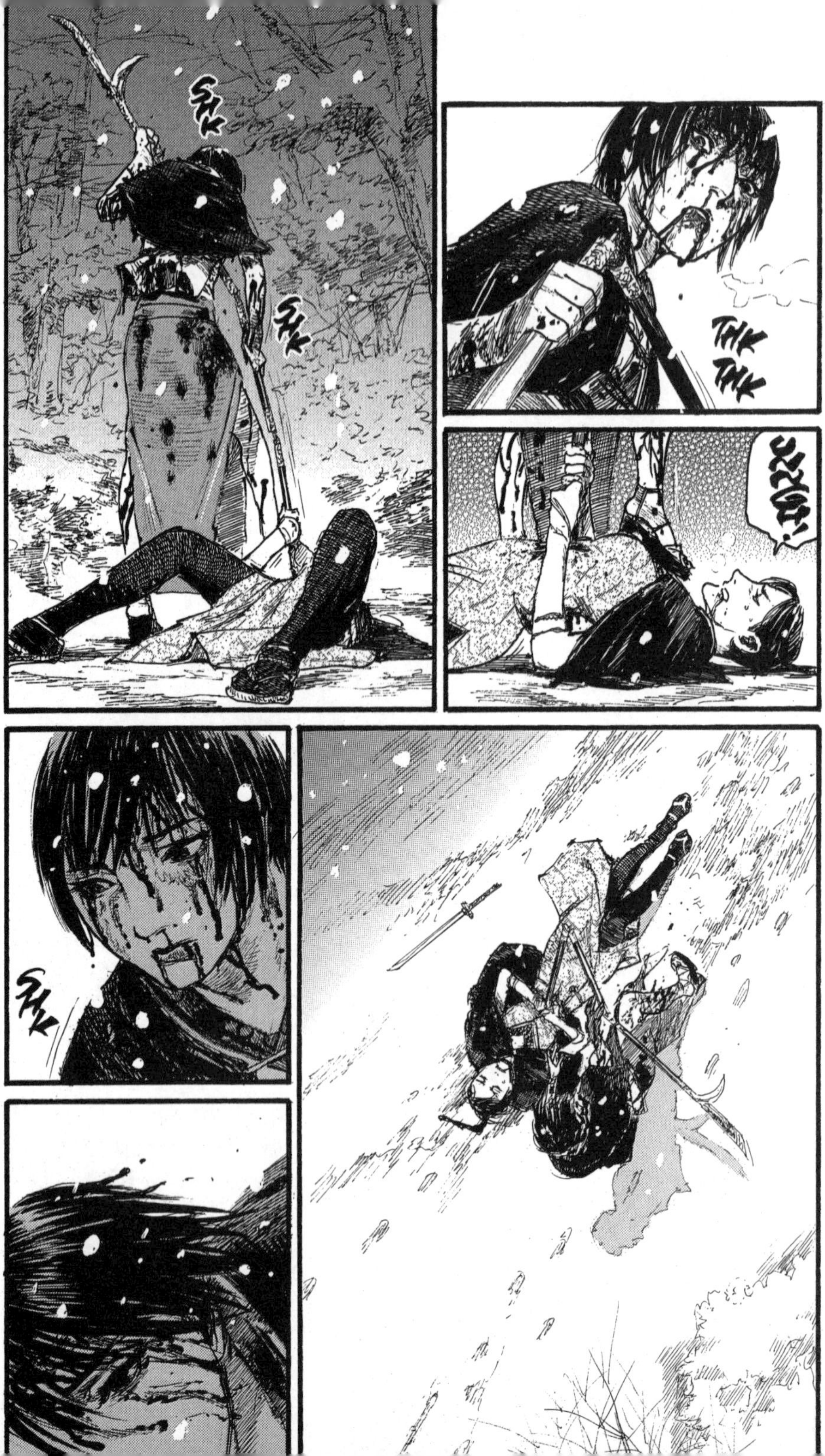
SHK
SHK
THK
THK
UKKGH!
SHK

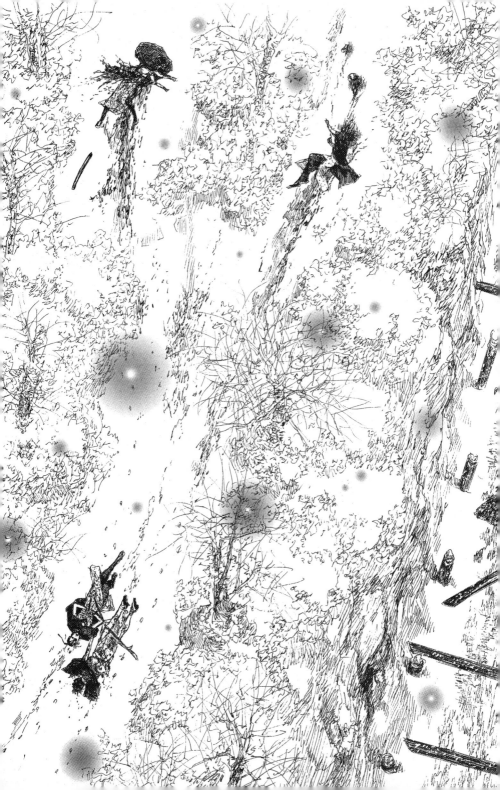

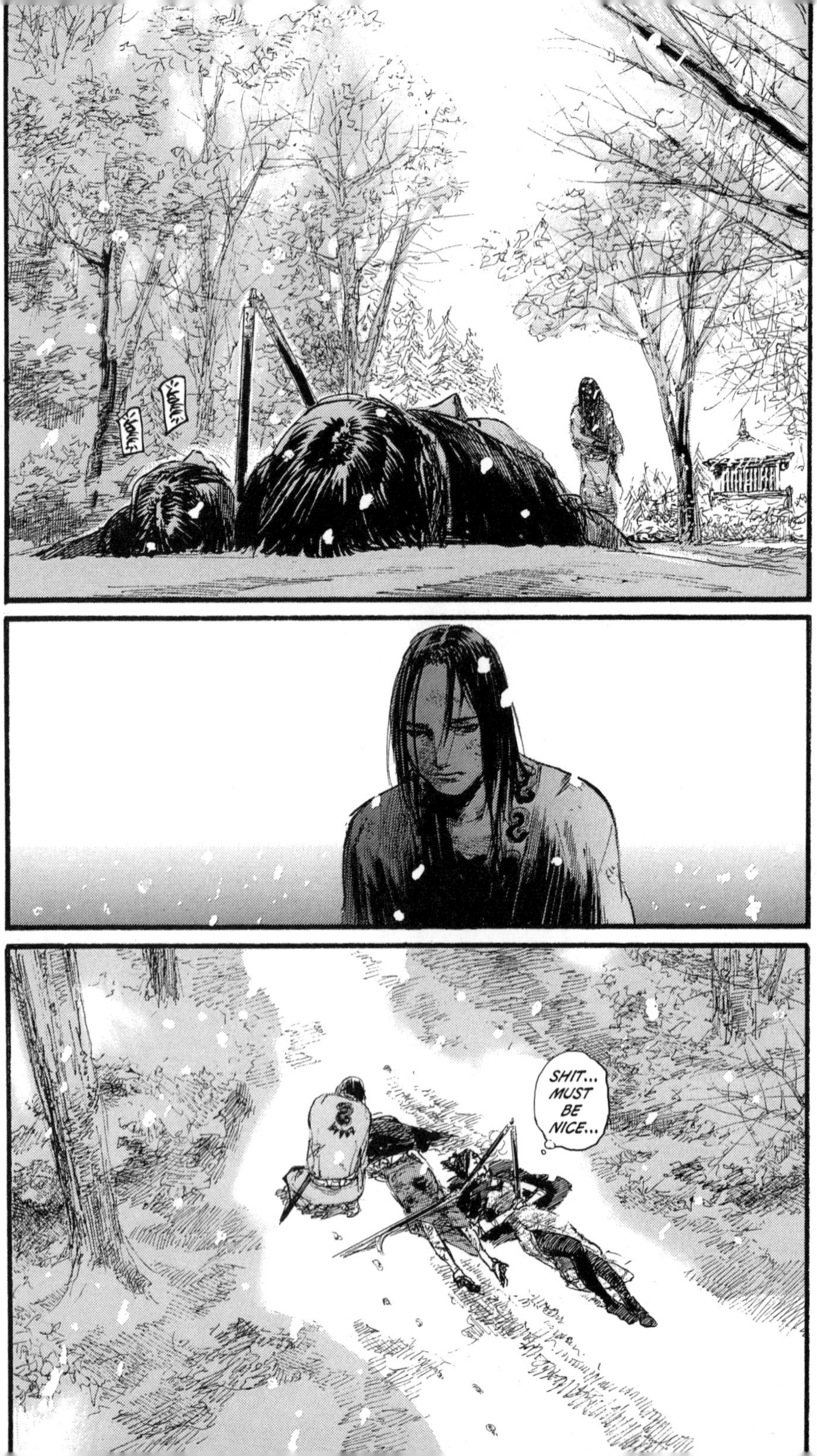
SHIT... MUST BE NICE...

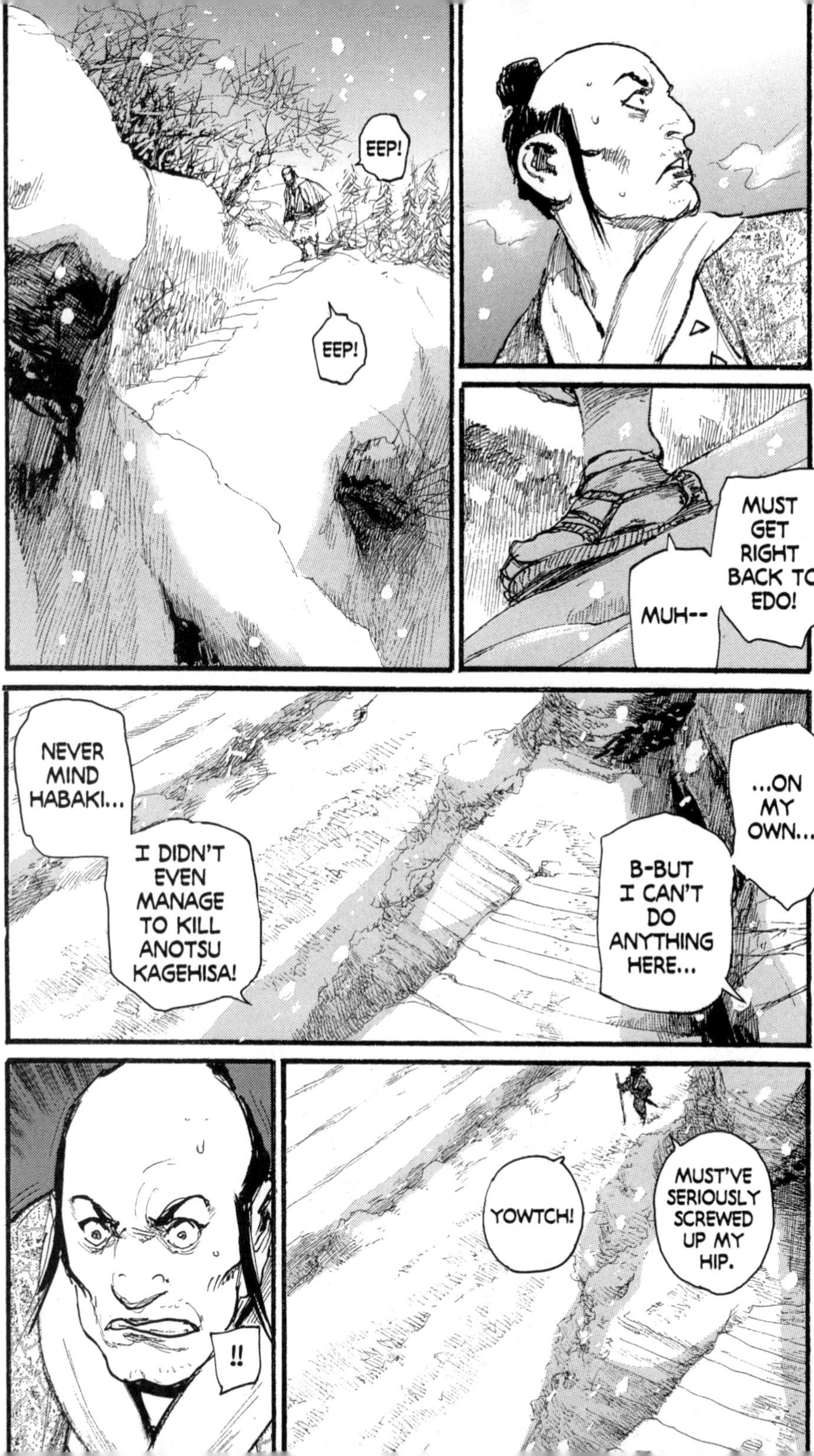
EEP!
EEP!
MUH--
MUST GET RIGHT BACK TO EDO!
NEVER MIND HABAKI...
I DIDN'T EVEN MANAGE TO KILL ANOTSU KAGEHISA!
B-BUT I CAN'T DO ANYTHING HERE...
...ON MY OWN...
!!
YOWTCH!
MUST'VE SERIOUSLY SCREWED UP MY HIP.

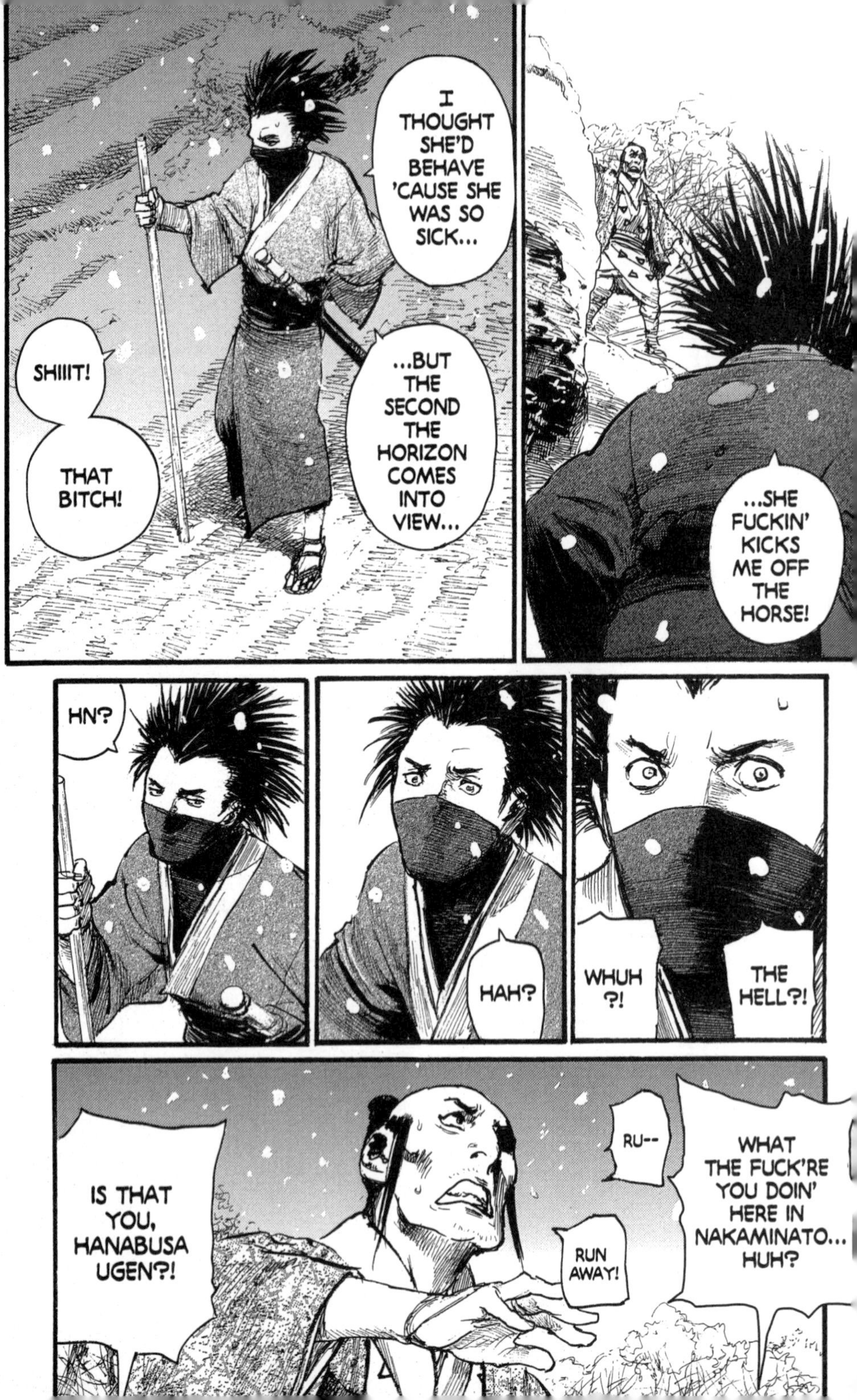
I THOUGHT SHE'D BEHAVE 'CAUSE SHE WAS SO SICK...
...BUT THE SECOND THE HORIZON COMES INTO VIEW...
SHIIIT!
THAT BITCH!
...SHE FUCKIN' KICKS ME OFF THE HORSE!
HN?
HAH?
WHUH ?!
THE HELL?!
IS THAT YOU, HANABUSA UGEN?!
RU--
RUN AWAY!
WHAT THE FUCK'RE YOU DOIN' HERE IN NAKAMINATO... HUH?

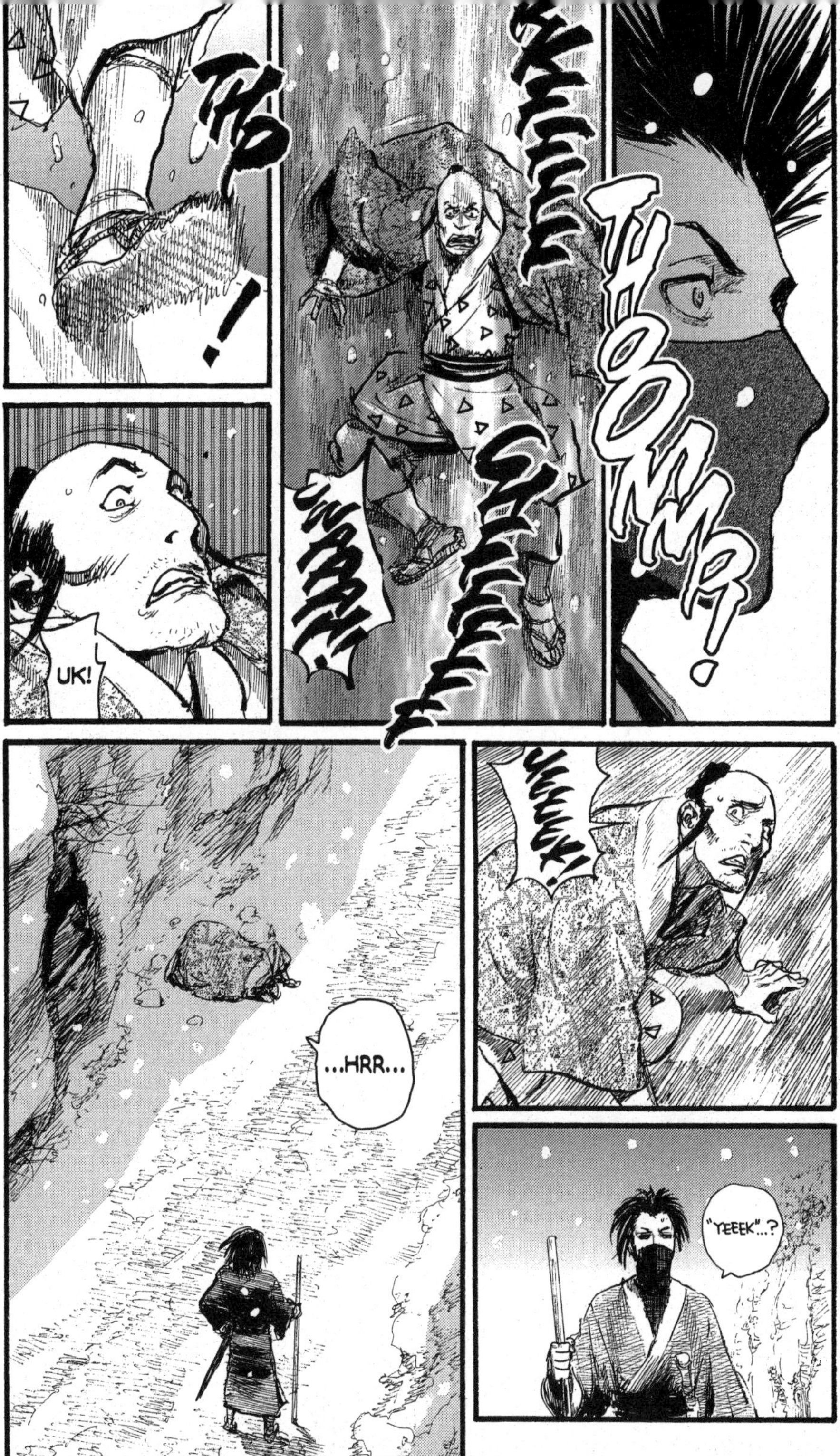
THP!
UK!
THOOMP!
...HRR...
"YEEEK"...?

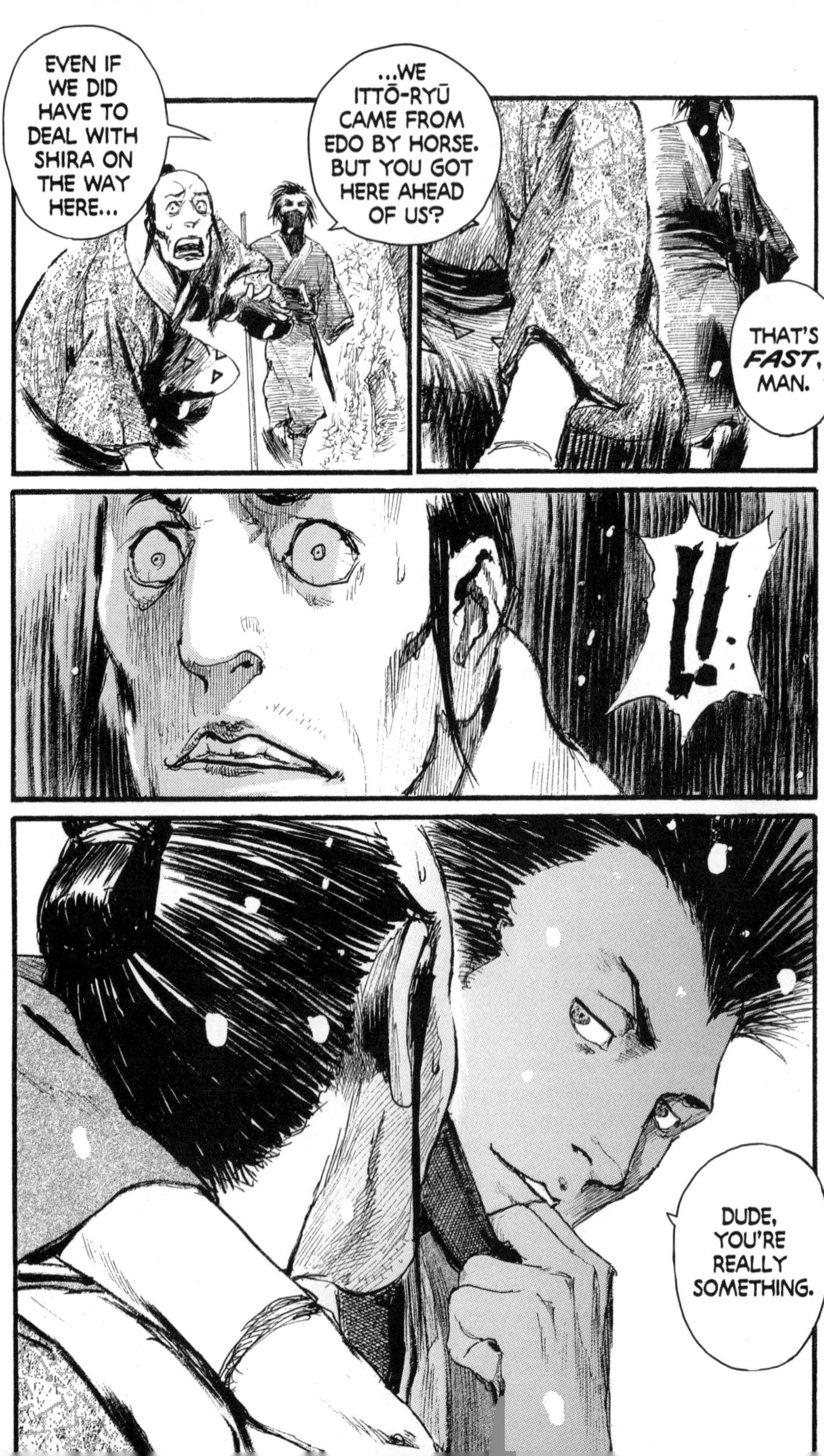
EVEN IF WE DID HAVE TO DEAL WITH SHIRA ON THE WAY HERE...
...WE ITTŌ-RYŪ CAME FROM EDO BY HORSE. BUT YOU GOT HERE AHEAD OF US?
THAT'S *FAST*, MAN.
!!
DUDE, YOU'RE REALLY SOMETHING.

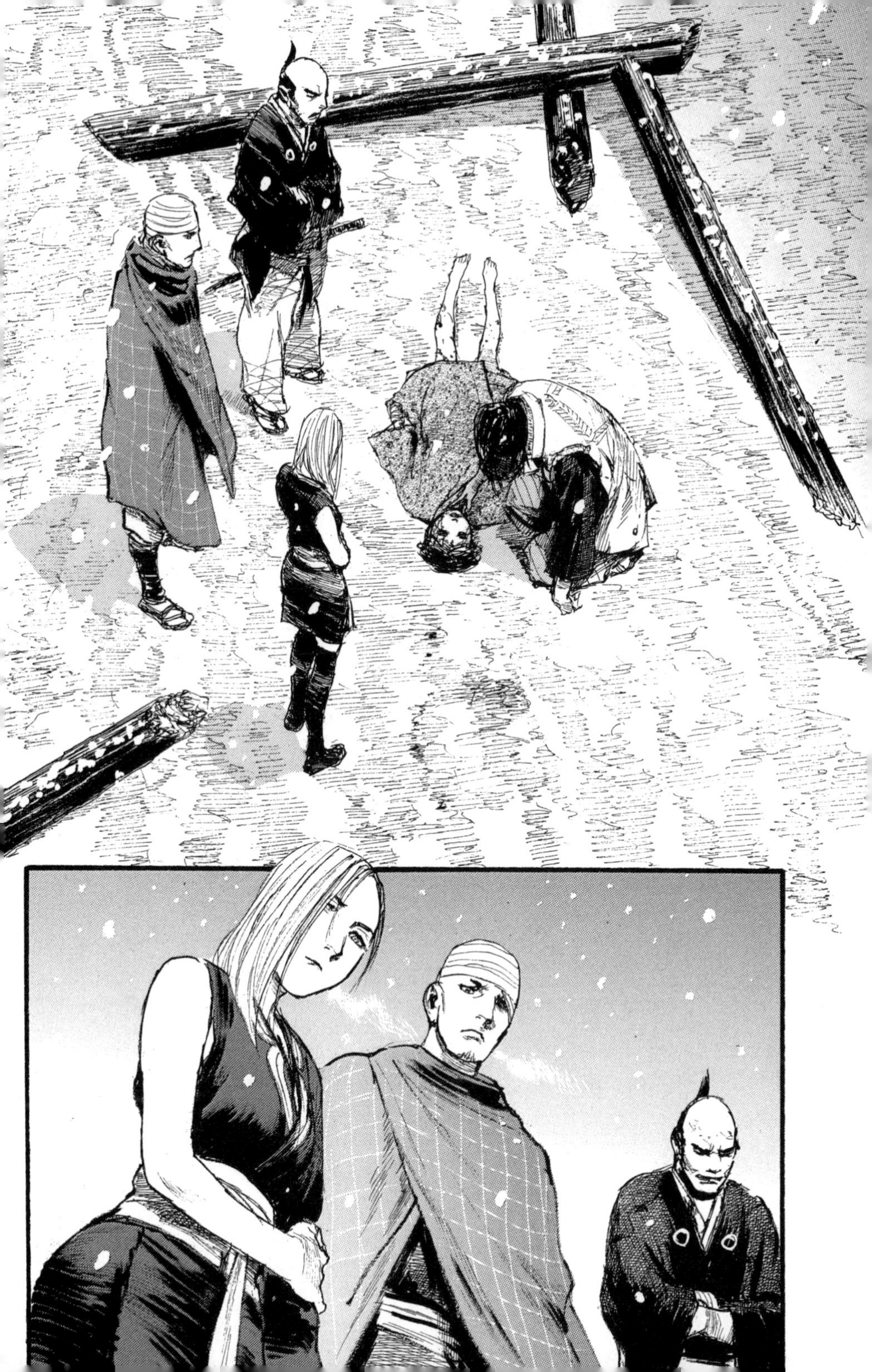

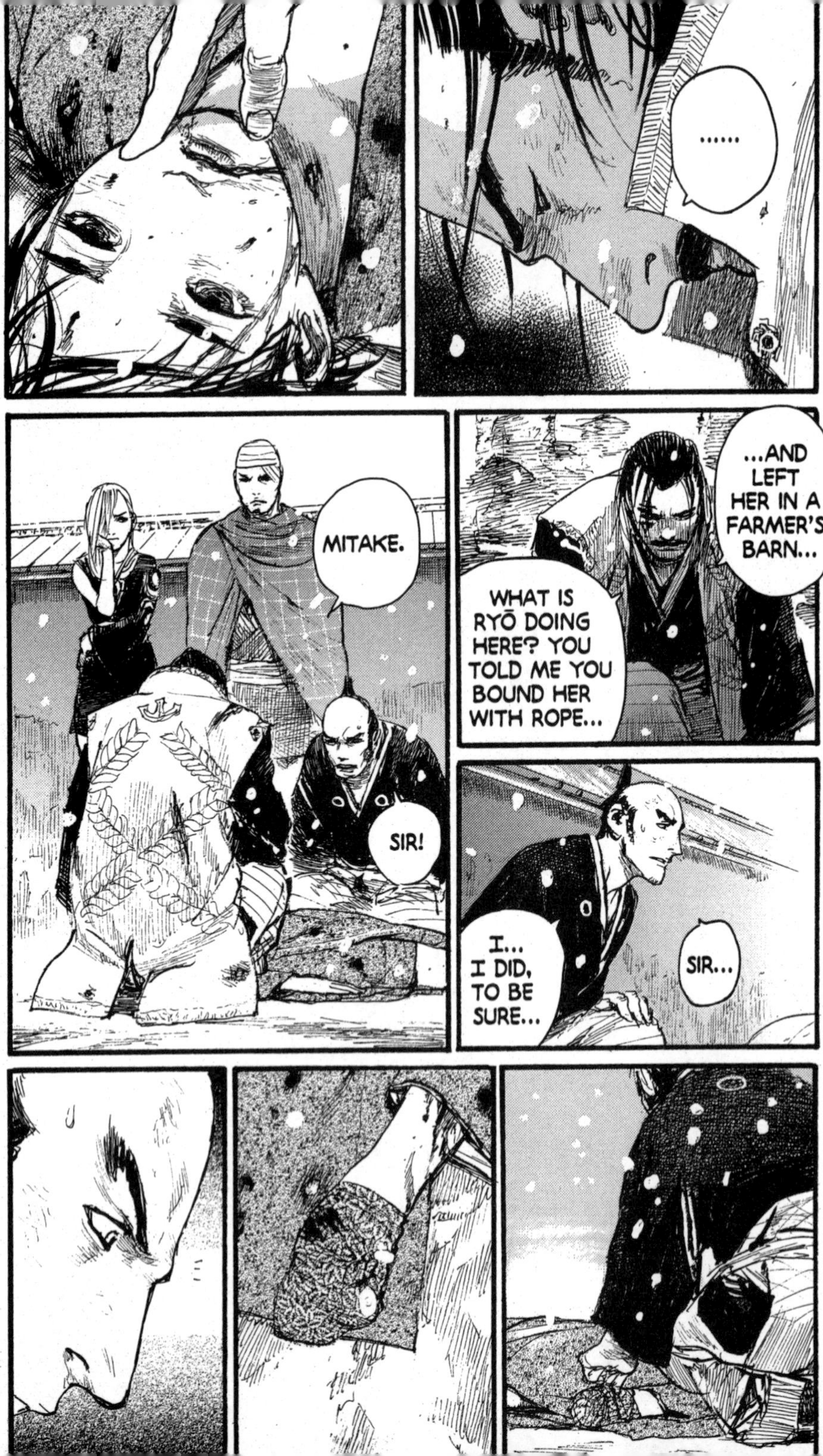
......
MITAKE.
SIR!
WHAT IS RYŌ DOING HERE? YOU TOLD ME YOU BOUND HER WITH ROPE...
...AND LEFT HER IN A FARMER'S BARN...
I... I DID, TO BE SURE...
SIR...

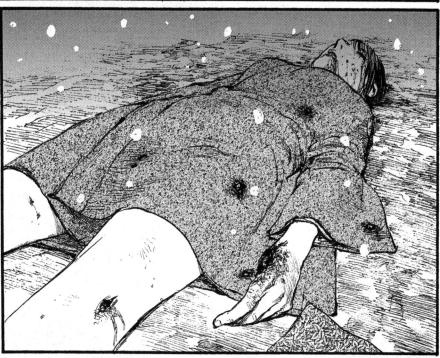

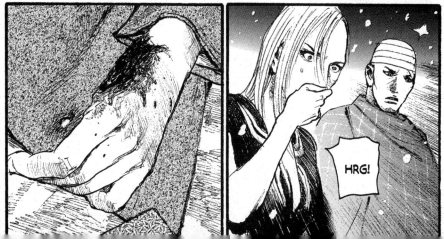

HRG!

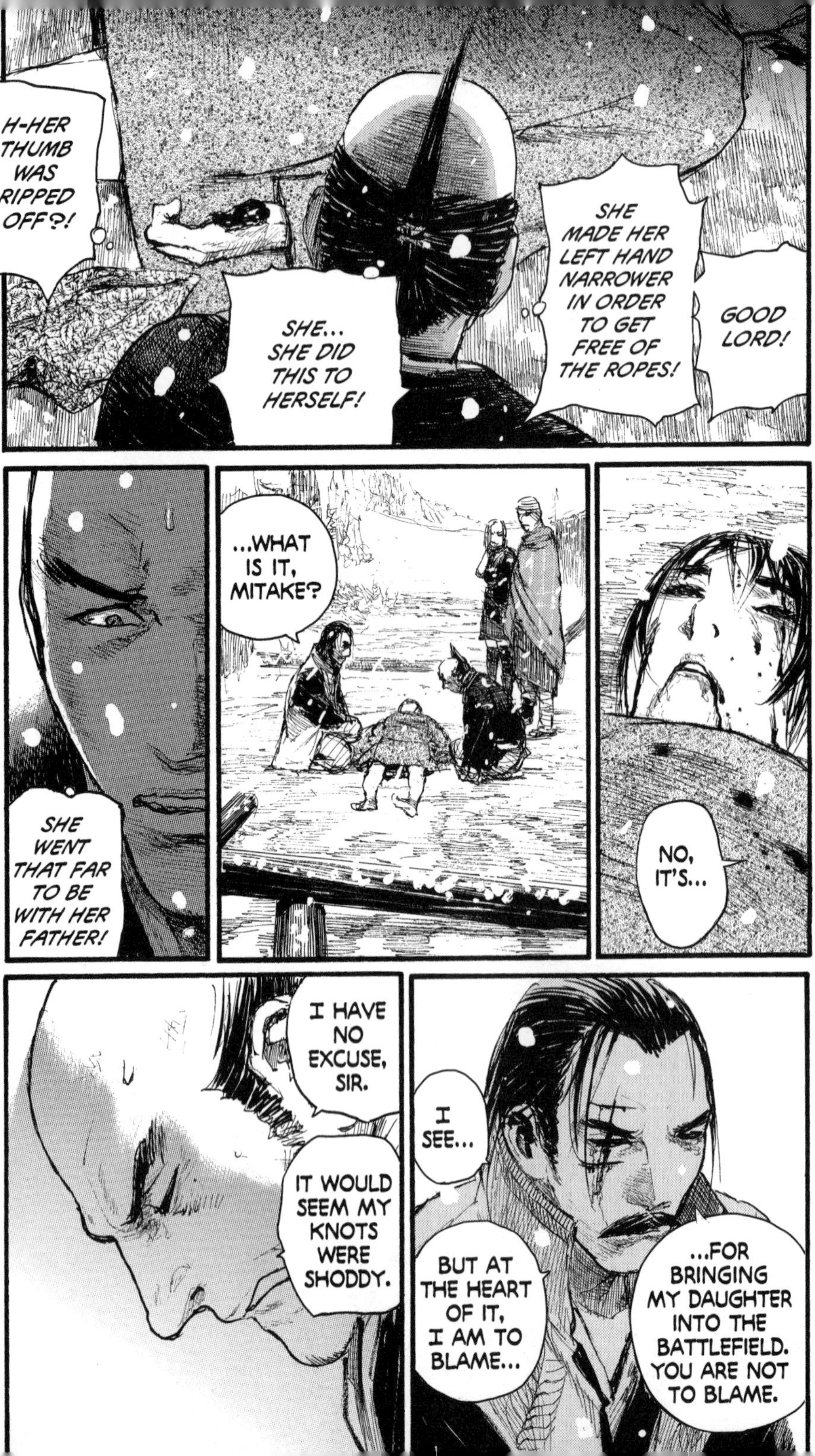
H-HER THUMB WAS RIPPED OFF?!
SHE... SHE DID THIS TO HERSELF!
SHE MADE HER LEFT HAND NARROWER IN ORDER TO GET FREE OF THE ROPES!
GOOD LORD!
SHE WENT THAT FAR TO BE WITH HER FATHER!
...WHAT IS IT, MITAKE?
NO, IT'S...
I HAVE NO EXCUSE, SIR.
IT WOULD SEEM MY KNOTS WERE SHODDY.
I SEE...
BUT AT THE HEART OF IT, I AM TO BLAME...
...FOR BRINGING MY DAUGHTER INTO THE BATTLEFIELD. YOU ARE NOT TO BLAME.

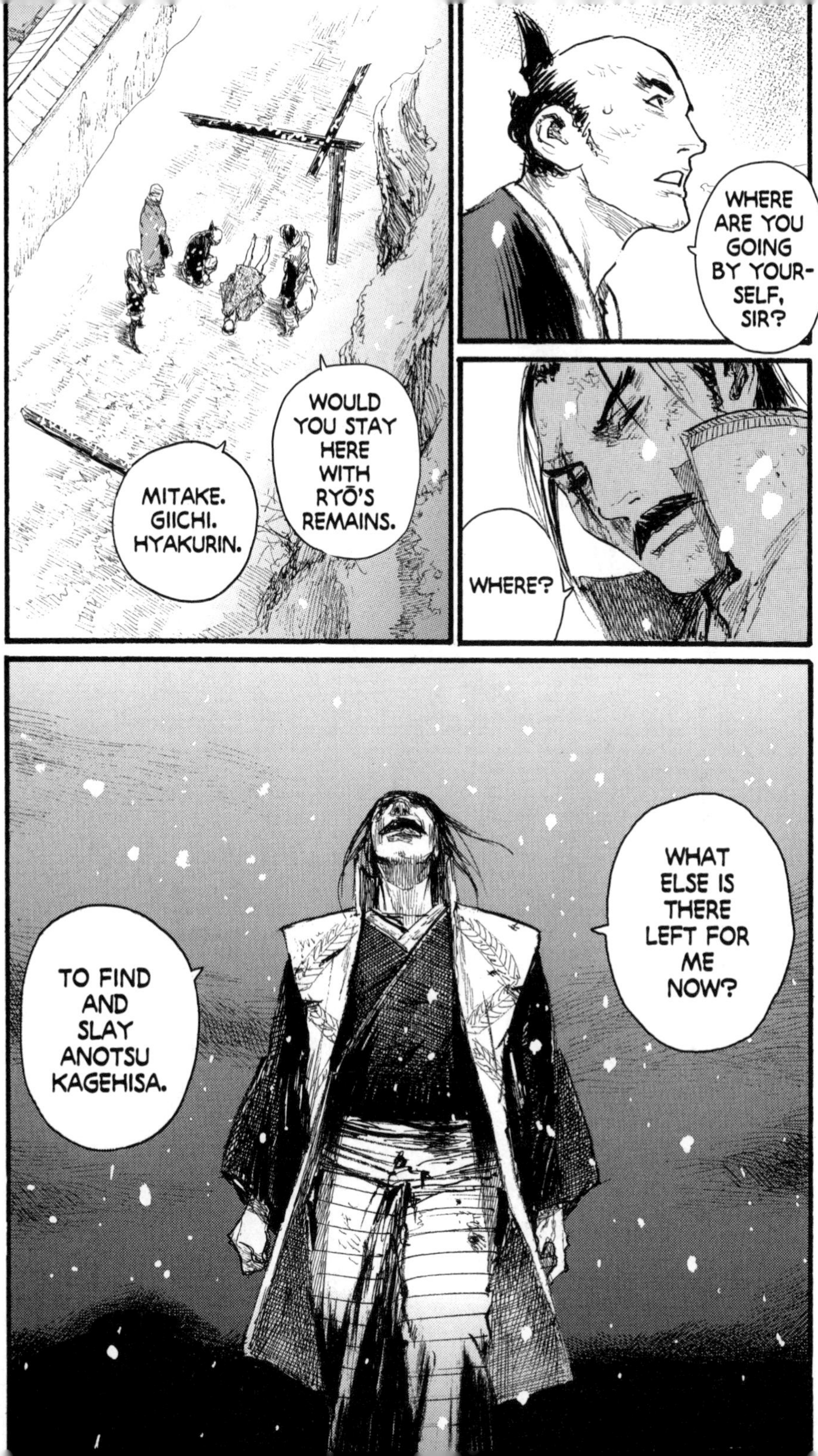
MITAKE. GIICHI. HYAKURIN.
WOULD YOU STAY HERE WITH RYŌ'S REMAINS.
WHERE ARE YOU GOING BY YOUR-SELF, SIR?
WHERE?
TO FIND AND SLAY ANOTSU KAGEHISA.
WHAT ELSE IS THERE LEFT FOR ME NOW?

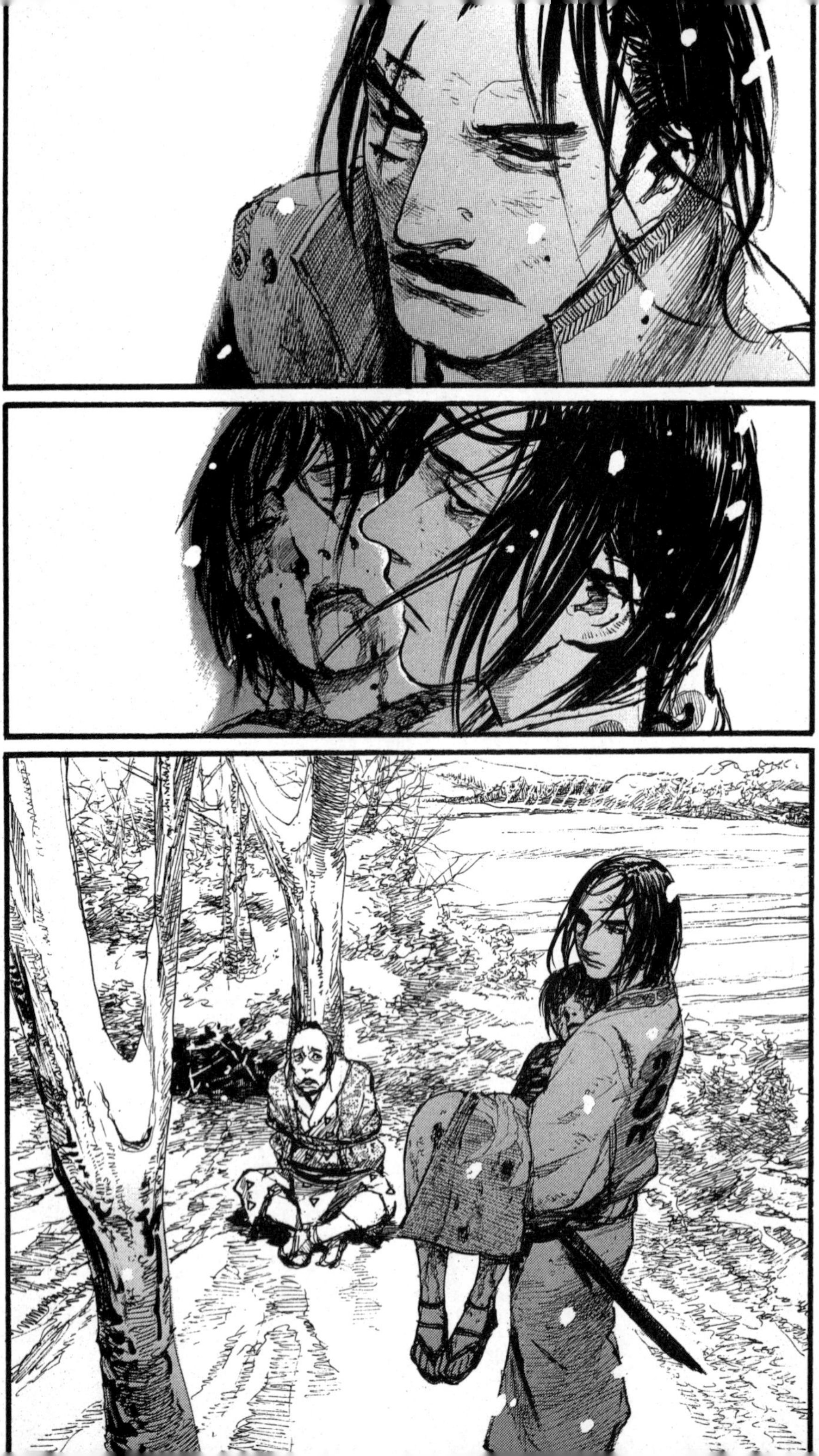

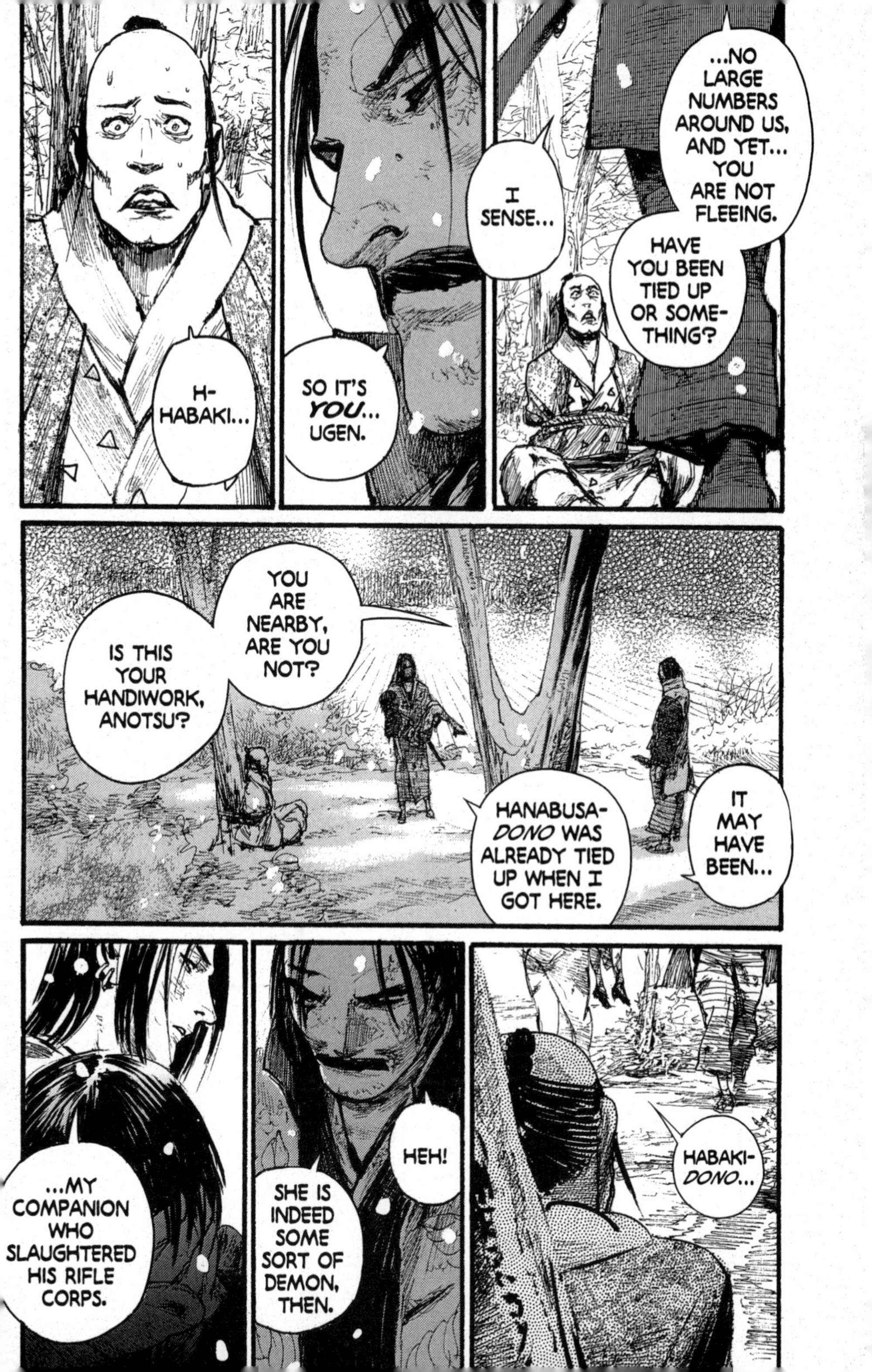
H- HABAKI...
SO IT'S *YOU*... UGEN.
I SENSE...
...NO LARGE NUMBERS AROUND US, AND YET... YOU ARE NOT FLEEING.
HAVE YOU BEEN TIED UP OR SOME- THING?
IS THIS YOUR HANDIWORK, ANOTSU?
YOU ARE NEARBY, ARE YOU NOT?
HANABUSA-*DONO* WAS ALREADY TIED UP WHEN I GOT HERE.
IT MAY HAVE BEEN...
...MY COMPANION WHO SLAUGHTERED HIS RIFLE CORPS.
HEH!
SHE IS INDEED SOME SORT OF DEMON, THEN.
HABAKI-*DONO*...

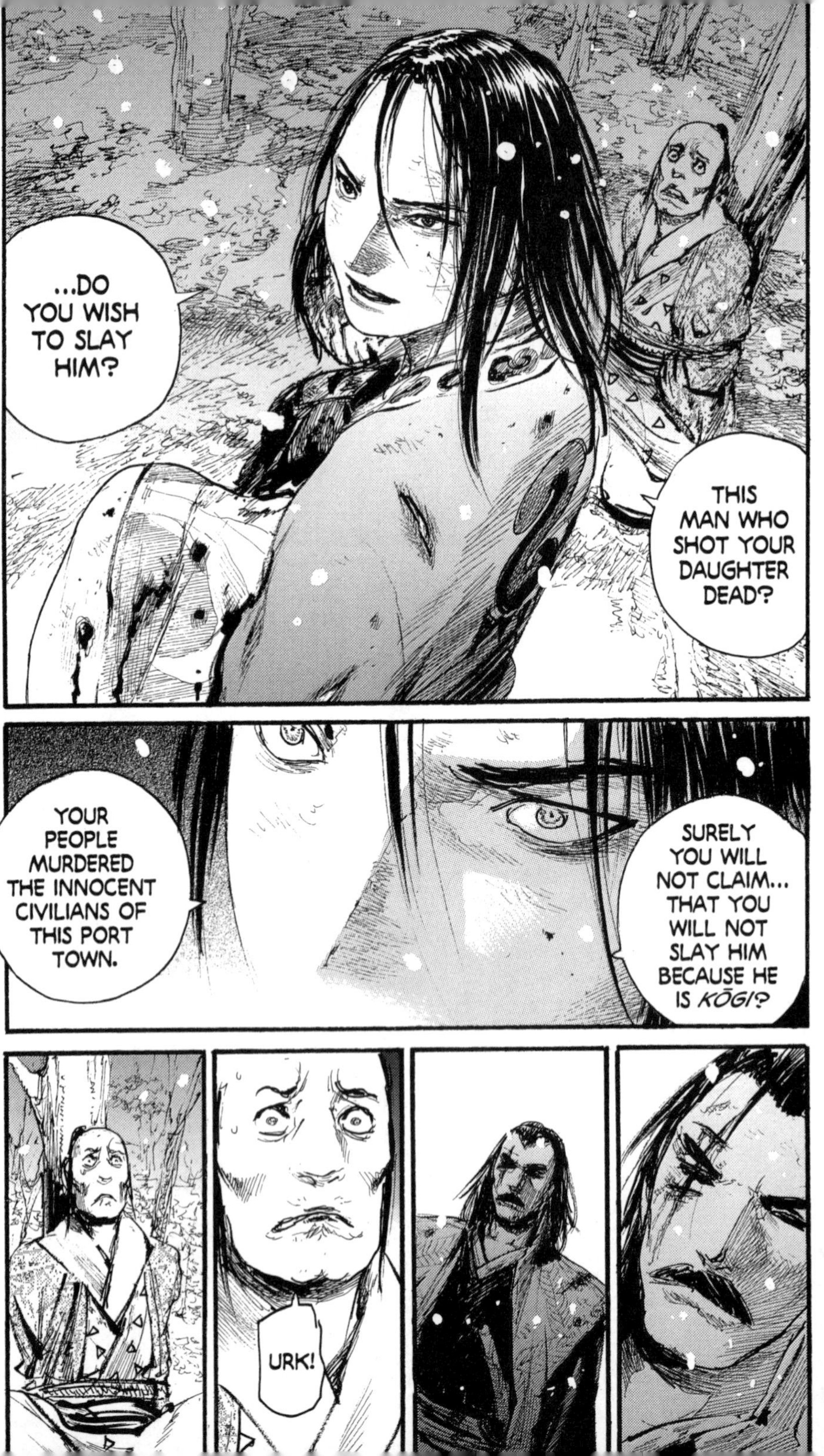
...DO YOU WISH TO SLAY HIM?
THIS MAN WHO SHOT YOUR DAUGHTER DEAD?
YOUR PEOPLE MURDERED THE INNOCENT CIVILIANS OF THIS PORT TOWN.
SURELY YOU WILL NOT CLAIM... THAT YOU WILL NOT SLAY HIM BECAUSE HE IS *KŌGI*?
URK!

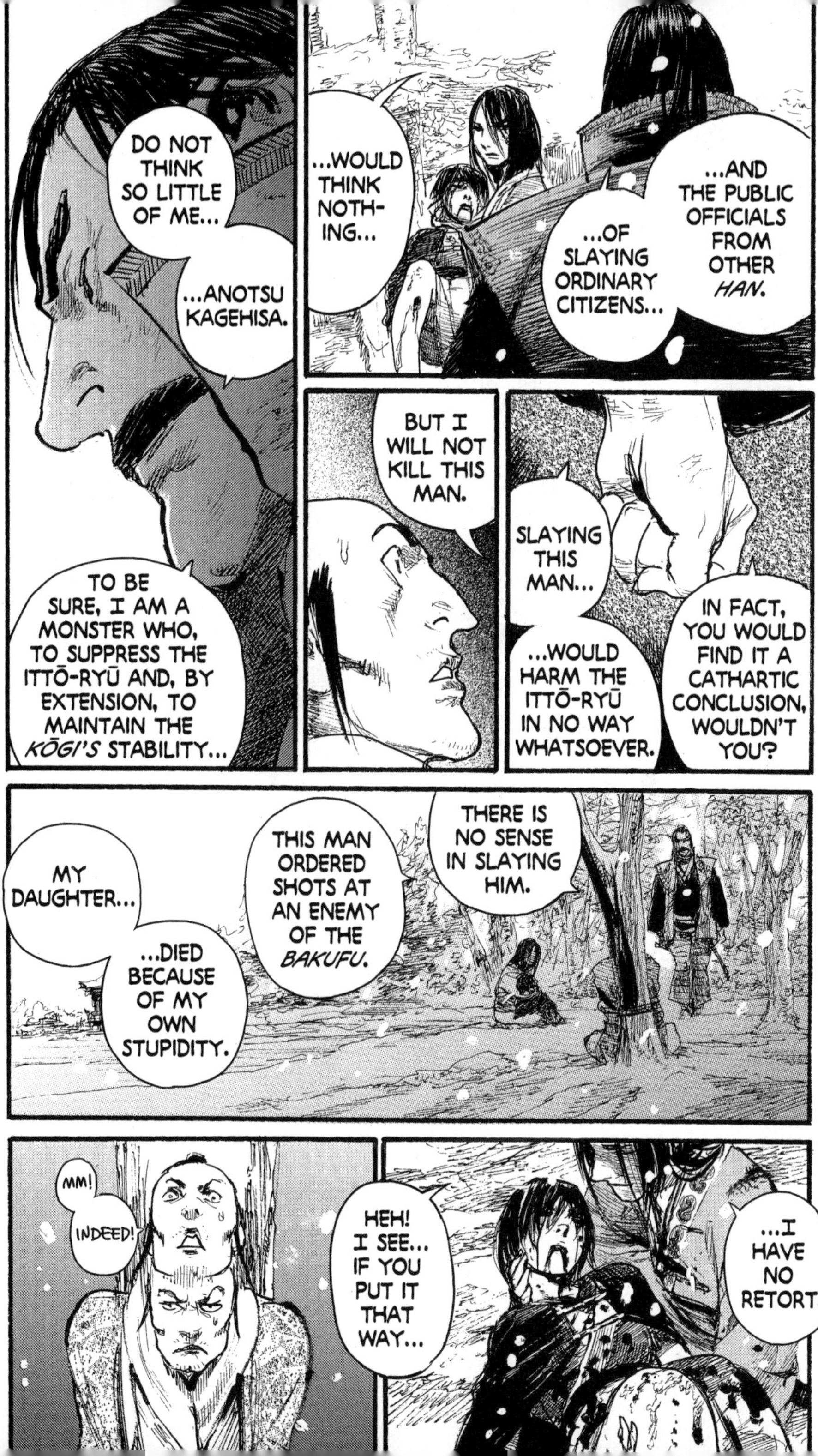
DO NOT THINK SO LITTLE OF ME...
...ANOTSU KAGEHISA.
TO BE SURE, I AM A MONSTER WHO, TO SUPPRESS THE ITTŌ-RYŪ AND, BY EXTENSION, TO MAINTAIN THE *KŌGI'S* STABILITY...
...WOULD THINK NOTHING...
...OF SLAYING ORDINARY CITIZENS...
...AND THE PUBLIC OFFICIALS FROM OTHER *HAN*.
BUT I WILL NOT KILL THIS MAN.
SLAYING THIS MAN...
...WOULD HARM THE ITTŌ-RYŪ IN NO WAY WHATSOEVER.
IN FACT, YOU WOULD FIND IT A CATHARTIC CONCLUSION, WOULDN'T YOU?
MY DAUGHTER...
...DIED BECAUSE OF MY OWN STUPIDITY.
THIS MAN ORDERED SHOTS AT AN ENEMY OF THE *BAKUFU*.
THERE IS NO SENSE IN SLAYING HIM.
MM!
INDEED!
HEH! I SEE... IF YOU PUT IT THAT WAY...
...I HAVE NO RETORT.

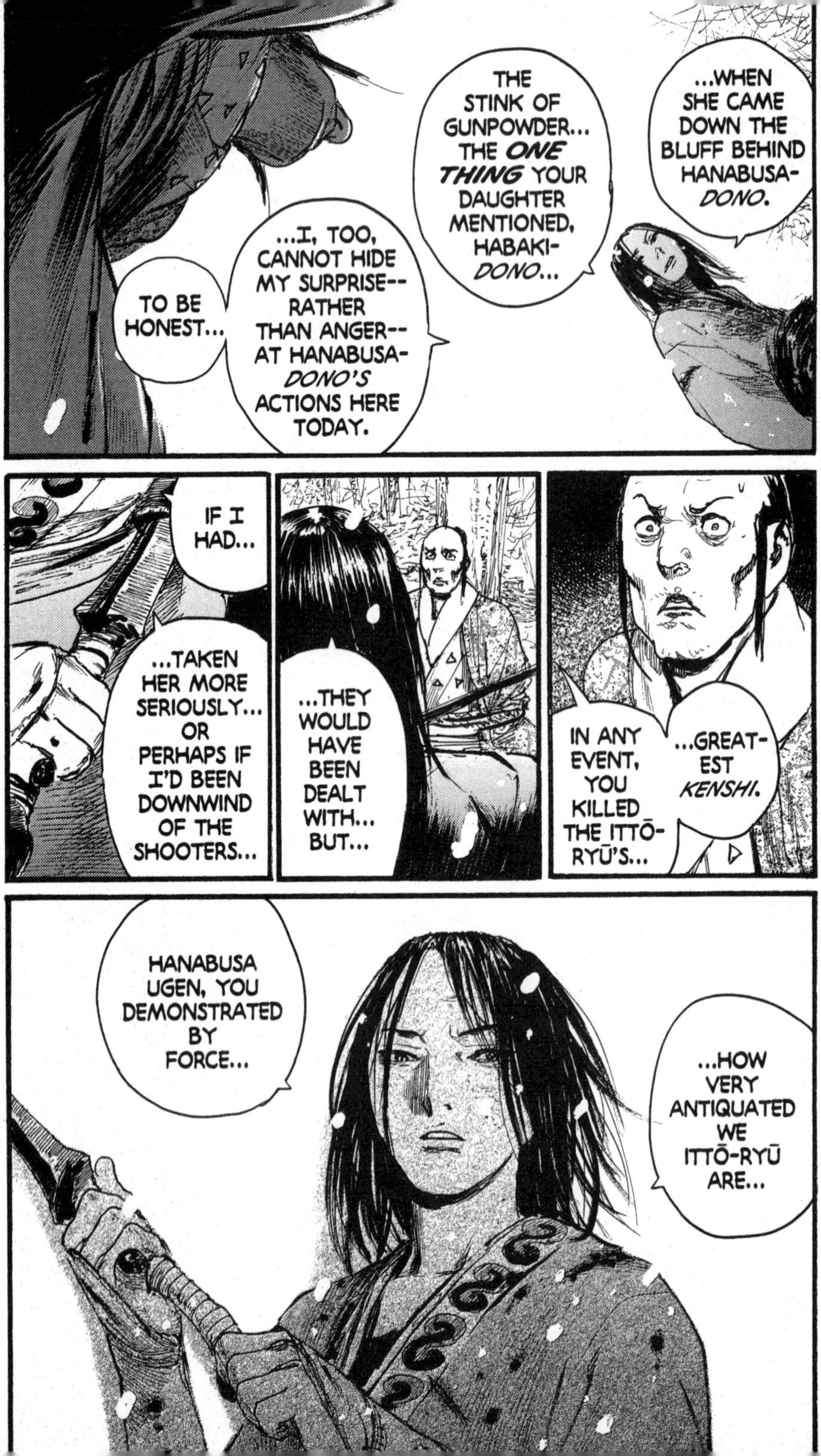
TO BE HONEST...
...I, TOO, CANNOT HIDE MY SURPRISE--RATHER THAN ANGER--AT HANABUSA-*DONO'S* ACTIONS HERE TODAY.
THE STINK OF GUNPOWDER... THE ***ONE THING*** YOUR DAUGHTER MENTIONED, HABAKI-*DONO*...
...WHEN SHE CAME DOWN THE BLUFF BEHIND HANABUSA-*DONO*.
IF I HAD...
...TAKEN HER MORE SERIOUSLY... OR PERHAPS IF I'D BEEN DOWNWIND OF THE SHOOTERS...
...THEY WOULD HAVE BEEN DEALT WITH... BUT...
IN ANY EVENT, YOU KILLED THE ITTŌ-RYŪ'S...
...GREATEST *KENSHI*.
HANABUSA UGEN, YOU DEMONSTRATED BY FORCE...
...HOW VERY ANTIQUATED WE ITTŌ-RYŪ ARE...

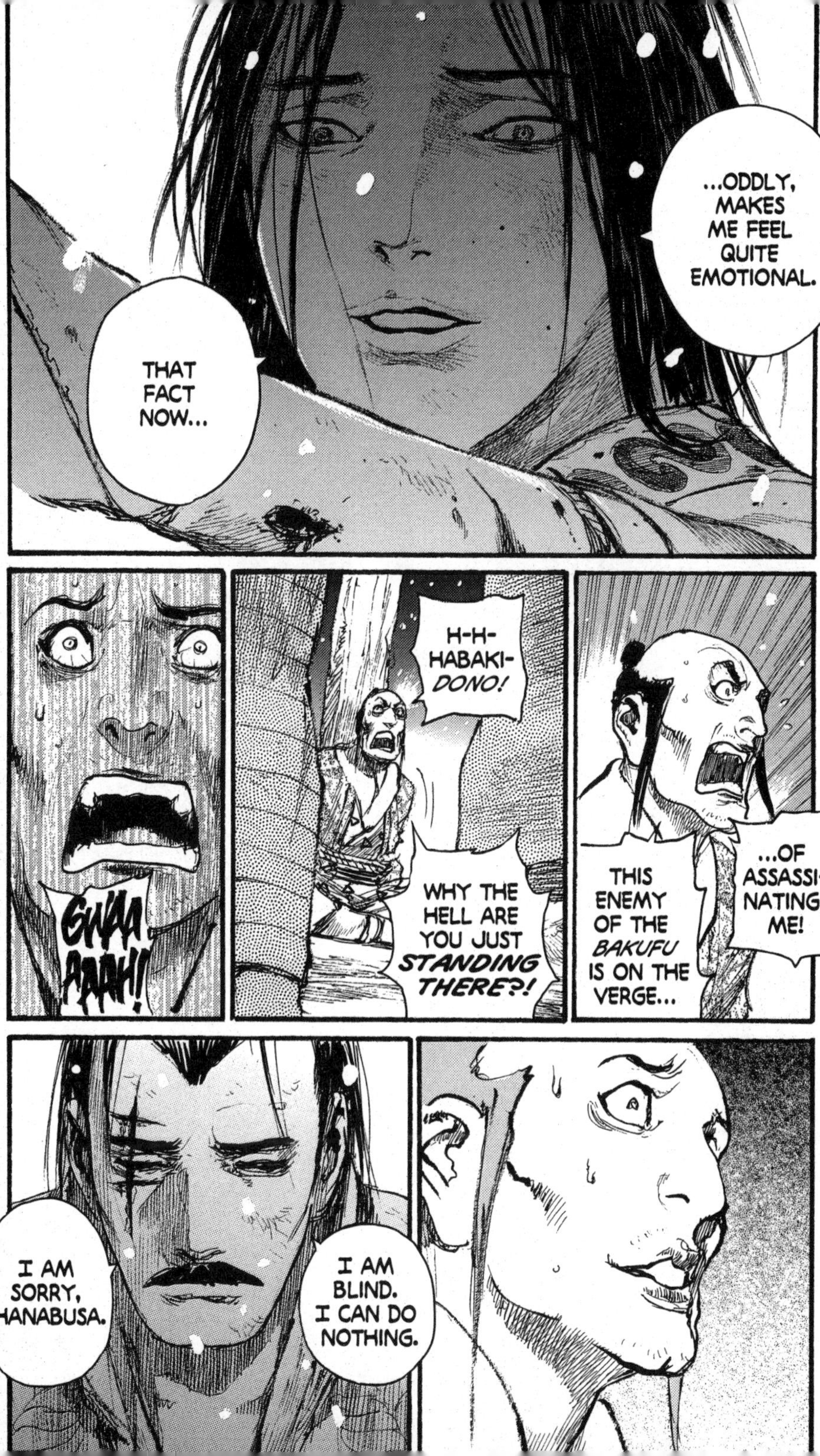
THAT FACT NOW...
...ODDLY, MAKES ME FEEL QUITE EMOTIONAL.
GWAAAAAH!!
H-H-HABAKI-*DONO*!
WHY THE HELL ARE YOU JUST ***STANDING THERE?!***
THIS ENEMY OF THE *BAKUFU* IS ON THE VERGE...
...OF ASSASSI-NATING ME!
I AM SORRY, HANABUSA.
I AM BLIND. I CAN DO NOTHING.

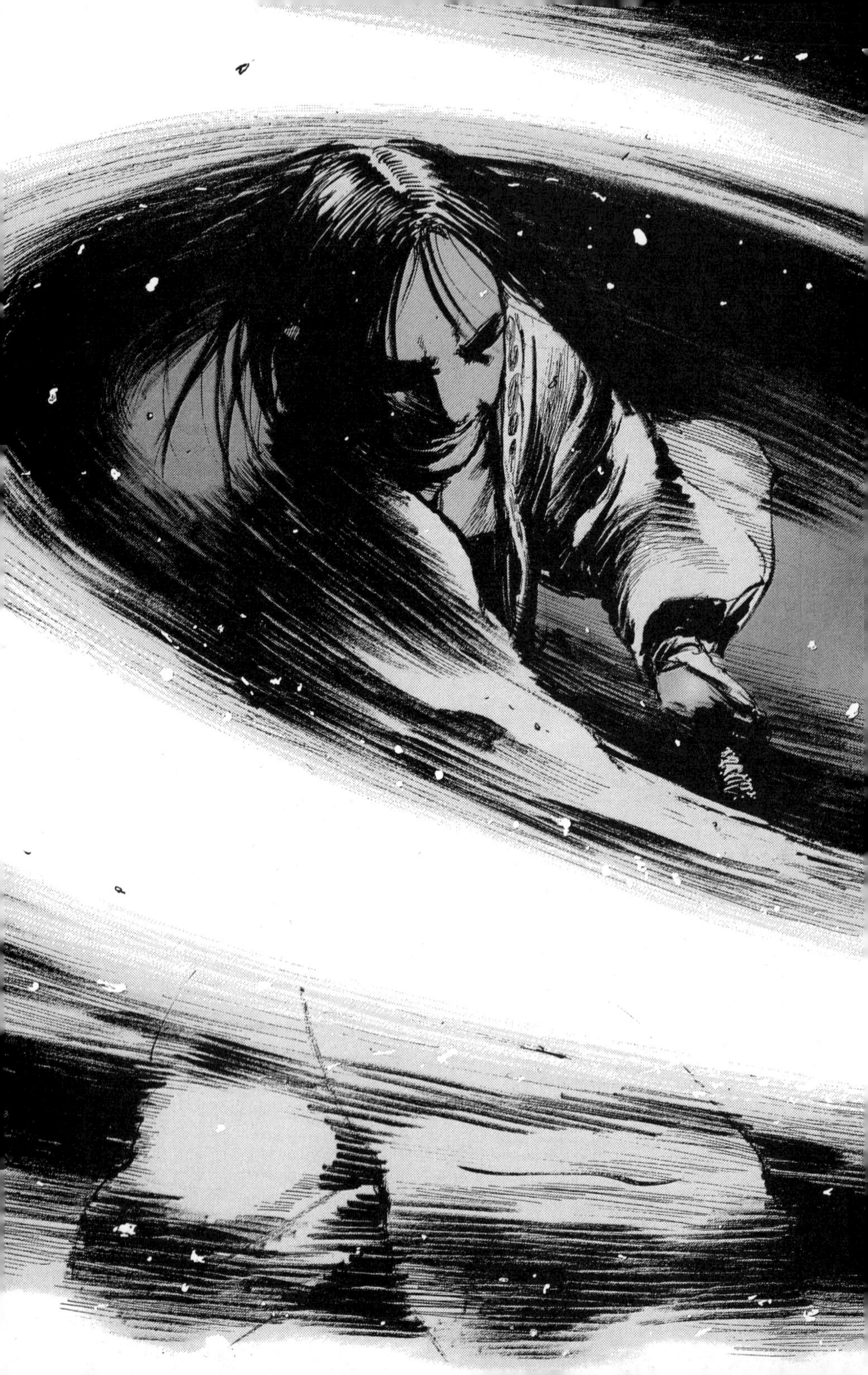

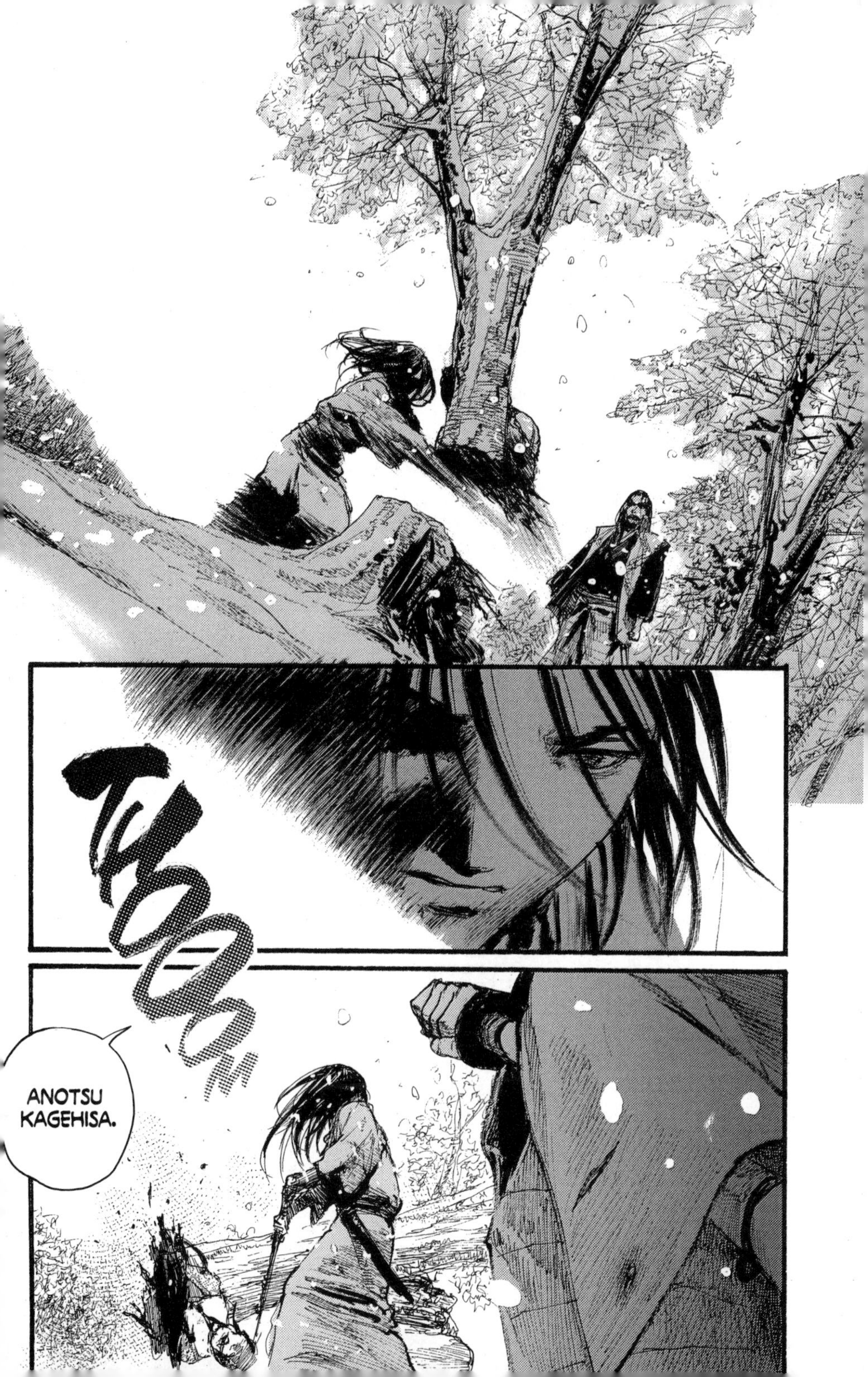
THOOOM
ANOTSU KAGEHISA.

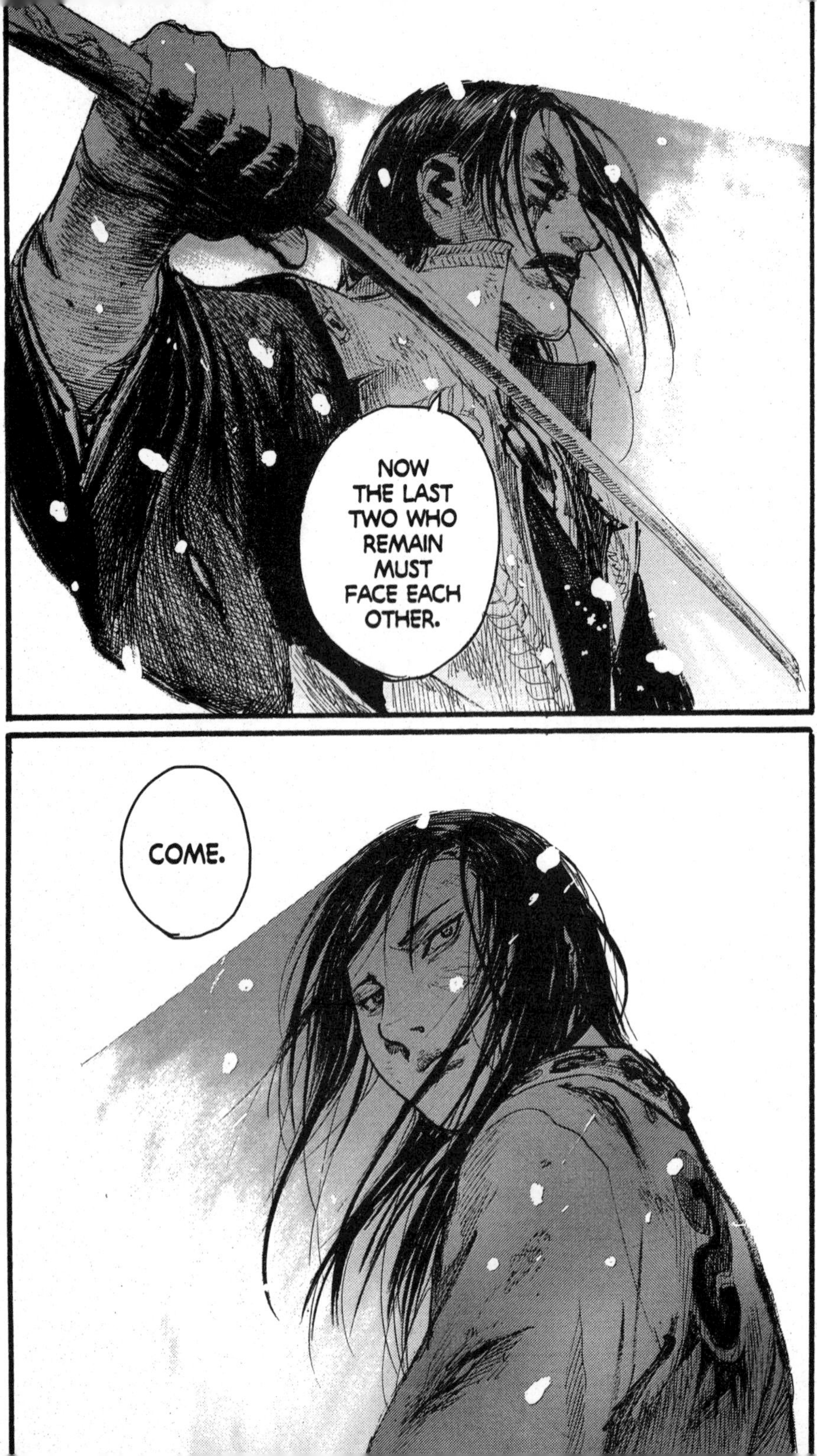
NOW THE LAST TWO WHO REMAIN MUST FACE EACH OTHER.
COME.

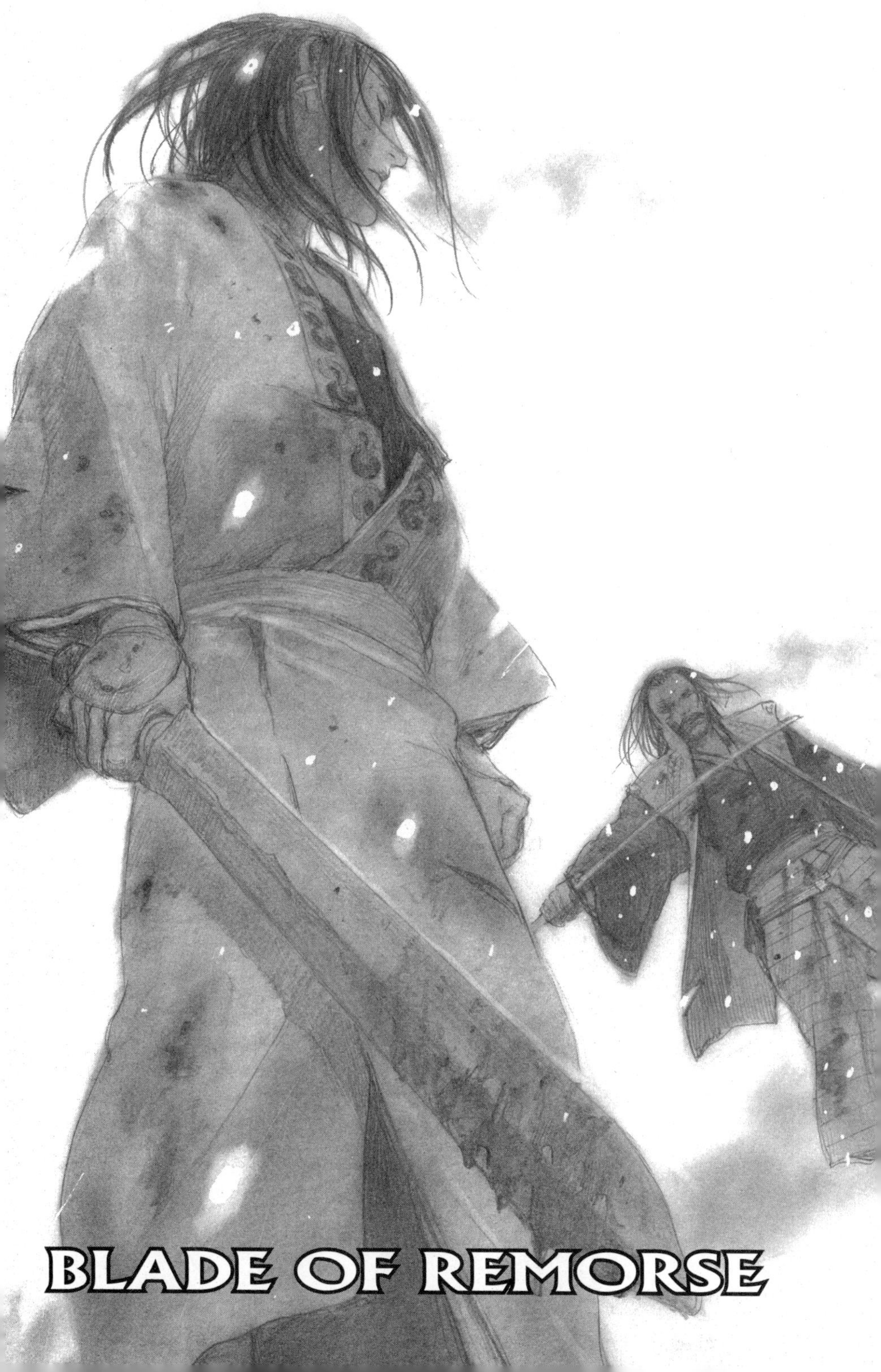

BLADE OF REMORSE

WELL, THEN...

...WE BECOME MERELY ANIMALS.

...HABAKI-DONO.

WHEN WE LOSE OUR SHACKLES TO HUMAN COMPASSION...

IT IS IMPERTINENT TO ASK... BUT YOU ARE NOT HOPING FOR ALLOWANCES OWING TO YOUR BLINDNESS...

...ARE YOU?

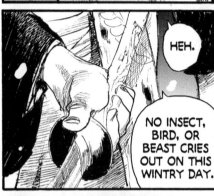

HEH.

NO INSECT, BIRD, OR BEAST CRIES OUT ON THIS WINTRY DAY.

THE LIVING ARE BY THE BLUFF.

WE ARE THE ONLY TWO BREATHING HERE.

HERE IN THIS PLACE... FROM YOUR BREATHING ALONE...

...AN IMAGE OF YOU FORMS IN MY MIND.

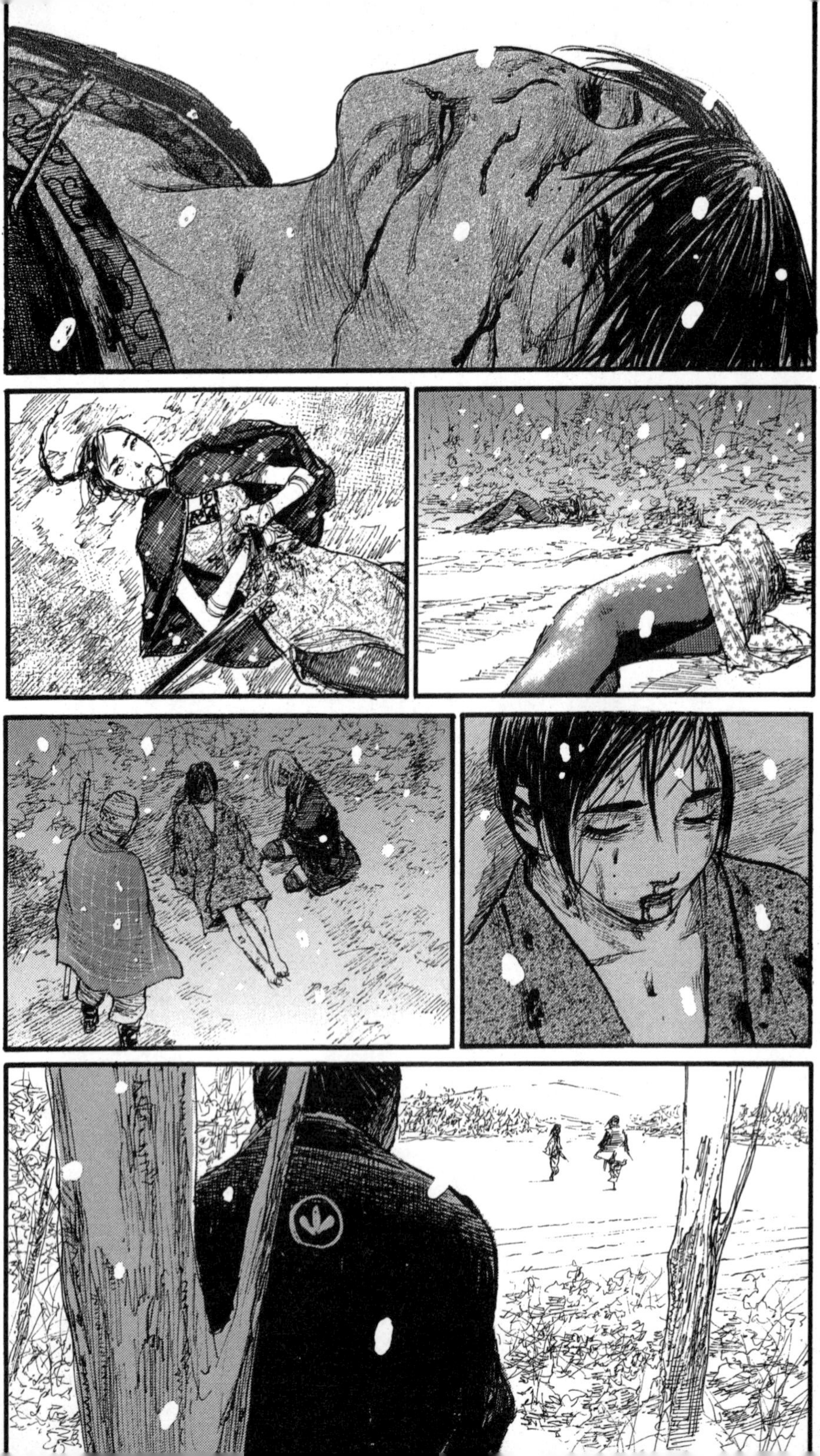

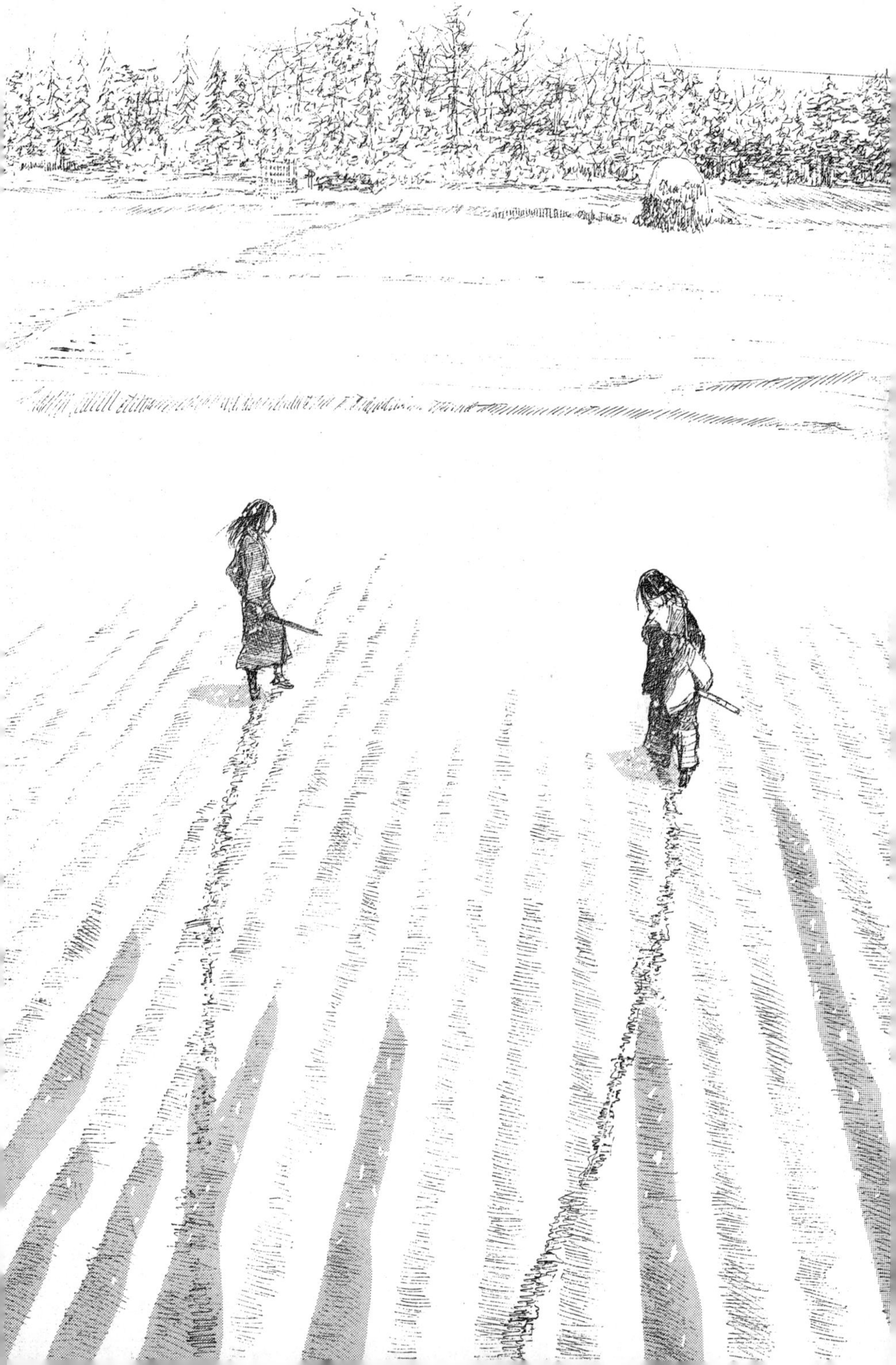

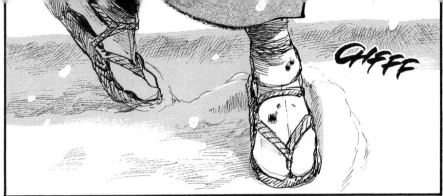

CHFFF

SKFF

...CULTIVATED
SOIL
UNDER
OUR FEET.

THAT
SHOULD
MEAN...
NO TREES
AROUND US
IN ANY
DIRECTION...

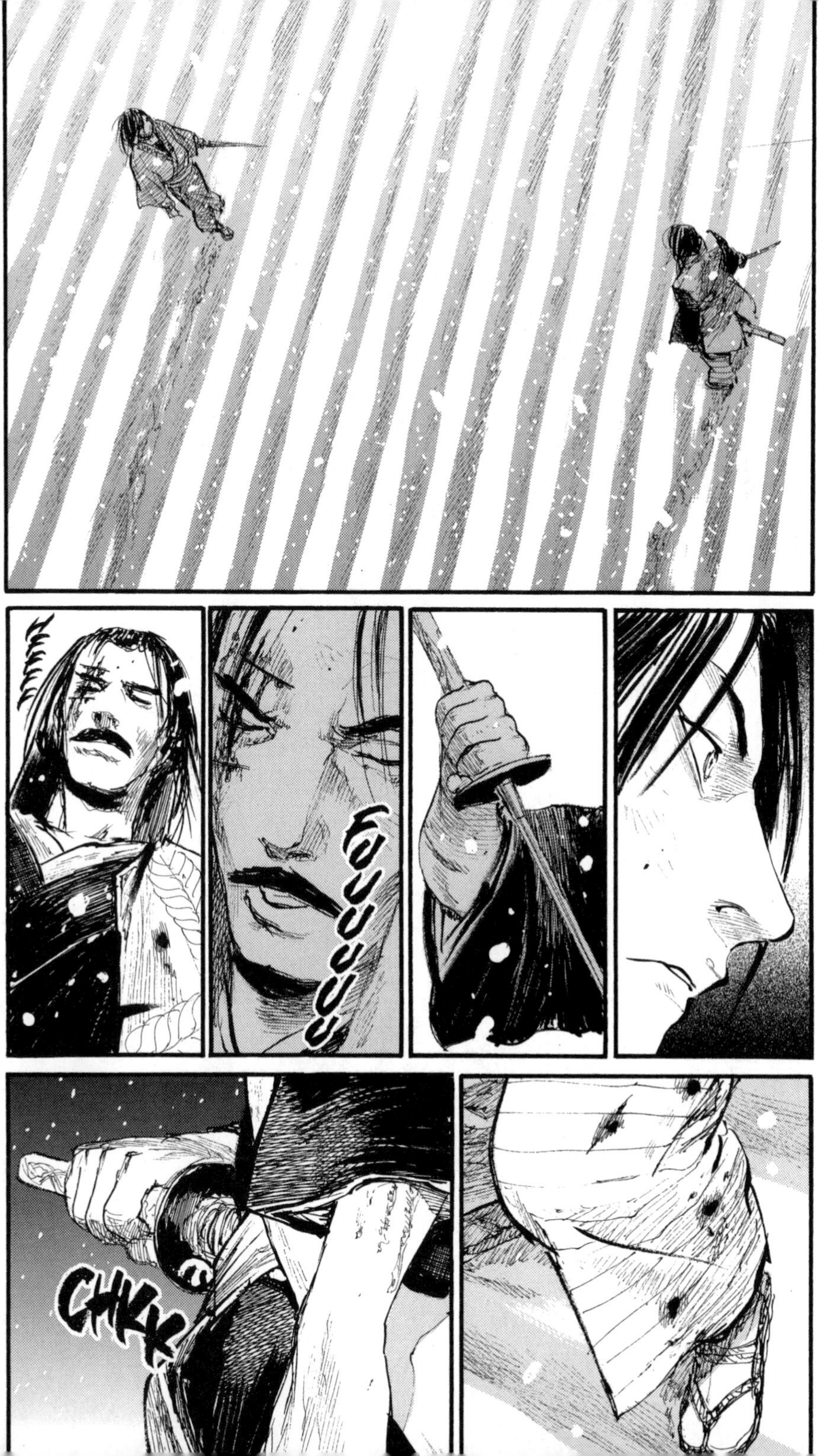
CHKK

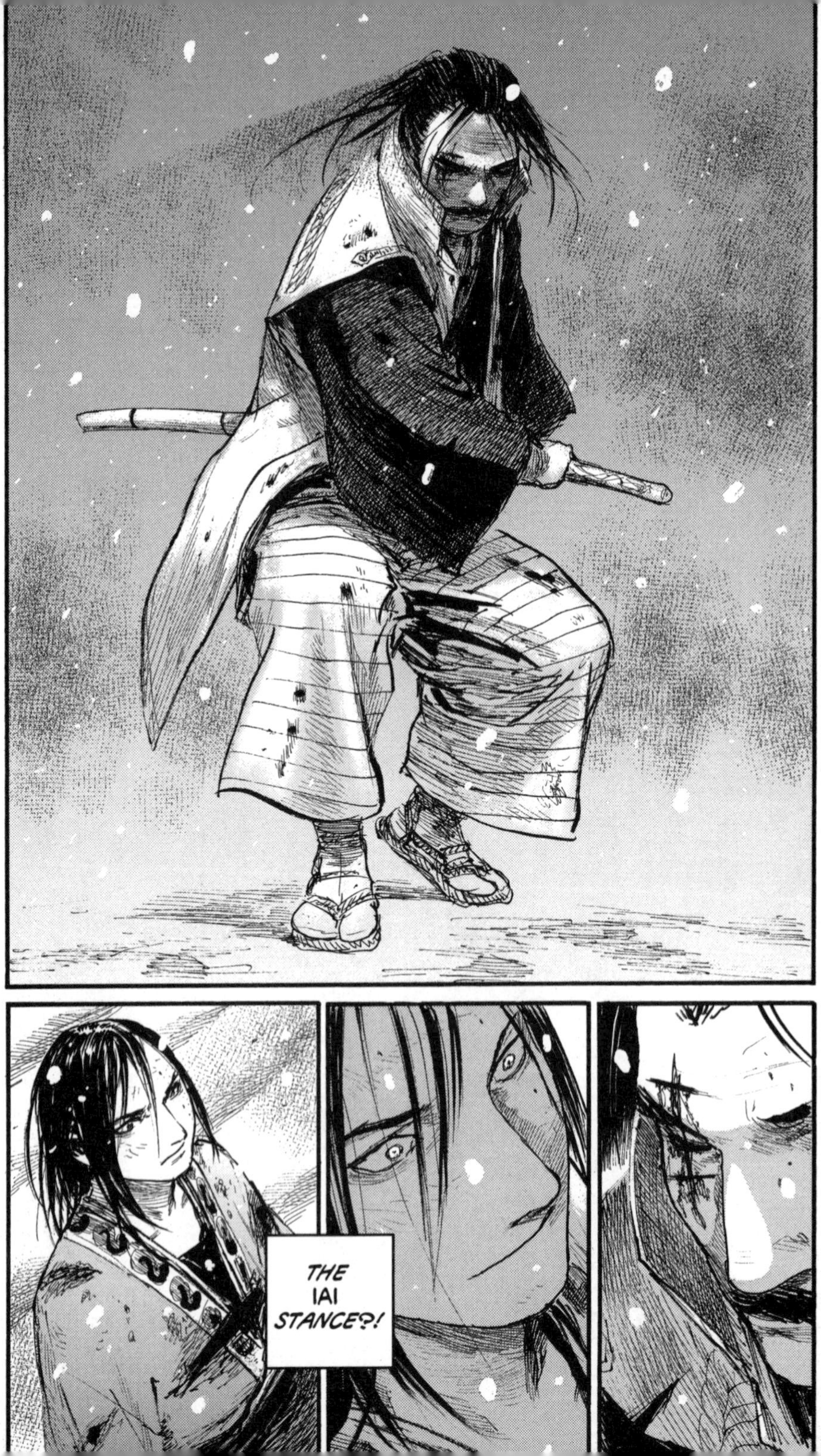
THE IAI STANCE?!

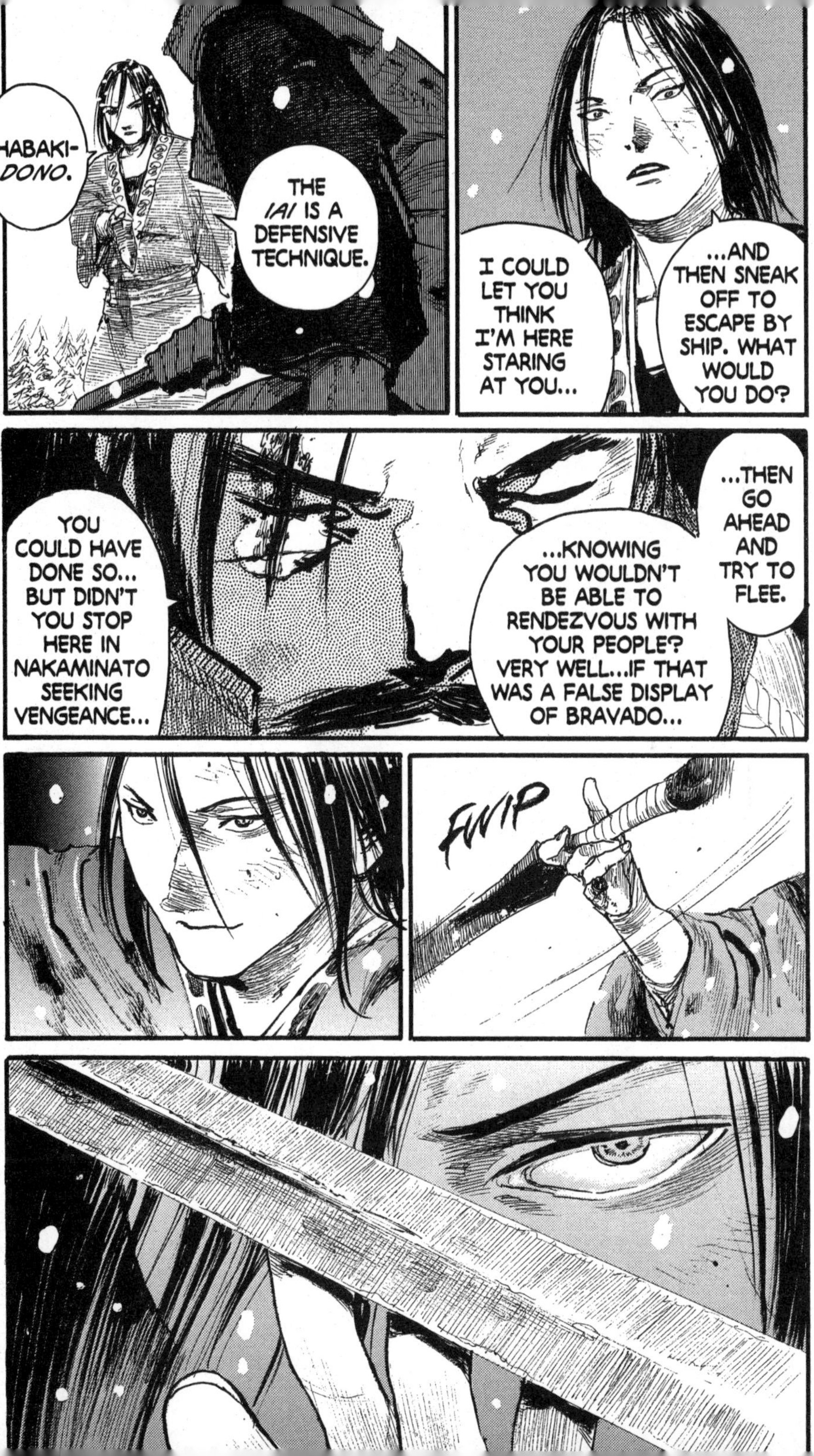
HABAKI-*DONO*.
THE *IAI* IS A DEFENSIVE TECHNIQUE.
I COULD LET YOU THINK I'M HERE STARING AT YOU...
...AND THEN SNEAK OFF TO ESCAPE BY SHIP. WHAT WOULD YOU DO?
YOU COULD HAVE DONE SO... BUT DIDN'T YOU STOP HERE IN NAKAMINATO SEEKING VENGEANCE...
...KNOWING YOU WOULDN'T BE ABLE TO RENDEZVOUS WITH YOUR PEOPLE? VERY WELL...IF THAT WAS A FALSE DISPLAY OF BRAVADO...
...THEN GO AHEAD AND TRY TO FLEE.
FWIP

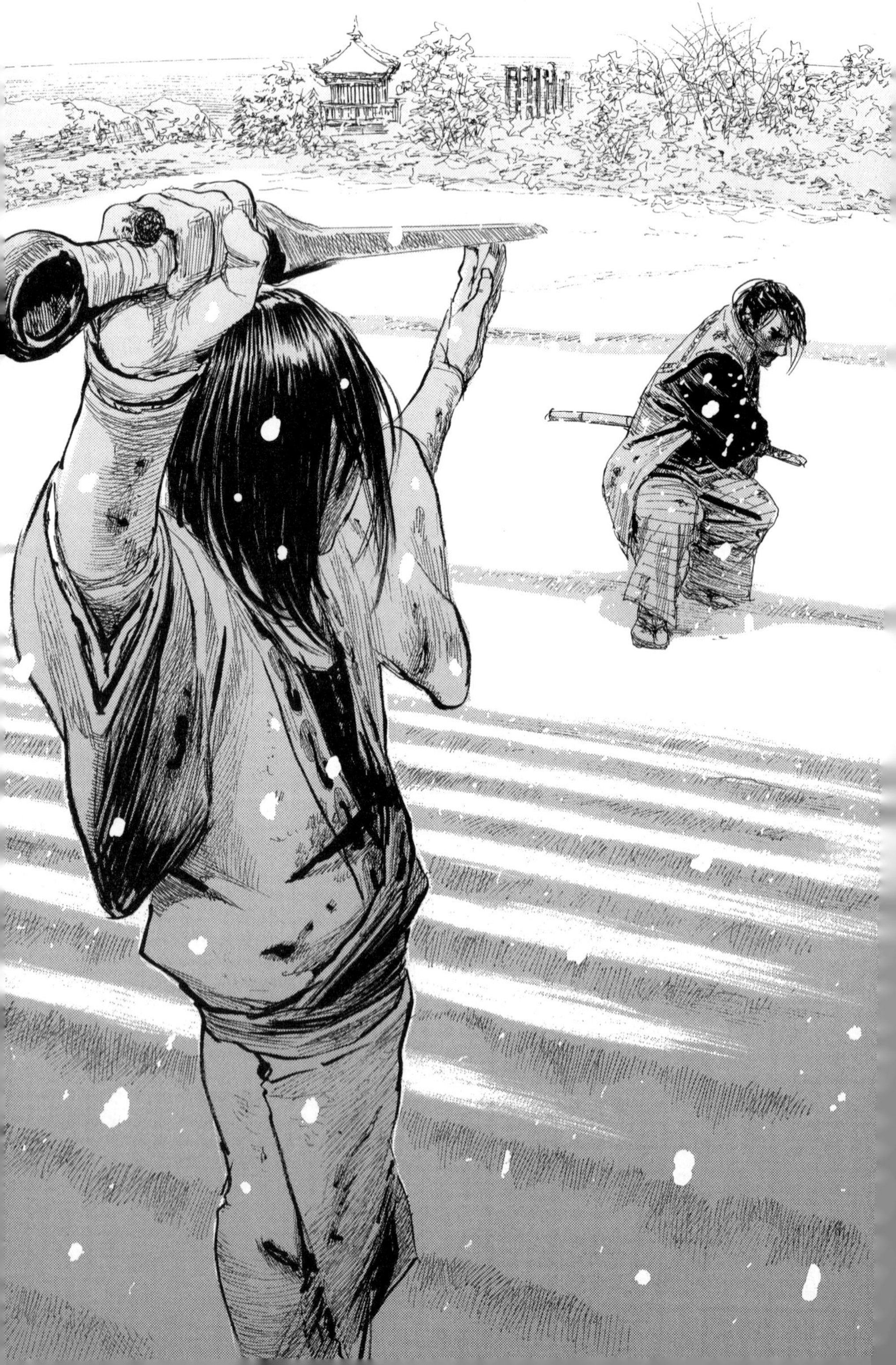

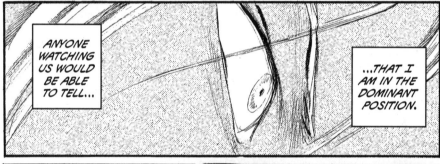

ANYONE WATCHING US WOULD BE ABLE TO TELL...

...THAT I AM IN THE DOMINANT POSITION.

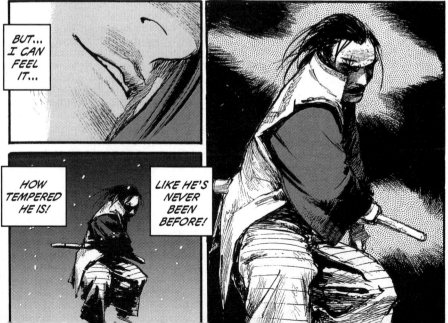

BUT... I CAN FEEL IT...

HOW TEMPERED HE IS!

LIKE HE'S NEVER BEEN BEFORE!

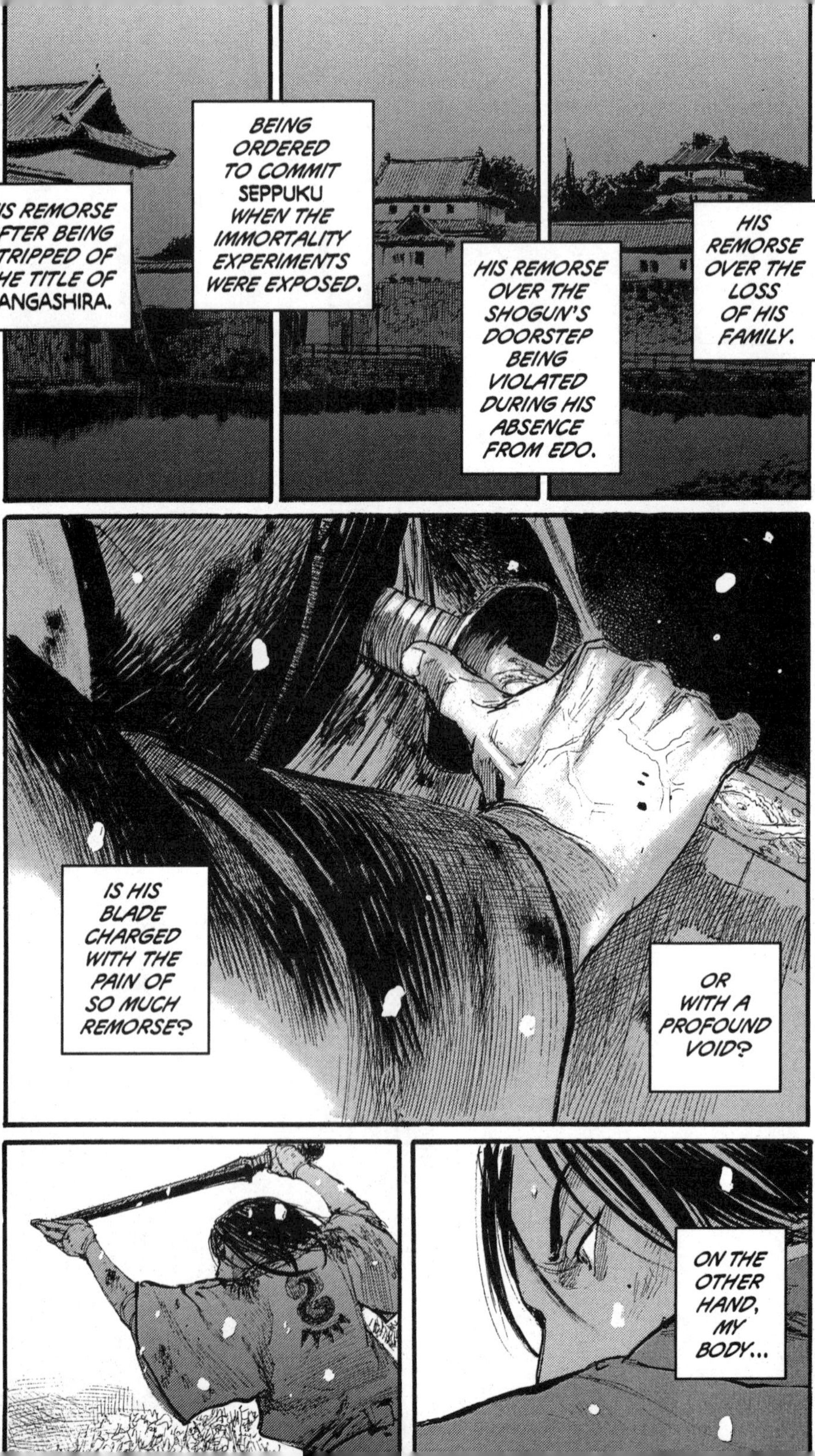
HIS REMORSE AFTER BEING STRIPPED OF THE TITLE OF BANGASHIRA.
BEING ORDERED TO COMMIT SEPPUKU WHEN THE IMMORTALITY EXPERIMENTS WERE EXPOSED.
HIS REMORSE OVER THE SHOGUN'S DOORSTEP BEING VIOLATED DURING HIS ABSENCE FROM EDO.
HIS REMORSE OVER THE LOSS OF HIS FAMILY.
IS HIS BLADE CHARGED WITH THE PAIN OF SO MUCH REMORSE?
OR WITH A PROFOUND VOID?
ON THE OTHER HAND, MY BODY...

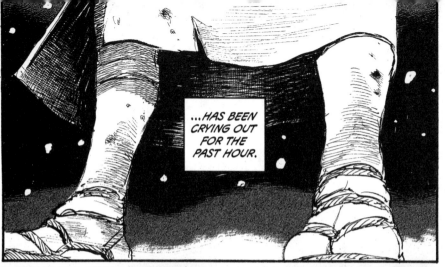

...HAS BEEN CRYING OUT FOR THE PAST HOUR.

IN THIS STATE...

...WHAT GAVE ME THE STRENGTH TO CUT THROUGH A MAN AND A TREE IN A SINGLE STROKE...

...WAS ANGER.

BUT FOR SOME REASON...

...STANDING HERE NOW, BEFORE A MAN I SHOULD DESPISE, IT WANES.

IS IT BECAUSE HE HAS NOW LOST EVERYTHING AND IS REDUCED TO BEING AN OBSTINATE BUSHI...?

OR IS IT BECAUSE I CAN'T HELP BUT REVERE HIS ASTONISHING MARTIAL DETERMINATION...?

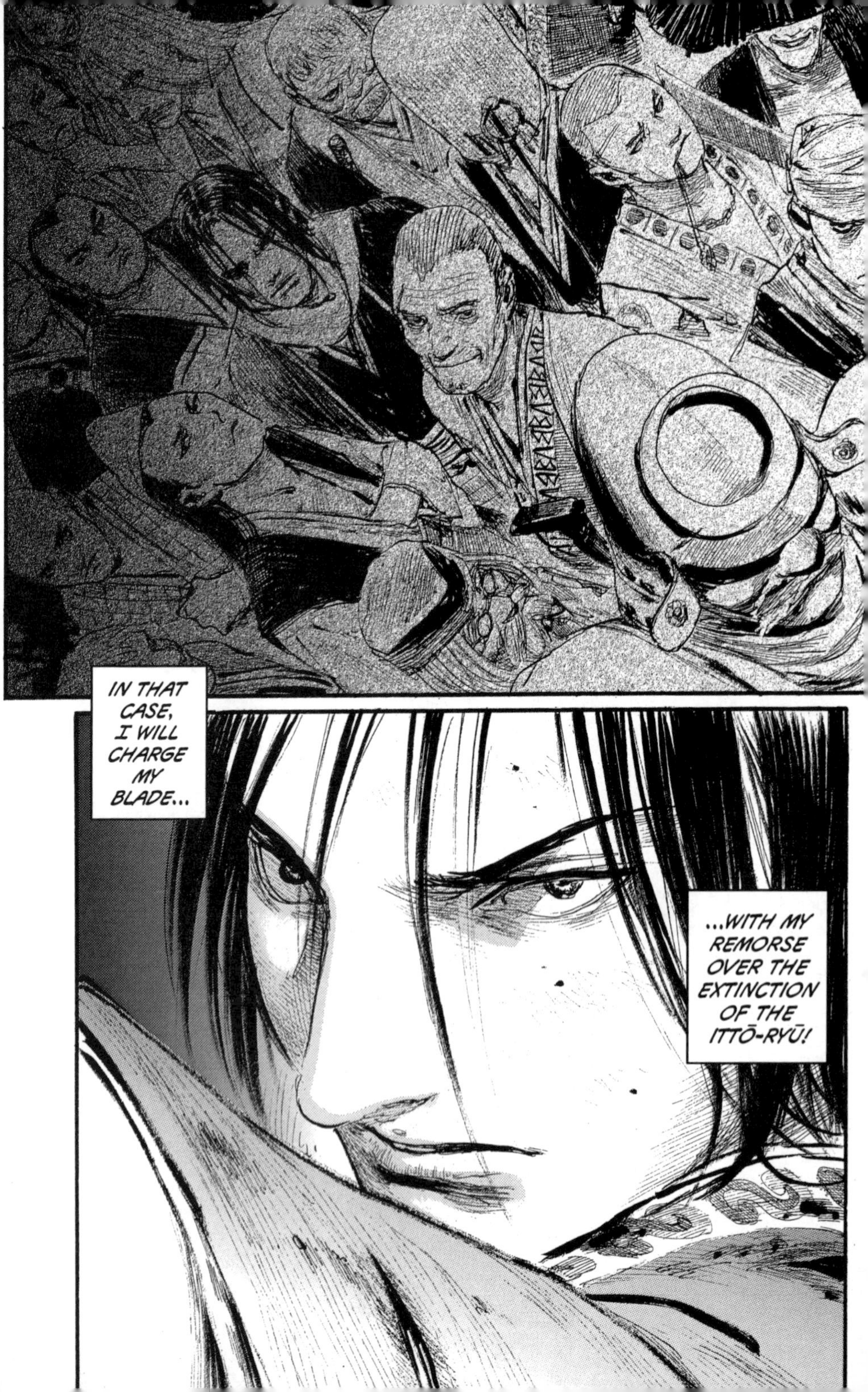
IN THAT CASE, I WILL CHARGE MY BLADE...
...WITH MY REMORSE OVER THE EXTINCTION OF THE ITTŌ-RYŪ!

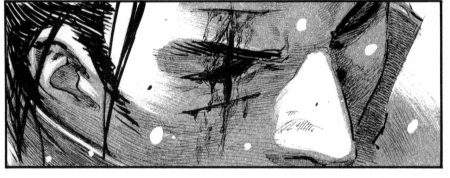

KUH

SHEE

FIRST STEP!

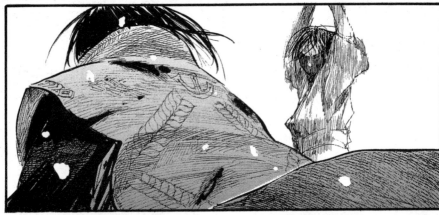

SECOND STEP!

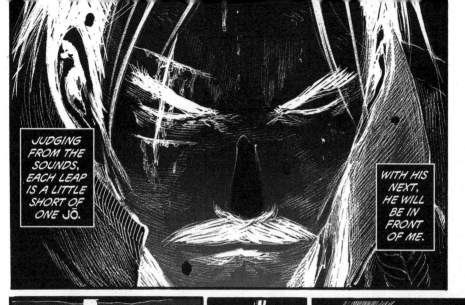

JUDGING FROM THE SOUNDS, EACH LEAP IS A LITTLE SHORT OF ONE JŌ.

WITH HIS NEXT, HE WILL BE IN FRONT OF ME.

I'VE GOT HIM!

YOUR BLOOD WILL SPRAY ACROSS THE SNOW--

--ANOTSU KAGEHISA!

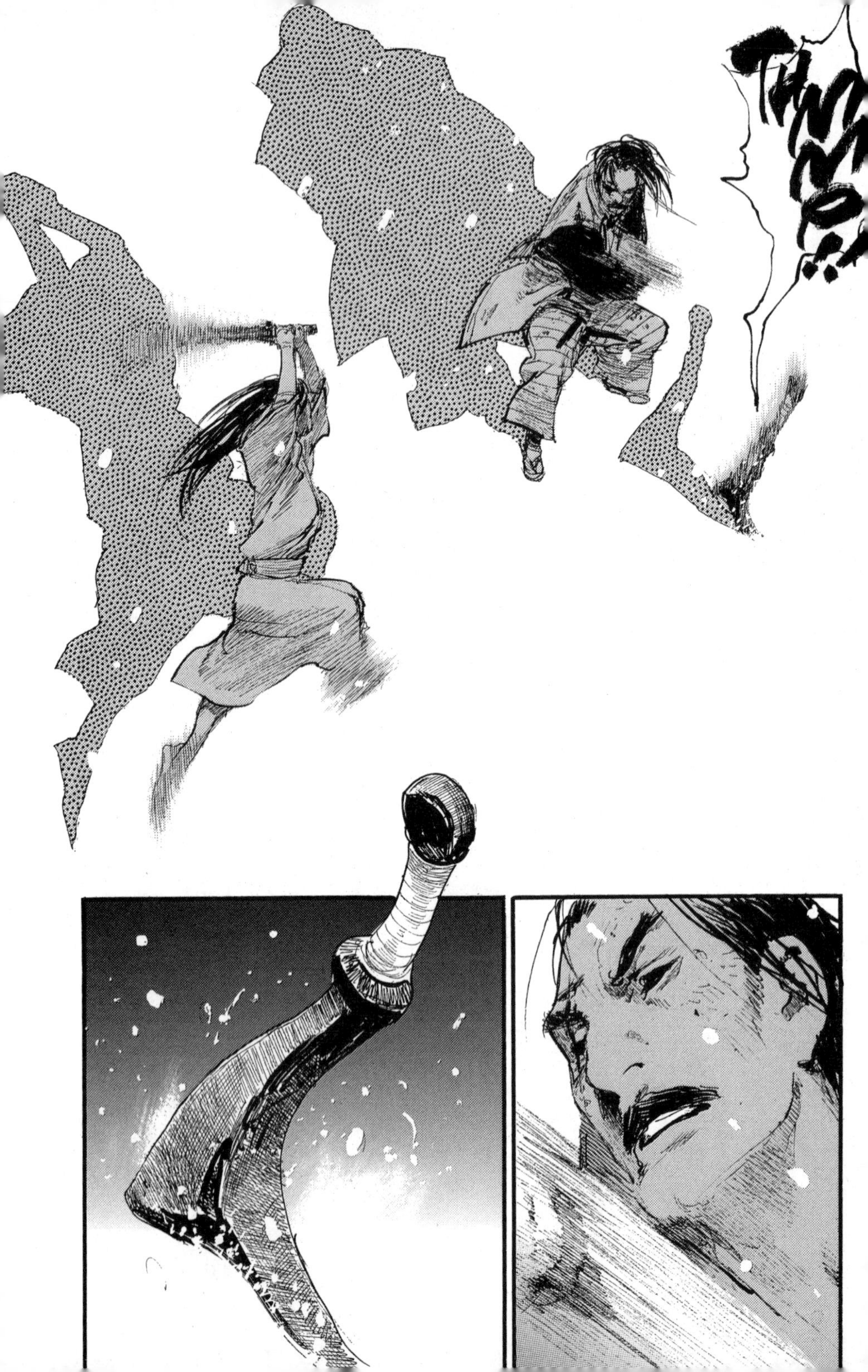

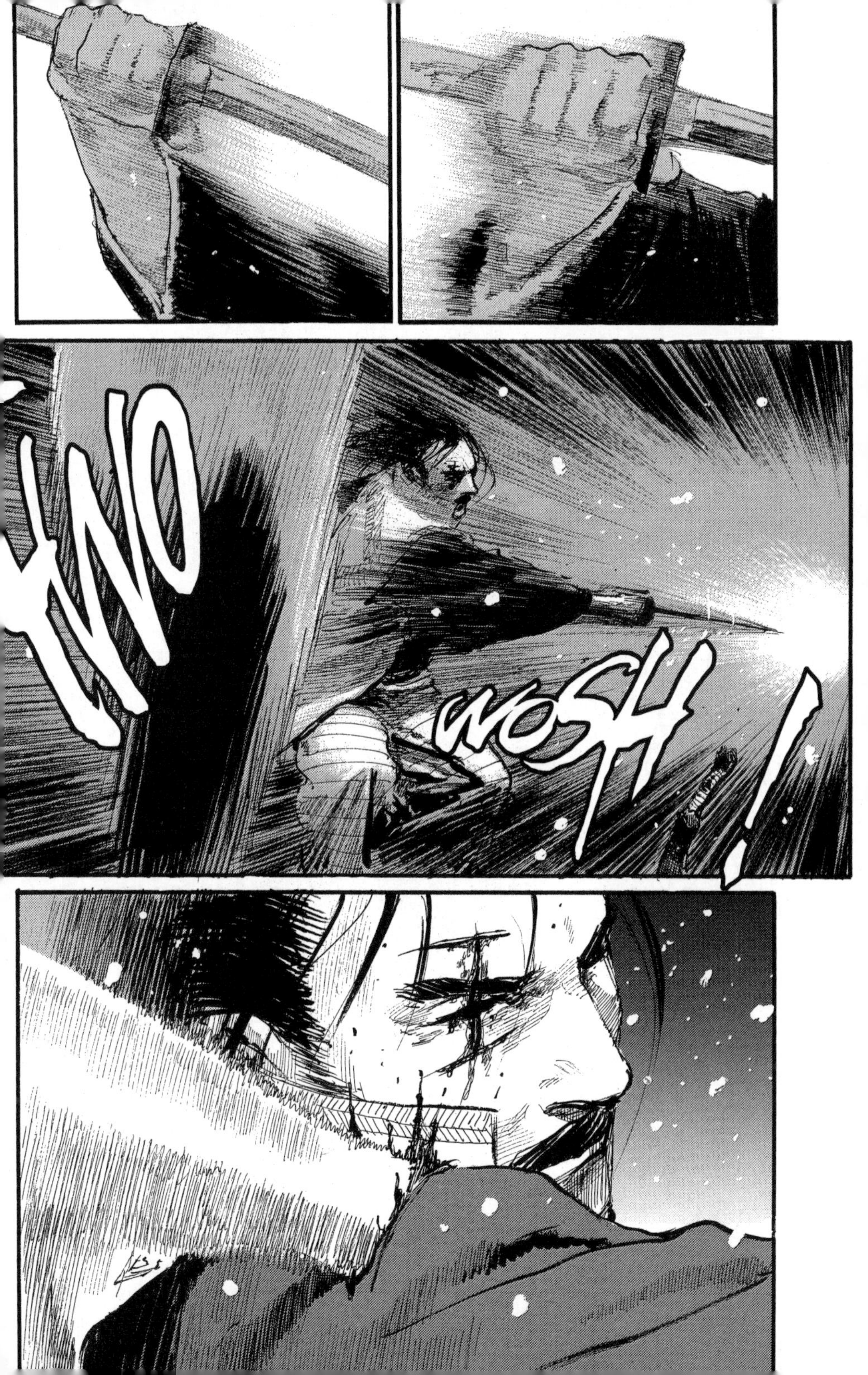
WOSH!

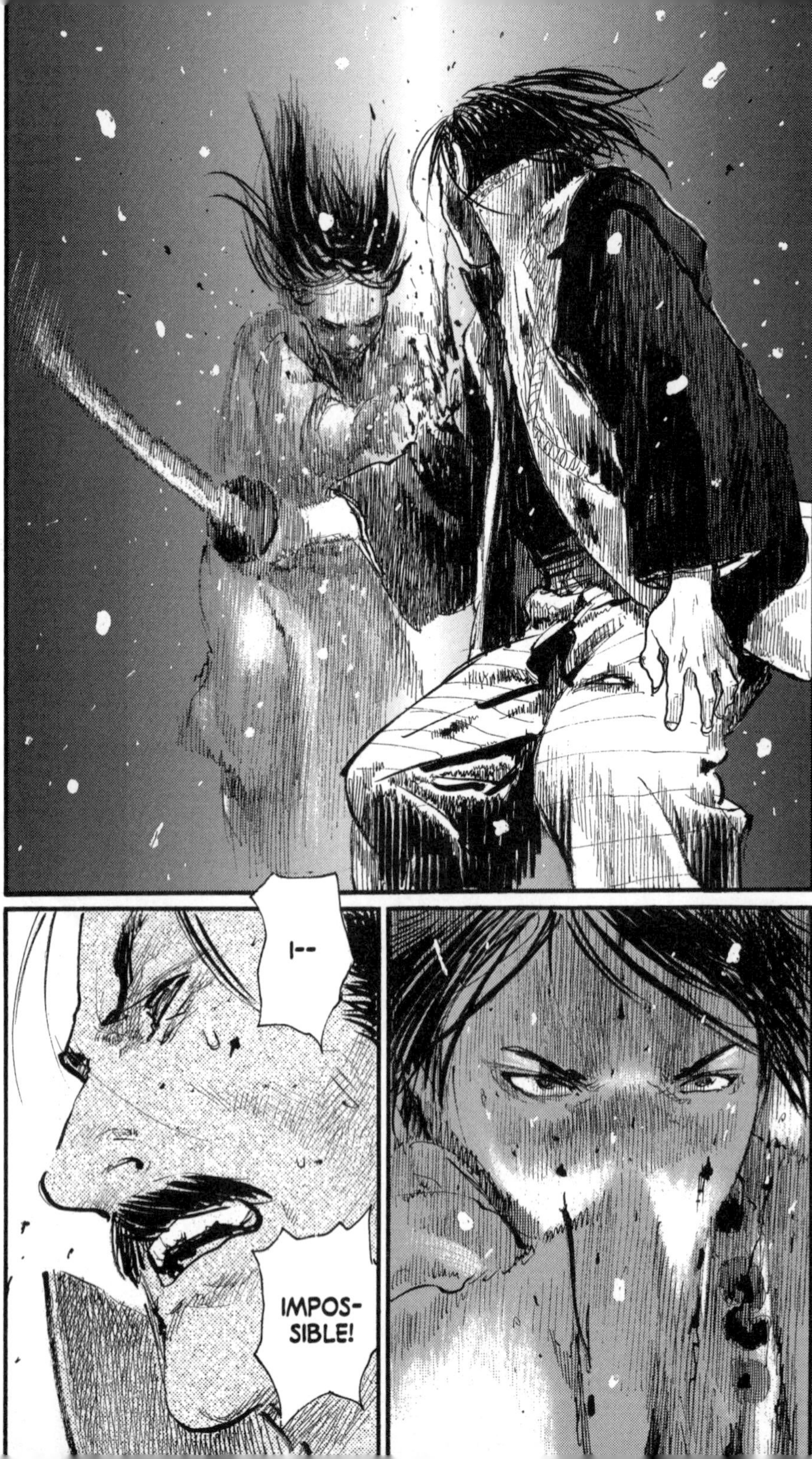
I--
IMPOS-
SIBLE!

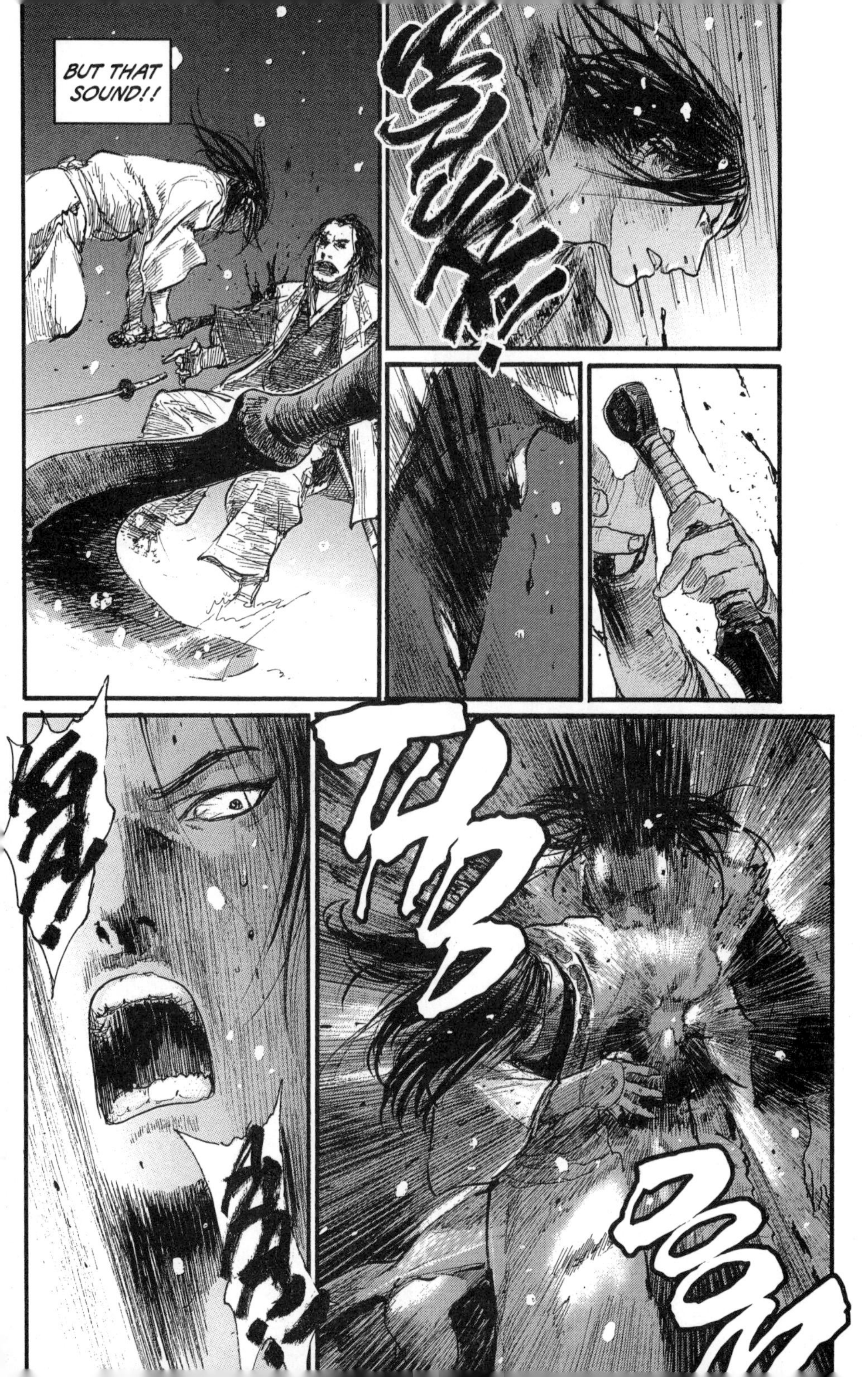
BUT THAT SOUND!!

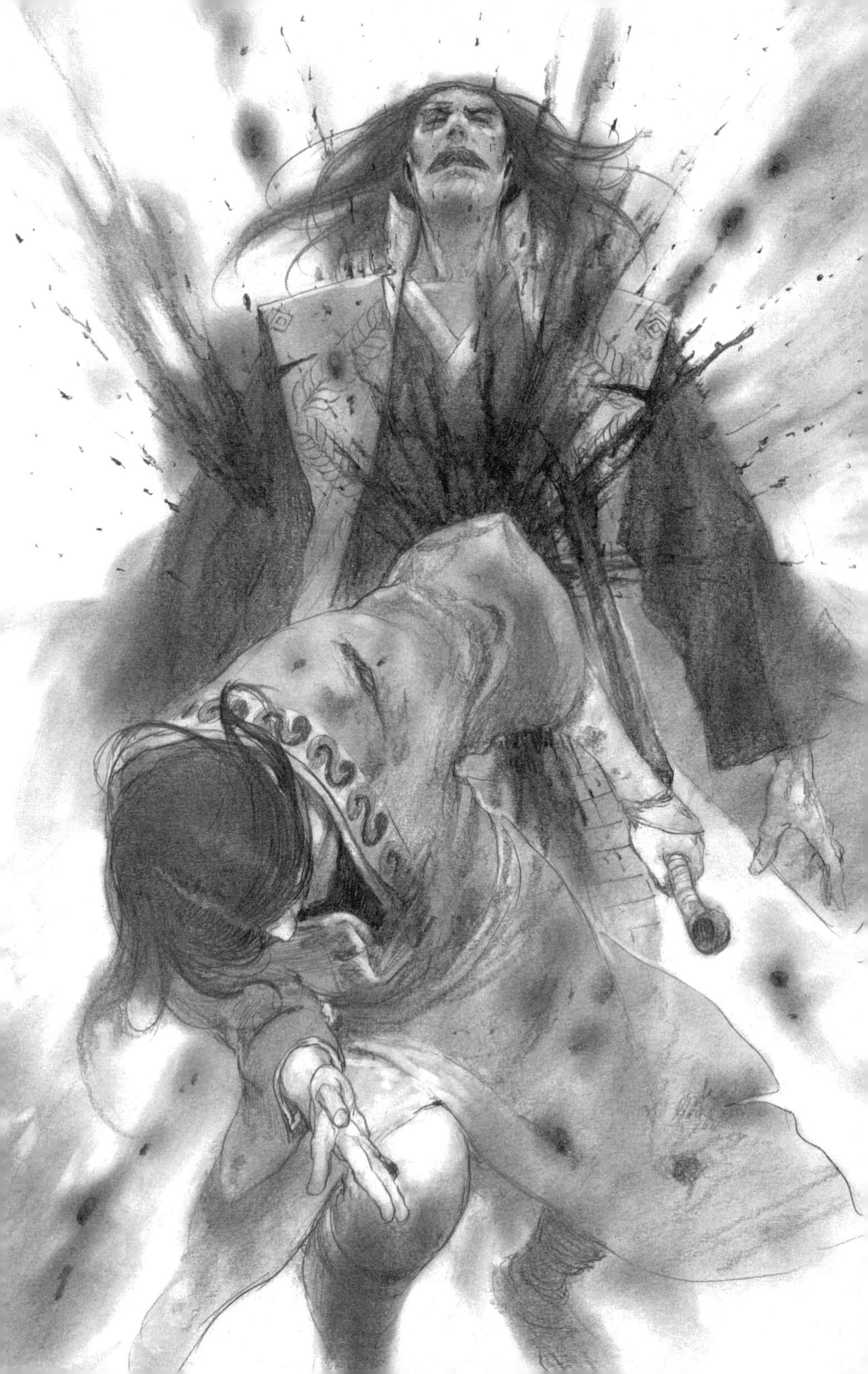

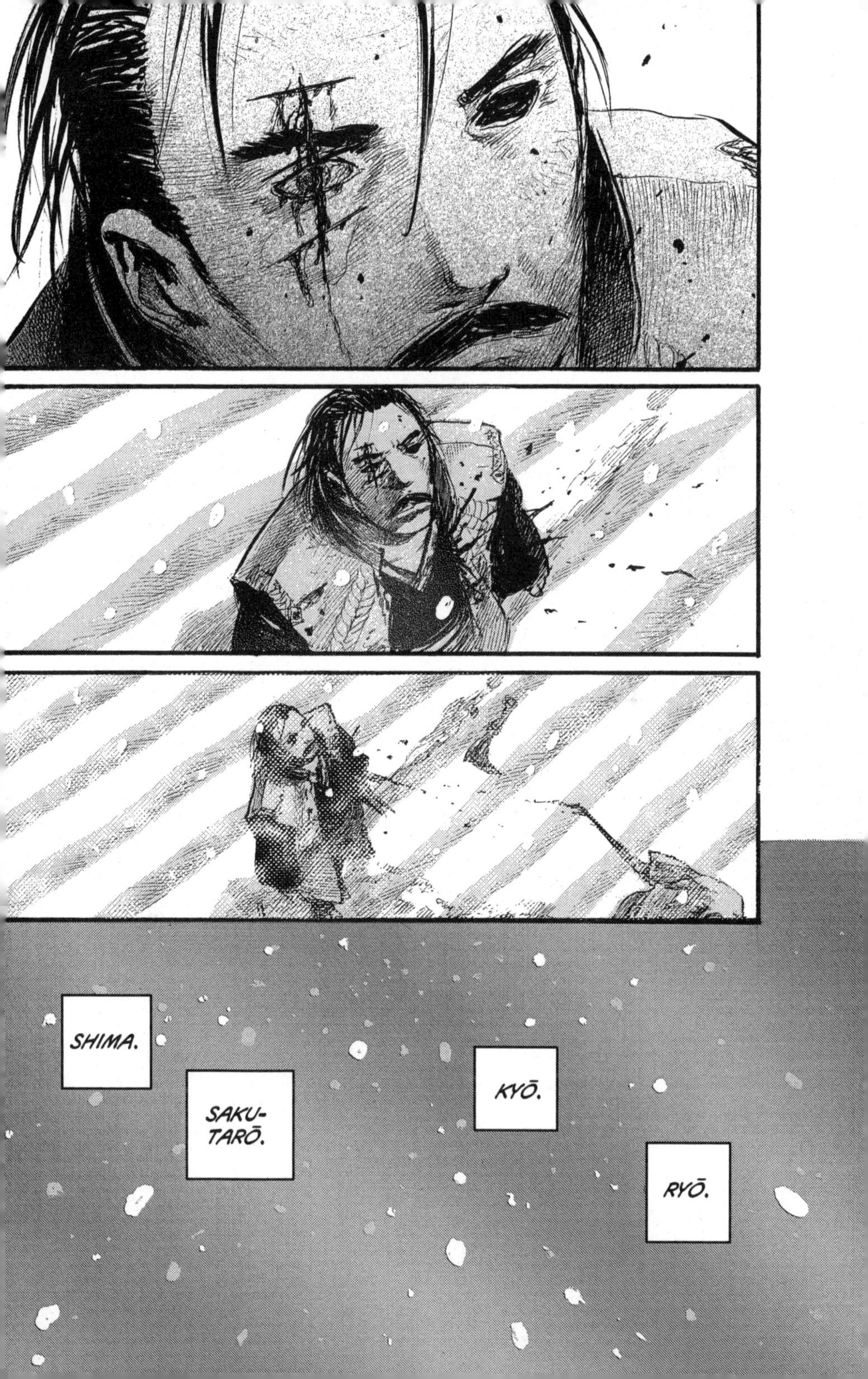
SHIMA.
SAKU-TARŌ.
KYŌ.
RYŌ.

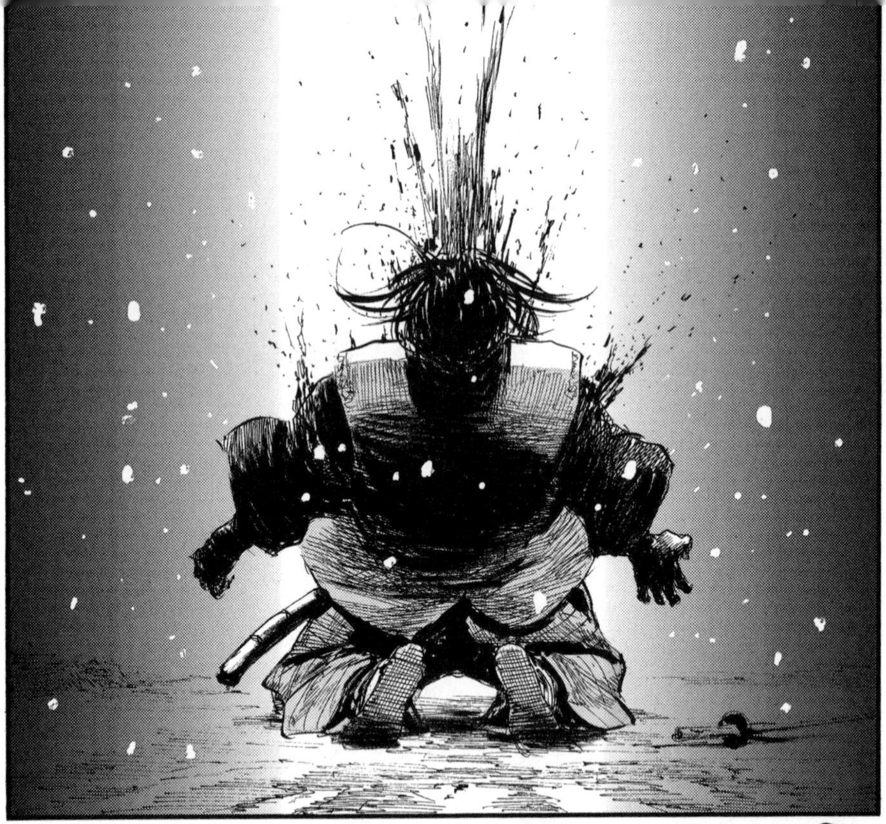

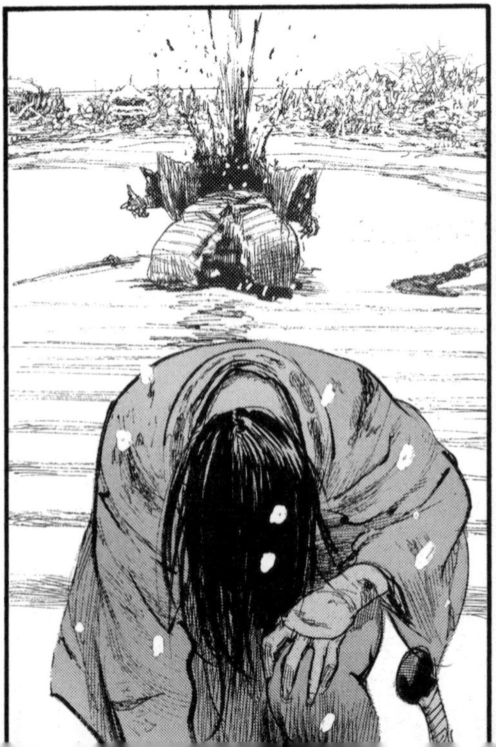

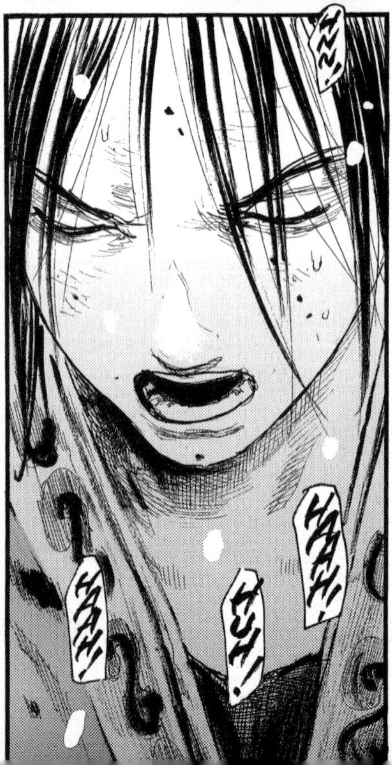
HNN!
HAAH!
HAAH!
KUH!

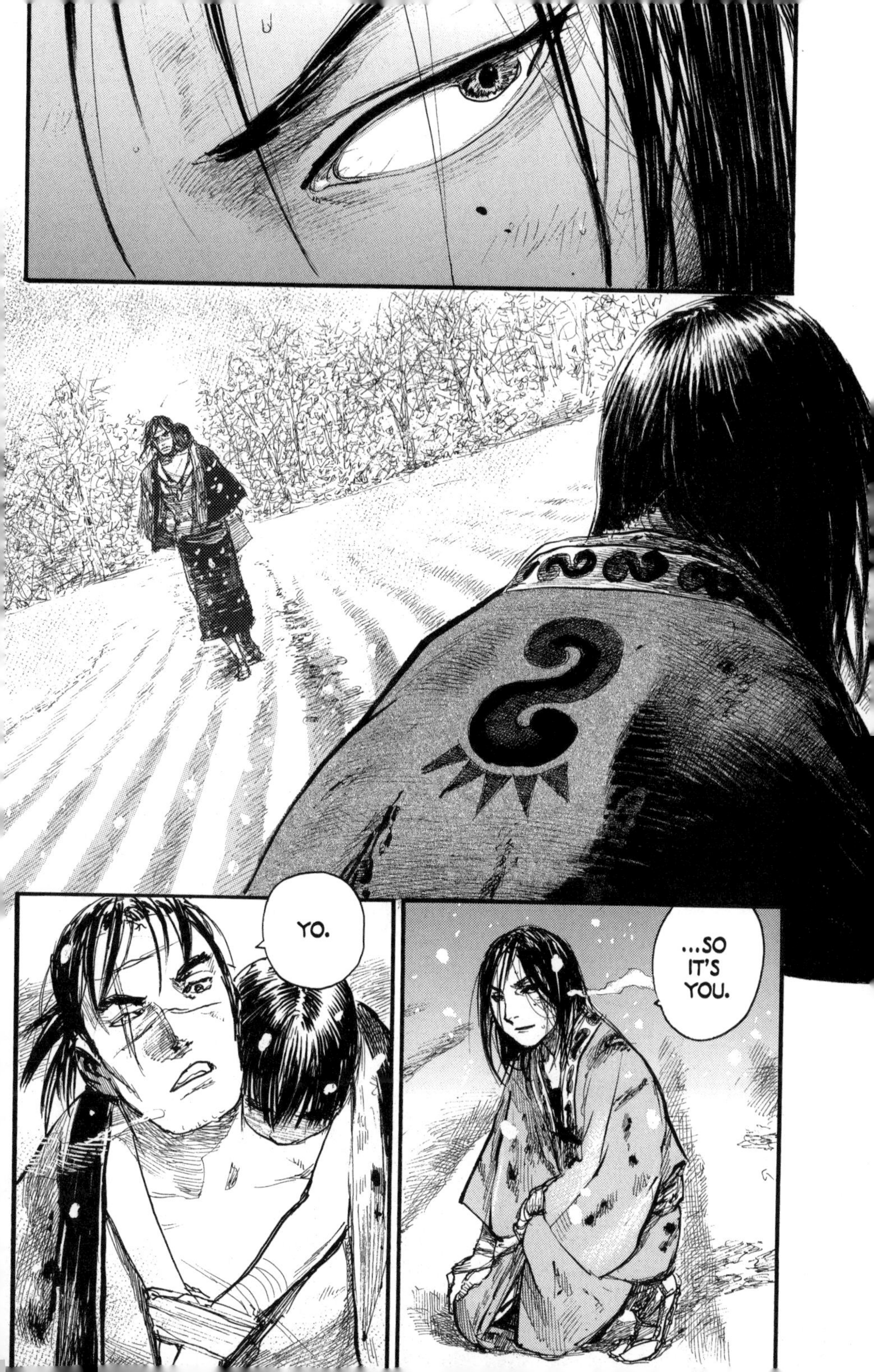
YO.
...SO IT'S YOU.

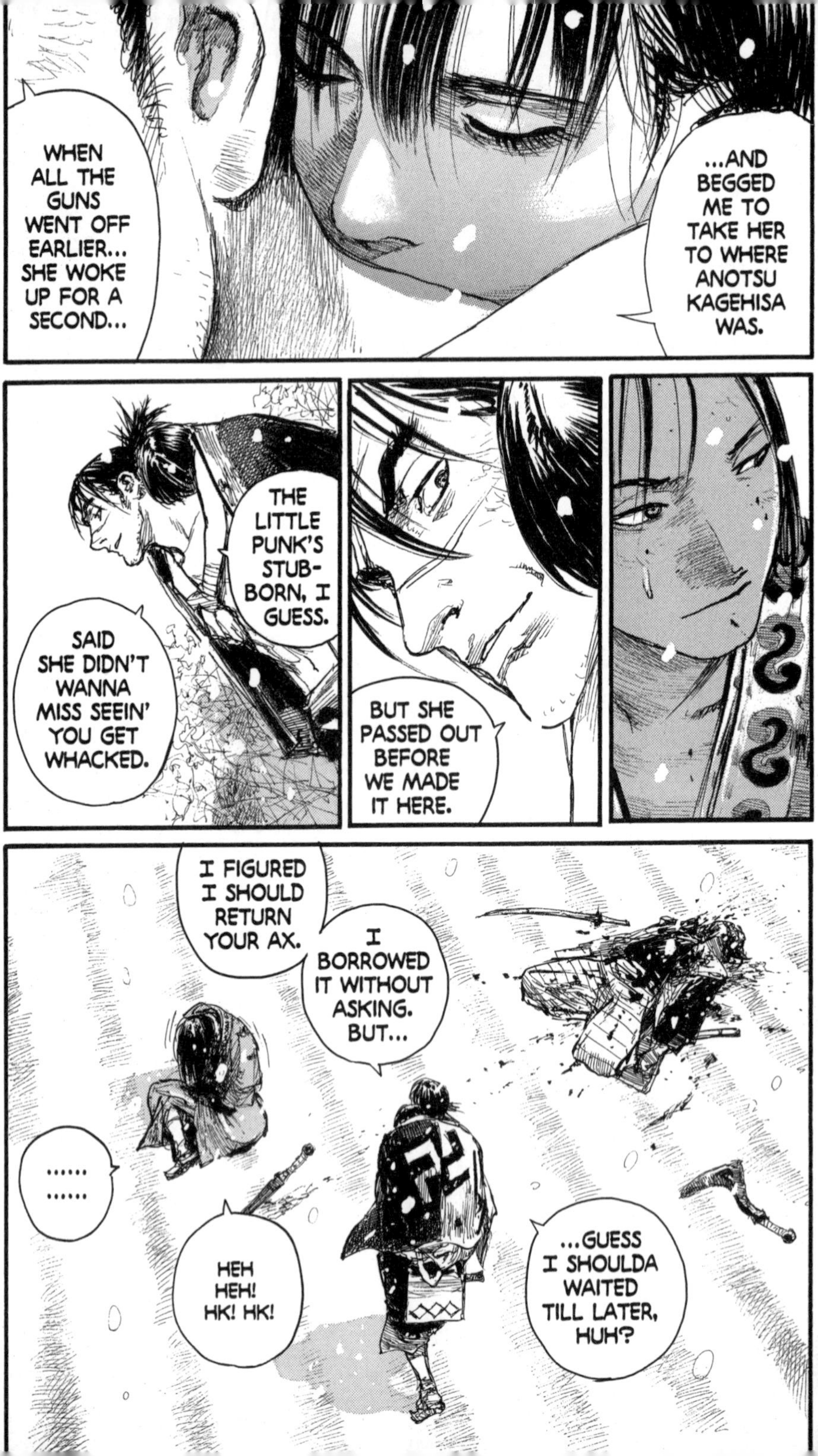

WHEN ALL THE GUNS WENT OFF EARLIER... SHE WOKE UP FOR A SECOND...
...AND BEGGED ME TO TAKE HER TO WHERE ANOTSU KAGEHISA WAS.
THE LITTLE PUNK'S STUBBORN, I GUESS.
SAID SHE DIDN'T WANNA MISS SEEIN' YOU GET WHACKED.
BUT SHE PASSED OUT BEFORE WE MADE IT HERE.
I FIGURED I SHOULD RETURN YOUR AX.
I BORROWED IT WITHOUT ASKING. BUT...
....
HEH HEH! HK! HK!
...GUESS I SHOULDA WAITED TILL LATER, HUH?

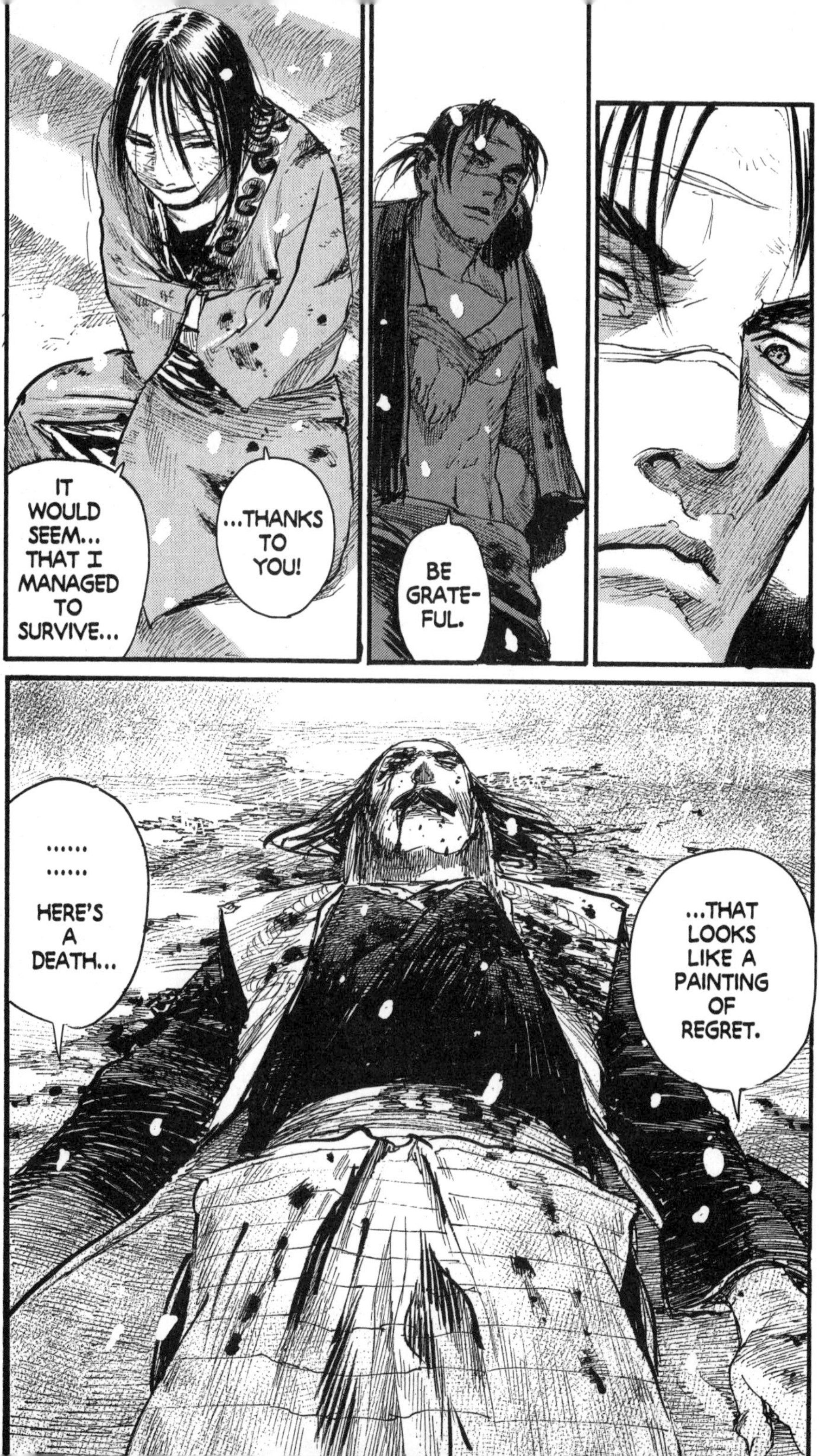
IT WOULD SEEM... THAT I MANAGED TO SURVIVE...
...THANKS TO YOU!
BE GRATE-FUL.
......
......
HERE'S A DEATH...
...THAT LOOKS LIKE A PAINTING OF REGRET.

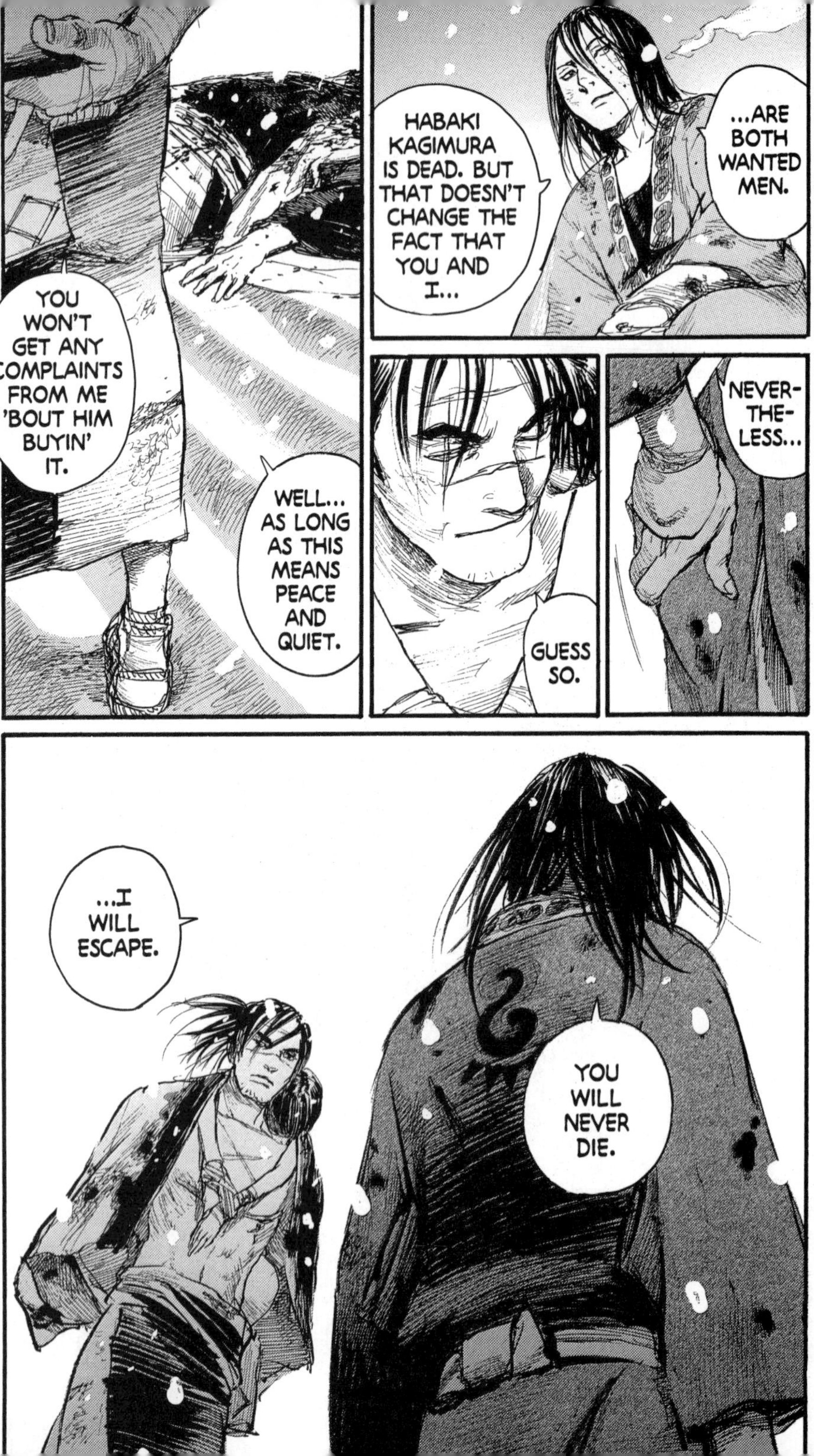
YOU WON'T GET ANY COMPLAINTS FROM ME 'BOUT HIM BUYIN' IT.
WELL... AS LONG AS THIS MEANS PEACE AND QUIET.
HABAKI KAGIMURA IS DEAD. BUT THAT DOESN'T CHANGE THE FACT THAT YOU AND I...
...ARE BOTH WANTED MEN.
GUESS SO.
NEVER-THE-LESS...
...I WILL ESCAPE.
YOU WILL NEVER DIE.

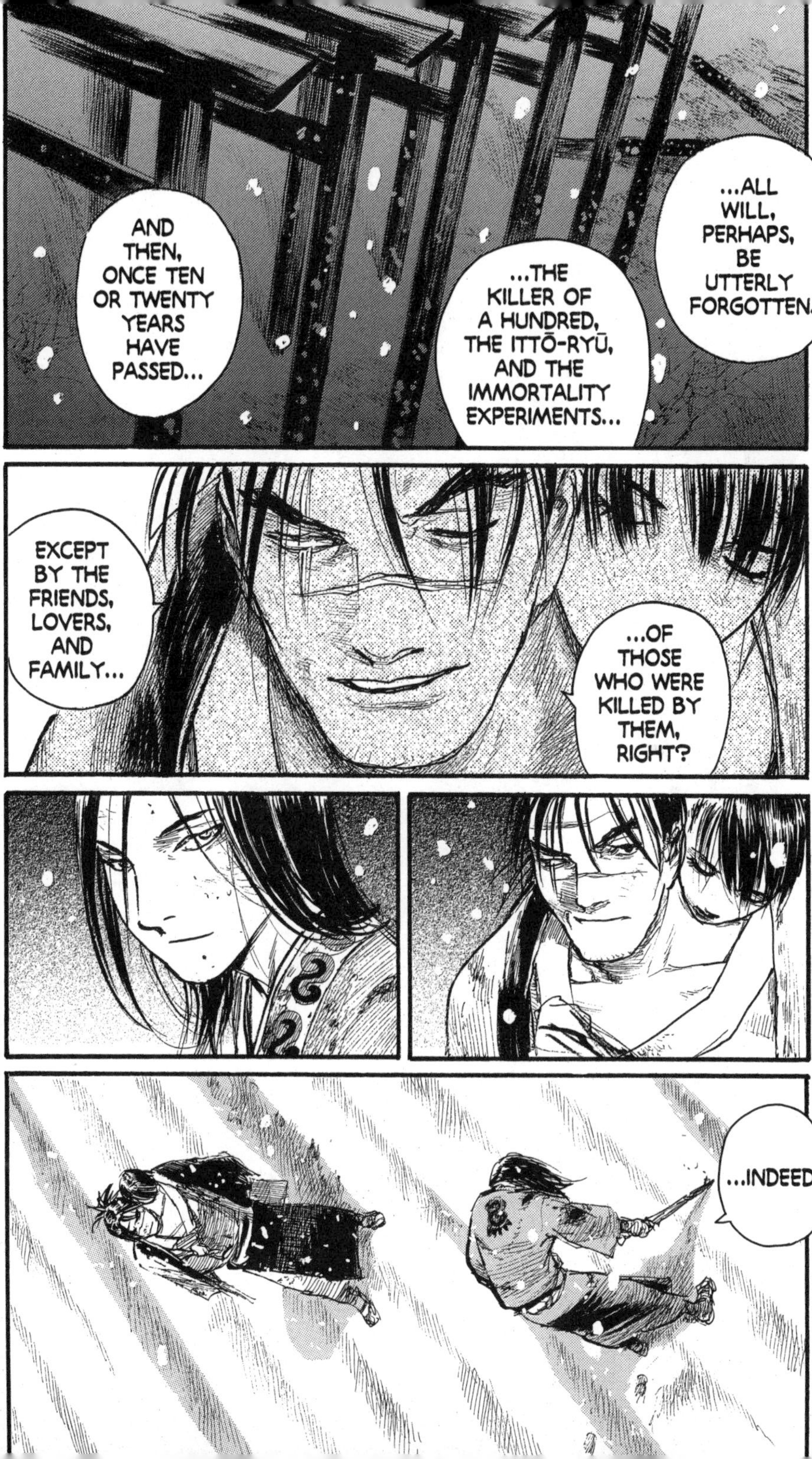
AND THEN, ONCE TEN OR TWENTY YEARS HAVE PASSED...
...THE KILLER OF A HUNDRED, THE ITTŌ-RYŪ, AND THE IMMORTALITY EXPERIMENTS...
...ALL WILL, PERHAPS, BE UTTERLY FORGOTTEN.
EXCEPT BY THE FRIENDS, LOVERS, AND FAMILY...
...OF THOSE WHO WERE KILLED BY THEM, RIGHT?
...INDEED.

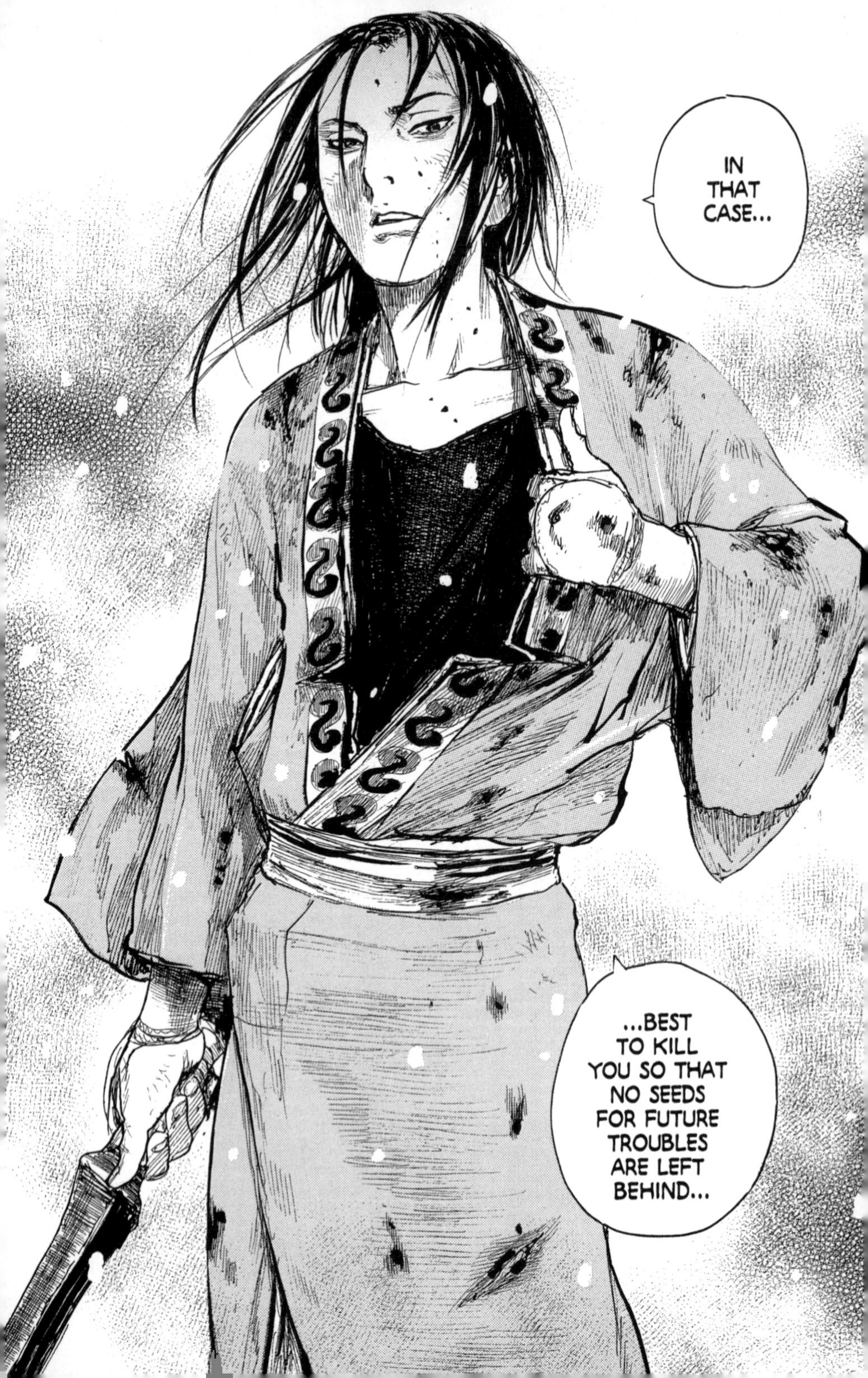
IN THAT CASE...
...BEST TO KILL YOU SO THAT NO SEEDS FOR FUTURE TROUBLES ARE LEFT BEHIND...

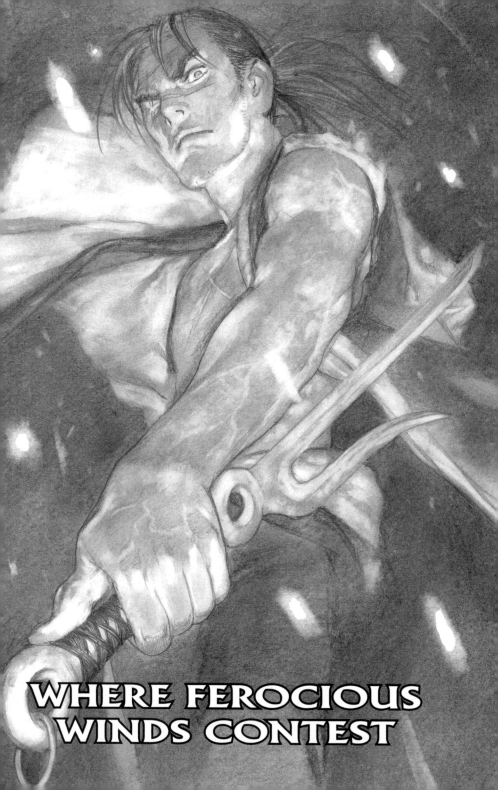

WHERE FEROCIOUS WINDS CONTEST

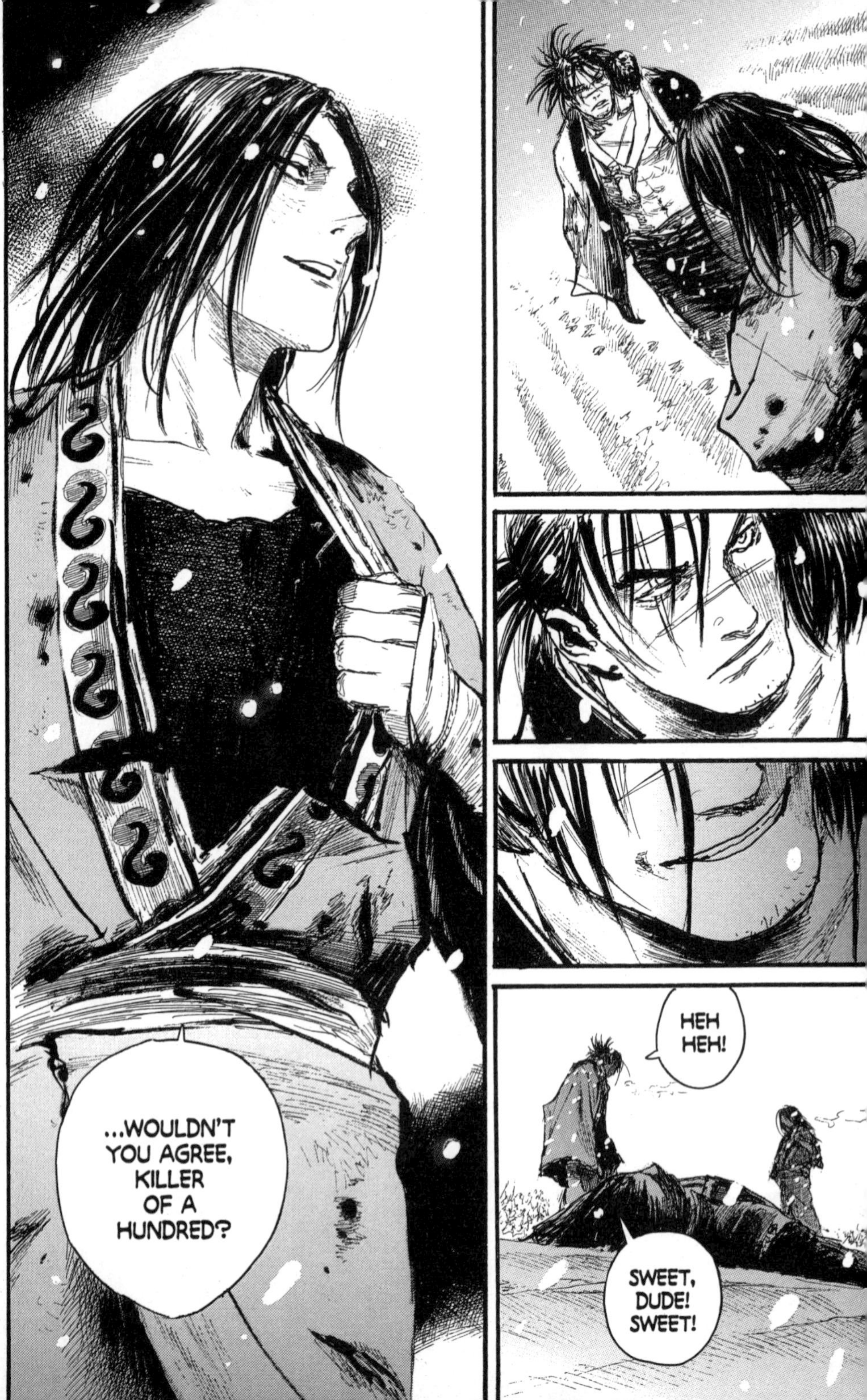
...WOULDN'T YOU AGREE, KILLER OF A HUNDRED?
HEH HEH!
SWEET, DUDE! SWEET!

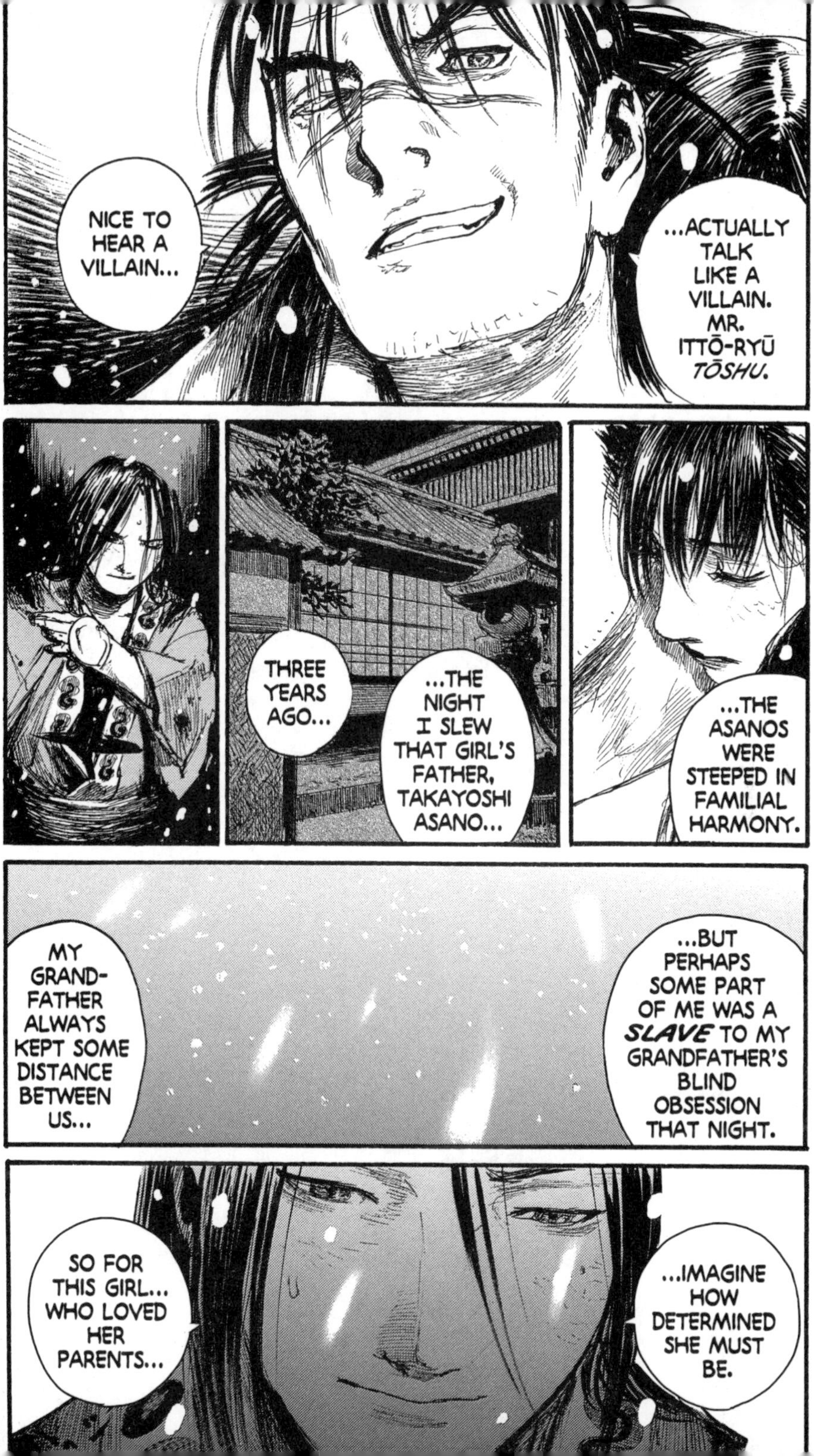
NICE TO HEAR A VILLAIN...
...ACTUALLY TALK LIKE A VILLAIN. MR. ITTŌ-RYŪ *TŌSHU*.
THREE YEARS AGO...
...THE NIGHT I SLEW THAT GIRL'S FATHER, TAKAYOSHI ASANO...
...THE ASANOS WERE STEEPED IN FAMILIAL HARMONY.
MY GRAND-FATHER ALWAYS KEPT SOME DISTANCE BETWEEN US...
...BUT PERHAPS SOME PART OF ME WAS A ***SLAVE*** TO MY GRANDFATHER'S BLIND OBSESSION THAT NIGHT.
SO FOR THIS GIRL... WHO LOVED HER PARENTS...
...IMAGINE HOW DETERMINED SHE MUST BE.

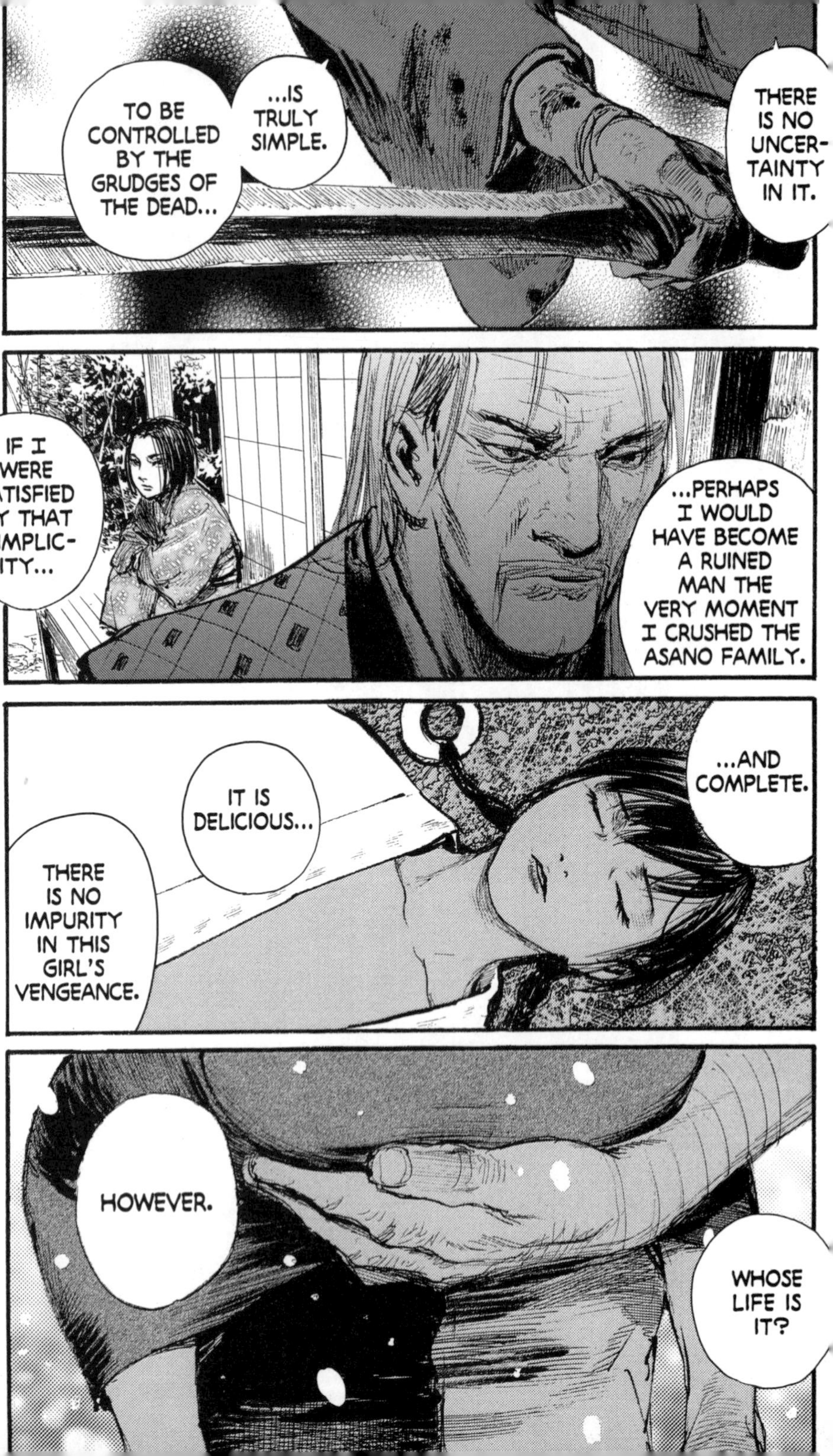
TO BE CONTROLLED BY THE GRUDGES OF THE DEAD...
...IS TRULY SIMPLE.
THERE IS NO UNCERTAINTY IN IT.
IF I WERE SATISFIED BY THAT SIMPLICITY...
...PERHAPS I WOULD HAVE BECOME A RUINED MAN THE VERY MOMENT I CRUSHED THE ASANO FAMILY.
THERE IS NO IMPURITY IN THIS GIRL'S VENGEANCE.
IT IS DELICIOUS...
...AND COMPLETE.
HOWEVER.
WHOSE LIFE IS IT?

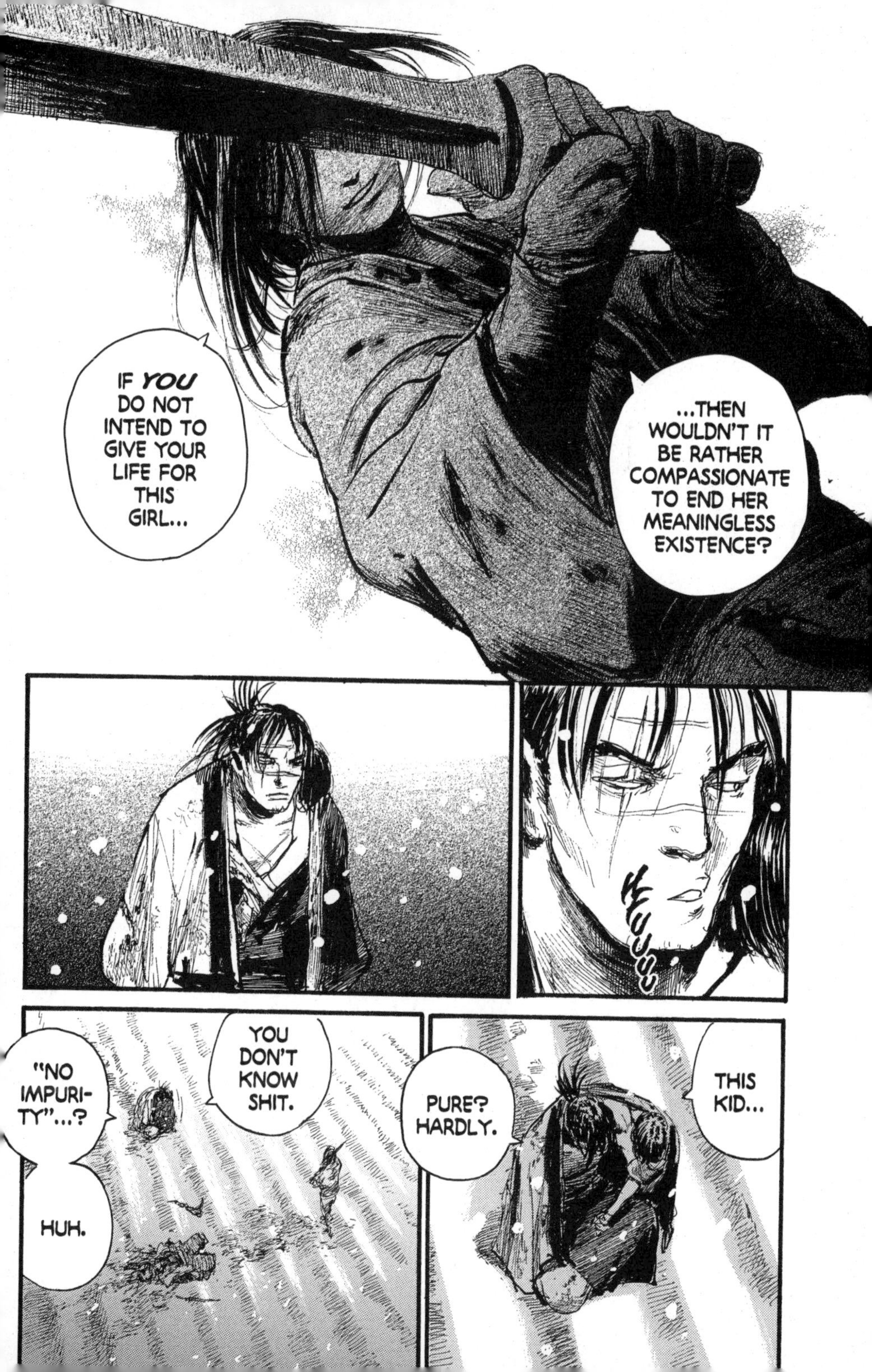
IF *YOU* DO NOT INTEND TO GIVE YOUR LIFE FOR THIS GIRL...
...THEN WOULDN'T IT BE RATHER COMPASSIONATE TO END HER MEANINGLESS EXISTENCE?
"NO IMPURITY"...?
HUH.
YOU DON'T KNOW SHIT.
PURE? HARDLY.
THIS KID...

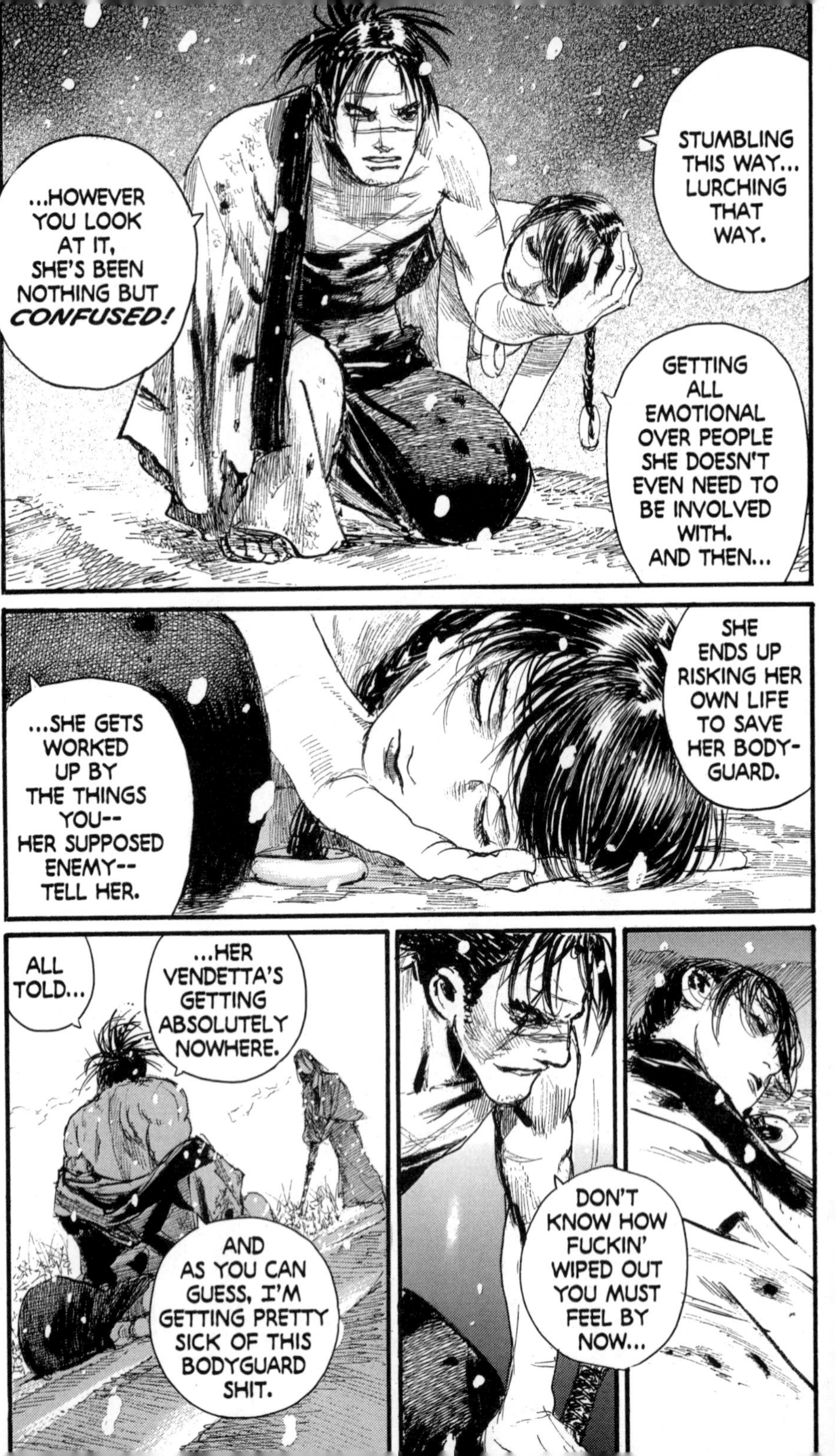
...HOWEVER YOU LOOK AT IT, SHE'S BEEN NOTHING BUT *CONFUSED!*
STUMBLING THIS WAY... LURCHING THAT WAY.
GETTING ALL EMOTIONAL OVER PEOPLE SHE DOESN'T EVEN NEED TO BE INVOLVED WITH. AND THEN...
...SHE GETS WORKED UP BY THE THINGS YOU-- HER SUPPOSED ENEMY-- TELL HER.
SHE ENDS UP RISKING HER OWN LIFE TO SAVE HER BODY-GUARD.
ALL TOLD...
...HER VENDETTA'S GETTING ABSOLUTELY NOWHERE.
AND AS YOU CAN GUESS, I'M GETTING PRETTY SICK OF THIS BODYGUARD SHIT.
DON'T KNOW HOW FUCKIN' WIPED OUT YOU MUST FEEL BY NOW...

...BUT I'M ALSO NOT TOO KEEN ON...

...WATCHIN' YOU WALK AWAY AGAIN, ANOTSU KAGEHISA.

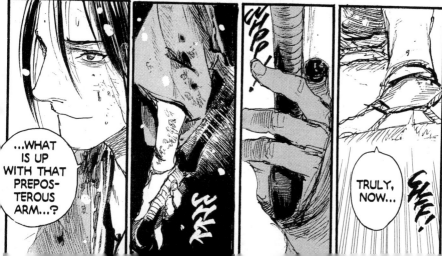

...WHAT IS UP WITH THAT PREPOSTEROUS ARM...?

TRULY, NOW...

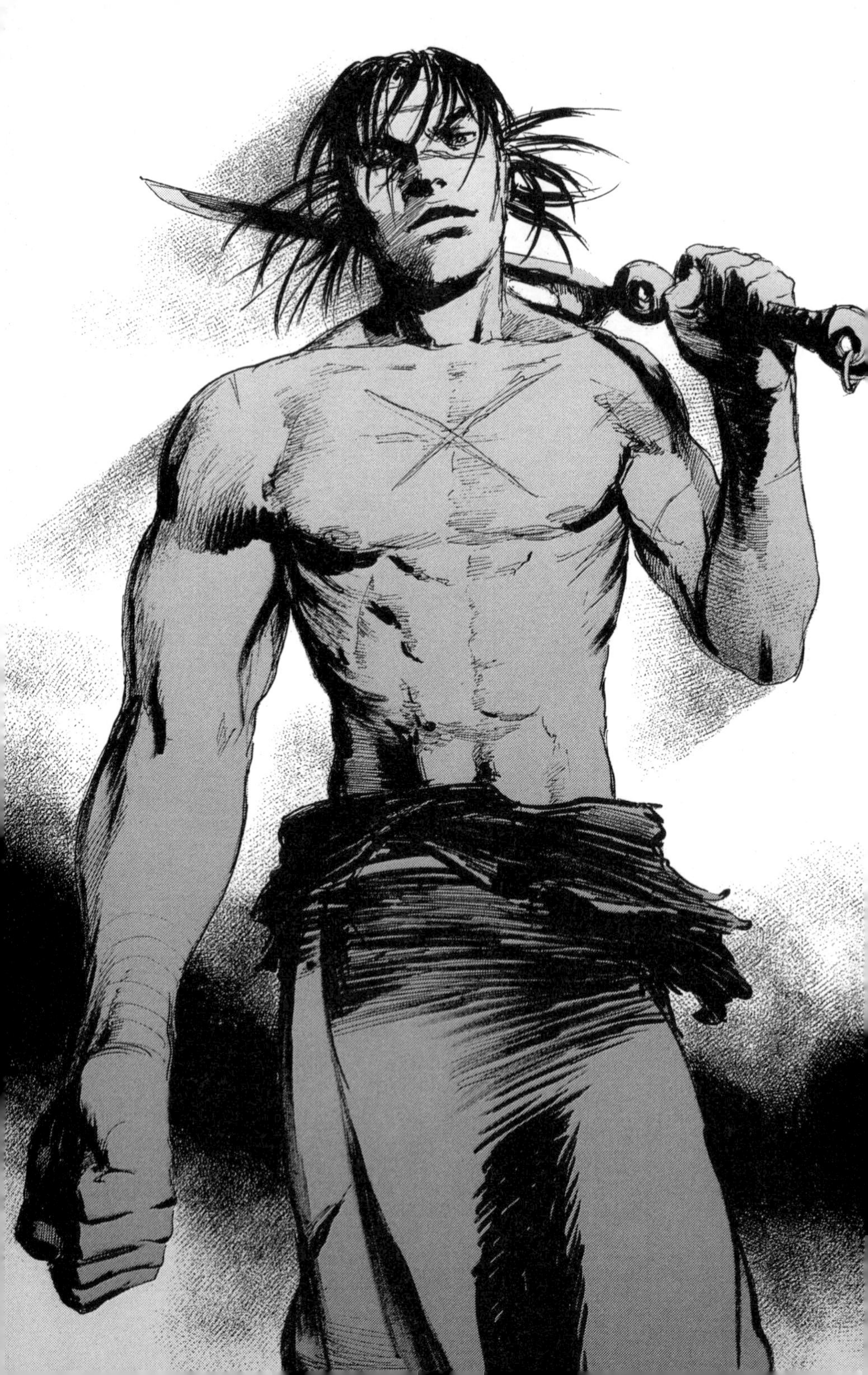

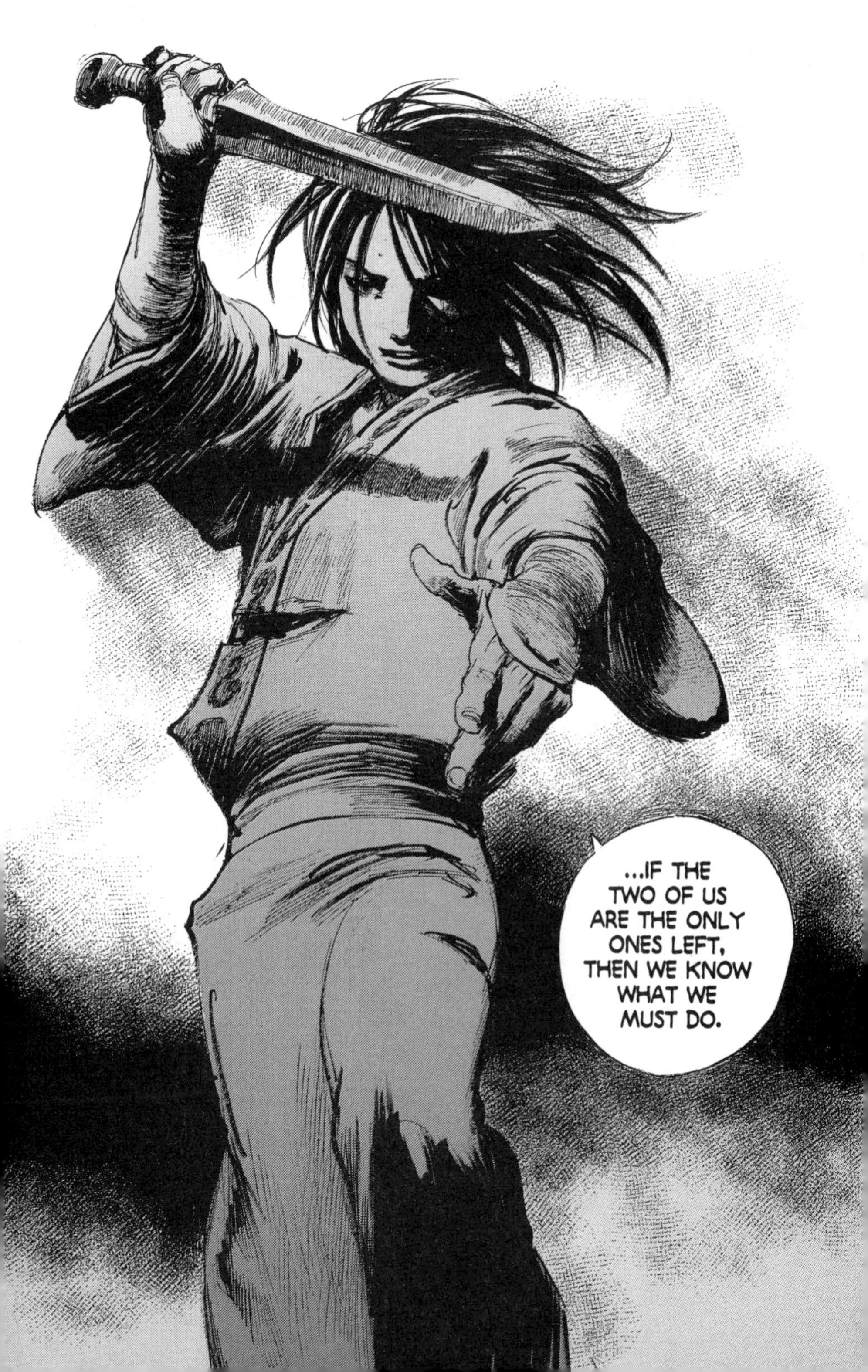
...IF THE TWO OF US ARE THE ONLY ONES LEFT, THEN WE KNOW WHAT WE MUST DO.

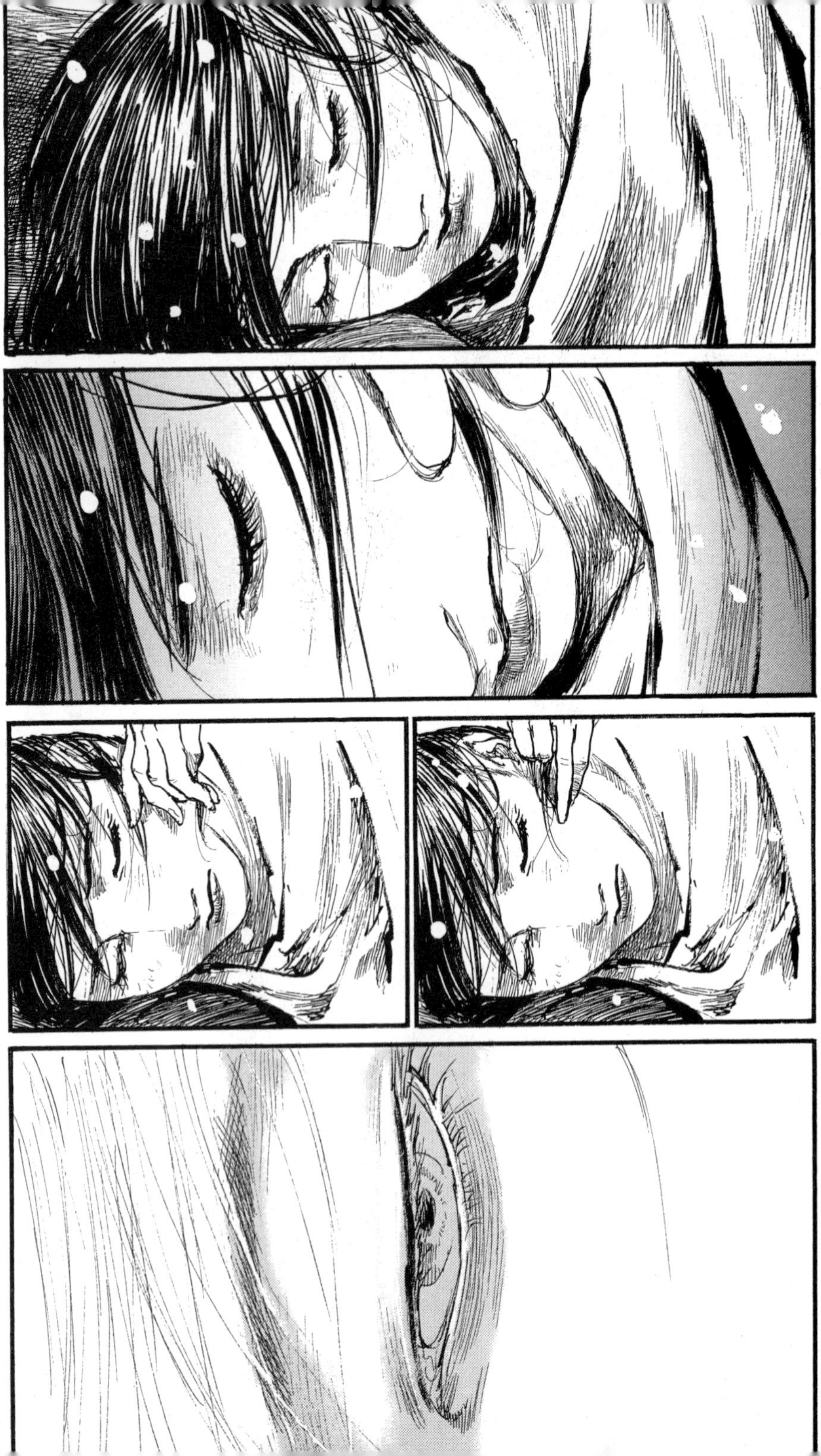

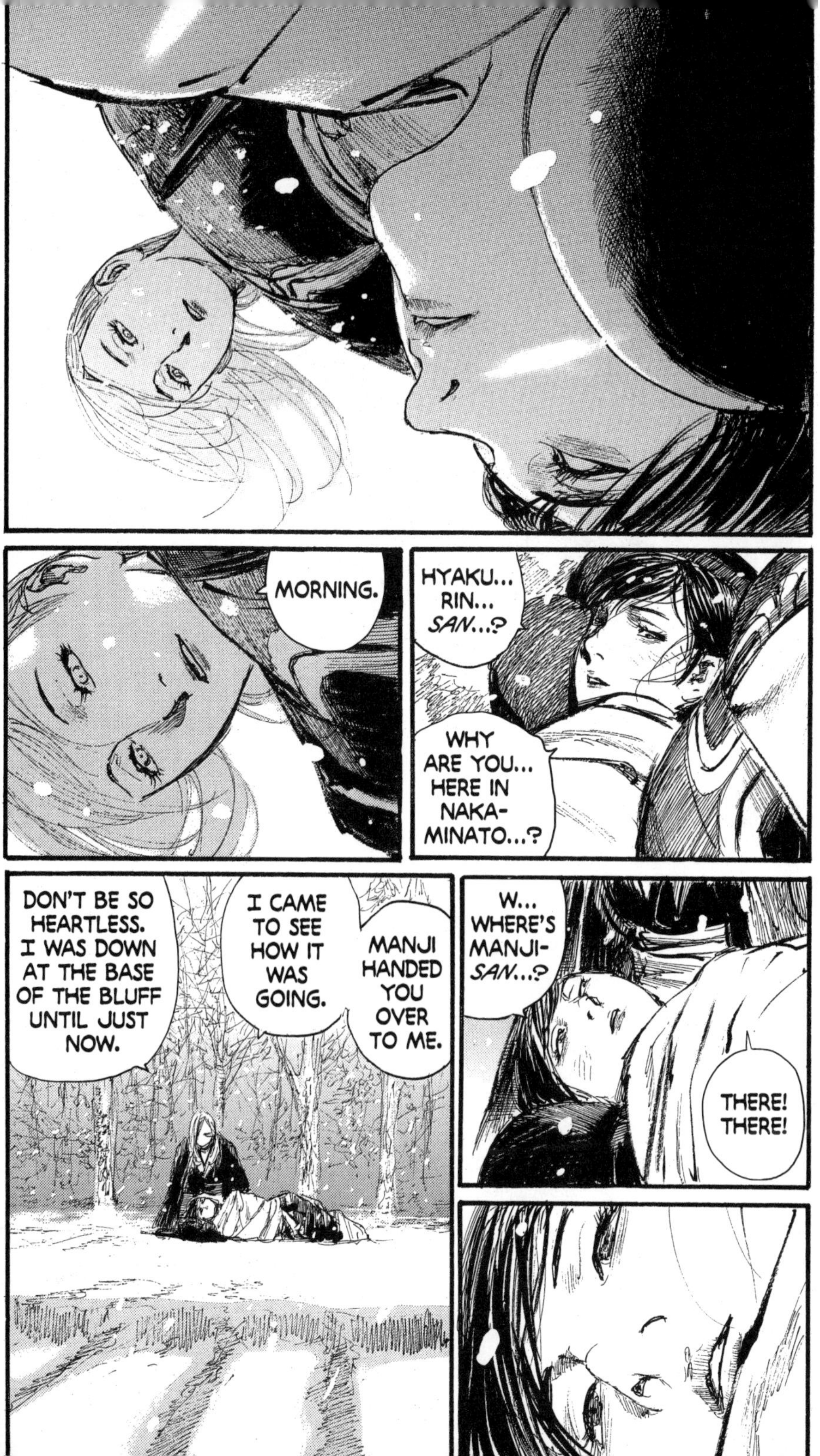
MORNING.
HYAKU... RIN... SAN...?
WHY ARE YOU... HERE IN NAKA-MINATO...?
DON'T BE SO HEARTLESS. I WAS DOWN AT THE BASE OF THE BLUFF UNTIL JUST NOW.
I CAME TO SEE HOW IT WAS GOING.
MANJI HANDED YOU OVER TO ME.
W... WHERE'S MANJI-SAN...?
THERE! THERE!

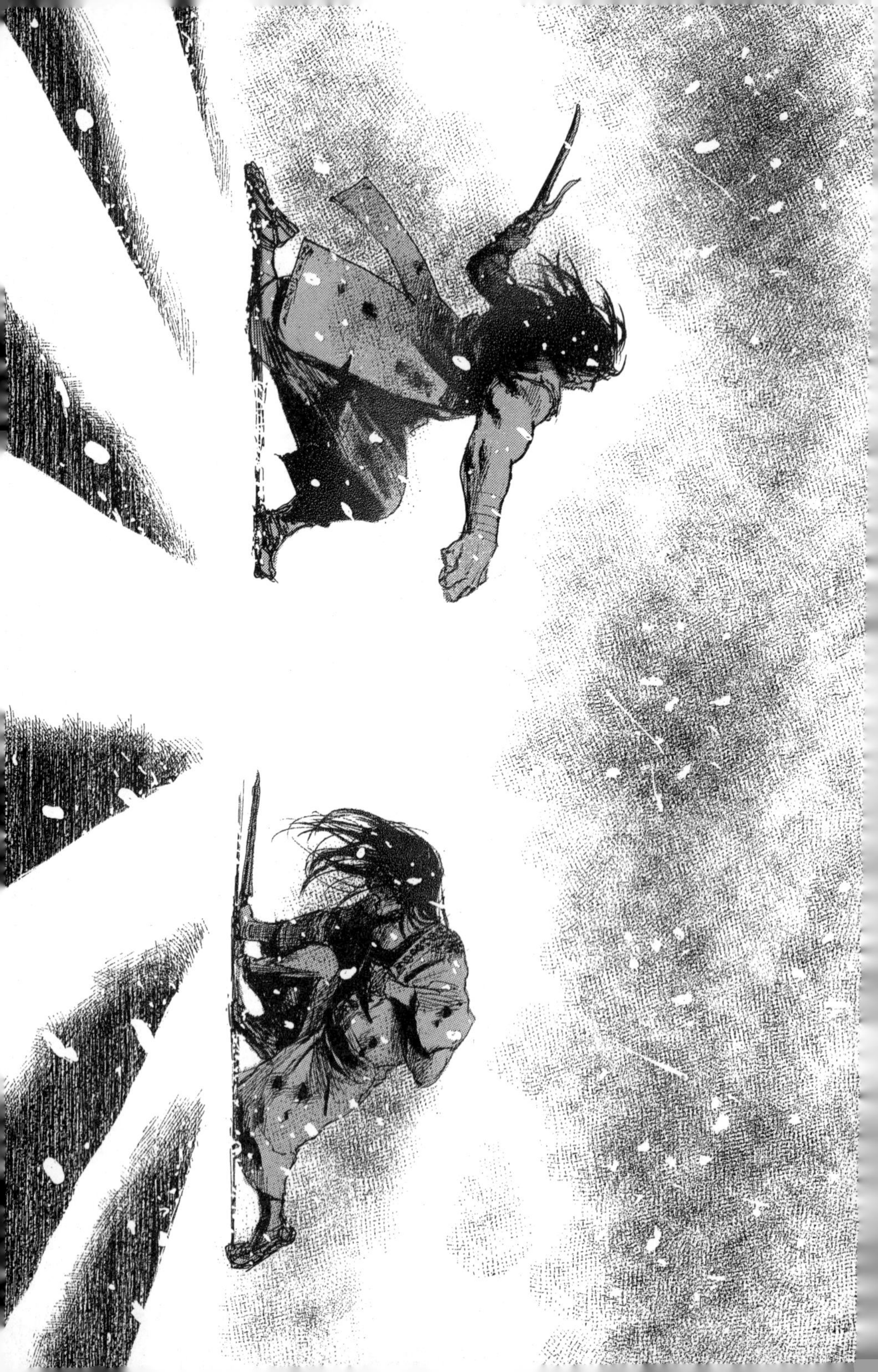

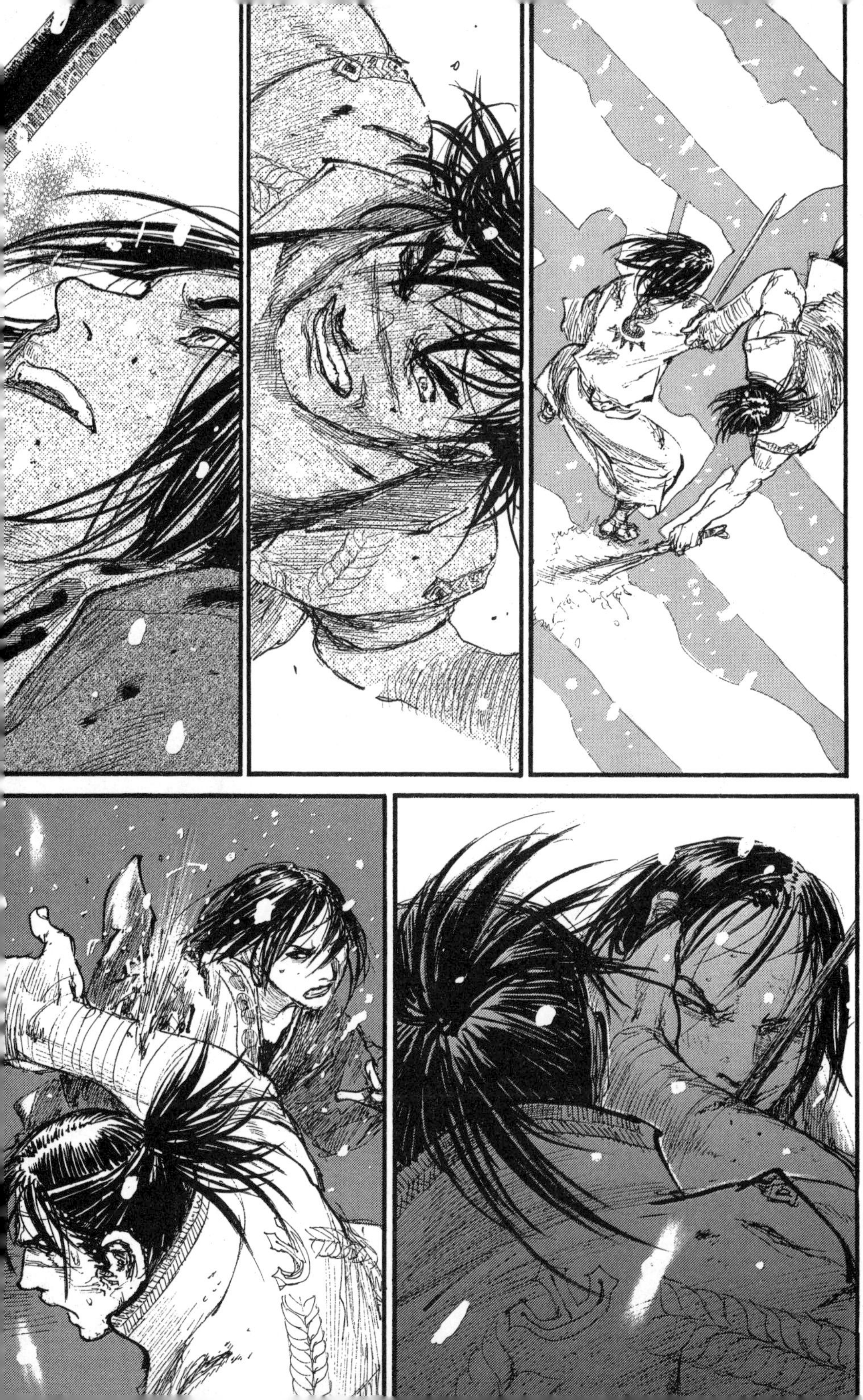

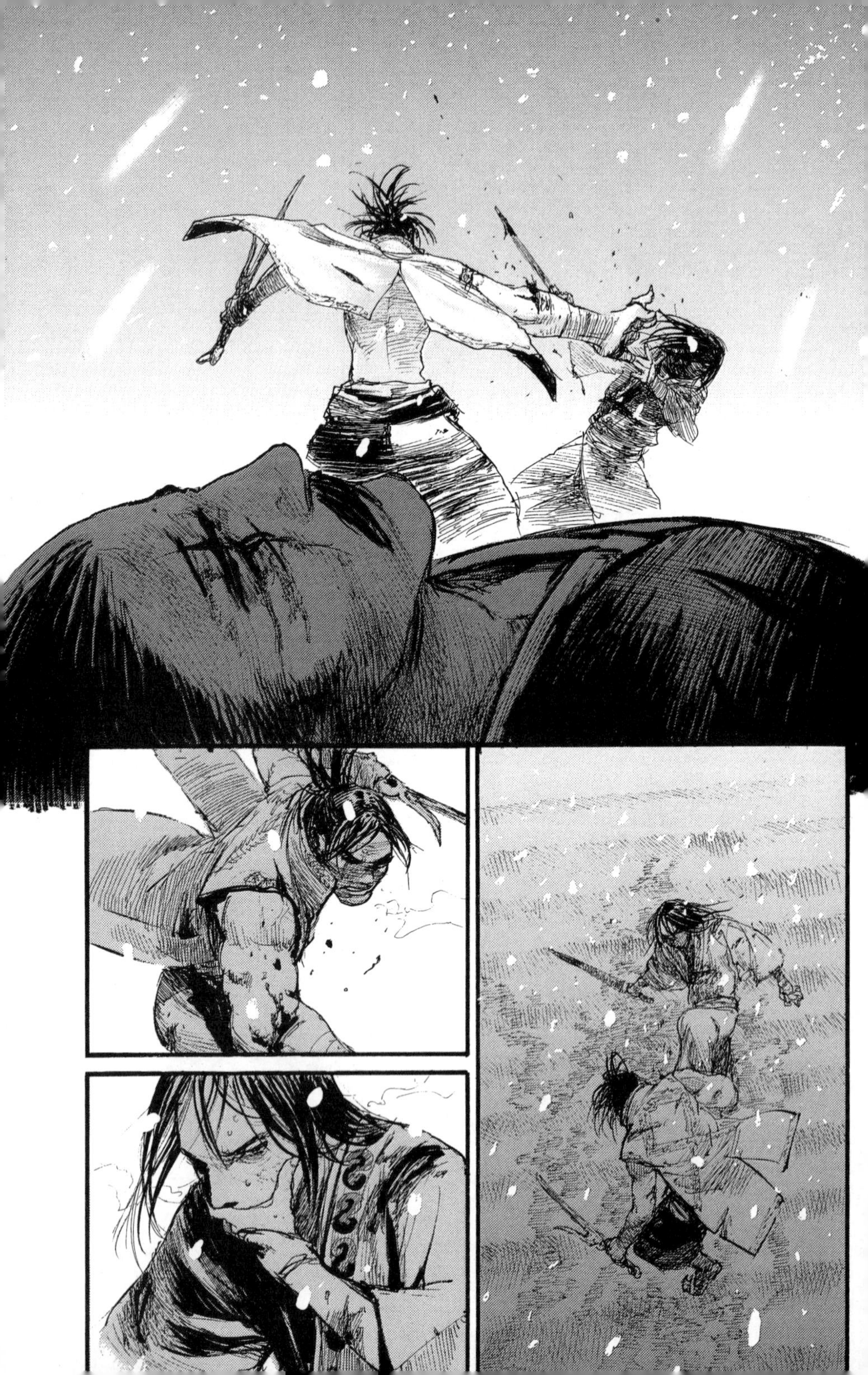

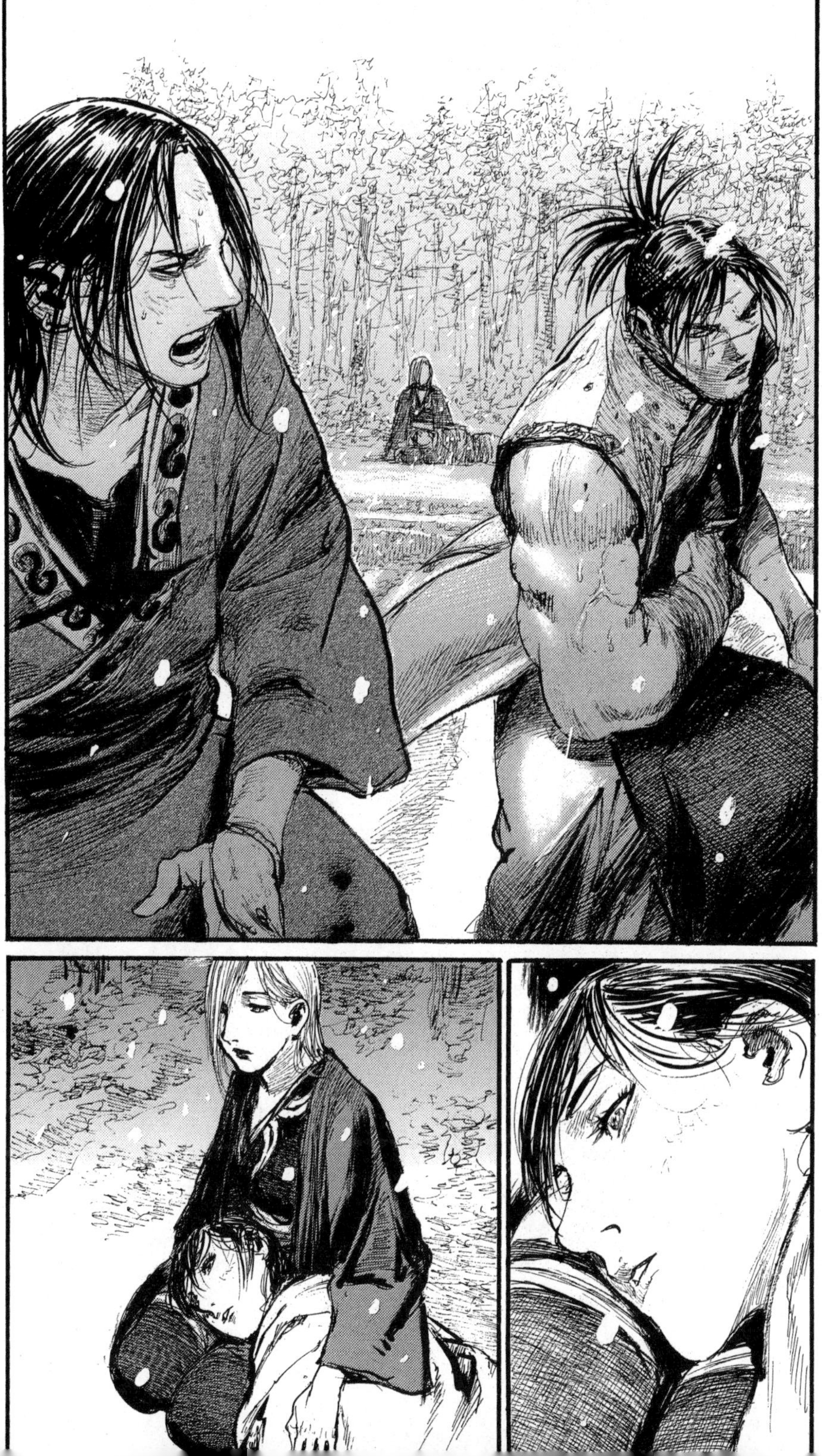

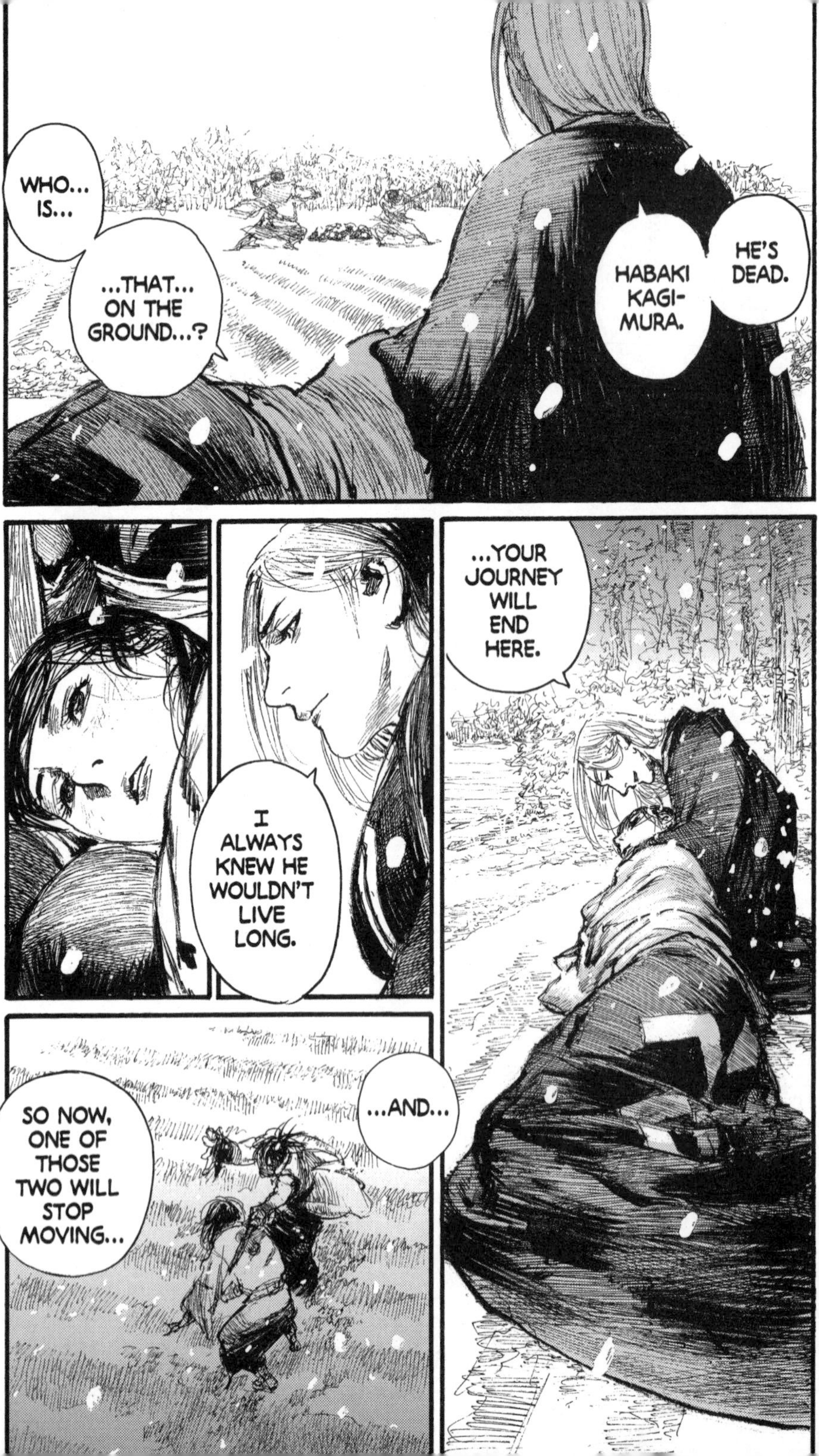
WHO... IS...
...THAT... ON THE GROUND...?
HABAKI KAGI-MURA.
HE'S DEAD.
I ALWAYS KNEW HE WOULDN'T LIVE LONG.
SO NOW, ONE OF THOSE TWO WILL STOP MOVING...
...AND...
...YOUR JOURNEY WILL END HERE.

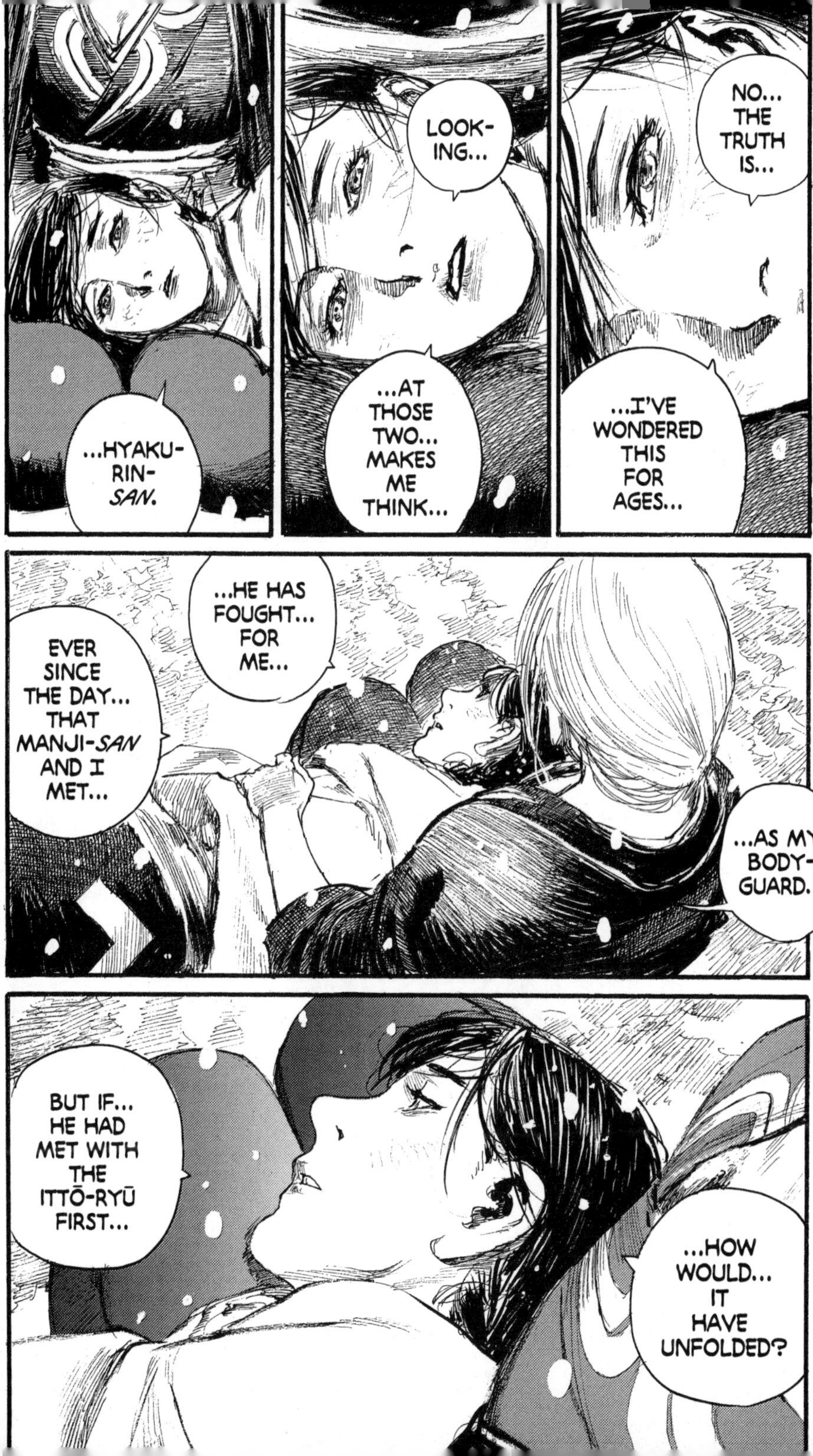
...HYAKU-RIN-*SAN*.
LOOK-ING...
...AT THOSE TWO... MAKES ME THINK...
NO... THE TRUTH IS...
...I'VE WONDERED THIS FOR AGES...
EVER SINCE THE DAY... THAT MANJI-*SAN* AND I MET...
...HE HAS FOUGHT... FOR ME...
...AS MY BODY-GUARD...
BUT IF... HE HAD MET WITH THE ITTŌ-RYŪ FIRST...
...HOW WOULD... IT HAVE UNFOLDED?

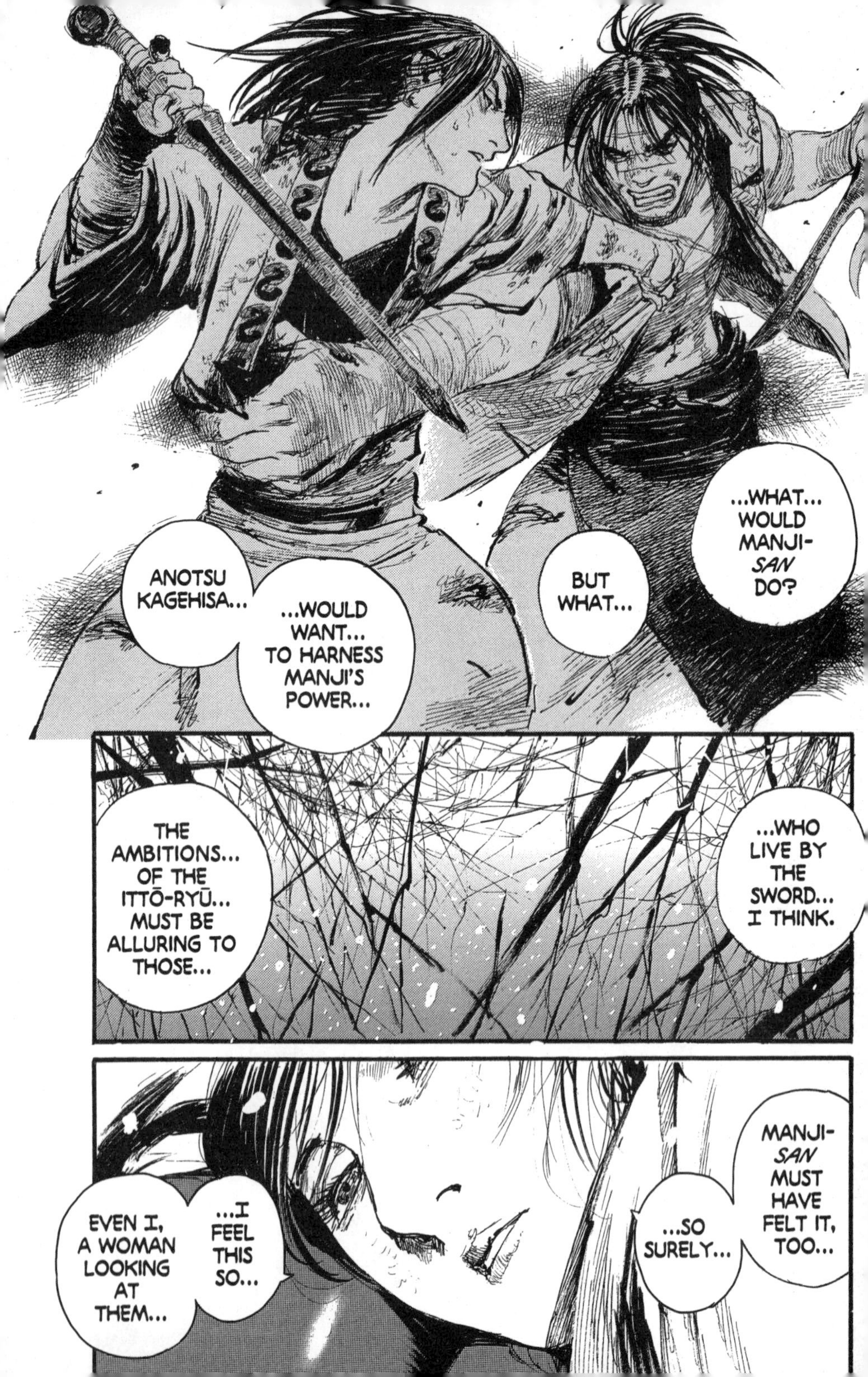
ANOTSU KAGEHISA...
...WOULD WANT... TO HARNESS MANJI'S POWER...
BUT WHAT...
...WHAT... WOULD MANJI-*SAN* DO?
THE AMBITIONS... OF THE ITTŌ-RYŪ... MUST BE ALLURING TO THOSE...
...WHO LIVE BY THE SWORD... I THINK.
EVEN I, A WOMAN LOOKING AT THEM...
...I FEEL THIS SO...
...SO SURELY...
MANJI-*SAN* MUST HAVE FELT IT, TOO...

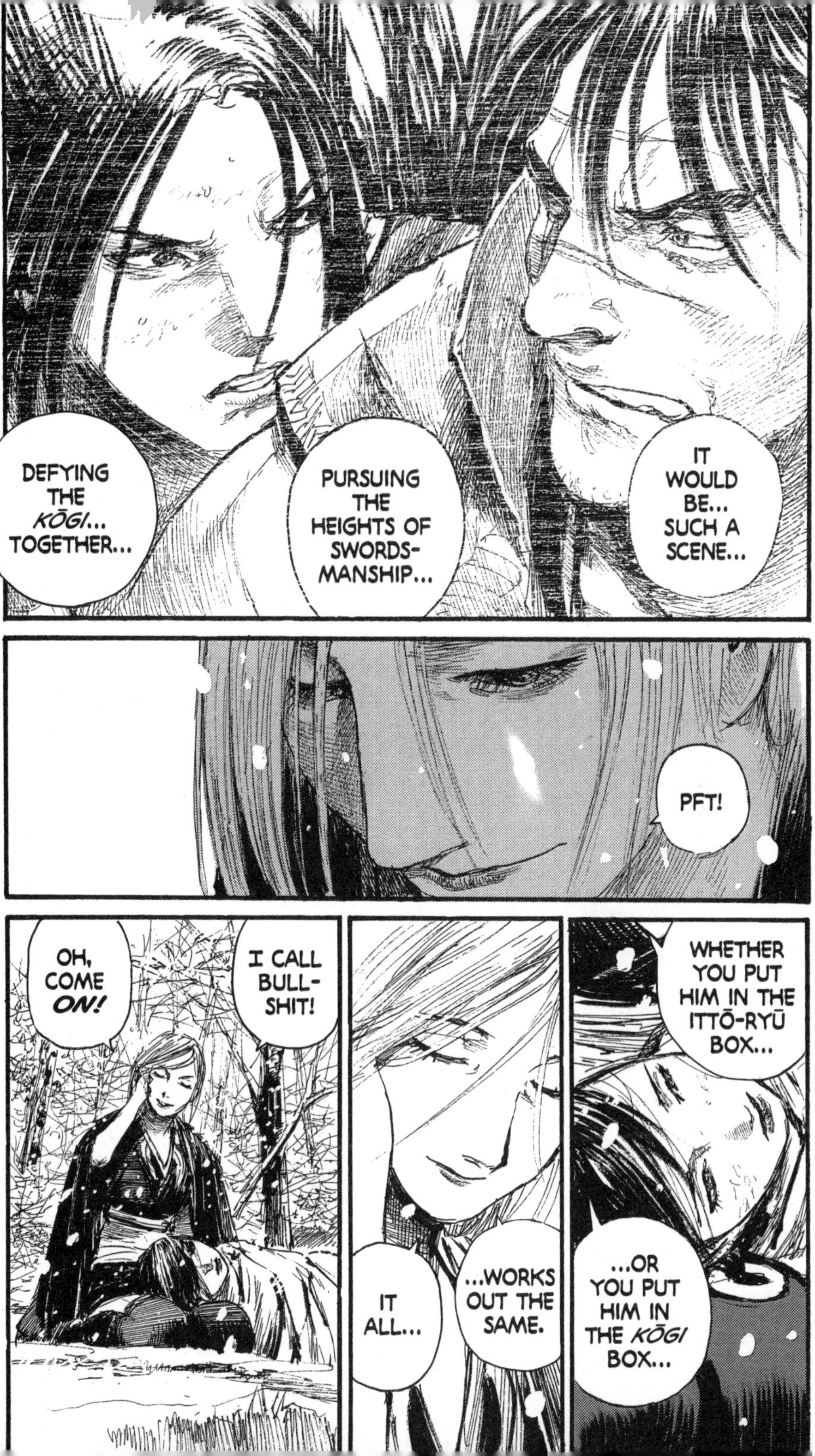
DEFYING THE *KŌGI*... TOGETHER...
PURSUING THE HEIGHTS OF SWORDS-MANSHIP...
IT WOULD BE... SUCH A SCENE...
PFT!
OH, COME *ON!*
I CALL BULL-SHIT!
IT ALL...
...WORKS OUT THE SAME.
WHETHER YOU PUT HIM IN THE ITTŌ-RYŪ BOX...
...OR YOU PUT HIM IN THE *KŌGI* BOX...

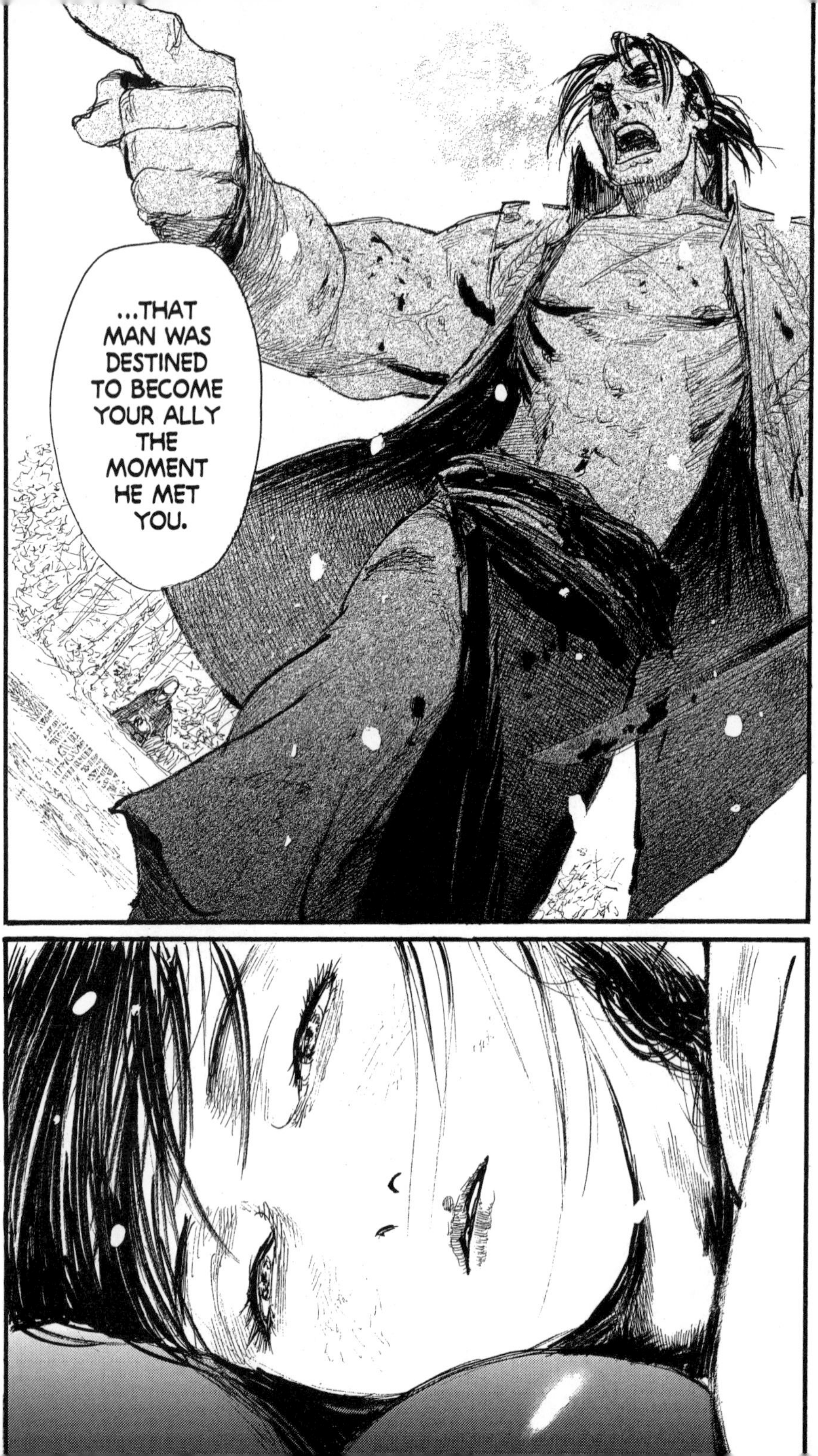
...THAT MAN WAS DESTINED TO BECOME YOUR ALLY THE MOMENT HE MET YOU.

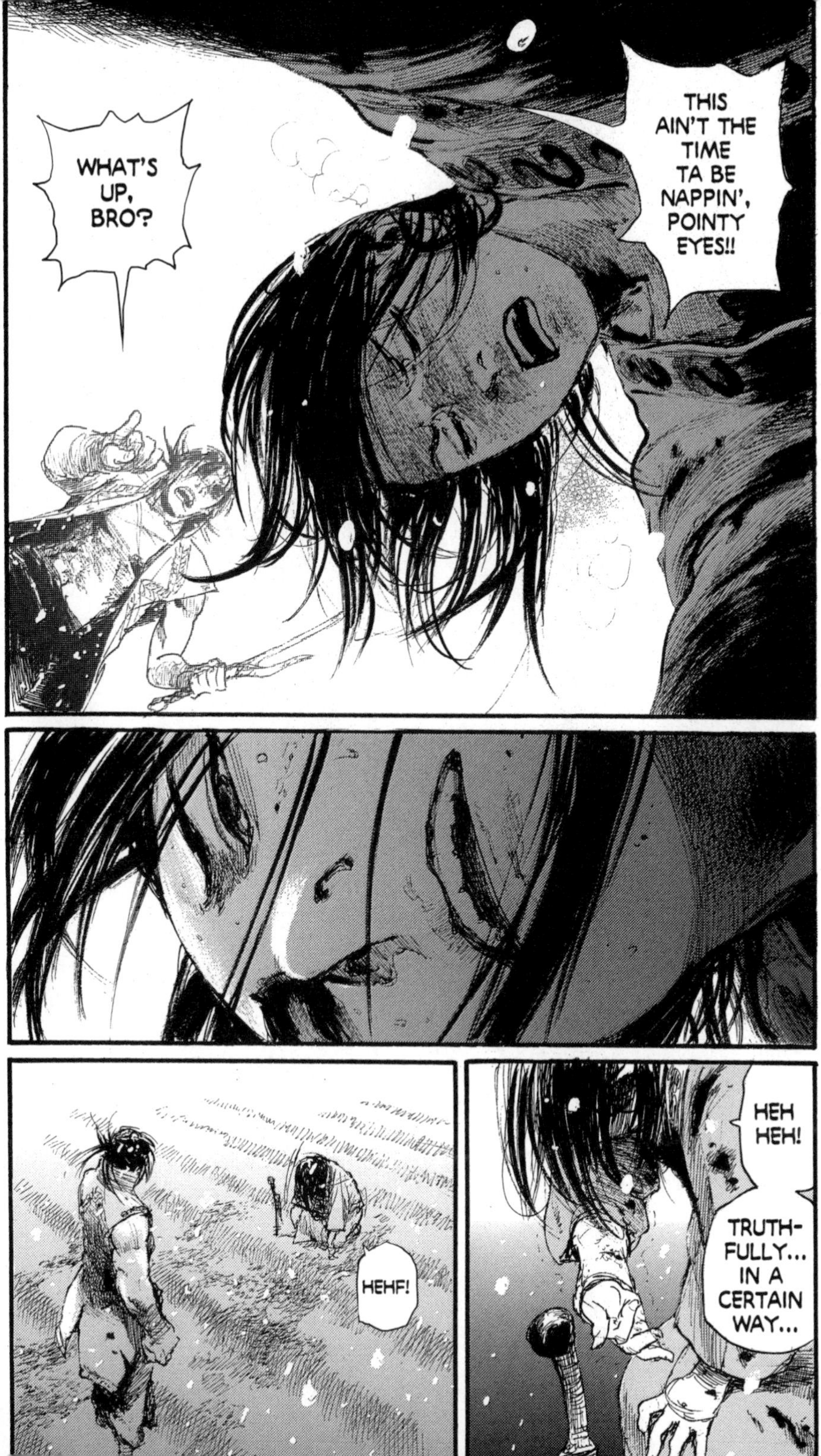
WHAT'S UP, BRO?
THIS AIN'T THE TIME TA BE NAPPIN', POINTY EYES!!
HEHF!
HEH HEH!
TRUTH-FULLY... IN A CERTAIN WAY...

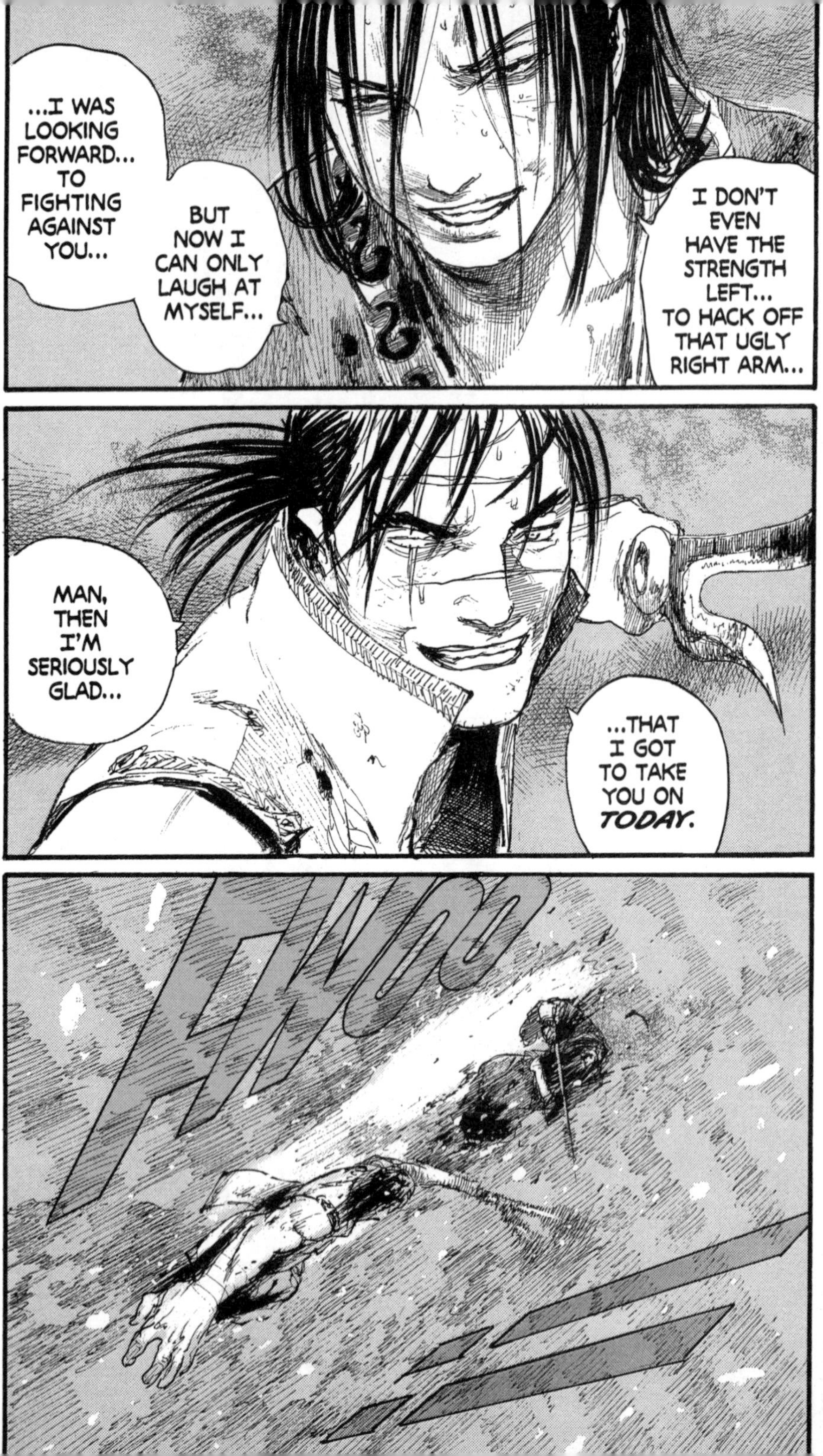
...I WAS LOOKING FORWARD... TO FIGHTING AGAINST YOU...
BUT NOW I CAN ONLY LAUGH AT MYSELF...
I DON'T EVEN HAVE THE STRENGTH LEFT... TO HACK OFF THAT UGLY RIGHT ARM...
MAN, THEN I'M SERIOUSLY GLAD...
...THAT I GOT TO TAKE YOU ON *TODAY*.

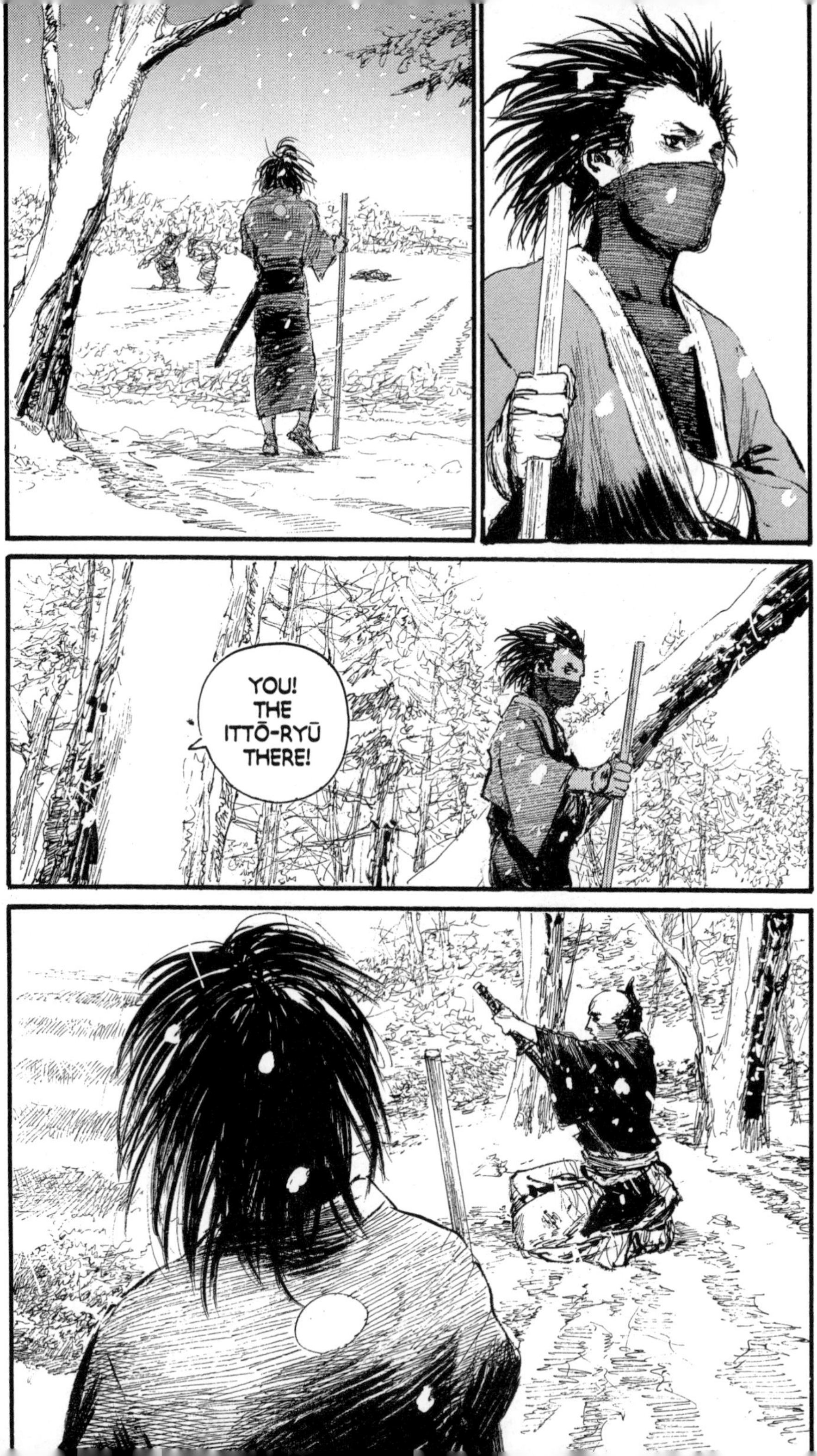
YOU! THE ITTŌ-RYŪ THERE!

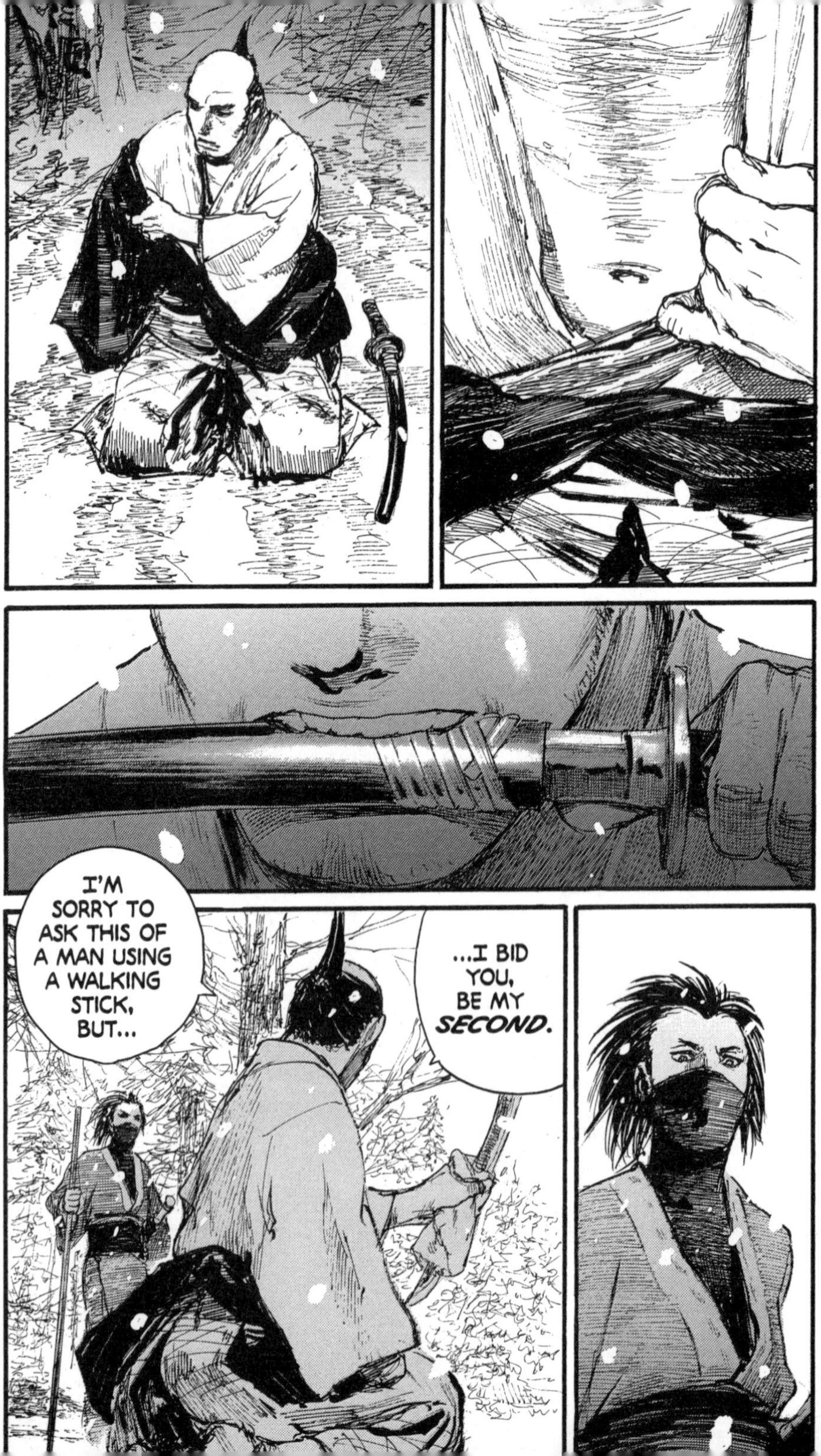

I'M SORRY TO ASK THIS OF A MAN USING A WALKING STICK, BUT...
...I BID YOU, BE MY *SECOND*.

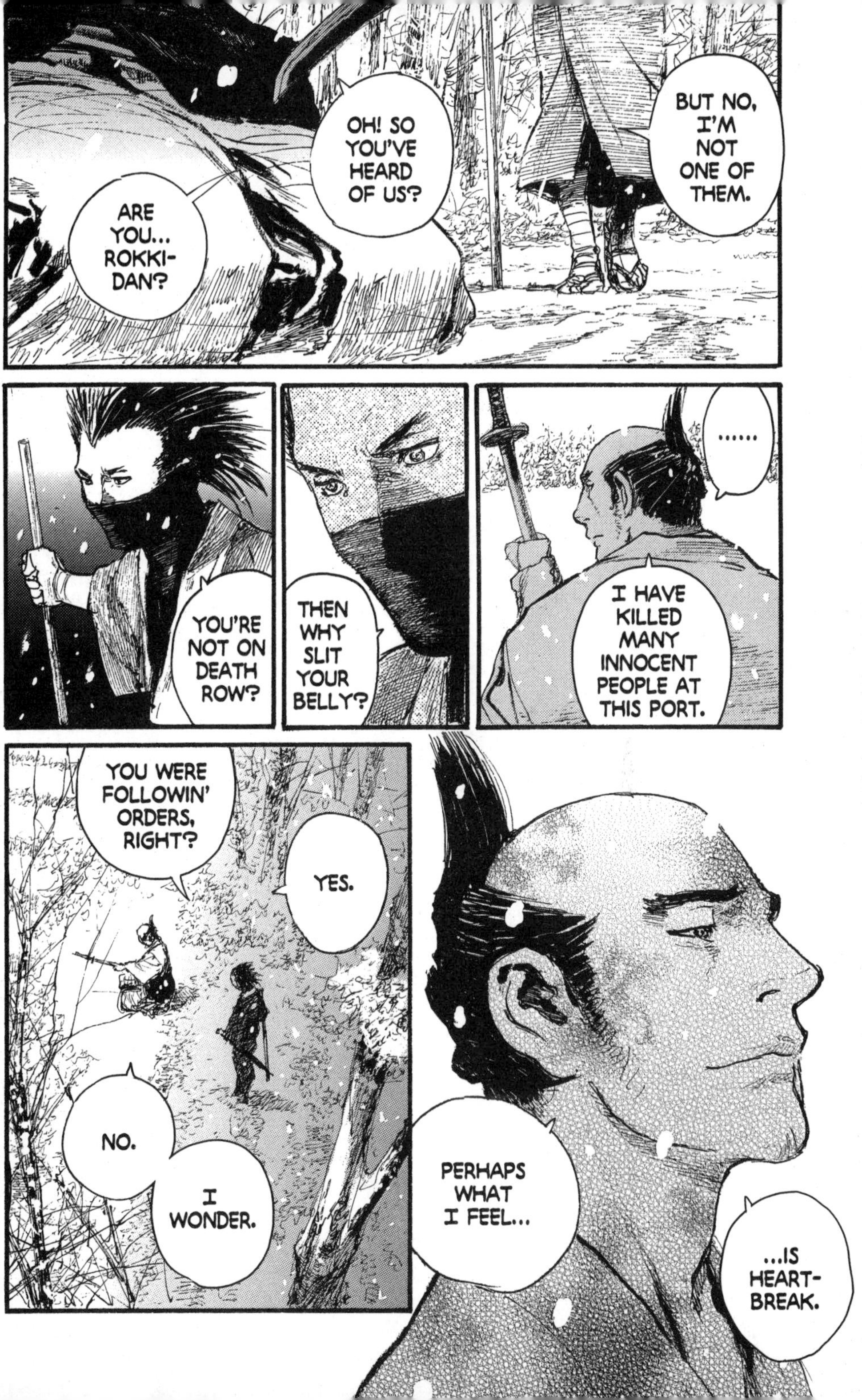
ARE YOU... ROKKI-DAN?
OH! SO YOU'VE HEARD OF US?
BUT NO, I'M NOT ONE OF THEM.
YOU'RE NOT ON DEATH ROW?
THEN WHY SLIT YOUR BELLY?
......
I HAVE KILLED MANY INNOCENT PEOPLE AT THIS PORT.
YOU WERE FOLLOWIN' ORDERS, RIGHT?
YES.
NO.
I WONDER.
PERHAPS WHAT I FEEL...
...IS HEART-BREAK.

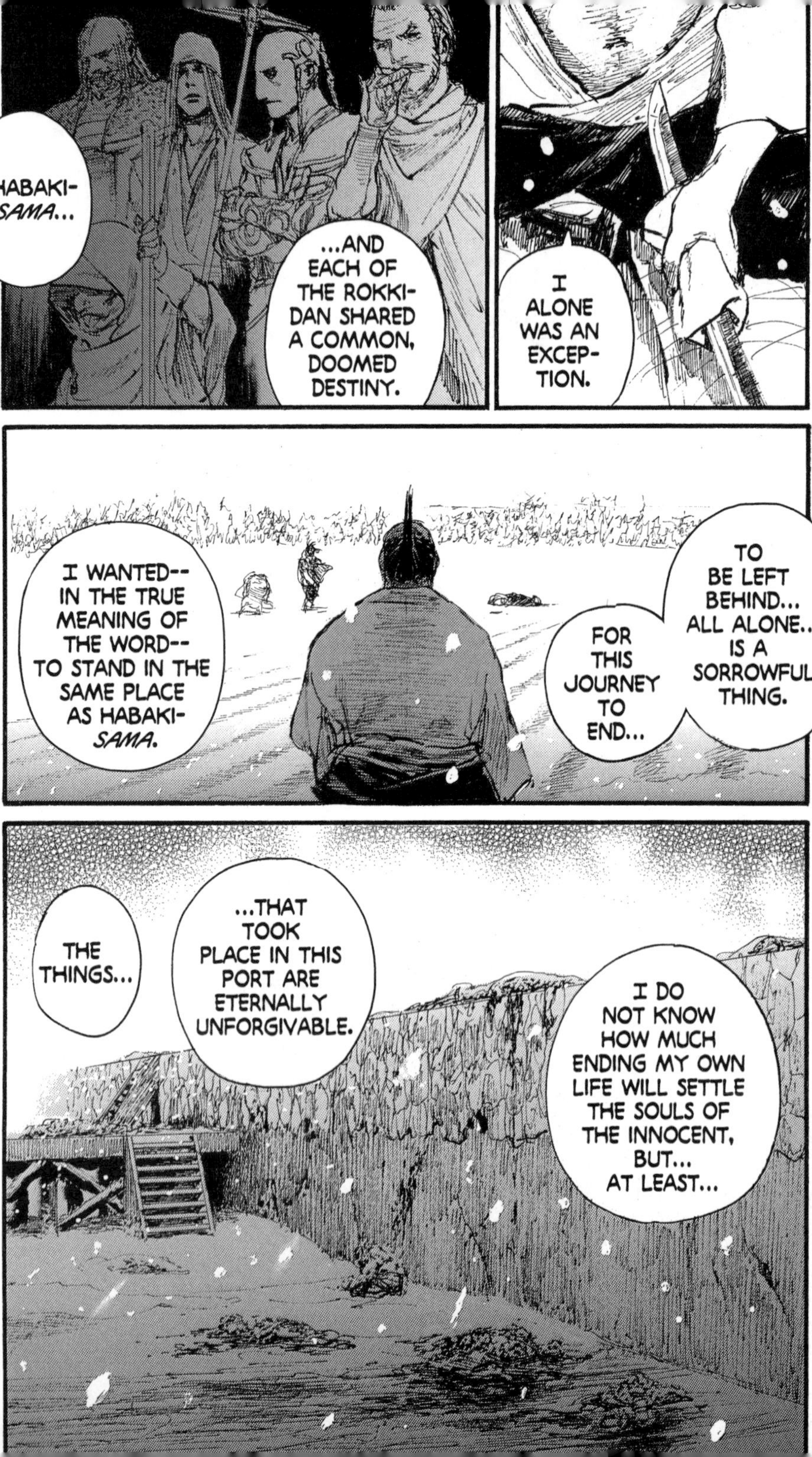
HABAKI-SAMA...
...AND EACH OF THE ROKKI-DAN SHARED A COMMON, DOOMED DESTINY.
I ALONE WAS AN EXCEPTION.
I WANTED-- IN THE TRUE MEANING OF THE WORD-- TO STAND IN THE SAME PLACE AS HABAKI-SAMA.
FOR THIS JOURNEY TO END...
TO BE LEFT BEHIND... ALL ALONE... IS A SORROWFUL THING.
THE THINGS...
...THAT TOOK PLACE IN THIS PORT ARE ETERNALLY UNFORGIVABLE.
I DO NOT KNOW HOW MUCH ENDING MY OWN LIFE WILL SETTLE THE SOULS OF THE INNOCENT, BUT... AT LEAST...

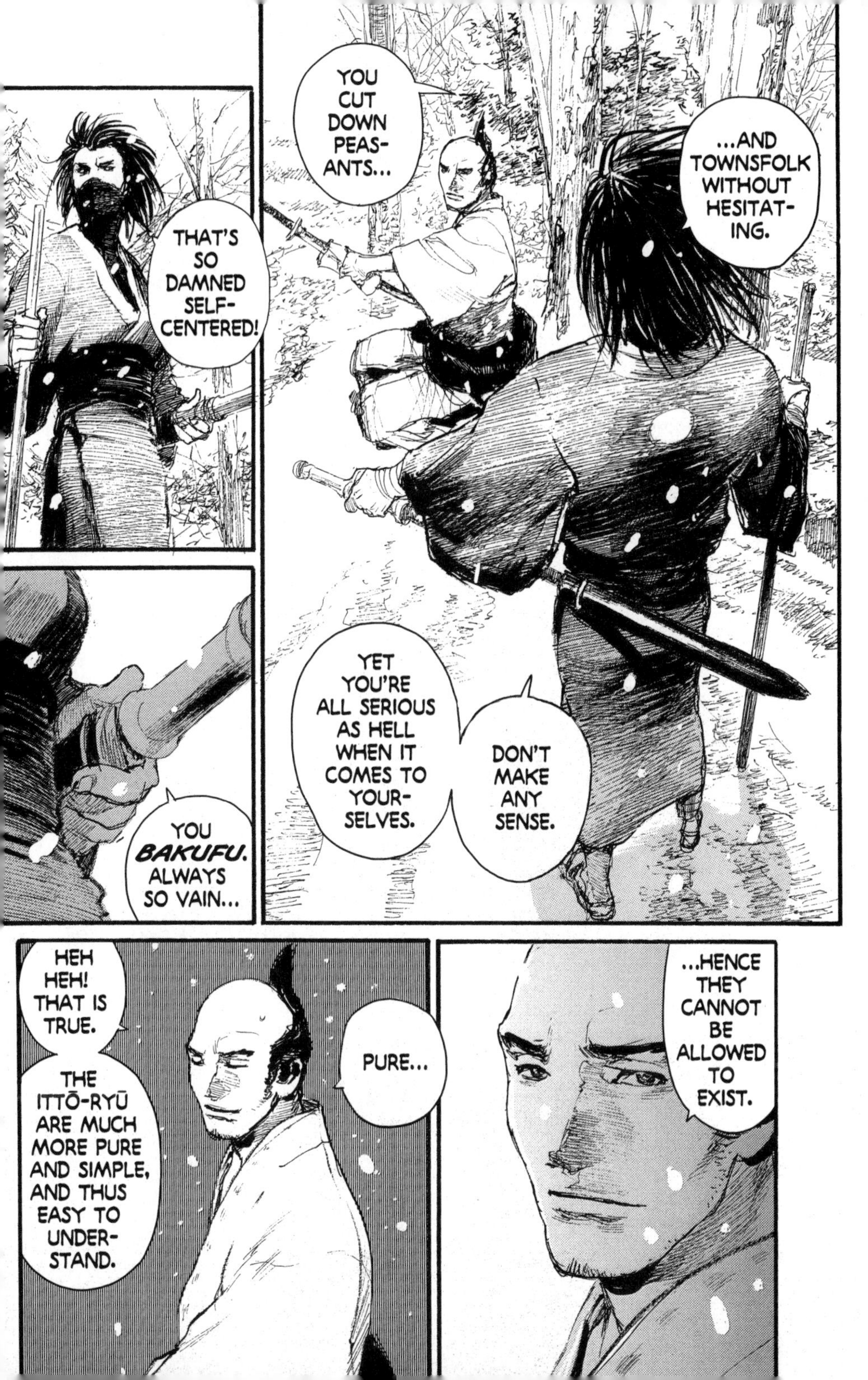
THAT'S SO DAMNED SELF-CENTERED!
YOU *BAKUFU*. ALWAYS SO VAIN...
YOU CUT DOWN PEASANTS...
...AND TOWNSFOLK WITHOUT HESITATING.
YET YOU'RE ALL SERIOUS AS HELL WHEN IT COMES TO YOURSELVES.
DON'T MAKE ANY SENSE.
HEH HEH! THAT IS TRUE.
THE ITTŌ-RYŪ ARE MUCH MORE PURE AND SIMPLE, AND THUS EASY TO UNDERSTAND.
PURE...
...HENCE THEY CANNOT BE ALLOWED TO EXIST.

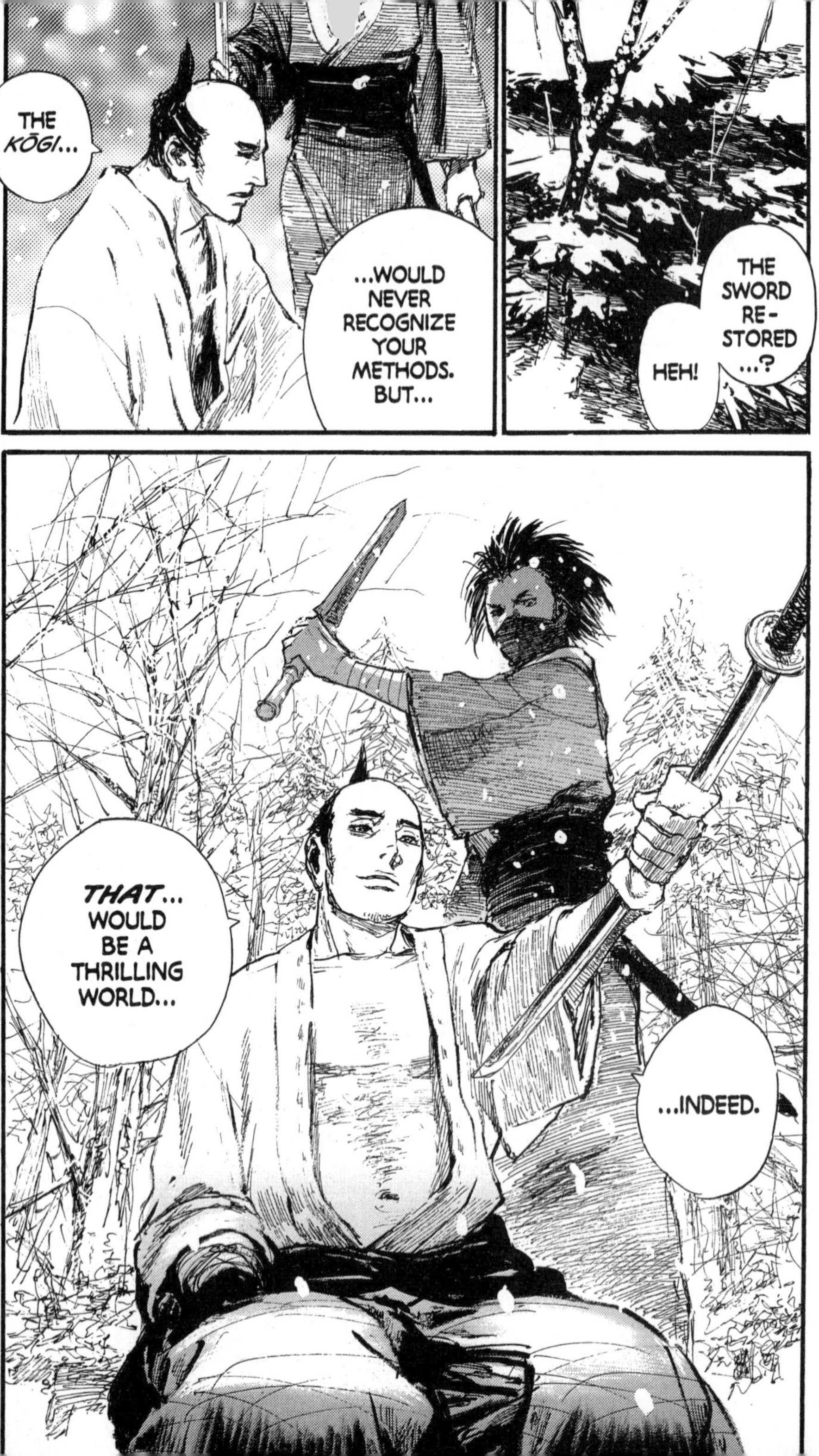
THE *KŌGI*...
...WOULD NEVER RECOGNIZE YOUR METHODS. BUT...
THE SWORD RE-STORED ...?
HEH!
THAT... WOULD BE A THRILLING WORLD...
...INDEED.

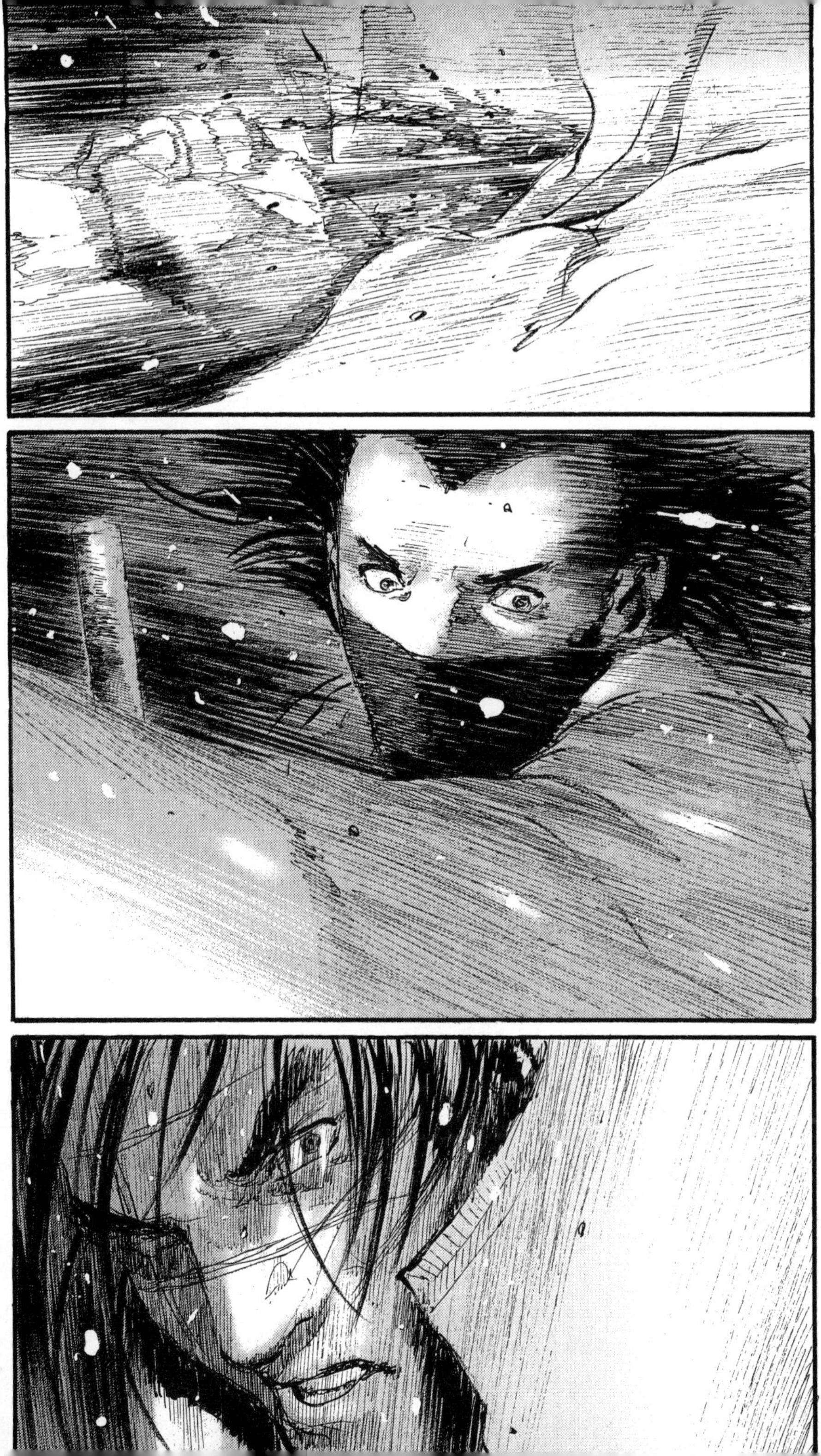

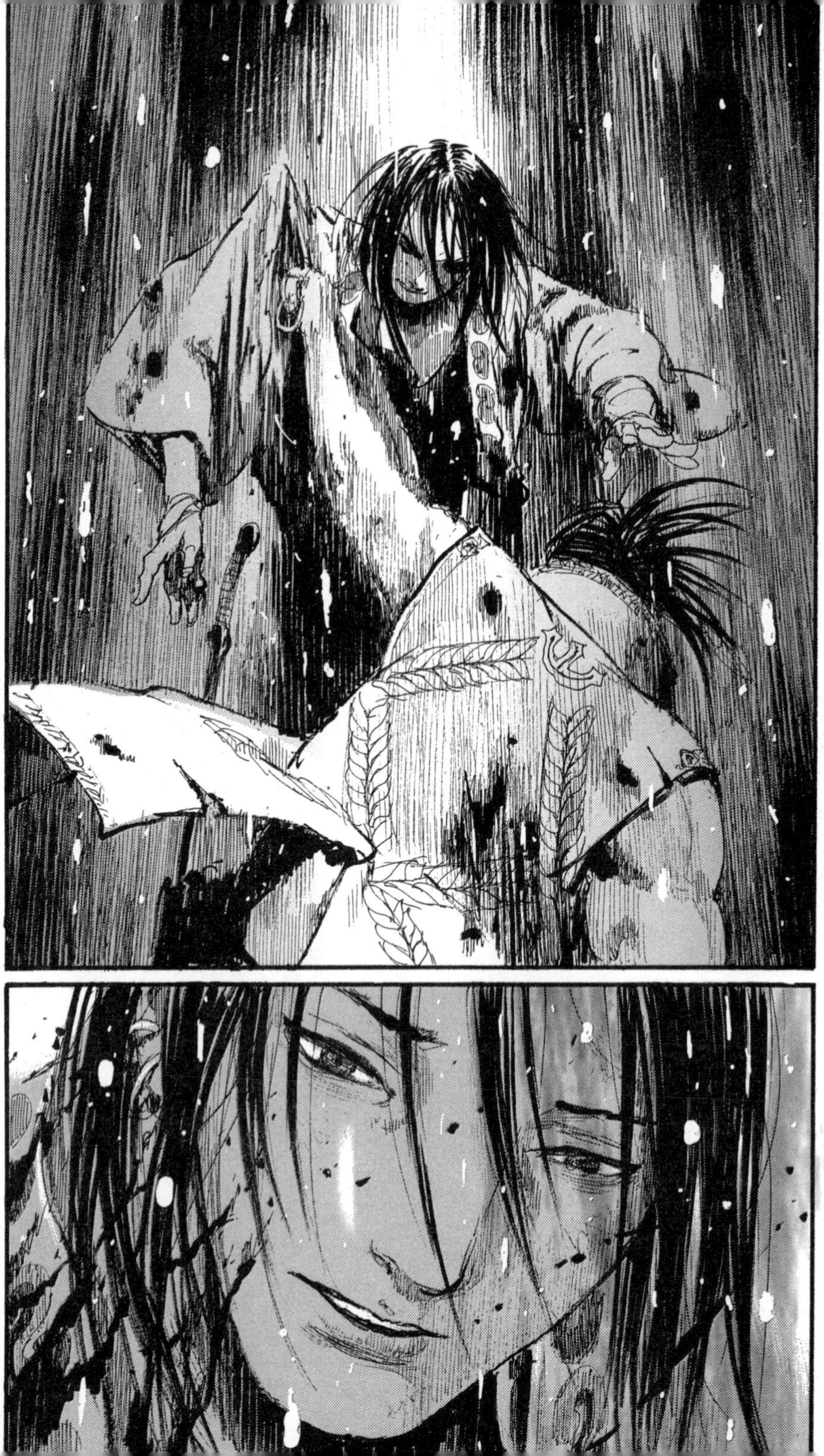

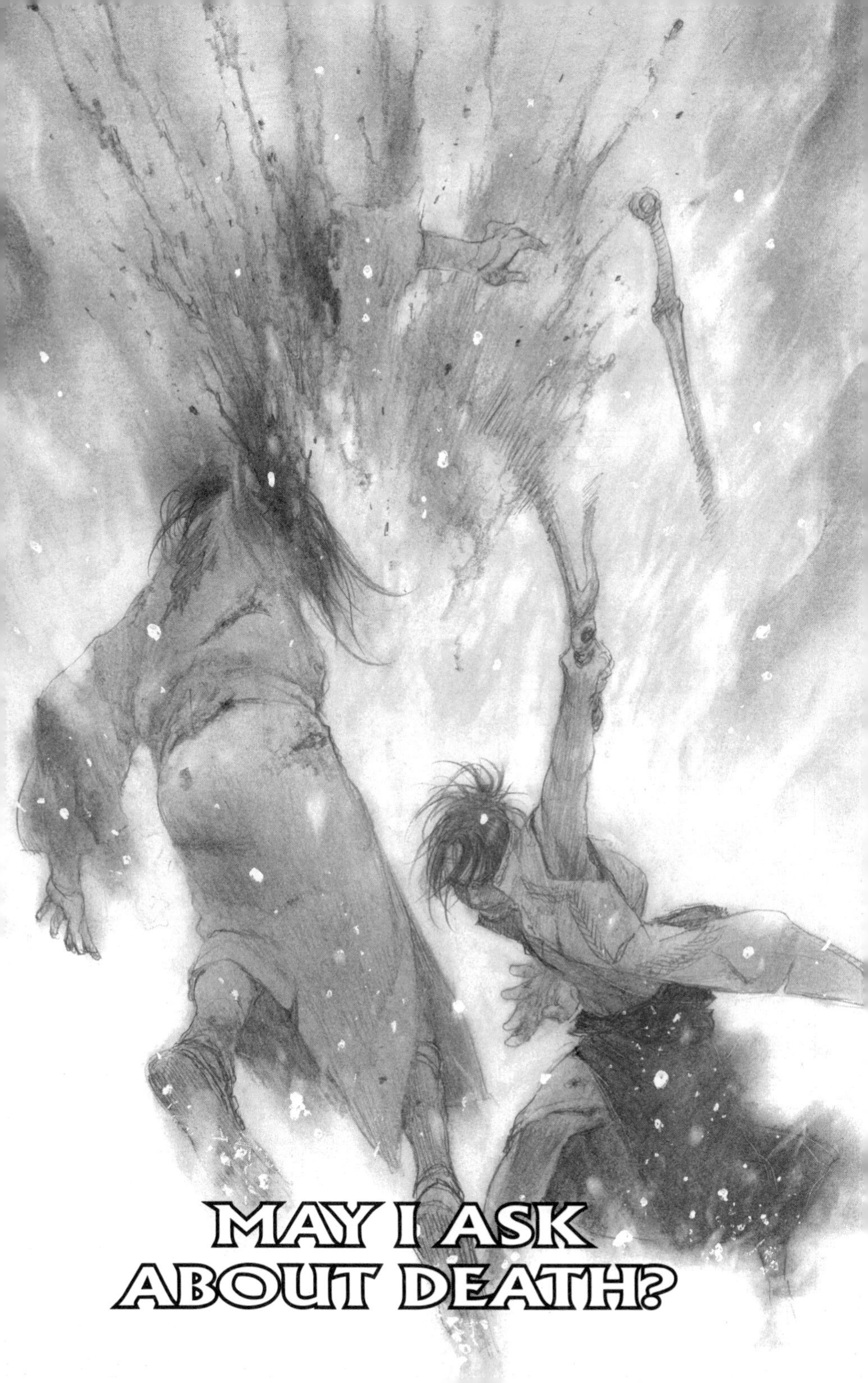

MAY I ASK ABOUT DEATH?

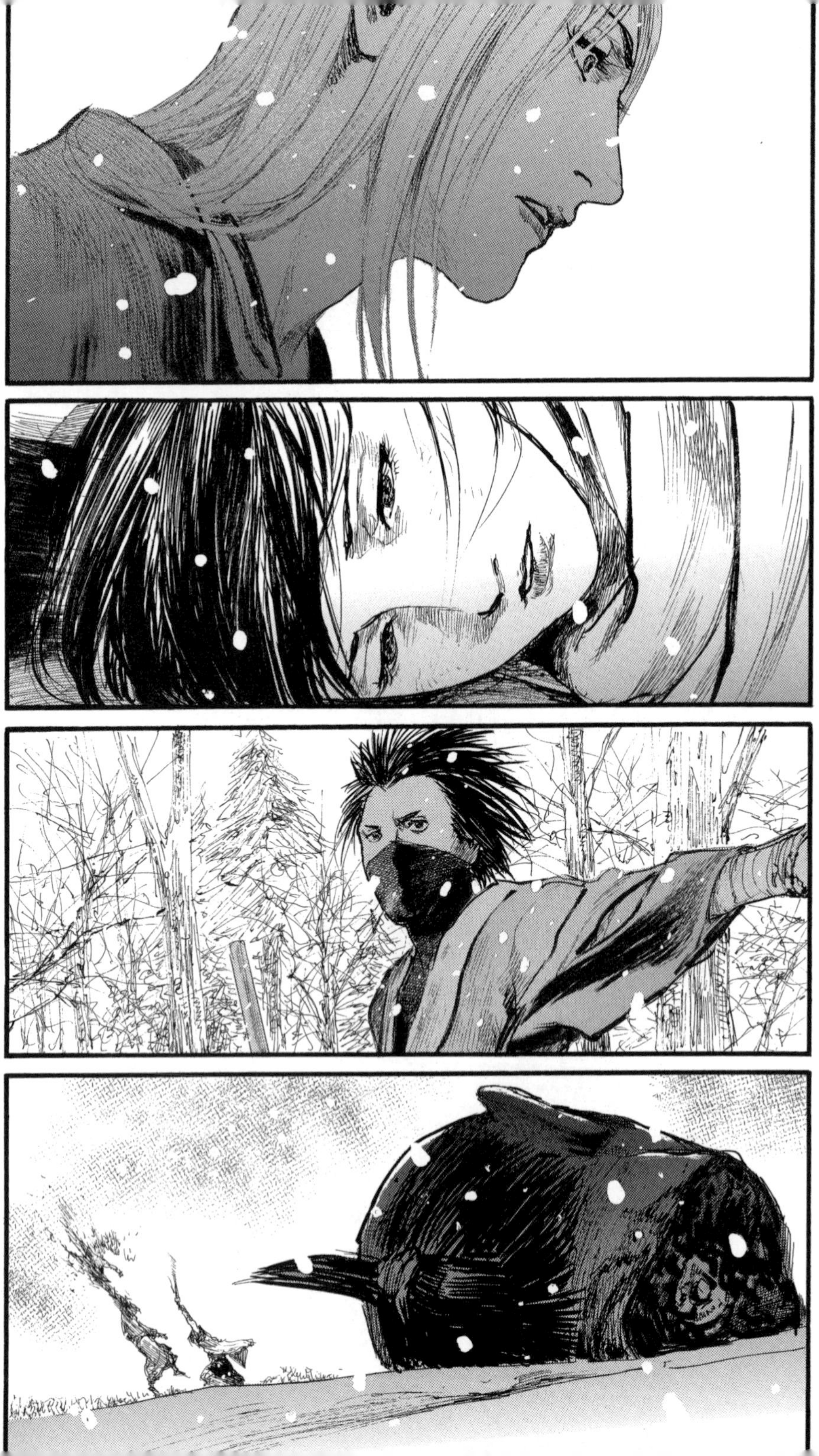

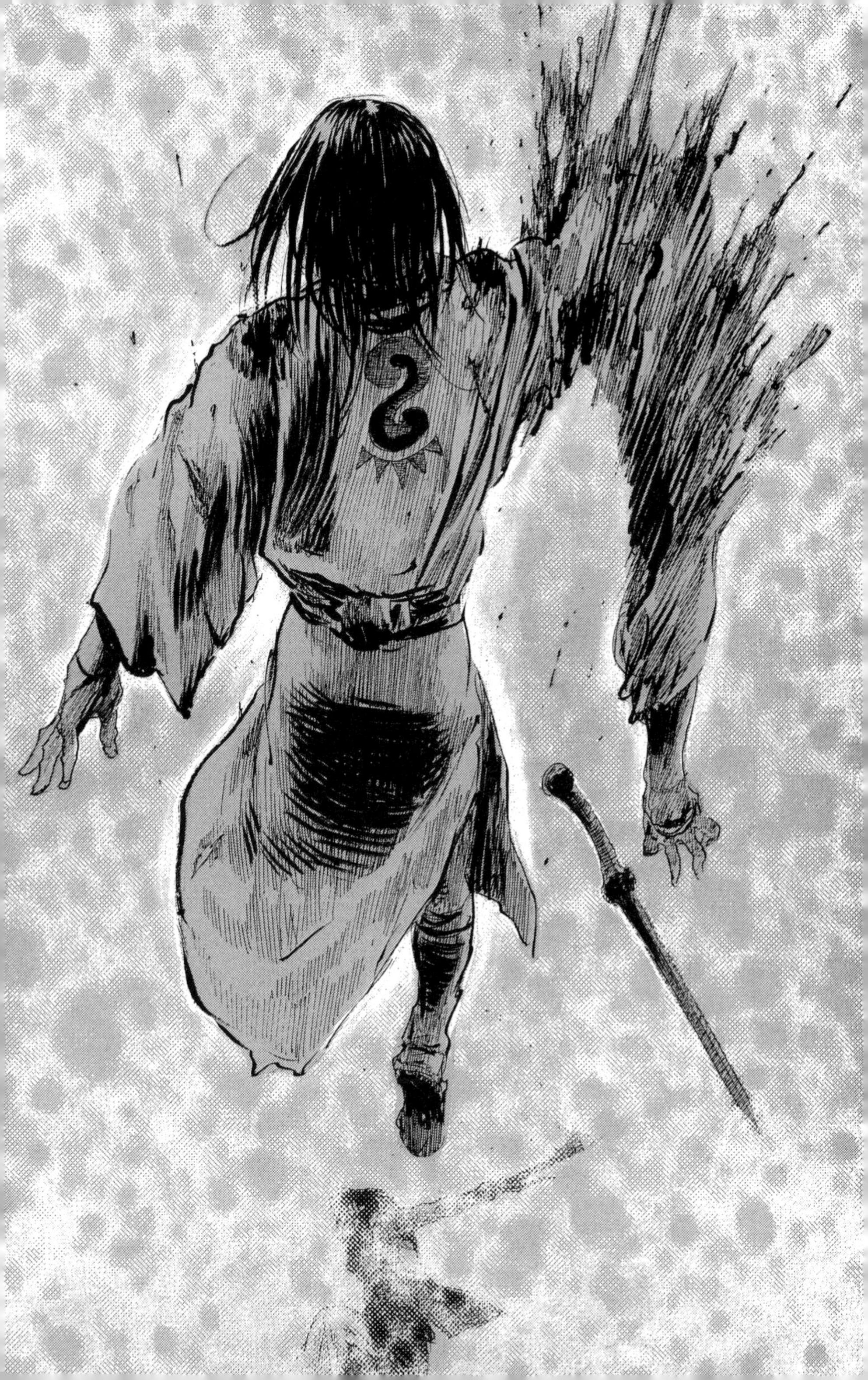

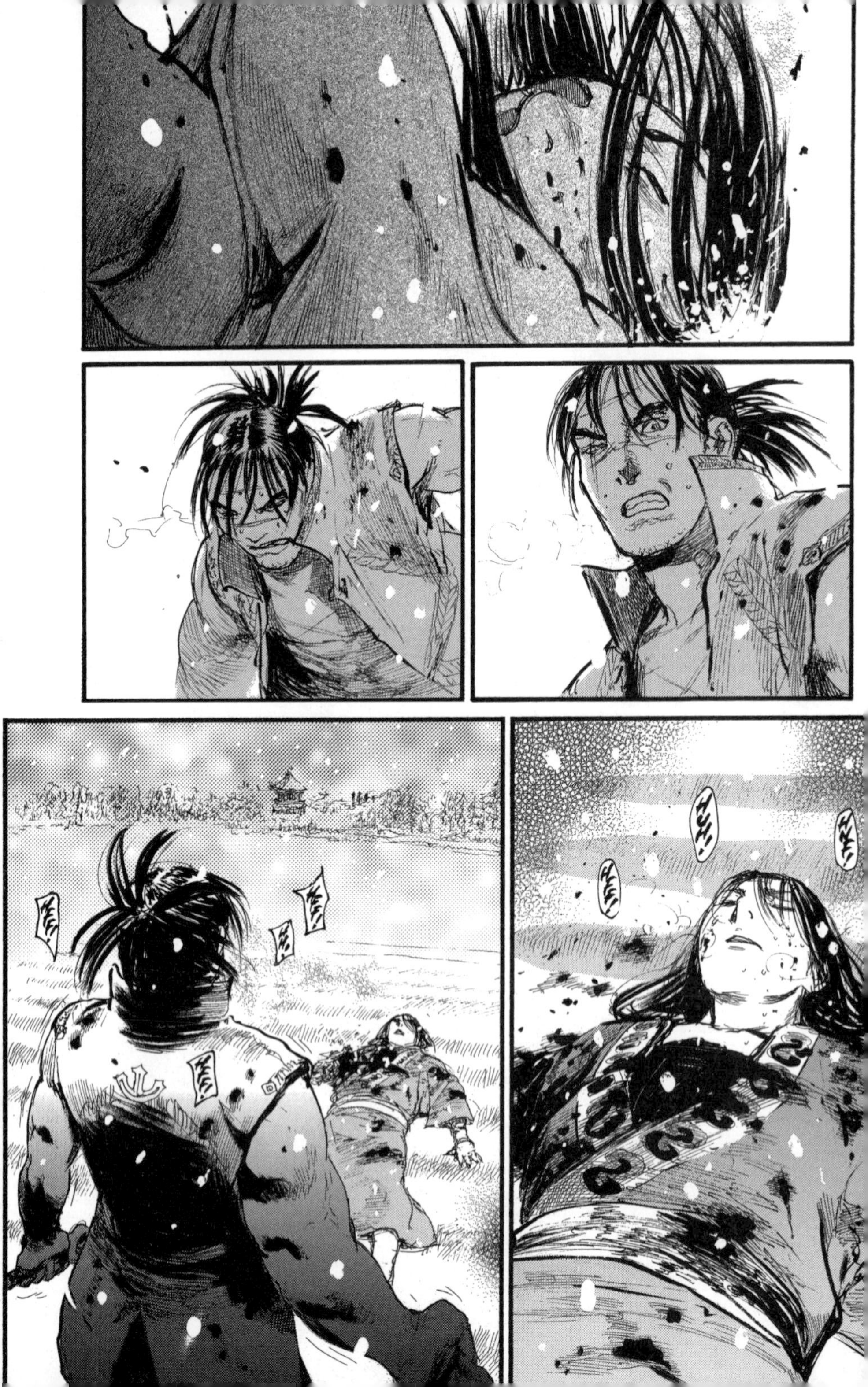

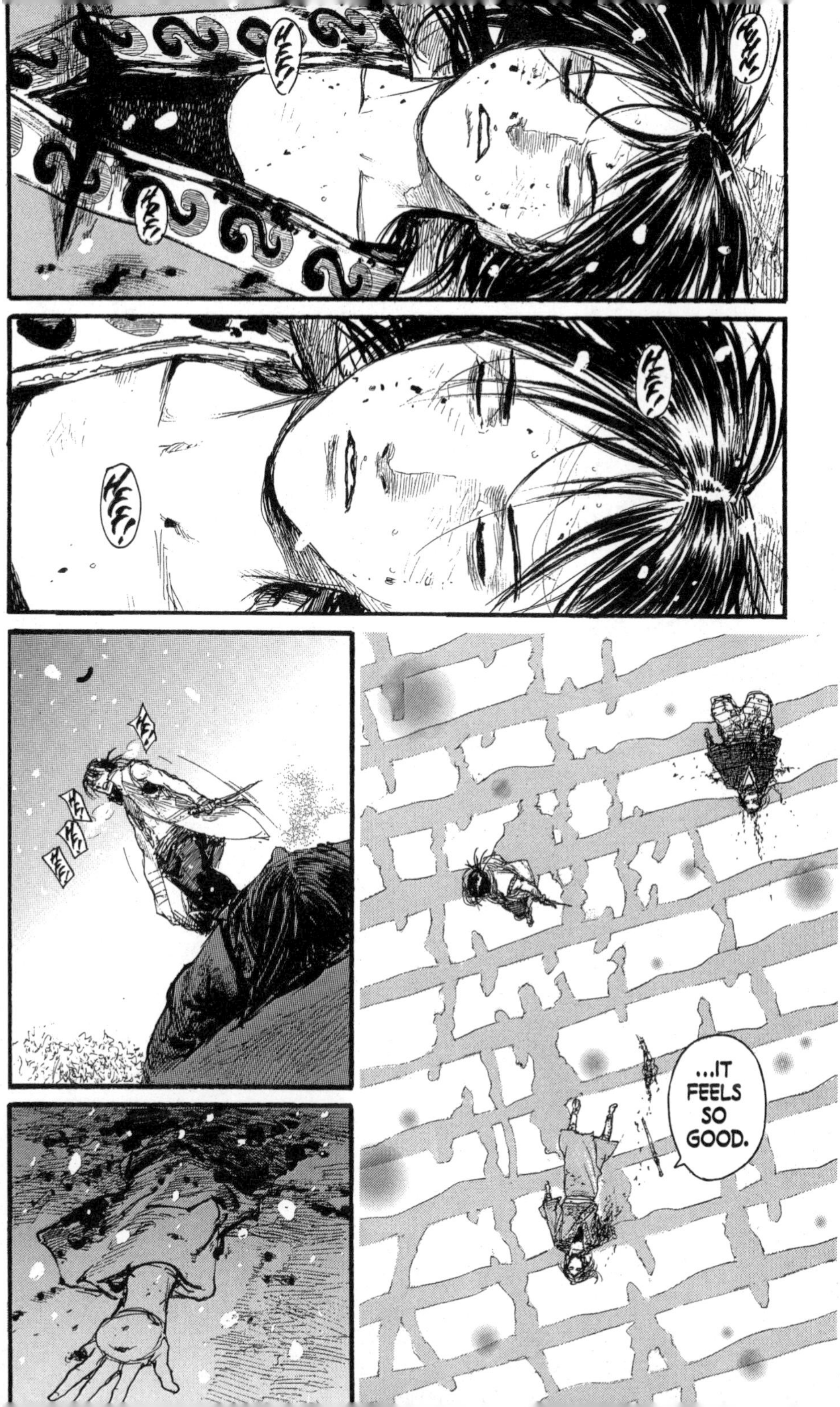
...IT FEELS SO GOOD.

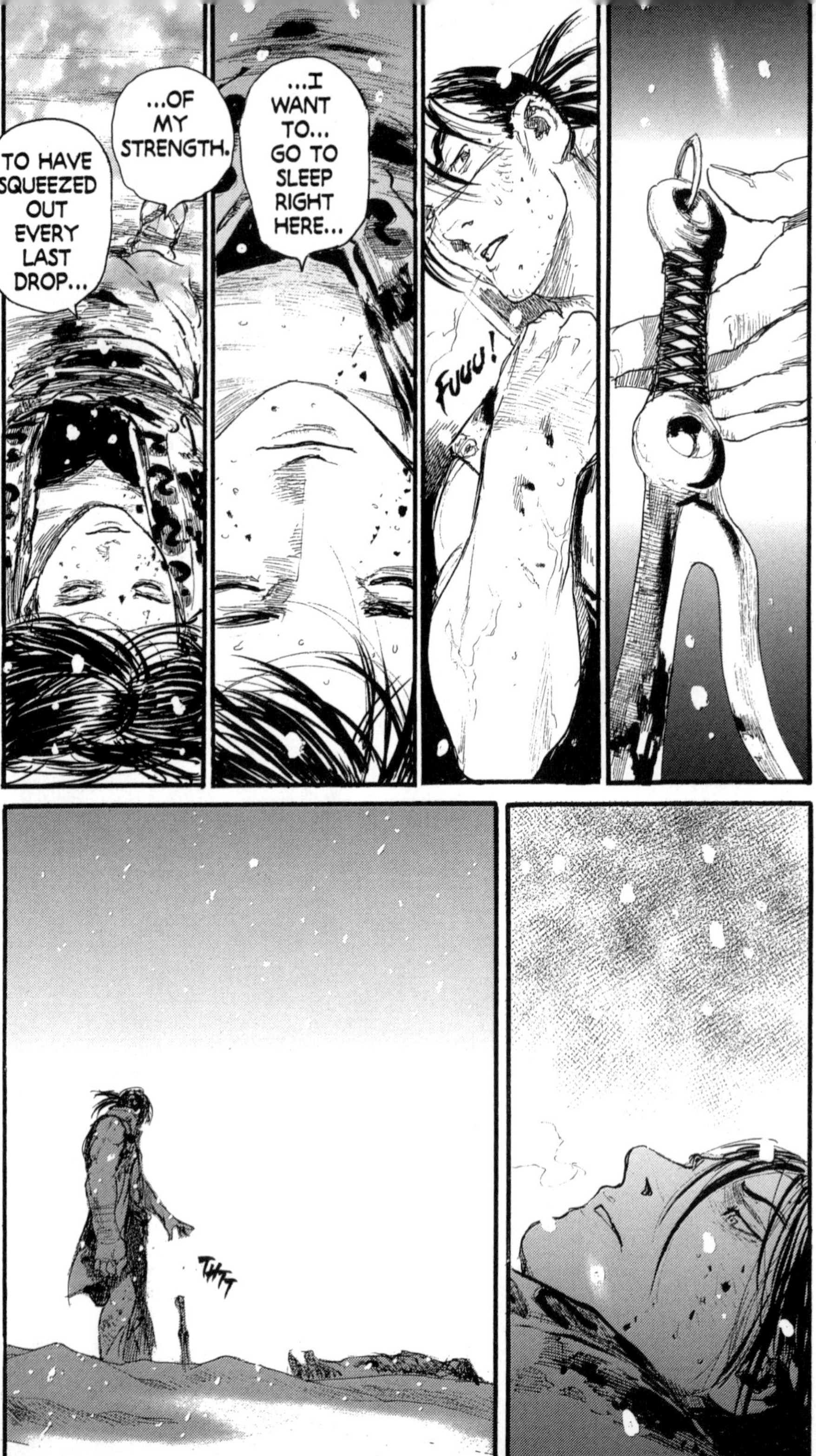
TO HAVE SQUEEZED OUT EVERY LAST DROP...
...OF MY STRENGTH.
...I WANT TO... GO TO SLEEP RIGHT HERE...
FUUU!
THTT

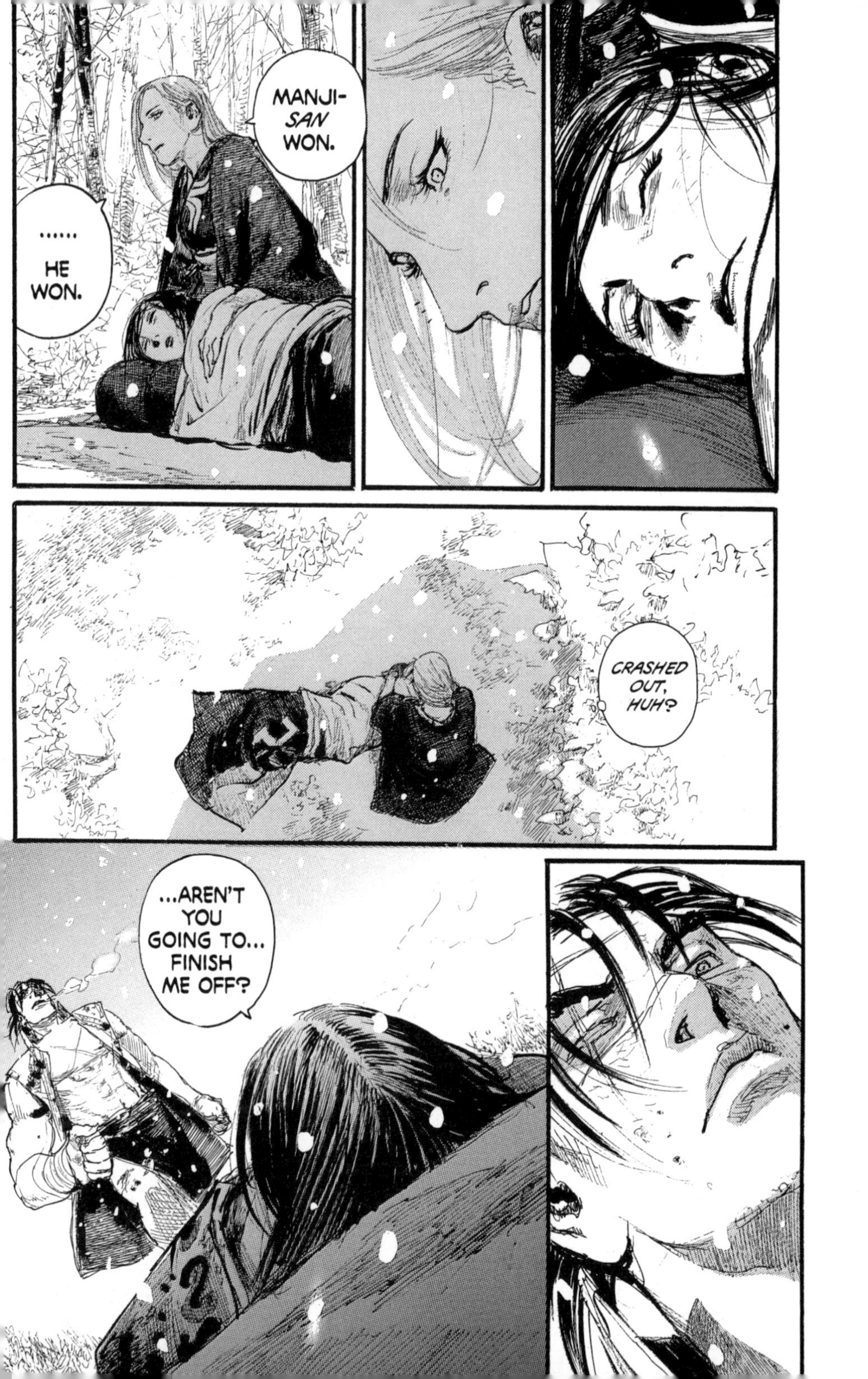
MANJI-SAN WON.
...... HE WON.
CRASHED OUT, HUH?
...AREN'T YOU GOING TO... FINISH ME OFF?

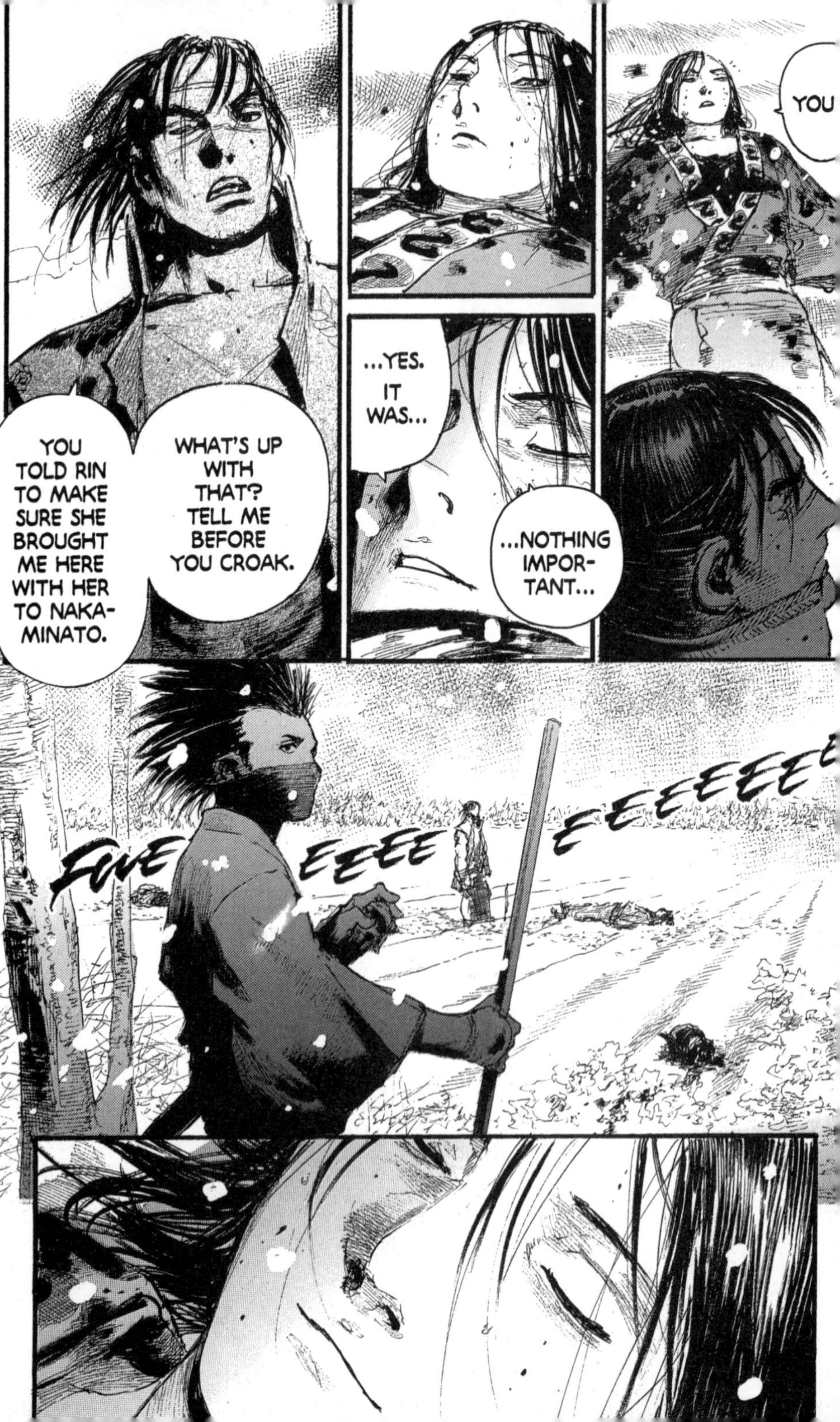
YOU TOLD RIN TO MAKE SURE SHE BROUGHT ME HERE WITH HER TO NAKA-MINATO.
WHAT'S UP WITH THAT? TELL ME BEFORE YOU CROAK.
...YES. IT WAS...
...NOTHING IMPOR-TANT...
YOU
FWEEEEEEEEEEEEEEEE

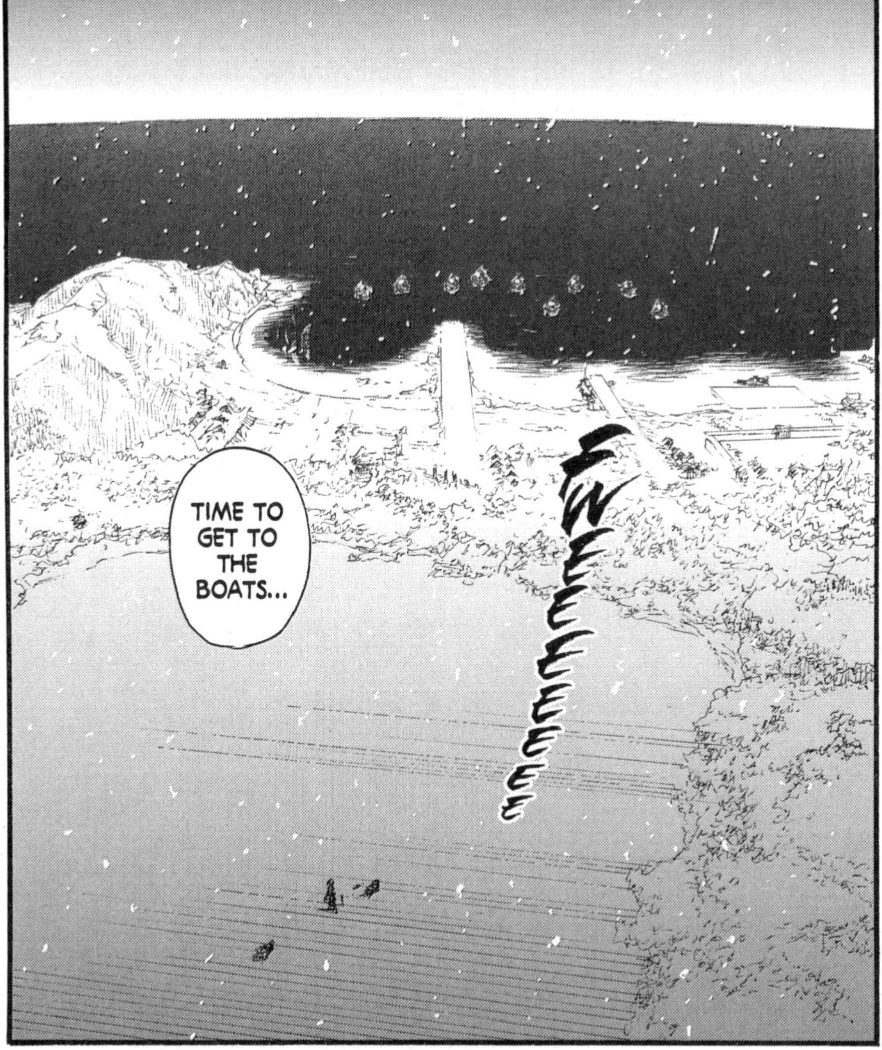
TIME TO GET TO THE BOATS...
FWEEEEEEEEEE
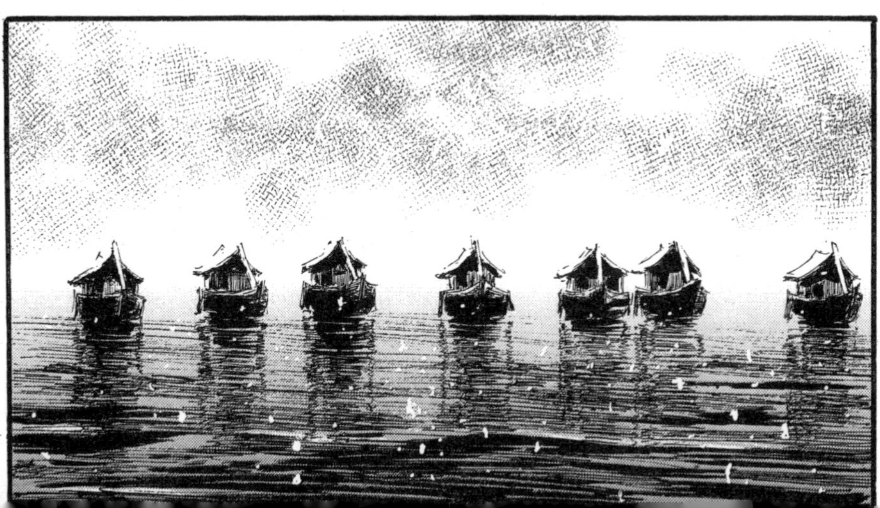

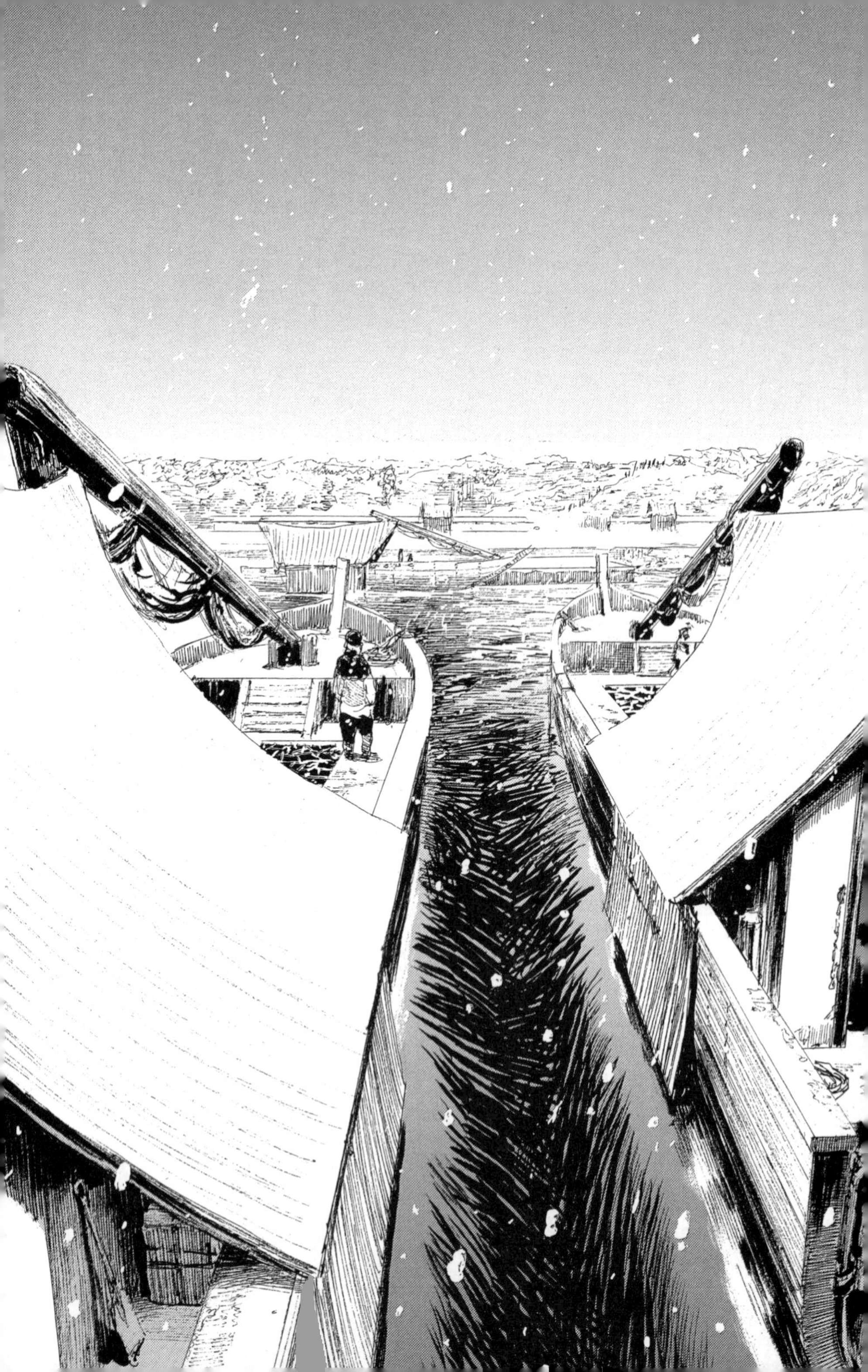

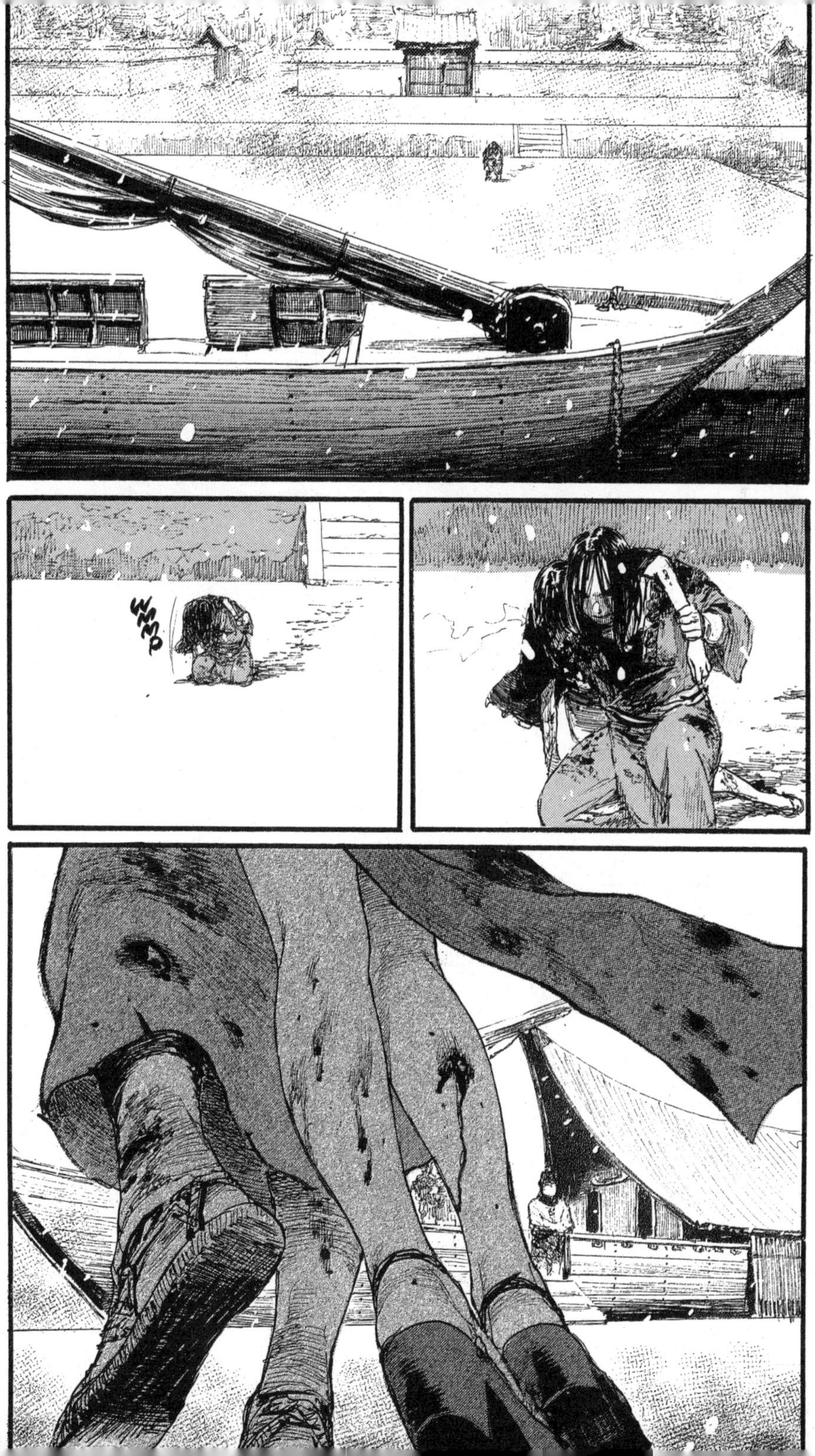
WMMP

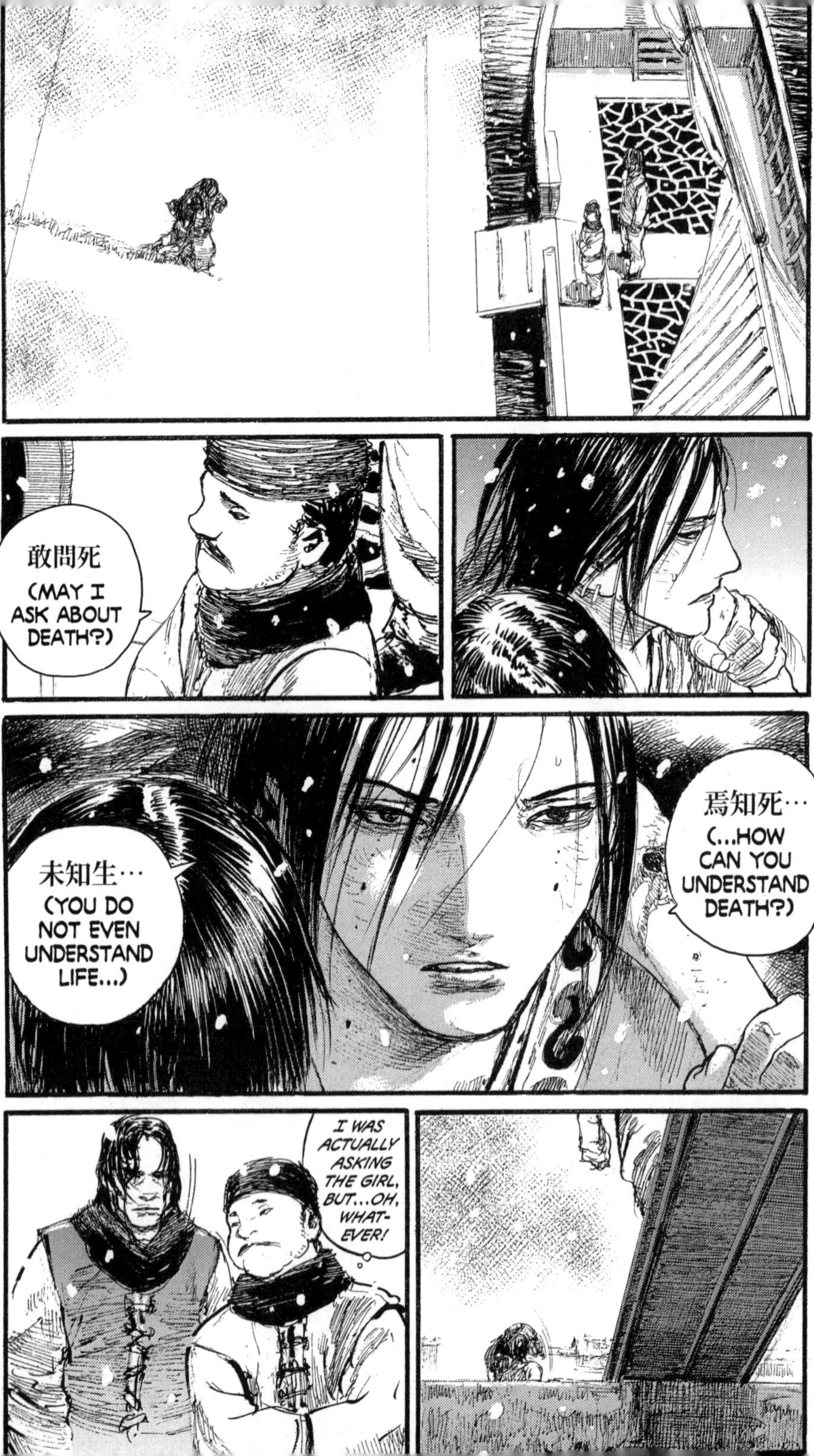

敢問死
(MAY I ASK ABOUT DEATH?)
未知生…
(YOU DO NOT EVEN UNDERSTAND LIFE...)
焉知死…
(...HOW CAN YOU UNDERSTAND DEATH?)
I WAS ACTUALLY ASKING THE GIRL, BUT...OH, WHATEVER!

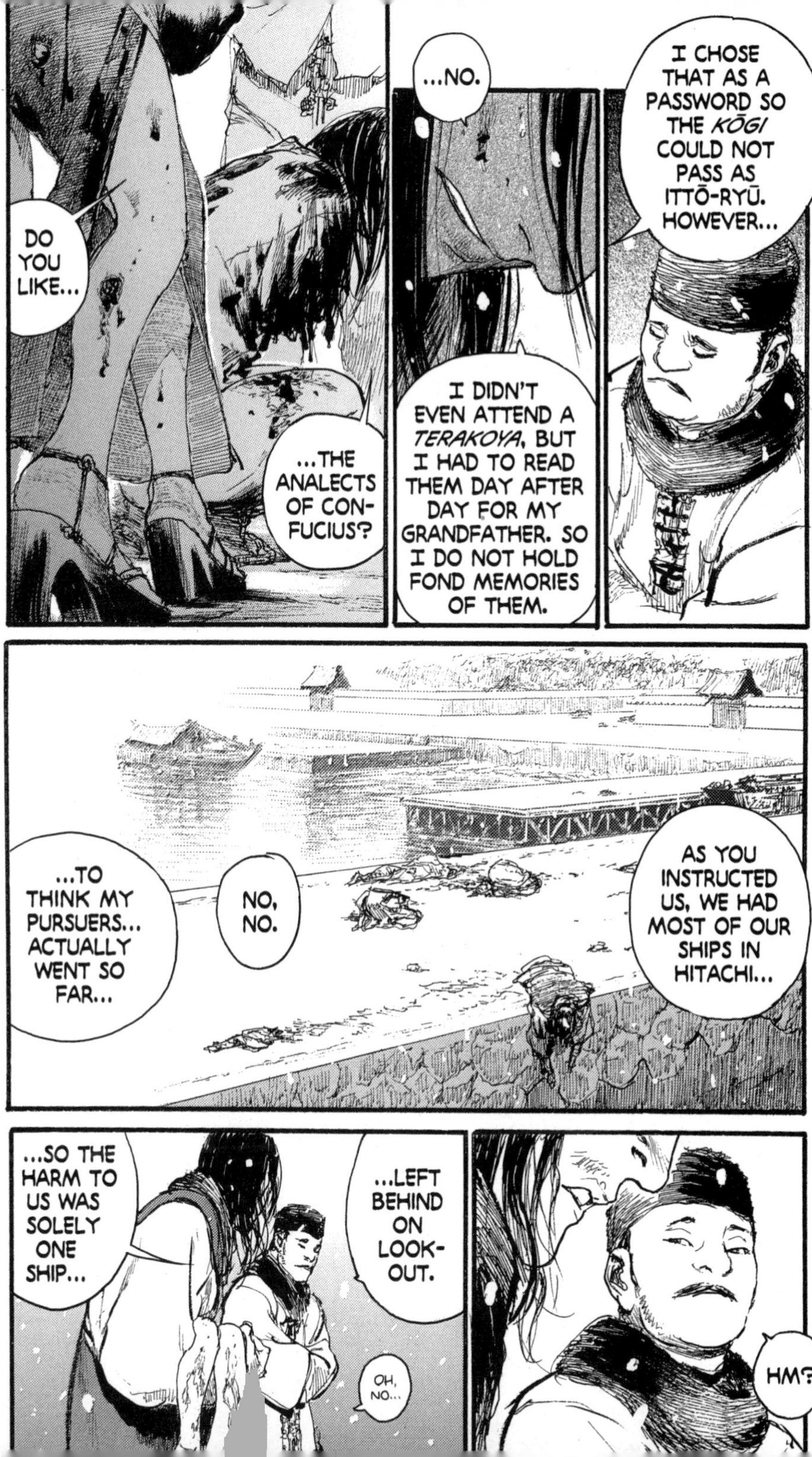
DO YOU LIKE...
...THE ANALECTS OF CON-FUCIUS?
...NO.
I DIDN'T EVEN ATTEND A *TERAKOYA*, BUT I HAD TO READ THEM DAY AFTER DAY FOR MY GRANDFATHER. SO I DO NOT HOLD FOND MEMORIES OF THEM.
I CHOSE THAT AS A PASSWORD SO THE *KŌGI* COULD NOT PASS AS ITTŌ-RYŪ. HOWEVER...
...TO THINK MY PURSUERS... ACTUALLY WENT SO FAR...
NO, NO.
AS YOU INSTRUCTED US, WE HAD MOST OF OUR SHIPS IN HITACHI...
...SO THE HARM TO US WAS SOLELY ONE SHIP...
...LEFT BEHIND ON LOOK-OUT.
OH, NO...
HM?

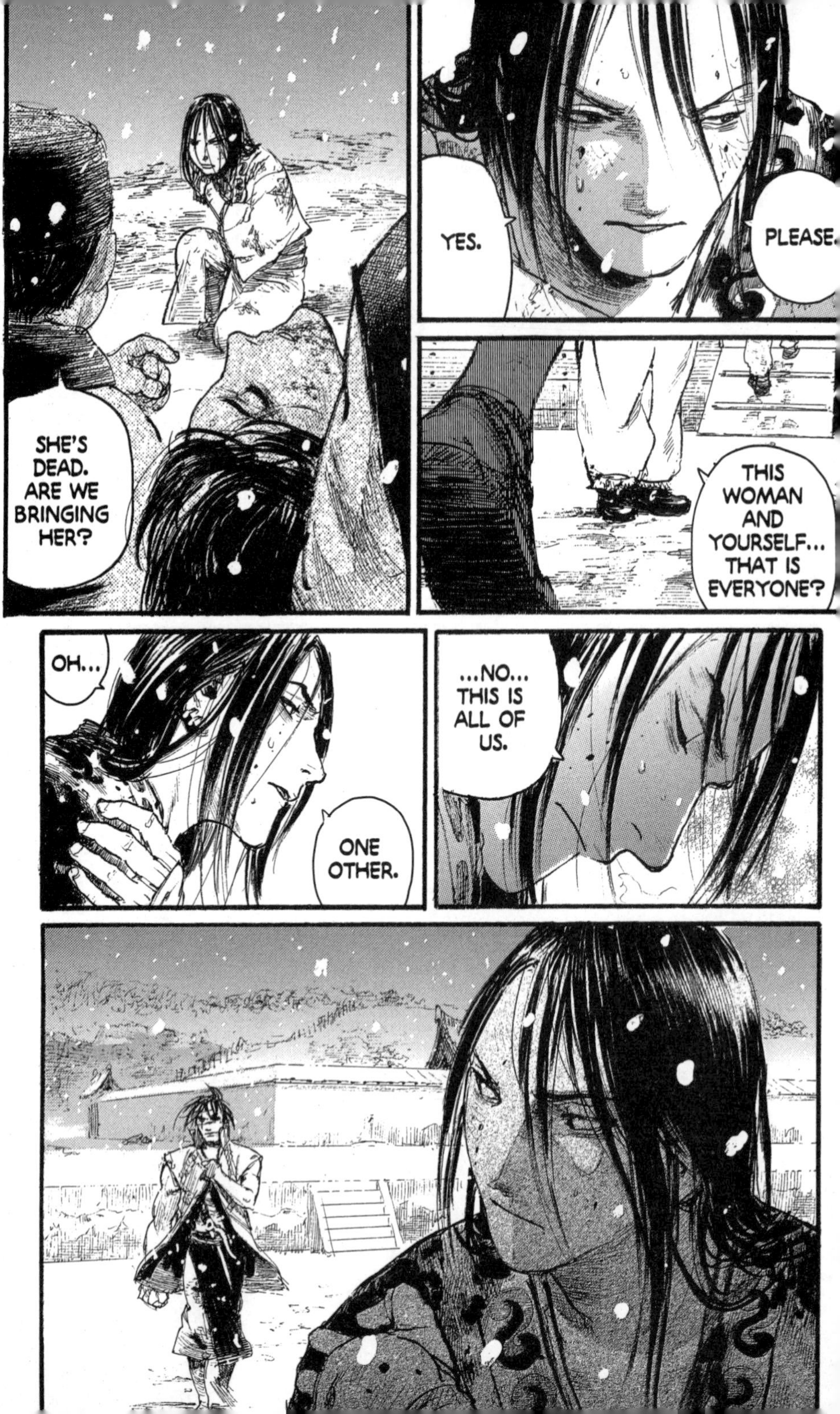
SHE'S DEAD. ARE WE BRINGING HER?
YES.
PLEASE.
THIS WOMAN AND YOURSELF... THAT IS EVERYONE?
OH...
ONE OTHER.
...NO... THIS IS ALL OF US.

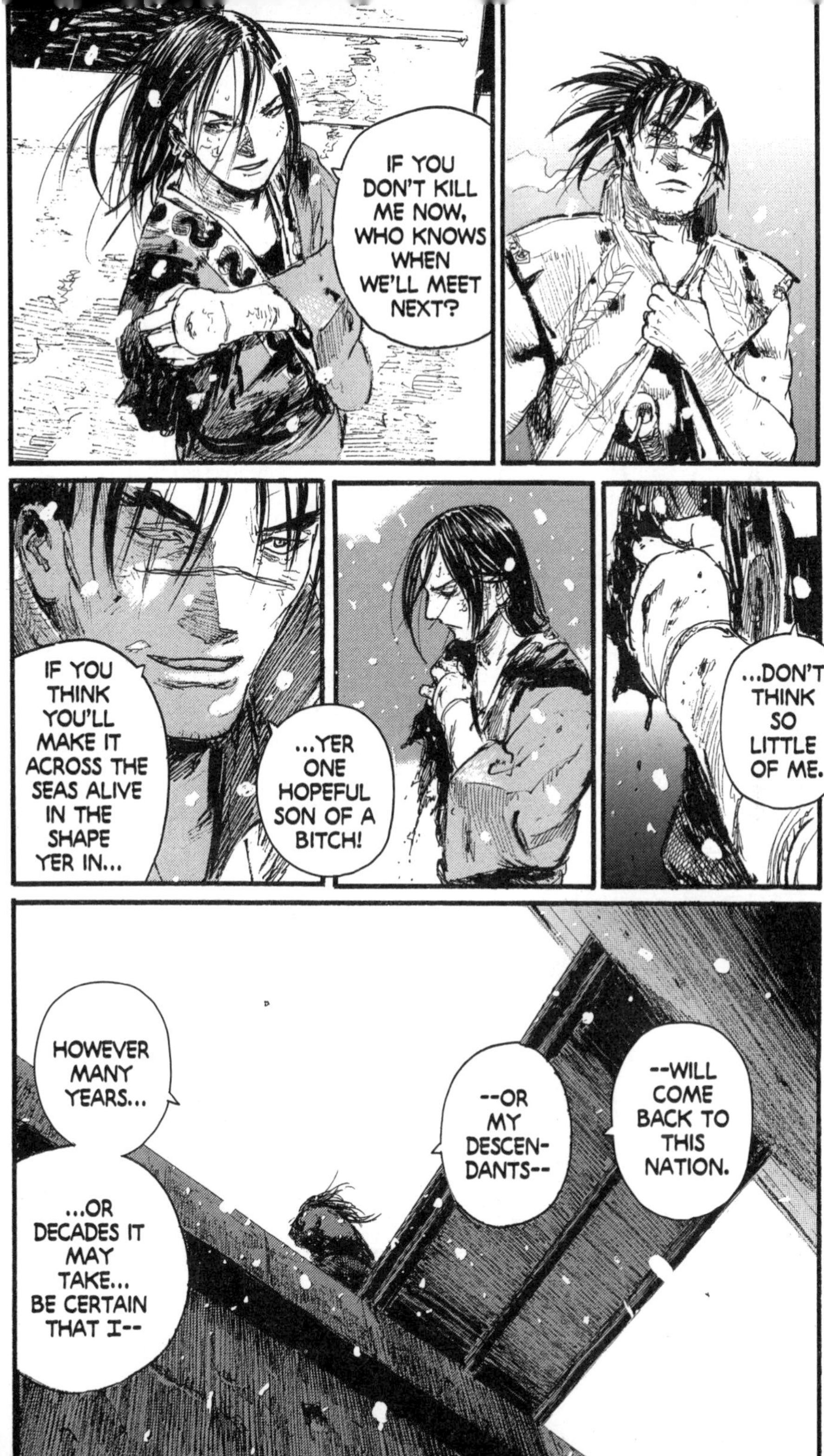
IF YOU DON'T KILL ME NOW, WHO KNOWS WHEN WE'LL MEET NEXT?
IF YOU THINK YOU'LL MAKE IT ACROSS THE SEAS ALIVE IN THE SHAPE YER IN...
...YER ONE HOPEFUL SON OF A BITCH!
...DON'T THINK SO LITTLE OF ME.
HOWEVER MANY YEARS...
...OR DECADES IT MAY TAKE... BE CERTAIN THAT I--
--OR MY DESCEN-DANTS--
--WILL COME BACK TO THIS NATION.

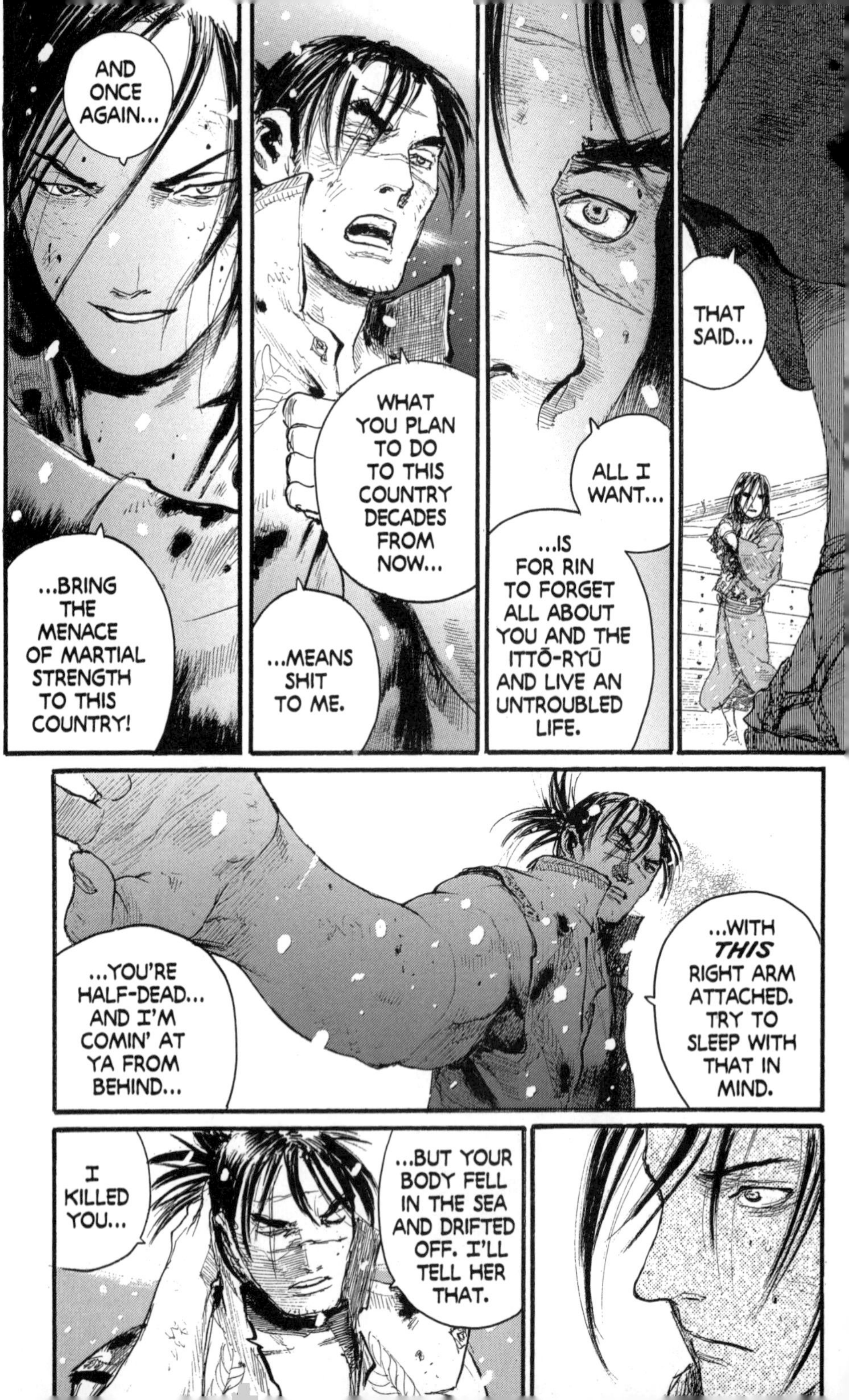
AND ONCE AGAIN...
...BRING THE MENACE OF MARTIAL STRENGTH TO THIS COUNTRY!
WHAT YOU PLAN TO DO TO THIS COUNTRY DECADES FROM NOW...
...MEANS SHIT TO ME.
ALL I WANT...
...IS FOR RIN TO FORGET ALL ABOUT YOU AND THE ITTŌ-RYŪ AND LIVE AN UNTROUBLED LIFE.
THAT SAID...
...YOU'RE HALF-DEAD... AND I'M COMIN' AT YA FROM BEHIND...
...WITH ***THIS*** RIGHT ARM ATTACHED. TRY TO SLEEP WITH THAT IN MIND.
I KILLED YOU...
...BUT YOUR BODY FELL IN THE SEA AND DRIFTED OFF. I'LL TELL HER THAT.

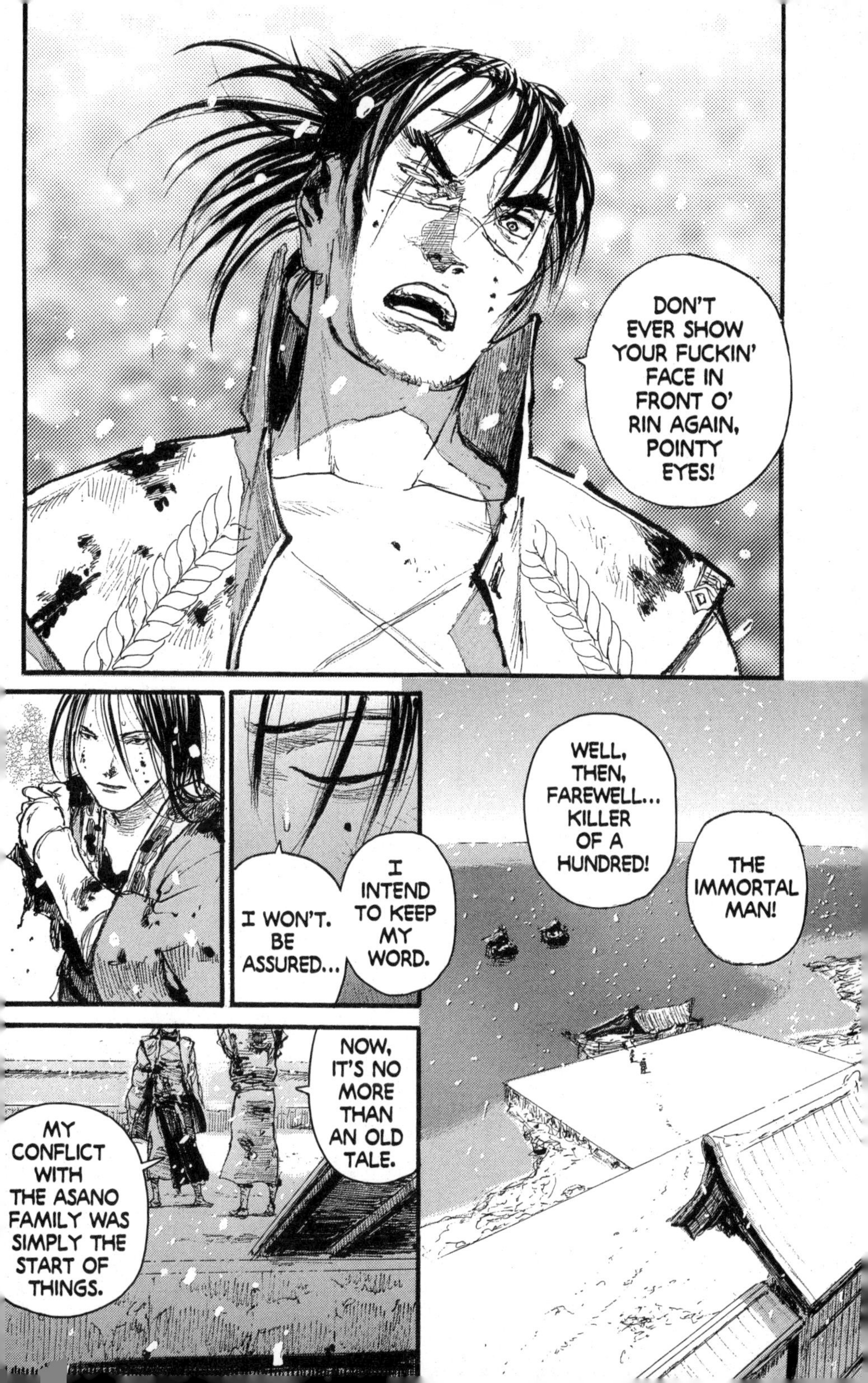
DON'T EVER SHOW YOUR FUCKIN' FACE IN FRONT O' RIN AGAIN, POINTY EYES!
I WON'T. BE ASSURED...
I INTEND TO KEEP MY WORD.
MY CONFLICT WITH THE ASANO FAMILY WAS SIMPLY THE START OF THINGS.
NOW, IT'S NO MORE THAN AN OLD TALE.
WELL, THEN, FAREWELL... KILLER OF A HUNDRED!
THE IMMORTAL MAN!

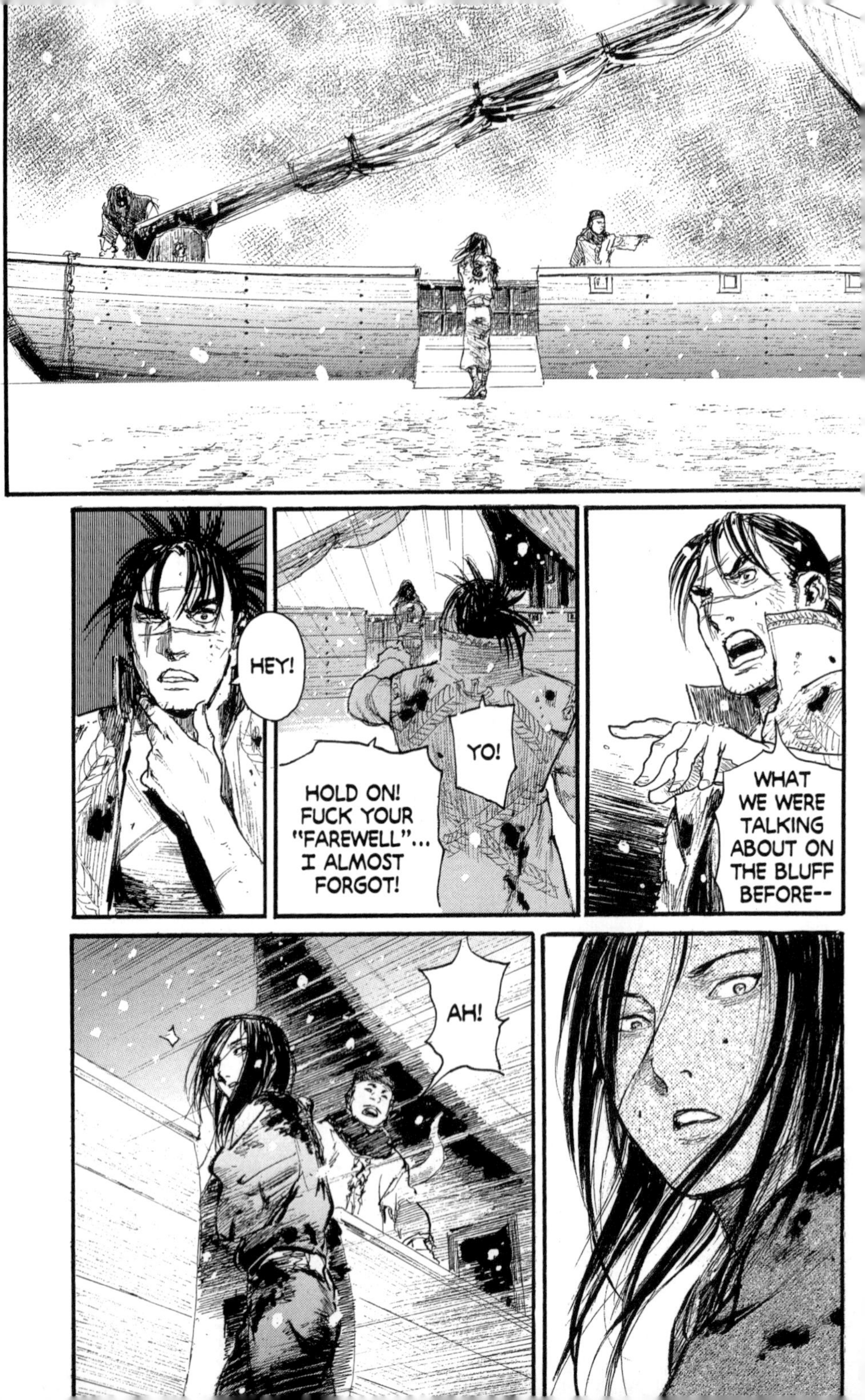
HEY!
HOLD ON! FUCK YOUR "FAREWELL"... I ALMOST FORGOT!
YO!
WHAT WE WERE TALKING ABOUT ON THE BLUFF BEFORE--
AH!

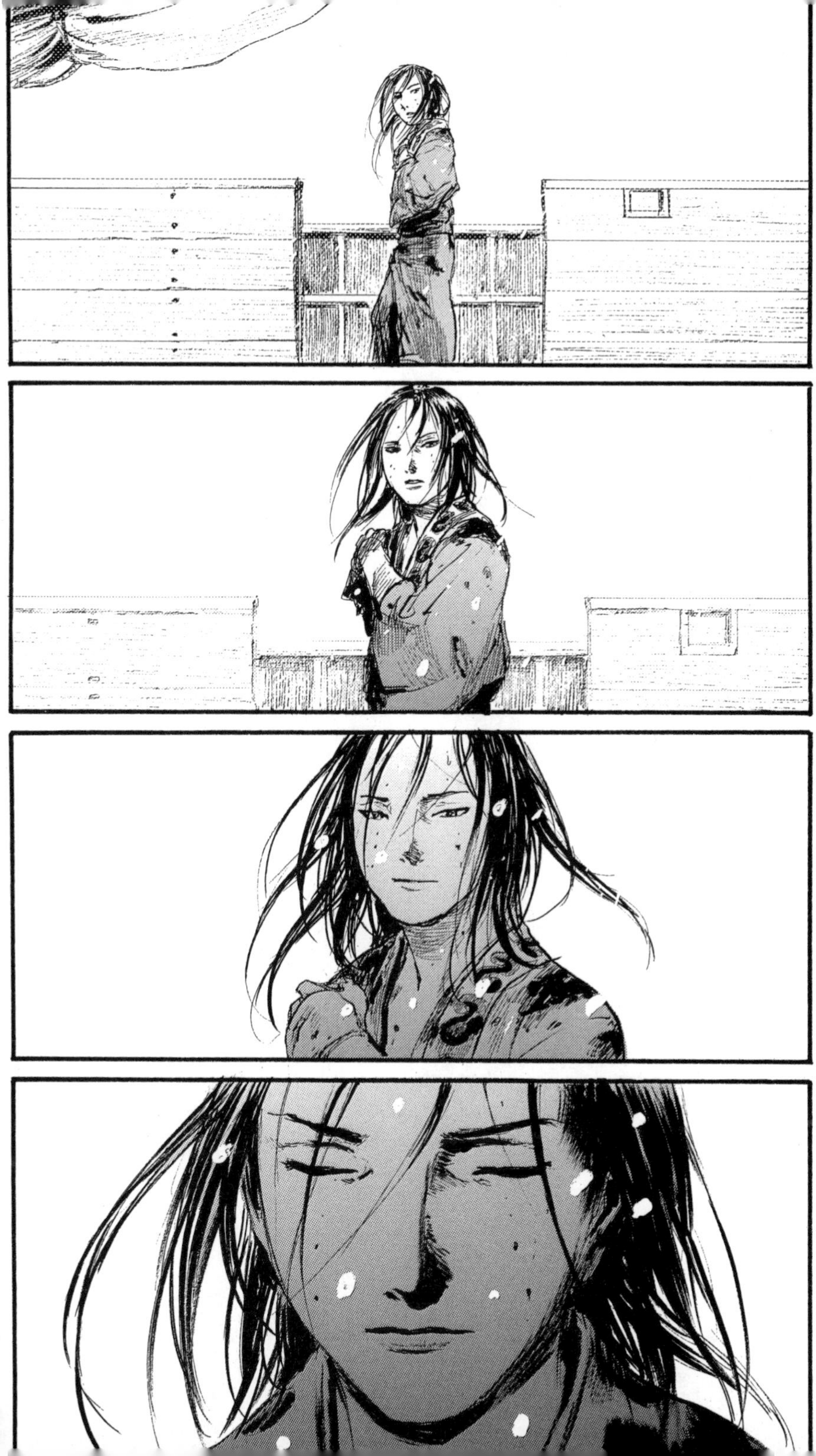

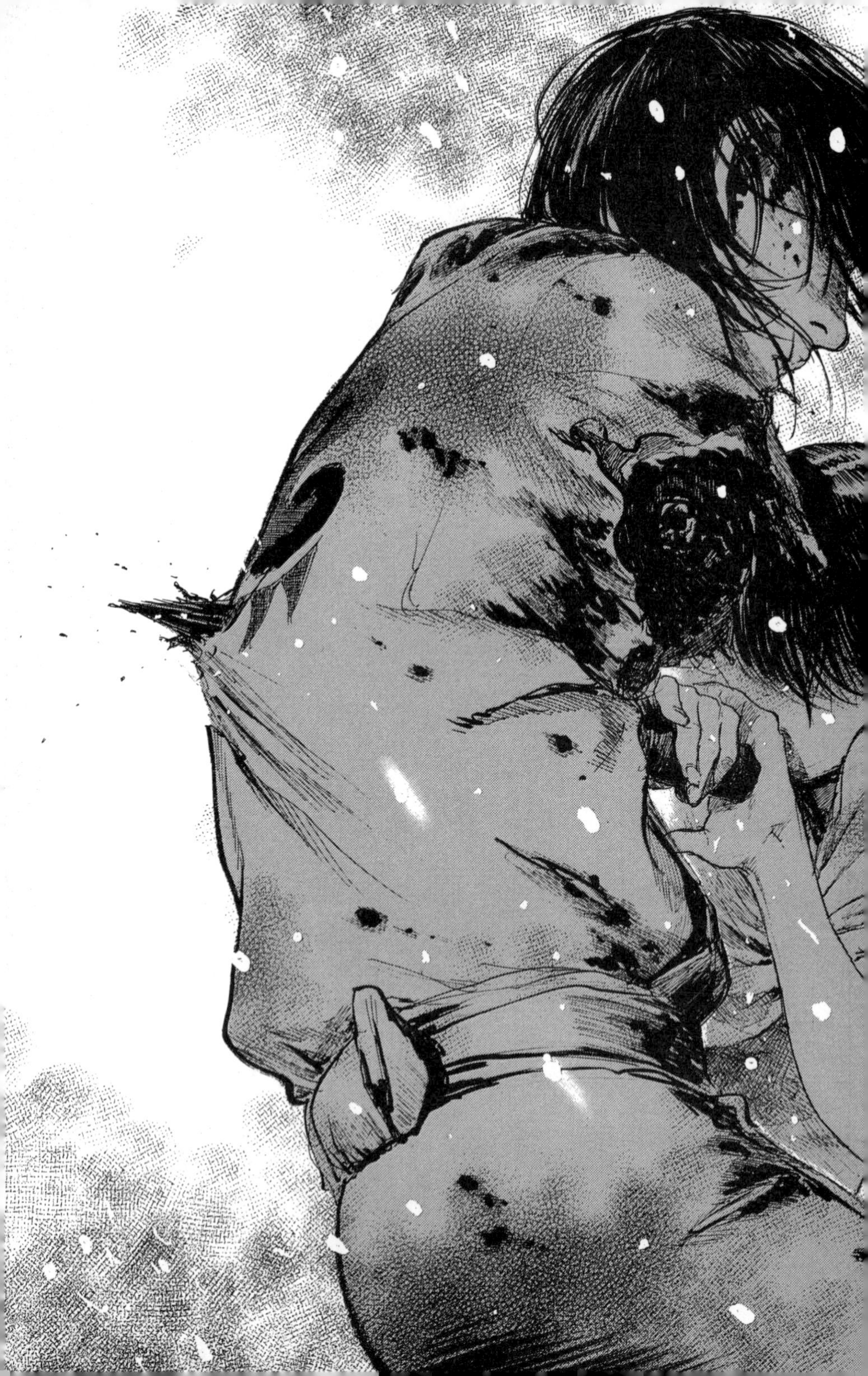

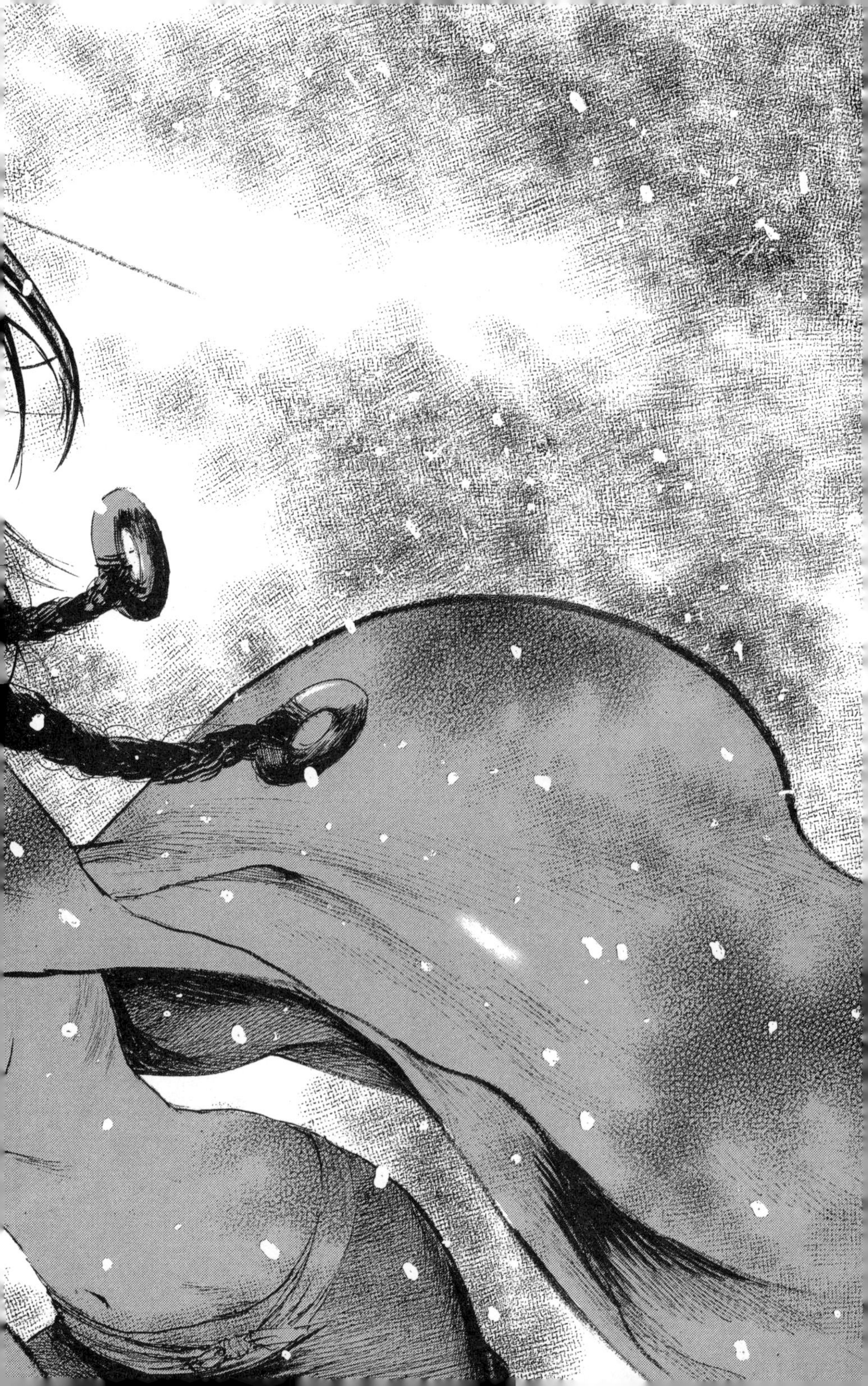

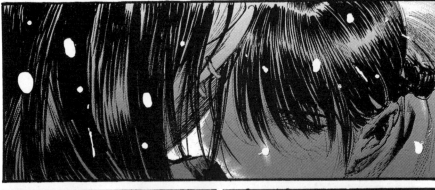

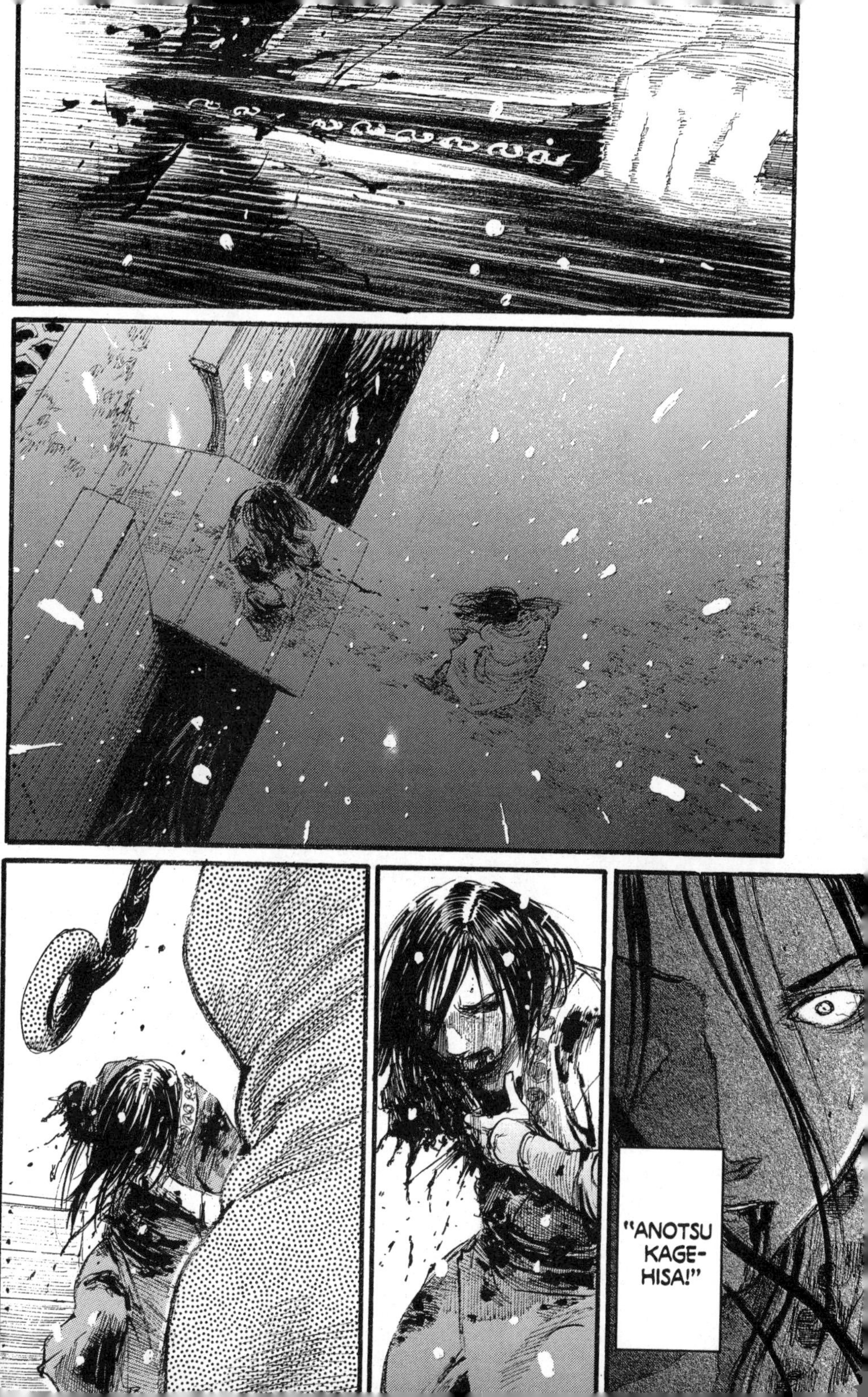
"ANOTSU KAGE-HISA!"

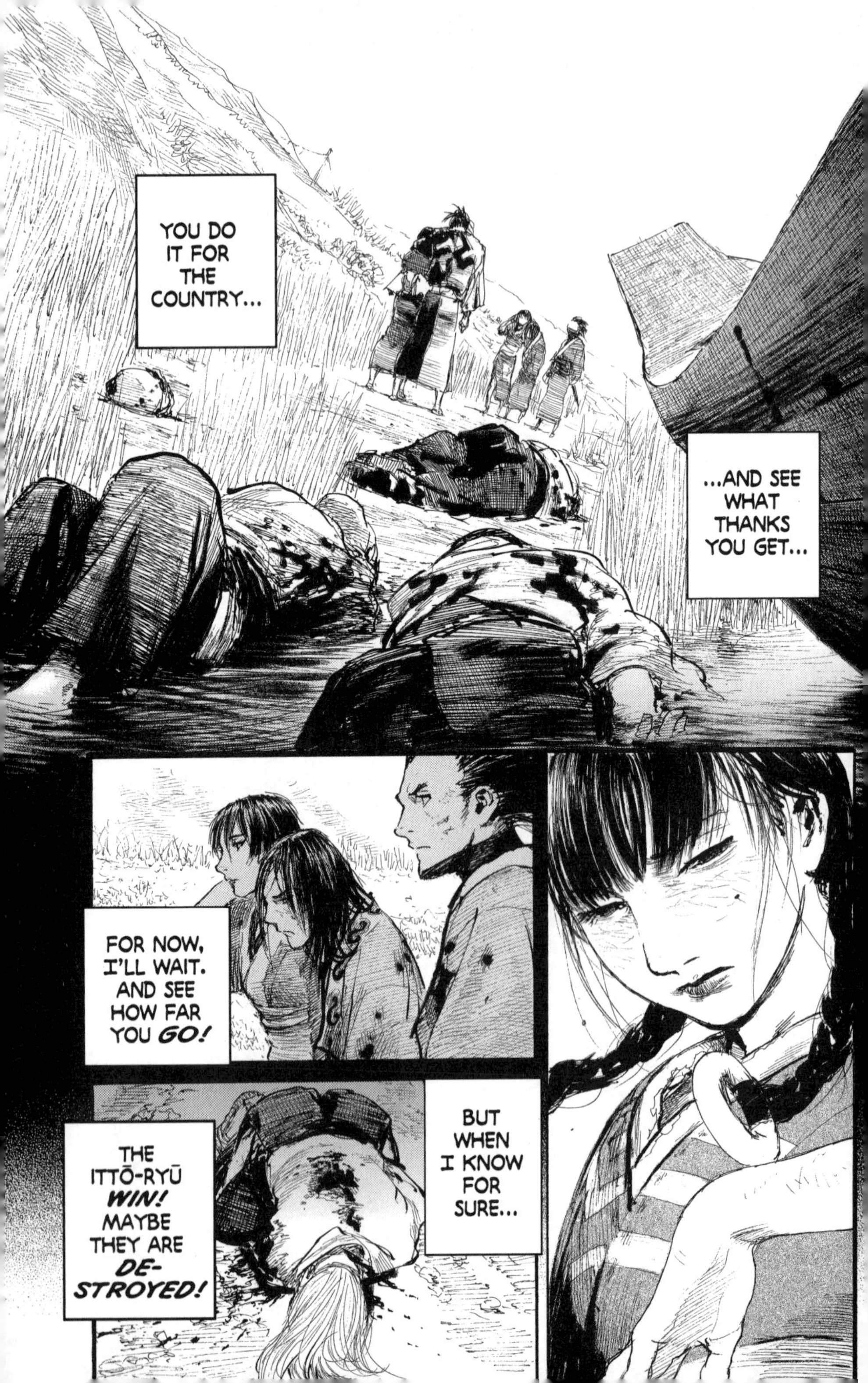

YOU DO IT FOR THE COUNTRY...
...AND SEE WHAT THANKS YOU GET...
FOR NOW, I'LL WAIT. AND SEE HOW FAR YOU *GO!*
THE ITTŌ-RYŪ *WIN!* MAYBE THEY ARE *DE-STROYED!*
BUT WHEN I KNOW FOR SURE...

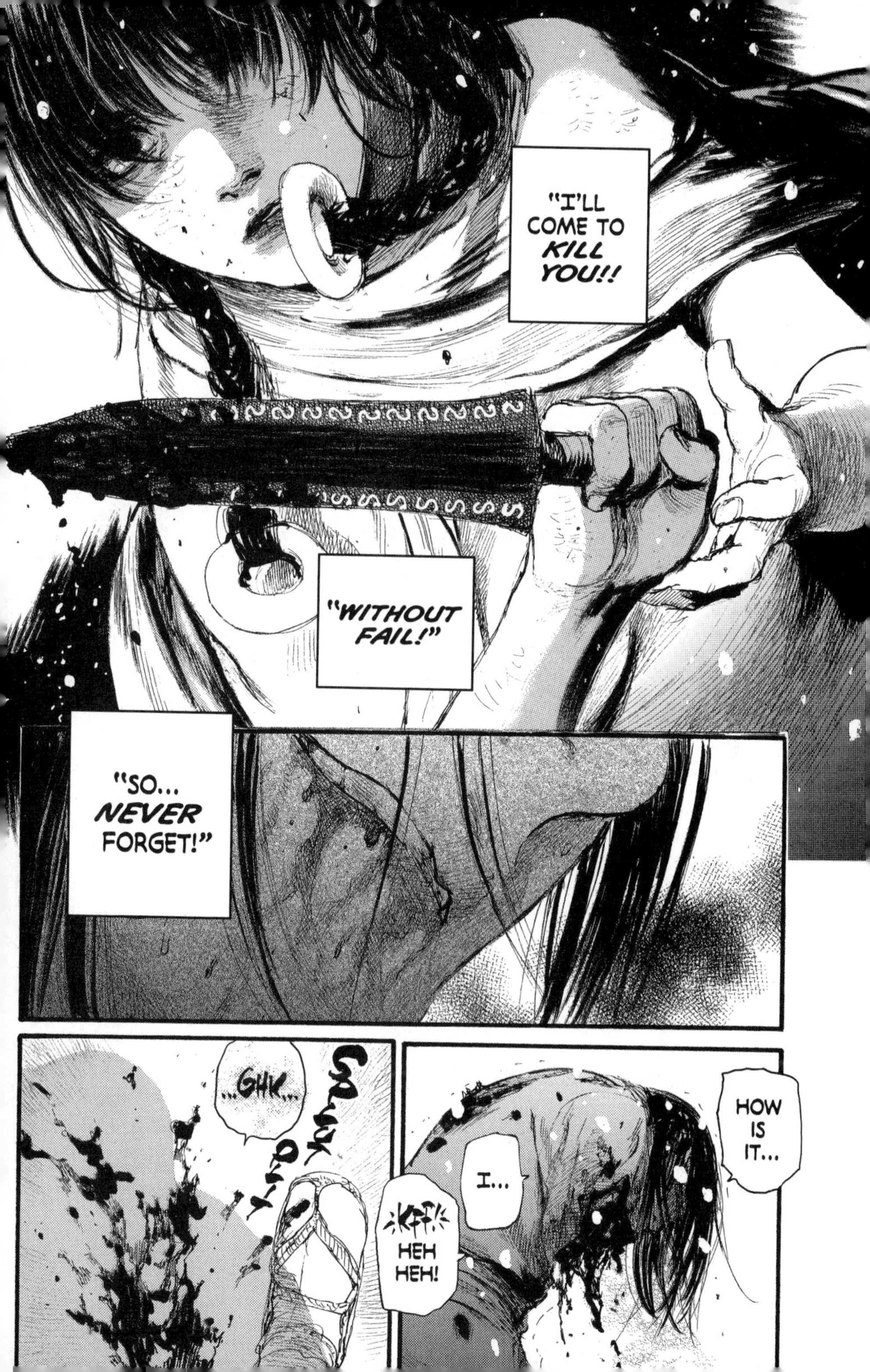
"I'LL COME TO KILL YOU!!
"WITHOUT FAIL!"
"SO... NEVER FORGET!"
...GHK...
SPLUK
HOW IS IT...
I...
KFF! HEH HEH!

...I COULD HAVE... FORGOTTEN...? ENTRUSTING MY AMBITIONS TO THE FUTURE...

TO MY DESCENDANTS...

SUCH FOOLISHNESS... SUCH SINFULNESS...

MANJI!

EARLIER... BEFORE...

...THE BATTLE... I...

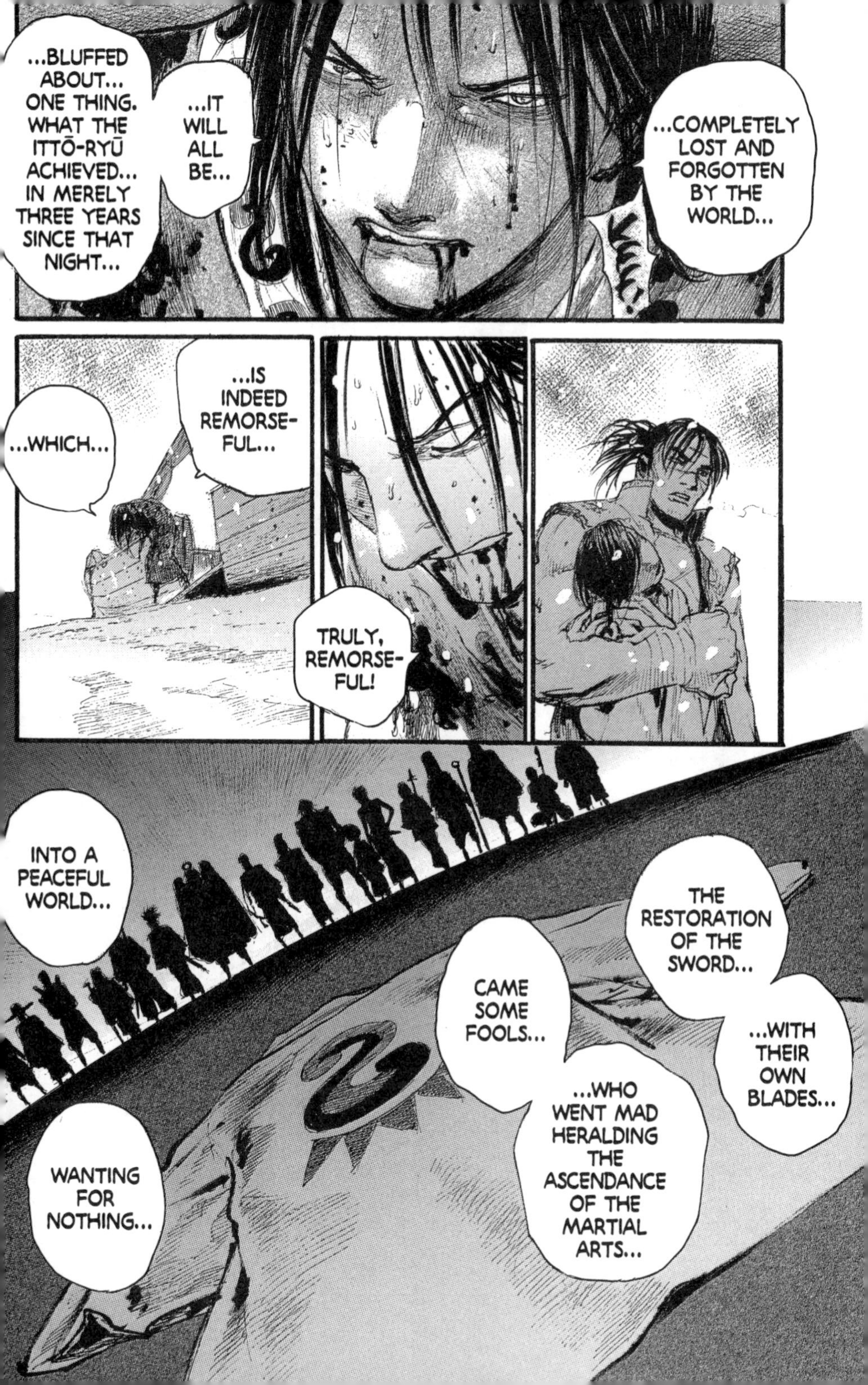
...BLUFFED ABOUT... ONE THING. WHAT THE ITTŌ-RYŪ ACHIEVED... IN MERELY THREE YEARS SINCE THAT NIGHT...
...IT WILL ALL BE...
...COMPLETELY LOST AND FORGOTTEN BY THE WORLD...
...WHICH...
...IS INDEED REMORSE-FUL...
TRULY, REMORSE-FUL!
INTO A PEACEFUL WORLD...
WANTING FOR NOTHING...
CAME SOME FOOLS...
...WHO WENT MAD HERALDING THE ASCENDANCE OF THE MARTIAL ARTS...
THE RESTORATION OF THE SWORD...
...WITH THEIR OWN BLADES...

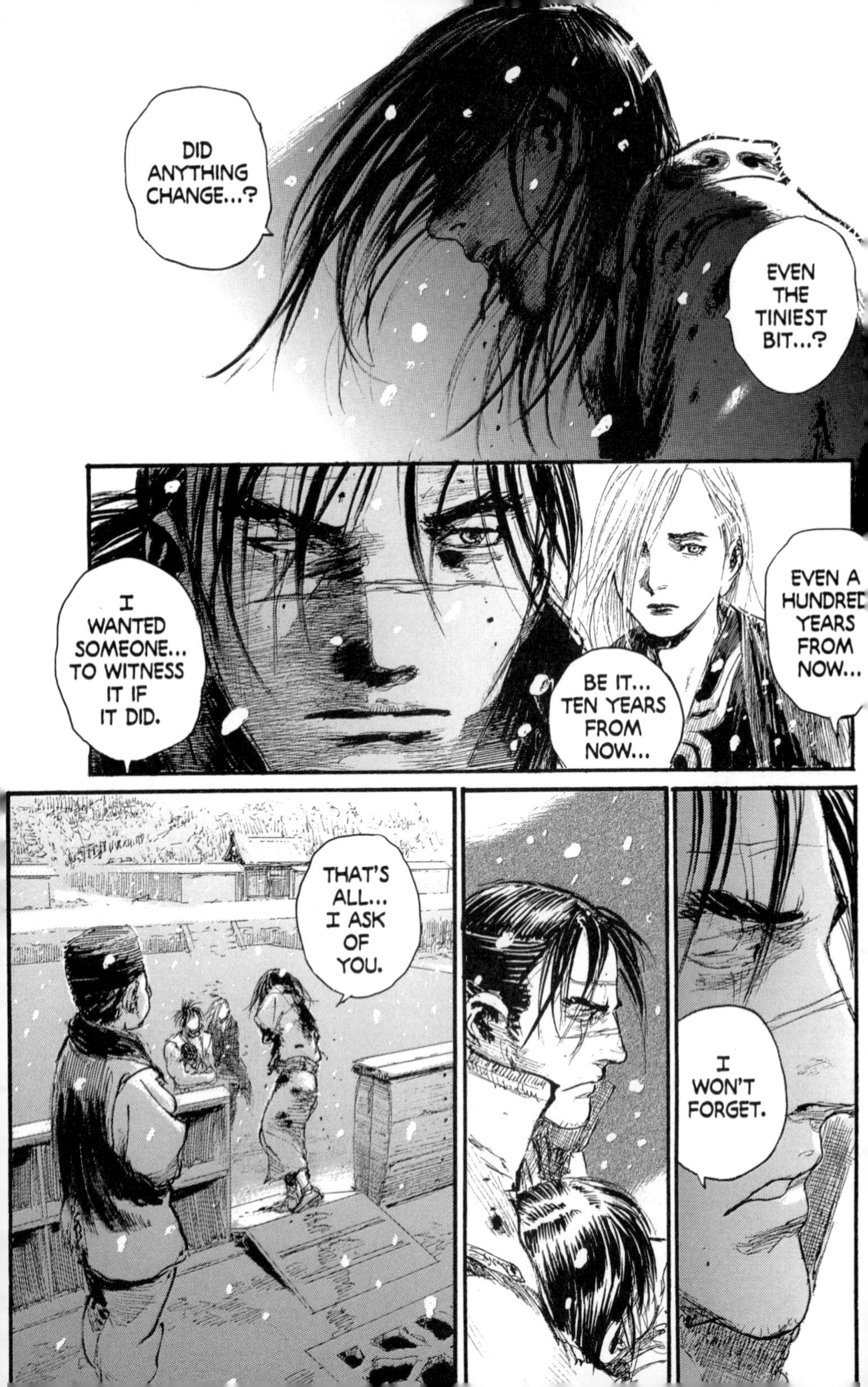
DID ANYTHING CHANGE...?
EVEN THE TINIEST BIT...?
I WANTED SOMEONE... TO WITNESS IT IF IT DID.
BE IT... TEN YEARS FROM NOW...
EVEN A HUNDRED YEARS FROM NOW...
THAT'S ALL... I ASK OF YOU.
I WON'T FORGET.

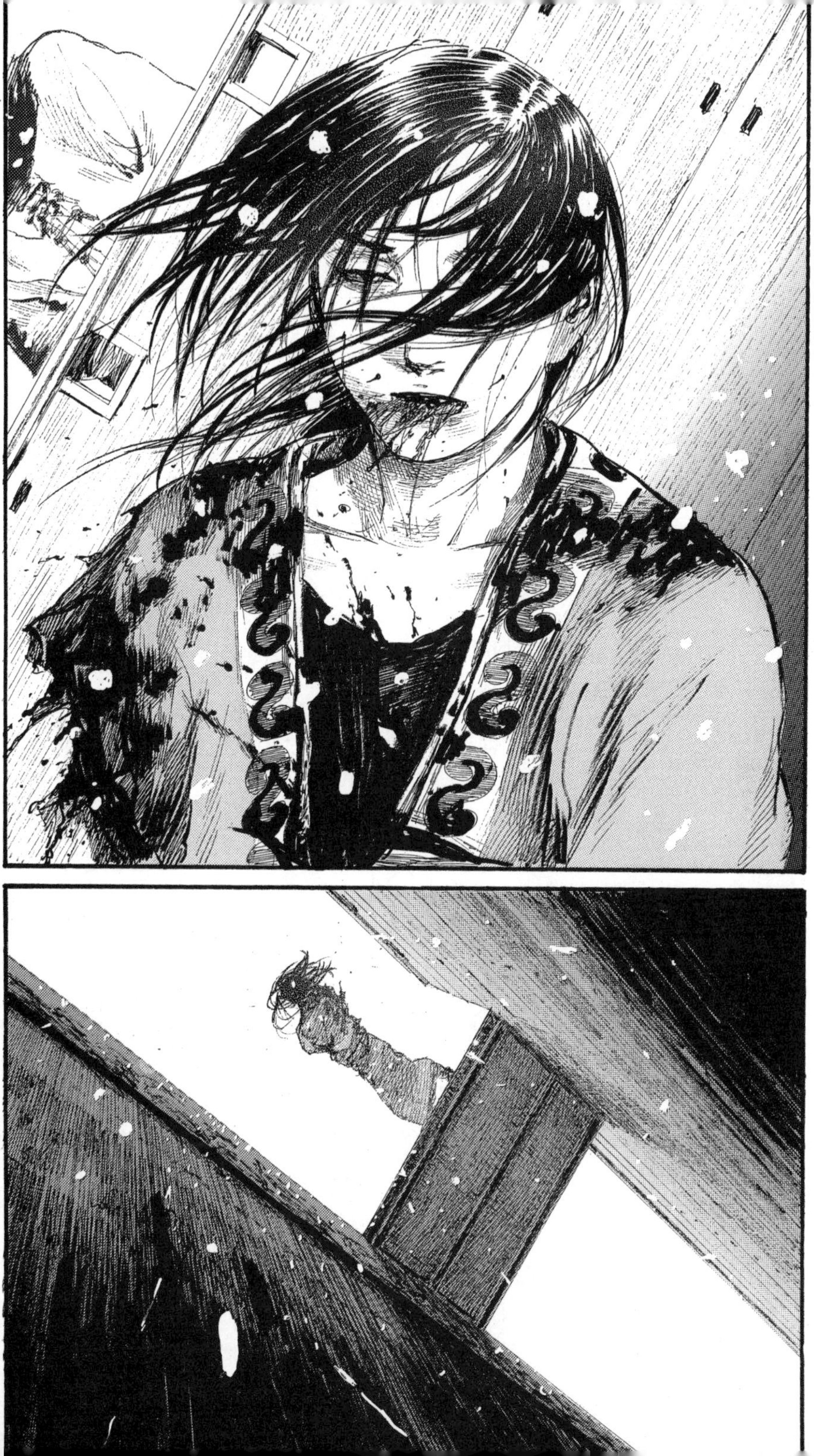

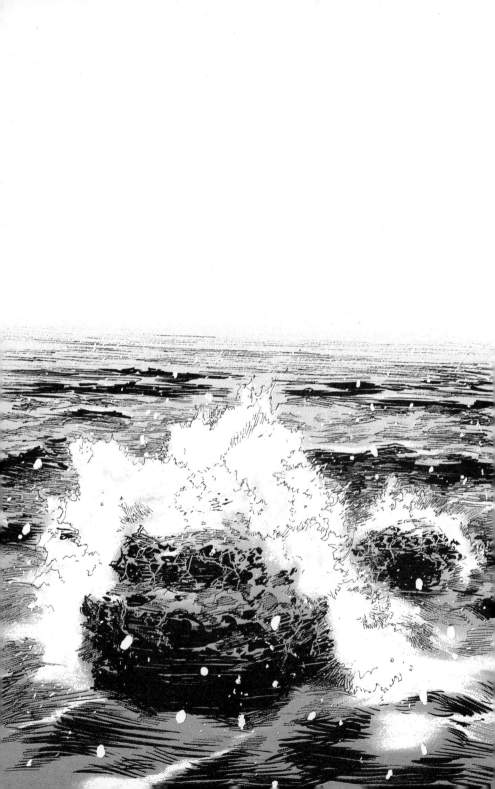

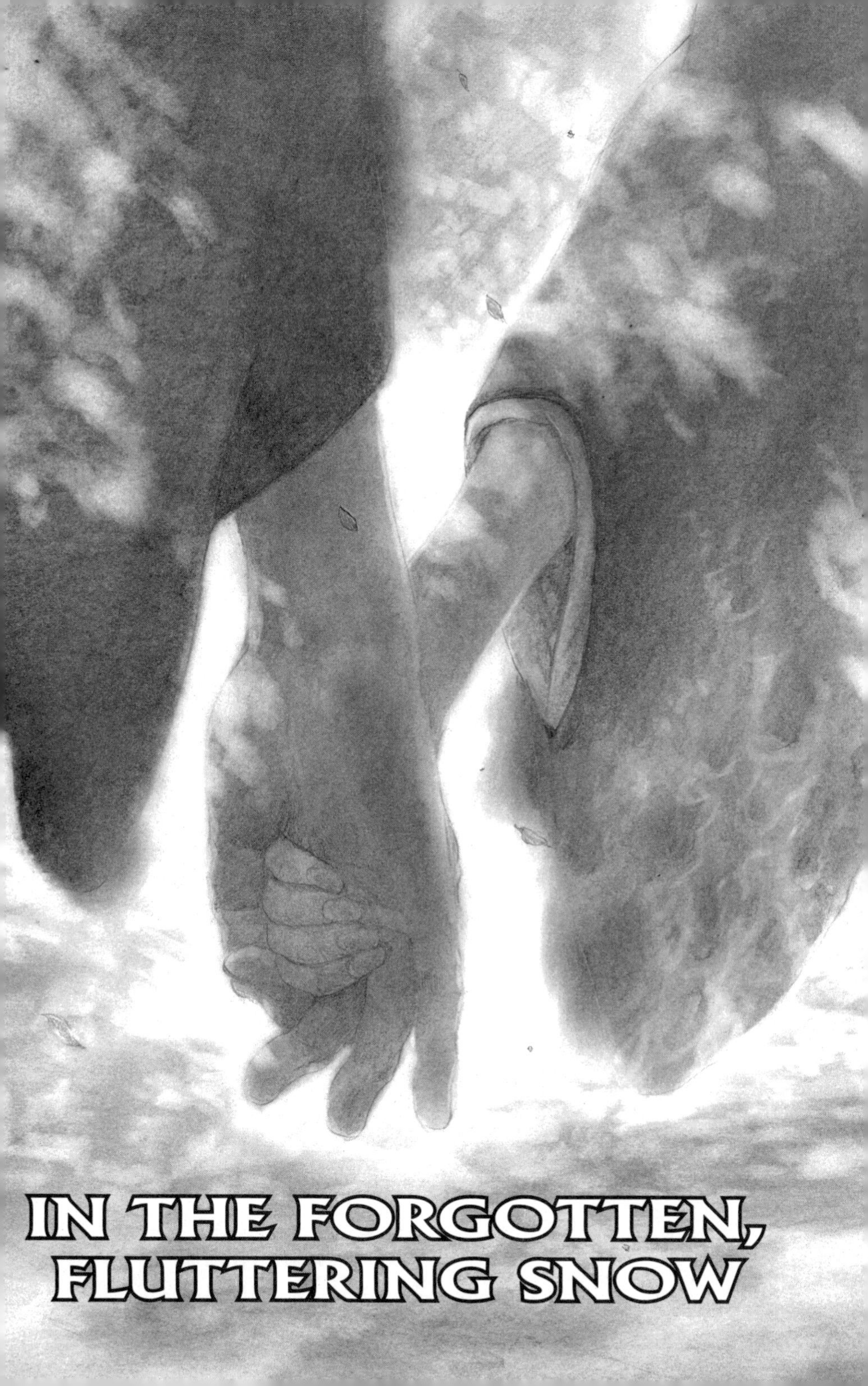
IN THE FORGOTTEN,
FLUTTERING SNOW

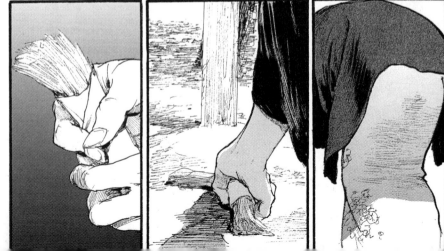

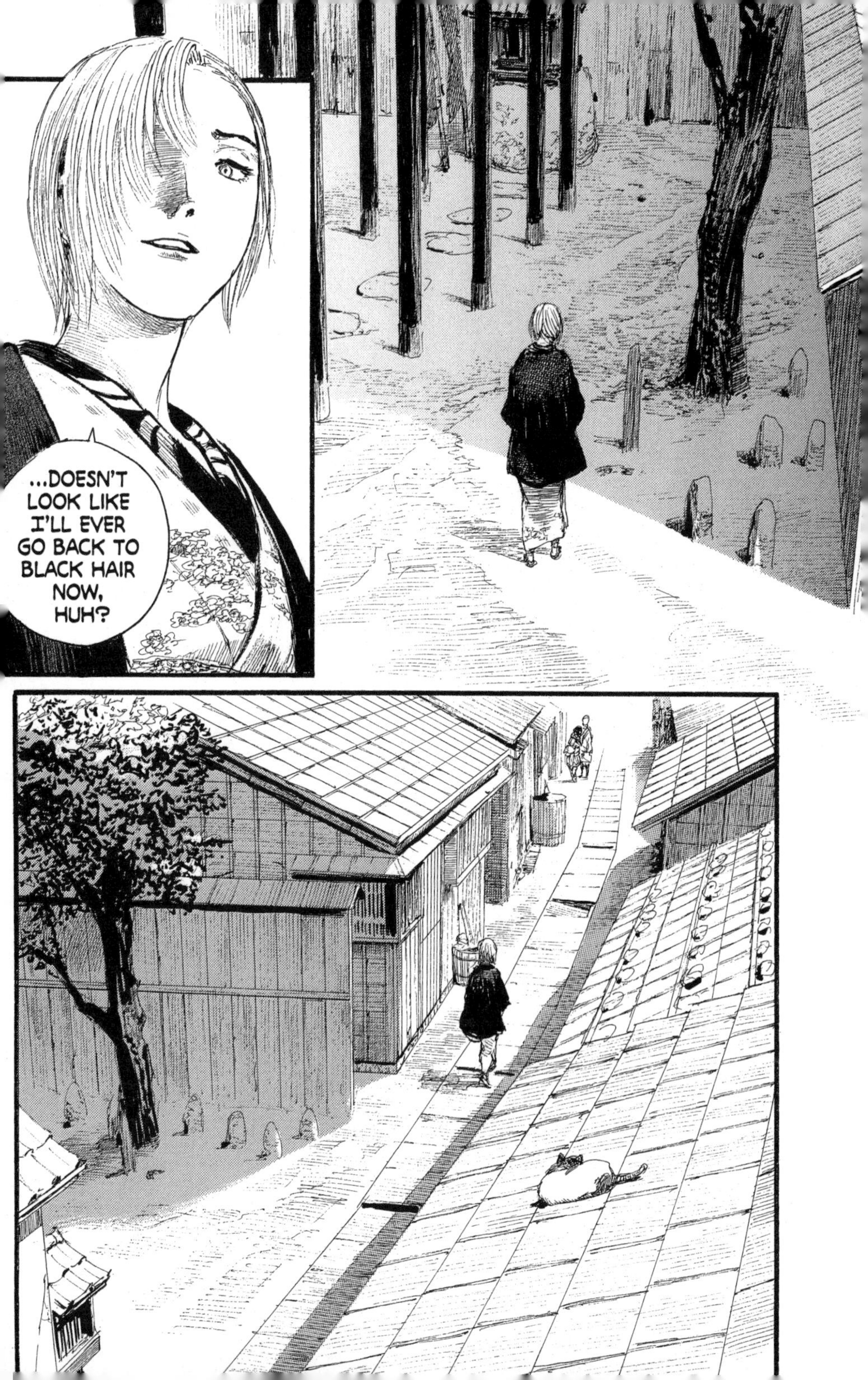
...DOESN'T LOOK LIKE I'LL EVER GO BACK TO BLACK HAIR NOW, HUH?

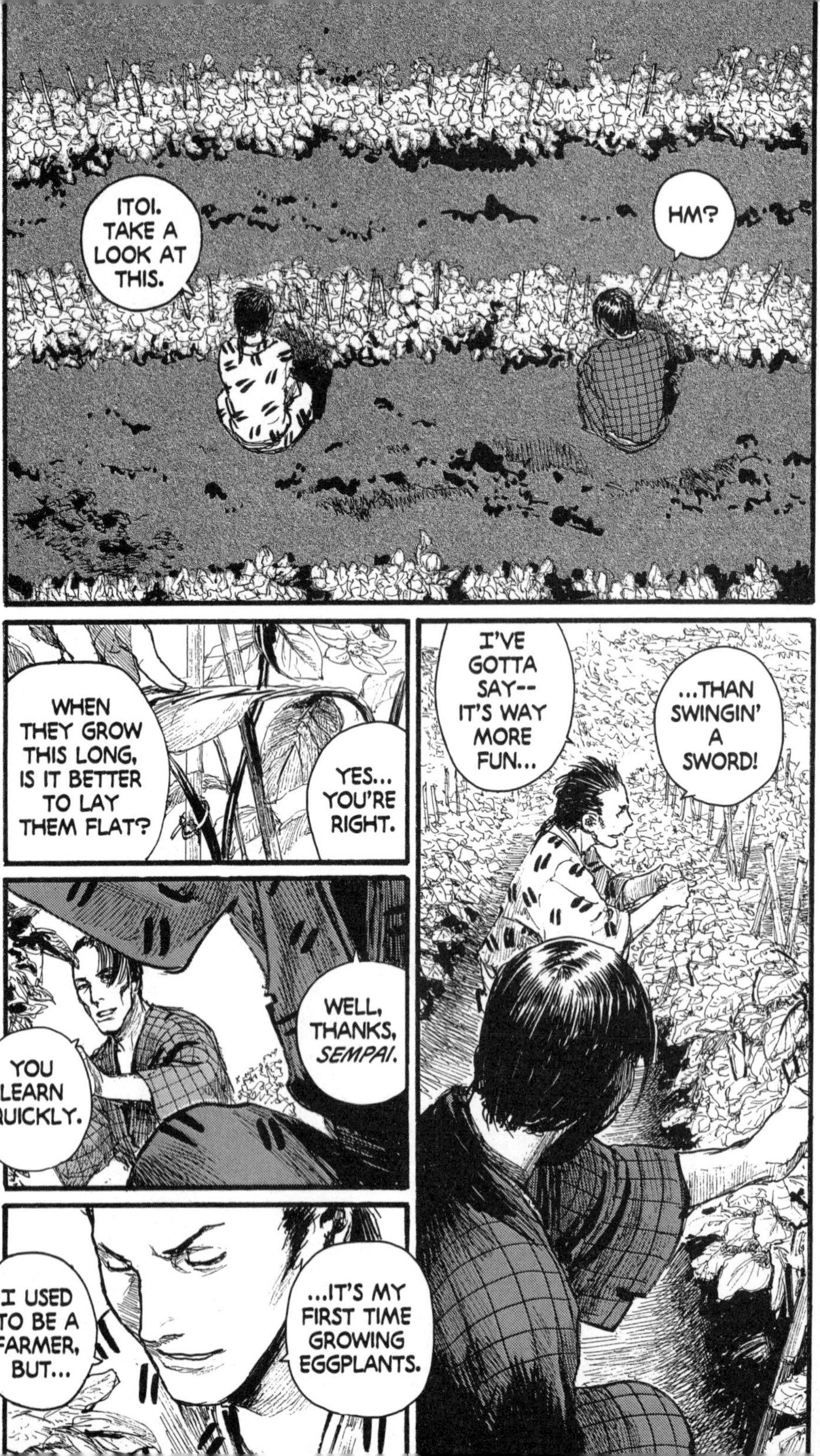
ITOI. TAKE A LOOK AT THIS.
HM?
WHEN THEY GROW THIS LONG, IS IT BETTER TO LAY THEM FLAT?
YES... YOU'RE RIGHT.
YOU LEARN QUICKLY.
WELL, THANKS, *SEMPAI*.
I USED TO BE A FARMER, BUT...
...IT'S MY FIRST TIME GROWING EGGPLANTS.
I'VE GOTTA SAY-- IT'S WAY MORE FUN...
...THAN SWINGIN' A SWORD!

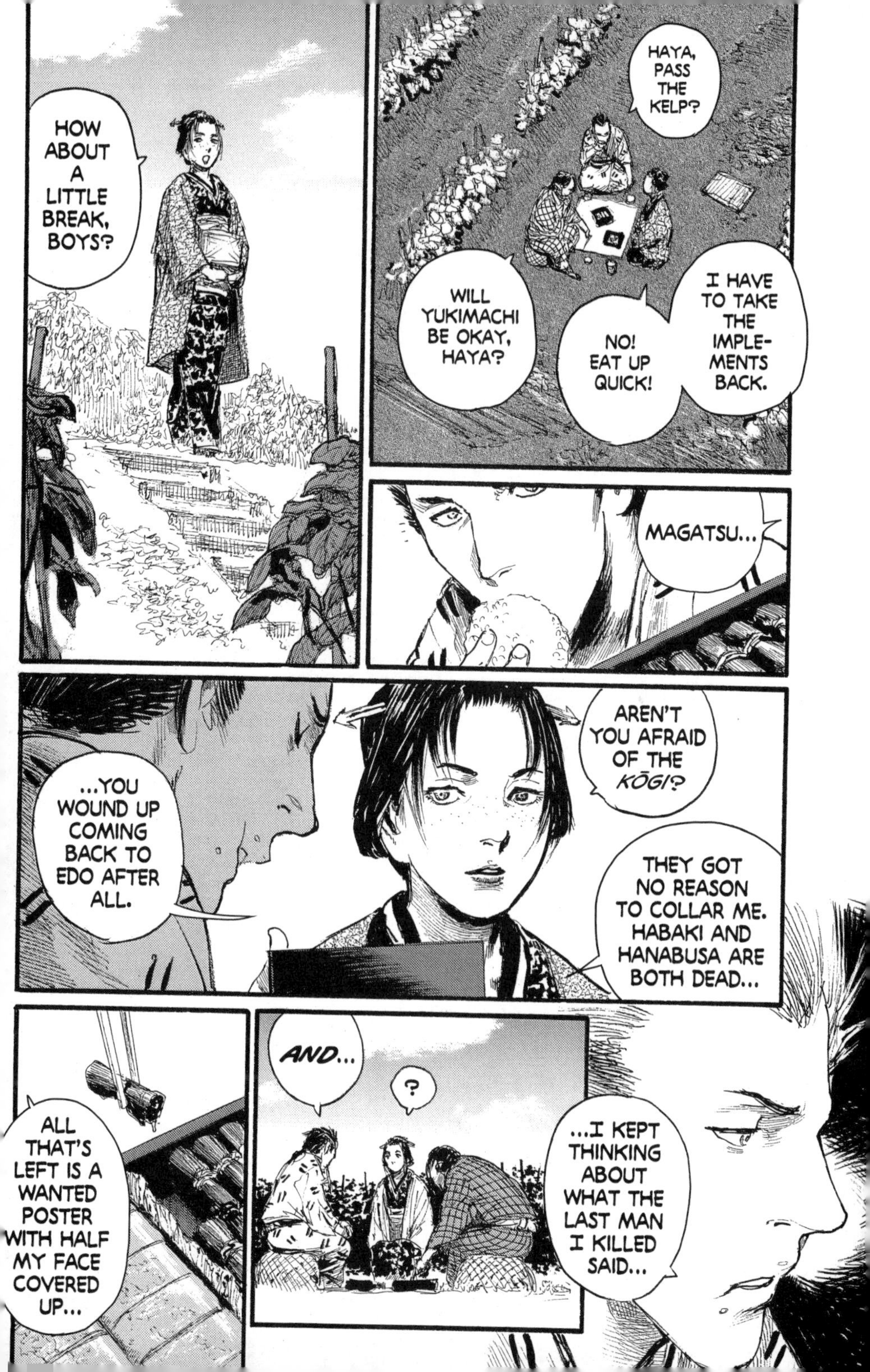
HOW ABOUT A LITTLE BREAK, BOYS?
HAYA, PASS THE KELP?
WILL YUKIMACHI BE OKAY, HAYA?
NO! EAT UP QUICK!
I HAVE TO TAKE THE IMPLE-MENTS BACK.
MAGATSU...
...YOU WOUND UP COMING BACK TO EDO AFTER ALL.
AREN'T YOU AFRAID OF THE *KŌGI*?
THEY GOT NO REASON TO COLLAR ME. HABAKI AND HANABUSA ARE BOTH DEAD...
ALL THAT'S LEFT IS A WANTED POSTER WITH HALF MY FACE COVERED UP...
AND...
?
...I KEPT THINKING ABOUT WHAT THE LAST MAN I KILLED SAID...

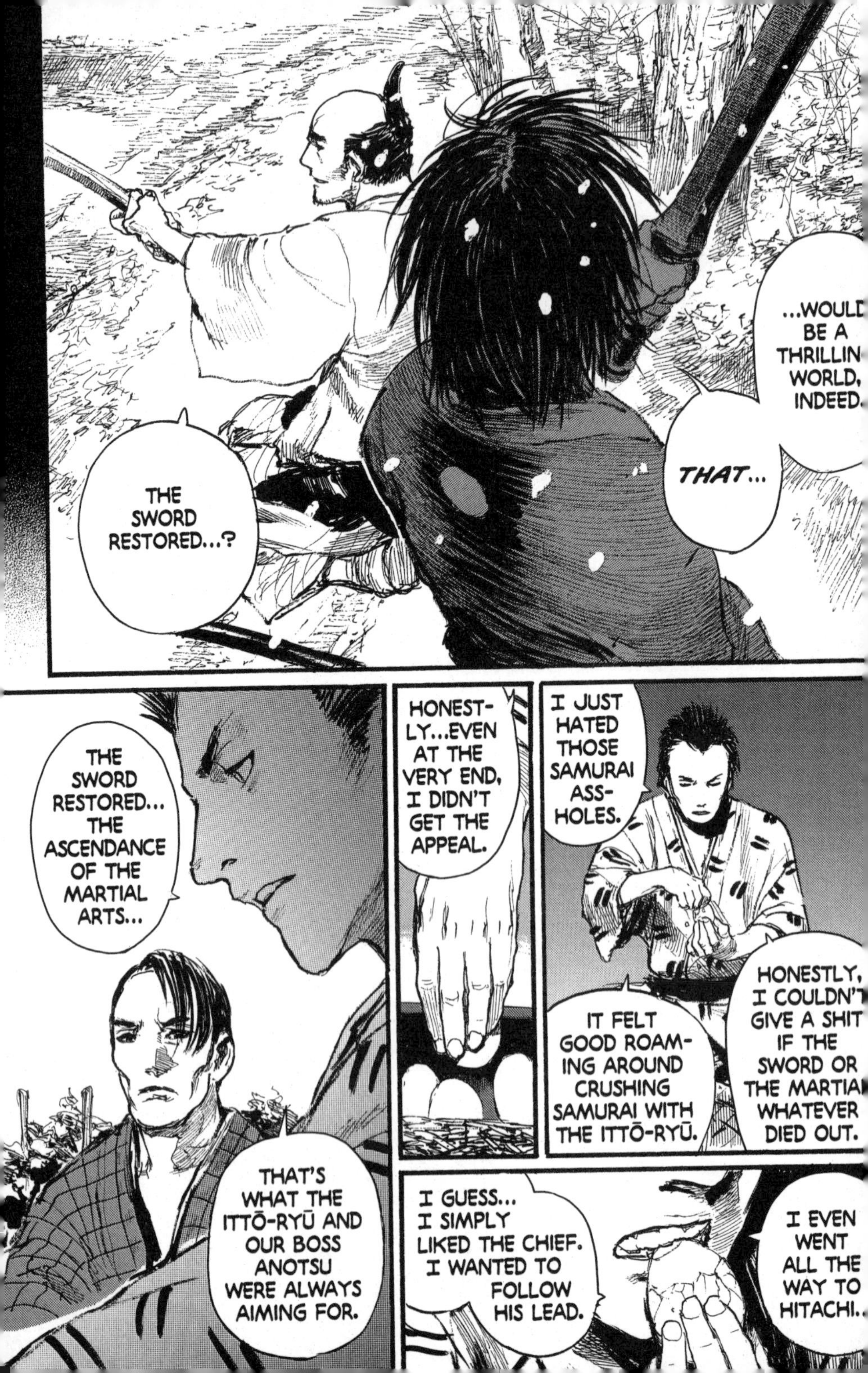
THE SWORD RESTORED...?
THAT...
...WOULD BE A THRILLIN WORLD, INDEED.
THE SWORD RESTORED... THE ASCENDANCE OF THE MARTIAL ARTS...
THAT'S WHAT THE ITTŌ-RYŪ AND OUR BOSS ANOTSU WERE ALWAYS AIMING FOR.
HONESTLY...EVEN AT THE VERY END, I DIDN'T GET THE APPEAL.
I JUST HATED THOSE SAMURAI ASSHOLES.
IT FELT GOOD ROAMING AROUND CRUSHING SAMURAI WITH THE ITTŌ-RYŪ.
HONESTLY, I COULDN'T GIVE A SHIT IF THE SWORD OR THE MARTIAL WHATEVER DIED OUT.
I GUESS... I SIMPLY LIKED THE CHIEF. I WANTED TO FOLLOW HIS LEAD.
I EVEN WENT ALL THE WAY TO HITACHI...

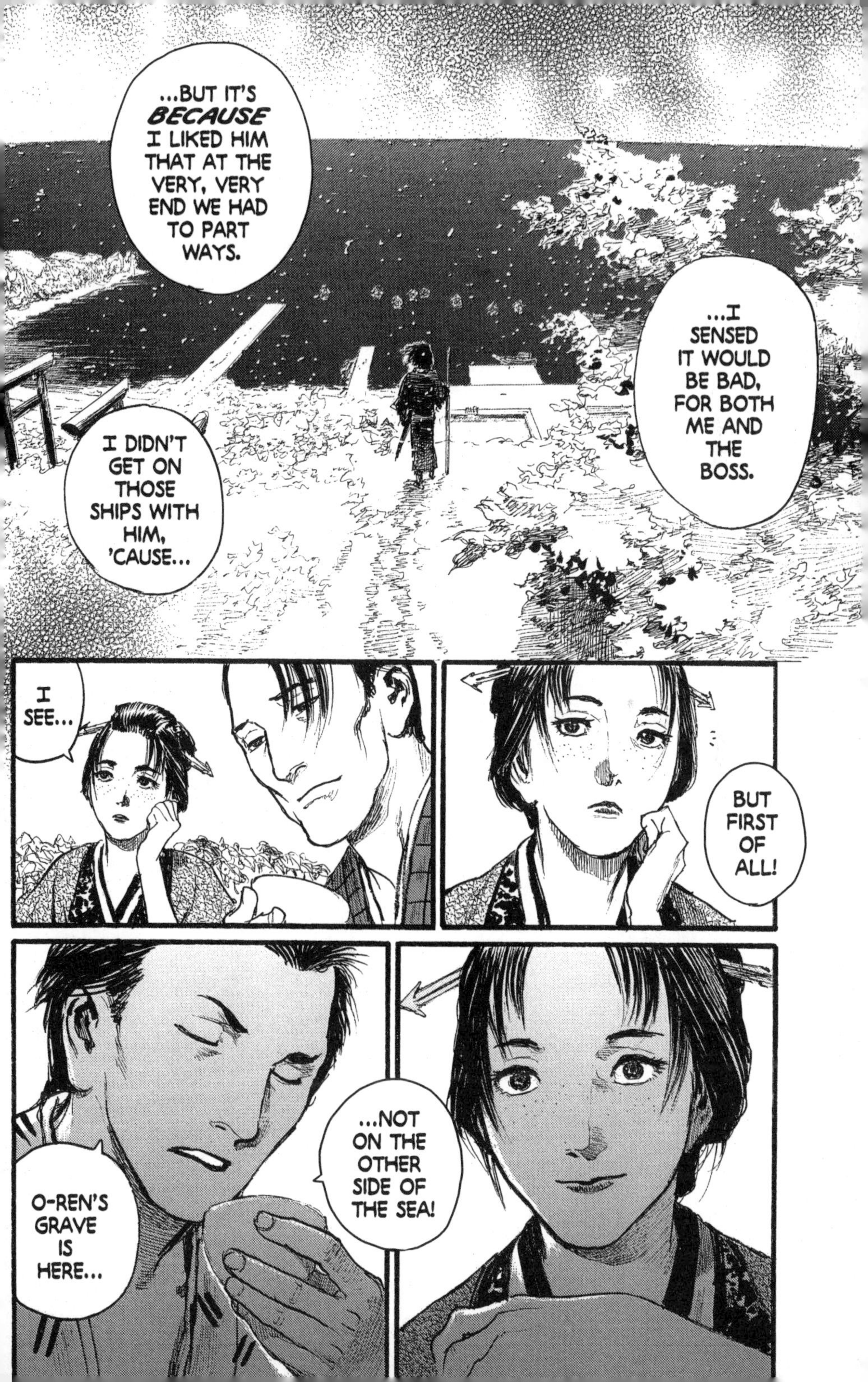
...BUT IT'S ***BECAUSE*** I LIKED HIM THAT AT THE VERY, VERY END WE HAD TO PART WAYS.
I DIDN'T GET ON THOSE SHIPS WITH HIM, 'CAUSE...
...I SENSED IT WOULD BE BAD, FOR BOTH ME AND THE BOSS.
I SEE...
BUT FIRST OF ALL!
O-REN'S GRAVE IS HERE...
...NOT ON THE OTHER SIDE OF THE SEA!

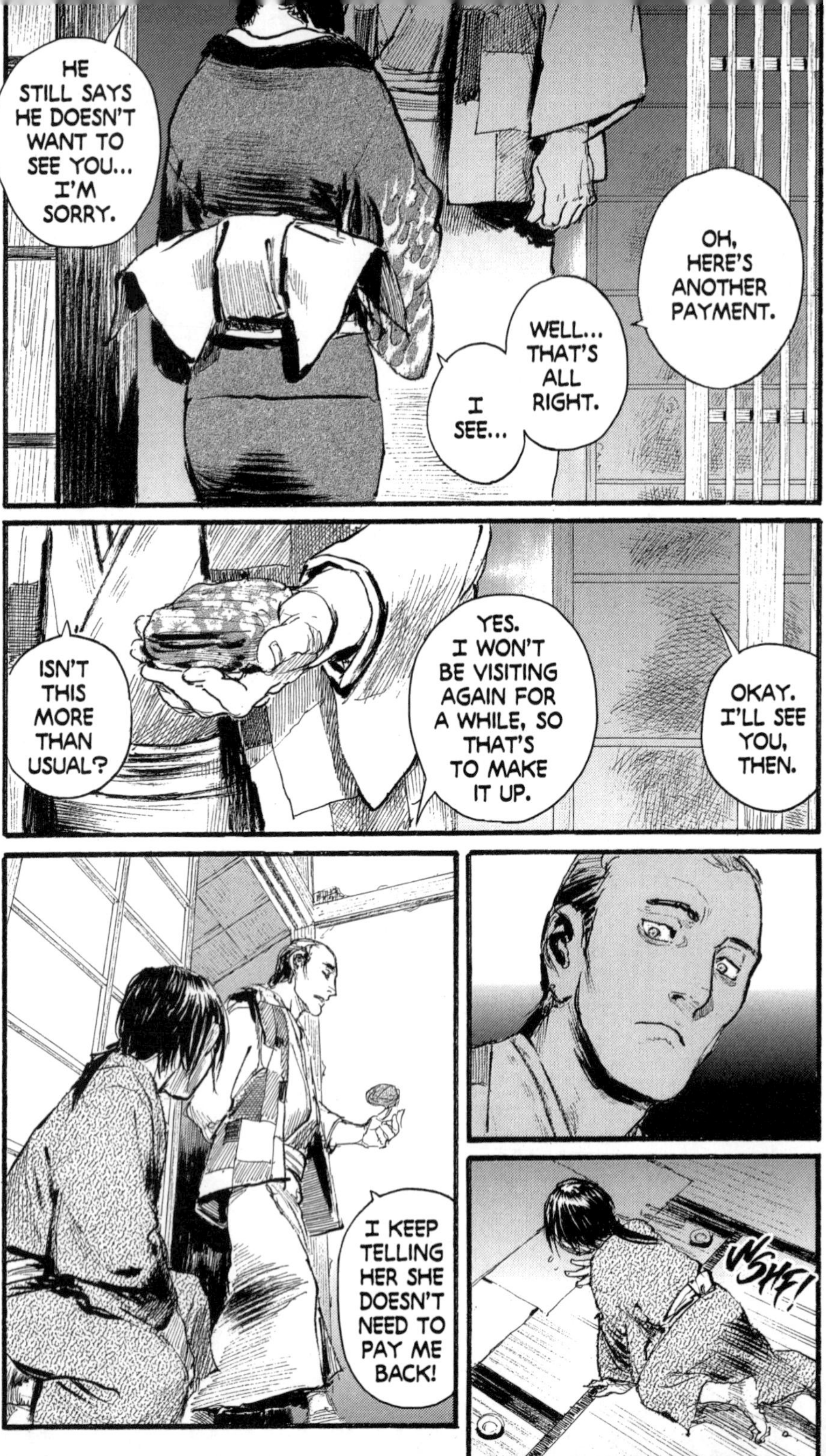
HE STILL SAYS HE DOESN'T WANT TO SEE YOU... I'M SORRY.
I SEE...
WELL... THAT'S ALL RIGHT.
OH, HERE'S ANOTHER PAYMENT.
ISN'T THIS MORE THAN USUAL?
YES. I WON'T BE VISITING AGAIN FOR A WHILE, SO THAT'S TO MAKE IT UP.
OKAY. I'LL SEE YOU, THEN.
I KEEP TELLING HER SHE DOESN'T NEED TO PAY ME BACK!
VSHF!

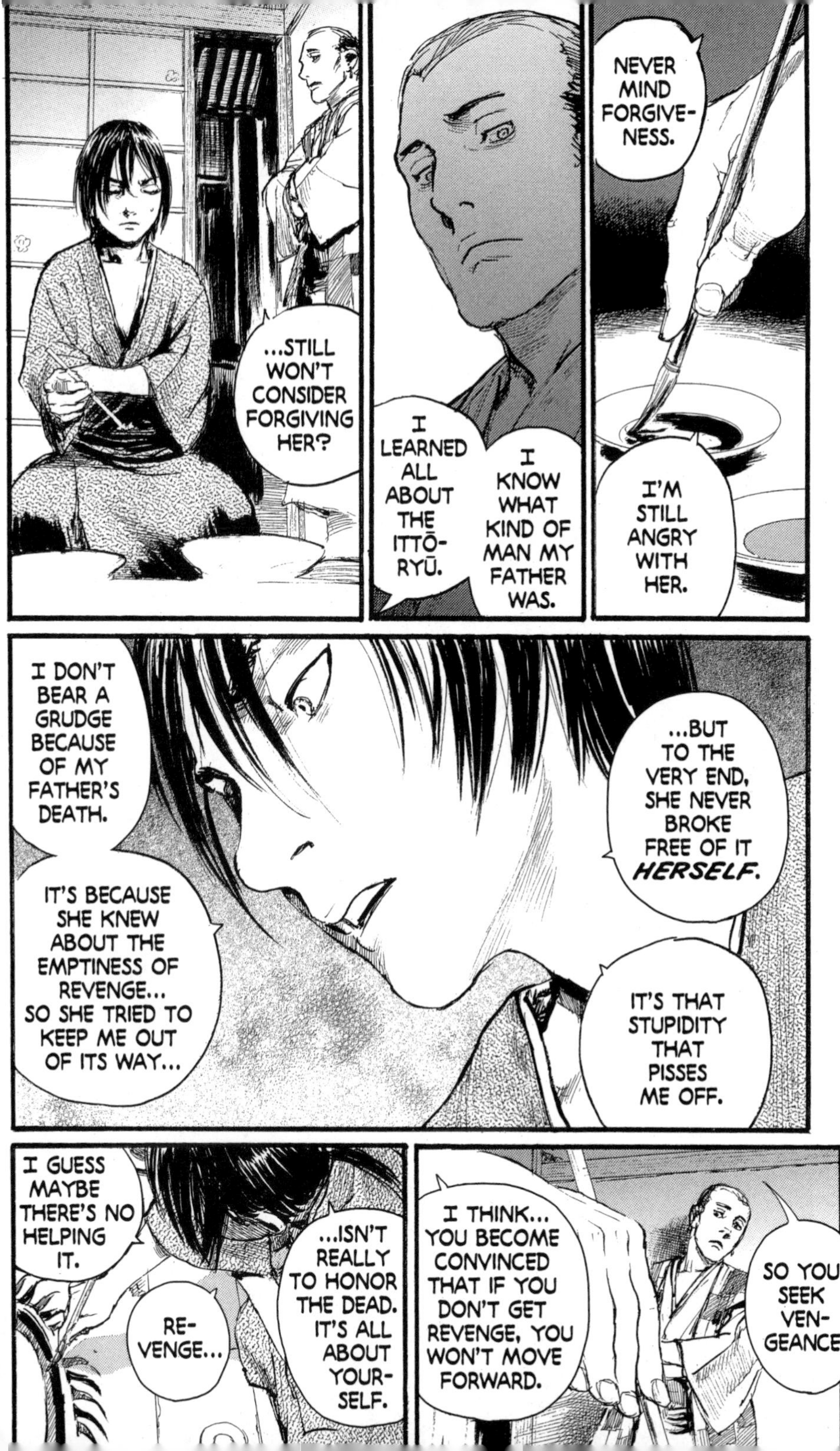
...STILL WON'T CONSIDER FORGIVING HER?
I LEARNED ALL ABOUT THE ITTŌ-RYŪ.
I KNOW WHAT KIND OF MAN MY FATHER WAS.
NEVER MIND FORGIVE-NESS.
I'M STILL ANGRY WITH HER.
I DON'T BEAR A GRUDGE BECAUSE OF MY FATHER'S DEATH.
IT'S BECAUSE SHE KNEW ABOUT THE EMPTINESS OF REVENGE... SO SHE TRIED TO KEEP ME OUT OF ITS WAY...
...BUT TO THE VERY END, SHE NEVER BROKE FREE OF IT ***HERSELF***.
IT'S THAT STUPIDITY THAT PISSES ME OFF.
I GUESS MAYBE THERE'S NO HELPING IT.
RE-VENGE...
...ISN'T REALLY TO HONOR THE DEAD. IT'S ALL ABOUT YOUR-SELF.
I THINK... YOU BECOME CONVINCED THAT IF YOU DON'T GET REVENGE, YOU WON'T MOVE FORWARD.
SO YOU SEEK VEN-GEANCE.

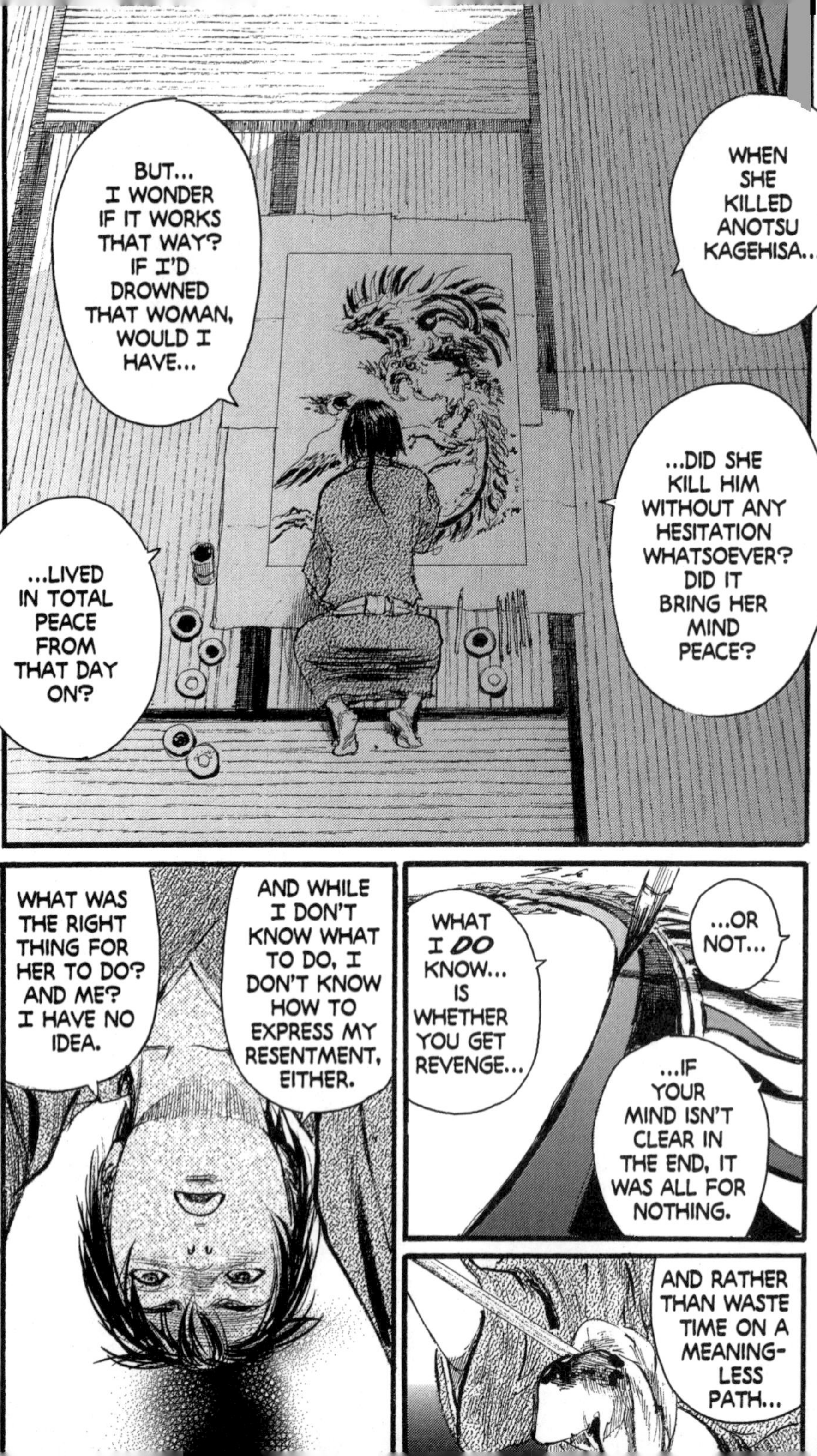
BUT... I WONDER IF IT WORKS THAT WAY? IF I'D DROWNED THAT WOMAN, WOULD I HAVE...
...LIVED IN TOTAL PEACE FROM THAT DAY ON?
WHEN SHE KILLED ANOTSU KAGEHISA...
...DID SHE KILL HIM WITHOUT ANY HESITATION WHATSOEVER? DID IT BRING HER MIND PEACE?
WHAT WAS THE RIGHT THING FOR HER TO DO? AND ME? I HAVE NO IDEA.
AND WHILE I DON'T KNOW WHAT TO DO, I DON'T KNOW HOW TO EXPRESS MY RESENTMENT, EITHER.
WHAT I *DO* KNOW... IS WHETHER YOU GET REVENGE...
...OR NOT...
...IF YOUR MIND ISN'T CLEAR IN THE END, IT WAS ALL FOR NOTHING.
AND RATHER THAN WASTE TIME ON A MEANING-LESS PATH...

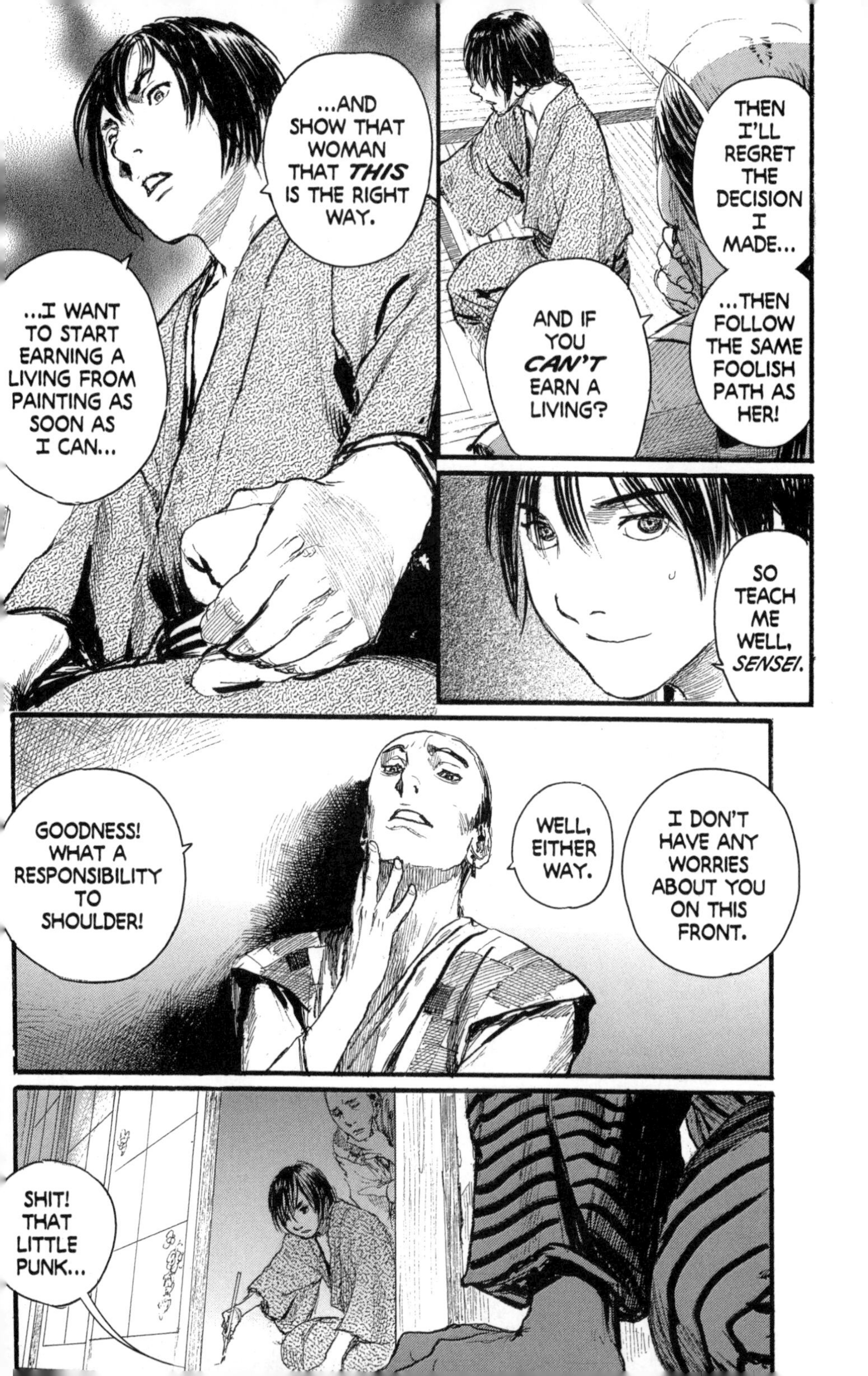
...I WANT TO START EARNING A LIVING FROM PAINTING AS SOON AS I CAN...
...AND SHOW THAT WOMAN THAT *THIS* IS THE RIGHT WAY.
AND IF YOU *CAN'T* EARN A LIVING?
THEN I'LL REGRET THE DECISION I MADE...
...THEN FOLLOW THE SAME FOOLISH PATH AS HER!
SO TEACH ME WELL, *SENSEI*.
GOODNESS! WHAT A RESPONSIBILITY TO SHOULDER!
WELL, EITHER WAY.
I DON'T HAVE ANY WORRIES ABOUT YOU ON THIS FRONT.
SHIT! THAT LITTLE PUNK...

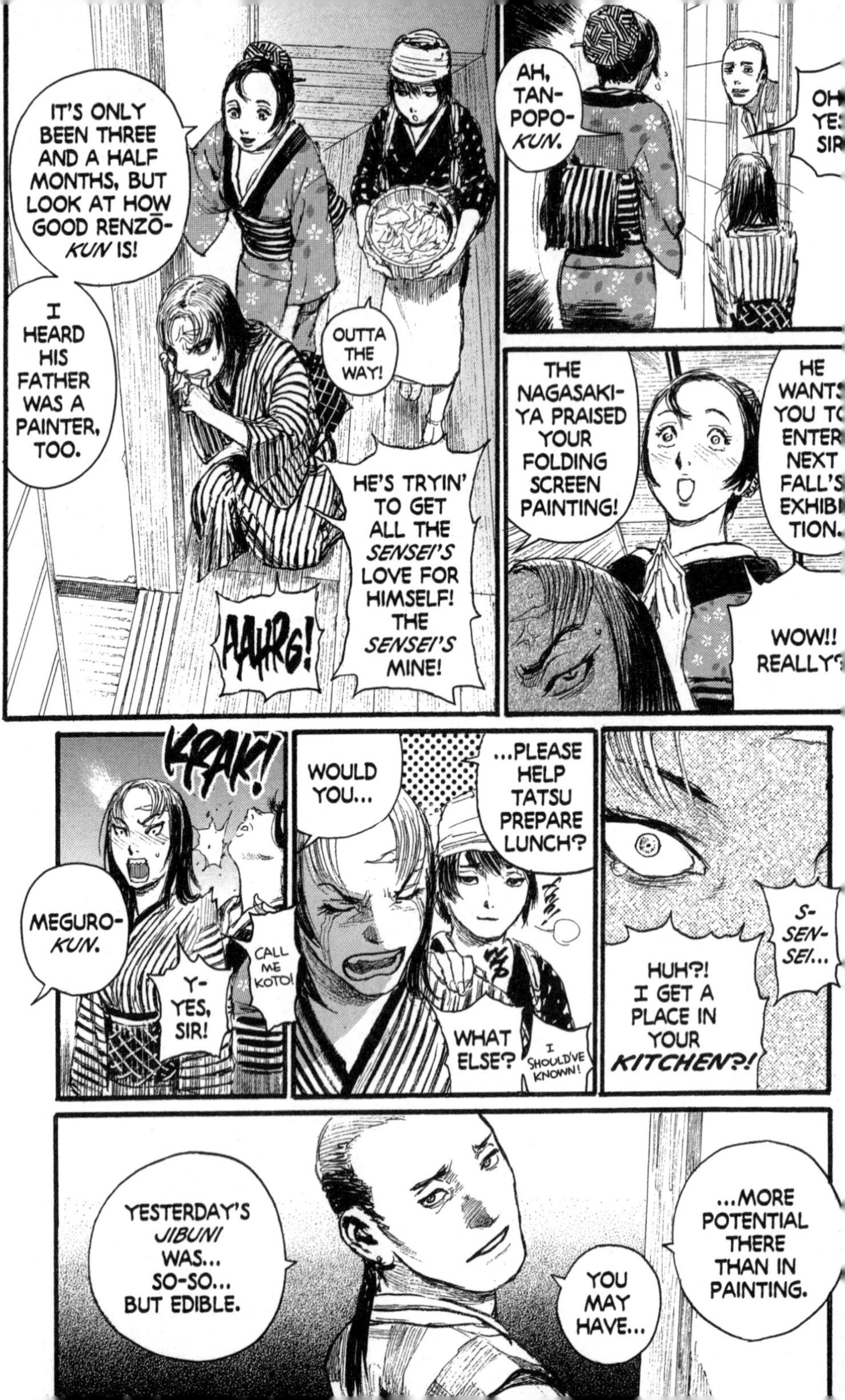
IT'S ONLY BEEN THREE AND A HALF MONTHS, BUT LOOK AT HOW GOOD RENZŌ-*KUN* IS!
I HEARD HIS FATHER WAS A PAINTER, TOO.
OUTTA THE WAY!
HE'S TRYIN' TO GET ALL THE *SENSEI'S* LOVE FOR HIMSELF! THE *SENSEI'S* MINE!
AAARG!
AH, TAN-POPO-*KUN*.
OH YES SIR
THE NAGASAKI-YA PRAISED YOUR FOLDING SCREEN PAINTING!
HE WANTS YOU TO ENTER NEXT FALL'S EXHIBITION.
WOW!! REALLY?
KRAK!
MEGURO-*KUN*.
Y-YES, SIR!
CALL ME KOTO!
WOULD YOU...
...PLEASE HELP TATSU PREPARE LUNCH?
WHAT ELSE?
I SHOULD'VE KNOWN!
S-SEN-SEI...
HUH?! I GET A PLACE IN YOUR *KITCHEN*?!
YESTERDAY'S *JIBUNI* WAS... SO-SO... BUT EDIBLE.
YOU MAY HAVE...
...MORE POTENTIAL THERE THAN IN PAINTING.

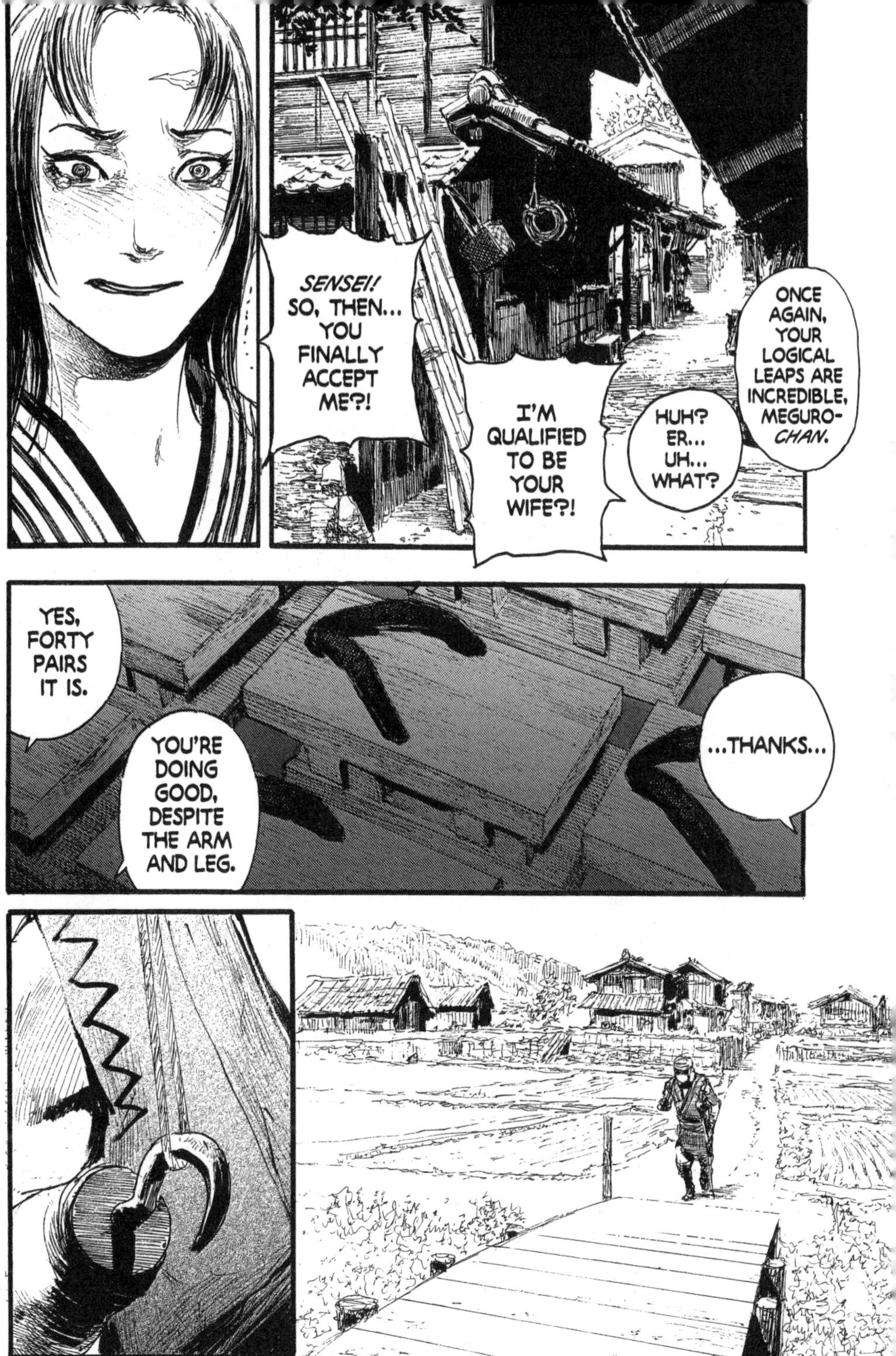
SENSEI!! SO, THEN... YOU FINALLY ACCEPT ME?!
I'M QUALIFIED TO BE YOUR WIFE?!
HUH? ER... UH... WHAT?
ONCE AGAIN, YOUR LOGICAL LEAPS ARE INCREDIBLE, MEGURO-CHAN.
YES, FORTY PAIRS IT IS.
YOU'RE DOING GOOD, DESPITE THE ARM AND LEG.
...THANKS...

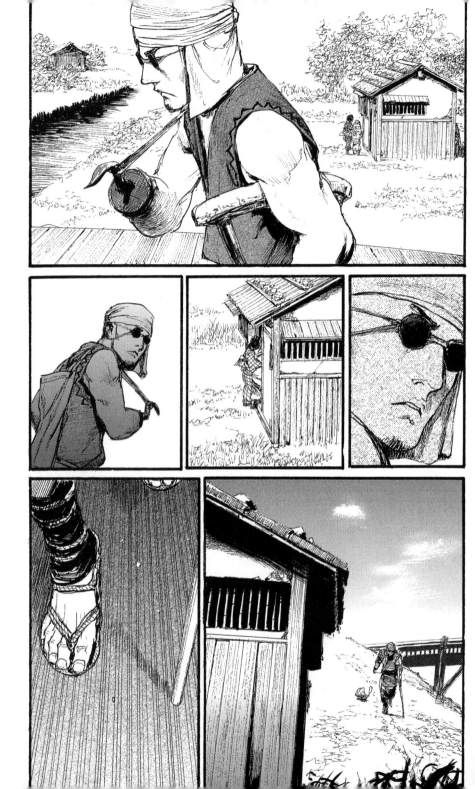

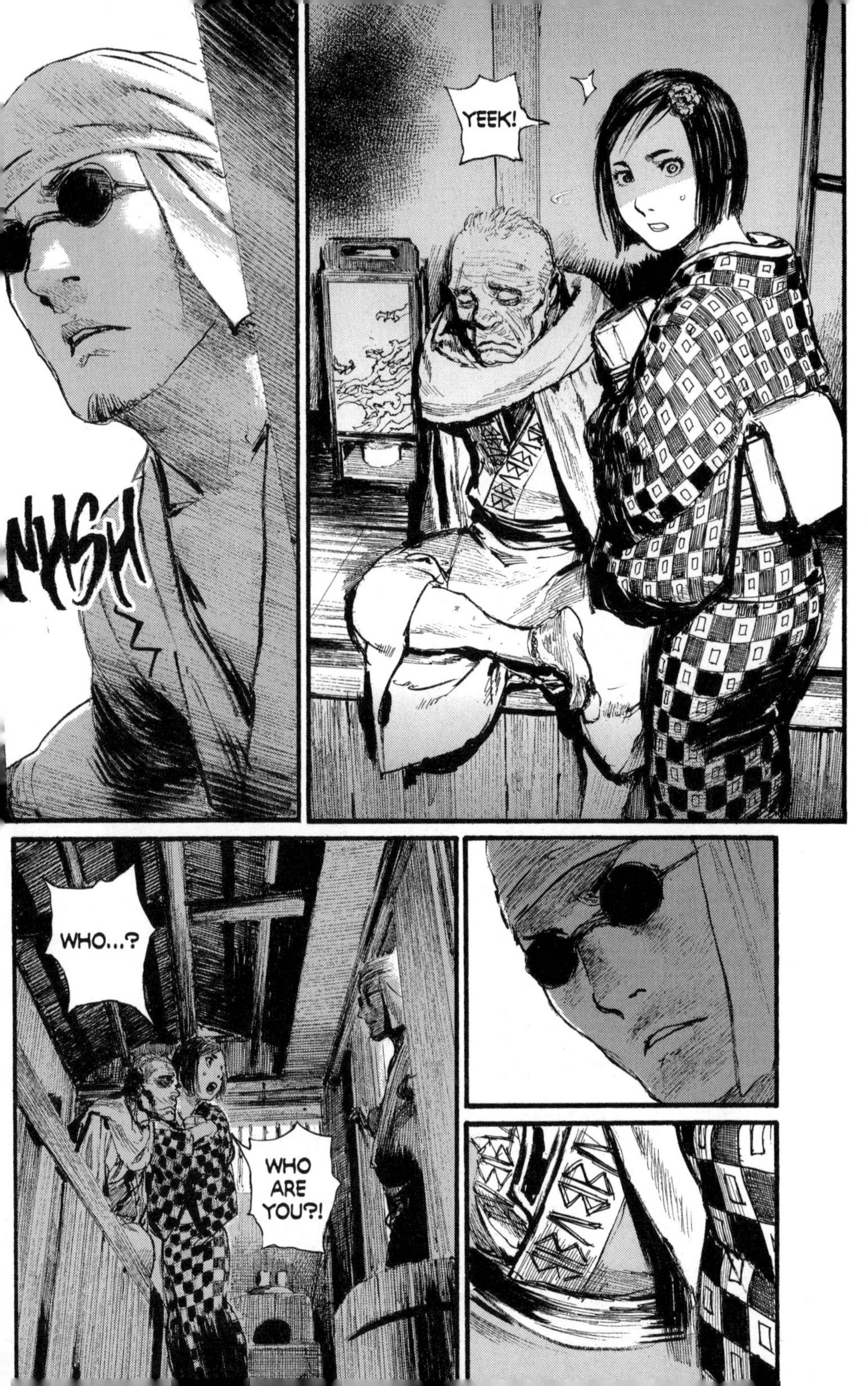
NYSH
YEEK!
WHO...?
WHO ARE YOU?!

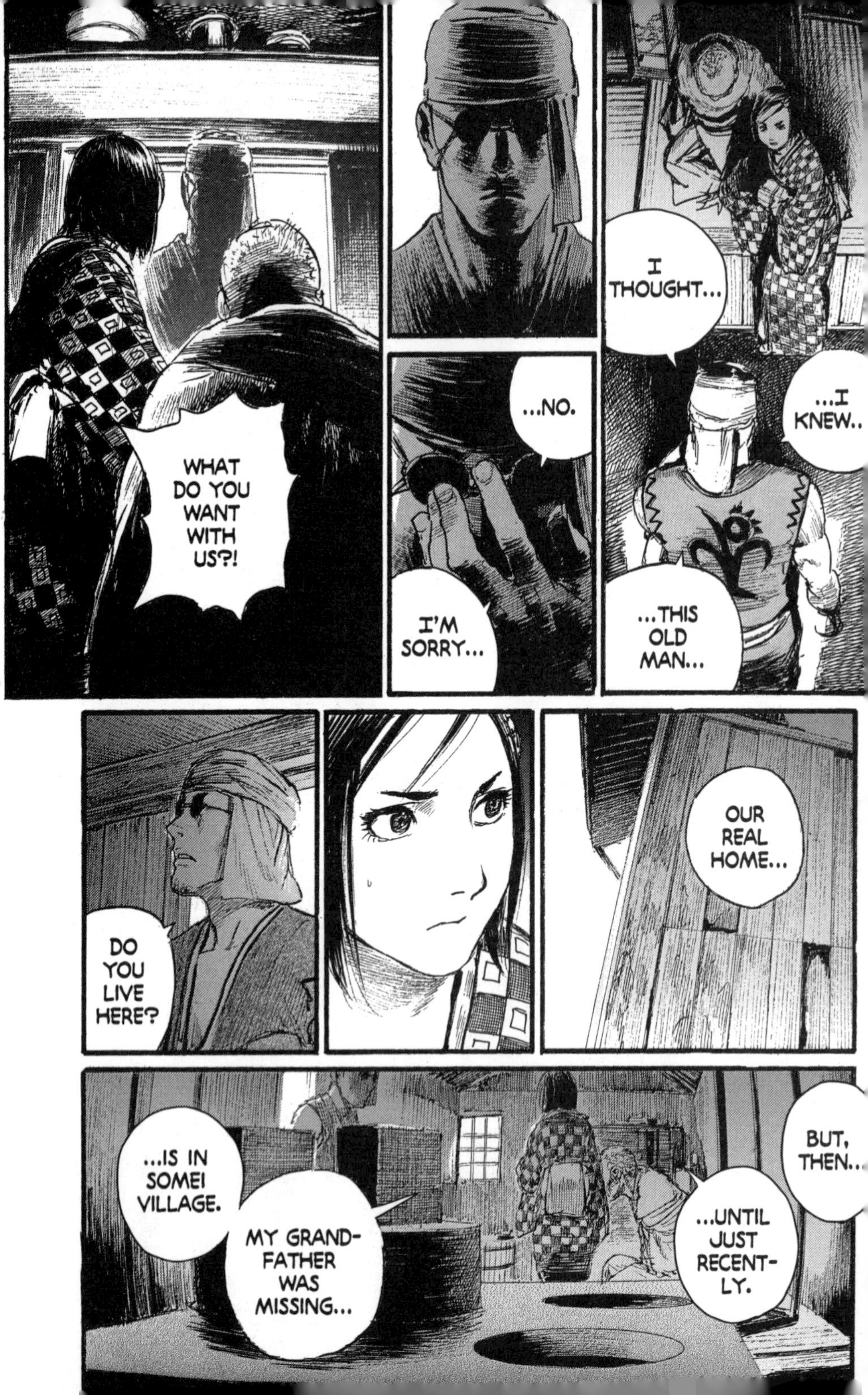
WHAT DO YOU WANT WITH US?!
...NO.
I'M SORRY...
I THOUGHT...
...I KNEW..
...THIS OLD MAN...
DO YOU LIVE HERE?
OUR REAL HOME...
...IS IN SOMEI VILLAGE.
MY GRAND-FATHER WAS MISSING...
...UNTIL JUST RECENT-LY.
BUT, THEN...

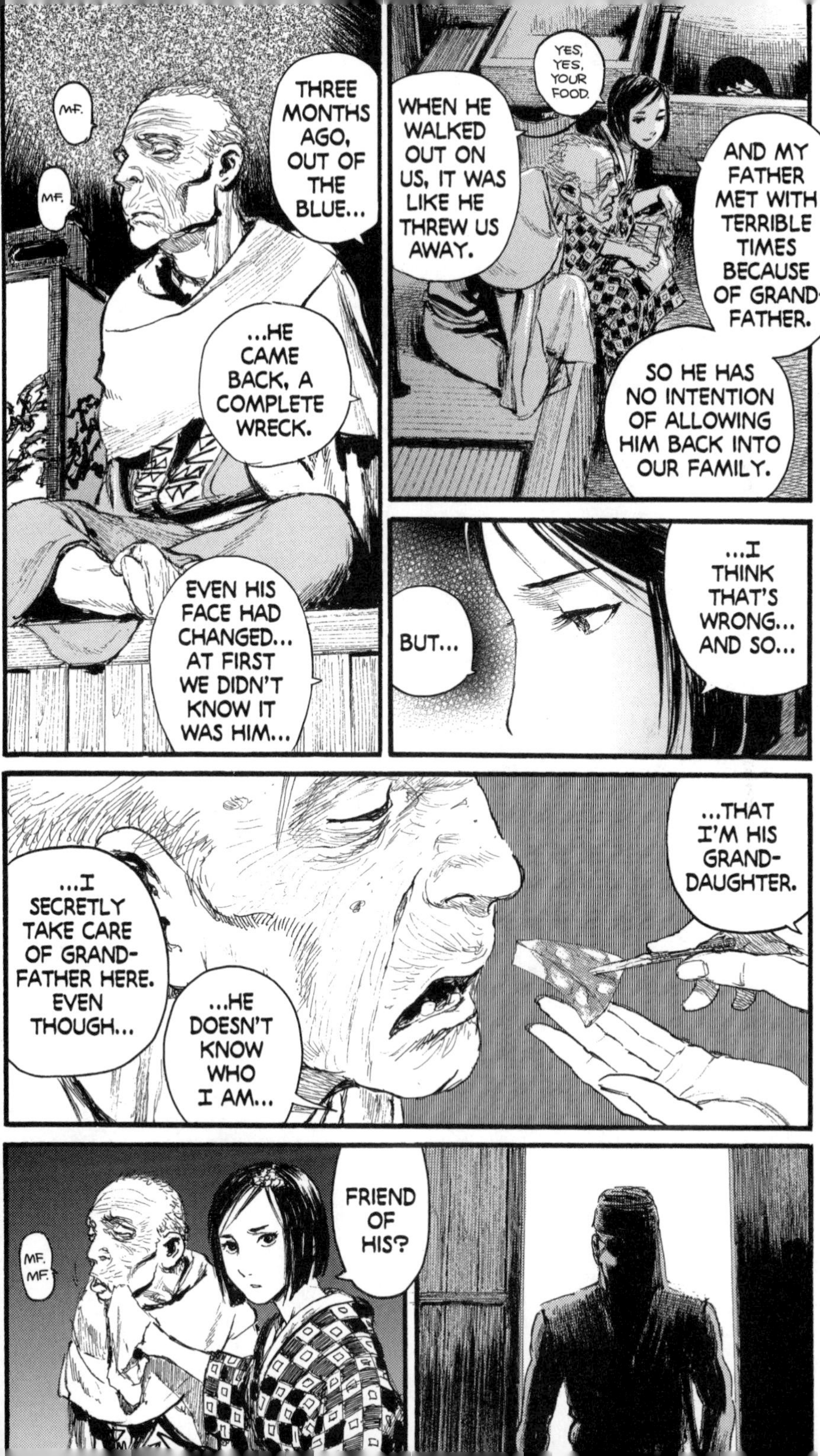
MF.
MF.
THREE MONTHS AGO, OUT OF THE BLUE...
...HE CAME BACK, A COMPLETE WRECK.
EVEN HIS FACE HAD CHANGED... AT FIRST WE DIDN'T KNOW IT WAS HIM...
WHEN HE WALKED OUT ON US, IT WAS LIKE HE THREW US AWAY.
YES, YES, YOUR FOOD.
AND MY FATHER MET WITH TERRIBLE TIMES BECAUSE OF GRAND-FATHER.
SO HE HAS NO INTENTION OF ALLOWING HIM BACK INTO OUR FAMILY.
BUT...
...I THINK THAT'S WRONG... AND SO...
...I SECRETLY TAKE CARE OF GRAND-FATHER HERE. EVEN THOUGH...
...HE DOESN'T KNOW WHO I AM...
...THAT I'M HIS GRAND-DAUGHTER.
MF. MF.
FRIEND OF HIS?

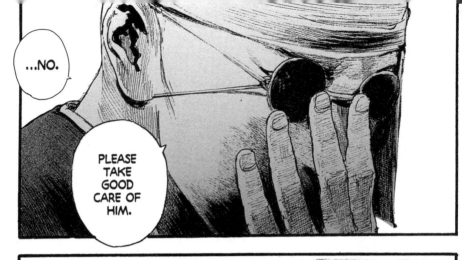

...NO.

PLEASE TAKE GOOD CARE OF HIM.

HIZEN PROVINCE, SHIMABARA *HAN*.

ISAKUUU!

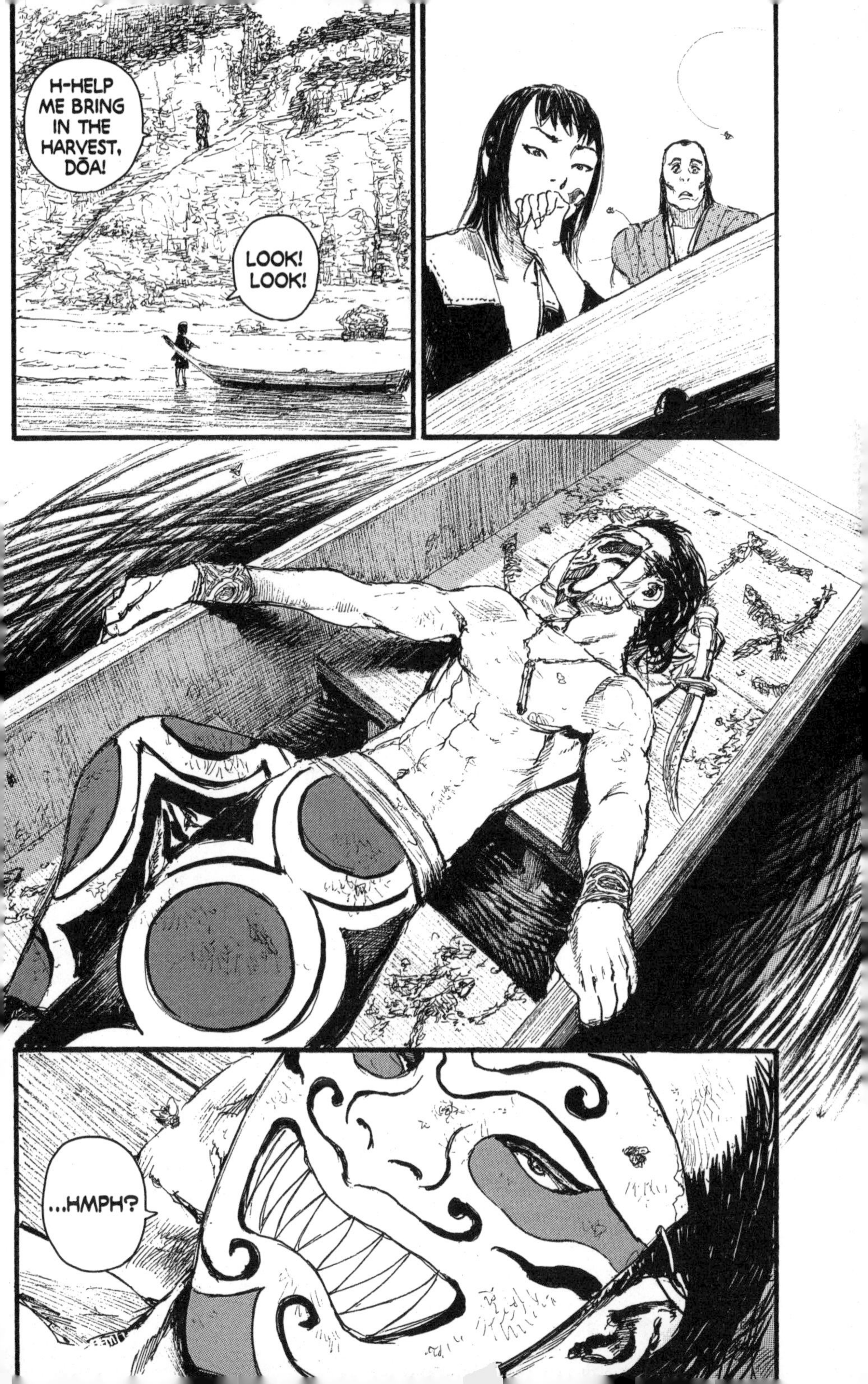
H-HELP ME BRING IN THE HARVEST, DŌA!
LOOK! LOOK!
...HMPH?

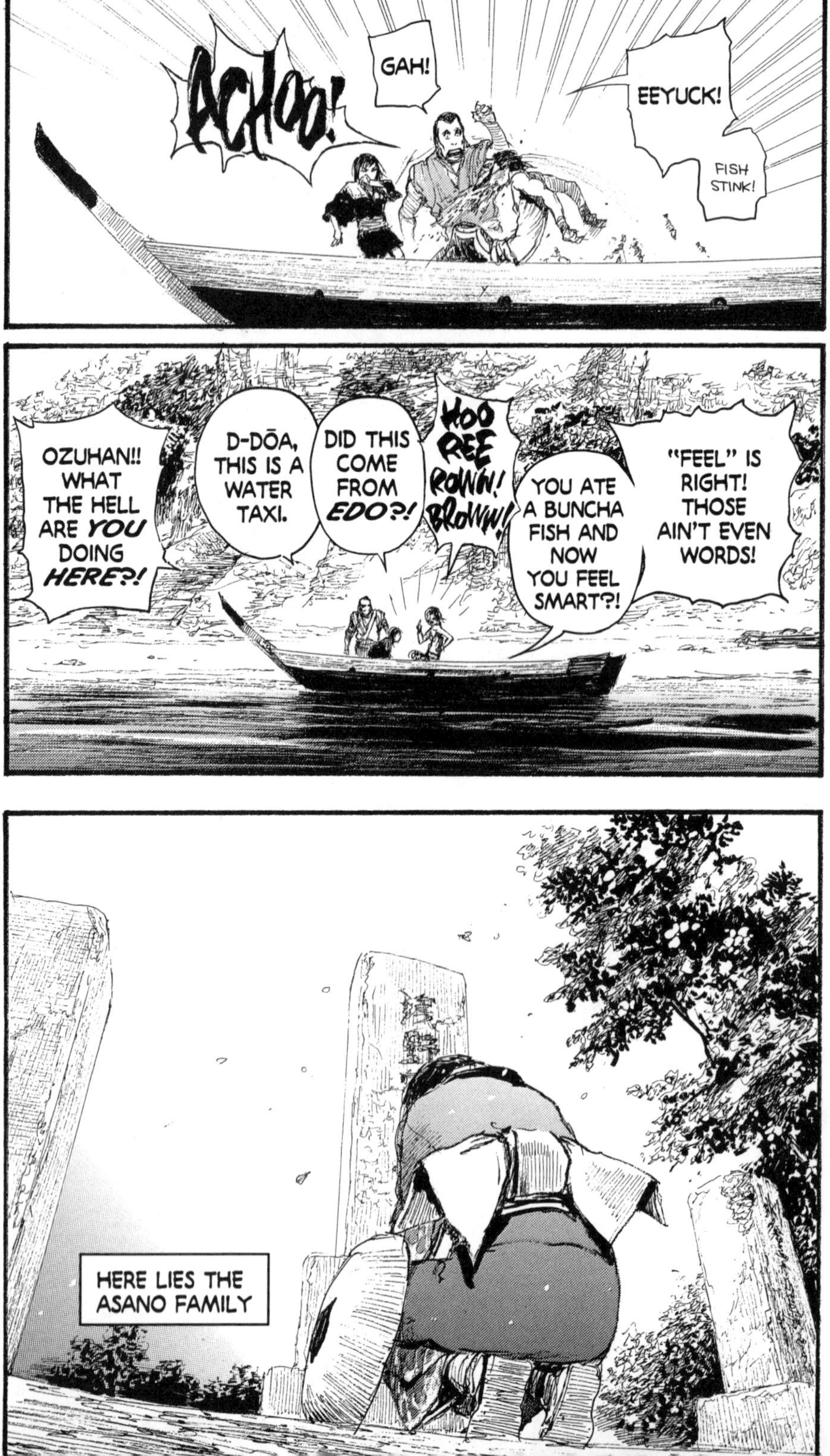
ACHOO!
GAH!
EEYUCK!
FISH STINK!
OZUHAN!! WHAT THE HELL ARE *YOU* DOING *HERE?!*
D-DŌA, THIS IS A WATER TAXI.
DID THIS COME FROM *EDO?!*
HOO REE ROWW! BROWW!
YOU ATE A BUNCHA FISH AND NOW YOU FEEL SMART?!
"FEEL" IS RIGHT! THOSE AIN'T EVEN WORDS!
HERE LIES THE ASANO FAMILY

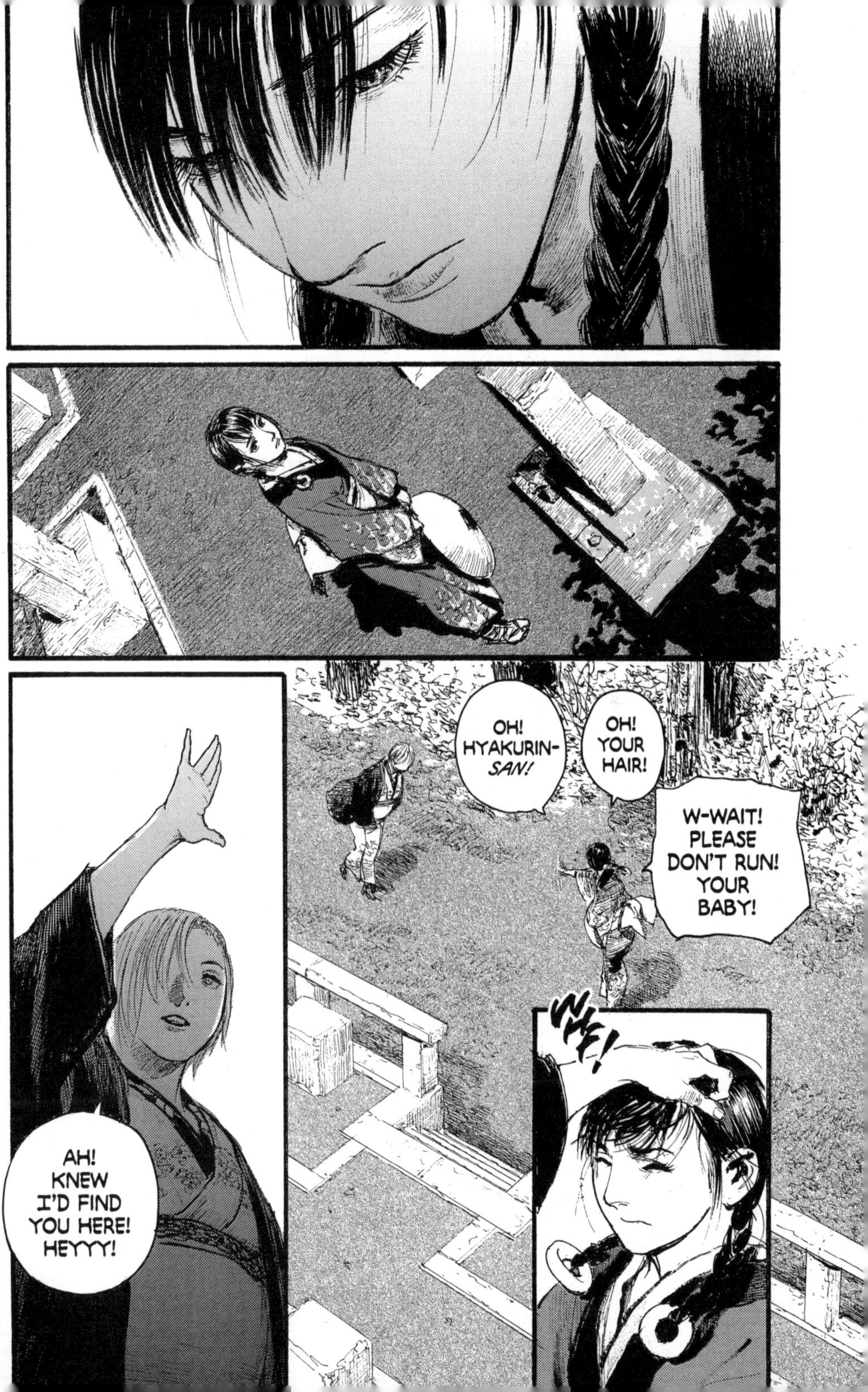
AH! KNEW I'D FIND YOU HERE! HEYYY!
OH! HYAKURIN-*SAN!*
OH! YOUR HAIR!
W-WAIT! PLEASE DON'T RUN! YOUR BABY!
WHF!

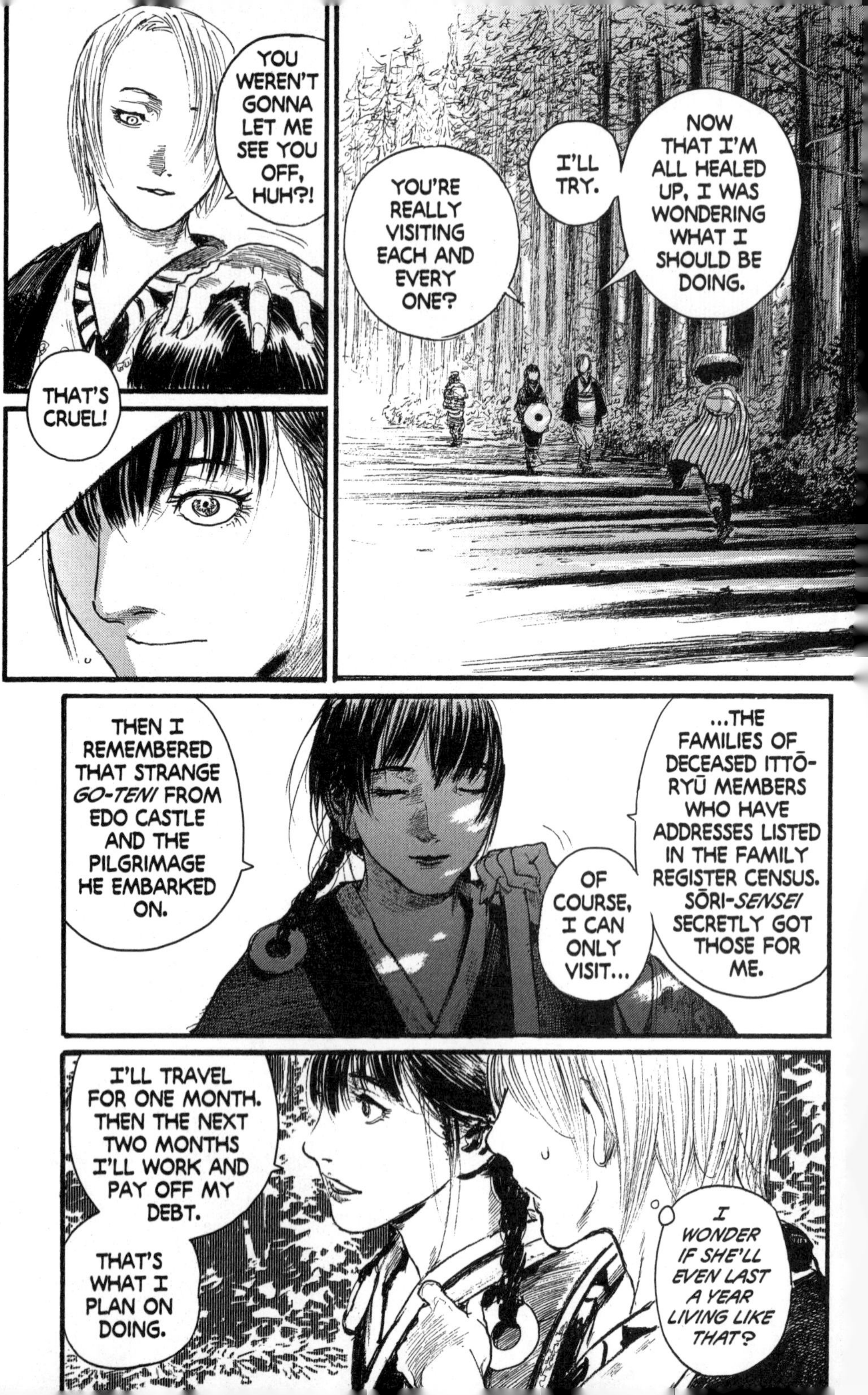
YOU WEREN'T GONNA LET ME SEE YOU OFF, HUH?!
THAT'S CRUEL!
YOU'RE REALLY VISITING EACH AND EVERY ONE?
I'LL TRY.
NOW THAT I'M ALL HEALED UP, I WAS WONDERING WHAT I SHOULD BE DOING.
THEN I REMEMBERED THAT STRANGE *GO-TENI* FROM EDO CASTLE AND THE PILGRIMAGE HE EMBARKED ON.
OF COURSE, I CAN ONLY VISIT...
...THE FAMILIES OF DECEASED ITTŌ-RYŪ MEMBERS WHO HAVE ADDRESSES LISTED IN THE FAMILY REGISTER CENSUS. SŌRI-*SENSEI* SECRETLY GOT THOSE FOR ME.
I'LL TRAVEL FOR ONE MONTH. THEN THE NEXT TWO MONTHS I'LL WORK AND PAY OFF MY DEBT.
THAT'S WHAT I PLAN ON DOING.
I WONDER IF SHE'LL EVEN LAST A YEAR LIVING LIKE THAT?

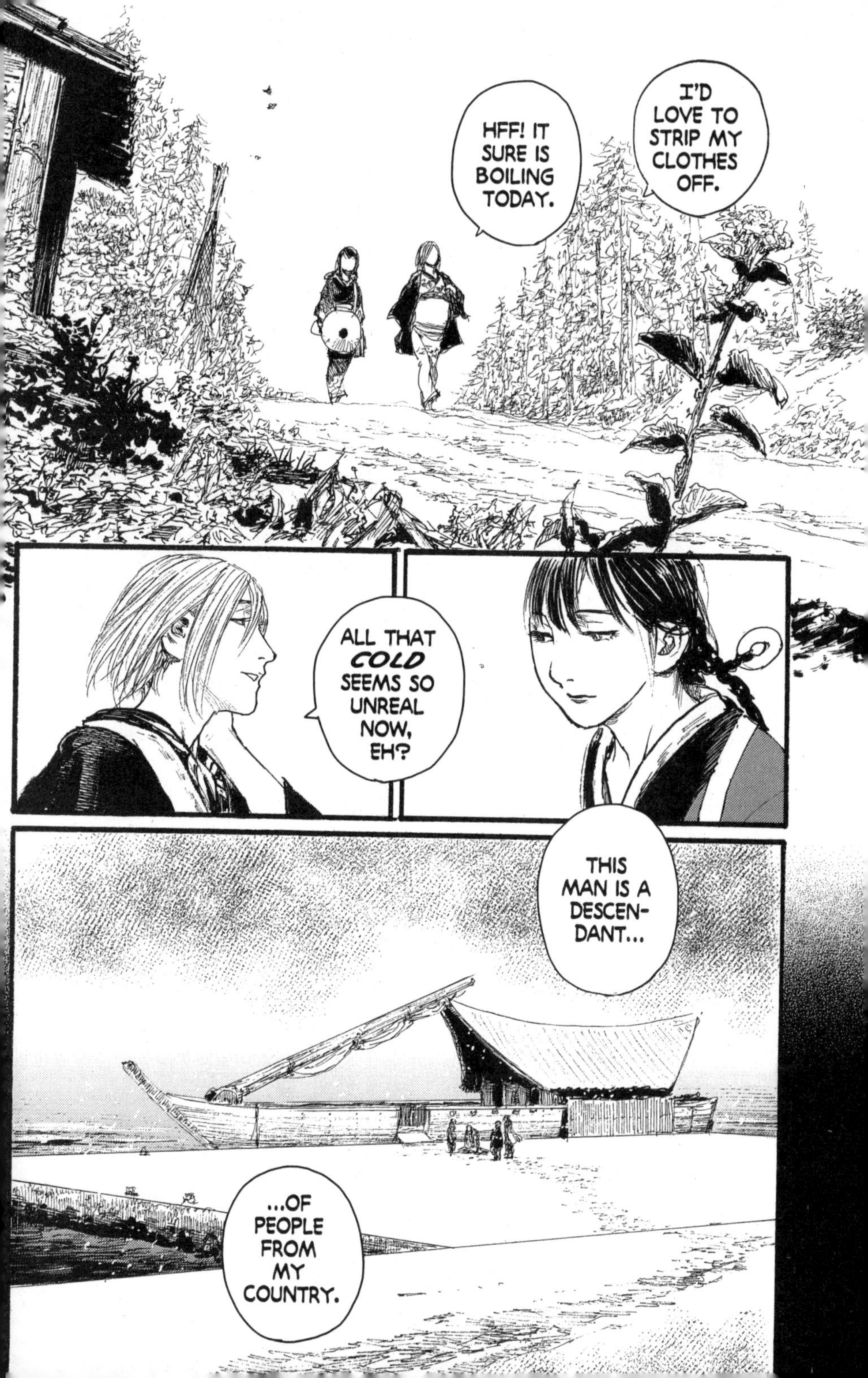
HFF! IT SURE IS BOILING TODAY.
I'D LOVE TO STRIP MY CLOTHES OFF.
ALL THAT *COLD* SEEMS SO UNREAL NOW, EH?
THIS MAN IS A DESCEN-DANT...
...OF PEOPLE FROM MY COUNTRY.

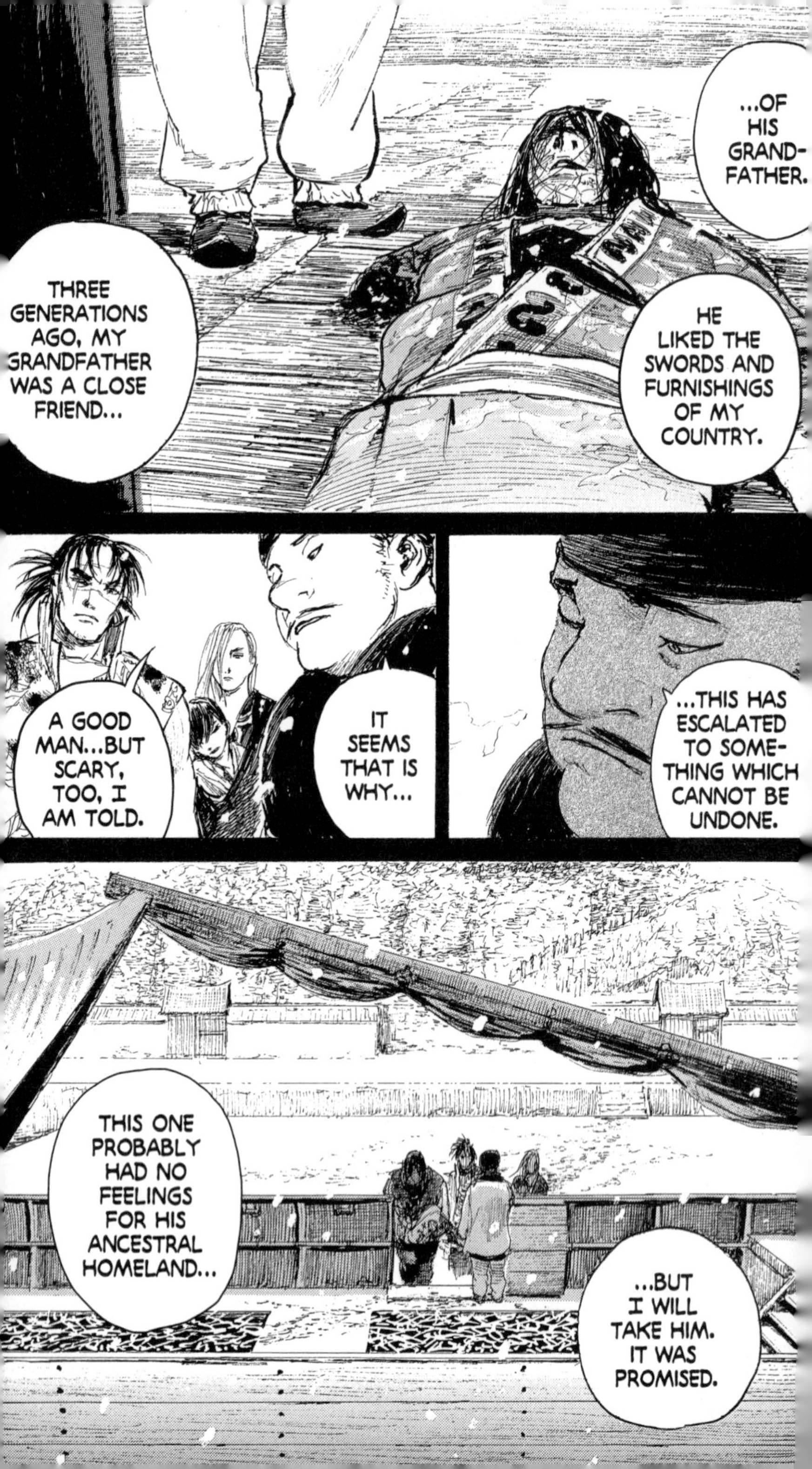
THREE GENERATIONS AGO, MY GRANDFATHER WAS A CLOSE FRIEND...
...OF HIS GRANDFATHER.
HE LIKED THE SWORDS AND FURNISHINGS OF MY COUNTRY.
A GOOD MAN...BUT SCARY, TOO, I AM TOLD.
IT SEEMS THAT IS WHY...
...THIS HAS ESCALATED TO SOMETHING WHICH CANNOT BE UNDONE.
THIS ONE PROBABLY HAD NO FEELINGS FOR HIS ANCESTRAL HOMELAND...
...BUT I WILL TAKE HIM. IT WAS PROMISED.

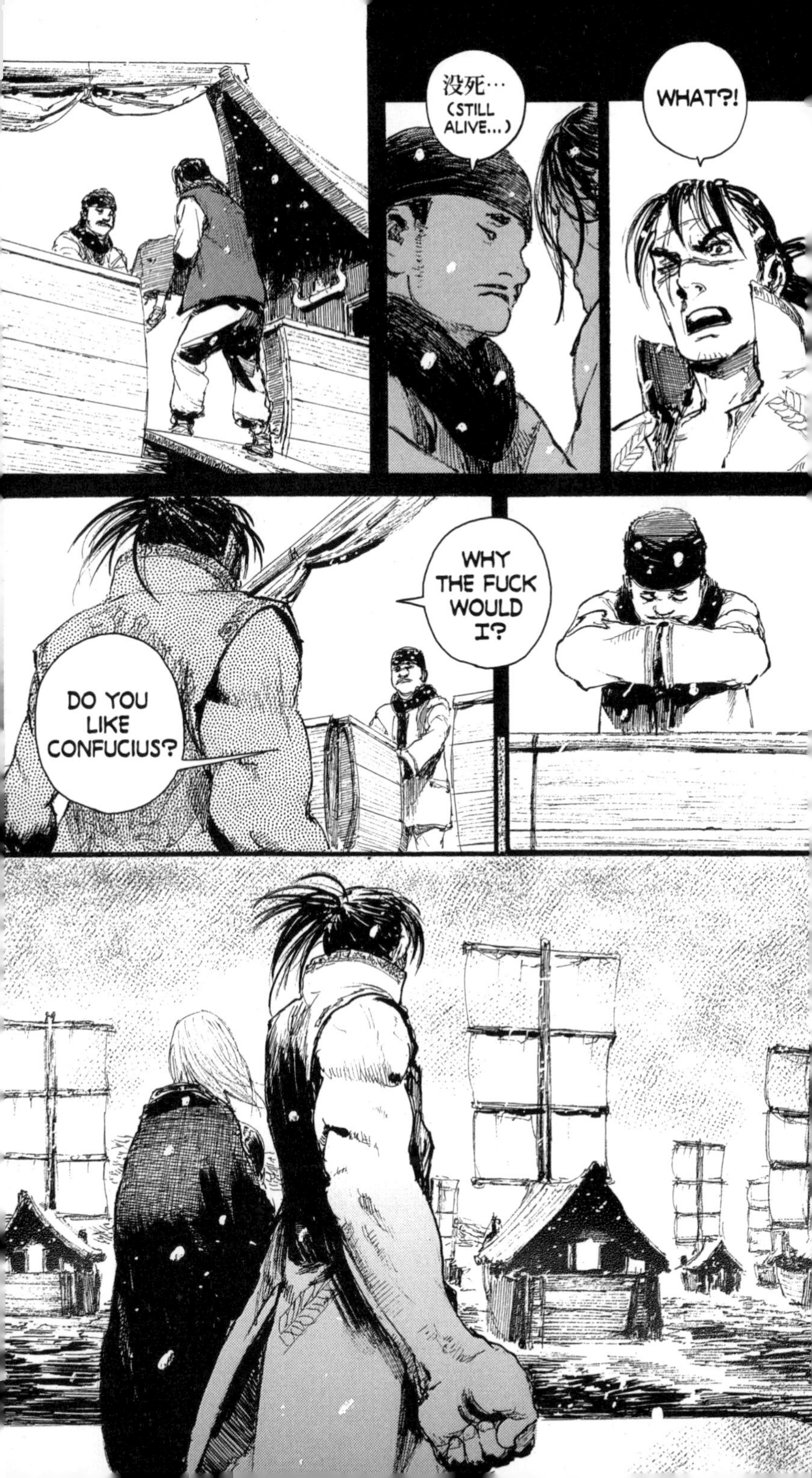
没死…
(STILL ALIVE...)
WHAT?!
DO YOU LIKE CONFUCIUS?
WHY THE FUCK WOULD I?

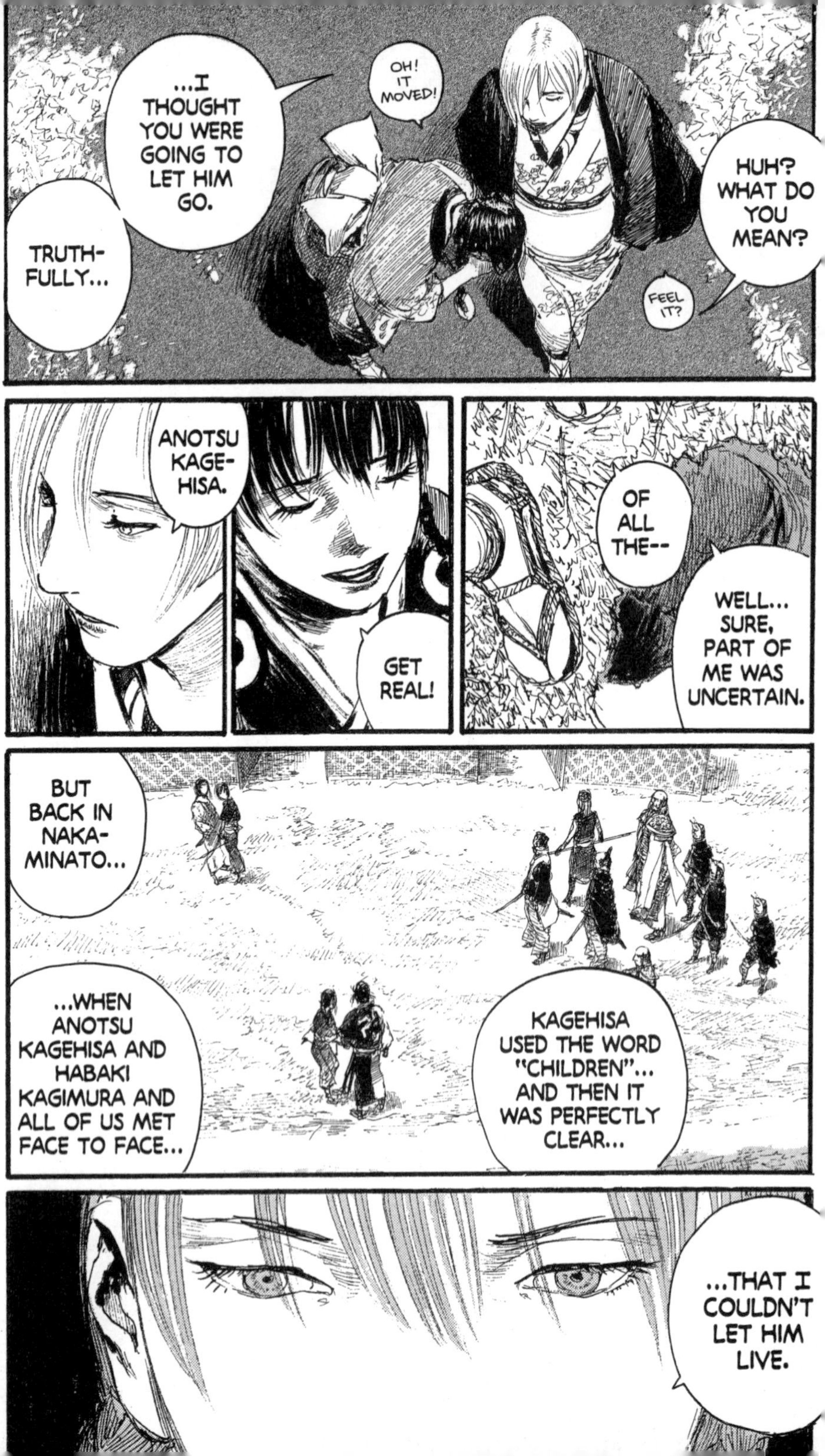
TRUTH-FULLY...
...I THOUGHT YOU WERE GOING TO LET HIM GO.
HUH? WHAT DO YOU MEAN?
FEEL IT?
OH! IT MOVED!
ANOTSU KAGE-HISA.
GET REAL!
OF ALL THE--
WELL... SURE, PART OF ME WAS UNCERTAIN.
BUT BACK IN NAKA-MINATO...
...WHEN ANOTSU KAGEHISA AND HABAKI KAGIMURA AND ALL OF US MET FACE TO FACE...
KAGEHISA USED THE WORD "CHILDREN"... AND THEN IT WAS PERFECTLY CLEAR...
...THAT I COULDN'T LET HIM LIVE.

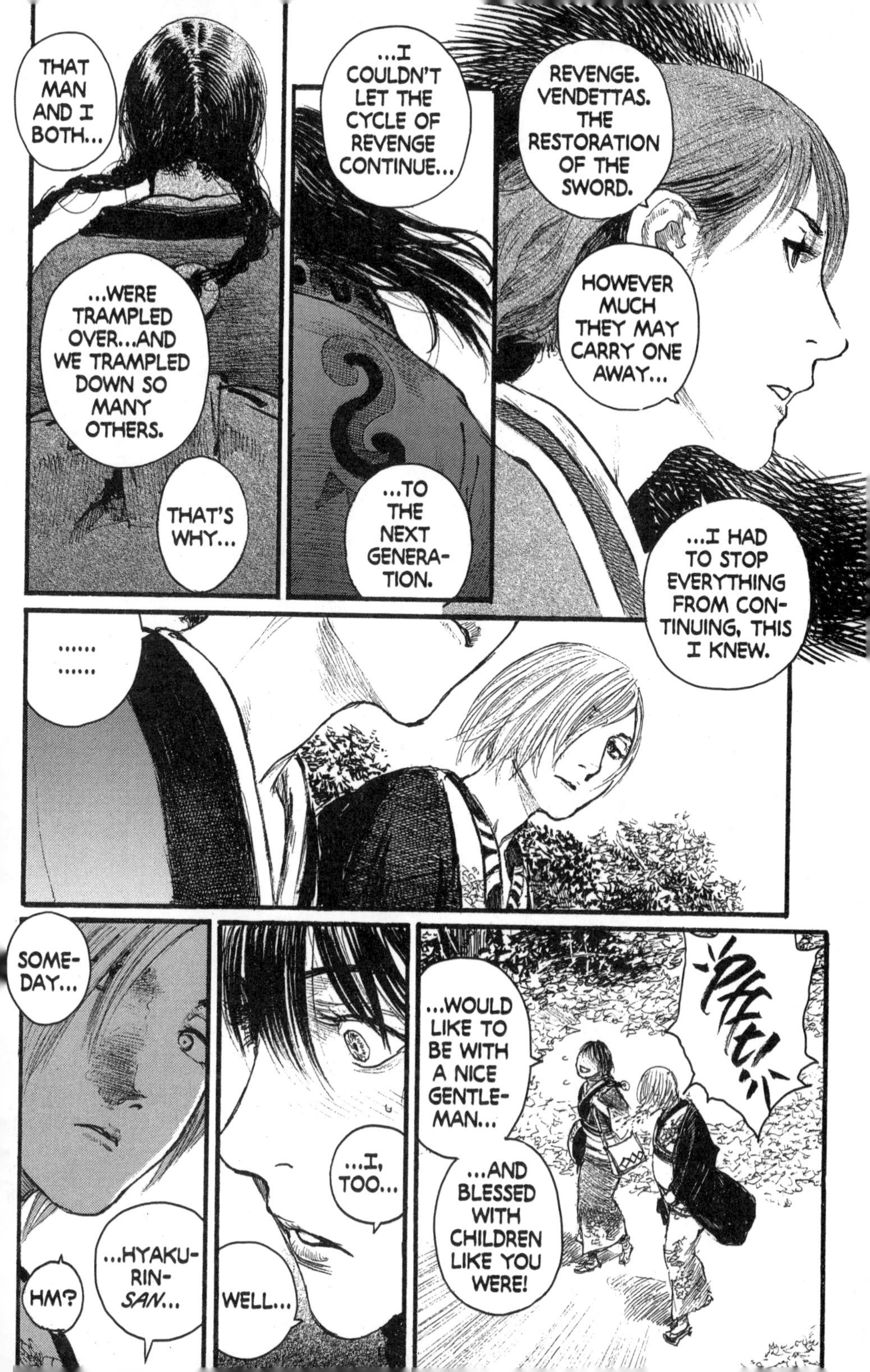
THAT MAN AND I BOTH...
...WERE TRAMPLED OVER...AND WE TRAMPLED DOWN SO MANY OTHERS.
THAT'S WHY...
...I COULDN'T LET THE CYCLE OF REVENGE CONTINUE...
...TO THE NEXT GENERATION.
REVENGE. VENDETTAS. THE RESTORATION OF THE SWORD.
HOWEVER MUCH THEY MAY CARRY ONE AWAY...
...I HAD TO STOP EVERYTHING FROM CONTINUING, THIS I KNEW.
....
SOME-DAY...
...HYAKU-RIN-*SAN*...
HM?
...I, TOO...
WELL...
...WOULD LIKE TO BE WITH A NICE GENTLE-MAN...
...AND BLESSED WITH CHILDREN LIKE YOU WERE!
PKU!

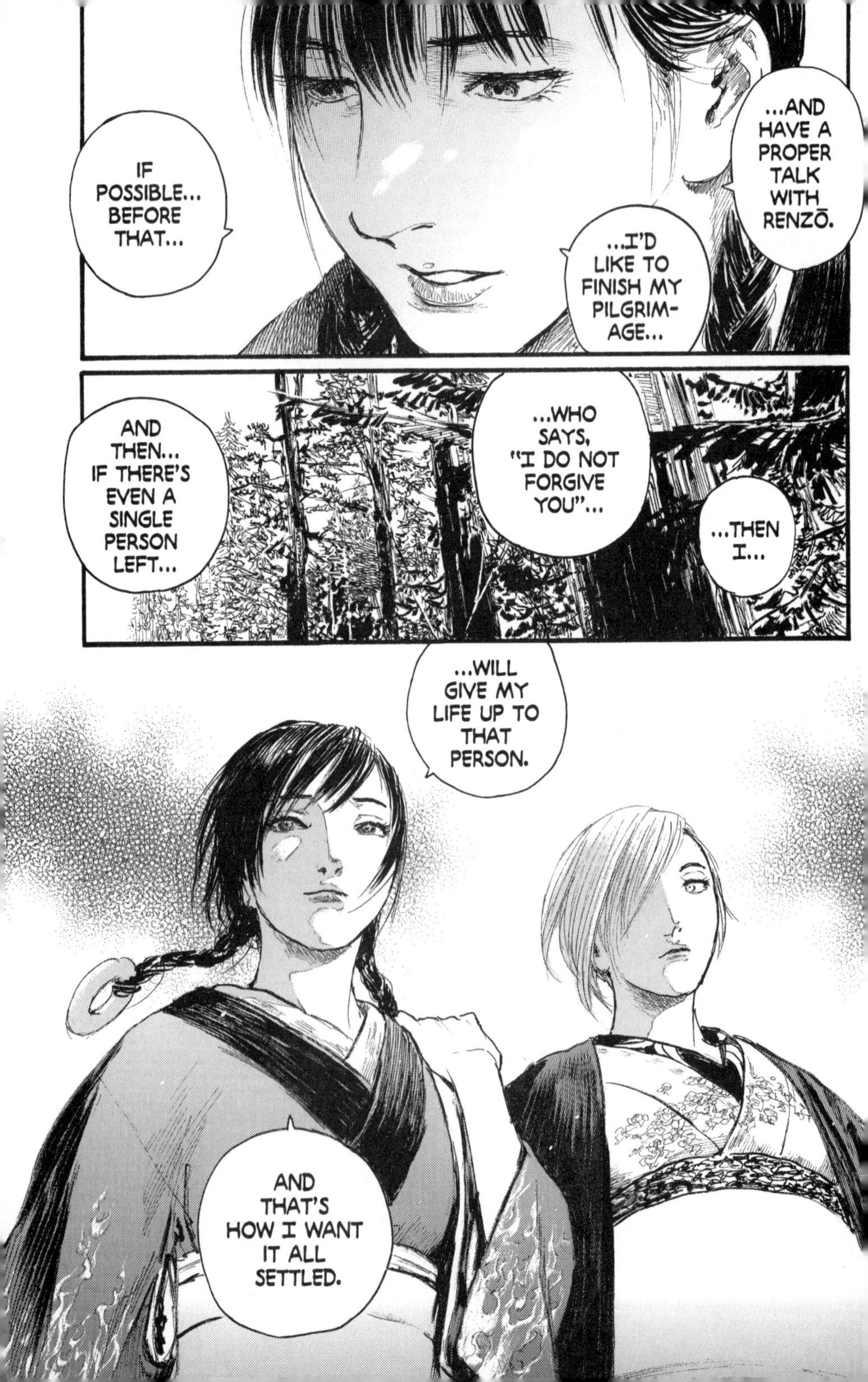
IF POSSIBLE... BEFORE THAT...
...I'D LIKE TO FINISH MY PILGRIM-AGE...
...AND HAVE A PROPER TALK WITH RENZŌ.
AND THEN... IF THERE'S EVEN A SINGLE PERSON LEFT...
...WHO SAYS, "I DO NOT FORGIVE YOU"...
...THEN I...
...WILL GIVE MY LIFE UP TO THAT PERSON.
AND THAT'S HOW I WANT IT ALL SETTLED.

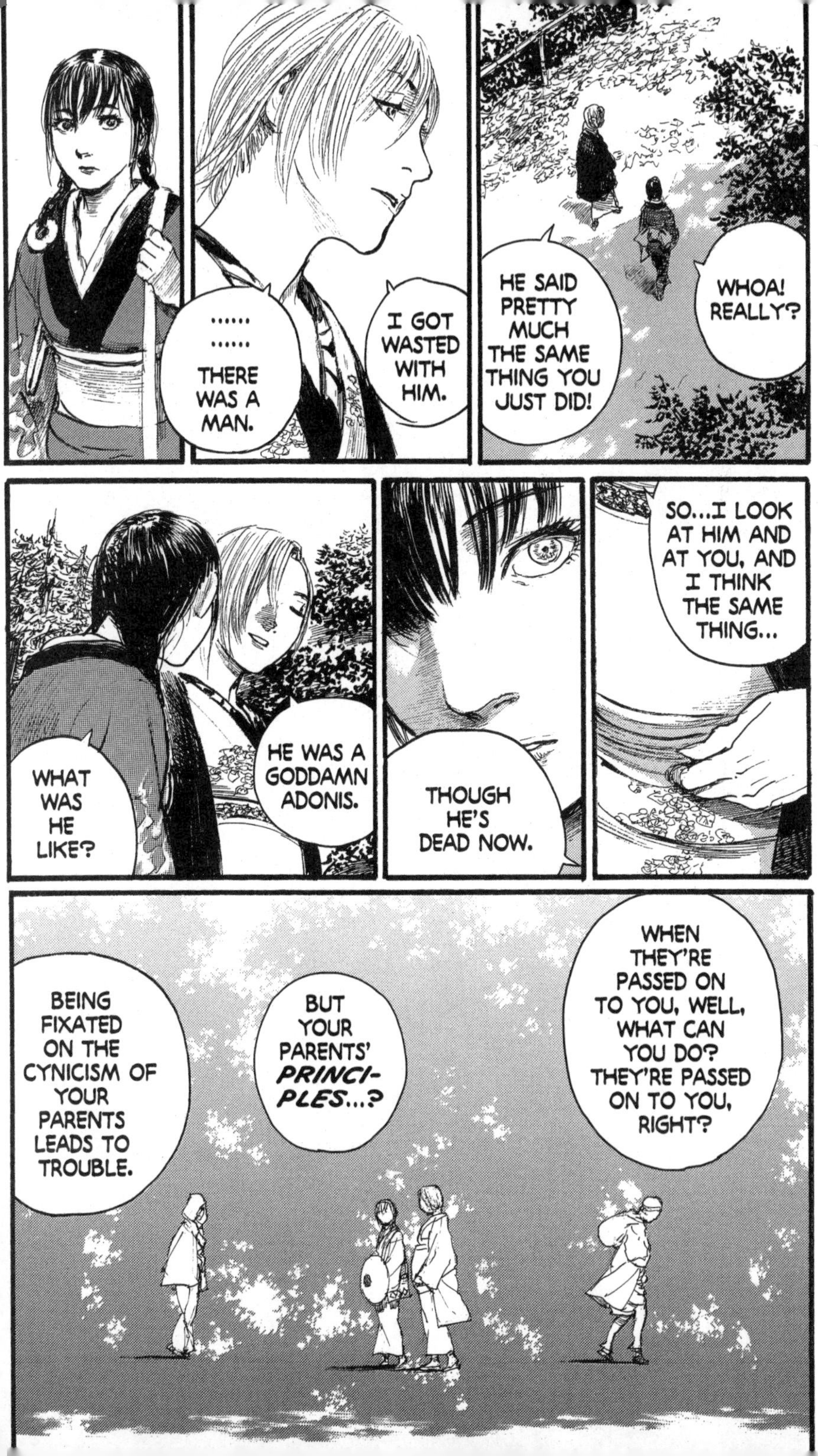
......
......
THERE WAS A MAN.
I GOT WASTED WITH HIM.
HE SAID PRETTY MUCH THE SAME THING YOU JUST DID!
WHOA! REALLY?
WHAT WAS HE LIKE?
HE WAS A GODDAMN ADONIS.
THOUGH HE'S DEAD NOW.
SO...I LOOK AT HIM AND AT YOU, AND I THINK THE SAME THING...
WHEN THEY'RE PASSED ON TO YOU, WELL, WHAT CAN YOU DO? THEY'RE PASSED ON TO YOU, RIGHT?
BUT YOUR PARENTS' *PRINCIPLES*...?
BEING FIXATED ON THE CYNICISM OF YOUR PARENTS LEADS TO TROUBLE.

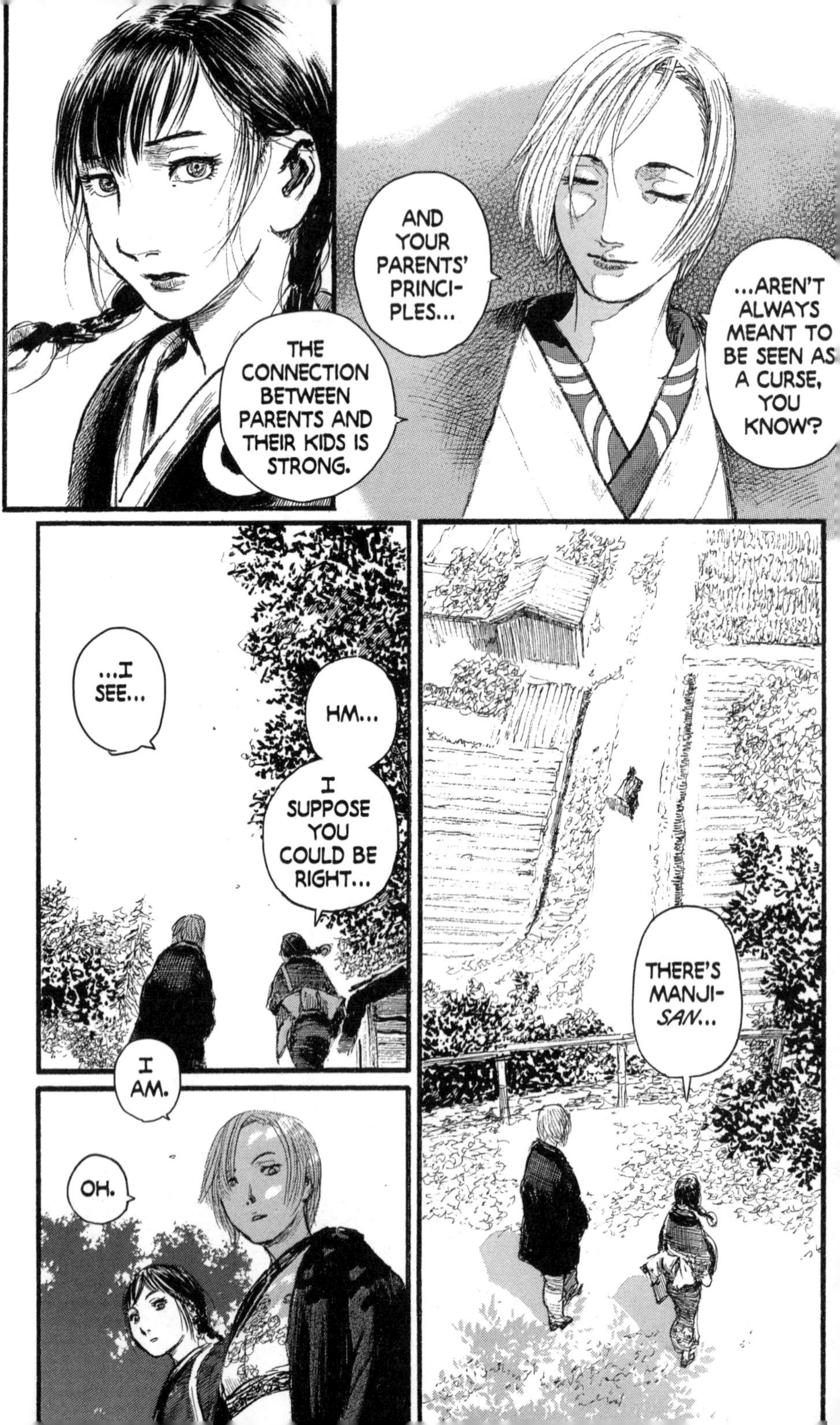
THE CONNECTION BETWEEN PARENTS AND THEIR KIDS IS STRONG.
AND YOUR PARENTS' PRINCIPLES...
...AREN'T ALWAYS MEANT TO BE SEEN AS A CURSE, YOU KNOW?
...I SEE...
HM...
I SUPPOSE YOU COULD BE RIGHT...
I AM.
OH.
THERE'S MANJI-*SAN*...

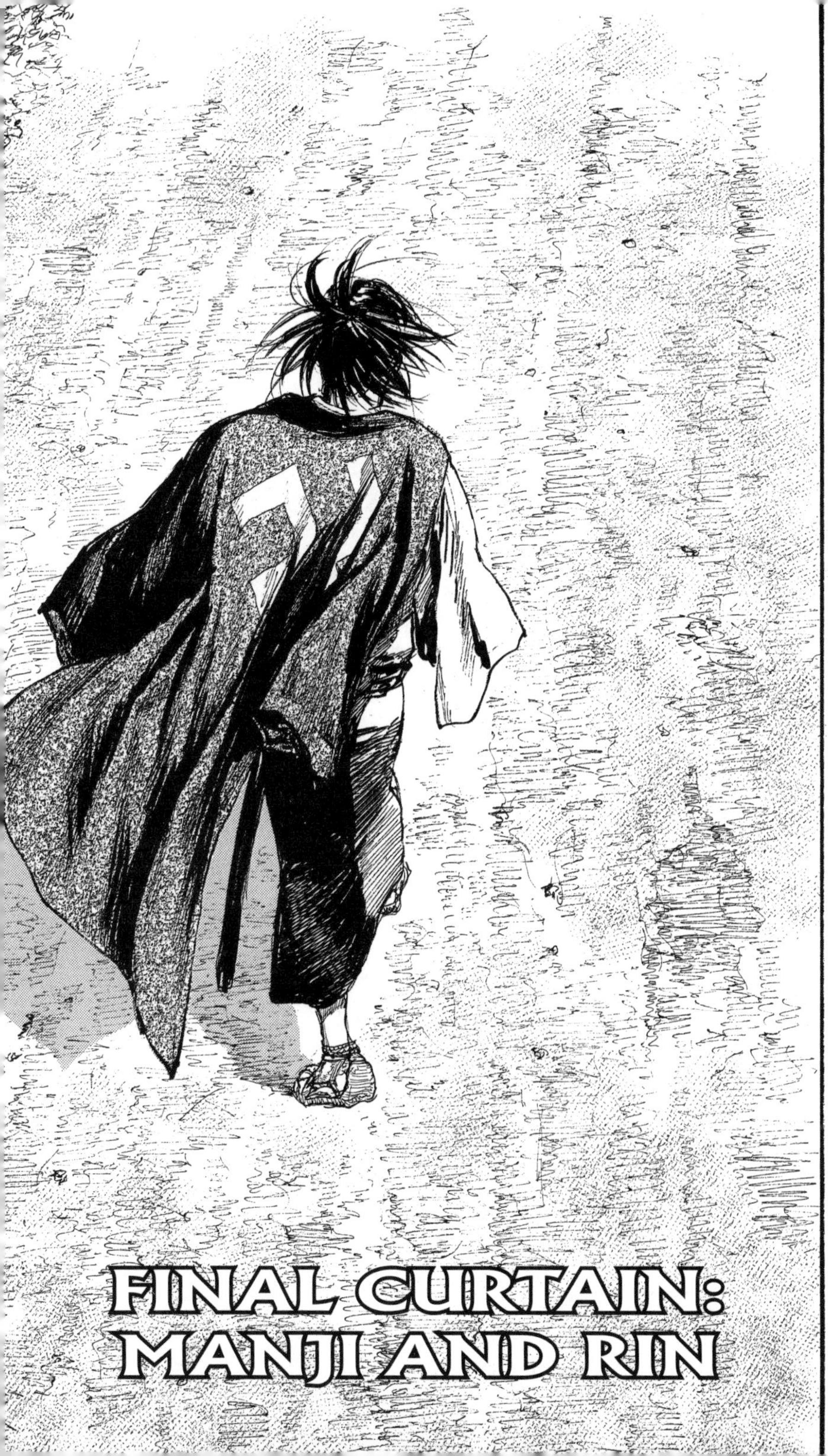

FINAL CURTAIN: MANJI AND RIN

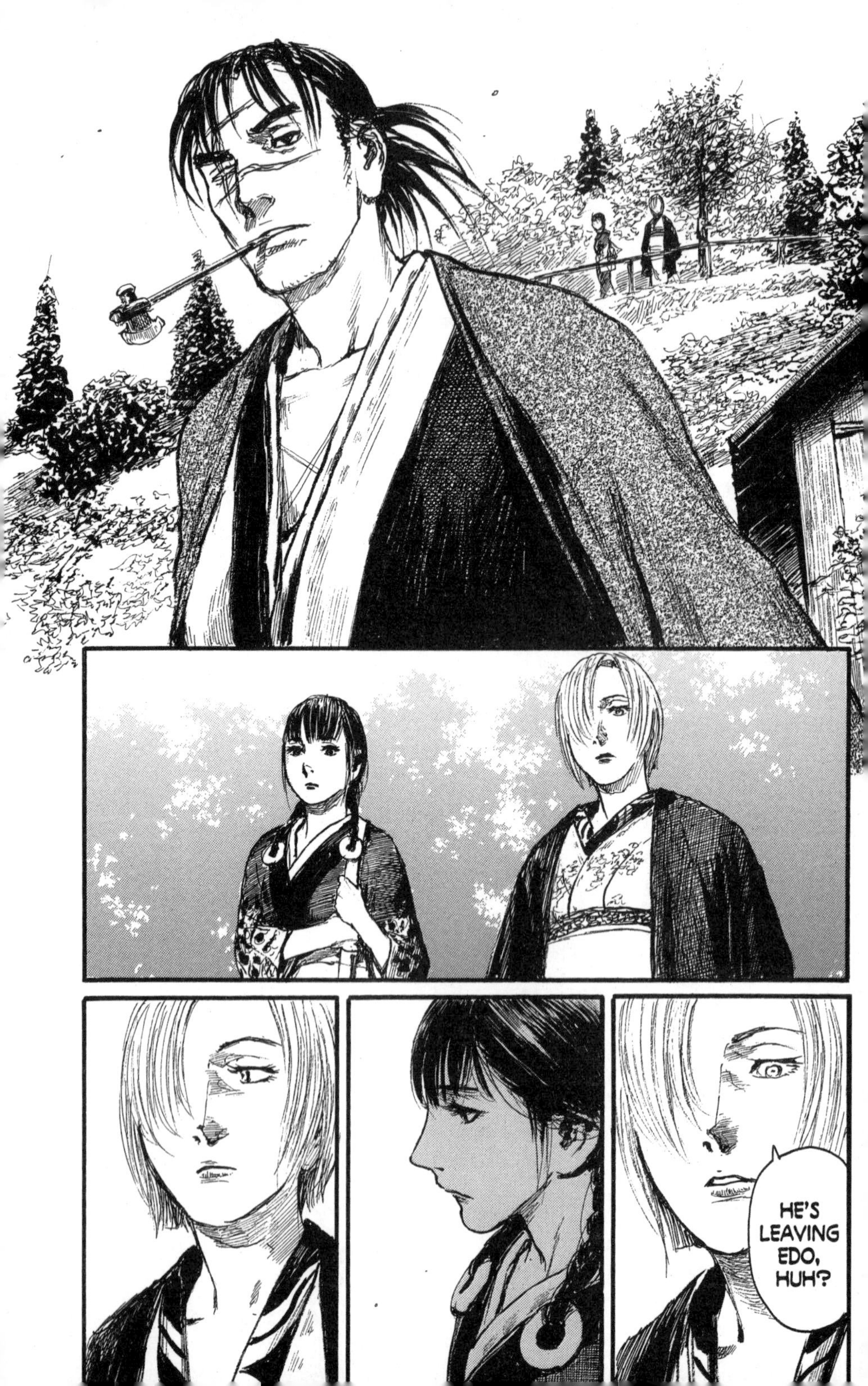
HE'S LEAVING EDO, HUH?

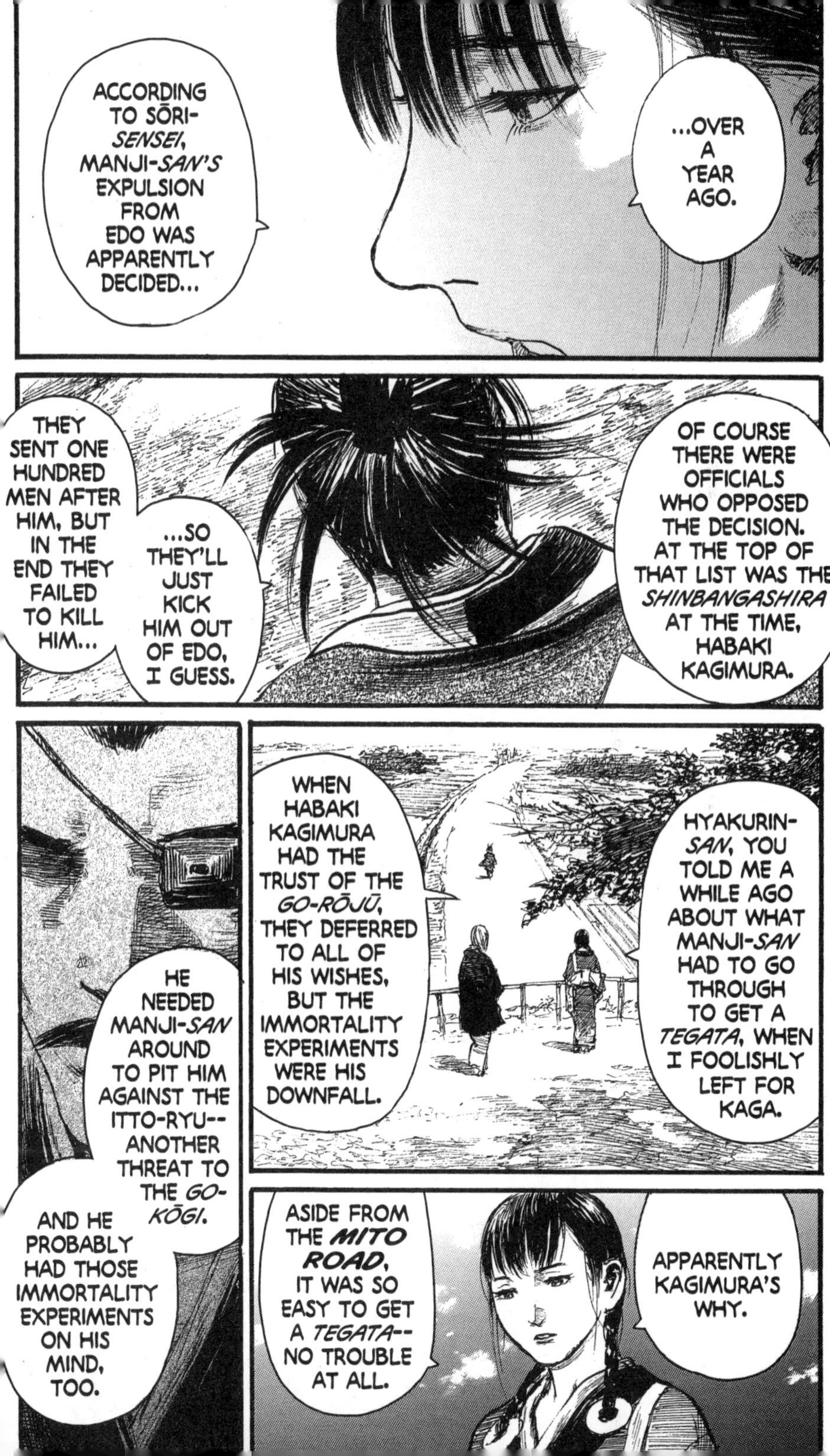
ACCORDING TO SŌRI-*SENSEI*, MANJI-*SAN'S* EXPULSION FROM EDO WAS APPARENTLY DECIDED...
...OVER A YEAR AGO.
THEY SENT ONE HUNDRED MEN AFTER HIM, BUT IN THE END THEY FAILED TO KILL HIM...
...SO THEY'LL JUST KICK HIM OUT OF EDO, I GUESS.
OF COURSE THERE WERE OFFICIALS WHO OPPOSED THE DECISION. AT THE TOP OF THAT LIST WAS THE *SHINBANGASHIRA* AT THE TIME, HABAKI KAGIMURA.
HE NEEDED MANJI-*SAN* AROUND TO PIT HIM AGAINST THE ITTO-RYU--ANOTHER THREAT TO THE *GO-KŌGI*.
AND HE PROBABLY HAD THOSE IMMORTALITY EXPERIMENTS ON HIS MIND, TOO.
WHEN HABAKI KAGIMURA HAD THE TRUST OF THE *GO-RŌJŪ*, THEY DEFERRED TO ALL OF HIS WISHES, BUT THE IMMORTALITY EXPERIMENTS WERE HIS DOWNFALL.
HYAKURIN-*SAN*, YOU TOLD ME A WHILE AGO ABOUT WHAT MANJI-*SAN* HAD TO GO THROUGH TO GET A *TEGATA*, WHEN I FOOLISHLY LEFT FOR KAGA.
ASIDE FROM THE ***MITO ROAD***, IT WAS SO EASY TO GET A *TEGATA*--NO TROUBLE AT ALL.
APPARENTLY KAGIMURA'S WHY.

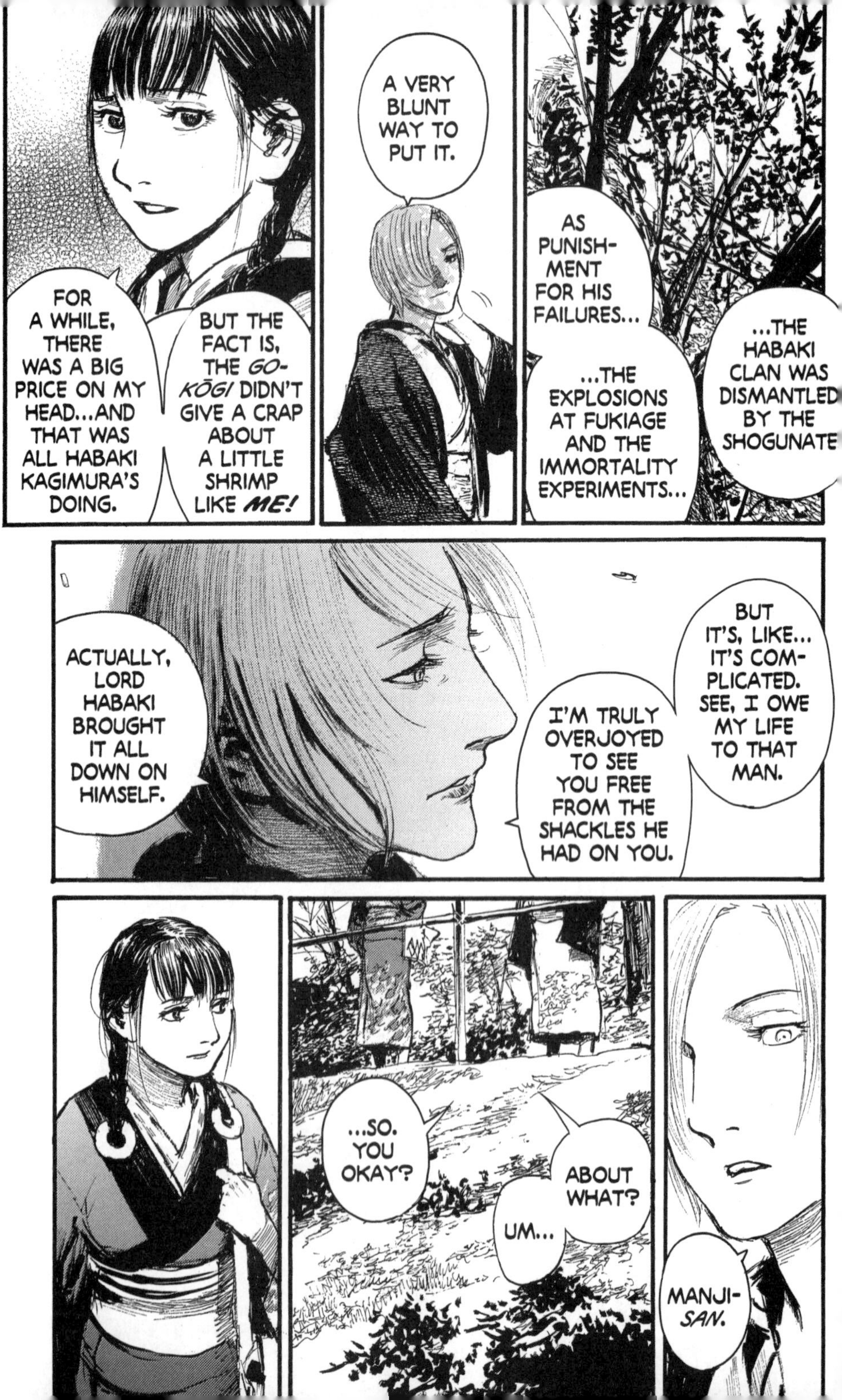
FOR A WHILE, THERE WAS A BIG PRICE ON MY HEAD...AND THAT WAS ALL HABAKI KAGIMURA'S DOING.
BUT THE FACT IS, THE GO-KŌGI DIDN'T GIVE A CRAP ABOUT A LITTLE SHRIMP LIKE ME!
A VERY BLUNT WAY TO PUT IT.
AS PUNISHMENT FOR HIS FAILURES...
...THE EXPLOSIONS AT FUKIAGE AND THE IMMORTALITY EXPERIMENTS...
...THE HABAKI CLAN WAS DISMANTLED BY THE SHOGUNATE
ACTUALLY, LORD HABAKI BROUGHT IT ALL DOWN ON HIMSELF.
I'M TRULY OVERJOYED TO SEE YOU FREE FROM THE SHACKLES HE HAD ON YOU.
BUT IT'S, LIKE... IT'S COMPLICATED. SEE, I OWE MY LIFE TO THAT MAN.
...SO. YOU OKAY?
ABOUT WHAT?
UM...
MANJI-SAN.

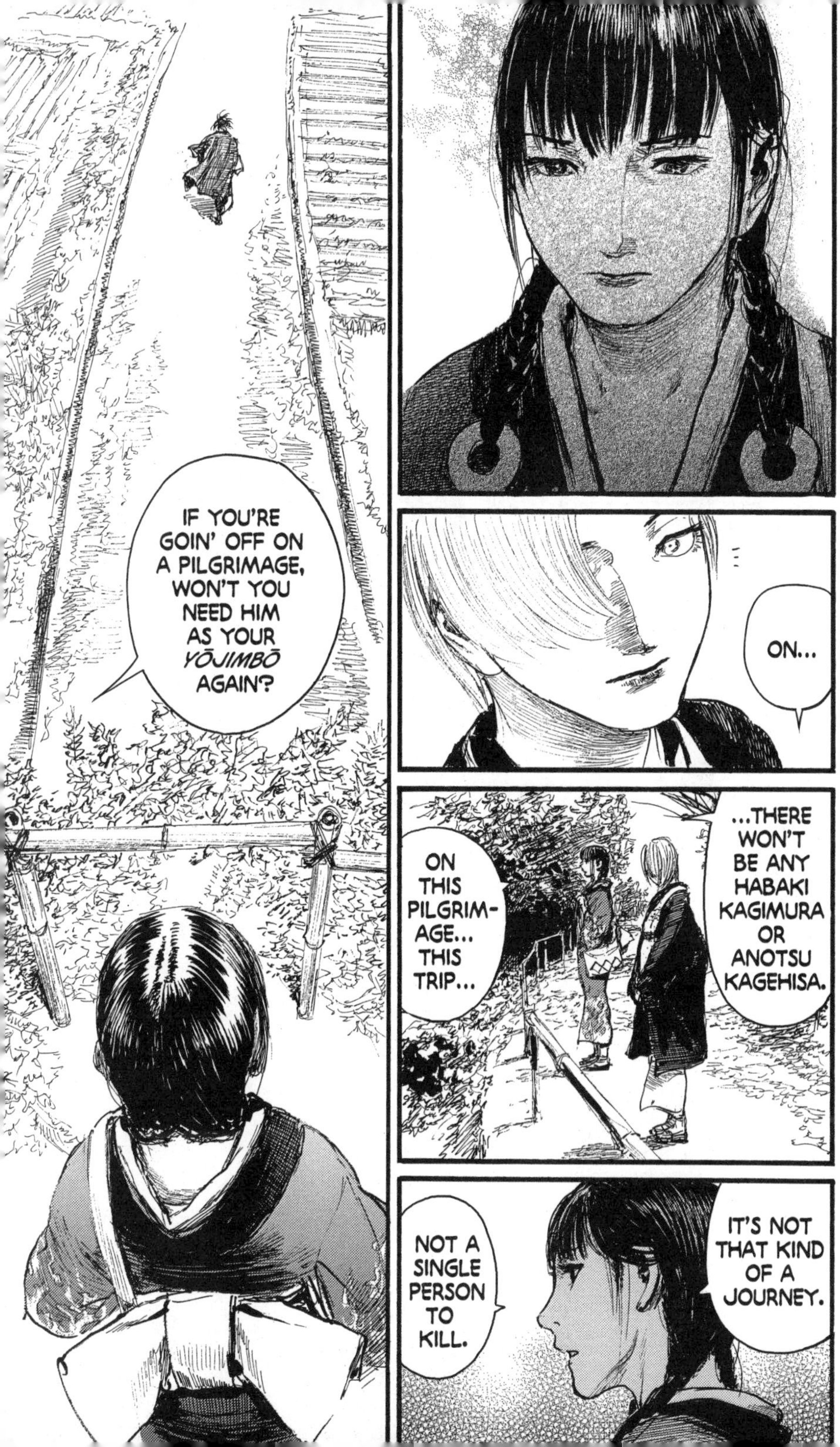
IF YOU'RE GOIN' OFF ON A PILGRIMAGE, WON'T YOU NEED HIM AS YOUR *YŌJIMBŌ* AGAIN?
ON...
ON THIS PILGRIM-AGE... THIS TRIP...
...THERE WON'T BE ANY HABAKI KAGIMURA OR ANOTSU KAGEHISA.
NOT A SINGLE PERSON TO KILL.
IT'S NOT THAT KIND OF A JOURNEY.

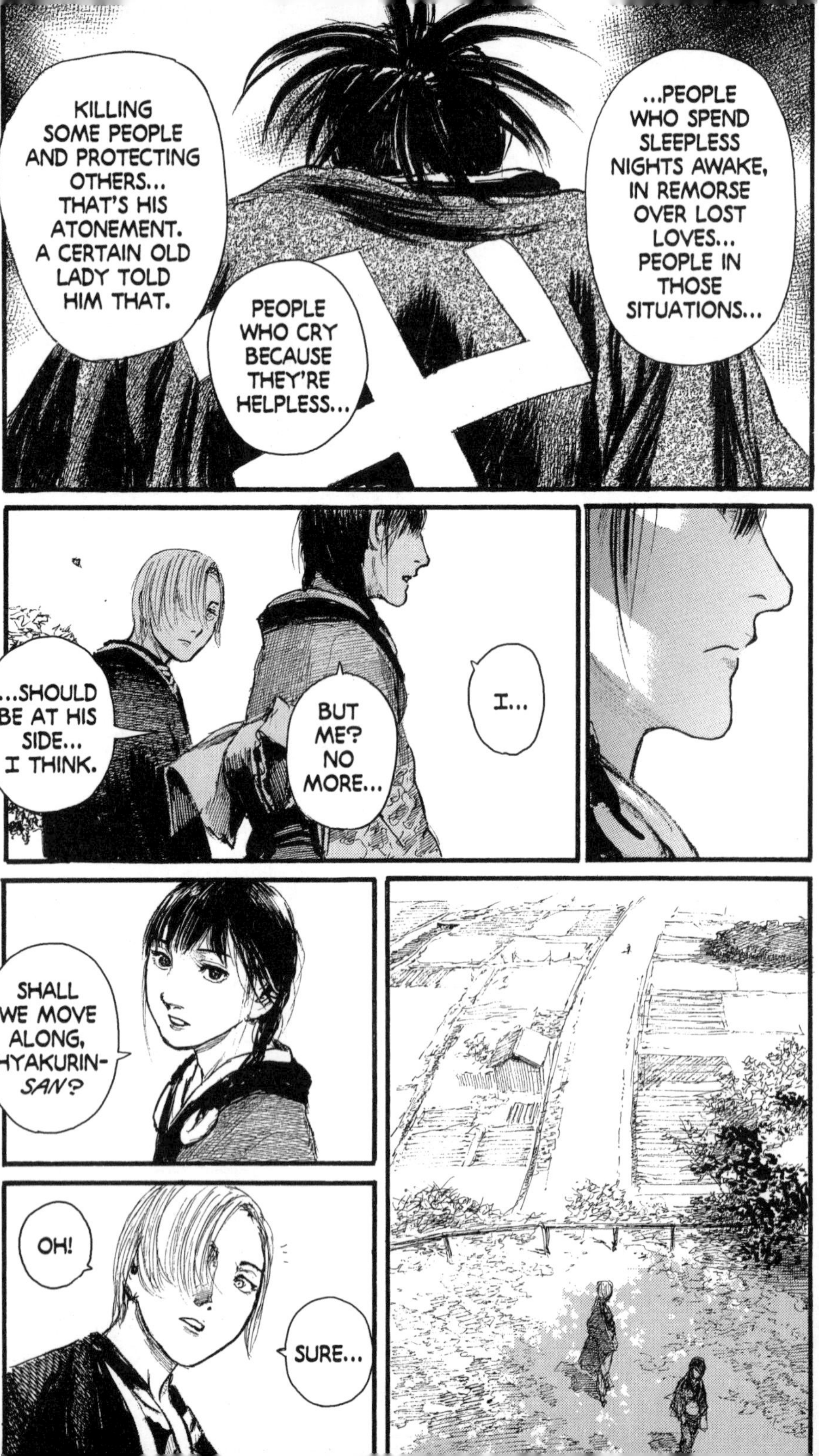
KILLING SOME PEOPLE AND PROTECTING OTHERS... THAT'S HIS ATONEMENT. A CERTAIN OLD LADY TOLD HIM THAT.
PEOPLE WHO CRY BECAUSE THEY'RE HELPLESS...
...PEOPLE WHO SPEND SLEEPLESS NIGHTS AWAKE, IN REMORSE OVER LOST LOVES... PEOPLE IN THOSE SITUATIONS...
...SHOULD BE AT HIS SIDE... I THINK.
BUT ME? NO MORE...
I...
SHALL WE MOVE ALONG, HYAKURIN-*SAN*?
OH!
SURE...

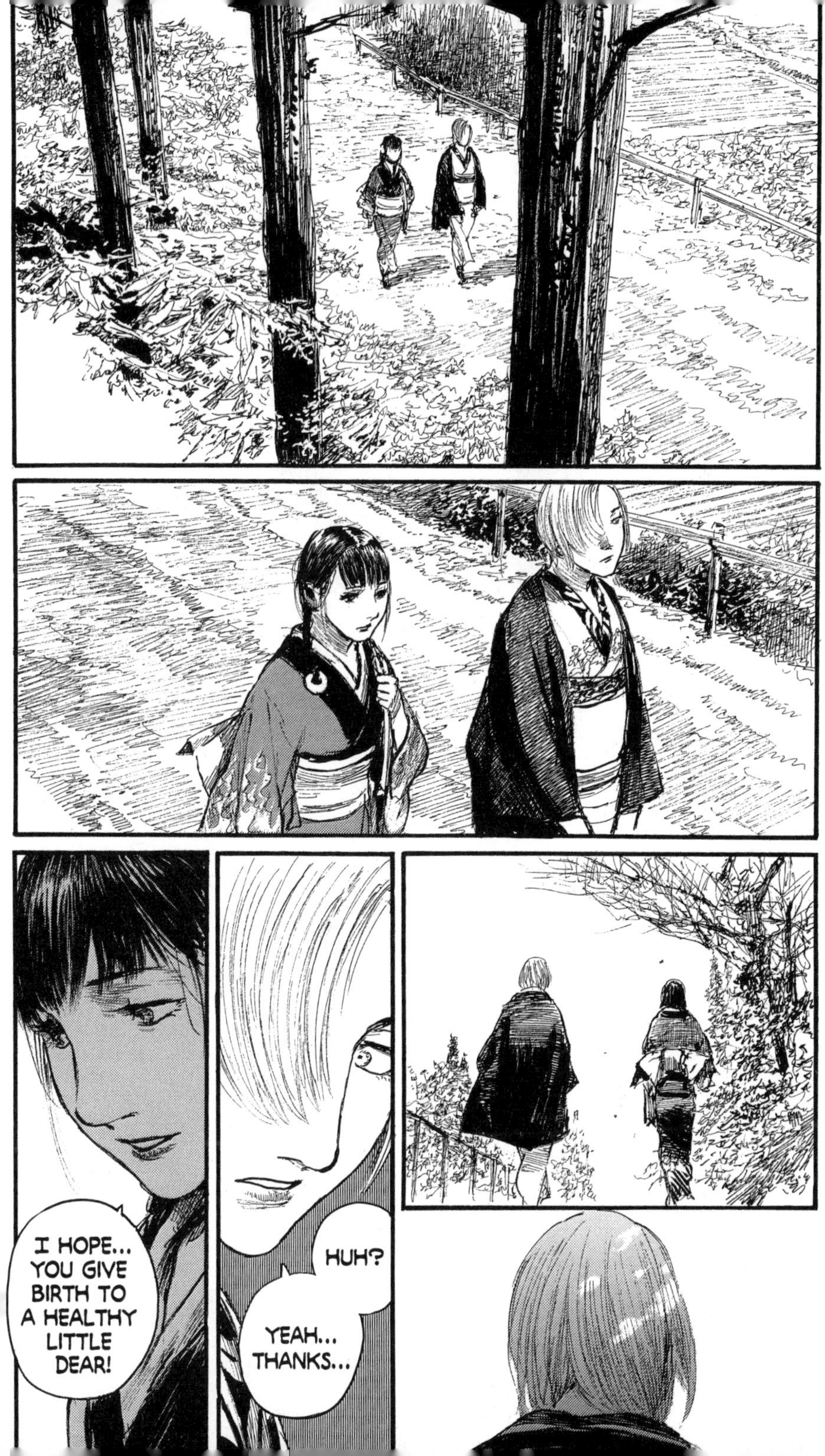
I HOPE... YOU GIVE BIRTH TO A HEALTHY LITTLE DEAR!
HUH?
YEAH... THANKS...

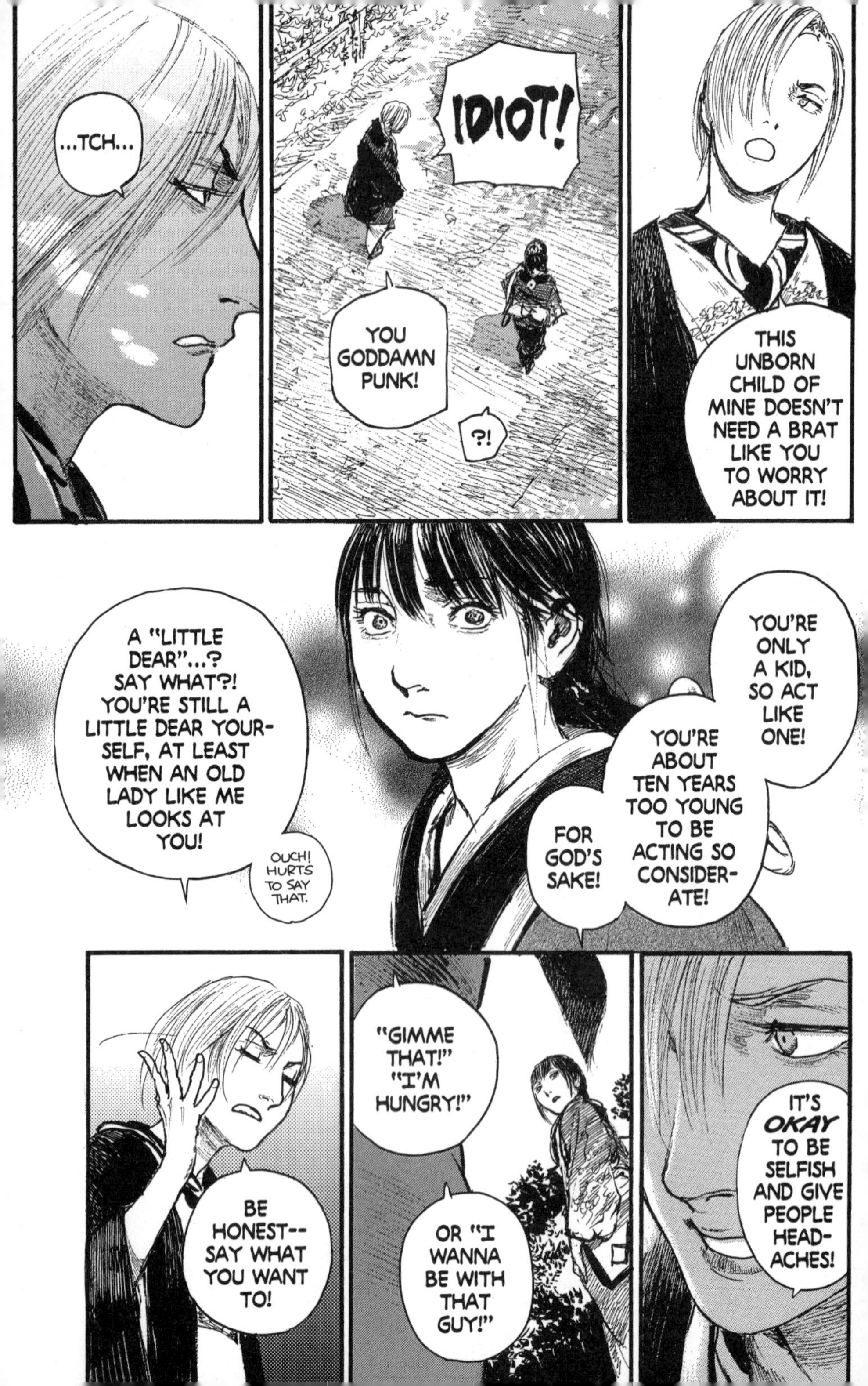
...TCH...
IDIOT!
YOU GODDAMN PUNK!
?!
THIS UNBORN CHILD OF MINE DOESN'T NEED A BRAT LIKE YOU TO WORRY ABOUT IT!
A "LITTLE DEAR"...? SAY WHAT?! YOU'RE STILL A LITTLE DEAR YOUR-SELF, AT LEAST WHEN AN OLD LADY LIKE ME LOOKS AT YOU!
OUCH! HURTS TO SAY THAT.
FOR GOD'S SAKE!
YOU'RE ABOUT TEN YEARS TOO YOUNG TO BE ACTING SO CONSIDER-ATE!
YOU'RE ONLY A KID, SO ACT LIKE ONE!
BE HONEST-- SAY WHAT YOU WANT TO!
"GIMME THAT!" "I'M HUNGRY!"
OR "I WANNA BE WITH THAT GUY!"
IT'S OKAY TO BE SELFISH AND GIVE PEOPLE HEAD-ACHES!

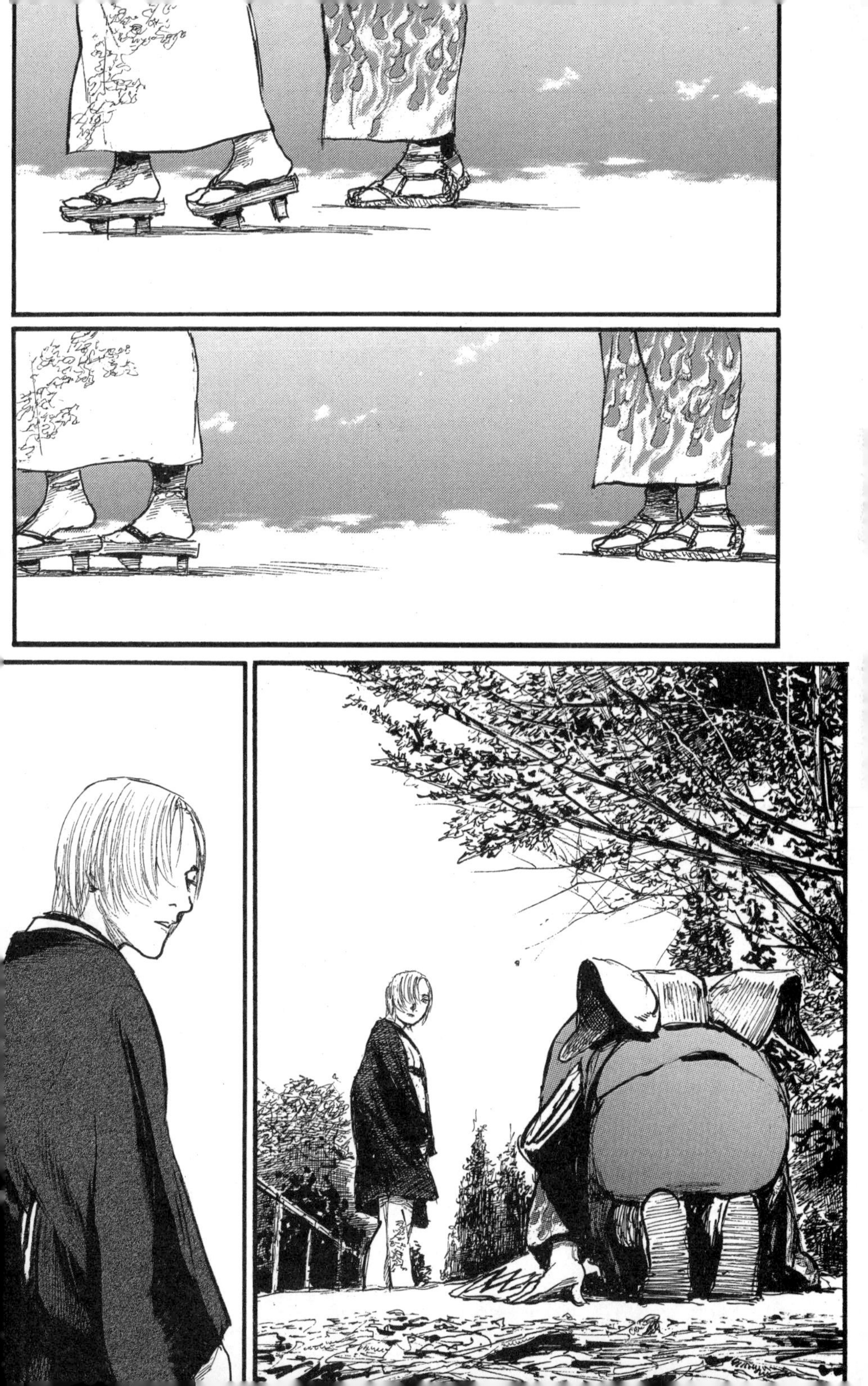

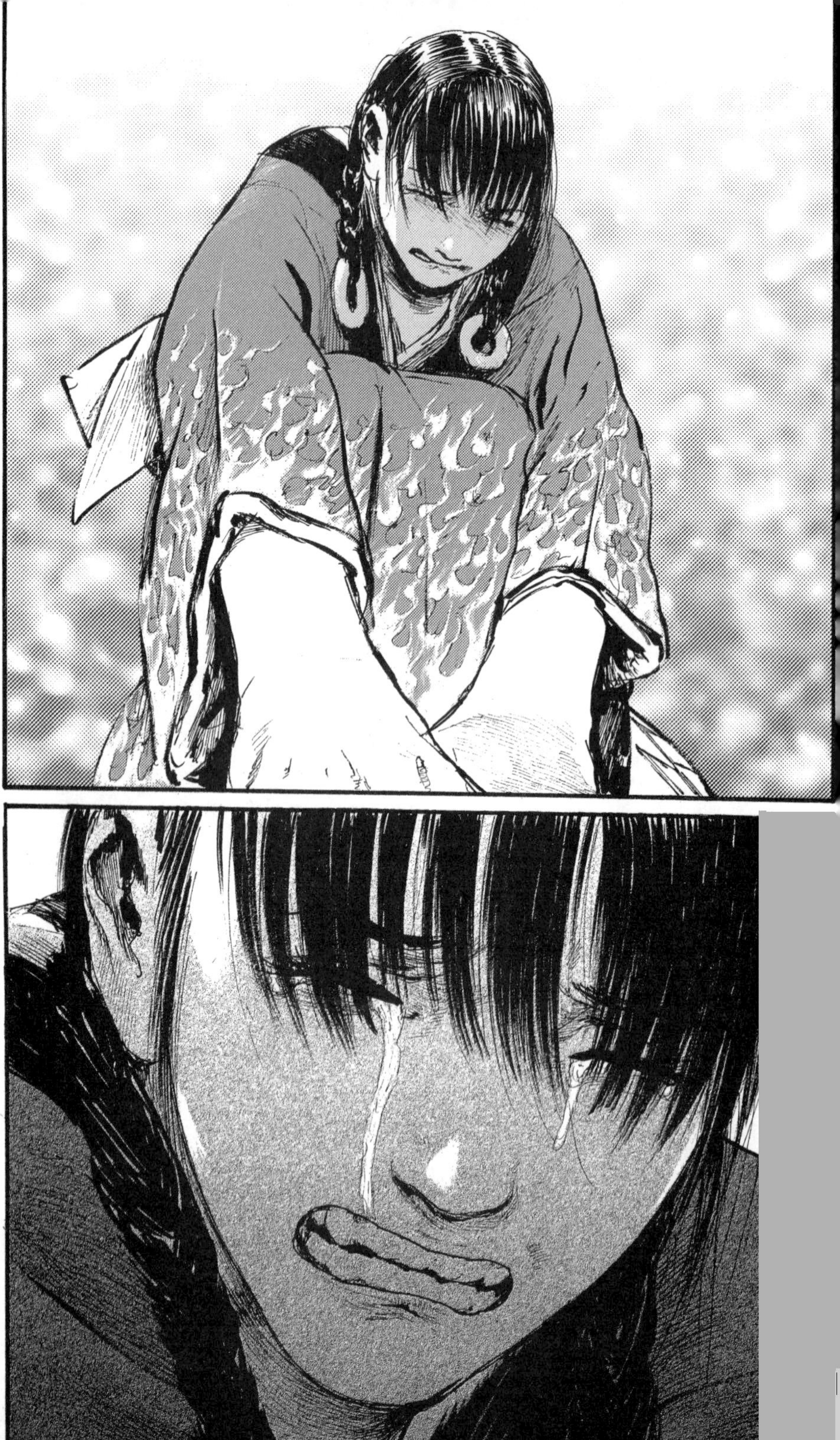

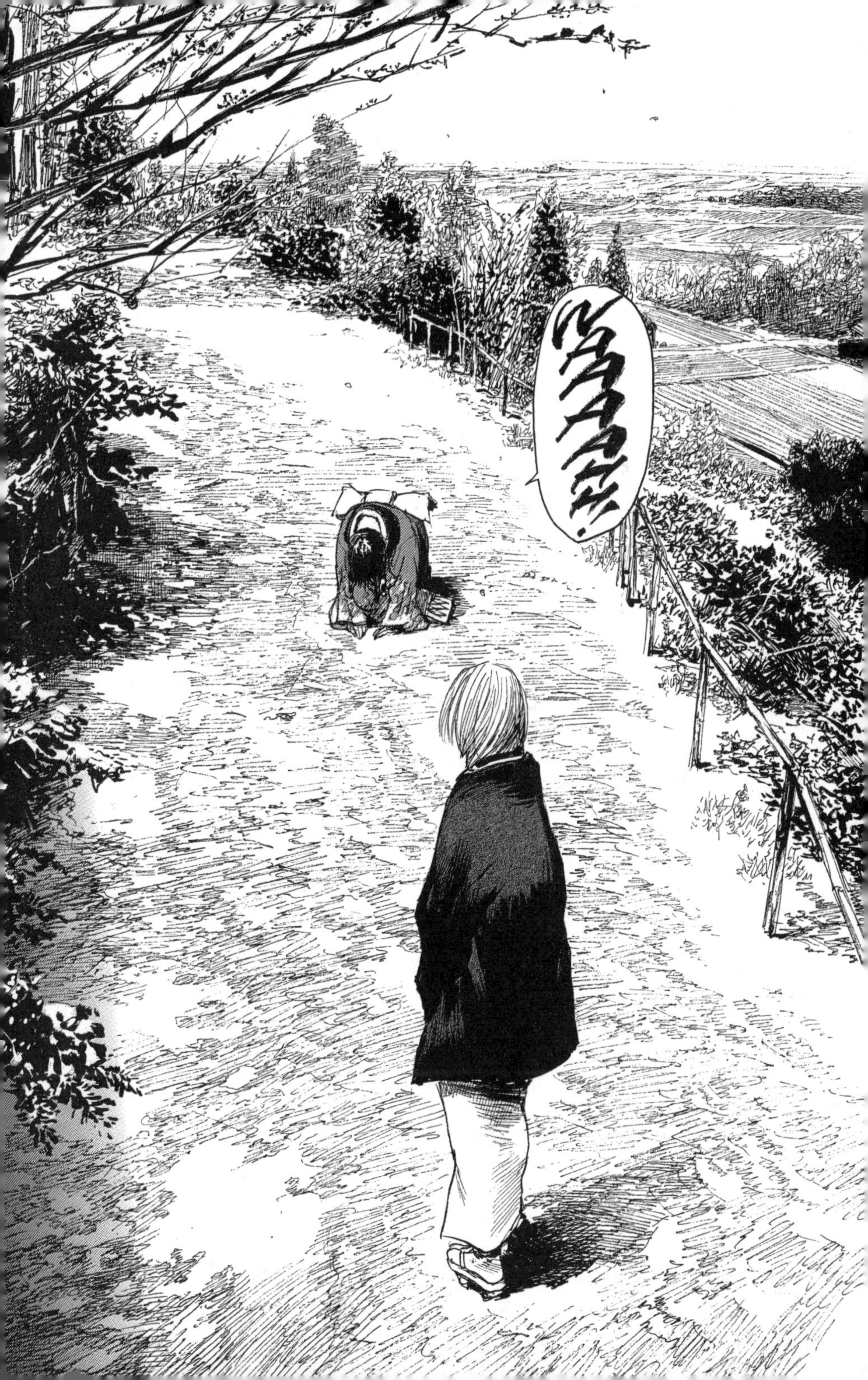

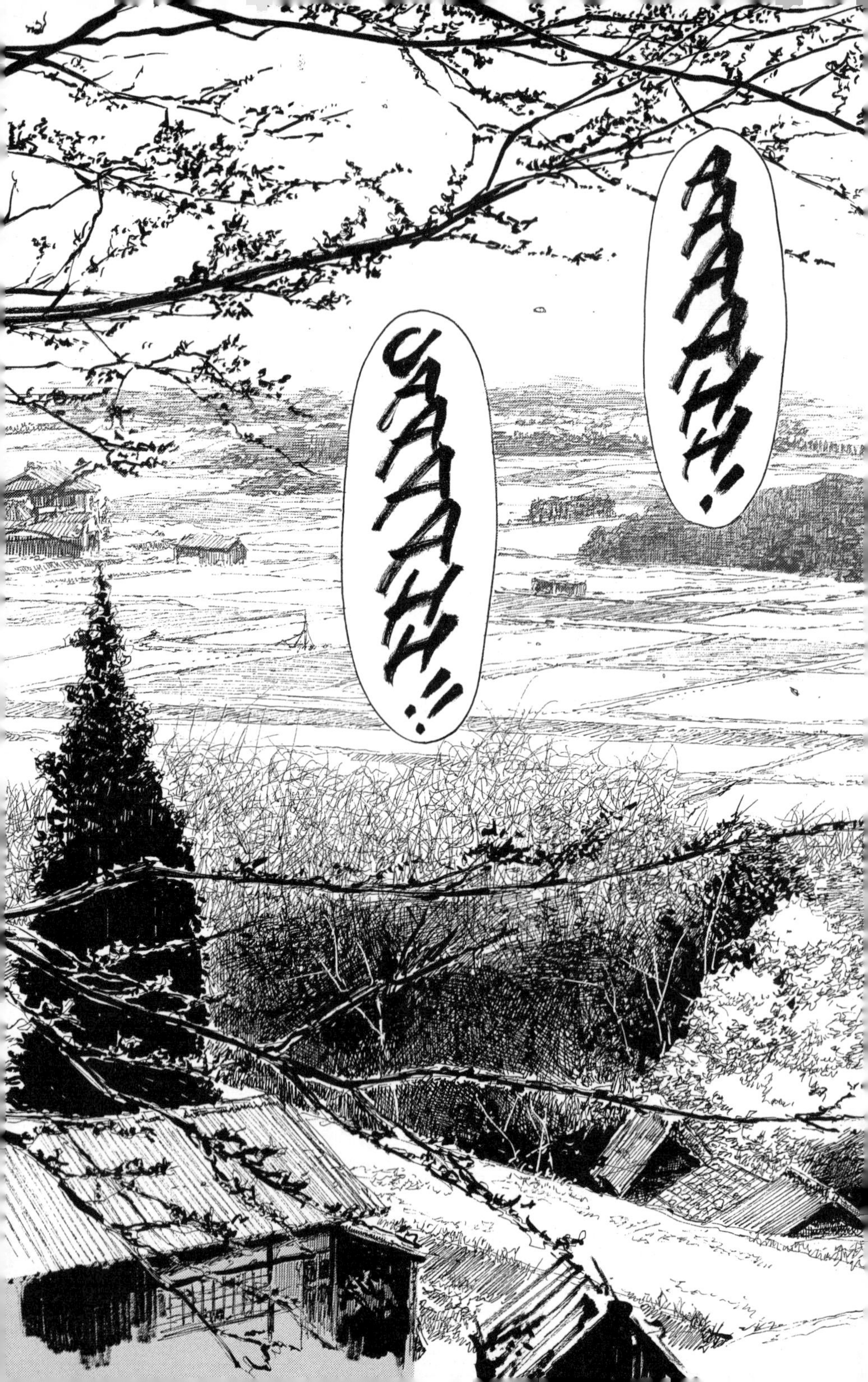
UAAAAHH!!
AAAAHH!

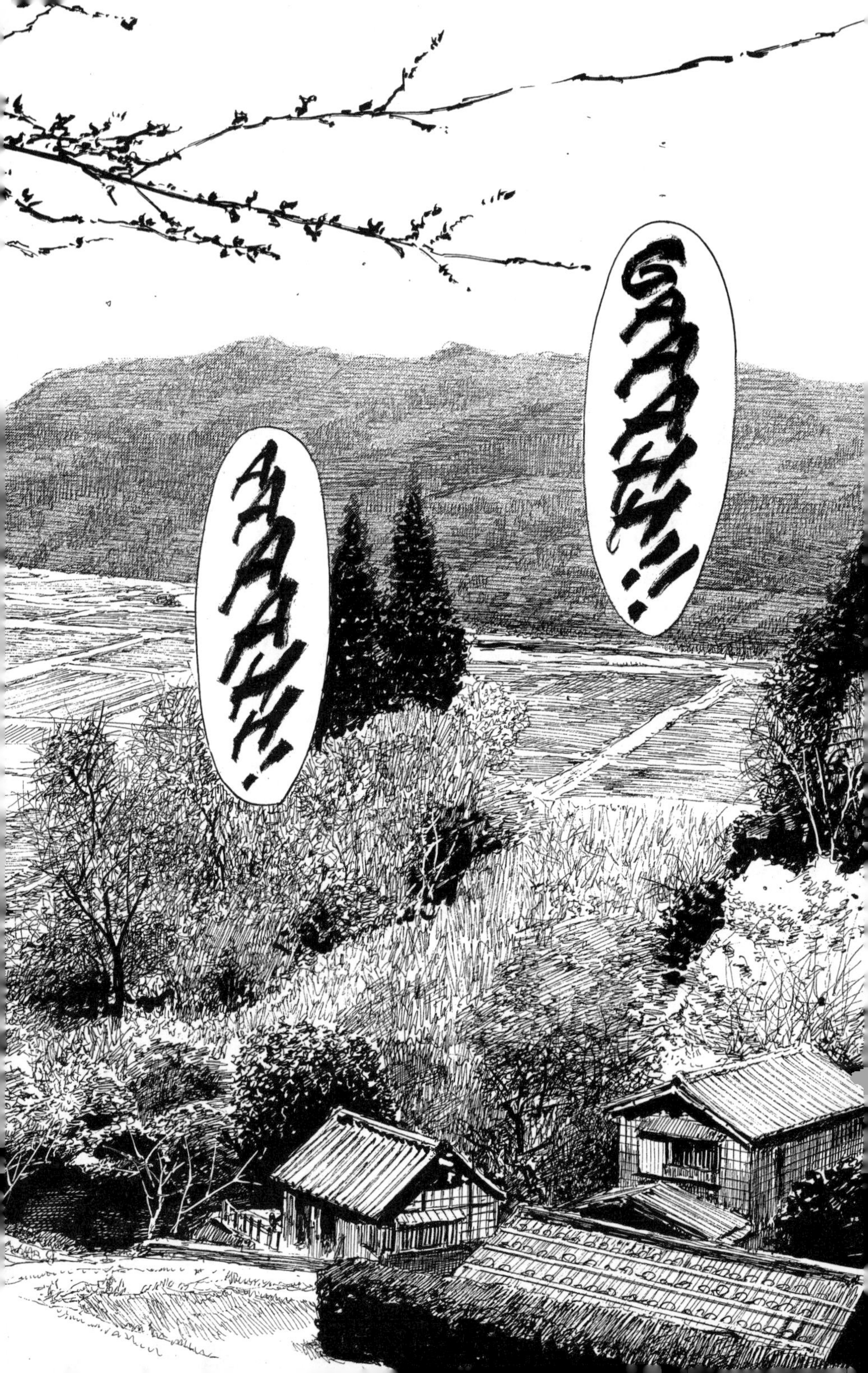
AAAAHHH!
GAAAHH!!

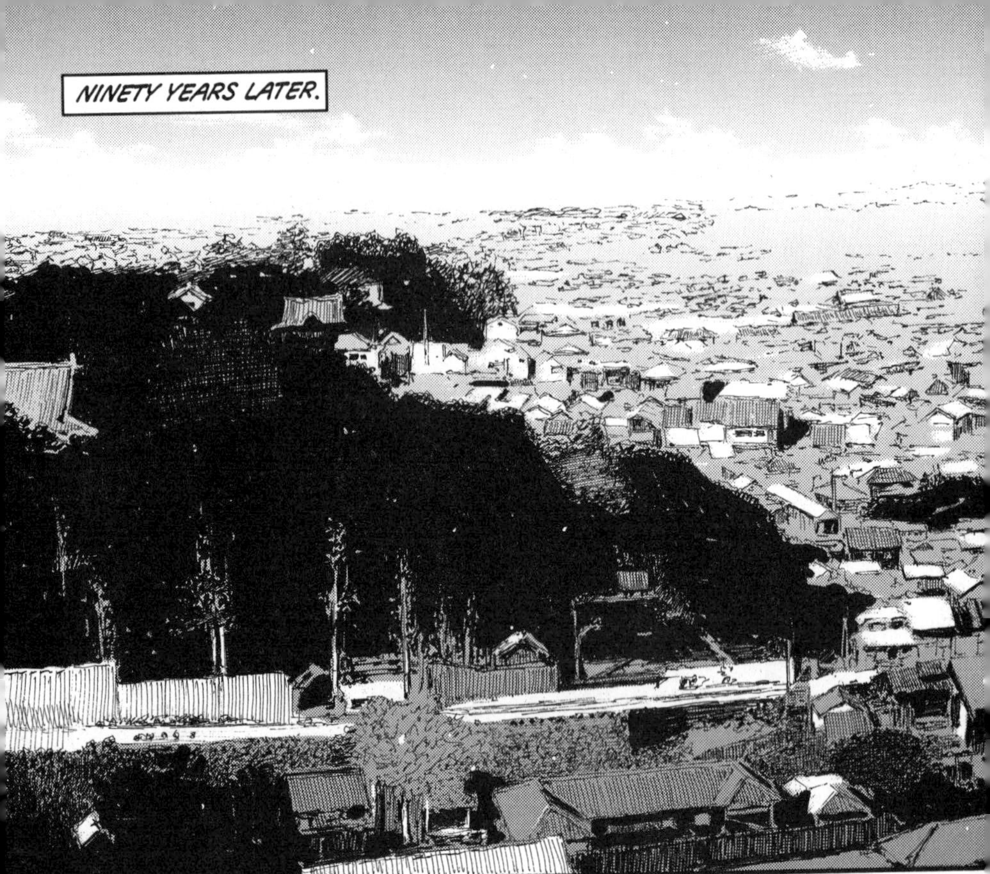
NINETY YEARS LATER.
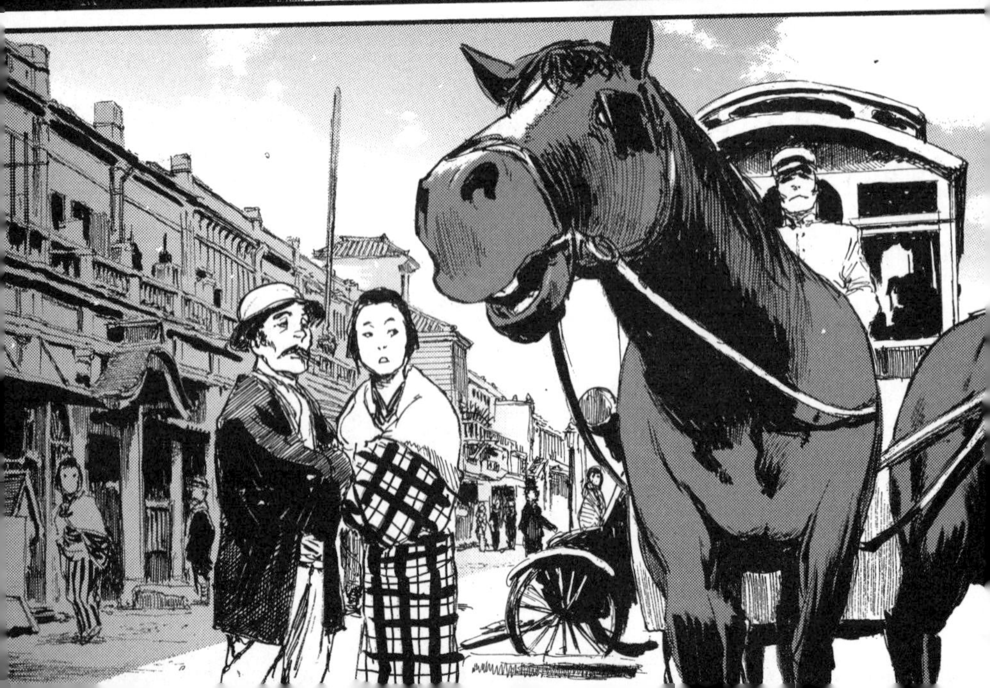

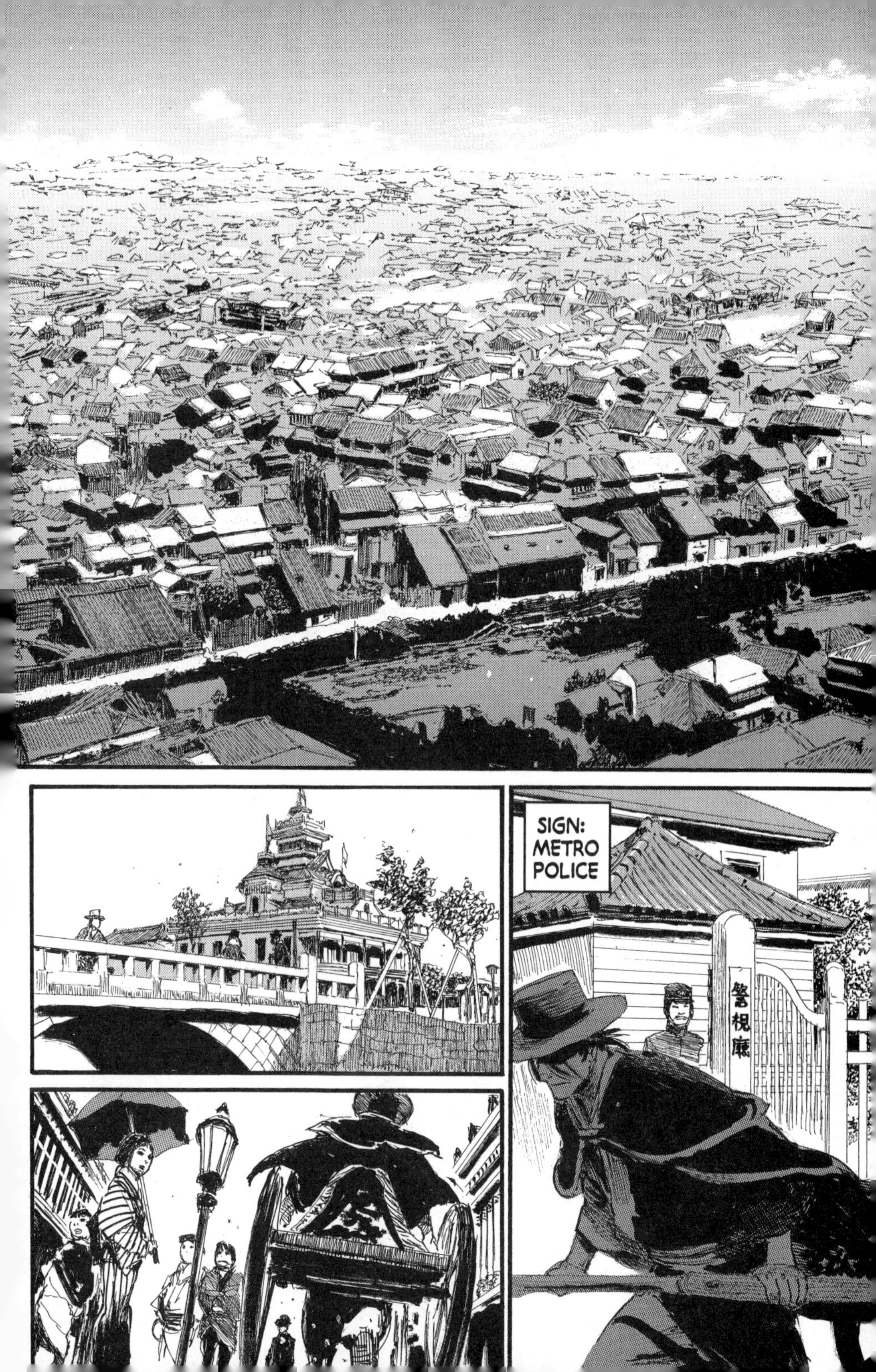
SIGN: METRO POLICE
警視庁

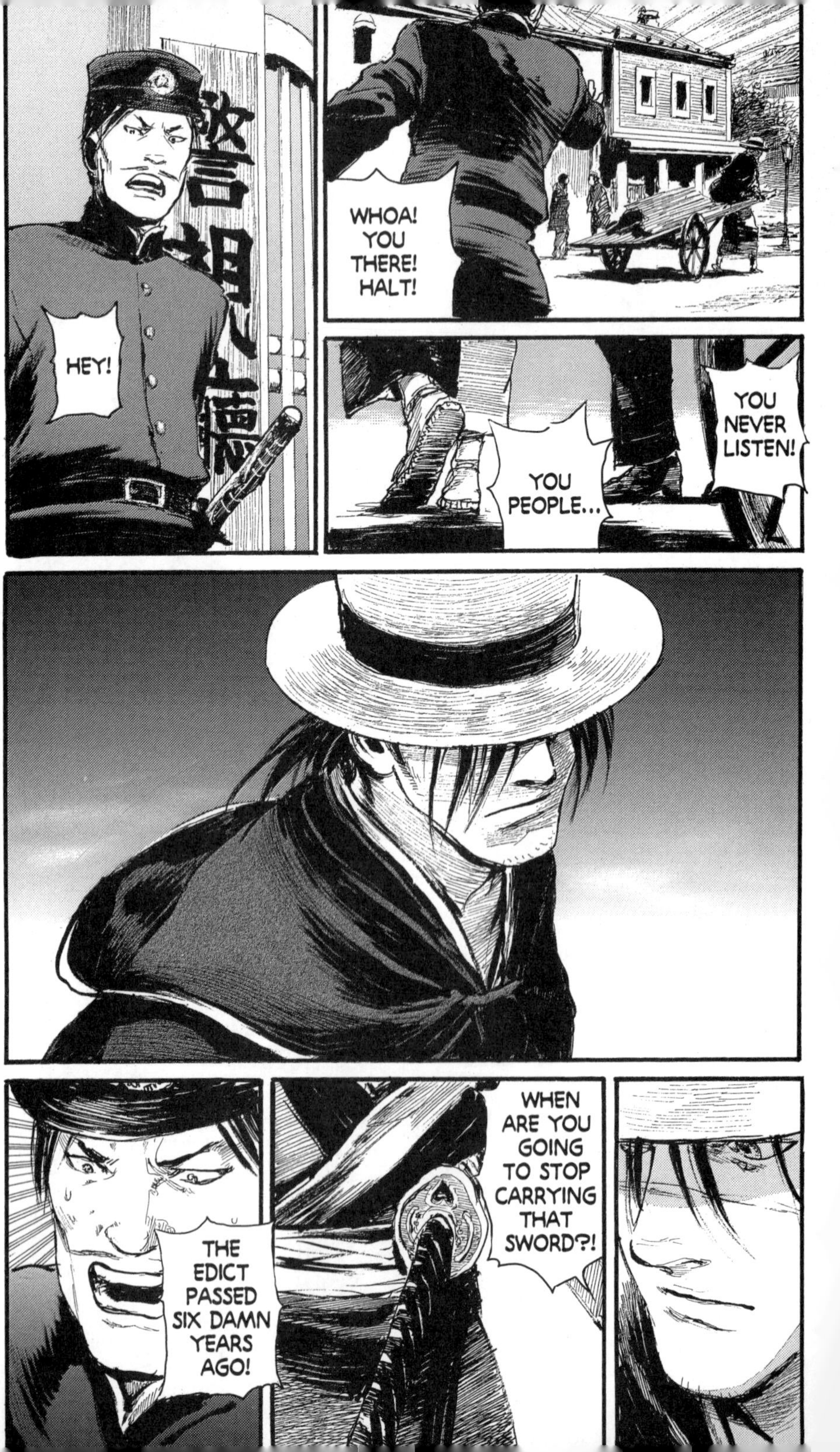
HEY!
WHOA! YOU THERE! HALT!
YOU PEOPLE...
YOU NEVER LISTEN!
THE EDICT PASSED SIX DAMN YEARS AGO!
WHEN ARE YOU GOING TO STOP CARRYING THAT SWORD?!

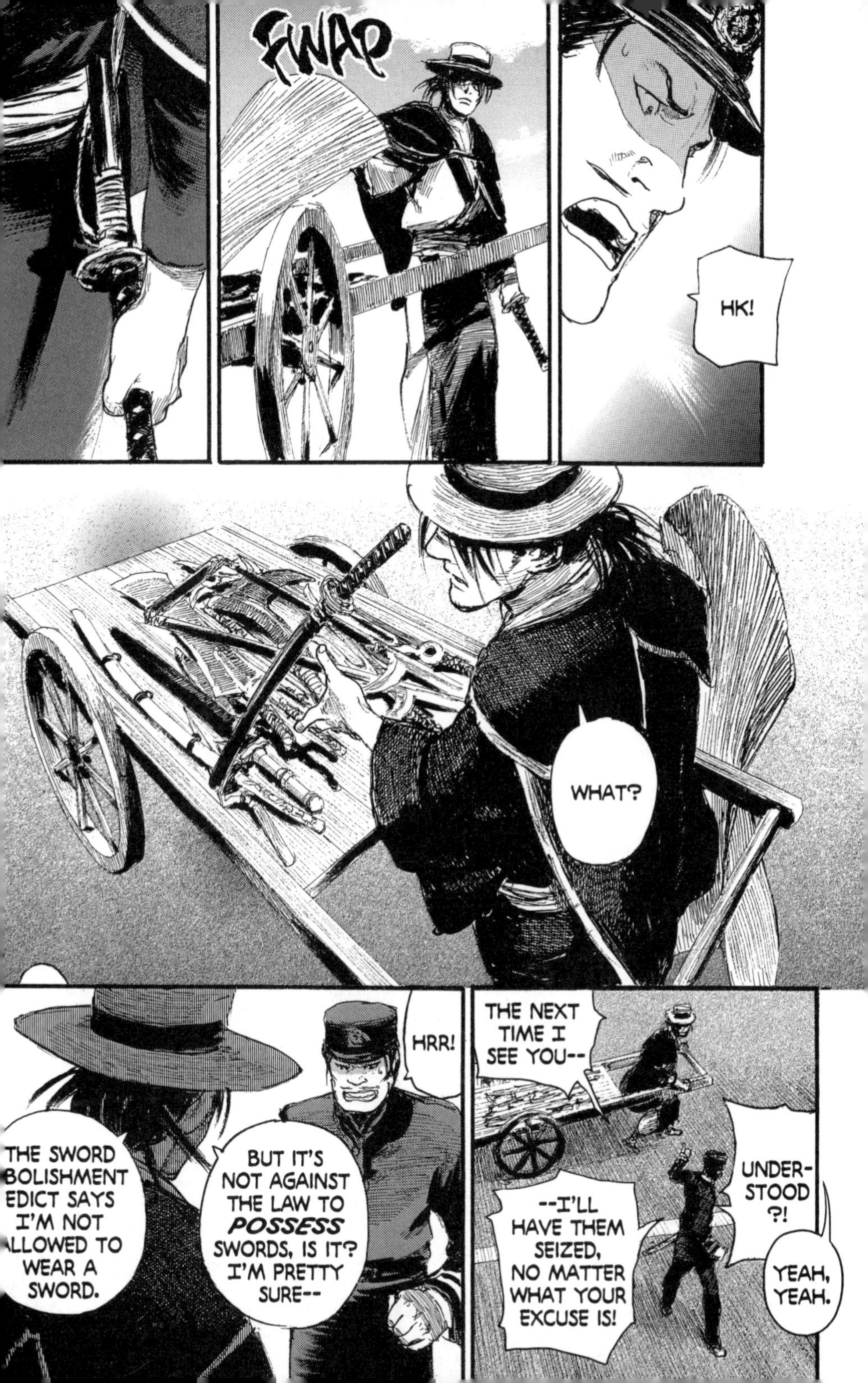
FWAP
HK!
WHAT?
THE SWORD BOLISHMENT EDICT SAYS I'M NOT LLOWED TO WEAR A SWORD.
BUT IT'S NOT AGAINST THE LAW TO *POSSESS* SWORDS, IS IT? I'M PRETTY SURE--
HRR!
THE NEXT TIME I SEE YOU--
--I'LL HAVE THEM SEIZED, NO MATTER WHAT YOUR EXCUSE IS!
UNDER-STOOD?!
YEAH, YEAH.

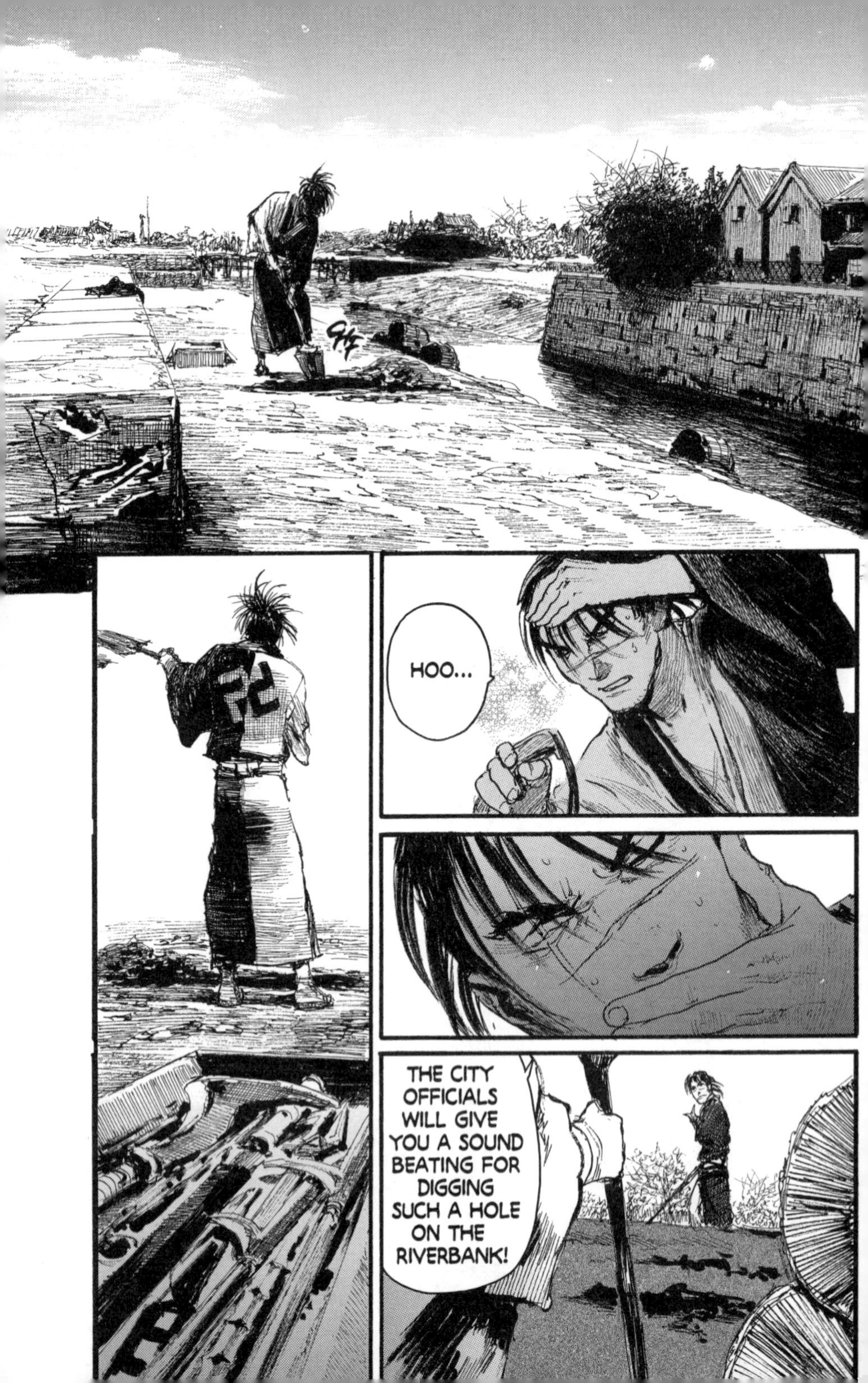
GAH
HOO...
THE CITY OFFICIALS WILL GIVE YOU A SOUND BEATING FOR DIGGING SUCH A HOLE ON THE RIVERBANK!

BEEN SEEIN' YOU A LOT LATELY, OLD LADY.

OH? IS THAT RIGHT?

OH! HO HO HO HO!

YOU GOING SENILE, GRANDMA?

I SAW YOU JUST TEN YEARS AGO...

...DIDN'T I?

I SAW ALL THAT COMMOTION, YOU KNOW.

HUH? OH.

THAT WAS HARDLY A "COMMOTION"...

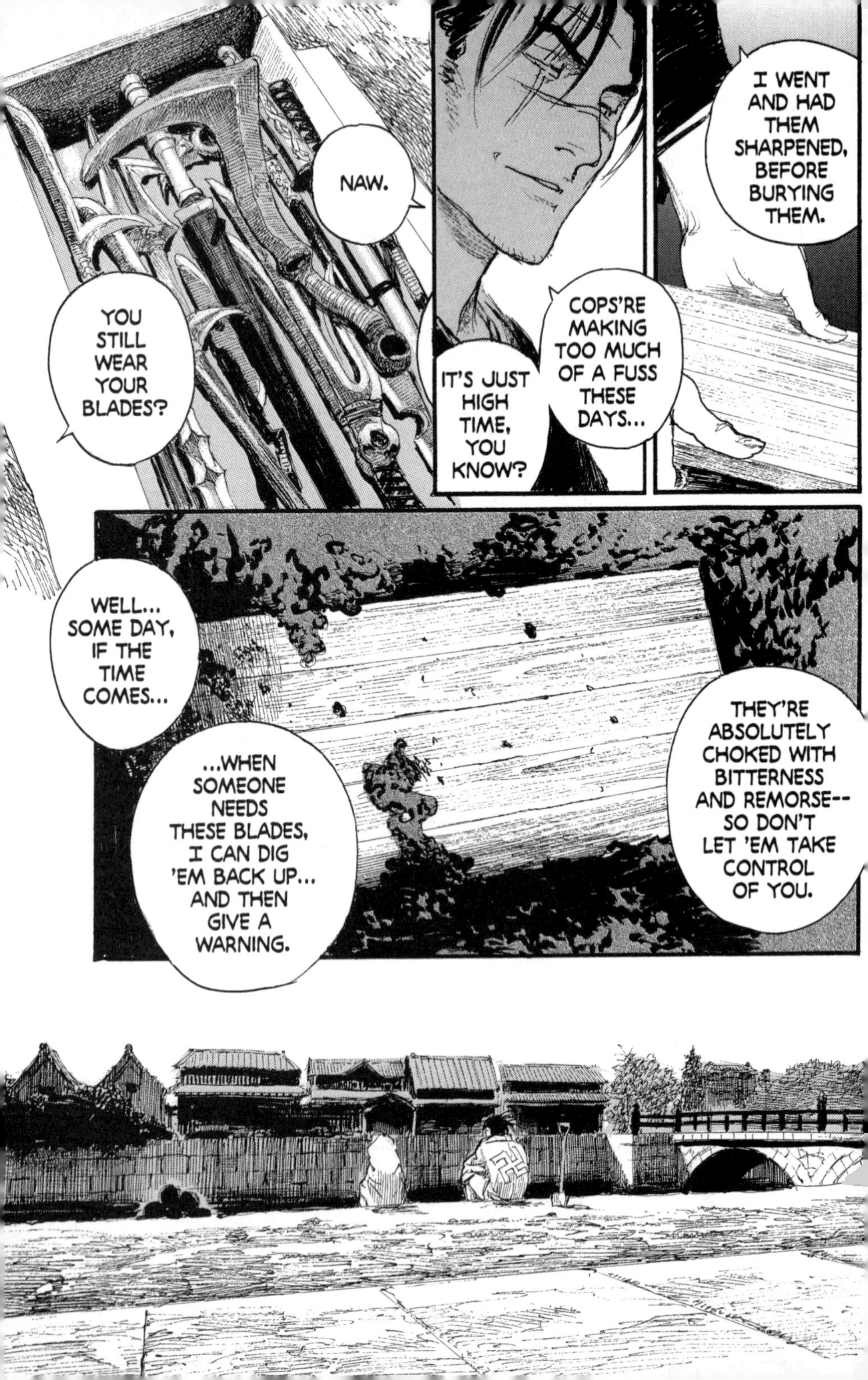
YOU STILL WEAR YOUR BLADES?
NAW.
IT'S JUST HIGH TIME, YOU KNOW?
COPS'RE MAKING TOO MUCH OF A FUSS THESE DAYS...
I WENT AND HAD THEM SHARPENED, BEFORE BURYING THEM.
WELL... SOME DAY, IF THE TIME COMES...
...WHEN SOMEONE NEEDS THESE BLADES, I CAN DIG 'EM BACK UP... AND THEN GIVE A WARNING.
THEY'RE ABSOLUTELY CHOKED WITH BITTERNESS AND REMORSE-- SO DON'T LET 'EM TAKE CONTROL OF YOU.

I DIDN'T ASK YOU LAST TIME, BUT WHERE'D YOU GO DURING THOSE EIGHTY YEARS...

...BEFORE THE *BAKUFU* WAS DISSOLVED?

WHERE? NOWHERE, REALLY...

HAD LOTSA FREE TIME. WENT TRUNDLING ALL OVER JAPAN.

WENT FISHING IN TOSA. GOT SHIP-WRECKED. WAS RESCUED BY AN AMERICAN SHIP.

AND WHEN I FINALLY GOT BACK TO JAPAN-- TWELVE YEARS LATER-- I WAS THROWN INTO HAGI PRISON.

HAD TO STUDY PHILOSOPHY. MENCIUS.

OH, I ENDED UP IN A BIG FIGHT OVER I DUNNO WHAT WITH SOME ITTŌ-RYŪ SORTA GUYS IN KYOTO...

I THOUGHT IT WOULD BE ONE ON ONE, BUT THE FOUR OF 'EM WORKED TOGETHER! HAD MY ASS HANDED TO ME...

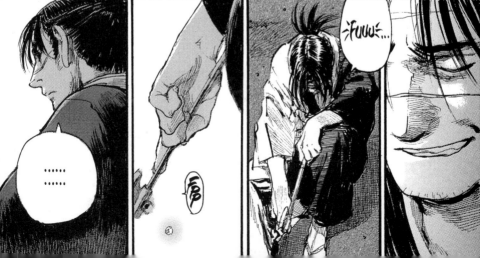

......
......

=FUUU=...

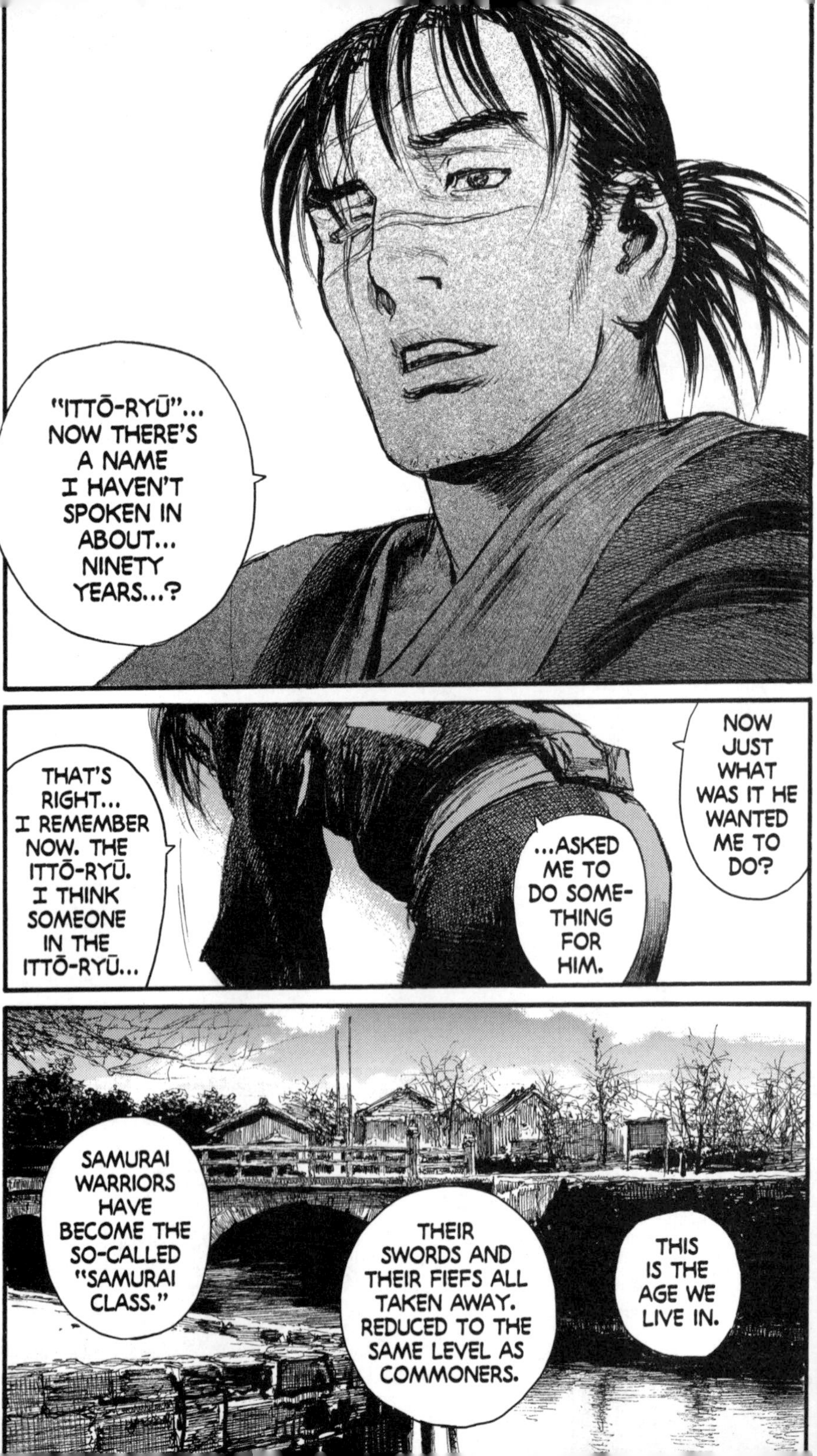
"ITTŌ-RYŪ"... NOW THERE'S A NAME I HAVEN'T SPOKEN IN ABOUT... NINETY YEARS...?
THAT'S RIGHT... I REMEMBER NOW. THE ITTŌ-RYŪ. I THINK SOMEONE IN THE ITTŌ-RYŪ...
...ASKED ME TO DO SOME-THING FOR HIM.
NOW JUST WHAT WAS IT HE WANTED ME TO DO?
SAMURAI WARRIORS HAVE BECOME THE SO-CALLED "SAMURAI CLASS."
THEIR SWORDS AND THEIR FIEFS ALL TAKEN AWAY. REDUCED TO THE SAME LEVEL AS COMMONERS.
THIS IS THE AGE WE LIVE IN.

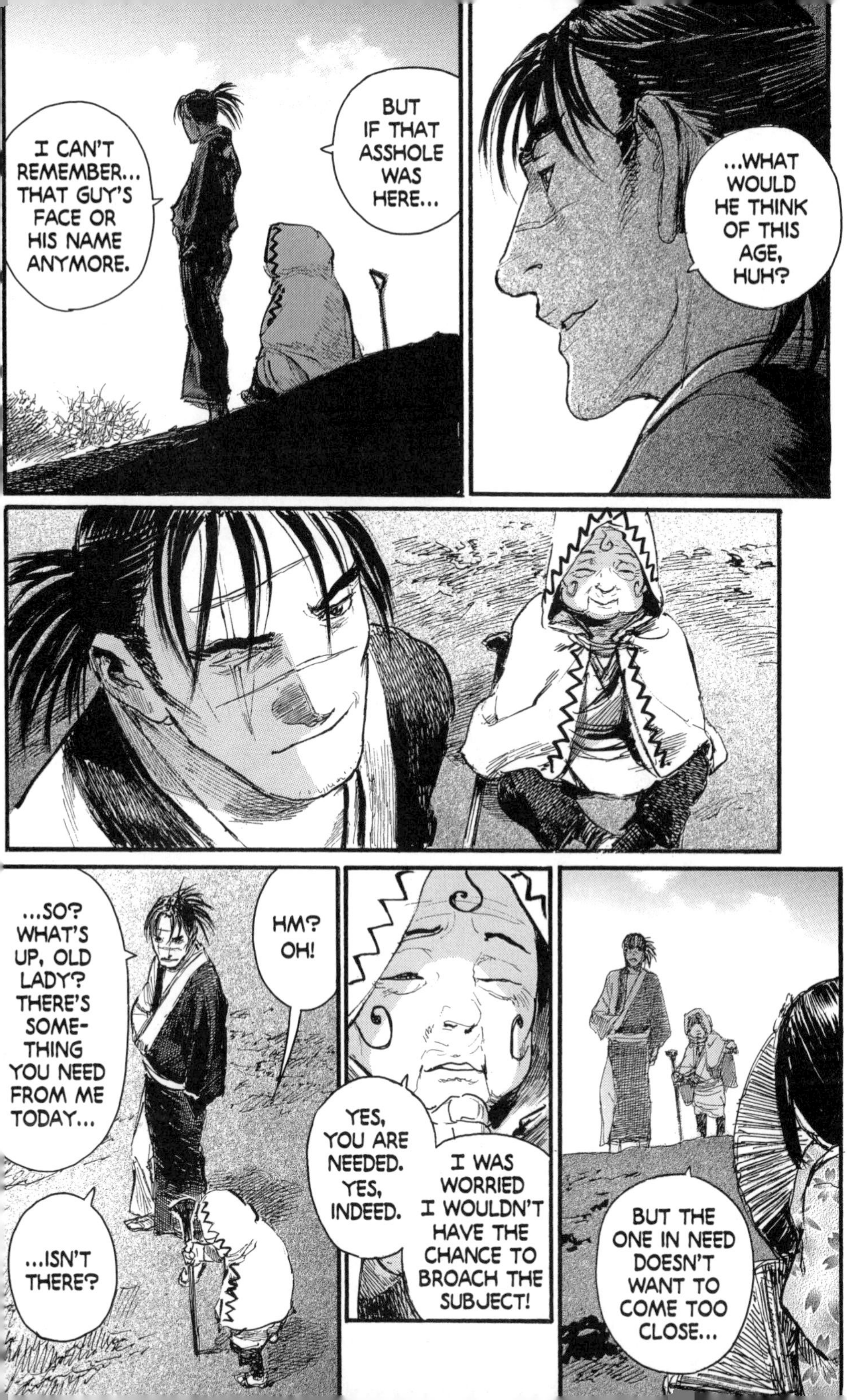
I CAN'T REMEMBER... THAT GUY'S FACE OR HIS NAME ANYMORE.
BUT IF THAT ASSHOLE WAS HERE...
...WHAT WOULD HE THINK OF THIS AGE, HUH?
...SO? WHAT'S UP, OLD LADY? THERE'S SOME-THING YOU NEED FROM ME TODAY...
...ISN'T THERE?
HM? OH!
YES, YOU ARE NEEDED. YES, INDEED.
I WAS WORRIED I WOULDN'T HAVE THE CHANCE TO BROACH THE SUBJECT!
BUT THE ONE IN NEED DOESN'T WANT TO COME TOO CLOSE...

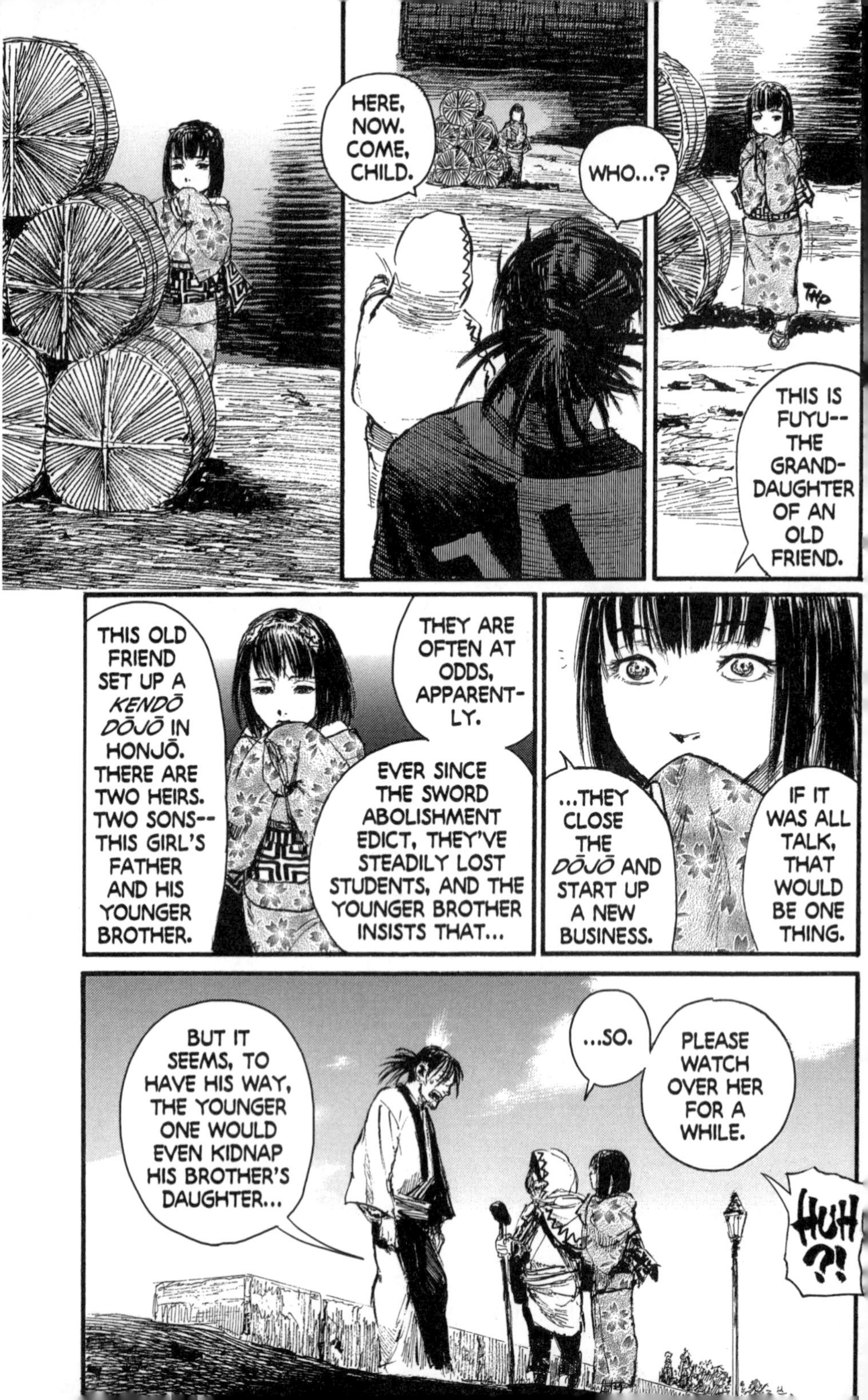
HERE, NOW. COME, CHILD.
WHO...?
THP
THIS IS FUYU--THE GRAND-DAUGHTER OF AN OLD FRIEND.
THIS OLD FRIEND SET UP A *KENDŌ DŌJŌ* IN HONJŌ. THERE ARE TWO HEIRS. TWO SONS--THIS GIRL'S FATHER AND HIS YOUNGER BROTHER.
THEY ARE OFTEN AT ODDS, APPARENT-LY.
EVER SINCE THE SWORD ABOLISHMENT EDICT, THEY'VE STEADILY LOST STUDENTS, AND THE YOUNGER BROTHER INSISTS THAT...
...THEY CLOSE THE *DŌJŌ* AND START UP A NEW BUSINESS.
IF IT WAS ALL TALK, THAT WOULD BE ONE THING.
BUT IT SEEMS, TO HAVE HIS WAY, THE YOUNGER ONE WOULD EVEN KIDNAP HIS BROTHER'S DAUGHTER...
...SO.
PLEASE WATCH OVER HER FOR A WHILE.
HUH?!

...HAT?

SO YOU'RE A *YŌJIMBŌ* BROKER, ARE YOU, OLD LADY? WHY ME...?

LOOK, I'M LIVIN' DAY TO DAY ON THE STREETS.

THAT'S TOO HARD FOR A KID!

I CAN HARDLY FEED MY-SELF!

I CAN'T LOOK AFTER HER!

JUST HOW THE-- HUH?

...HERE...

?

WHAT IS THIS?

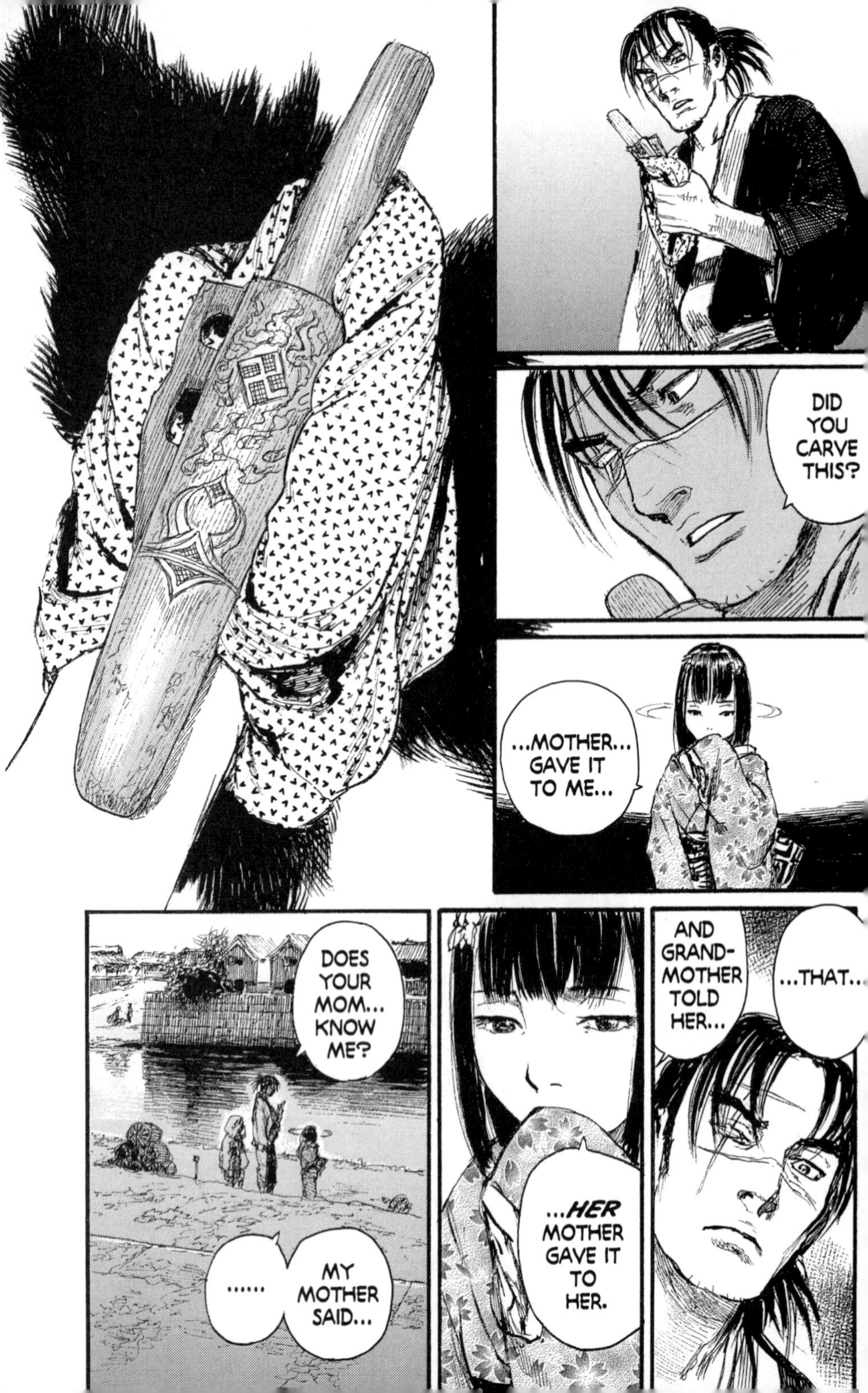
DID YOU CARVE THIS?
...MOTHER... GAVE IT TO ME...
DOES YOUR MOM... KNOW ME?
......
MY MOTHER SAID...
...*HER* MOTHER GAVE IT TO HER.
AND GRAND-MOTHER TOLD HER...
...THAT...

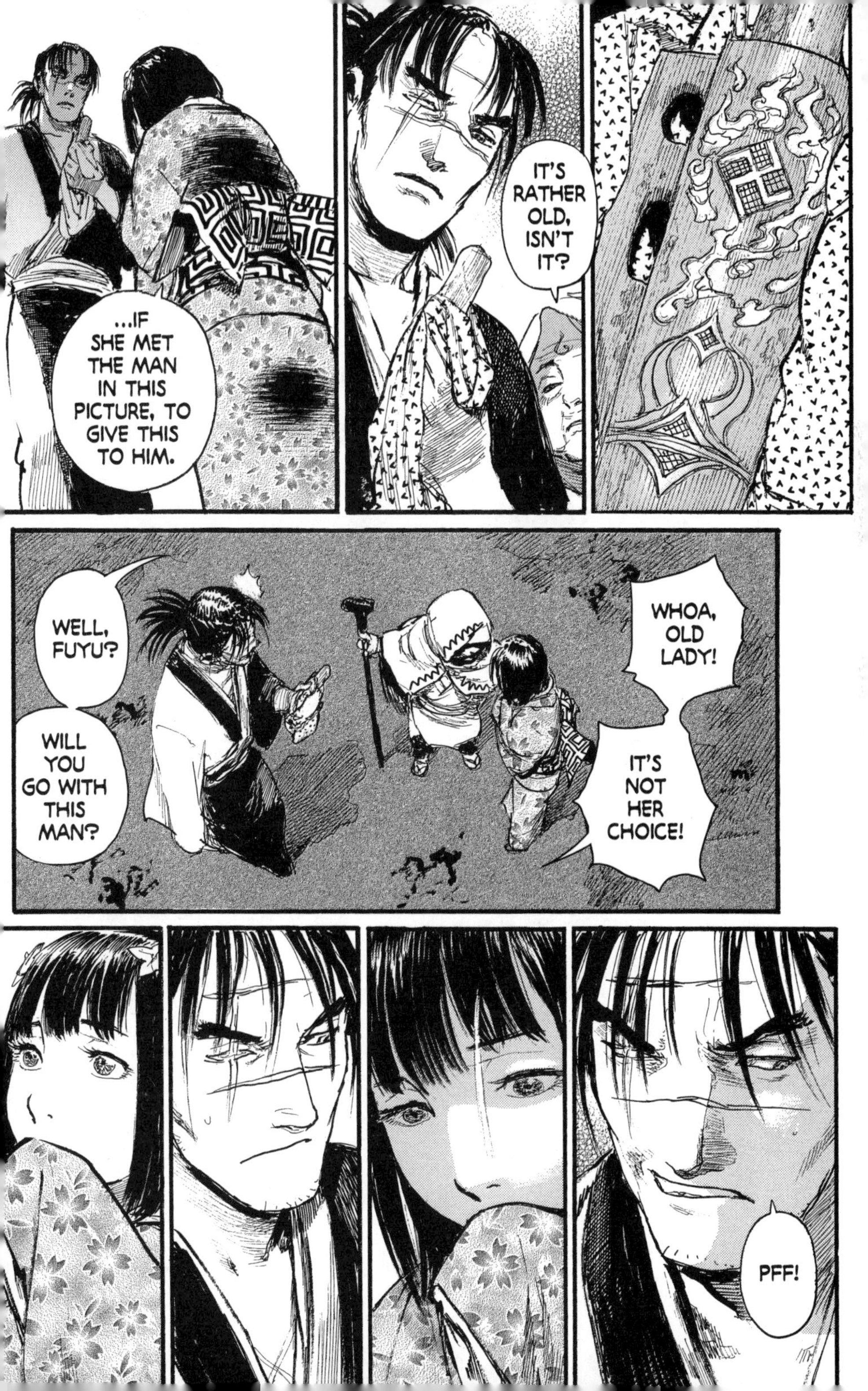
...IF SHE MET THE MAN IN THIS PICTURE, TO GIVE THIS TO HIM.
IT'S RATHER OLD, ISN'T IT?
WELL, FUYU?
WILL YOU GO WITH THIS MAN?
WHOA, OLD LADY!
IT'S NOT HER CHOICE!
PFF!

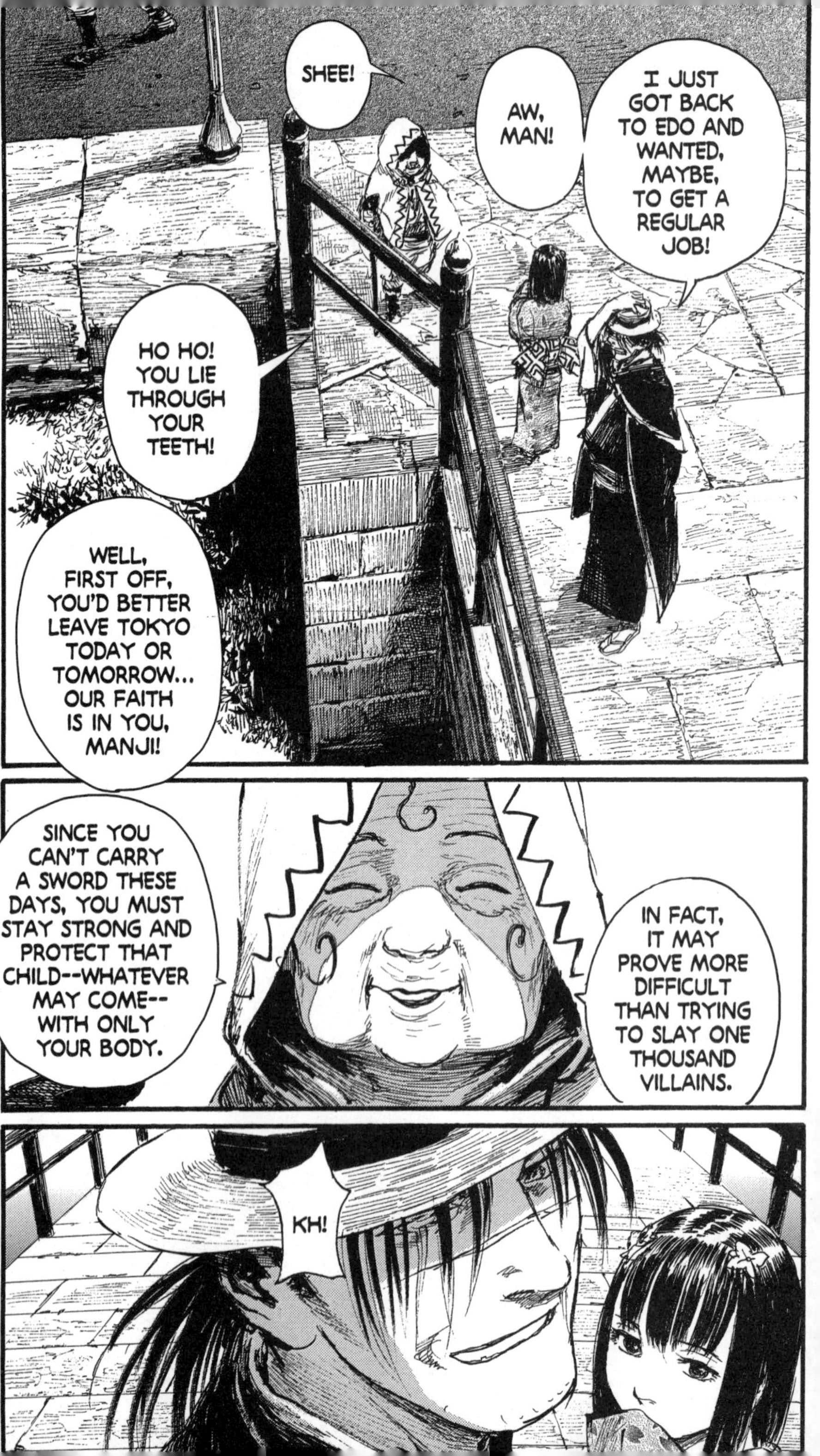
SHEE!
AW, MAN!
I JUST GOT BACK TO EDO AND WANTED, MAYBE, TO GET A REGULAR JOB!
HO HO! YOU LIE THROUGH YOUR TEETH!
WELL, FIRST OFF, YOU'D BETTER LEAVE TOKYO TODAY OR TOMORROW... OUR FAITH IS IN YOU, MANJI!
SINCE YOU CAN'T CARRY A SWORD THESE DAYS, YOU MUST STAY STRONG AND PROTECT THAT CHILD--WHATEVER MAY COME--WITH ONLY YOUR BODY.
IN FACT, IT MAY PROVE MORE DIFFICULT THAN TRYING TO SLAY ONE THOUSAND VILLAINS.
KH!

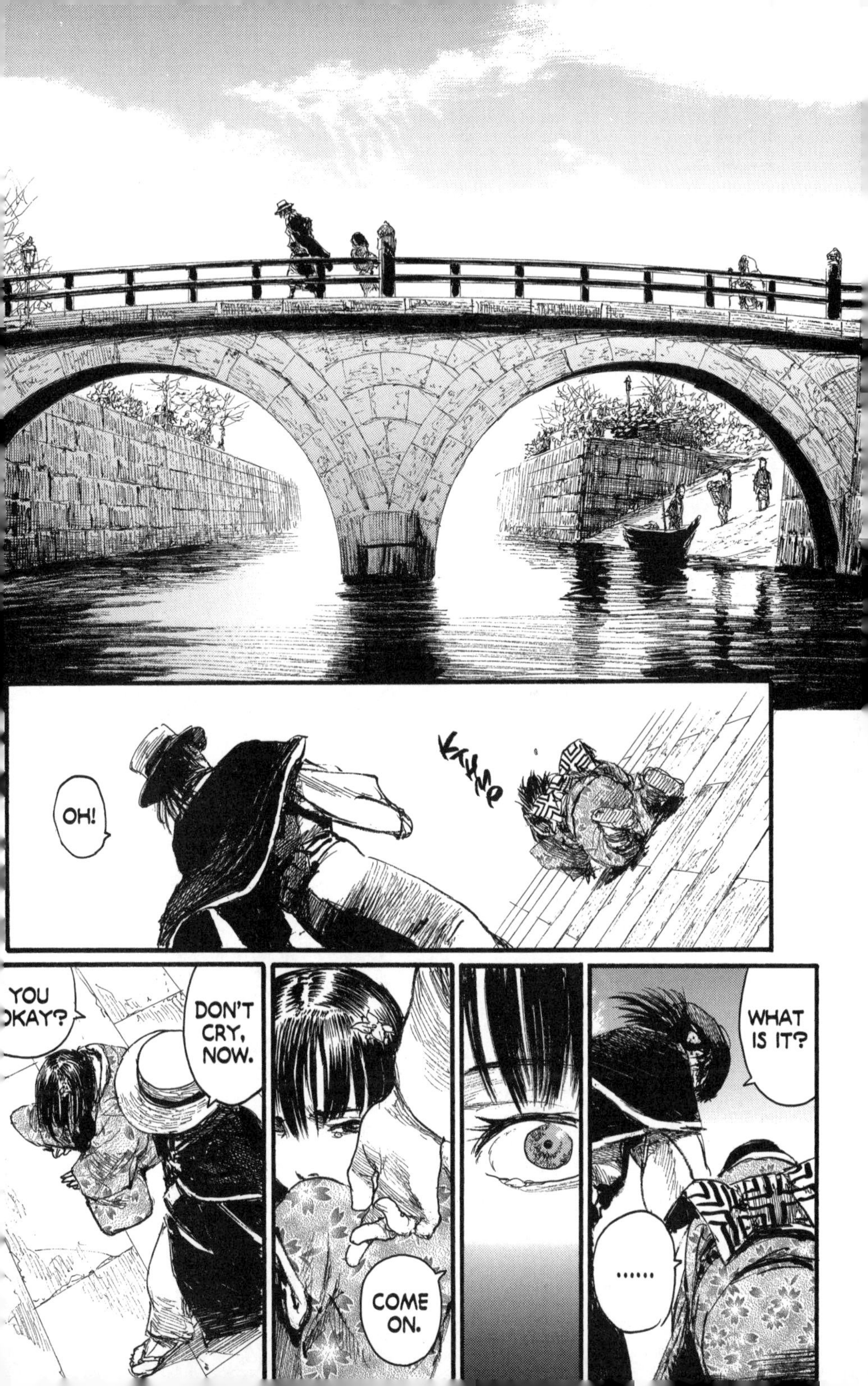
OH!
KTHMP
YOU OKAY?
DON'T CRY, NOW.
COME ON.
WHAT IS IT?
......

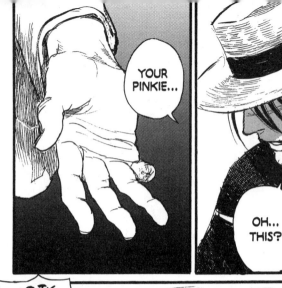

YOUR PINKIE...

OH... THIS?

≥PHT!≤
GAH!
HA HA
HA HA!

≥ULP!≤

EH...?

HELL!

THANKS TO YOU, I FINALLY REMEMBERED HIS NAME!

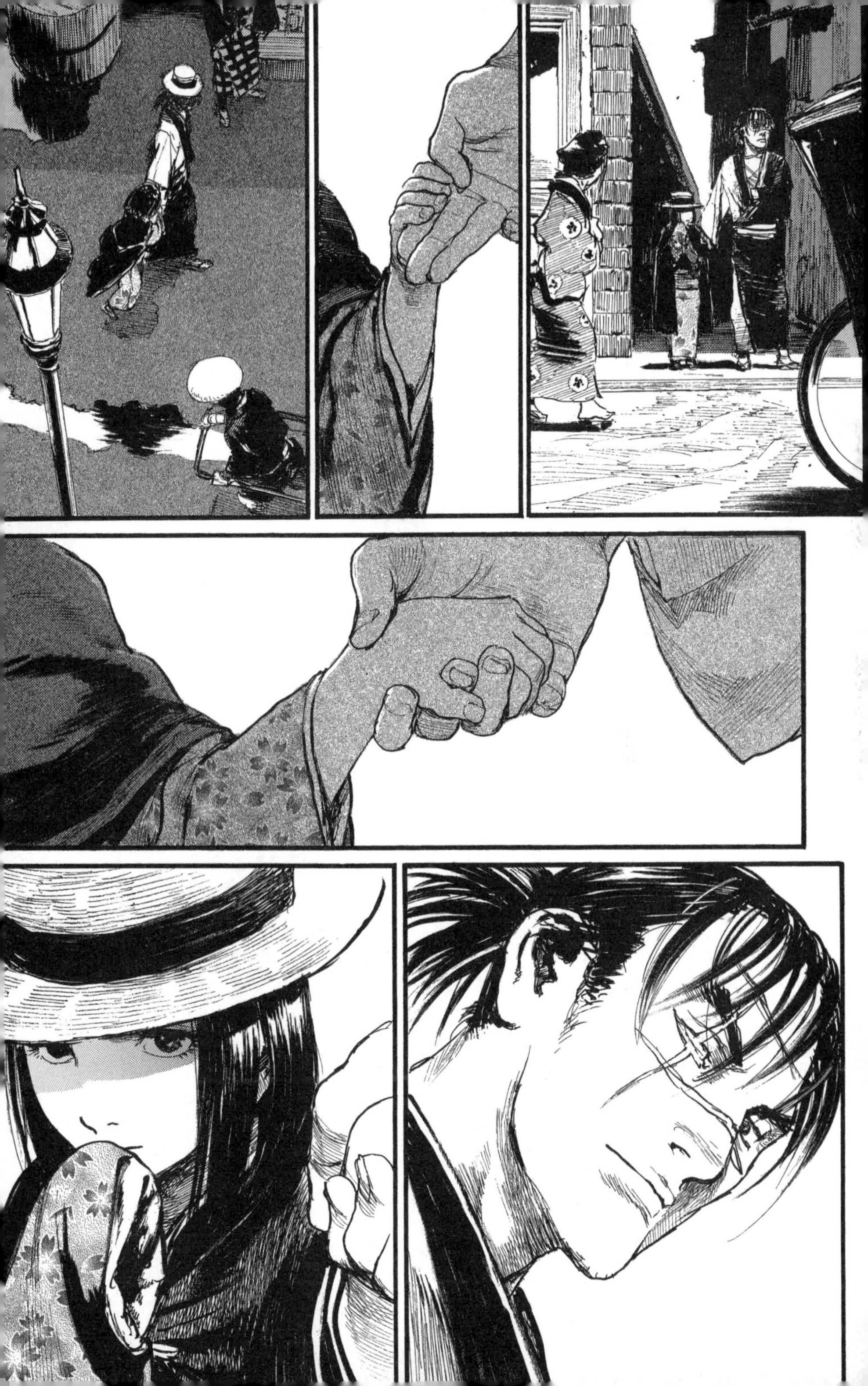

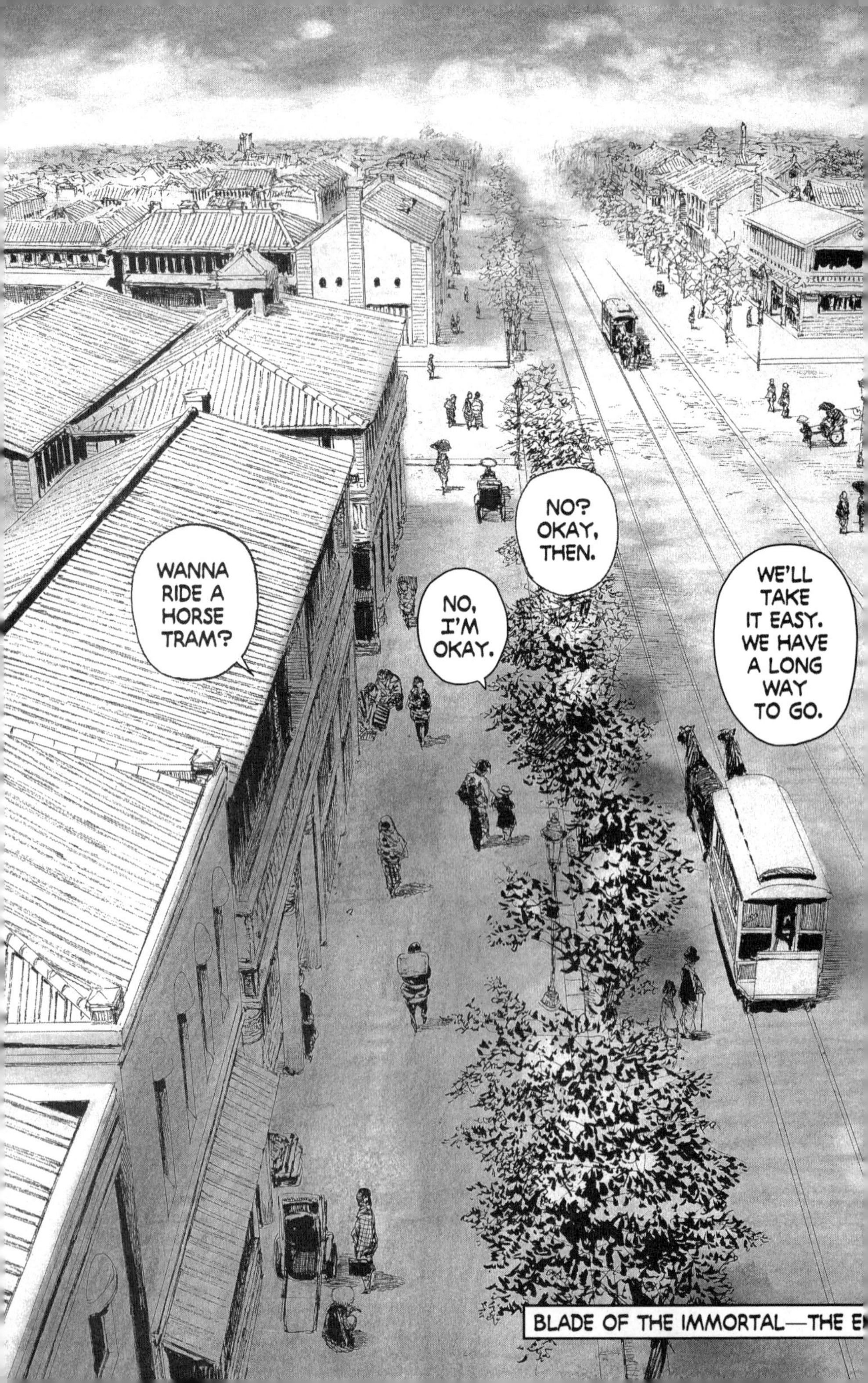
WANNA RIDE A HORSE TRAM?
NO, I'M OKAY.
NO? OKAY, THEN.
WE'LL TAKE IT EASY. WE HAVE A LONG WAY TO GO.
BLADE OF THE IMMORTAL—THE E

GLOSSARY

bakufu: (1) The central government originally established in Edo (today's Tokyo) by the warlord Tokugawa Ieyasu. (2) The bureaucracy that grew up around the Tokugawa shoguns.

bangashira: Head of the banshū.

banshū: Officers serving under the shogun, usually assigned to Edo Castle to defend the shogun himself.

bushi: Warriors; samurai.

chan: Honorific used to show affection, most often toward young people and sometimes between close friends.

chōkibune: Edo-period water taxi. Ozuhan seems to have hijacked one in this volume.

daimyō: Ruler of a *han*, or feudal fiefdom. By the late-Edo period of *Blade of the Immortal*, the shogunate had evolved into a de facto central government, with only a few unruly *han* resisting assimilation.

dōjō: A school for combat and self-defense training in martial arts; here, a training center for swordsmanship.

dono: Archaic honorific used to show respect, usually for someone of higher rank.

Edo: Capital of premodern Japan, later renamed Tokyo.

go-rōjū: Senior councilors to the shogun, picked from the most trusted *daimyō*.

go-sanke: One of the three branches of the Tokugawa clan.

go-teni: Doctors employed by the feudal lords who served under the shogun.

han: A feudal estate or fiefdom.

hana-gumi: The "flower group" or "flower team" that Habaki Kagimura has put together to help him kill off the Ittō-ryū—these are the more elite fighters.

hara-kiri: Ritual suicide by disembowelment, also known as *seppuku*.

hebi-gumi: The "snake group" or "snake team" that Habaki Kagimura has put together to help defeat the Ittō-ryū—these are the less-skilled fighters in Kagimura's small army.

Honjō: One of the Shitamachi, a group of low-lying districts in eastern Tokyo near Tokyo Bay.

iai stance: A position that allows a swordsman to simultaneously draw and slash, in a single movement, from a sitting or crouched position.

Ittō-ryū: The radical sword school of Anotsu Kagehisa.

jibuni: Boiled and seasoned duck with vegetables, a Kanazawa city and Ishikawa Prefecture specialty.

jō: A length of approximately three meters.

kasha: A cat-like monster in Japanese myths who, it is said, causes fires at funerals, steals corpses, and is sometimes a representative from hell.

kenshi: A swordsman or swordswoman, not necessarily born into the samurai caste.

kessen-chū: The "sacred bloodworms." A person infected by them cannot die but feels pain like a mortal.

kōgi: The Tokugawa shogunate, which is also referred to as the Tokugawa *bakufu* and the Edo *bakufu*.

kun: Honorific mainly—but not exclusively—

used when addressing male children or males of much lower status. Can also be used to show affection between close friends, depending on the situation.

Mugai-ryū: Sword school of the Akagi assassins; literally, "without form." Created and then disbanded by Habaki Kagimura, the Mugai-ryū included Giichi, Hyakurin, the evil Shira, and the deceased Shinriji.

Mutenichi-ryū: The sword school led by Rin's father (now deceased), destroyed by Anotsu Kagehisa.

Nagasaki-ya: In Edo, the Nagasaki-ya inn catered to envoys of foreign merchants. The hereditary managers of this inn were named Nagasaki-ya Gen'emon, which Sori shortens to Nagasaki-ya in this volume.

palanquin: An enclosed travelers' litter carried on poles on the shoulders of bearers.

Rokki-dan: *Rokki* means "six demons," and *Rokki-dan* means "band of six demons." They are Habaki Kagimura's new group of warriors—a small army set to take down Anotsu Kagehisa and the Ittō-ryū.

ryō: A high-value gold coin.

ryū: A sword school.

sama: Honorific used to show respect, mainly referring to people who are much higher in rank and sincerely admired.

san: Honorific used to show respect, usually when addressing equals.

second: Mitake asks Magatsu to be his "second," or his *kaishaku*, the beheader for someone who commits *hara-kiri* (*seppuku*).

sempai: A more modern Japanese honorific that means "mentor" or refers to a senior member in an organization.

sensei: A teacher, a master.

seppuku: Ritual suicide by disembowelment, also known as *hara-kiri*.

shidō: The samurai code.

shinbangashira: Meaning the same thing as *shinbangata*, the *shinbangashira* was the leader of the officers serving under the shogun, usually assigned to Edo Castle to defend the shogun himself.

shogun: Title for the former military dictator of Japan.

tegata: Official travel passes in Edo-era Japan.

tengu: A mythical Japanese creature.

terakoya: Edo-era private schools that taught reading and writing to the children of commoners.

Tori no Machi: Originally known as *Tori no Ichi* (rooster market), this is an open-air fair held at *otori-jinja* shrines around the country on the Days of the Rooster in November every year.

torii: Shrine gates. In *Blade of the Immortal* Volume 30: *Vigilance*, a row of torii are hacked down by Anotsu Kagehisa and Habaki Kagimura.

tōshu: Leader; master.

Yamada Asaemon: Nicknamed Kubikiri Asa, the shogun's executioner was a master swordsman, a sword tester, and an expert at beheading and cutting human bodies.

yōjimbō: Bodyguard.

"Manji and Rin" bonus art by longtime
Blade of the Immortal letterer Tomoko Saito.

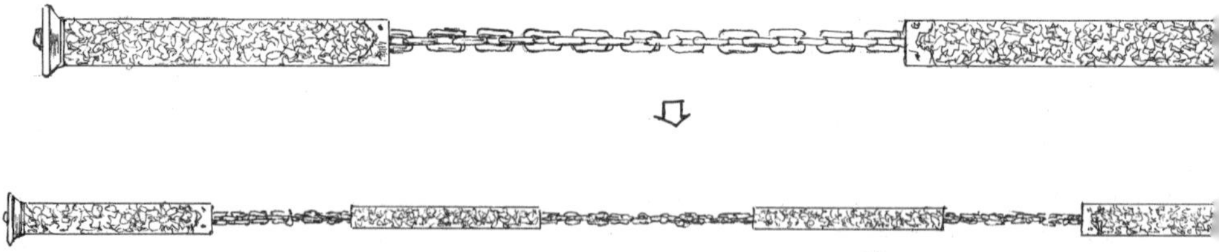

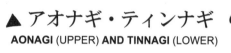

▲アオナギ・ティンナギ
AONAGI (UPPER) **AND TINNAGI** (LOWER)

DŌMA

I guess Tinnagi is kind of like Aonagi's "awakened state"—it's Aonagi's true form. It's got a long reach, but the handles are hollow, so they don't actually do much damage. Bruce Lee, who brought the appeal of nunchakus to the world, supposedly said (though I don't know if he actually did or not), "They look great, but they're not really a practical weapon"…Well, they were meant to be more of a concealable weapon than a lethal one anyway.

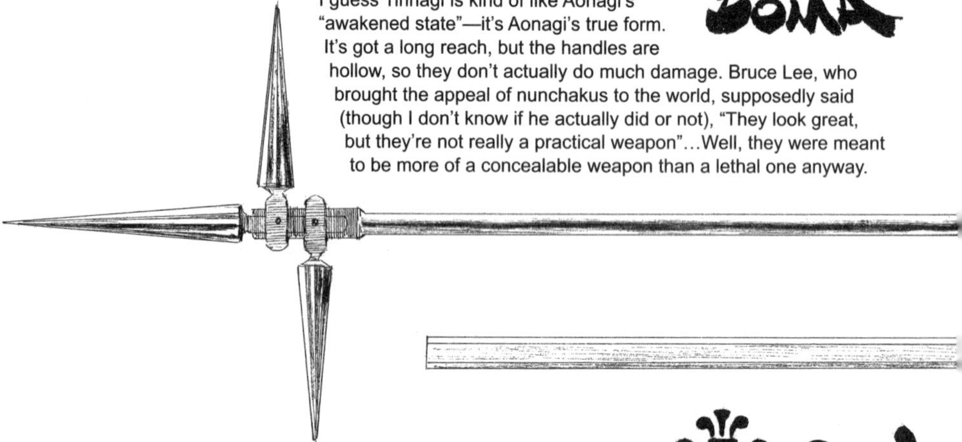

BAN

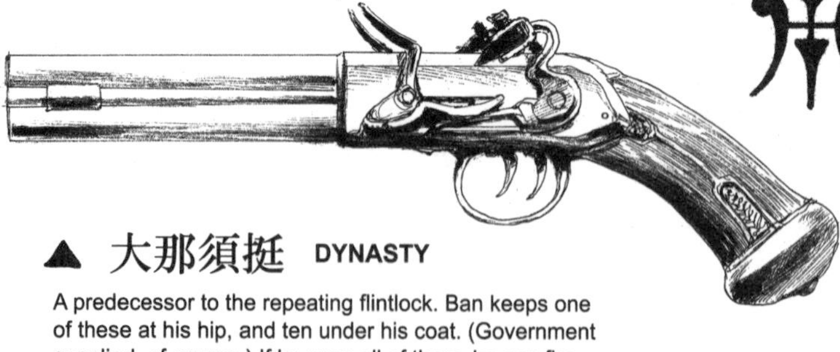

▲ 大那須挺 **DYNASTY**

A predecessor to the repeating flintlock. Ban keeps one of these at his hip, and ten under his coat. (Government supplied, of course.) If he uses all of them, he can fire twenty-two times without reloading, but after that he's in trouble.

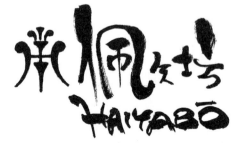

HAIYABŌ

▼二十拳之槍
HATETSUKA NO YARI ("Twenty-Hands Pike'

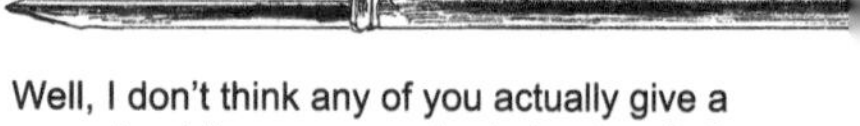

Well, I don't think any of you actually give a crap about the weapon of a dude who died at the very start of the final act, but hey…

SAMURA'S WEAPON SHOP OPEN 24 HOURS

~PLOPPY YOUTH~

TARIESHIN

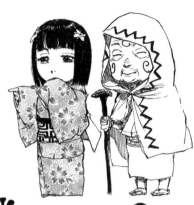

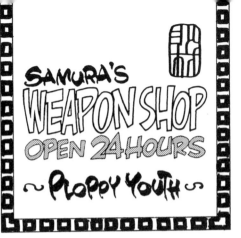

▼ヴォーホルベルス フリッカー

VOGELVERSCHRIKKER

How unfortunate. He simply named his weapon "scarecrow" in Dutch, but to our ears it sounds like something a geeky teenager would come up with to sound cool. After Rin, he's the second character to scream out a lethal attack move.

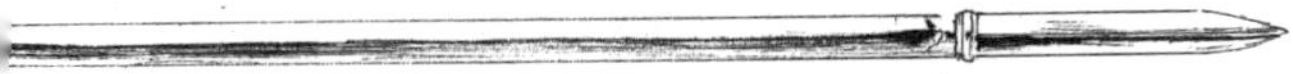

↑ The shape of the ferrule is the same as on Hai Yabō's weapon. It also was furnished by the *go-kōgi*.

▲ 悪杖・雨甘露

EVIL STAFF—UKANRO ("Rain of Nectar")

MURASAKI

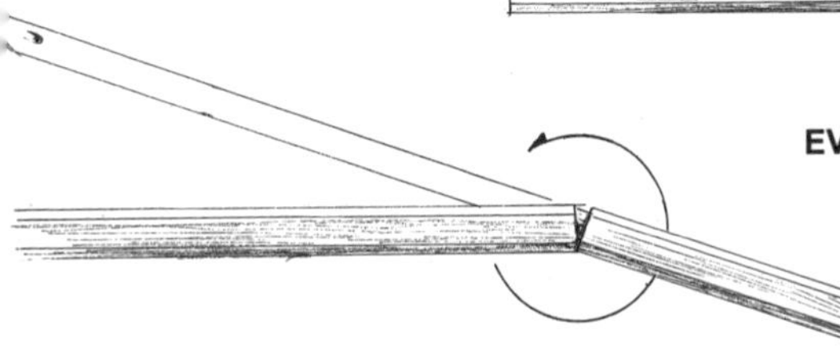

◀ 悪玉・叢咲海胆

EVIL ORB—MURASAKI UNI ("Purple Sea Urchin")

Rokki-dan chief interrogator Murasaki Shōzō. He fights with acid, which is super scary. What's really scary is the control needed. When he wipes the blood off the blade, he could accidentally melt his fingers. Or if he has the Murasaki Sea Urchin still hidden in his shirt and he accidentally falls over, he could get major burns on his chest. If he keeps doing that over and over again, he'll look the way he does now. (Yes, he's dead now.)

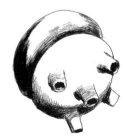

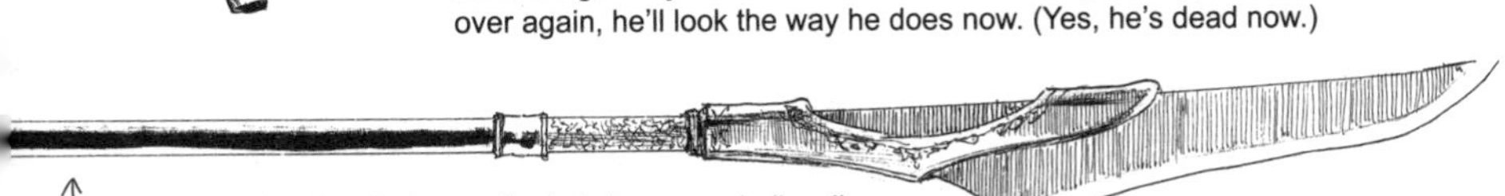

↑ In the story, this is called a *naginata* (a japanese halberd), but it's a *naginata* in no way whatsoever.

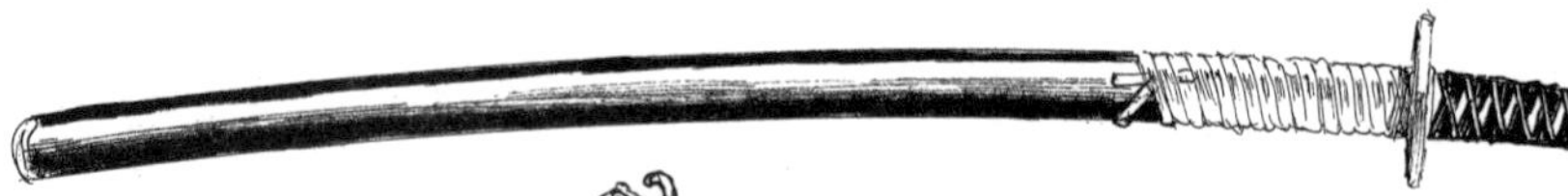

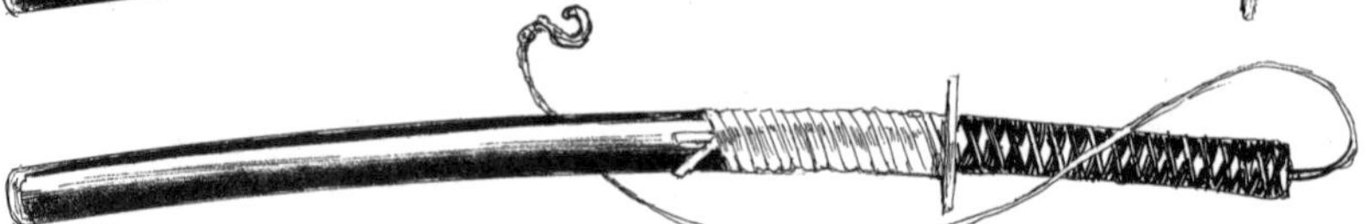

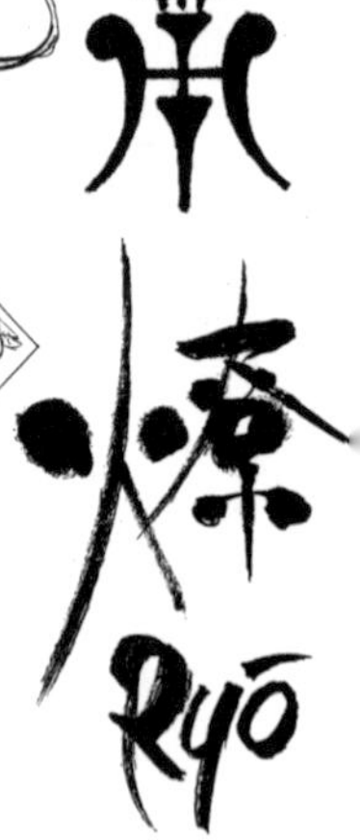
RYŌ

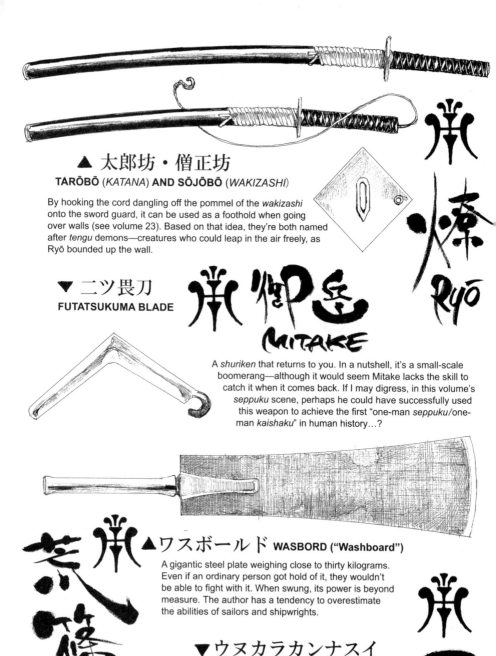

▲ 太郎坊・僧正坊

TARŌBŌ (*KATANA*) **AND SŌJŌBŌ** (*WAKIZASHI*)

By hooking the cord dangling off the pommel of the *wakizashi* onto the sword guard, it can be used as a foothold when going over walls (see volume 23). Based on that idea, they're both named after *tengu* demons—creatures who could leap in the air freely, as Ryō bounded up the wall.

▼ 二ツ畏刀

FUTATSUKUMA BLADE

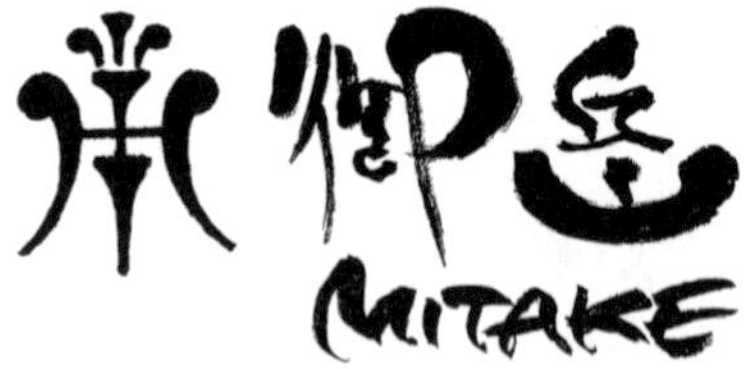
MITAKE

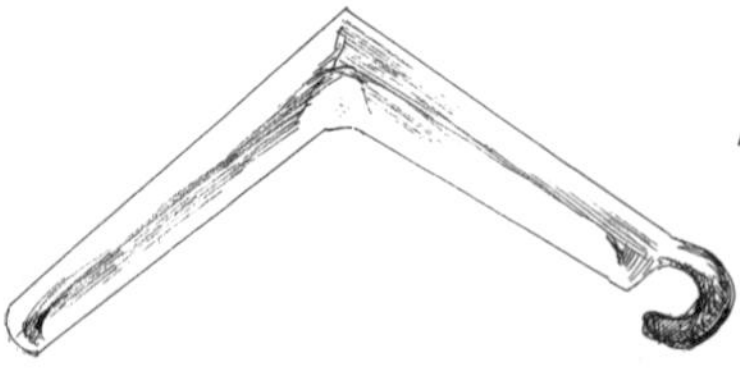

A *shuriken* that returns to you. In a nutshell, it's a small-scale boomerang—although it would seem Mitake lacks the skill to catch it when it comes back. If I may digress, in this volume's *seppuku* scene, perhaps he could have successfully used this weapon to achieve the first "one-man *seppuku*/one-man *kaishaku*" in human history…?

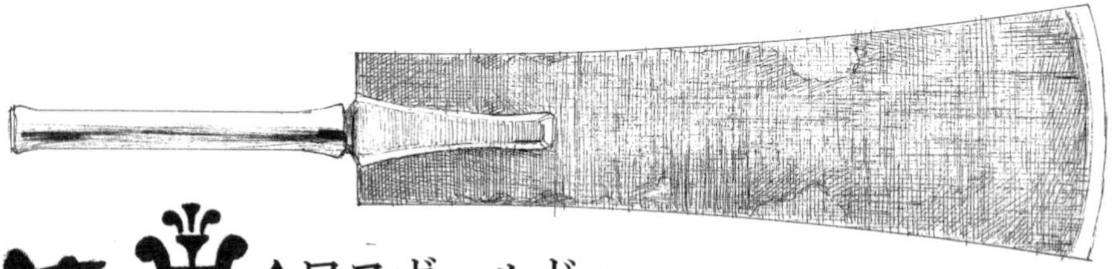

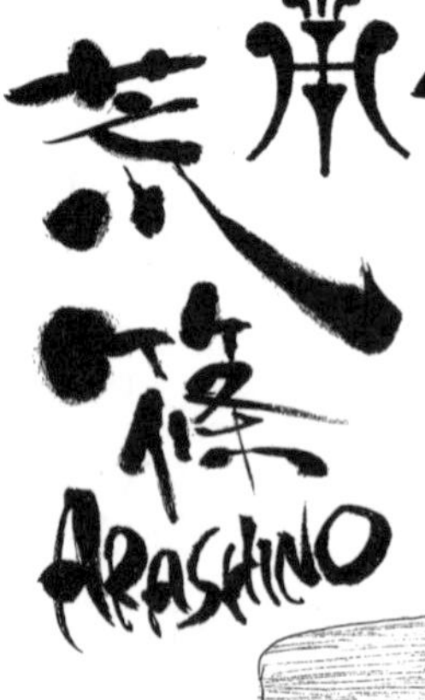
ARASHINO

▲ワスボールド **WASBORD ("Washboard")**

A gigantic steel plate weighing close to thirty kilograms. Even if an ordinary person got hold of it, they wouldn't be able to fight with it. When swung, its power is beyond measure. The author has a tendency to overestimate the abilities of sailors and shipwrights.

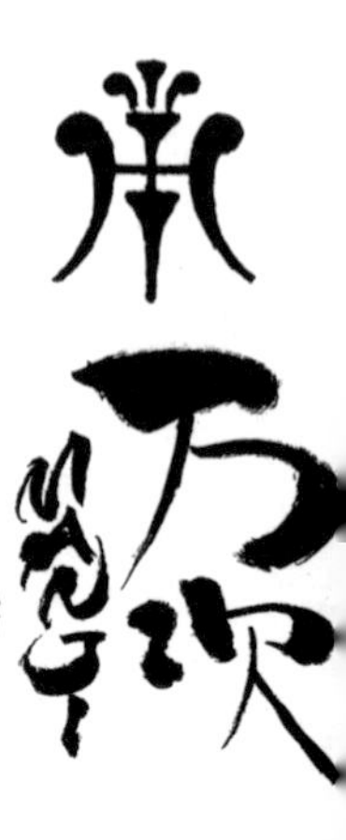

▼ウヌカラカンナスイ

UNUKAR KANNA SUY

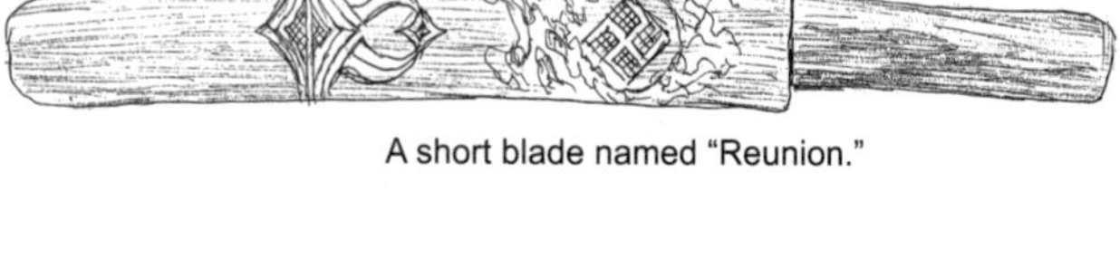

A short blade named "Reunion."

AFTERWORD

My debut story ran in *Afternoon* in June 1993, and the first chapter of ongoing serialization began in December of the same year. The final chapter ran in December 2012, so when you work it out, I've been drawing *Blade of the Immortal* for nineteen and a half years.

It's not that I really like period dramas. In high school, the subject I hated the most was Japanese history, and second was world history.

When I was in university, I bought a book of illustrations from prewar novels at a used bookstore. One of them was a piece featuring Tange Sazen (a famous fictional swordsman who first appeared in a series of novels by Fubo Hayashi) by Shimura Tatsumi. It was just totally cool . . . and *that* was what started it. I've said it a hundred times: Manji's design was a total swi—I mean, homage to Tange Sazen. While we're on the subject, I've never read a single Tange Sazen novel. Because I don't like period dramas.

Even so, the more I learned about the Edo era, the more I thought, "That was a pretty great time to live!"

To Mr. Y-da, my first editor (presently head editor of *Young Magazine*)—who, more than twenty years ago, when I submitted my drafts and manga from my university manga club publication, said to me, "How about if you try a period drama?" To Mr. O-gawa in Editorial, who gave me advice about fight scenes and the like. To my subsequent editors, Mr. I-ue, Mr. N-tani, Mr. O-kawau-chi (name not censored), Mr. M-shita, and Mr. I-mura. To Professor Hongō Kazuto of the University of Tokyo's Historiographical Institute, for teaching me about the minimal bits of historical authenticity that actually appear in this half-baked manga. To everyone in the sales departments and bookstores who sold my collections. To all the readers who have stuck with me for so long, thank you for everything . . . I should be writing more of those kinds of things in my afterword, but the more I think about it, for those of you who have been following this series and are going to follow my post-*Blade* work anyway, I figure I don't really need to make too much of a big deal about this.

Oh, to those readers who say, "I read *Blade* but don't give a crap about your other stuff," I say, "Is that so . . . ? Well, thanks, anyway."

I'll see you again sometime.

—Hiroaki Samura

Hiroaki Samura's Eisner Award–winning manga epic

BLADE OF THE IMMORTAL

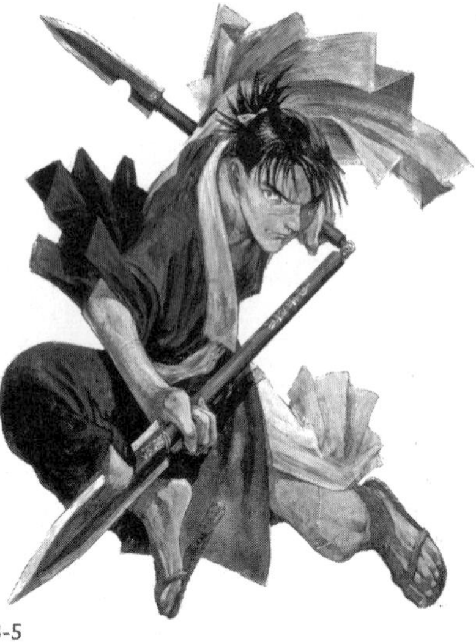

Volume 1: Blood of a Thousand
ISBN 978-1-56971-239-9
$14.99

Volume 2: Cry of the Worm
ISBN 978-1-56971-300-6
$14.99

Volume 3: Dreamsong
ISBN 978-1-56971-357-0
$14.99

Volume 4: On Silent Wings
ISBN 978-1-56971-412-6
$14.99

Volume 5: On Silent Wings II
ISBN 978-1-56971-444-7
$14.99

Volume 6: Dark Shadows
ISBN 978-1-56971-469-0
$14.99

Volume 7: Heart of Darkness
ISBN 978-1-56971-531-4
$16.99

Volume 8: The Gathering
ISBN 978-1-56971-546-8
$15.99

Volume 9: The Gathering II
ISBN 978-1-56971-560-4
$15.99

Volume 10: Secrets
ISBN 978-1-56971-746-2
$16.99

Volume 11: Beasts
ISBN 978-1-56971-741-7
$14.99

Volume 12: Autumn Frost
ISBN 978-1-56971-991-6
$16.99

Volume 13: Mirror of the Soul
ISBN 978-1-59307-218-6
$17.99

Volume 14: Last Blood
ISBN 978-1-59307-321-3
$17.99

Volume 15: Trickster
ISBN 978-1-59307-468-5
$16.99

Volume 16: Shortcut
ISBN 978-1-59307-723-5
$16.99

Volume 17: On the Perfection of Anatomy
ISBN 978-1-59307-782-2
$16.99

Volume 18: The Sparrow Net
ISBN 978-1-59307-871-3
$19.99

Volume 19: Badger Hole
ISBN 978-1-59307-969-7
$17.99

Volume 20: Demon Lair
ISBN 978-1-59582-199-7
$19.99

Volume 21: Demon Lair II
ISBN 978-1-59582-323-6
$19.99

Volume 22: Footsteps
ISBN 978-1-59582-443-1
$19.99

Volume 23: Scarlet Swords
ISBN 978-1-59582-671-8
$19.99

Volume 24: Massacre
ISBN 978-1-59582-751-7
$19.99

Volume 25: Snowfall at Dawn
ISBN 978-1-59582-883-5
$19.99

Volume 26: Blizzard
ISBN 978-1-61655-098-1
$19.99

Volume 27: Mist on the Spider's Web
ISBN 978-1-61655-215-2
$19.99

Volume 28: Raining Chaos
ISBN 978-1-61655-321-0
$19.99

Volume 29: Beyond Good and Evil
ISBN 978-1-61655-337-1
$19.99

Volume 30: Vigilance
ISBN 978-1-61655-484-2
$19.99

Volume 31: Final Curtain
ISBN 978-1-61655-626-6
$19.99

Also by Hiroaki Samura:

Hiroaki Samura's Emerald and Other Stories
ISBN 978-1-61655-065-3
$12.99

Ohikkoshi
ISBN 978-1-59307-622-1
$12.99

The Art of Blade of the Immortal
ISBN 978-1-59582-512-4
$29.99

AVAILABLE AT YOUR LOCAL COMICS SHOP OR BOOKSTORE • To find a comics shop in your area, call 1-888-266-4226
For more information or to order direct visit DarkHorse.com or call 1-800-862-0052 Mon.–Fri. 9 AM to 5 PM Pacific Time.
*Prices and availability subject to change without notice

DARK HORSE MANGA
DarkHorse.com